A Global Sourcebook in Protestant Political Thought, Volume I: 1517–1660

This first volume of *A Global Sourcebook in Protestant Political Thought* provides a window into the early Protestant world, and the ways in which Protestants wrestled with politics and religion in the wake of the Reformation.

This period saw political authorities and church hierarchies challenged and defended by scholars, clerics, and laypeople alike. The volume engages the full spectrum of Protestants, with reference to theology, geography, ethnicity, historical importance, socio-economic background, and gender. This diversity highlights how Protestants felt pulled towards differing political positions and used several maps to chart their course – conscience, custom, history, ecclesiastical tradition, and the laws of God, nature, nation, or community. On most important issues, Protestants lined up on opposing sides. Additionally, Catholic and Eastern Orthodox political thought, as well as interactions with Jewish and Muslim texts and thinkers, profoundly influenced different directions taken in the history of Protestant political thought. Even as our own time is fraught with deep disagreement and political polarisation, so too was early modern Europe, and we might read it in the anxieties, uncertainties, hopes, and expectations that the sources vividly express.

This sourcebook will enrich both research and classroom teaching in politics, theology, and history, whether geared towards general political or religious history, or towards more specialised courses on colonialism, warfare, gender, race, or religious diversity.

Matthew Rowley, FRHistS, is Visiting Assistant Professor of History at Fairfield University. His publications include *Trump and the Protestant Reaction to Make America Great Again* (Routledge, 2020), *God, Religious Extremism and Violence* (2024), and *Godly Violence in the Puritan Atlantic World* (2024).

Marietta van der Tol is College Lecturer in Politics at Lincoln College, University of Oxford. She is Principal Investigator of the Protestant Political Thought project and is the author of the book *Constitutional Intolerance: The Fashioning of the Other in Europe's Constitutional Repertoires* (2024).

A Global Sourcebook in Protestant Political Thought, Volume I: 1517–1660

Edited by Matthew Rowley
and Marietta van der Tol

LONDON AND NEW YORK

Designed cover image: *Still Life with Books*, Jan Lievens, c. 1627–c. 1628. Purchased with the support of the Foundation for the Promotion of the Interests of the Rijksmuseum. Public Domain.

First published 2024
by Routledge
4 Park Square, Milton Park, Abingdon, Oxon OX14 4RN

and by Routledge
605 Third Avenue, New York, NY 10158

Routledge is an imprint of the Taylor & Francis Group, an informa business

© 2024 selection and editorial matter, Matthew Rowley and Marietta van der Tol; individual chapters, the contributors

The right of Matthew Rowley and Marietta van der Tol to be identified as the authors of the editorial material, and of the authors for their individual chapters, has been asserted in accordance with sections 77 and 78 of the Copyright, Designs and Patents Act 1988.

All rights reserved. No part of this book may be reprinted or reproduced or utilised in any form or by any electronic, mechanical, or other means, now known or hereafter invented, including, photocopying and recording, or in any information storage or retrieval system, without permission in writing from the publishers.

Trademark notice: Product or corporate names may be trademarks or registered trademarks, and are used only for identification and explanation without intent to infringe.

British Library Cataloguing-in-Publication Data
A catalogue record for this book is available from the British Library

ISBN: 978-1-032-16209-6 (hbk)
ISBN: 978-1-032-16210-2 (pbk)
ISBN: 978-1-003-24753-1 (ebk)

DOI: 10.4324/9781003247531

Typeset in Sabon
by codeMantra

Contents

Acknowledgements	*xv*
Author Biographies	*xvii*
Preface	*xix*

PART I
Introductions 1

1 **Introduction** 3
MATTHEW ROWLEY AND MARIETTA VAN DER TOL

2 **Early Modern Biographies as a Window into Political Thought** 15
BRUCE GORDON

3 **Natural Law and Divine Law** 23
SARAH MORTIMER

4 **Resistance and Rebellion** 30
KARIE SCHULTZ

5 **The Use of the Sword: Violence, Empire, and Slavery** 37
MATTHEW ROWLEY

6 **Toleration, Coexistence, and the Place of 'The Other'** 44
MARIETTA VAN DER TOL

7 **The Hebrew Bible and Politics** 50
JOHN COFFEY

8 **Islam and Protestantism** 60
MEHMET KARABELA

vi *Contents*

PART II
Sources   69

Note on Symbols in Titles   71

1 *Martin Luther,* To the Christian Nobility
   of the German Nation *(1520) 73*
2 *Philip Melanchthon,* Natural, Divine and Human Laws
   (1521) 79
3 Reports Concerning the Zwickau Prophets *(1521) 85*
4 Social Welfare Legislation for the City of Wittenberg
   (1522) 87
5 *Andreas Karlstadt,* On the Abolition of Images and
   Poverty *(1522) 89*
6 *Martin Luther,* Temporal Authority: To What Extent it
   Should Be Obeyed *(1523) 91*
7 *Argula von Grumbach,* Against Coercion in the
   University *(1523) 94*
8 *Huldreich Zwingli,* The Sixty-Seven Articles *(1523) 97*
9 *Huldreich Zwingli,* Divine and Human Righteousness
   (1523) 99
10 *Gustav Vasa,* Test Luther with Scripture *(1524) 101*
11 *Thomas Müntzer,* Sermon to the Princes *(1524) 103*
12 Conrad Grebel to Thomas Müntzer on Separation and
   Violence *(1524) 107*
13 *Peasants of Upper Swabia,* Twelve Articles *(1525) 110*
14 *Thomas Müntzer,* Letter to the People of Allstedt
   (1525) 113
15 *Christoph Schappeler,* To the Assembly of the Common
   Peasantry *(1525) 115*
16 *Urbanus Rhegius,* Serfdom and the Kingdom of Christ
   (1525) 117
17 *Zürich,* Order to Drown Anabaptists *(1526) 119*
18 *Martin Luther,* Whether Soldiers, Too, Can Be Saved
   (1526) 121
19 *Ordinance of the Diet of Odense (1527) 125*
20 *Michael Sattler,* The Schleitheim Articles *(1527) 127*
21 *Hans Denck,* Concerning True Love *(1527) 130*
22 King Gustav Vasa Renounces the Crown *(1527) 132*
23 Diet of Västerås Elevated the Swedish King Above the
   Church *(1527) 134*
24 *Balthasar Hubmaier,* On the Sword *(1527) 136*
25 *William Tyndale,* The Obedience of a Christian Man
   (1528) 143

Contents vii

26 The Protestation at Speyer *(1529)* 146
27 The First Peace of Kappel *(1529)* 148
28 *Johannes Bugenhagen,* Whether One Can Wage War for the Sake of the Gospel *(1529)* 150
29 *Johannes Brenz,* The Case for State-Established Lutheranism *(1529)* 153
30 *Olaus Petri,* Rules for Judges *(c.1520–1540)* 156
31 *Andreas Osiander,* Against Incredible Antisemitic Accusations *(1529)* 159
32 *Anonymous,* Whether Secular Government Has the Right to Wield the Sword in Matters of Faith *(1530)* 161
33 Copenhagen Confession *(1530)* 164
34 Augsburg Confession *(1530)* 165
35 German Theologians on the Legal Grounds for Resistance *(1530)* 168
36 Founding of the Schmalkaldic League *(1531)* 170
37 *Ambrosius Blaurer,* Memmingen Resolution Against Persecuting Anabaptists *(1531)* 172
38 *Huldreich Zwingli,* A Short Exposition of the Christian Faith *(1531)* 174
39 *Michael Servetus,* Human Frailty and Religious Liberty *(c.1531)* 177
40 *Johannes Eisermann,* The Body of Christ and the Body Politic *(1533)* 179
41 Violence, Polygamy and Theocracy in the Anabaptist Kingdom of Münster *(1534)* 184
42 *Menno Simons,* The Blasphemy of Münster's King David *(1535)* 189
43 *John Calvin,* Dedication to Francis I *(1536)* 191
44 *Marie Dentière,* Defence of Women *(1539)* 195
45 *David Joris,* Plea for the End of Persecution in Holland *(1539)* 198
46 *Peter Riedemann,* Account of our Religion, Doctrine and Faith *(1541)* 200
47 *John Calvin,* Ecclesiastical Ordinances for Geneva *(1541)* 203
48 *Martin Luther,* On the Jews and Their Lies *(1543)* 207
49 *Abraomas Kulvietis,* Confession Fidei *(1543)* 210
50 *Aonio Paleario,* Indictment Against the Roman Pontiffs *(1544)* 215
51 Anabaptist Appeal to Moravian Nobility *(1545)* 220

viii *Contents*

52 *Miles Coverdale*, Biblical Israel and the Righteous Use of the Sword *(1547) 222*

53 *Thomas Cranmer*, A Speech at the Coronation of Edward VI *(1547) 225*

54 *Mikael Agricola*, On the Importance of a Finnish Translation of the New Testament *(1548) 228*

55 *Edward VI*, Act to Take Away All Positive Laws Against the Marriage of Priests *(1549) 231*

56 *Thomas Cranmer*, Notes on Rebellion *(1549) 233*

57 *Thomas Cranmer*, What Is Thy Duty towards Thy Neighbour? *(1549, rev. 1662) 236*

58 *Martin Bucer*, On the Reign of Christ *(1550) 237*

59 Magdeburg Pastors on Resistance to Authority *(1550) 241*

60 *Katharina von Bora*, Appeal to the King of Denmark *(1550) 243*

61 *Menno Simons, Magistrates*, Marriage and Rebellion *(c.1552) 245*

62 *Hugh Latimer*, Obedience to God's Will Requires Submission *(1553) 249*

63 *Sébastien Castellion*, Concerning Heretics and Those Who Burn Them *(1554) 251*

64 *Theodore Beza*, The Authority of the Magistrate in Punishing Heretics *(1554) 254*

65 *Heinrich Bullinger*, Obedience to Lawful Female Magistrates *(1554) 257*

66 The Peace of Augsburg *(1555) 261*

67 *John Calvin*, International Relations and National Boundaries *(1555) 264*

68 Philip Melanchthon to King Sigismund II Augustus of Poland *(1556) 267*

69 John Łaski to King Sigismund II Augustus of Poland *(1556) 270*

70 *John Ponet*, On Deposing or Killing a Tyrant *(1556) 272*

71 *Christopher Goodman*, The People May Disobey, Resist and Dethrone Magistrates *(1558) 275*

72 *John Knox*, Letter to the Commonality of Scotland *(1558) 278*

73 *John Knox*, Outline for the Second Blast of the Trumpet *(1558) 281*

74 *Elizabeth I*, Proclamation Forbidding Preaching *(1558) 283*

Contents   ix

75 John Calvin to William Cecil on Female Authority
    (1559) 285
76 Elizabeth I as Deborah *(1559) 288*
77 The French Confession of Faith *(1559) 290*
78 *Geneva Bible,* Dedication to Elizabeth I and Notes
    on Tyranny *(1560) 293*
79 The Scottish Confession of Faith *(1560) 297*
80 *Erik XIV,* Edict Concerning Religious Refugees
    (1561) 299
81 *Casiodoro de Reina,* Confessio Hispanica
    (1560/1561) 301
82 *Peter Martyr Vermigli,* Gideon and the Godly
    Commonwealth *(1561) 304*
83 John Calvin's Letters to Jeanne III *(1561–1563) 308*
84 *Sébastien Castellion,* Advice to a Desolate France
    (1562) 312
85 *John Foxe,* To the Persecutors *(1563) 315*
86 Heidelberg Catechism *(1563) 317*
87 *Bernardino Ochino,* On the Toleration of Heretics
    (1563) 320
88 *Jacopo Aconcio,* Satan's Strategy of Persecution
    (1565) 326
89 *George Buchanan,* Romans 13 and the Limits
    of Lawfull Magistracy *(1567) 330*
90 *Edict of Torda (1568) 333*
91 *Iwie Synod,* On Christians Holding Slaves *(1568) 335*
92 The Protestation of Louis de Bourbon, Prince of Condé
    (1568) 338
93 Jeanne III to Catherine De Medici on Religious
    Toleration *(1568) 340*
94 *Thomas Erastus,* State Power and Excommunication
    (1568) 342
95 *Niels Hemmingsen,* On Obeying Idolatrous Princes
    (1569) 349
96 Protestant Peace Terms in the French Wars of Religion
    (1569) 352
97 *Synod of Sandomierz,* Consensus of Sandomierz
    (1570) 354
98 A Defence and True Declaration of the Things Lately
    Done in the Low Country *(1570) 357*
99 *Zacharias Ursinus,* Commentary on the Heidelberg
    Catechism *(c.1570) 360*

x *Contents*

100 A Homily Against Disobedience and Wilful Rebellion *(1570) 367*

101 *Jeanne III,* The Magistrate's Duty to Further Christ's Rule *(1571) 370*

102 The Thirty-Nine Articles of Religion of the Church of England *(1571/1801) 372*

103 *Confederation of Warsaw,* Pax Dissidentium *(1573) 374*

104 *François Hotman,* Francogallia *(1573) 376*

105 *Edmund Grindal,* Preaching, Rebellion and the Limits of Royal Authority *(1576) 378*

106 *Innocent Gentillet,* Against Machiavelli's Amoral Politics *(1576) 381*

107 *Peter Walpot,* Non-Violence in the Gospels *(1577) 386*

108 *Peter Beutterich,* Catholicism and Tyranny over the Conscience *(1578) 389*

109 Union of Utrecht *(1579) 391*

110 Vindiciæ Contra Tyrannos *(1579) 393*

111 *Fausto Sozzini,* On Pacifism and the Love of Country *(1581) 397*

112 The Declaration of the States General of the United Provinces *(1581) 400*

113 *William Cecil,* The Execution of Justice in England *(1583) 402*

114 *Richard Hakluyt,* A Discourse Concerning Western Planting *(1584) 404*

115 Elizabeth I to the King of Poland on Religious Refugees *(1591) 407*

116 *Richard Hooker,* Of the Laws of Ecclesiastical Polity *(c.1593) 410*

117 The Decree of Uppsala *(1593) 413*

118 *Alberico Gentili,* International Laws of War *(1598) 415*

119 *Ministers of England,* The Millenary Petition *(1603) 429*

120 Regulating the Dutch Reformed Faith in Asia *(1607–1642) 431*

121 Forming the Protestant Union *(1608) 435*

122 *William Perkins,* A Discourse of the Damned Art of Witchcraft *(1608) 437*

Contents xi

123 *Edward Coke,* The Abrogation of Infidel Laws
(1608) 441

124 *Hugo Grotius,* On the Freedom of the Seas
(1609) 443

125 *Jacobus Arminius,* On Magistracy *(1603–1609) 451*

126 *James I,* Speech on Divine Right Kingship *(1609) 455*

127 *Lubbert Gerritsz and Hans de Ries,* Mennonite
Confession of Faith *(c.1610) 457*

128 *Thomas Helwys,* A Call for Toleration
(1611–1612) 459

129 *Virginia Colony,* Laws Divine, Moral and Martial
(1612) 463

130 *John Smyth,* Magistrates Should Leave Christian
Religion Free *(c.1612) 467*

131 *Leonard Busher,* Certain Reasons Against Persecution
(1614) 469

132 *Johannes Althusius,* Politics, Community and
Covenant *(1614) 472*

133 The Irish Articles of Religion *(1615) 475*

134 *People of Zizers,* Local Religious Co-Existence
(1616) 478

135 *David Pareus,* The Politics of Opposing the Antichrist
(1618) 480

136 The Belgic Confession *(1561, rev. 1619) 483*

137 Sacred and Mundane Politics in Plymouth Colony
(1620–1622) 485

138 *Gustav II Adolf,* Letters Patent to the Newly
Established Swedish South Company *(1622) 490*

139 *James I,* Directions Concerning Preachers *(1622) 492*

140 *William Ames,* The Duty Towards Our Neighbour
(1623) 494

141 *John Robinson,* On Killing American Indians
(1623) 499

142 *Hugo Grotius,* Warfare and the Law of Nations
(1625) 501

143 Demands of the Peasants of Austria *(1626) 514*

144 Algonquians and Africans in New Netherland
(1628–1660) 516

145 *Robert Filmer,* Patriarchal Rule in Home and State
(c.1628) 523

146 *Gustav II Adolf,* On Marching to War *(1630) 526*

xii *Contents*

147 *John Winthrop*, A Model of Christian
    Charity *(1630)* *528*

148 Battle Hymn from the Thirty Years' War *(1631)* *531*

149 *Johan Crell*, The End of Miracles and the Beginning of
    Toleration *(1632)* *533*

150 Religion and Military Discipline in Sweden
    (1632) *536*

151 Hero Worship, Humility and the Death of Gustav
    II Adolf *(1632)* *538*

152 *Jan Amos Komenský*, Politics, Piety and Universal
    Childhood Education *(c.1632)* *540*

153 Targeting Civilians in the Pequot War *(1637)* *543*

154 *French Reformed Churches*, On the Legality of
    Slavery *(1637)* *546*

155 *Anne Hutchinson*, Female Authority and Divine
    Revelation *(1637)* *548*

156 *Godfried Udemans*, Slavery as Godly Commerce
    (1612, 1638) *553*

157 Women's Right to Liberty of Conscience
    (1638–1641) *558*

158 *Anna Maria van Schurman*, Whether a Woman
    Should be Educated in Politics and Government
    (1638) *561*

159 Begrudged Toleration in New Netherland
    (1638–1674) *564*

160 *Amalia Elisabeth*, Fighting for Freedom of Thought
    and Religion in Germany *(1639)* *570*

161 *Massachusetts Bay Colony*, Body of Liberties
    (1641) *572*

162 Solemn League and Covenant of Scotland *(1643)* *577*

163 *Edmund Calamy*, Souldier's Pocket Bible *(1643)* *580*

164 *György I Rákóczi*, Reasons for Going to War
    (1644) *583*

165 *John Milton*, Freedom of the Press *(1644)* *585*

166 *Particular Baptists*, The First London Confession
    of Faith *(1644)* *592*

167 *Roger Williams, The Bloody Tenent of Persecution*
    (1644) *596*

168 *Samuel Rutherford*, Lex, Rex, or, The Law and the
    Prince *(1644)* *599*

Contents   xiii

169 *Massachusetts Bay*, American Indians and Blasphemy *(1646)* 606
170 An Agreement of the People for the Restoration of Native Rights *(1647)* 609
171 The Westminster Confession of Faith *(1647)* 612
172 *Mary Pope*, A Treatise of Magistracy *(1647)* 615
173 Slavery in Dutch Brazil *(1637–1650)* 617
174 The Windsor Prayer Meeting and the Execution of the King *(1648)* 621
175 *Congregationalists of New England*, The Cambridge Platform *(1648)* 623
176 Religious Clauses of the Peace of Westphalia *(1648)* 626
177 Act Abolishing the Office of King in England *(1649)* 629
178 *John Milton*, Biblical Israel and God's Displeasure at Monarchy *(1649)* 632
179 *Alexander Ross*, The Alcoran of Mahomet *(1649)* 635
180 *Gerrard Winstanley*, On the True Levelling of Social Difference *(1649)* 638
181 *Johanna and Ebenezer Cartwright*, Petition for the Readmission of the Jews *(1649)* 641
182 A Petition of Women to the English Parliament *(1649)* 643
183 Colonisation and Slavery in Dutch South Africa *(1649–1685)* 646
184 *John Eliot*, The Christian Commonwealth among Algonquians *(c.1649)* 651
185 *Oliver Cromwell*, Plea to Avoid War *(1650)* 654
186 *Thomas Hobbes*, Political Obedience and Eternal Salvation *(1651)* 657
187 *Doll Allen*, Petition of an Enslaved Christian Girl in Bermuda *(1652)* 663
188 *Frederick William*, On Tolerating Contentious Protestants *(1652)* 665
189 *Mary Cary*, Twelve Humble Proposals to the Supreme Governours of the Three Nations *(1653)* 667
190 *Roger Williams*, Toleration and Compulsion in the Ship of State *(1655)* 669

xiv *Contents*

191 Resenting and Restricting the Jewish Community
of New Netherland *(1655–1656) 671*
192 *Michael Wendeler,* Politics of the Turkish Republic
(1655) 675
193 The Confession of the Waldenses *(1655) 678*
194 *John Phillips,* Humanitarian Conquest
in the Caribbean *(1656) 680*
195 *James Harrington,* Commonwealth of Oceana
(1656) 683
196 *Richard Baxter,* Directions to Justices of the Peace
(1657) 687
197 Flushing Remonstrance Against Persecuting Religious
Outsiders *(1657) 691*
198 *Edward Sexby and Silius Titus,* Killing No Murder
(1657) 694
199 *Congregational Churches of England,* The Savoy
Declaration *(1658) 696*
200 *Pieter Corneliszoon Plockhoy,* An Ideal and Loving
Society *(1659) 699*
201 *Andrzej Wissowatius and Joachim Stegman,* Preface
to the Racovian Catechism *(1659) 701*
202 *George Fox,* Friends Must Refuse Violence
(c.1660) 707

Acknowledgements

This volume has been produced with generous support from the Protestant Political Thought project at the University of Cambridge (2019–2021) and the University of Oxford (2021–2023), with funds originally made available by the Harold C. Smith Foundation. The project started with a number of reading groups geared towards undergraduate as well as graduate students, convened by Marietta van der Tol and Jonathan Chaplin in 2017–2018. This project has since included more than 200 scholars from around the world to debate, discuss, and criticise the relationship between Christianity and the rise of right-wing populism, and has branched out to include Orthodox and Catholic scholars. The Sourcebook in Protestant Political Thought is the project's chief academic output, aiming to recover the wider range of thinking in historical traditions of Protestantism and to include often forgotten sources. The hope is that the Sourcebook may enrich contemporary reflection on politics and religion, and reinvigorate an interest in the political writing that emanates from within Protestant traditions.

Editors express their gratitude to a number of scholars who have contributed to the volume through themed contributions, suggesting sources, and sharing their insights. The editors would like to thank Odile Panetta in particular for providing new translations of sources in Latin by Ochino, Paleario, and Kulvietis. Her work is acknowledged in the bibliographic details of the relevant sources. Our gratitude also goes to Sarah Mortimer, Bruce Gordon, Karie Schultz, Mehmet Karabela, and John Coffey, whose contributions and ongoing interest in the sourcebook have been greatly appreciated. Source-specific guidance has been gratefully received from Dainora Pociūtė, Mika Vähäkangas, and Niklas Antonsson. We are thankful for the guidance and interest of Alexandra Walsham, John Morrill, Alec Ryrie, Joel Dodson, Randall C. Zachman, Petr Kratochvíl, Joshua Rowley, and Manfred Svensson. Matthew would like Alathia and Keira for the strength of their love and the joy of being their father.

Lastly, the editors have tremendously benefitted from access to libraries at Duke, Yale, Cambridge, and Oxford, as well as from support in the completion of the project from the Inez and Julius Polin Institut for Theological Research at Åbo Akademi (Finland). Editors are grateful for permissions xvi *Acknowledgements*

granted for the use of original source material, where this material was not already publicly available or otherwise covered under fair use. Details of permissions are included in individual source material. Every effort has been made to identify copyright holders and obtain permission for the use of copyrighted material.

Author Biographies

John Coffey is Professor of History at the University of Leicester. Among his publications are *Persecution and Toleration in Protestant England, 1558–1689* (2000), and *Exodus and Liberation: Deliverance Politics from John Calvin to Martin Luther King Jr* (2014). He is currently Director of the Wilberforce Diaries Project.

Bruce Gordon is Titus Street Professor of Ecclesiastical History at Yale Divinity School and teaches in the History Department and Early Modern Studies. He is the author of *The Swiss Reformation* (2002), *Calvin* (2009), *John Calvin's Institutes of the Christian Religion* (2016), and *God's Armed Prophet: Zwingli* (2021). His forthcoming book, *The Bible: A Global History*, will appear in 2024.

Mehmet Karabela is the author of *Islamic Thought Through Protestant Eyes* (Routledge, 2021) which examines the engagement of early modern Protestant scholars with Islam. Karabela's writings have appeared in edited books and journals. His research interests include Islamic intellectual history, Islam and the Reformation, and political theology. He teaches at Queen's University, Canada.

Sarah Mortimer is Professor of Early Modern History at Christ Church, University of Oxford, where her research explores religious and political ideas and the relationships between them. She has published widely on these themes, and her most recent book is *Reformation, Resistance, and Reason of State: The Oxford History of Political Thought 1517–1625* (2021).

Matthew Rowley, FRHistS, is Visiting Assistant Professor of History at Fairfield University. He has authored and edited several books, including *Trump and the Protestant Reaction to Make America Great Again* (Routledge, 2020), *God, Religious Extremism and Violence* (2024), and *Godly Violence in the Puritan Atlantic World* (2024).

Karie Schultz is Leverhulme Early Career Fellow and Associate Director of the Institute of Intellectual History at the University of St Andrews.

xviii *Author Biographies*

Her research interests include early modern political thought, theology, and university education. She is currently working on a project about Catholic and Reformed student migration throughout Europe.

Marietta van der Tol is Alfred Landecker Postdoctoral Research Fellow at the Blavatnik School of Government and College Lecturer in politics at Lincoln College, University of Oxford. She is Principal Investigator of the Protestant Political Thought project and is the author of the book *Constitutional Intolerance: The Fashioning of the Other in Europe's Constitutional Repertoires* (2024).

Preface

Beneath it all, there was a trick question, and an answer that was, according to taste, either a brilliant piece of lateral thinking or an infuriating dodge. Jesus was asked if it was legitimate to pay taxes. *No* would mean rebellion and suicide; *yes* would mean submission and surrender to a pagan power. So he replied: give to Caesar what is Caesar's, and to God what is God's.

During the first Christian centuries, this riddling piece of evasion became the seed of an entire political philosophy. Early Christians faced the exact same dilemma continually: they were subjects of a vast empire that they could neither openly challenge nor fully obey. Threading this needle, they developed a set of solutions which seem obvious to modern eyes, but which were startlingly new in theirs – to declare themselves apolitical, carving out a space in which they could practice their rites, revere their Lord, and still honour the emperor, affirming their *worldly* allegiance to Rome but asserting their *spiritual* independence. And their community, their 'church', became almost a self-governing state within the state, insisting on its own freedom while also sedulously refusing to offer any open political challenge. This paradoxical ethic found its fullest expression in that weirdest and most characteristic of early Christian political acts: martyrdom, in which Christians freely yielded their bodies to Caesar and their souls to God.

When Christianity's political situation was transformed by the conversion of Constantine, this distinctive political ethic receded, and, in the Eastern churches, all but disappeared. Even in the medieval West, where the distinction between spiritual and temporal power persisted and became institutionalised, its expression was very different, with popes and bishops far more politically involved and ambitious than their pre-Constantinian predecessors.

It was only with the Protestant Reformation, when a new set of Christian theologians found themselves confronting a political situation not entirely unlike that of the first centuries, that the old principles came back to the fore. The Protestant thinkers were intensely conscious of that ancient history and were actively attempting to recover it. Yet, their circumstances were *not* the same, nor could 12 centuries of post-Constantinian experience simply be shrugged off. This was their dilemma: the only way they could truly recover the spirit and practice of the early church was to do something new.

xx *Preface*

This was how Martin Luther came, during the earliest, most chaotic and creative years of the Reformation, to formulate his doctrine of the 'two kingdoms', an idea so seminal that its original radicalism is hard to recover: since most modern political thought can ultimately be traced back to it, his bold innovations now seem like banal truisms. In arguing for a profound separation between church and state, Luther asserted that the authority of secular rulers – even of secular rulers who happened to be Christians – was inherently limited. They existed to hold the ring, to maintain some semblance of order, and to punish notorious or egregious crimes – and these were God-given roles, for which those rulers should be honoured. But they could not govern their subjects' consciences, hearts, or minds, not even, he argued, to the point of regulating the preaching of the church or the writing and publication of books.

As so often with Luther, this idea was built from a baffling set of paradoxes. He lauded secular authorities with one breath and damned them as corrupt and depraved with the next; and as for the practicalities of how such an arrangement might actually be made to work, well, Luther never had much patience with legal and administrative details of that kind. And yet, as this book shows, the rich paradoxes that Luther sketched provided an arena within which his contemporaries and successors could thrash out what being a Protestant believer and also a political animal meant in practice. Could Christian kings wield some degree of spiritual authority? What matters must be reserved for the consciences of churches and of individual believers, and in what matters must they be subject to their rulers? When might (and must) Protestants disobey their rulers, and what forms might that disobedience take? What, in the end, is due to Caesar, and what is due to God?

In these disputes, we can see most of modern political thought in embryo. There is certainly an authoritarian streak to Protestant political thought, emphasising the moral right and duty of (supposedly) godly rulers to punish religious crimes such as heresy and witchcraft, and insisting that since secular powers are given their authority by God, the Christian's duty to obey is almost (never wholly) limitless. But there is also a radically egalitarian streak, in which the longstanding Christian assertion of the spiritual equality of all souls before God is brought into this world's affairs and, at times, weaponised. When John Knox told the people of Scotland that 'all man is equal', he was not declaring equal *rights* in the modern sense, but he was declaring that they had an equal *responsibility* to obey God, a responsibility which they could not evade by passing the buck to their rulers. Knox insisted that all Scots were obliged to act in God's cause, and to obey God rather than their idolatrous queen. When that queen's son and successor, the Protestant King James VI, warned that 'some fiery spirited men in the ministry' were plotting a 'Democratic form of government', he was exaggerating, but not inventing. As this book shows, half a century later some Protestants were speaking of democracy in earnest.

But alongside the authoritarianism and the egalitarianism comes another, even more pervasive and radical idea: apoliticism, or the doctrine that the authority of any secular government must be limited. This is the space of conscience that Luther carved out for himself; the conviction that not everything is due even to the most righteous Caesar; and the mulish insistence of Protestants that *they* will be the ones who decide what they do and do not owe, and to whom. Both in the ancient world and in the modern world, rulers and states have a way of demanding total allegiance and absolute loyalty from their people, but Protestants' loyalty, while real, is always limited and hedged. There are some things rulers cannot do, and some spheres – including, in the end, everything that is of any real or enduring worth – into which they cannot stray.

As befits what we call the 'early modern' age, the ideas and debates collected in this book are both distant from our world and part of it. The editors of this collection have quite rightly assembled a set of texts which reflect the most pressing ideas of the sixteenth and seventeenth centuries, rather than concocting some dubious selection oriented towards modern concerns, and so modern readers will at times need to do the hard and invigorating imaginative work needed to put themselves in that alien world, with very different preoccupations to our own. And yet, throughout these texts, disconcertingly familiar issues and problems bubble to the surface, and we hear echoes between the world of the Reformation and the modern world that is its direct descendant.

Protestant political thought will not tell us everything we need to understand the world and times we live in. But we cannot understand this world and these times without it. That is why this book is indispensable.

Professor Alec Ryrie
Durham, 19 September 2023

Part I
Introductions

1 Introduction

Matthew Rowley and Marietta van der Tol

In studying Protestant political thought, one enters into a cacophony of debates about politics, law, and religion. In this first volume of *A Global Sourcebook in Protestant Political Thought*, we put the spotlight on the period from Luther's rise in 1517 to the mid-seventeenth century. Around 200 sources provide a rich window into a period of early modern history, known as the Reformation, which saw political authorities and church hierarchies challenged and defended by scholars, clerics, and laypeople. Even as our own time is fraught with deep disagreement and political polarisation, so too was early modern Europe, and we might read it in the anxieties, uncertainties, hopes, and expectations that the sources vividly express.

The roots of these debates about politics, law, and religion stretch into Roman Catholic and Eastern Orthodox thought, and further back into the worlds of Roman, Greek, and Jewish thought and reflection. The Renaissance humanist reorientation of ancient sources deeply informed the rise of early Protestantism, as well as early political writings emanating from it. Its chief source, at least for most Protestants, was the Bible, the translation of which into vernacular languages allowed scholars, clerics, and laypeople to read the stories that had shaped a centuries-old tradition for themselves, and to identify with them.

Uncovering a wider range of sources in Protestant political writing than the traditional canons in the history of political thought allow for helps us to understand the sheer variety of responses articulated to both everyday problems and major political events. Some of this writing is deeply systematic and scholarly, while other writings may be incidental, highly local, and a bit incoherent. All of the sources are contextual, in that the author and their experiences, the places in which they lived, the difficulties they faced, and the audience they addressed all influenced the style of their writing. Some of it was bold and proclamatory, while other writing might strike as particularly shrewd or strategic. Studying the history of Protestant political thought is no exercise in self-satisfaction. Even if read 'within' their time, there will be aspects in these writings that will strike the reader as problematic, and perhaps rightly so.

DOI: 10.4324/9781003247531-2

The rapid dissemination of ideas through the novel technology of the printing press allowed them to spread far and wide. Centres in Wittenberg, Geneva, Königsberg, Emden, and Cambridge connected Reformers from across the continent, with strong bonds of solidarity developing between like-minded groups, such as between the Hungarian, Swiss, Dutch, and English reformed movements. Puritans who set out to settle in New England passed through Cambridge, Norwich, and Leiden. Lesser-known connections existed between centres of learning in northern Italy, present-day Lithuania, and Königsberg, as the Italian-born queen of Poland-Lithuania Bona Sforza supported major Reformers such as **Abraomas Kulvietis**, some of whose work is translated into English for the first time in this volume.[1]

These networks of scholars, churches, and universities also facilitated places of refuge. The Palatinate became such a place for Huguenots, as did London, which had a number of refugee churches, and the Americas, where dissenting Protestants attempted to settle with the support of the English monarchy. Stories about martyrdom have shaped the identity and memory across the Protestant traditions, sometimes with reference to ancient biblical Israel and the early church, and sometimes with reference to the wars of religion and the experience of persecution. These stories play an important role in creating a sense of historical lineage and legitimacy. The movement of people, ideas, and books also imprinted on Protestantism a transnational ethos, which was nevertheless grounded in a strong sense of local and personal piety.[2]

The geographical, confessional, and political diversity of Protestant political thought is not as visible as it perhaps should be. The relative dominance of Anglo-American voices in the history of Protestant political thought has come at the cost of voices from central, northern, and eastern Europe, while indigenous voices from elsewhere in the world, and indeed the voices of women and people of colour have often been ignored. Perhaps this is a by-product of a canon-focused ethos in the wider field of intellectual history, as much as a result of certain biases within Protestant traditions privileging well-educated men, and in particular those in active ministry. Another constraint comes from the need to translate sources from a number of languages. Some of the sources in this book have been freshly translated, or re-translated, so as to increase the accessibility of lesser-known sources.

An awareness of the breadth and depth of Protestant writing is important to ongoing reflection on political thought both within and beyond Protestant traditions. The rise of right-wing populism and the revival of nationalist politics lend an urgency to delving into this historical tradition – first, to show that radical voices have always existed on the spectrum of Protestant political thought; and second, to show that many voices provide a more robust intellectual foundation to the criticism of right-wing populism and Protestant support thereof. For those identifying with Protestant traditions, it might be important that a genuinely Protestant voice is preserved, and that political theology is not overshadowed by the overpublication of familiar conservative (or indeed liberal) tropes.

Introduction 5

Recovering the depth of Protestant traditions of thinking about politics will require a basic interest in the sources themselves, as well as emotional intelligence to try to understand who the people behind those sources were, what their hopes and expectations, their fears and desperations were, and to ask: what was it like to walk in their shoes? The task of the reader is not to ascertain who was right at a particular moment in time, but rather to read the sources deeply so as to uncover some of the complexity of their ideas and their personalities, and to reflect on them. The editors very much hope that the sourcebook will function as the starting point for research projects for students and scholars, and will prompt further specialist writing about the authors and issues presented here.

The sources have been arranged chronologically rather than thematically. This order allows the reader to pick up on developments in different parts of Europe and the wider world, and to discern their historical interrelation. All sources have been supplemented by a short introduction. These introductions draw on existing literature by subject or author specialists as indicated through endnotes, and which the reader might want to consult for further reading. The introductions also highlight possible connections to other pieces of writing in bold. Keywords have been added for ease of usage, especially for the digital edition of the sourcebook.

Several eminent scholars have provided thematic introductions, which provide themed roadmaps through the volume, explaining some of the key concepts and pointing to a number of particularly relevant sources. These include the following: Bruce Gordon on the importance of biographies and context; Sarah Mortimer on the relationship between natural and divine law; Karie Schultz on the issue of resistance and rebellion; Matthew Rowley on the use of the sword through violence, empire, and slavery; Marietta van der Tol on practices of toleration; John Coffey on the reception of the Hebrew Bible; and Mehmet Karabela on the relationship between Protestantism and Islam. These thematic introductions will no doubt enhance the experience of the users of this volume.

Selection of the Sources: What Makes Them Protestant?

This sourcebook has deliberately cast the net of Protestantism wide to include Lutheran, Reformed, Anabaptist, Presbyterian, Anglican, and anti-Trinitarian thought, and eschews a particular definition of Protestantism. Much like Alec Ryrie, it takes Protestantism as a 'whole family of squabbling identities, that people define themselves by, hold to, fight for, and sometimes abandon'.[3] This includes cultures and practices, doctrines and ideas, and daily lived experiences. Many of the Protestants whose work is reproduced in this volume would not have considered other Protestants (whose work is also reproduced here) to be *true* Protestants or *true* Christians. As the sources themselves indicate, the labels of 'Protestant' and 'Christian' are very easily politicised.[4] For this reason, it is perhaps more appropriate to talk about 'Protestantisms'

6   Matthew Rowley and Marietta van der Tol

and 'Reformations', much like scholars have come to speak about multiple Enlightenments, including Catholic and Jewish Enlightenments.[5]

Protestantism in this volume refers to writings that reference and build on the Bible as an authoritative source of knowledge. Some of the sources will only refer to the Bible, whereas others might use biblical examples alongside rich references to other scholars and sources from antiquity. The editors of this volume have inserted the biblical references where they were assumed to be known, and thus not specifically listed. The Protestant emphasis on a personal as well as communal understanding of the Bible often hindered Protestants from acknowledging other interpretations or arguments as legitimate, both among themselves and vis-à-vis Catholic and Jewish writers. However, much some sources say about political others, they always tell us something about the author, and how they understood their place in the world.

For example, those whose imaginations were strongly occupied with the apocalypse tended to have complicated relationships with their present circumstances. Minorities that existed under pressure tended to spiritualise their faith, or to focus on heavenly citizenship rather than earthly or political belonging. The radicalisation of some strands of Protestantism indicates something of this cycle of persecution and spiritualisation. Whereas some thought that resistance, and even armed resistance, could be a possibility, for others, their resignation to being persecuted led them to accept death. On the contrary, Protestants who enjoyed the support of princes and monarchs were quick to argue for the use of violence against Catholics, for example, or against Jews and heretics. A careful reader of the sources will find that much political thought reflects such circumstances, rather than a definitive biblical approach to one situation or another.

Another example of the fluidity of ideas that were often assumed to be rigid is in the matter of marriage, divorce, and bigamy. The story of Henry VIII is well known, but similarly, the professors of Wittenberg (including **Martin Luther**) were asked whether their prince could have a second wife, and ended up concluding he could so long as this second marriage remained a well-kept secret! The issue of marriage also touched upon the lives of those who produced political writing. As the introductions will detail, many of them had been previously ordained and committed themselves to celibacy, but may have ended up breaking their vows. This is also true for some of the women. The story of **Katharina von Bora**, a former nun, and Martin Luther, a former monk, is well known, but lesser known is the story of **Marie Dentière**, a former prioress from Belgium who married a Protestant theologian and became **John Calvin's** begrudged critic in the city of Geneva.

To bring out a range of Protestant voices representing rather different lives and lifestyles has required the editors to look beyond traditional political tracts, such as those produced by the famous legal scholar **Hugo Grotius**, or **Samuel von Pufendorff**, or **Johannes Althusius**, to name a few. While scholarly tracts remain of great interest, other political writings can be found in

Introduction 7

pamphlets, poems, songs, letters, in which the less educated frequently expressed themselves. Some legal documents, such as the so-called 'toleration treaties', have been included, the earliest being the **Edict of Torda** from 1568. These legal documents tend to bridge ideas about coexistence with (legal) reality, and bring out the perspectives of those charged with administrative responsibility. This volume aims to recover the diversity in Protestant political thought, and this diversity exists in six senses: theology, geography, ethnicity, influence, socio-economic background, and gender.

Theological diversity was present from the earliest days of the Reformation. However, most accounts focus on the main strands of Protestant thought and fail to include a wide range of theological convictions. Reformation *geography* tends to focus on a Europe within a Europe (Germany, Switzerland, France, the Low Countries, England, and Scotland). This focus has often left out the vibrant and eclectic Protestant traditions in Italy, Poland-Lithuania, Hungary, Denmark, and Sweden. These regions influenced the course of the Reformation, and we would do well to remember them. During the Reformation, political boundaries were in flux. Additionally, to borrow another phrase from Alec Ryrie, Protestants were 'a footloose people, forever on the move'.[6] Persecution accounted for much of this. But Protestants moved for many different reasons, and ideas cross-pollinated throughout Protestant Europe and even across Catholic, Orthodox, and Protestant communities.

Almost all Protestants in the first 200 years after the Reformations might be classified today under the heading of 'European' or 'Western', even as those labels veil something of the ethnic and cultural diversity present throughout European history. It took a considerable time for Protestantism to spread across the globe, and often longer for those around the world to start writing on politics from a Protestant perspective. This gradual widening of discourse will become especially apparent in the chronological arrangement of the sources in this volume, as well as in the next, where the global moorings of Protestant political thought begin to take shape. This global character necessitates a cross-cultural interest and imagination. 'It would take a special kind of cultural arrogance', write John Witte and Frank Alexander, 'for Western and non-Western Christians to refuse to learn from each other'.[7]

The volumes include authors who vary in their *influence*. Some lived their lives on the margin and remain relatively unknown to the modern reader. Others were influential in their lifetime, but have been largely forgotten today. Yet, others have grown in their importance over the centuries, and we can study the reception of their work across different times and contexts. Protestants came in many *socio-economic* shapes and sizes. Some were wealthy, well educated, and connected to power. Others lacked all these things or were of a middling sort. Older histories of the Reformation, and many modern ones, focus almost exclusively on influential men.

8 Matthew Rowley and Marietta van der Tol

This volume also highlights the importance of *gender*. Women contributed greatly to debates on conscience and coercion, hierarchy and submission, accountability and confrontation, and the interpretation of the Bible. They were largely left out of later accounts of the Reformation, but several notable figures are included in this volume. As Merry E. Wiesner puts it:

> Women were not simply passive recipients of the Reformation message, but left convents, refused to leave convents, preached, prophesied, discussed religion with friends and family, converted their husbands, left their husbands, wrote religious poems, hymns, and polemics, and were martyred on all sides of the religious controversy.[8]

Kristin Waters rightly notes the breadth of topics that women covered, they wrote 'not just about women and "women's issues"'[9] – and many did so from an explicitly Protestant perspective. Protestant women were defenders of garrisons (not to forget *Fidei Defensatrix*), printers, editors, letter-writers, petitioners, novelists, playwrights, spies, poets, agitators, and martyrs.

What Makes the Sources Political?

Many sources in these two volumes are overtly political, and yet some are only implicitly political. What exactly it means to write something that is 'political' is a thorny question – an issue that lies below the surface of many debates but is rarely answered. And how should one discuss political matters: by appeals to power, reason, emotion, scripture, law, or custom? The political nature of theology is guided here by a discussion of the five *solae* (*solas*): scripture alone, Christ alone, grace alone, faith alone, and to the glory of God alone. These *solae* were not systematised until centuries after the Reformation, but they are present in the writings of the Reformers. These *solae* are read in relation to political events and issues, whether these were addressed directly or indirectly, and they provide a window into the controversial, contradictory, and subversive character of much of Protestant political thought.

Sola Scriptura

Since the patristic age, scripture and theology 'dominated the way political discussion was conducted'.[10] Scripture was so common that it can be easy to ignore how central it is. Mark Noll cautions against viewing the ubiquitous use of scripture as 'wallpaper'. Instead, he says, 'Scripture should be viewed as a sturdy piece of furniture smack in the middle of the room'.[11] Many Reformers, like other Renaissance humanists, researched textual traditions and produced translations aimed at providing a faithful rendering of the text. They echoed many in the Catholic tradition who made scripture the rule for faith and practice. Unlike most Catholics, they often employed scripture against tradition. 'Tradition', like 'toleration' and 'innovation', generally carried negative connotations. Tradition was still useful when subordinated to scripture, most Protestants thought. *Sola Scriptura*, writes Carlos M. N. Eire, was Luther's 'most basic hermeneutical principle'. The term became 'the chief battle cry of his war against the Romanists'.[12]

Reformers paired the belief in the perspicuity (or clarity) of scripture with the conviction that scripture interpreted itself. Thus, scripture itself could rebuke centuries of the 'fallible' reception of the Bible. Yet though the text was supposed to interpret itself, when humans approached it, they saw it interpreting itself in different ways. Peter Matheson says 'it may be helpful to think of each of the Reformers as having a personalised canon in their head which linked together texts from Psalms and Paul, Numbers and Revelation'.[13] In their own way, they embraced the entire canon, but made different connections between the parts. Hans-Jürgen Goertz rightly notes that 'the Holy Scriptures were [not] read in the same way by all. Luther, Zwingli, and Melanchthon read them differently than Karlstadt and Müntzer, the spiritualists and Anabaptists differently than the peasant revolutionaries'.[14] Each of these, and the confessions they wrote or influenced became – ironically–extra-scriptural sources of authority.

Scripture alone, however, raised more questions than it answered – and many of these had unmistakably political implications. The appeal to *Sola Scriptura*, intended to end debate, opened up new theatres of conflict. What does it mean to turn to scripture alone as the rule for belief and practice? Is it possible, or desirable, to rid oneself of other influences (church tradition, like-minded peers, personal bias, or the prevailing *Zeitgeist*)? What role should be given to nature, conscience, or the moving of the Holy Spirit? Are the educated more qualified interpreters? Does scripture speak clearly and univocally on political matters? What parts of scripture should be emphasised? Does one part supersede another? How does one move from exegesis to application (for an individual, church, or society)? Behind all these questions lay a more problematic one: who has the authority to decide which group stands on scripture alone, and where did this authority come from? *Sola Scriptura*, by vesting authority in one source, in some ways attributed authority to interpret the Bible to everyone, leading to all sorts of squabbles.

Solus Christus

For Protestants across this volume, the Bible alone was the highest rule and guide, not least because scripture revealed the redemption of creation in Christ. If his sacrifice on the cross sufficiently covered the sins of humanity, there was no need for additional dependence on Rome, the prayers of the clergy, the intercession of saints, or even the good works of believers. In one stroke, this severed the believer from the past (no longer praying for or to the deceased) and atomised the believer's relationship with God. Christ, not the clergy, mediated between God and man. At judgement day, every person stood alone before God, and the only acceptable plea was the one made in Christ's name.

The primacy of Christ raised fundamental political questions. If it is Christ alone who saves, and if there is no salvation outside of Christ, how should the redeemed act towards the unredeemed or the not-yet redeemed, whether in one's own community or elsewhere? How should one respond to those who openly reject Christ or ridicule Christians? Do unbelievers jeopardise a covenantal relationship between Christ, his people, and security in their land? Does reliance on Christ make one a better leader, subject, or citizen? Are magistrates and ministers like Christ? Does God mediate his will through magistrates? A final implication was perhaps the most overtly political. Since all authority was granted to Christ, all owed ultimate allegiance to him. The New Testament confession that Jesus is Lord, κύριον Ἰησοῦν (Rom. 10:9), has long been considered subversive.

Sola Fide and Sola Gratia

Sola Fide, the other main pillar of Luther's thought, was simple to understand. As Eire summarises, 'salvation is never earned; it is simply and freely granted by God to those who have faith in the saving sacrifice of Jesus Christ'.[15] Closely related with this was *Sola Gratia* – the conviction that grace was a free gift of God to be received independently of good works. Both doctrines had a levelling effect because God granted salvation to all in the same way – irrespective of social or ecclesiastical rank, and even in disregard to the behaviour of the individual. *Sola Fide* and *Sola Gratia*, although not overtly political, raised fundamental questions about authority, obedience, conscience, and how one should live. If faith is a gift from God, can godly society and laws move one closer to faith? Can ungodly leaders stymie or subdue God's free gift of faith? Should a godly magistrate encourage faith, and if so, by what means? Does regeneration free one from human law or bind one in closer obedience to it? Does the imputation of grace make one a better subject or citizen? If believers are saved by grace – an unmerited gift from God – do good works matter? Do the eyes of faith provide special insight into political matters?

Soli Deo Gloria

The Reformed tradition emphasised the glory of God – a theme that was also present in, but not foundational to, Lutheranism. Nothing was exempted from the duty to glorify God, and a Christian should glorify God in everything. As Luther streamlined authority by elevating scripture, the Reformed posited the same *telos* for all actions and institutions. States, laws, vocations, marriage, pleasure: all had a similar aim – the glorification of God. If God was not glorified, these pursuits were warped, defunct, and possibly idolatrous. To the glory of God, Christians fought slavery, championed the cause of the poor, worked for the humane treatment of prostitutes, advocated sensible working conditions, and endeavoured to hold governments to account, to name just a few. As with *Sola Scriptura*, this doctrine carried with it the seeds of fragmentation: the glory of God seemed to be in the eye of the beholder. The magistrate and the martyr might agree that their actions should be done to the glory of God. With this belief in hand, the one lights the pyre and the other offers their body as kindling.

The political implications of *Soli Deo Gloria* are many. Should all the functions of the state, including taxation, war, incarceration, or execution be carried out to the glory of God? Does glorifying God in political affairs heighten the guilt or increase the sanctity of the endeavour? Is God glorified because a policy is righteous, or is a policy made righteous because Christians glorify God in it? How does one balance ultimate allegiance to God with duties to neighbours and superiors? If the government dedicates its endeavours to God, does this mean God owns the undertaking? If obedience to a command from a superior would fail to bring glory to God, is the Christian free to disobey authority? Might removing an ungodly magistrate be God-glorifying? Again, fundamentally, who decides what beliefs and institutions glorify God? The resort to *Sola Scriptura* begs the question.

The significance of these five *solae* is not that these doctrines are primarily or exclusively political, but that they carried political significance. For the reader of this sourcebook, it is important to note how doctrines that are seemingly unconnected to politics can have significant political implications. For example, a strong focus on the Book of Revelation often informed creative and controversial military decisions. If one identified their historical moment with the slain under the altar (6:9–11), this seemed to guard against many martial applications. Identification with the heavenly army (τὰ στρατεύματα τὰ ἐν τῷ οὐρανῷ, 19:14) that accompanied the slaying rider often had the opposite effect. Or consider the parable of the wheat and the tares in Matthew 13: if one identified with the reaping angel (ἄγγελος, v. 39) who separated good from bad, it was possible to justify the banishment or execution of the religiously impure. If one believed God removed the tares through supernatural messengers, then the application of this parable was markedly different. Even minor doctrinal differences could separate persecution from toleration, and massacre from martyrdom.

The Politics of Paradox

In *The Freedom of a Christian* (1520), Martin Luther put forward two theses: 'A Christian is a perfectly free lord of all, subject to none. A Christian is a perfectly dutiful servant of all, subject to all'.[16] The statement that 'freedom in Christ made one a subject to all' is perhaps easy to comprehend, but difficult to carry out, and the political implications of this assertion are legion.

12 Matthew Rowley and Marietta van der Tol

What would it mean for a subject to be 'lord of all, subject to none' or for a magistrate to be 'dutiful servant of all, subject to all'? Does this mean a Christian is free from all laws or bound to all laws – or somehow both? Although Luther admitted the 'theses seem to contradict each other', he used the tension to support Christian practice. He built politics on paradox.

Scripture is bursting with juxtaposed proclaimed truths, counterintuitive realities, and seemingly conflicting commands. If not all 'paradoxes', many of the following 'tensions' form part of the scaffolding of political thought: God is sovereign over all, yet holds humans responsible; humans resemble God, but are marred by depravity; believers are in the world, but not of it; they obey human laws, but owe allegiance to God; they walk in the light, but not after the devil's radiance; they leave judgement to God, and judge all things. Scripture teaches them to practise good works because they are unnecessary, to hate their family and love their enemies, to lose their lives to find them, and to see the unseen. They are to consider weakness as strength, foolishness as wisdom, affliction as blessing, poverty as wealth, humiliation as exaltation, and death as gain. Faith tussles with reason; divine sovereignty with human causality; the demands of justice with those of mercy; and the world as it is with the world as God would have it. The reader of this sourcebook is invited to enter into these tensions, with their different and often contradictory ways of relating faith to politics, some of which may be deeply personal.

Previous Readers of Protestant Political Thought

There are numerous readers and handbooks on Protestant history and theology. Many were published around the 500th anniversary of the Reformation in 2017. Some of these books are more thematically expansive than these volumes, while others offer a more specialist and precise reading of a smaller number of authors. For example, some major Protestant political writings are printed in series like the *Oxford Classics* or the *Cambridge Texts in the History of Political Thought*. Many are also reproduced for free online by the Liberty Fund. These editions are indispensable for in-depth research.[17] Even though many of the primary texts are pared down for these editions, they are still of such a length (and often price) that they make general readership unlikely. As this volume fills a sizeable gap between general readership and a range of historical sources, it is intentionally more diverse in its selections and more expansive in its chronology than other readers in Protestant political thought.

Two readers serve as models for these volumes: *From Irenaeus to Grotius: A Sourcebook in Christian Political Thought, 100–1625* by Oliver O'Donovan and Joan Lockwood O'Donovan, and *The Teachings of Modern Protestantism on Law, Politics, & Human Nature* by John Witte and Frank Alexander. Most of the earlier volume is dedicated to Roman Catholic and Eastern Orthodox political thought, with a strong emphasis on Roman Catholicism. This book is the go-to source on the rich tradition of political reflection before the Reformation, providing many of the antecedents of authors included in this sourcebook. O'Donovan's volume stops at 1625 with the publication of Hugo Grotius' *De Jure Belli et Pacis*, but they were keenly aware that Protestant political thought extends to the present. Many subsequent Christian thinkers 'have been forgotten to all but specialists. Their thinking on law, politics, and society needs to be retrieved, restudied, and reconstructed for our day'.[18]

On the other end, few studies consider Protestant political thought in the eighteenth and nineteenth centuries, and there is no general reader for the vast period in between. There certainly has been an uptick in interest starting in the late eighteenth century, likely owing to the World Wars, as well as interest in the rise of nation-states and decolonisation. John Witte Jr. and Frank S. Alexander edited a major sourcebook discussing a number of eminent thinkers from the late nineteenth century. They produced a three-volume set on Christian political thought, with volumes devoted to Eastern Orthodox, Roman Catholic, and Protestant thought respectively. Their volume on Protestantism includes contributions by Abraham Kuyper, Susan B. Anthony, Karl Barth, Dietrich Bonhoeffer, Reinhold Niebuhr, Martin Luther King Jr., William Stringfellow, and John Howard Yoder.

This sourcebook bridges these two comprehensive collections, spanning the long and multifaceted period between the sixteenth and nineteenth centuries. This period witnessed the beginnings of Protestantism, its initial fragmentation, early Protestant colonialism, the 'wars of religion', the Westphalian attempt to curb religious conflict, the Enlightenments, the transatlantic slave trade, the age of revolutions and independence movements, and the romantic nationalism that played a key role in the twentieth-century World Wars. The sheer variety of sources highlights how differently Protestants have responded to these events by contributing to them, by arguing against them, and sometimes by remaining silent about them.

Notes

1 Dainora Pociūtė, "Abraomas Kulvietis: Humanistic Origins of the Early Reformation in the Grand Duchy of Lithuania", in *Latinitas in the Polish Crown and the Grand Duchy of Lithuania: Its Impact on the Development of Identities*, ed. Giovanna Siedina (Florence: Firenze University Press, 2014), 161–175.

2 John F. Bosher, "Huguenot Merchants and the Protestant international in the Seventeenth Century", *The William and Mary Quarterly* 52, no. 1 (1995): 77–102.

3 Alec Ryrie, *Protestants: The Faith that Made the Modern World* (London: Penguin, 2017), 467.

4 Matthew Bowman, *Christian: The Politics of a Word in America* (Cambridge, MA: Harvard University Press, 2020).

5 James E. Bradley and Dale K. Van Kley, *Religion and Politics in Enlightenment Europe* (University of Notre Dame Press, 2001), 2; Jonathan I. Israel, "Enlightenment! Which Enlightenment?", *Journal of the History of Ideas* 67, no. 3 (2006): 528.

6 Alec Ryrie, *Protestants: The Faith that Made the Modern World* (London: Penguin, 2017), 132.

14 *Matthew Rowley and Marietta van der Tol*

7 John Witte and Frank Alexander, eds., *The Teachings of Modern Protestantism on Law, Politics, and Human Nature* (New York: Columbia University Press, 2007), xxxi.
8 Merry E. Wiesner, "Beyond Women and the Family: Towards a Gender Analysis of the Reformation", *The Sixteenth Century Journal* 18, no. 3 (1987): 313–314.
9 Kristin Waters, "Introduction", in *Women and Men Political Theorists: Enlightened Conversations* (Oxford: Blackwell, 2000), 1.
10 Oliver O'Donovan, and Joan Lockwood O'Donovan, eds., *From Irenaeus to Grotius* (Grand Rapids, MI: William B. Eerdmans Publishing, 1999), xv.
11 Mark Noll, *In the Beginning Was the Word: The Bible in American Public Life, 1492–1783* (Oxford: Oxford University Press, 2016), 19.
12 Carlos M.N. Eire, *Reformations: The Early Modern World, 1450–1650* (New Haven, CT: Yale University Press, 2016), 173.
13 Peter Matheson, *Imaginative World of the Reformation* (Edinburgh: T&T Clark, 2000), 44.
14 Hans-Jürgen Goertz, "Radical Religiosity in the German Reformation", in *A Companion to the Reformation World*, ed. R. Po-chia Hsia (Oxford: Blackwell, 2004), 73.
15 Carlos M.N. Eire, *Reformations: The Early Modern World, 1450–1650* (Yale University Press, 2016), 174.
16 Martin Luther, *The Freedom of a Christian, 1520: The Annotated Luther Study Edition* (Minneapolis, MN: Fortress Press, 2016).
17 J.M. Porter, *Luther: Selected Political Writings* (Eugene, OR: Wipf and Stock, 2003). Other readers focus on individual strands of Protestantism (e.g., Anabaptist political thought): for example, Andrew Bradstock and Christopher Rowland's edited *Radical Christian Writings: A Reader* (Oxford: Blackwell, 2002), does not include contributions from a host of influential political thinkers (e.g., Luther, Zwingli, Calvin, Knox). Their volume highlights the voices that are often overlooked, as do these two present volumes.
18 John Witte and Frank Alexander, eds., *The Teachings of Modern Protestantism on Law, Politics, and Human Nature* (New York: Columbia University Press, 2007), xxx.

2 Early Modern Biographies as a Window into Political Thought

Bruce Gordon

Biographies of pre-modern figures pose a particular challenge for historians.[1] At one level, it is generally possible to determine the basic facts about a life, although that is not always straightforward. It is amazing how little we know about William Shakespeare, for example, the most well-known English literary figure. For most prominent men and women (mostly men), we are able to piece together the bare bones of their backgrounds, education, family, and achievements. Sometimes the sources are plentiful. But where does that get us? What can we actually know about those who lived in the sixteenth and seventeenth centuries?[2]

Modern biographical writing seeks to enter into the worlds of distant lives to offer narratives and interpretations. But the obstacles are formidable. Is it even possible to know the inner thoughts and intentions of a historical figure? How do we tell the stories of the lives of persons who had no conception of what we might want to know? How do we talk about those who thought very differently about themselves than we do about them? Early modern people had a distinctive understanding of the self, and one that contemporary readers are challenged to enter into.

What do we expect of a good modern biography? Some of the elements that come to mind include a pacey, compelling story, and deep insights into the character of the protagonist. We want to know why they did or wrote what they did and how they interacted with the world around them. Context is crucial. We need to understand how they were shaped by the cultures in which they lived in order to assess their impact. Family, friendships, and social, religious, and political relations of all sorts remind us that no life was lived in isolation. Each person is shaped by the complex web of relationships that can shift over a lifetime.

All of this is desirable but elusive for a number of interlocking reasons. On the whole, biographical information from the early modern period largely exists for those who mattered: rulers, reformers, scholars, and military leaders, most of whom were part of the educated elites. For the vast majority of people, we have little to no information, except perhaps in remarkable circumstances. Records of birth, baptism, marriage, taxes, and death provide a sense of the lives lived, but about which we can know very little else. Judicial

DOI: 10.4324/9781003247531-3

16 *Bruce Gordon*

and church records throw some light on otherwise obscure figures, but only briefly. They were subjects, often living in remote rural regions and have almost no historical voice.

We can talk about the men and women who appear in this collection precisely because they were for the most part educated, possessed status, and were well connected. They are studied because they possessed various forms of authority or notoriety, often leaving a trail of writings. Although the field has expanded greatly to include greater attention to material and visual cultures, historians continue to focus mostly on textual evidence, which can only give us a partial perspective on the early modern world.

Textual evidence from the period is by no means monolithic, and those pursuing biographical information have learned to be deft in sifting through a wide variety of sources for echoes of lives. In some cases, we have biographical and autobiographical accounts that form a crucial but problematic foundation for studying a life. But early modern writers are present in many types of writings if we are prepared to engage in textual archaeology.[3] Many of the documents in this collection arose out of personal experiences and observations of society, religion, and politics. The writers were often participants in the events they describe. Letters are a crucial source of biographical information, as are historical chronicles, biblical and theological texts, sermons, and political tracts.

Crucial to mining texts for biographical information is context. There is a long tradition of reading theological and political treatises purely in terms of the history of ideas, including confessions, of which there are numerous examples in this collection. Such an approach privileges the central arguments and looks for connections between thinkers and theologians with little interest in the contexts in which these documents were written. Biographical information often resides in the crucial situations that helps to illuminate the author's complex relationships to current events. Questions such as why men and women chose to write at particular moments and in specific genres through which they presented their arguments yield a good deal of information not only about convictions and tensions, but also about the anxieties and concerns of both writers and their intended audiences.

Biographical information is often most richly gathered from the contingent moments of a life. The historian needs to employ the skills of literary studies in considering issues of authorship, style, and language. Each document in this collection tells a range of stories in which authors, readers, and the wider public were participants. Identifying the various roles played by each offers biographical insights. Where texts are absent or silent, we may have recourse to other forms of evidence that can be revealing. Clothing, for example, was a powerful indication of status and aspirations. In the public sphere, one's outward appearance was a clear statement not only of who you were and your place at court or in wider society, but also of who you wanted to be. It was central to the phenomenon of 'self-fashioning' to which I shall return.

Early Modern Biographies as a Window into Political Thought   17

Often, such information is available through art, notably portraits of royalty and nobility, as well as of merchants and clerics. The portraits of the great humanist Erasmus by Hans Holbein were a deliberate effort to present the Dutchman as St Paul and St Jerome, the translator of the Bible for his age. In the Netherlands, the paintings of Rembrandt offer a view of the complexities of Dutch society, including his representation of biblical figures as contemporary Jews in Amsterdam. Again, context is crucial: who chose to be painted by whom, and where the picture was to be seen. But it was not only the elites. In the paintings of the Breughels, father and son, we are offered a rich perspective on the lives of common people, such as in *The Battle between Carnival and Lent*.

Scientific advances have also been rewarding for biographers. Forensic analysis of human remains makes available precious information about early modern lives with information about diet and diseases. We are able to learn more about the afflictions suffered, medical practices, and food consumed. While such information might seem a long way from political or theological writing, the connections can be important. Take, for example, the French Reformer **John Calvin** in Geneva, who died in 1564. For much of his last years, he was bed-bound by serious illness and was forced to dictate his texts to scribes who gathered around him. There is no doubt that his works from these years, and his views on the frailty of the body, were moulded by the extreme pain he suffered.[4]

Biography must be undertaken with a broad mind about the ways in which we can gather information about people's lives. Yet, at all times we have to maintain a critical attitude towards the sources regarding what they can and cannot tell us. The question we always have to have in mind is, what is our relationship to the subject of our investigation. This brings us back to the issue of texts; a degree of scepticism is essential.

Why? Because early modern biographical and autobiographical sources were written with intentions distant from our understanding of objectivity. Biography was not primarily about providing factual information, but about the portrayal of a life to particular ends. Whether writing about the self or about others, the primary purpose was exemplarity.[5] That is, the representation of a life often served as an example or embodiment of certain ideals and beliefs. Biographical writing was intended to be didactic, instructing the readers about desired religious and political norms to be emulated. The same could also work in reverse. Bad lives were morality tales in how not to lead your life. The authors of biographical information often claimed their authority based on eyewitness accounts or personal acquaintance. Early modern writers drew heavily from the classical tradition of biography and historical writing that believed that history is a teacher, that the past is instructive for the present. The assumption was of a certain constancy of human behaviour.

Another crucial source was the antique and medieval traditions of hagiography, presenting the lives of saints as models for the contemporary faithful.[6] Like the accounts of saints, early modern writers often highlighted the way a

18   Bruce Gordon

person died. The lives of the Protestant Reformers **Martin Luther** and John Calvin both emphasised that they died well, peacefully in their beds, as a sign of their sanctity. The early modern world, Catholic and Protestant, inherited the medieval tradition of the 'good death', which involved preparation for one's end of life and peaceful resignation to the Lord. Protestants shifted the focus of the vast body of literature on how to die well towards an emphasis on good living.[7] The spiritual diaries of Puritans, often written by women, scrupulously document daily events in terms of biblical virtues. These diaries are a wonderful source of information on the lives of men and women, but we must be aware that their primary purpose was spiritual.

These spiritual diaries lead us to a fundamental challenge for us when we read the documents in this collection in terms of biographical information.[8] That is the question of the self.[9] Here, in our world we stand at considerable distance from early modern culture. In our Western, post-Freudian, postmodern societies, we tend towards an understanding of the self in terms of individuality and agency. That is a broad statement, but it helps to understand that the early modern self was constructed differently. To begin with, despite the fragmentation of Christianity following the Reformation, there was a shared belief that each person was essentially a religious being, created by God, and whose primary relationship was with the divine. The self did not belong to the individual, but to God. This does not mean there was uniformity of belief – that was by no means the case – but almost universally the self was understood in terms of divine creation. Each person negotiated their life in a world under the auspices of an omnipotent deity who was the primary source of identity and authority.

In the contemporary Western world, institutions and societal structures are increasingly held in contempt, or at least deep suspicion. Recent events in the United States have evidenced widespread anxiety about the 'deep state', and the development of AI and other technologies has bred suspicions that our lives are increasingly monitored and controlled, whether by government or by consumer culture. Rebelling against systems of authority has become an important part of some modern conceptions of the self. At the same time, gender norms and attitudes towards patriarchy have transformed our views of individuality, families, and communities. These current attitudes play an important role in how we address early modern texts by opening themes not previously considered, such as masculinity, pre-modern conceptions of race, societal violence, and sexualities.

The early modern world was defined by fixed social and political hierarchies, patriarchal families and communities, and the belief that each person existed within a web of relationships and not as an individual agent. Community rather than individuality was the ideal. In assessing biographical information from the early modern world, we should be cautioned against too much emphasis on independent individuals. That is not how they saw themselves. Even remarkable figures such as Martin Luther or **John Milton** who

Early Modern Biographies as a Window into Political Thought 19

gained widespread fame never understood themselves as societal outsiders in the sense of living apart. They believed that their distinctive roles ultimately served the communities in which they lived.

The documents in this collection also reveal the different voices that early modern writers assumed. There was no more brutal hostility in the early Reformation than between **Martin Luther** and **Thomas Müntzer**.[10] Although both were former Catholic clerics and embraced scripture as the sole authority for Christians, their personalities played an enormous role in their mutual animosity. As we see from both Luther and Müntzer's texts, they write as self-acknowledged prophets who possess a special spiritual authority to interpret scripture and current events. In speaking to princes in interpreting the dreams of Daniel as well as to the people of Allstedt in 1525, Müntzer presents himself as uniquely able to discern God's will. That authority was not based on any office or educational status, but rather upon the direct revelation of God. Müntzer's hostility to Luther arose in good part out of their rival claims to the gospel grounded in their own sense of being chosen.

Prophetic character became an essential part of Reformation biography. By setting aside the authority of the church and its traditions and claiming that the people should have direct access to the Bible, the Reformers created an enormous problem. What was to be done with multiple and contradictory interpretations of scripture? The Reformers, including Luther, **Huldreich Zwingli**, Müntzer, and later Calvin, looked to models of biblical prophecy to shape their own sense of self as chosen interpreters of God's word. Luther's sense of being Elijah played out in his responses to the German peasants, who he claimed had misrepresented scripture to justify a political and social revolution.

In writings on politics and religion, it is essential that we continue to ask how authors understood their position of authority and how it is expressed in their texts. **Elizabeth I's** proclamation forbidding preaching, issued at the beginning of her reign, speaks of how the gospel is to be spread without interpretation or addition.[11] Who is able to determine what that meant? She was the model Protestant ruler. Elizabeth wove a careful sense of identity out of her Protestantism, gender, and the precarious state of her kingdom. Protestant Reformers often identified their rulers in terms of biblical judges and kings. The pious were Hezekiah and Josiah. Elizabeth very much made this tradition her own in her close identification with the biblical judge Deborah, which conveyed her with a sacred authority and model for female rule.

Such delicate identities, so important for our sense of biography, were easily threatened. **John Knox's** infamous *First Blast* was interpreted by Elizabeth as an attack on her as a queen.[12] The consequences were enormous. She turned against Geneva and Calvinism, ensuring that the Reformation in England would continue on its distinctive course. The text is an excellent example of how contested origins led to radically different readings and receptions. Knox believed that he was attacking Mary Queen of Scots, the

20   *Bruce Gordon*

hated Catholic monarch. Calvin, who did not share Knox's view of female rulers, had dedicated his Isaiah commentary to Elizabeth, but she was so offended by the *First Blast* that she refused to accept the dedication of the commentary.

The relationship between individual personhood and authority emerges clearly in the famous case of **Anne Hutchinson** of New England and her trial in 1637, shortly before her death.[13] Like Elizabeth, Hutchinson faced the question of how a woman could hold religious and political authority. Elizabeth, naturally, could appeal to the Bible and the tradition of sacred monarchy, but Hutchinson raised a more ominous spectre for the sixteenth and seventeenth centuries: she connected divine revelation directly to her person as her source of self and authority. Further, she invoked her conscience, a crucial part of Reformation religious culture, as shaping her identity as an interpreter of divine will. Hutchinson continued in the highly gendered, biblically based tradition of construction of the self around ideas of prophecy and immediate divine revelation that shaped the auto/biographical material of the period.

As mentioned, many of the documents included in this collection of political writings reflect the personal experiences of the authors. An excellent example is the two selections from **Sebastien Castellio**, the Savoyard humanist and leading voice against **John Calvin** in Geneva.[14] A brilliant scholar, one of the greatest of his day, Castellio lived much of his life in poverty, wandering across French and German lands. He became well connected with other refugees, many from Italy and Eastern Europe, who embraced the evangelical reform but not entirely in the manner of Luther and Calvin. Many were inspired by Erasmus to a more sceptical view of doctrine and church authority. They also believed in reading the Bible in a less dogmatic way, which led some, including Castellio, to reject certain tenets of the Protestant faith, such as infant baptism and the doctrine of the Trinity.

Castellio rose to prominence in the scandal unleashed by the execution of the Spaniard **Michael Servetus** in early 1554.[15] The burning of a condemned heretic raised for Castellio the question of what right ruling magistrates possess to interfere in matters of faith. The Savoyard and his supporters did not argue for toleration in our modern sense, but they put forward a notion of the private space of belief or non-belief that could not be judged by the institutional powers of church and state. Castellio made the same arguments in his passionate *Advice to a Desolate France*, in which remarkably he speaks to both Catholics and Protestants, finding fault with both. The *Advice*, like the debate with Calvin, was highly personal for Castellio for several reasons. Firstly, Calvin and Castellio had known one another in Geneva and quarrelled, making their textual exchange particularly personal. Secondly, Castellio knew many of the key protagonists in France, and his *Advice* was drawn from those relationships. Once more, we see how texts have a strong biographical character.

As a final example from the collection, let us turn to the irascibly brilliant poet John Milton.[16] A dominant figure of the Western literary canon, Milton has received a great deal of attention in recent debates about how to read the established figures of English writing. The text on press censorship offers rich insights into Milton's character, reflecting both his contradictions and the power of his convictions. As *Paradise Lost* and *Paradise Regained* demonstrate, Milton did not shy away from dangerous, even heterodox ideas. An excoriating critic of institutional religion, his arguments for the freedom of ideas reflect the sources of his powerful imagination, including the Bible, music, and popular culture. There is a great deal of Milton's self in the text as we see how he struggles with necessity and limitations of what should be contained as well as his belief that the dangerous is essential to human flourishing.

Although the focus of this document collection is on political writings, the biographical information yielded by these texts opens up the world in which the sources were written, revealing their authors' complex relationships to ideas, beliefs, and events. The search for information about the self in early modern writings is not limited to the specifically biographical sources, but through careful examination of a wide body of sources.

Notes

1 Some recent work of early modern biography include Klaus-Dieter Beims, "On the Limits of an Early-Modern Biography", *Daphnis* 46 (2018): 346–426; David Farr, *Oliver Cromwell's Kin, 1643–1726: The Private and Public Worlds of the English Revolution and Restoration* (New York: Routledge, 2024); Camilla Russell, *Being a Jesuit in Renaissance Italy: Biographical Writing in the Early Global Age* (Cambridge, MA: Harvard University Press, 2022); Andrea Walkden, *Private Lives Made Public: The Invention of Biography in Early Modern England* (Pittsburgh, PA: Duquesne University Press, 2016).
2 Katherine MacDonald, *Biography in Early Modern France, 1540–1630: Forms and Functions* (London: Legenda, 2007).
3 Ronald Bedford, *Early Modern English Lives: Autobiography and Self-Representation, 1500–1660* (Burlington: Ashgate, 2007).
4 Bruce Gordon, *Calvin* (New Haven, CT: Yale University Press, 2009).
5 Michael Ullyot, *The Rhetoric of Exemplarity in Early Modern England* (Oxford: Oxford University Press, 2022).
6 Jenni Kuuliala, Rose-Marie Peake, and Päivi Räisänen-Schröder, eds., *Lived Religion and Everyday Life in Early Modern Hagiographic Material* (Oxford: Oxford University Press, 2015).
7 Austra Reinis, *Reforming the Art of Dying: The Ars Moriendi in the German Reformation (1519–1528)* (Burlington: Ashgate, 2007).
8 Miriam Nandi, *Reading the Early Modern English Diary* (Cham: Palgrave Macmillan, 2021).
9 Udo Thiel, *The Early Modern Subject: Self-Consciousness and Personal Identity from Descartes to Hume* (Oxford: Oxford University Press, 2011); Alexandra Shephard, *Accounting for Oneself: Worth, Status, and the Social Order in Early Modern England* (Oxford: Oxford University Press, 2015).

22 *Bruce Gordon*

10 Tom Scott, *Thomas Müntzer: Theology and Revolution in the German Reformation* (Basingstoke: Macmillan, 1989).
11 Peter Marshall, *Heretics and Believers: A History of the English Reformation* (New Haven, CT: Yale University Press, 2017).
12 Jane Dawson, *John Knox* (New Haven, CT: Yale University Press, 2015).
13 Eva LaPlante, *American Jezebel: The Uncommon Life of Anne Hutchinson, The Woman Who Defied the Puritans* (New York: Harper Collins, 2004).
14 Hans R. Guggisberg, *Sebastian Castellio, 1515–1563: Humanist and Defender of Religious Toleration in a Confessional Age*, trans. Bruce Gordon (Burlington: Ashgate, 2003).
15 Roland H. Bainton, *Hunted Heretic: The Life and Death of Michael Servetus, 1511–1553* (Boston, MA: Beacon Press, 1953).
16 Nicholas McDowell, *Poet of Revolution: The Making of John Milton* (Princeton, NJ: Princeton University Press, 2020).

3 Natural Law and Divine Law

Sarah Mortimer

Protestant political thought was built upon the foundations provided by the Reformers' account of natural law. The early Reformers emphasised the divine origins of natural law, engraved upon the human mind by God himself, and they appealed to natural law to provide the conceptual and theological underpinnings for magistracy, morality, and human social life. Soon, however, this account was challenged by Christians who began to separate more clearly the laws of nature and the laws of God, a position that gained considerable momentum in the seventeenth century. The definition of natural and divine laws, and their relationship to each other, became some of the most crucial and contested issues as Protestant political thought developed.[1]

Law and the Magistrate

The first systematic discussion of natural law was offered by **Philip Melanchthon** in his *Loci Communes* (1521). Here, he explained that 'natural law is a judgment common to all and suited to the formation of morals', pointing to St Paul's words in the Letter to the Romans (2:14–15) as evidence that the law was inscribed upon the minds of human beings. For Melanchthon, the law of nature commanded all the duties of morality and set out all our obligations to our fellow humans – it bound Christians and non-Christians alike, and the content of law was not in any way altered by the teaching of Christ. This commitment to the universality and the binding force of natural law was then taken up by other writers, for example, **John Ponet**, one of those Protestants who fled England when the Catholic queen Mary ascended the throne. Like Melanchthon, he appealed to Romans 2:14–15 to demonstrate that natural law was 'common to all' and 'grafted in the hearts of men'. Similarly, the Genevan Reformer **John Calvin** insisted in his *Institutes of Christian Religion* (1536) that the natural law was accessible to all and that its principles were those of true Christian charity.

It was important to the Reformers that natural law did not simply concern relationships between human beings but that it also included provision for the true worship of God. Again, Melanchthon used the Letter to the Romans to make this point, writing that 'We have taken the first law about

DOI: 10.4324/9781003247531-4

worshipping God from Romans 1, where Paul unmistakably counts it among natural laws'. This theme was developed by others, including the Genevan pastor and theologian **Theodore Beza**, for whom it was axiomatic that 'the chief end of human society is for God to be honoured by humans as he ought to be'. For Beza, the natural law that underpinned human society also imposed religious obligations upon those societies – there could be no purely secular human community.[2]

Although these Protestants believed that natural law was given by God directly, they held that humans' knowledge of the law had been damaged by the Fall. God had, however, provided his people with scripture and particularly with the Ten Commandments (or Decalogue), widely seen as a summary of the law of nature. In his commentary on the *Heidelberg Catechism* (c.1570), **Zacharias Ursinus** set this out clearly, explaining that the Decalogue was 'the renewal and re-enforcing of the natural law', necessary as a result of sin and of the corruption of human nature in its fallen state. In this way, Ursinus could show that the moral principles of natural law were also commanded in scripture, and thus underline that the law of nature was the standard for human life given by God and to which all human beings were obliged. Of course, no one could fulfil the duties of the law of nature, given that humans were fallen and sinful, but Protestants looked to the Gospel rather than the law for forgiveness and salvation.

In his commentary, Ursinus was keen to point out that natural law was not the only law that God had given to human beings, however. Like most of his contemporaries, he held that the scriptures contained many laws given by God to the people of Israel, which had since been abolished with the coming of Christ. On the whole, the Reformers distinguished natural law, whose moral principles held for all people, from ceremonial and judicial laws, given specifically to the people of Israel to regulate their religious and civil life. Ceremonial laws, the rites and rituals of Jewish religious practice, were seen as no longer binding; indeed, the Reformers insisted that the liberty of Christ meant the abolition of these laws. The status of the judicial laws of the Old Testament was less straightforward, for while Christian societies could dispense with ceremonial laws, they still needed laws to govern relationships between people and to ensure that those who violated these laws would be punished. Mainstream Protestant theologians tended to argue that while the specific mandates of the Old Testament law need not be adopted, the underlying moral principles of these laws were still valid, for these principles were themselves part of the natural law.

This early Protestant account of natural and divine laws then helped to shape the Reformers' approaches to the duties and legitimacy of magistrates. The basic contours of the Protestant argument were laid down by Melanchthon in the early 1520s, but it became especially important to defend Christian magistracy in the wake of the **German Peasants' War** (1524–1525), when human hierarchies were challenged in the name of Christian liberty.

On Melanchthon's reading, human authority was grounded in the natural and divine laws, and it included the ability to shape laws and constitutions according to the laws given by God and nature. Indeed, Melanchthon was keen to emphasise that a 'good man will fashion civil constitutions according to a just and good rule, that is, with both divine and natural laws'. It was not necessary that these laws replicate the laws of Moses or the Old Testament, but only that they reflect the same core principles of morality and religion. Where people violated these laws, then the magistrate must take action to punish them, for the ruler was, as Beza explained, 'established as the guard and governor' of human societies. Like many Protestants, Beza saw the authority of human rulers as anchored in a divinely given natural law, affirmed in the scripture in passages like the famous opening words of Romans 13: 'obey the powers that be'.

Natural Law and Resistance Theory

If the initial impetus for discussing natural law came from the need to uphold magisterial authority, soon similar ideas were also being used to advocate resistance to powers seen as tyrannical or idolatrous. Because natural law offered a standard by which magistrates could be judged, those who violated this law were seen as illegitimate and resistance to them could be cast as a Christian duty. Furthermore, because for Protestants the natural law demanded the true worship of God, any attempt to prescribe 'idolatrous' practices would be seen as unlawful and impermissible. Some writers, such as the Scottish minister **John Knox**, developed radical theories of resistance demanding that such unnatural rulers must be deposed. Knox was particularly exercised by the regimes of Mary of Guise in Scotland and Mary I in England, where Catholicism and female rule went hand in hand. In his view, these governments were affronts to all laws, divine and natural – not only because they were imposing idolatry but also because they were headed by queens and for women to hold authority over men was contrary to all natural and divine laws. Others, such as the author of the **Vindiciae Contra Tyrannos** (1579), appealed to natural and divine laws, refracted through the lens provided by Roman law principles and classical authors, to justify resistance.

By invoking a legal standard that was natural and divine, rather than specific to any particular country or people, Protestants could justify intervention in the lands of others, across national borders. They were well aware that their cause was fragile, and to withstand Catholic opposition, it was necessary to create alliances and to encourage people to help their co-religionists elsewhere in Europe. A particularly forceful and clear statement of this position was offered in the Fourth Question of the *Vindiciae*, written to drum up European support for the French Huguenots; here, the author argued that princes had a duty to prevent tyranny wherever it may be found – to fail to help fellow Christians was, it was claimed, a grave sin.[3]

26   Sarah Mortimer

Not everyone was supportive of this position, however, and some Christians were sceptical of this alliance between natural and divine laws – particularly as it was used to justify warfare and resistance. Many Anabaptist, Mennonite, and Socinian Christians believed that to follow Jesus's teaching, it was necessary to avoid warfare and violence, and even to eschew participation in the structures of earthly government, which were tainted by their association with human sin. They pointed to Jesus's words, especially in the Sermon on the Mount, as evidence that he called his followers to a way of life more excellent than natural human morality. Perhaps the most articulate proponent of this position was the Italian anti-Trinitarian **Faustus Socinus**, who challenged the Protestant insistence on the unity of divine and natural laws on the grounds that Christ had revealed new and more stringent laws for his followers. Socinus defended a pacifist position and counselled against involvement in the murky world of politics. In a similar way, the Mennonites explained in their *Confession of Faith* (c.1610) that they could not engage in magistracy as so much of what it entailed contravened the laws of Christ.

From the late sixteenth century, Protestants found themselves exploring the relationship between natural and divine laws with real urgency. Given this scriptural critique of the legitimacy of magistracy and of warfare and resistance, many Protestant leaders were concerned to show that the fundamental demands of natural law and Christianity were not in conflict, and that the natural law principles that underpinned human social life had not been altered or undermined by Christ's teaching. But the radical potential of natural law was also recognised, and some Protestant rulers began to portray themselves as ruling by divine right – most obviously **James VI and I**, who used scriptural and natural law arguments in the service of this claim.

Natural Law between the Nations

At this time, Protestants also began to consider the implications of natural law in the international sphere. They could draw upon generations of Catholic reflection, for the Spanish conquests in the Americas had stimulated intense discussion about the rights and status of non-Christians and the duties and obligations owed under natural law. Though some Protestant writers like the lawyer Sir **Edward Coke** were dismissive of non-Christians or 'infidels', claiming that their laws were necessarily invalid, others began to develop a more nuanced approach. Often, it was scholars writing about just war theory who began to consider natural law more systematically, and to draw upon classical and Catholic writing in order to do so.

The Italian Protestant **Alberico Gentili** discussed the laws of war in lectures given at Oxford in the 1580s and in a treatise on the same subject published in 1598. Gentili saw natural law as crucial to his argument, but he distinguished this law, which regulated human interactions, from religion or divine law, which concerned God and humans. He acknowledged that all societies needed some kind of religious belief, but he denied that the kind of religion practised could be a cause for intervention or warfare. His was in some ways quite a sharply Protestant argument, because it denied the Catholic Church any grounds on which to intervene in the civil or secular sphere. But it also challenged the widespread Protestant desire to hold natural and divine laws together.

Protestant discussion of natural law and warfare was accelerated by the outbreak of what became known as the **Thirty Years' War**, and in this context, the Dutch scholar **Hugo Grotius** offered one of the most ambitious Protestant accounts of natural and international laws, *Of the Rights of War and Peace* (1625). At the heart of his theory was a separation between the natural law that flowed from human sociability, and the positive law whose source was the will of a lawgiver, be they human or divine. For Grotius, crucially, much of the teaching of Jesus had to be seen as divine positive law; it did not contravene natural law, but it was not identical to it, and the human obligation to obey and to uphold the natural law did not mean enforcing Christianity. Grotius insisted on what he acknowledged to be a highly unusual position: that 'in that most holy Law [of Christ] a greater Sanctity is enjoined us, than the meer Law of Nature in itself requires'. In this way, Grotius sought to limit the grounds for war on the basis of religion or confession, while also providing some standards for the conduct of war, which could be traced back to the demands of natural sociability. Grotius's account of natural law would prove particularly influential in the Protestant world and was widely read and discussed at the universities.

Natural Law and National Churches

Although, as we have seen, early Reformers like Melanchthon believed civil rulers had a duty to promote the glory of God, by the seventeenth century many Protestants had begun to argue instead that human magistrates must limit themselves to preserving earthly peace and stability. For some, notably the Puritans, this led to an insistence on the purity and independence of the church, and an unwillingness to obey what they saw as the 'Popish' rules of the Church of England. Others began instead to develop theories of toleration, often adopting elements of Grotius' arguments about the difference between natural law and Christianity. The Socinian **Johan Crell**, for example, claimed that because civil society was founded on the natural law principle of keeping covenants rather than upon shared religious belief, religious diversity would not undermine political stability. Indeed, he argued that commonwealths would be stronger if they allowed people freedom of religion. A similar distinction between the civil and Christian spheres underlay the arguments for toleration generated by the Dutch Remonstrants and, later, by **John Locke**.

Meanwhile, those who defended the power of the magistrate over religion began to consider in more detail the implications for their position of new ideas about natural law. One of the most subtle and sophisticated accounts came from the English theologian **Richard Hooker,** whose conception of the relationship between divine and natural law allowed him to explain and defend the Royal Supremacy. Hooker argued that God gave humans many different kinds of laws, some of which were known through scripture and others through reason, and some of which directed people to spiritual ends and others to natural or temporal ends. For him, this was a way of defending rules whose sources were reason and nature rather than scripture, particularly in the face of the Puritan challenge. But it also allowed him to argue that in a Christian kingdom such as England, the church and commonwealth could be both distinct and united. They were distinct insofar as the church's purpose was spiritual and the commonwealth's temporal, but they were made up of the same people and could share the same supreme head.[4]

Hooker's careful synthesis won him many English admirers, but even in England Protestants continued to debate how natural law and divine positive law or Christian ethics might or might not cohere. Many readers questioned just how natural law could oblige people in conscience, if its dictates were different from Christianity, and Grotius's work in particular helped to spark a wider debate about the duties and obligations of law. In Germany, the key figure was the Lutheran **Samuel Pufendorf,** but from Paris, the English exile **Thomas Hobbes** offered a striking contribution in his *Leviathan.* Hobbes was concerned to show the identity between natural law and the laws of God, at least within human commonwealths; while he acknowledged that God could give additional laws, he explained that these were only applicable to the kingdoms of God in the past (when God ruled the people of Israel) and in future (when Christ would rule as king). Hobbes's theory of natural law gave to the ruler great power over the church, although on natural law rather than spiritual grounds.

It was, however, in the Americas that some of the most heated arguments about toleration and the scope and limits of magisterial authority took place. For **Roger Williams,** persecution was a 'bloody tenent'; no civil magistrate had the right to interfere in matters of conscience or faith because their power was confined to temporal matters. In a truly Christian society, the state must allow religious freedom. On the contrary, men like **John Elliot** stood in the tradition of Melanchthon and Beza when they claimed that magistrates had responsibility for the religious as well as political affairs of their community. These different visions of the Christian commonwealth continued to clash even as the European presence in the so-called 'New World' grew greater and more powerful.

Conclusion

Into the late seventeenth century, Protestants continued to question how far the gospel and teaching of Christ might reflect the law of nature, and thus how compatible Christianity might be with political office, or even political life. For some, the answer was to be found from the scriptures, especially

Paul's Letter to the Romans, while others saw in the writing of their contemporaries new ways of analysing and addressing these issues. In the final texts of this collection, we see the contrasting positions of **George Fox** and **George Lawson;** whereas Fox called on Christians to step away from the sinful practices of a fallen world, Lawson saw it as the magistrate's duty to ensure the practice of true faith. This disagreement among Protestants remained lively, shaping their political and ecclesiological thinking for centuries to come.

Notes

1 These themes are developed further in Sarah Mortimer, *Reformation, Resistance, and Reason of State: the Oxford History of Political Thought 1517–1625* (Oxford: Oxford University Press, 2021).
2 Odile Panetta, "Heresy and Authority in the Thought of Théodore de Bèze", *Renaissance and Reformation* 45 (2022): 33–72.
3 *Vindiciae, Contra Tyrannos: Or, Concerning the Legitimate Power of a Prince over the People, and of the People over a Prince.* edited by G. Garnett (Cambridge: Cambridge University Press, 1994).
4 Peter Lake, *Anglicans and Puritans? Presbyterianism and English Conformist Thought from Whitgift to Hooker* (Boston: Unwin Hyman, 1988).

4 Resistance and Rebellion

Karie Schultz

In the wake of the sixteenth-century Reformation, Protestant intellectuals across Europe advanced new ideas about political power to complement their attempts at religious reform. Roman Catholics had regarded the temporal world as a place where human beings exercised their rationality and participated in civic life, with the distinct aim of attaining human flourishing (in the Aristotelian sense of *eudaimonia*). To this end, the church existed as an independent institution governed by the Pope, not by civil rulers. In contrast, Protestants believed that societies existed to honour and glorify God, and for this reason often sought closer cooperation between civil and ecclesiastical authorities.[1] Civil magistrates played an essential role in advancing the godly commonwealth by upholding both tables of the Decalogue, or the Ten Commandments. The first table included commandments from divine law that regulated worship, while the second table included commandments from natural law that governed human relationships, such as injunctions against adultery, theft, and murder. The civil magistrate's duty was thus twofold: preserving temporal peace and punishing spiritual crimes (such as heresy and blasphemy) to maintain religious orthodoxy across society.

The distinctly Protestant desire to attain a 'godly commonwealth' could only be achieved if civil magistrates fulfilled their duties and defended the true religion across their lands. Yet, the religious wars that raged across Europe and the British Isles during the sixteenth and seventeenth centuries demonstrated that this did not always happen, especially in multi-confessional states where rulers remained hostile to reform. The violence and destruction wrought by the **French Wars of Religion** (1562–1598), the **Dutch Revolt** (1566/1568–1648), the **Thirty Years' War** (1618–1648), and the **British Civil Wars** (1639–1651) forced Protestants to reconsider how subjects should react to rulers who threatened their lives, liberties, or faith. But the ideas that Protestants developed about how best to respond to tyrannical or idolatrous rulers were far from static. The increasing intensity of violence during the early modern period prompted some to change their minds on the legitimacy of resistance, or to develop increasingly radical ideas.

As a result, a diverse body of Protestant thought about resistance and rebellion emerged. Some individuals legitimised taking up arms against

DOI: 10.4324/9781003247531-5

idolatrous rulers on the basis of divine law, arguing that God commanded Christians to defend the true religion, even by force. Others justified resistance on legal-constitutional grounds, claiming that subjects could lawfully rise against a magistrate who ruled tyrannically in opposition to the laws of the land. In contrast, other Protestants rejected resistance entirely, claiming that taking up arms constituted a seditious rebellion against God's anointed rulers or that it contravened biblical commands for pacifism. They thus advocated a policy of total non-resistance or obedience instead. This introductory chapter examines the central themes that emerged within these various intellectual traditions as early modern Protestants either justified armed resistance as a legitimate action or condemned it as an unlawful rebellion.

Divine Right, Passive Disobedience, and Non-resistance

First and foremost, some Protestants argued that subjects must never resist their magistrates, regardless of how they governed, since God directly appointed all rulers and bestowed absolute power upon them. Resistance to any magistrate (even a wicked, ungodly, or tyrannical one) thus constituted rebellion against God. This perspective depended, in large part, upon the divine right theory of kingship.[2] According to this theory, Romans 13:1–2 proved that God ordained all civil magistrates and commanded Christians only to obedience.[3] If subjects resisted their rulers for any reason, they challenged the hand of God. King **James VI and I** (1566–1625) was a leading proponent of this theory. He defended divine right kingship in multiple works on politics, but most famously in *The Trew Law of Free Monarchies* (1598). The Gunpowder Plot (1605), a Roman Catholic assassination attempt, reinvigorated his commitment to absolute monarchical power. In his 1609 speech, he maintained that kings were synonymous with gods and that they exercised divine power on earth. Kings held unchallengeable authority over their subjects and answered to God alone for their actions. It could therefore never be lawful for subjects to challenge or resist political authorities.

For Protestants who believed in such absolute political power, subjects could respond to tyranny only through 'passive disobedience'. This meant that if a civil magistrate issued a commandment contrary to natural or divine law, subjects must refuse to follow it since their duty to obey God surpassed their duty to obey temporal authorities. However, they must also bear all punishments that resulted from this refusal. Since God permitted wicked rulers as a punishment for sin, subjects should respond with prayers, tears, and repentance, but never with the force of arms. The Archbishop of Canterbury, **Thomas Cranmer** (1489–1556), exemplified this approach in his 1549 notes on rebellion. He argued that God directly appointed all magistrates and entrusted them (not the people) with the power of the civil sword. As a result, God commanded Christians to obey their magistrates in all worldly matters, for these had no bearing upon salvation. Lest subjects bring about the greater scourge of civil war and unrest, subjects should obey in all instances rather than take up arms.

32 Karie Schultz

Other Protestant intellectuals articulated a doctrine of non-resistance on different grounds. For example, the century of violent religious conflict across Europe prompted **Thomas Hobbes** (1588–1679) to offer a modified view of God's commandment to obedience, one that diminished the preeminent role of the 'godly commonwealth'. Wearied by the **Wars of the Three Kingdoms** (1639–1653) – ones that resulted in large part from tensions between Protestants within the British Isles – Hobbes justified obedience to Christian and infidel magistrates alike. In the third part of *Leviathan* (1651), he argued that all civil magistrates, whether Christian or unchristian, constituted legitimate rulers to whom subjects owed unconditional obedience. He accordingly decreased the importance of the true religion by arguing that even if a king led his subjects astray in religious matters, he did not threaten their salvation. They therefore had no reason to disobey given that their salvation was not at stake. Hobbes thus rejected resistance on religious grounds and removed any potential conflict between God's commands and those of a civil ruler, a conflict that had provoked the destructive civil wars of the 1640s.

Other Protestant groups emerged during the radical Reformation of the sixteenth century and derived theories of non-resistance based upon their spirituality and scriptural injunctions against violence. For instance, the Anabaptists (and especially Mennonites) rejected all resistance to political authorities, even unjust or tyrannical ones, on the grounds that scripture prohibited Christians from taking up arms. Only non-violent methods could be used to achieve justice, for the sword did not pertain to the perfection of Christ. By belonging to a group of the 'elect' on earth, Christians must bear any consequences for their non-resistance. These might include persecution, exile, or even death. Other Protestant groups that appeared in the seventeenth century, such as the Quakers, similarly embraced pacifism and viewed any violence against authorities as unbiblical rebellion. Significant diversity therefore existed in the arguments that early modern Protestants used to reject resistance, such as the divine right theory of kingship, the need to eradicate the evils of religious warfare, or biblical commandments for pacifism.

Idolatry and the True Religion

In contrast, widespread religious persecution and political violence prompted other Protestants to justify armed resistance through appeals to divine and natural laws. Although some Reformers believed that scripture prohibited Christians from taking up arms, others conversely claimed that armed conflict might be necessary to enact God's will on earth. One central component of Protestant resistance theory comprised the divinely mandated duty to root out idolatry. In an ideal godly commonwealth, civil magistrates would defend and advance the true religion themselves by punishing blasphemy and heresy. As Article 36 of the **Belgic Confession** (1561) stated, magistrates must 'remove and prevent all idolatry and false worship' while ensuring the preaching of the gospel. However, if they failed to do so (or if they turned towards the active persecution of Protestants), this duty devolved to their Christian subjects. The importance of eradicating idolatry as a justification for resistance was especially prominent during the sixteenth century, a time when Roman Catholic rulers frequently resisted the Protestant Reformation of their lands. Under these conditions, some Protestants argued that God commanded them to resist rulers who forced idolatry or 'popery' upon their subjects.

During the reign of Catholic Queen Mary I (1516–1558), a group of English Protestants known as the 'Marian exiles' fled to mainland Europe where they advanced revolutionary legitimisations of resistance in terms of idolatry.[4] This group included **John Ponet** (c.1514–1556) and **Christopher Goodman** (c.1521–1603), in addition to the Scottish Reformer **John Knox** (c.1514–1572) who fled to Geneva during the reign of Catholic Mary, Queen of Scots (1542–1587). These authors broadly agreed that Christian subjects should lawfully resist their superiors to extirpate idolatry and establish the true religion. According to Ponet, civil magistrates ruled for their subjects' temporal and spiritual good, while God permitted subjects to redress the vices of a ruler who failed to do so. As the Old Testament demonstrated, God's people might execute divine judgement upon wicked rulers. The Bible thus provided precedents for the whole commonwealth to depose an ungodly magistrate. Likewise, Goodman argued that magistrates must defend God's glory and protect the laws of the land. If they failed, subjects must resist to extirpate idolatry and advance the glory of God. Knox also articulated ideas about political power to support the Protestant Reformation of Scotland. He maintained that the nobility (in particular) should advance Protestantism against the wishes of their Catholic monarch, Mary, Queen of Scots. Their zeal for church reform in the British Isles, coupled with their experience of exile and persecution, thus prompted the Marian exiles to defend resistance to monarchs using the language of idolatry.

Covenants and the Origins of Political Power

While some Protestants justified resistance as a divinely mandated duty to defend the true religion (even with violent force), others turned towards legal-constitutional ideas about a covenant between the ruler, subjects, and God as the standard for good rule.[5] By arguing that rulers had a contractual relationship with their subjects, these individuals asserted that the people could recall the political power that they originally held. For example, the Scottish historian and civic humanist **George Buchanan** (c.1506–1582) justified resistance in terms of a covenant between the king and subjects. He is most well known for *De jure regni apud Scotos* (1579), a treatise in which he reflected on Aristotelian ideas about political authority and civil government. But in his earlier exposition of Romans 13 (1567), he also used scripture to argue that God ordained the 'office' of magistracy to eradicate evil and preserve temporal peace. Political power derived from God in a general sense, but the people elected their individual rulers. Contrary to the divine right theory of kingship, God did not grant magistrates licence to rule arbitrarily. If they did, subjects could recall their original power and replace a tyrannical ruler with a just one.

Furthermore, if the people elected their rulers, they could restrict the authority of these magistrates through covenantal obligations imposed at the coronation. Ideas about a binding covenant between the king, subjects, and God instituted through the coronation oath appeared in the *Vindiciae Contra Tyrannos* (1579). This famous resistance tract appeared following the St. Bartholomew's Day Massacre (1572), an episode of Catholic mob violence against the French Huguenots in Paris. According to this treatise, as God's delegates on earth, princes formed a covenant with their subjects similar to the contract between a lord and a vassal. This covenant came into being through the coronation oath and resulted in reciprocal obligations between the king and his subjects. The people swore to worship God properly by faithfully obeying the prince, while the prince promised to serve God above all else and rule for the good of his subjects. If he broke the terms of this covenant, either by ruling idolatrously or by threatening his subjects' lives and liberties, God commanded subjects to resist and elect a new king who would better fulfil his duties. Kings who broke the terms of this covenant could therefore be deprived of power and replaced by the people, even through the force of arms.

Ideas about the covenantal relationship between the king and subjects called into question the origins of political power. Whereas divine right theorists maintained that God directly appointed rulers, many resistance theorists argued that the people themselves possessed the power of election. Although God retained ultimate authority to make and unmake kings, humans mediated this power. One example of this perspective appeared in the work of **Johannes Althusius** (c. 1557–1638), a German Calvinist jurist. Responding to the religious conflicts of the sixteenth century and the rise of absolutist monarchies throughout Europe, Althusius promoted a theory of federalism that gave greater authority to the people or the majority in the commonwealth (rather than to their rulers). In *Politica* (1604), he advanced a symbiotic theory of politics to explain how humans came to live peacefully in different levels of society. He argued that the commonwealth – the highest level of political association – comprised smaller social units that voluntarily combined in pursuit of the common good. The administrators of the commonwealth included the supreme magistrate and the ephors (inferior rulers who checked the power of their superior). Althusius opposed tyranny precisely because it negated the benefits that humans hoped to attain by entering different types of association. Since tyranny equated to a corruption of political power, ephors could remove a supreme magistrate who failed to exercise their office appropriately. While Althusius's symbiotic theory laid foundations for developments in federalist political thought, it also informed early modern theories of resistance through its stipulation that magistrates derived their authority from (and could thus be held accountable to) the people.

Althusius' theory addressed another core theme within Protestant resistance theories: the authority of 'inferior' or 'lesser' magistrates. Inferior magistrates were rulers who represented the people but who were below the supreme magistrate in power, such as the nobility or members of Parliament. A broad consensus existed among Protestant resistance theorists that only inferior magistrates (not individual subjects) could resist superiors. Early modern Protestants tended to reject an individual right to resistance as anarchical and destabilising. Although the idea of 'inferior magistrates' has been regarded as a distinctly Reformed concept established by **John Calvin** in Book IV, Chapter 20 of the *Institutes of the Christian Religion* (1536), Lutherans also expounded upon this category. Luther himself had been ambiguous in his support for resistance, initially opposing it but seeming to favour its legitimacy later in his life. However, the clearest articulation of Lutheran resistance theory appeared in 1550 when nine **Magdeburg Pastors** issued a statement of faith in response to the Augsburg Interim (1548), an imperial decree issued by Charles V, Holy Roman Emperor, that imposed reconciliation between Roman Catholics and German Protestants. The Magdeburg Pastors argued that if a supreme magistrate forced subjects into idolatry, lower magistrates had a duty to resist and preserve true worship. While a more populist right of resistance occasionally appeared in Protestant thought, such as in Buchanan's writings, this was not a standard position for most early modern Protestants.[6] Instead, the perspective that Calvin, the Magdeburg pastors, and Althusius took regarding the authority of inferior magistrates (rather than individual subjects) was most prevalent.

Althusius's ideas about origins of authority and the role of inferior magistrates also informed the work of **Samuel Rutherford** (c.1600–1661), a Reformed theologian and Scottish Covenanter. In 1644, Rutherford authored *Lex, Rex; or, the Law and the Prince* to defend the Scots' resistance to King Charles I in the Wars of the Three Kingdoms.[7] Echoing Buchanan, Rutherford argued that God ordained only the 'office' of magistracy. The people mediated God's power when they elected specific rulers using Old Testament criteria for good kings. Once the people elected their king, he took the coronation oath and entered a threefold covenant with his subjects and swore to rule for their temporal good and defend the true religion. As Rutherford argued, Charles broke this covenant when he ruled arbitrarily and forced idolatrous reforms upon the Scottish church, such as the *Book of Common Prayer*. As a result, God permitted inferior magistrates (in this case, the parliamentary estates) to resist his innovations with violence. Crucially, Rutherford claimed that the Scots' resistance constituted a defensive, not offensive, act. He asserted that Charles threatened his subjects' lives by raising an army against them during the Bishops' Wars (1639–1640). As a result, natural law permitted humans to defend their own lives by repelling force with force. The Scots' resistance therefore constituted an act of self-defence, one intended to protect their lives and liberties after the king broke the covenant with his people.

36 *Karie Schultz*

Conclusion

When faced with intensifying religious and political violence throughout the sixteenth and seventeenth centuries, Protestants throughout mainland Europe and the British Isles developed a diverse body of ideas about resistance and rebellion. On the one hand, many Reformers combined arguments from scripture and natural law to justify taking up arms against an idolatrous or tyrannical ruler. Some capitalised upon the concept of idolatry, arguing that God commanded Christians to militantly defend the true religion. Others turned towards legal-constitutional arguments, maintaining that subjects elected their magistrates and that these magistrates had a contractual obligation to uphold God's word and the laws of the land. Such assertions about the people's power to elect magistrates and hold them accountable thus laid foundations for later developments in constitutionalism. On the other hand, some Protestants viewed resistance as a rebellious, seditious, and treasonous act. They rejected resistance by reiterating the divine right of kingship or appealing to scriptural precedents for pacifism. They tended to uphold God's direct sovereignty over the commonwealth, giving human beings little recourse against a tyrannical or idolatrous ruler beyond passive disobedience, prayers, and repentance. Regardless of the position that early modern Protestants took on the legitimacy of resistance, they ultimately ushered in significant new ways of thinking about the relationship between rulers and their subjects, ones that had important implications for the later emergence of political ideas underlying the modern state.

Notes

1 Ian Campbell and Floris Verhaart, "Introduction: Calvinism, Warfare, and the Politics of Duty", in *Protestant Politics Beyond Calvin: Reformed Theologians on War in the Sixteenth and Seventeenth Centuries* (Abingdon: Routledge, 2022), 2–20; Sarah Mortimer, *Reformation, Resistance and Reason of State (1517–1625)* (Oxford: Oxford University Press, 2021), 64.
2 Glenn Burgess, "The Divine Right of Kings Reconsidered", *English Historical Review* 107, no. 425 (1992): 837–861.
3 Romans 13:1–2 (KJV): 'Let every soul be subject unto the higher powers. For there is no power but of God: the powers that be are ordained of God. Whosoever therefore resisteth the power, resisteth the ordinance of God'.
4 Jane Dawson, "Revolutionary Conclusions: The Case of the Marian Exiles", *History of Political Thought* 11, no. 2 (1990): 257–272.
5 David Henreckson, *The Immortal Commonwealth: Covenant, Community, and Political Resistance in Early Reformed Thought* (Cambridge: Cambridge University Press, 2019).
6 John Coffey, "George Buchanan and the Scottish Covenanters", in *George Buchanan: Political Thought in Early Modern Britain and Europe*, ed. Caroline Erskine and Roger Mason (Farnham: Routledge, 2012), 189–203.
7 Karie Schultz, "Catholic Political Thought and Calvinist Ecclesiology in Samuel Rutherford's *Lex, Rex* (1644)", *Journal of British Studies* 61 (2022): 162–184.

5 The Use of the Sword
Violence, Empire, and Slavery

Matthew Rowley

Few aspects of early modern religious and political life were free from association with (lethal) force, coercion, or violence. Sometimes the use or threat of violence was overt; at other times, it was more subtle. The sword often defended orthodoxy, civil laws gained their force through the state's monopoly on violence, and slavery relied on daily acts of violation. Reformers expressed divergent attitudes towards warfare, peace, and non-violence in the first few decades after the Reformation, and more differences continued to emerge over time. For example, **Martin Luther** sanctified warfare, provided the proper authorities commanded it and did not ask the soldier to commit acts that clearly contradicted scripture. Early Anabaptists reached back to the days before Constantine baptised the Roman state, and they rejected Christian participation in government and prohibited the use of the sword. Other early Anabaptists in the German city of Münster thought weapons were essential to ushering in the kingdom of God. Reformed groups often sought greater power for the church in deciding when violence was righteous, even as many sought to separate those who fought with physical weapons from those who fought with spiritual weapons. Further, the proliferation of colonies and slavery intensified old debates about if and when force might be used against a non-European or non-Christian other.

As the Reformation progressed, many came to believe that religious difference was ineradicable and not for lack of trying to manufacture uniformity. The **Schmalkaldic War** (1546–1547) was followed by a recognition of Lutheran and Catholic regions in Germany. A series of **French religious wars** (1562–1598) eventually carved out a limited space for Protestants within Catholic France. The **Dutch revolt** (1568–1648) led to the establishment of a largely Protestant republic that afforded limited toleration for Catholics and other religious minorities. The **British Civil Wars** (1639–1651) saw Protestants and Catholics – and Protestants and Protestants – remake the British Isles at the cost of neighbour-stained steel.

Exploration and colonisation further widened the pool of 'religious others' that Protestants interacted with. Their relationship with far-flung peoples ranged from separation to cooperation to subjugation to expulsion, sometimes blending all four. The threat or experience of violence often drove

DOI: 10.4324/9781003247531-6

38 *Matthew Rowley*

Protestant refugees far from home. Viewing themselves as victims of injustice, they often came to perpetrate injustice against the Indigenous peoples they encountered.

Protestant ideas about violence were never monolithic, be they related to persecution, warfare, slavery, or colonisation. The costs of armed conflict are often unimaginably high, even for wars considered just, defensive, restrained, or necessary. A tremendous burden often falls on relatively powerless people, be they the poor soldiers, women, or children. Wars can affect entire communities as violence impacts the relationships between majorities and minorities, and leads to the disintegration of local churches and the destruction of the natural environment. Then as now, after the dust of war settles, the effects of war can linger. As such, debates over the legitimacy of war carry a particular significance. Protestants approached the biblical text with different hopes, fears, and historical circumstances that informed the questions they asked, the methods of exegesis they employed, and the parts of scripture they identified as foundational for Christian society. This introduction offers a few vignettes illustrating Protestant beliefs and practices regarding war, peace, non-violence, and slavery.

Martin Luther and Magistrate-Directed Warfare

When Martin Luther (1483–1546) objected to the sale of indulgences in 1517, he could not have imagined the extent to which his ideas would become intertwined with foreign power struggles. Theological disagreements were quickly enfolded into conflicts between the Holy Roman Emperor, Charles V (r.1519–1556), and Pope Leo X (r.1513–1521). Some German territorial princes sympathised with Luther's call for reform and found his arguments useful when asserting religious and political autonomy from the Holy Roman Emperor and the Pope. Armed conflict with non-Christian powers also shaped the early Reformation. Luther's challenge emerged in the context of the shrinking of Christendom on its eastern border. The ancient Byzantine Empire, home to the Eastern Orthodox Church, dissolved after the fall of Constantinople in 1453, and by 1517, the Ottoman Empire pressed deeper into Roman Catholic Europe. A disgruntled Augustinian friar was initially considered of minor concern when compared to the military advances of Suleiman the Magnificent (r.1520–1566).

Although Luther wrote many works of varying lengths on warfare, his writings were occasional and prompted by the moment's needs. He wrote his most notable works on the subject as responses to what he saw as a misapplication of his theology. Luther had a penchant for writing things that were difficult to understand and even harder to apply. For example, in *The Freedom of a Christian* (1520), Martin Luther put forward two theses: 'A Christian is a perfectly free lord of all, subject to none. A Christian is a perfectly dutiful servant of all, subject to all'. He packed radical equality and submission into one punchy couplet. Luther envisioned spiritual equality

The Use of the Sword: Violence, Empire, and Slavery   39

and submission; however, many German serfs and peasants translated his ideas about equality into the social sphere. Although Luther was sympathetic to the plight of the peasants, after the lower classes took up arms against what he saw as God-ordained authority, Luther argued for their ruthless suppression. Many fighting in the **German Peasants' War** (1524–1525) found inspiration in Luther's ideas; however, he recoiled at their social agenda and emphasised the role of authorities in promoting, defining, and defending orthodoxy and public order.

For Luther, the individual Christian soldier was not authorised to kill simply because they were righteous and their enemies were ungodly, nor was their killing itself a meritorious act that brought them closer to God. However, Luther argued that the obedience involved in following orders and that trusting God in battle was a praiseworthy act of worship. Warfare might bring one closer to God, because fighting required obedience to God-ordained authority and dependence on God. Further, because warfare jeopardised temporal wellbeing and focused thoughts on eternal wellbeing, the crucible of war might spur genuine faith. However, divine wrath principally fell on the magistrate if they commanded participation in an unjust cause. In most cases, individual soldiers were not in the position to decide on matters of foreign affairs, and thus, their trust in their sovereign would be taken by God as an act of faith. If, however, a superior commanded what was manifestly unjust, the Christian soldier could disobey and accept judgement from man and reward from God. Armed resistance was not an option for the individual soldier, although Luther later embraced resistance by lesser magistrates on legal rather than biblical grounds.

Pacifist and Violent Anabaptists

Early modern warfare often sat awkwardly with the violence that was patiently endured by Christ, as well as the ethics of the Sermon on the Mount (Matt. 5–7). Moreover, the stories of the early church narrate an acceptance of persecution, a disinterest in political power, and the glorification of martyrdom. Although the New Testament employed the language of spiritual warfare, the writers did so before the first Christians used physical force to kill or developed sophisticated theories that justified participation in combat. Reformers within the Catholic Church sought to restore aspects of belief and practice from antiquity, peeling away what they saw as layers of corruption that accumulated over the centuries. Whereas many Catholics and Protestants viewed Constantine's conversion as an example of the triumph of the Gospel, Anabaptists viewed this merging of church and state as another corruption that led Christians from the purity and simplicity of the early church. Thus, these Anabaptists rejected any Christian involvement in wielding political power, especially if it involved lethal force.

The Schleitheim Articles (1527), formulated by **Michael Sattler** (c.1490–1527), challenged all Christian uses of the sword. Sattler, like many Anabaptists, believed that God ordained the civil magistrates to maintain order

40 *Matthew Rowley*

and execute justice on evildoers. Christians, however, belonged to a spiritual kingdom, and their allegiance to Christ meant that Christians could not hold office or employ physical force. Many Anabaptists argued for similar principles in greater detail, including **Hans Denck** (1527), **Balthasar Hubmaier** (1527), **Menno Simons** (after the mid-1530s), and **Peter Walpot** (1577). Other Protestants indirectly echoed similar claims, including the Italian anti-Trinitarian **Fausto Sozzini** (1581) and the leader of the Society of Friends (Quakers) **George Fox** (c.1660). Minor variations in beliefs often contribute to major differences in how individuals and communities act upon beliefs, as the twin trajectories of the Anabaptists illustrate. Some eschewed violence, and others embraced it. Whereas pacifist Anabaptists anchored their vision of government and attitude towards violence in the New Testament, violent Anabaptists drew greater inspiration from the portions of the Hebrew Bible related to governance and warfare. Pacific and violent Anabaptists shared similar beliefs, including an eschatological orientation, an impulse to reform Christian living, and a conviction that holiness required separation from the corrupt world – but disagreed over the use of the sword.

Under the conviction that Christ would return in the early 1530s, several Anabaptists endeavoured to reform society radically, first in the German city of Strassburg, then in the German city of Münster. At the **Münster commune** in 1533 and 1534, those claiming prophetic authority donned the mantle of biblical prophets and political leaders. They argued that the city would be the site of the long-anticipated New Jerusalem. They remodelled society and called for Anabaptists across Europe to come to the city that Jan van Leiden, the new King David, would rule over. The leaders turned to the Pentateuch for its legal code, expelled the ungodly, executed the recalcitrant, and instituted polygamy. Catholics and Lutherans each looked on with great alarm. They laid siege to the city, toppled the reign of prophets, and displayed the bodies of executed leaders in cages that still hang over from the cathedral of Münster to this day.

The debacle at Münster taught a powerful lesson: mixing prophecy, apocalypticism, and an emphasis on the internal leading of God with political aspirations was a potent mixture. For example, Luther denounced the **Zwickau prophets** in 1521. He was also critical of **Thomas Müntzer** (d.1525), who advocated the cause of the poor and oppressed. In 1524, Müntzer argued that godliness created the right to decide who deserved to live. He linked apocalypticism with a strong sense of the internal leading of God, coupling these convictions with the belief that God would fight supernaturally for peasants. Like the leaders of Münster commune, Thomas Müntzer was executed after a military defeat. Following Luther's caution, many Protestants have been suspicious of the destabilising nature of new prophetic utterances. Centuries after the Münster commune, Protestants continued to invoke this event as a cautionary tale. The ongoing fear of radical prophets partly explained why Massachusetts Bay expelled **Anne Hutchinson** in 1638 and why England violently suppressed the Fifth Monarchists in the late 1650s and early 1660s.

Empire and Slavery

Clergy often waded into discussions about the relationship between political powers, as when **John Calvin** argued in 1555 that God did not permit people to expand their territory through warfare unless they were first unjustly attacked. Modern theories of international law and the laws of war trace their origins to three theorists: Francisco de Vitoria (Spanish Catholic), **Alberico Gentili** (Italian Protestant in England), and **Hugo Grotius** (Dutch Protestant). They theorised about practices common to all or most peoples that might form part of the basis for international law. They also discussed what to do in response to grave injustices between peoples, how to conduct warfare between those of different faiths, and what one could do with a conquered population.

Theories about international relations and warfare emerged in the context of the shrinking of Europe due to the Ottoman threat and the expansion of Europe's power overseas. Vitoria developed his theories against the backdrop of Spanish expansion. Gentili did the same for England and Grotius for the Dutch and the French. All three, in various ways, tried to undermine colonial conquest for religious reasons, but they often justified warfare based on a right to international trade. Those involved firsthand in trading and colonising often made decisions without reference to academic theories. However, some had considered how colonisation might be both just and holy. Many Protestants argued that their colonies would be more humane than Spanish and Portuguese ones. However, they often ended at a similar destination: warfare, land dispossession and enslavement, and promises to 'civilise' and evangelise those under their 'paternal' care.

In the context of early modern Europe, the legality of one human owning another was often assumed – however, a critical theological difficulty related to whether Christians could enslave other Christians. The 1568 **Iwie Synod** in the Grand-Duchy of Poland-Lithuania might be 'the first substantive Christian debate on slavery', even as their discussion was not about race, but about the question whether one Christian could bind a theological sibling.[1] Their debate took place against the backdrop of centuries of Europeans being enslaved and sold south, often to peoples with darker skin. As Protestants gained more colonies, they held more humans and bondage and developed legal and theological rationales to justify what they were doing. Towards the end of the time period covered in this volume, slavery was increasingly written into law. Not only did the 1641 'Body of Liberties' produced by **Massachusetts Bay Colony** enshrine limited slavery, but also many others argued in its favour, even if they had some reservations.

Ministers played an important role in the embrace of slavery. For example, **Godfried Udemans** argued that slavery should benefit the enslaved by bringing them closer to Christ and 'civility', but foremost, that Christian masters ought to remember that they have a master in God. Other Dutch Reformed Protestants in **Brazil**, **South Africa**, and **New Netherland** argued

42 Matthew Rowley

similarly. Confessional statements like the one written by the **French Reformed churches** in 1637 gave slavery a theological grounding. Many Protestants wanted to enslave people and convert them, but these twin desires destabilised justifications for bondage. If enslaved persons converted to Christianity, they might argue that faith purchased their freedom. In 1652, **Doll Allen,** an enslaved girl in Bermuda, challenged the entire basis on which slavery rested when she argued that her faith had freed her. Allen's conversion complicated justifications for slavery that were based on religious differences. As the number of enslaved converts grew, slave status became increasingly justified in terms of racial – rather than religious – difference.[2]

Religious Wars in Europe

Protestants and Catholics regularly faced each other in war within Europe, first in the Swiss fields near Kappel. Some Swiss cantons remained Catholic, while others implemented reforms under the influence of **Huldreich Zwingli** and others. The execution of a reform-minded priest led Reformed cantons to take up arms, and Catholic forces met them on the battlefield. However, they managed to avert war. The **First Peace of Kappel** (1529) recognised the autonomy of the cantons and the right of majorities in each canton to decide on religious policy. The fragile peace at Kappel did not last, and Zwingli died in battle in 1531, but religious differences in Switzerland outlasted this war.

Germans also stumbled into the begrudging recognition of some religious differences, not because peace was ideal but because peace seemed a necessary practical solution to intractable differences. After the Schmalkaldic Wars (1546–1547), the **Peace of Augsburg** (1555) gave greater authority to princes to settle religious matters within their realm, provided those princes were Catholic or Lutheran. The peace was fragile for several reasons. First, since the Holy Roman Emperor remained Catholic, there was a delicate balance between the rights of Protestant princes and those of the emperor. Second, the conversion of princes, often from Catholic to Protestant, proved challenging to accept in practice, and some Catholics attempted to reclaim lands lost through conversion. Third, the toleration afforded at Augsburg was limited. Subjects were limited by the religion of their prince, and the Calvinists and other Protestant groups were not included in the terms of the agreement.

The tension between the rights of the emperor and the rights of local authorities erupted several times: most notably, the Dutch struggle for independence (the **Eighty Years' War,** 1568–1648) and the Bohemian revolt that sparked the **Thirty Years' War** (1618–1648). Both long and bloody wars ended in 1648 with the twin peace agreements signed in Münster and Osnabrück (known collectively as the **Peace of Westphalia** of 1648). This peace recognised the rights of the Reformed alongside Lutherans and Catholics, and some religious minorities within a realm were granted greater rights.

Although the peace tried to prevent religious differences from spilling into warfare, post-Westphalian Europe experienced continual warfare with ever-larger armies. Conflicts became increasingly global as European political struggles involved far-flung colonies in war.

Although Christians in the sixteenth and seventeenth centuries believed that peace was God's ideal, most came to justify warfare when they thought the cause was righteous and necessary. The inability to resolve religious differences through warfare contributed to the growth of de facto toleration. Many tolerationists pushed further, arguing that tolerance was required by scripture and necessary for genuine faith to flourish. Protestant tolerationists also theorised about the prevention of war. Most notably, in 1693 the Quaker, **William Penn**, proposed a parliament for the peace of Europe where disputes were settled in court rather than on the battlefield. Centuries later, Immanuel Kant made a similar argument in 1795 essay *On Perpetual Peace*.

Notes

1 Michael W. Bruening, *A Reformation Sourcebook: Documents from an Age of Debate* (New York: University of Toronto Press, 2017), 264–265.
2 Michael J. Jarvis, *Isle of Devils, Isle of Saints: An Atlantic History of Bermuda, 1609–1684* (Baltimore, MD: Johns Hopkins University Press, 2022), 1–17, 244–245.

6 Toleration, Coexistence, and the Place of 'The Other'

Marietta van der Tol

Early modern political imagination was profoundly influenced by religion. Early moderns inherited from the medieval church the central organising idea of the *corpus christianum,* symbolising the transcendental oneness of state, church, and society under Christendom. This entwinement had historically triggered tension between church and state about the appointment of senior clerical offices, known as the Investiture Controversy. During the Reformation, this oneness of state, church, and society came under increasing pressure of new ideas, as tensions exacerbated about the relationship between society and the authority of both cleric and crown. These ideas did not necessarily stem from a closer reading of scripture, rather, they reflected major changes in early modern Europe to which Christians of all sorts responded, using the cultural and religious repertoires that were available to them. The sources in this book show something of the breadth and depth of thinking of early Protestantism. A few Protestant thinkers produced systematic accounts of church and state, doctrine and law, such as **Balthasar Hubmaier, Johannes Bugenhagen, Johannes Althusius, Johannes Brenz,** and **Hugo Grotius.** Other sources read like highly personal accounts, singling out specific biblical stories with which they may have identified. Scripture could be referenced in myriad contexts, contradictorily so, offering a unique window into the lives of people who lived in the early modern era.

The idea of the *corpus christianum* remained pervasive in Protestant thought emerging from local majorities, where the idea of oneness could be projected onto a local or regional community, or indeed where Protestants thought that their ideas should gain prevalence. **John Calvin**'s repeated appeals to the French King and to the noblewoman **Jeanne III** echo such hopes. Minorities living under immediate pressure tended to spiritualise their sense of belonging. The further a Protestant movement developed away from state authority, the more spiritual their political theology tended to be. Anabaptists are a good example, as they tended to disregard temporal authority and often refused to engage in physical violence. Their position is relatively well known. Even so, Anabaptists too were divided over the question how far this spiritualisation of belonging ought to go, and how close they thought they were to the return of Christ and the dawning of the new heaven and new

DOI: 10.4324/9781003247531-7

earth. After the drama of the **Münster Commune**, Anabaptists elsewhere, such as in the Duchy of Poland-Lithuania, were at pains to assure their rulers that they would be good subjects.

Among Protestants, memories of the Reformation often emphasised the virulent persecution of Protestants by Catholic kings, princes, and religious authorities. The Inquisition, the St. Bartholomew's Day Massacre, and the anti-Protestant actions of Queen Mary of England contributed to the identification of Protestants with persecution and martyrdom. These memories have imprinted suspicion within Protestantism towards clerical and political authorities and catalysed thinking about some fundamental freedoms, such as the freedom of conscience, the freedom of religious belief, and the freedom of association.[1] While the development of these ideas can be partially credited to Protestant thinkers, it is important to remember that Protestants wholeheartedly engaged in violence and persecution too. This violence was not limited to Catholics, as somehow uniquely in response to Catholic violence. Protestants persecuted Jews, and both anti-Catholic and anti-Semitic propaganda proliferated. Throughout this volume, one can see the double standards that Protestants held to be suitable for rulers that were similarly Protestant and for those who were not. Sometimes, someone was courageous enough to call out their fellow Protestants. **Andreas Osiander** called out other Protestants for spreading blood libels about the Jews, and **Godfried Udemans** scathed slaveholders for the poor treatment of their enslaved workers.

The asymmetry can be largely attributed to a pattern of binary thinking of good and evil, church and world, the self and the other. The association of the ultimate good with the peace and security of the *corpus christianum* necessitates the projection of evil onto the other, both outside and inside the community. As Europe's Christendom began to disintegrate, meaningful questions were raised about the potential to coexist in the *saeculum*, and to what extent the presence of evil would cause harm to the integrity of the Christian community. This was intensified by a sense of apocalyptic immediacy, which spurned ideas about personal and communal purity, so as to be ready for the second coming of Christ. The question of coexistence thus became a question about the potential of the other to become a good Christian, first to conform outwardly, but, ultimately, to be transformed inwardly so as to fully belong to the story of Christendom. This placed Catholics, Jews, and Muslims on different temporal scales, similarly to medieval canon law.[2] For example, Muslims along with the inhabitants of the New World needed to be evangelised, Jews were yet to embrace the story of Christ, and Catholics and other 'heretics' got to Christ, but got him wrong. At what point would their fault justify violence against them?

The matter of toleration uniquely demonstrates a continuity of thought between medieval and early modern political thought.[3] Much scholarship will situate the development of toleration in the time leading up to the 'superior' thought produced in the Enlightenment, and perhaps underscore the

46 *Marietta van der Tol*

importance of a *modus vivendi* after societies were ripped apart by war and violence.[4] What is underexplored, however, is the continuity of thought that built on the imaginary of the *corpus christianum,* as well as existing canonical resources to think through practical questions of coexistence. Canonical resources, and the reception thereof in the medieval philosophical school of Scholasticism, had long since introduced toleration as a discretionary administrative power, predicated on a number of norms, including public peace and order, the measure of deviation from truth, the proximity and duration of evil, economic considerations, the possibility of outward conformity, and perceived loyalty. Many of these norms play a role in 'toleration treaties', such as the **Edict of Torda** (1568) – which was echoed in **The Consensus of Sandomierz** (1570) – as well as the **Union of Utrecht** (1579), the Edict of Nantes (1598), and the **Westphalian Treaties** (1648).[5]

The sources in this book often engage one or more of these norms, but the level and sophistication thereof varies greatly, depending on the profession and degree of learning. For example, those trained in law tended to be more attuned to political and legal aspects of this question, ranging from the substantiation of public peace and order to major philosophical distinctions between natural and divine laws. Some of the most eminent Protestant theologians had previous training in law, and vice versa, many Protestant legal scholars had meaningful knowledge of theology. The ones at the crossroads of both disciplines often were the ones capable of producing systematic political thinking. This was only rivalled by philosophers who questioned the very foundations of the knowledge of truth and challenged the ethics of forced conformity, thus challenging the epistemic foundations of political order. Such philosophical challenges must be situated in Renaissance humanism and the epistemic transformation that it engendered.[6] Many of the learned Protestants were humanists themselves and prided in their ability to engage with humanists across Europe.

The interest in the sources and substantiation of truth is revealed in the precision with which aspects of the Christian faith were increasingly debated for their self-evidence. Knowledge of the truth was constitutive of the logic of administrative toleration. The distinction between core aspects of faith and matters of opinion was one mechanism through which the level of self-evidence was mediated: if certain beliefs were a matter of opinion, the administration had little justification to interfere, unless, for example, public peace and order were at risk. At the same time, philosophers tended to hold on to the idea of the Christian truth, at least on an ontological level. What people could know about this truth and how they arrived at it was another matter. Protestant thinkers took from Renaissance humanism the recognition that knowledge could be fallible and the necessity of critically engaging the epistemic foundations of knowledge. This led them to challenge their Catholic opponents, but famously, Protestants argued bitterly among each other and yet rarely showed a profound capacity to question their own ideas.

But toleration was not simply about who was right and who was wrong. Toleration was about finding a way of living with difference, so long as the presupposed evils of the other were redeemable, judged by the measures of gravity, proximity, and transience. Toleration is different from tolerance, in that it focuses on the role of state authorities in ascertaining peace and order in towns, villages, regions, and states.[7] Toleration was about the restraint of the sword, whereas intolerance pertains to the use of power against religious minorities. The canonical notion of toleration is mirrored by the notion of dissimulation, which refers to practices of concealing one's true identity, often termed pejoratively as 'Nicodemist' behaviour. Dissimulation is about the extent to which dissent is visible or invisible in day-to-day life of a community: it is about the governance of differences in space.[8]

Benjamin Kaplan in his book *Divided by Faith* recounts practices of toleration in particular communities, which leads us to consider the importance of space.[9] For example, the bottom line of toleration was toleration of difference within private spaces, such as the home, or, at the time, in certain universities. This invisibility echoes in the recommendation that the Wittenberg Reformers made to Philip of Hesse regarding his bigamy: his marriage should remain secret (**Founding of the Schmalkaldic League**). Other practices include the relative invisibility of churches and synagogues that were built in barns, attics, or otherwise hardly recognisable places of worship, or that were built outside of the original city walls. Places that learned to live with differences may have had churches and cemeteries with separate entrances and different times of worship so that congregations could limit their exposure to each other on a Sunday morning. The strongest form of toleration was perhaps parity, where different Christian congregations coexisted in the same town, sharing institutions and sharing citizenship. But this coexistence was beholden to those who were significant enough in number and economic power, and it could still coexist with the marginalisation of Jews in separate neighbourhoods, known as the ghettos. Toleration never was for everyone, and those who benefitted from it had it only as a non-permanent privilege.

Several of the sources hint at the realities of rolled-back toleration, demonstrating that the history of toleration cannot be told as a neat linear story.[10] For the Habsburg Empire, religious dissent was a matter of international security. The Ottoman Empire's ambitions for Vienna made the Habsburg monarchy wary of religious dissent and the political instability that would come with it. The revocation of toleration led to the **Protestation at Speyer**, where German princes defended their own competing interests, including that of the toleration of Lutherans. In the meantime, Protestant Transylvanian rulers in pursuit of greater autonomy bargained with the Ottomans, the Catholic French, and the Lutheran Swedes in their fight against the Catholic Habsburg monarchy (**György I Rákóczi**). A similar interest in unity arose under the English monarchies of the sixteenth century. The consolidation of the Church of England under **Elizabeth I** and the standardisation of the

48 Marietta van der Tol

liturgy under **Oliver Cromwell** provoked all sorts of dissent, not only from Catholics, but also from those for whom the reforms did not go far enough. Violent crackdown on dissent could be motivated by the English equivalent of toleration, namely, moderation, as described by Ethan Shagan in *The Rule of Moderation*.[11]

The 'discovery' of the New World also brought new possibilities for toleration. Puritans from England set out to build local communities with their religion in power, in a way that was impossible in England. Jews settled in Dutch Brazil, where they would gain a degree of religious freedom that was unthinkable even in the 'tolerant' city of Amsterdam.[12] Some of the French Huguenots who found refuge in England would resettle in the Americas. Several of the American states would later go on to adopt state constitutions with explicit references to 'tolerant', only years before the drafting of the American Constitution in the 1770s and its First Amendment. However, toleration had not been for everyone in the colonies either. Fierce arguments arose over the treatment of Native populations, from which **Roger Williams** gained his fame, even as he too was open to violence against American Indians who did not eventually convert to Christianity.[13] Moreover, the rapid growth of the transatlantic slave trade also proliferated racist political writings, which have too often been branded as simply a product of their time, rather than an integral part of many Protestant traditions.

There are some wonderful but largely unfamiliar sources to explore on this topic: **Bernardo Ochino,** part of whose work is newly translated for this sourcebook; the local solutions found by **The People of Zizers;** and the pleas for toleration coming from a number of women. The latter include writings by **Johanna and** (her son) **Ebenezer Cartwright** on the toleration of Jews in England; (Roger Williams on) **Jane Verin and Katherine Chidley** on the liberty of conscience for women; **Amalia Elisabeth** on the inclusion of the Reformed in the **Peace of Westphalia;** and finally, the **Petition of Women to the English Parliament** on state violence against the Levellers.

Notes

1 John Witte Jr., "Law, Religion and Human Rights: A Historical Protestant Perspective", *The Journal of Religious Ethics* 26, no. 2 (1998): 257–262.

2 Julia Costa Lopez, "Beyond Eurocentrism and Orientalism: Revisiting the Othering of Jews and Muslims through Medieval Canon Law", *Review of International Studies* 42, no. 3 (2016): 450–470.

3 István P. Bejczy, "Tolerantia: A Medieval Concept", *Journal of the History of Ideas* 91, no. 4 (1997): 365–384.

4 Rainer Forst, *Toleration in Conflict: Past and Present* (Cambridge: Cambridge University Press, 2013).

5 Marietta Van Der Tol, "Politics of Religious Diversity: Toleration, Religious Freedom and Visibility of Religion in Public Space", chapter 2 (PhD diss., University of Cambridge, 2021), doi:10.17863/CAM.64125.

6 Gary Remer, *Humanism and the Rhetoric of Toleration* (State College, PA: The Pennsylvania State University Press 1996); Stefania Tutino, *Uncertainty*

Toleration, Coexistence, and the Place of 'The Other' 49

    in Post-Reformation Catholicism: A History of Probabilism (Oxford: Oxford University Press, 2018).

7 Jeffrey R. Collins, "Redeeming the Enlightenment: New Histories of Religious Toleration", *The Journal of Modern History* 81, no. 3 (2009): 607–636.

8 Filomena Viviana Tagliaferri, *Tolerance Re-shaped in the Early-Modern Mediterranean Borderlands: Travellers, Missionaries and Proto-journalists (1683–1724)* (New York: Routledge, 2018); Miriam Eliav-Feldon and Tamar Herzig, eds., *Dissimulation and Deceit in Early Modern Europe* (New York: Palgrave Macmillan, 2015); Peter Zagorin, *Ways of Lying: Dissimulation, Persecution and Conformity in Early Modern Europe* (Cambridge, MA: Harvard University Press, 1990).

9 Benjamin J. Kaplan, *Divided by Faith: Religious Conflict and the Practice of Toleration in Early Modern Europe* (London: Belknap Press, 2007).

10 Alexandra Walsham, *Charitable Hatred: Tolerance and Intolerance in England 1500–1700* (Manchester: Manchester University Press, 2006); Alexandra Walsham, "Culture of Coexistence in Early Modern England: History, Literature, and Religious Toleration", *The Seventeenth Century* 28, no. 2 (2013): 115–137. Compare Wayne P. Te Brake, *Religious War and Religious Peace in Early Modern Europe* (Cambridge: Cambridge University Press, 2017).

11 Ethan H. Shagan, *The Rule of Moderation: Violence, Religion and the Politics of Restraint in Early Modern England* (Cambridge: Cambridge University Press, 2011).

12 Jonathan Israel, "Religious Toleration in Dutch Brazil (1624–1654)", in *The Expansion of Tolerance: Religion in Dutch Brazil (1624–1654)*, ed. Jonathan Israel and Stuart B. Schwartz (Amsterdam: Amsterdam University Press, 2007).

13 Teresa M. Bejan, "The Bond of Civility: Roger Williams on Toleration and its Limits", *History of European Ideas* 37, no. 4 (2011): 409–420.

7 The Hebrew Bible and Politics

John Coffey

At first glance, the Hebrew Bible might not seem of central importance to the Reformation. Protestantism was fundamentally a Pauline Renaissance: its greatest theologians drew on the Epistles of St Paul to formulate their doctrines of justification by faith, union with Christ, and assurance of salvation. Debates with Roman Catholics and with other Protestants turned on the interpretation of the New Testament. Moreover, **Martin Luther's** fundamental distinction between law and gospel drove a sharp wedge between Moses and Christ, between works of the law and the gift of faith. In Lucas Cranach's visual *Allegory of Law and Grace* (c.1529), an encapsulation of Lutheran doctrine, the legal preaching of Moses (who points to the Decalogue) drives sinners to despair and to hell, while the gospel preaching of John the Baptist (who points to Christ crucified and risen) reveals the divine gift of forgiveness. On this account, Roman Catholic priests were like the 'Judaizers' whom Paul castigated in his Epistle to the Galatians: instead of trusting in Christ alone for justification, they relied on their performance, both of good deeds and religious rituals. Indeed, the Reformation can be seen as part of the anti-Judaic strain in Western thought, reinforcing supersessionist dichotomies between the flesh and the spirit, the external and the internal, the sword and the word, the old and the new. Historians continue to debate the relationship between the theological anti-Judaism of the early Luther and the political anti-Semitism of his late writings against the Jews.[1]

Yet, Luther was not like the ancient heretic Marcion, who restricted the canon of scripture to the Gospel of Luke and the Epistles of Paul. The Protestant canon included the Hebrew scriptures. In fact, Protestants diverged from Catholic and Orthodox Christians by distinguishing sharply between the Hebrew texts of the Tanakh ('the Old Testament') and inter-testamental Greek-language Jewish texts ('the Apocrypha'). Luther's 1534 Bible placed the Apocrypha in a separate section after the Old Testament, marking it as 'useful' but not as equally divinely inspired. The Hebrew Bible, in contrast, was part of the Protestant scriptures, though it was no longer divided into three sections (Torah, Prophets, Writings), and its 24 books were divided into 39. Moreover, these books were freshly translated and bound up with the New Testament, signalling a different hermeneutical relationship: one can

DOI: 10.4324/9781003247531-8

The Hebrew Bible and Politics   51

argue that Protestants (like Catholics) read 'the Old Testament' rather than 'the Hebrew Bible'. The two terms point us in different directions: either towards the Christian character of the Protestant Bible or towards the inclusion of pre-Christian Jewish texts in the Protestant canon.

As the text became part of the Protestant canon, the principle of *sola scriptura*–that the Bible was the sole infallible authority in religion–summoned the reader into utmost reverence. When translating into the vernacular, Protestants usually prioritised the New Testament, but the Old Testament duly followed.[2] Luther's distinction between law and gospel was never a simple case of Old versus New Testaments, for the New Testament contained law and the Old Testament proclaimed the gospel. Covenantal thinking provided the texture of interpretation, especially in the Abrahamic covenant, which according to Paul had been about justification by faith alone. Christ was foreshadowed in the typology of the Old Testament: he was the second Adam and the greater David. Protestants did not dismiss the value of the law either. It had two, perhaps three, uses. First, insofar as the Decalogue corresponded with natural law, it applied to all people and served to keep order in society. Second, the preaching of the law forced sinners to recognise their own moral failings and their desperate need for divine grace and mercy. Finally, the moral law had a role to play in the sanctification (though not the justification) of believers.

The Old Testament was also an indispensable resource for Protestant political thought. Of course, Protestants made much of political prooftexts from the New Testament: 'Render unto Caesar the things that are Caesar's, and unto God the things that are God's' (Matt. 22:21); 'We ought to obey God rather than men' (Acts 5:29); 'The powers that be are ordained of God' (Rom. 13:1); and 'Submit yourselves to every ordinance of man for the Lord's sake' (1 Pet. 2:13). For relatively positive views of secular authority, Protestants could turn to the Roman governors in the book of Acts; for devastating indictments, they could turn to the book of Revelation. The Old Testament, however, contained a far greater wealth of relevant material: political narratives, legal codes, and prophetic texts that addressed nations and empires. Thus from the outset of the Reformation, Protestants studied the Old Testament to inform their political thought.

Political Uses of the Hebrew Bible

To begin with, the Hebrew Bible contained examples of godly magistrates: Moses, Joshua, Gideon, Deborah, David, Hezekiah, Josiah. This was not the case with the New Testament, where the civil authorities were at best indifferent and at worst hostile to Jesus and the primitive church. So the Old Testament proved especially useful to the mainstream Reformers, whose Reformation was a magisterial Reformation, one that sought, and often found, support from magistrates. Unlike medieval heretics, Lutherans and Calvinists thrived under the protection of dukes, princes, kings, and city-states. In

52 John Coffey

England, **Miles Coverdale** argued that Moses and Joshua were not simply shadowy types of Christ, but models for Christian kings. England was a new Israel. **Thomas Cranmer's** coronation sermon for Edward VI compared the boy king to Josiah, while **Elizabeth I** was seen as 'England's Deborah'.

This is often labelled 'political typology', but strictly speaking, typology has a one-to-one referent. In reading the Old Testament politically, Protestants looked to it for models or *exempla* that could be fulfilled in various figures and situations. In the Protestant international community, there was more than one new Israel, and Old Testament analogues were evoked in political sermons preached in German, French, English, Dutch, Swedish, Hungarian, and other languages. As a result, the Hebrew Bible and its Protestant readers played a significant role in the formation of national identities in early modern Europe. This would have an ambivalent and often unhappy legacy. The instrumental use of the Old Testament to forge national identities involved 'patterns of othering' that excluded Jews, Catholics, Muslims, and other minorities.[3]

Yet, the richness of the Hebrew Bible allowed it to resonate in a multitude of situations. Preachers were able to transport their congregations into various episodes in Israel's story. The Exodus narrative had been foundational for Jewish identity, and Protestants were quick to read themselves into the story. The Reformation itself was seen as a deliverance from popish bondage, a new Exodus with Luther as a new Moses. In the Dutch republic, fighting for its independence from Spanish rule, the Exodus loomed larger still, with William of Orange being hailed as the Dutch Moses. In early modern Dutch culture, the Exodus story was depicted in sermons, songs, silver plaques, engravings, wall tiles, paintings, and the stage. In Hungary too, Reformed clergy drew biblical parallels between the Hungarians and the Israelites: ancient Hungarians had migrated from Asia like the Jews from Egypt, and Reformed Hungarians were embarking on a new Exodus to the Promised Land. In England, the title page of the **Geneva Bible** (1560) displayed a woodcut of the Israelites preparing to cross the Red Sea, Pharaoh's army behind them. During the 1640s, radical Puritans depicted the Civil War as England's Exodus from civil and ecclesiastical bondage. Two later revolutions in the Anglophone Atlantic world – the so-called '**Glorious Revolution**' of 1688 and the American Revolution of 1776 – were each legitimised and celebrated as a new Exodus.[4]

Later episodes in Israel's history also served political purposes. The conquest of Canaan recorded in the book of Joshua was a wartime favourite, employed during confessional conflicts with Catholic powers and in colonial wars against the Indigenous peoples of North America. In Protestant minds, there was a blurred line between just and holy wars. During times of political instability, Protestants could turn to the book of Judges: 'In those days there was no king in Israel: every man did what was right in his own eyes' (Judges 21:25). Monarchists sought to bolster royal authority by comparing

Protestant kings to Moses or David or Josiah; those who took up arms against princes or kings were compared to Old Testament rebels, such as Korah or Absalom. Yet, resistance theorists had their prooftexts too: the Geneva Bible cited the Hebrew midwives and their passive resistance to Pharaoh's genocidal commands, as well as Jehu's rising against the wicked Queen Jezebel; the Huguenot author of the *Vindiciae Contra Tyrannos* (1579) argued that the authority of biblical kings was based on a conditional covenant with God and the people; the Scottish Covenanter **Samuel Rutherford** agreed that in Israel and Judah, the power of kings derived from the people, whose lawful representatives could reclaim that power if a king turned tyrannical; in 1649, godly officers of the New Model Army concluded at the **Windsor Prayer Meeting** that King Charles I was 'that man of blood' (Num. 35:33; 2 Sam. 16:7–8), who had forfeited his own life by plunging the nation into a second civil war.

But what was to be done if Protestants found themselves powerless? Here too, Old Testament narrative could be useful. In an age of religious refugees, when Protestant minorities found themselves persecuted or exiled, readers were inexorably drawn to the archetypal story of the Judean exiles in Babylon. Luther had lamented the 'Babylonian captivity' of the Christian Church, and Huguenots in Louis XIV's France saw themselves as outsiders in a new Babylon. For those returning from exile (whether physical or metaphorical), the story of Ezra and Nehemiah resonated: both Elizabethan Reformers in the 1560s and Puritans in the 1640s repeatedly preached on the rebuilding of Jerusalem.

Of course, there was more to the Old Testament than history, and other genres were mined for the purposes of political thought. The creation stories of Genesis were foundational for theological anthropology and for theories about the origins of political authority. **Robert Filmer** traced the absolute authority of kings to the patriarchal authority of Adam; **John Locke** responded in the first of his *Two Treatises of Government* (1689), offering a very different view of humanity's original state, one of freedom and equality. Locke, like most Protestant thinkers since **Philip Melanchthon**, appealed to the law of nature, but its principles could be confirmed by scripture. The doctrine of the Fall, rooted in Genesis 3, was also foundational. Filmer wrote that 'the desire for Liberty was the first Cause of the Fall of Adam', but the fallenness of all men, including rulers, was used as an argument to limit the power of magistrates. For the Digger **Gerrard Winstanley**, the early chapters of Genesis revealed how a world designed as 'a Common Store-house for all' had been partitioned and privatised by 'Covetousness and Pride'.

Mosaic law was another important source for Protestant political thought. Protestants agreed that much of the Old Testament law had been abrogated by the coming of Christ – the sacrificial system and ritual food and purity laws were types fulfilled and superseded in the gospel. Reformers disagreed over what elements of the law were still binding. Most believed that the

54 John Coffey

Decalogue was still in force, and it was widely seen as a republication of natural law. Indeed, the Ten Commandments were prominently displayed in parish churches across Protestant Europe, and expounded in countless catechisms. The problem lay with a grey zone between the Decalogue and the ritual code. Protestants developed a taxonomy, one articulated by **Zacharias Ursinus**, between moral laws (of permanent validity), ceremonial laws (now abrogated), and judicial laws (which, while not binding, might have enduring equity). It was this third category that caused most dispute. Some Mosaic penal laws were incorporated into the legal code of the **Virginia Colony** and into a proposed **Massachusetts Body of Liberties**. Such importation of Mosaic penal law could (in theory if not in practice) result in capital punishment for blasphemy, adultery, sodomy, witchcraft, and Sabbath-breaking, though it could also yield more egalitarian and humane laws, especially around property crimes. Yet, few Protestant states favoured full-scale implementation of the Mosaic judicial law, and it met with resistance from professional lawyers, who were heavily invested in existing traditions of Roman or common law.

The writings of the Hebrew prophets were also grist to the mill of Protestant political thought. Prophecy involved both 'forthtelling' and 'foretelling': speaking truth to power and predicting the future. Protestant leaders, including Luther and **John Calvin**, but also **Thomas Müntzer**, developed a prophetic identity and persona, thundering against idolatry or injustice like their Old Testament counterparts.[5] From the beginning, Protestants were also fascinated by predictive prophecy, and while their primary focus was on the book of Revelation, they increasingly sought to harmonise it with the book of Daniel. Both texts were subjected to historicist interpretation, and read as a preview of the whole of church history, including the rise and ultimate fall of the Church of Rome (Daniel's fourth kingdom before the fifth monarchy of God). In the sixteenth century, Protestants accepted the standard view that Old Testament prophecies about 'Israel', 'Judah', 'Jerusalem', and 'Zion' were fulfilled in the Christian church, but in the seventeenth century, a new mode of Judeo-centric interpretation arose that insisted on applying such prophecies to the Jews. This was a hermeneutical revolution, changing the way that some Reformed Protestants read the Old Testament, and giving the Jews a starring role in the end-times. It is here that we find the roots of Christian Zionism.[6]

The book of Psalms was also politically charged, especially in its focus on Israel's God and Israel's enemies. Psalms were an integral element of Lutheran and Reformed liturgy, and were sung by congregations across Protestant Europe. As Diarmaid MacCulloch puts it, they became 'the secret weapon of the Reformation'.[7] They forged a powerful corporate identity, especially in the face of persecution or attack. Among French Calvinists, the vernacular-metrical psalms, pioneered by Clément Marot, championed by Calvin, and completed by Theodore Beza, were sung by crowds and by armies during the French wars of religion. Psalm 68 was the Huguenot 'song of battles': 'Let God arise, let his enemies be scattered'. Psalm 128 was another favourite: 'If it had not been the Lord who was on our side, now may Israel say...'.[8] In England, in 1649, the regicide of Charles I was justified by appeal to Psalm 149: 'To bind their kings with chains, and their nobles with fetters of iron; To execute upon them the judgment written; this honour have all his saints'.

Given the importance of the Hebrew Bible to Protestant theology and Protestant politics, it naturally became the site of intensive scholarship. While some early translations into the vernacular relied on the Latin Bible, Protestant translators such as **Melanchthon, Tyndale,** and the Hungarian István Székely worked directly from the Hebrew. There was a great flowering of Christian Hebraism, disproportionately concentrated in Protestant universities, where humanist scholars studied and translated a vast array of rabbinic texts. This led to the rise of political Hebraism and to a new genre of works on the Hebrew republic, which used Jewish commentaries to advance new readings of Old Testament texts. Exposure to rabbinic readings of Old Testament texts had a tangible impact on European political thought, not least in England, where the Hebraic learning of figures like **John Milton** and **James Harrington** fostered fresh ideas about republicanism, toleration, and the redistribution of property. In Amsterdam, with its prosperous Sephardic community, there were remarkable intellectual exchanges between Jewish rabbis and Reformed pastors. To some extent, however limited, Hebraism encouraged more sympathetic attitudes towards the Jews. There is much debate over whether Christian Hebraism was good for the Jews, but there are good grounds for seeing the seventeenth century as 'the Hebrew century' in European political thought.[9]

A Hermeneutical Spectrum

There was, however, a spectrum of Old Testament interpretation among Protestant Reformers. At one end stood radical sects who maximised the *continuity* between the Old Testament and the New; at the other end stood radical sects who maximised the *discontinuity*, stressing the degree of abrogation and supersession. Most Protestants, including Lutherans and Calvinists, occupied a middle ground. This oversimplifies the relationship between these parts of the Bible, since the balance between continuity and discontinuity could vary within confessional traditions, even within the thought of a single theologian. The pacifist theologian, **Menno Simons**, for example, accused the Münster Anabaptists of trading the spirit of the new covenant for the fleshly politics of the old, yet elsewhere he could turn to the Hebrew Bible for examples of humble rulers. And in some texts, both Testaments were cited opportunistically, with little sign of a consistent hermeneutic. Nevertheless, we can identify some basic patterns.

On the wilder fringes of the radical Reformation, in both sixteenth-century Europe and seventeenth-century England, a tiny minority of Christian Judaizers embraced Jewish rituals that had long been consigned to the age of

56   John Coffey

ancient Israel: the observance of a Saturday Sabbath, food laws, and even circumcision. On rare occasions, radical sectarians found a political stage on which to enact their Old Testament literalism. In the city of **Münster** in 1534, radical Anabaptists established a theocracy under the leadership of **Jan van Leiden**, who, as the new David, was crowned King of the New Jerusalem. Twelve Elders, representing the Twelve Tribes of Israel, instituted a set of Mosaic penal laws. In Interregnum England, during the 1650s, **Fifth Monarchists** lobbied unsuccessfully for the incorporation of Mosaic judicial code into English law. Paradoxically, both Münsterites and many Fifth Monarchists rejected infant baptism, a position that depended on a sharp disjunction between old and new covenants, circumcision and baptism.

The Reformed, guided by erudite theologians like Calvin and **Martin Bucer**, aimed to avoid such extremes, but compared to the Lutherans, they were arguably more emphatically oriented towards Old Testament Israel. They generally eschewed hymnody in favour of exclusive psalmody. They stressed the third use of the law (in the life of the believer), and often took a more positive view of the Mosaic judicial law. As a humanist scholar, Calvin was accused of Judaising because he read the Psalms in their historical context, in contrast to Luther's relentlessly Christological interpretations.[10] The Reformed tradition was defined by iconophobia, based on the centrality of idolatry in Old Testament history, a history re-enacted in bouts of Calvinist iconoclasm directed at religious images, murals, and stained glass. The Reformed even numbered the Ten Commandments differently to Catholics and Lutherans so that the Second Commandment concerned graven images. From **Huldreich Zwingli** onwards, the Reformed were preoccupied by the project of civic Reformation, and the concept of the covenant played an important role to their political as well as theological thought. They sought to create new Israels.[11] And they were leading proponents of Christian Hebraism. The Jewish political theorist, Michael Walzer, has argued that English Puritans can plausibly be seen as 'Judaizers': 'they defend the "carnality" of the promise; they seek a worldly kingdom'.[12]

In contrast, Luther drew a sharper divide between the temporal and the spiritual, the legal and the evangelical, and the old covenant and the new. His writings contain a running polemic against the Judaistic legalism of rabbis and Pharisees – ancient and modern, Jewish and Christian. His reading of the Psalms was so Christological that the historical David faded from view so that the psalmist's enemies frequently become the Jews who persecuted Christ.[13] Ironically, this sharp disjunction between Old Testament externality and New Testament interiority underpinned his early tolerationist argument (in 1523) against the use of force in matters of religion. Under the old dispensation, religious coercion was legitimate, but in the era of the new covenant, the church must not depend on 'carnal weapons' – faith must be freely chosen.[14] However, Luther himself soon shifted ground on this point, and by 1529, the Lutheran Reformer **Johannes Brenz** was citing Old

Testament kings to justify a system of enforced religious uniformity. The Lutheran tradition, like the Reformed, was variegated, and it cannot be reduced to the writings of Luther himself (who, in any case, produced a complex and evolving body of work). Lutheranism nurtured a thriving culture of Christian Hebraism, led by scholars such as Melanchthon, Wilhelm Schickard, and Solomon Glassius.[15] And in their political sermons, Lutheran divines (like their Reformed counterparts) envisaged Protestant polities as new Israels.[16]

It is in the theology of Anabaptists and other radical Reformers that we find the sharpest discontinuity between the Testaments. Anabaptists rejected the analogy with circumcision that justified infant baptism. In **Conrad Grebel, Balthasar Hubmaier,** and Menno Simons, a new doctrine of Christian pacifism emerged out of the dichotomy between old and new, flesh and spirit, sword and word. Anabaptist theology was concentrated on the restoration of the early church, a community separated from the corrupt world of political power. The sword was necessary to maintain social order, but the true Christian (always in a marginal minority) must obey Christ's Sermon on the Mount, and that ruled out the use of force, whether in self-defence or to promote true religion. The Socinian **Johann Crell** adopted the same view, adding that Old Testament magistrates punished idolatry and blasphemy in an age when the truth was vindicated by miracles; in the church age, there was no justification for compulsion in matters of religion. Radical Puritans such as **Roger Williams** and the **Levellers** concurred: biblical Israel was 'figurative and ceremonial' and 'no pattern nor precedent for any kingdom or civil state in the world to follow'. The only sword Christians could use against heresy was the Bible, the sword of the Spirit. **George Fox**, the Quaker leader, took the argument one stage further, embracing a strict pacifism based on Christ's ethical teaching, a position that resembled that of Mennonites and Socinians. Levellers and Quakers could still invoke the Hebrew prophets' call for social justice, but theirs was not a magisterial Reformation based on the model of ancient biblical kings.

Conclusion

Karl Marx once remarked that in eighteenth-century bourgeois England, 'Locke supplanted Habbakuk'.[17] There was indeed a contrast with 'the Hebrew century'. Already, in the writings of **Thomas Hobbes** and **Benedict Spinoza,** a sceptical biblical criticism had emerged, which openly questioned the Mosaic authorship of the Pentateuch. The eighteenth century would prove relatively inhospitable to Christian Hebraism, and French *philosophes*, in particular, would be contemptuous of Old Testament 'barbarism'. Catholics and Protestants had cited the Hebrew Bible to justify holy wars, blasphemy laws, witch-hunts, slavery, and draconian penal laws. Locke, like other tolerationists, invoked the principle of abrogation to nullify the Old Testament case for religious coercion.

58 John Coffey

Yet, the story of early modern Protestants and the Hebrew Bible cannot be reduced to a simple morality tale, and the legacy of post-Reformation hermeneutics has lasted longer than Marx suggested. Christian Hebraism could be polemically anti-Judaic, but it also fostered sympathy and respect for Jews and the Jewish tradition in some respects. The Old Testament (and Hebraic scholarship) was cited in support of religious toleration, popular sovereignty, republicanism, economic redistribution, social justice, and female monarchs. Milton's Hebraic argument against monarchy (based on rabbinic readings of I Samuel 8) was popularised by Tom Paine in *Common Sense* (1776), the bestseller of the American Revolution and a major inspiration for American republicanism.[18]

Moreover, modern Protestants still wrestle with the relationship between the two Testaments. Whether they recognise it or not, Christian nationalists, Christian Zionists, and liberation theologians all draw on the Hebrew Bible in ways that are recognisably early modern. Global Protestantism still catches visions of a magisterial Reformation and godly nations, but it is also the child of the radical Reformation and early modern tolerationists, whose doctrines owed much to biblical interpretation. Contemporary Protestantism, so often bereft of a sense of history, would benefit from becoming historically (and hermeneutically) self-aware. 'Reading the Bible with the dead' can be a salutary exercise, especially when readers eschew easy answers and wrestle with difficult problems.[19] The tradition of Protestant political thought, so contested and multivocal, remains a significant intellectual resource.

Notes

1 For different perspectives, see David Nirenberg, *Anti-Judaism: The Western Tradition* (New York: W.W. Norton & Co, 2013), chapter 7; Heiko Oberman, *The Roots of Anti-Semitism in the Age of Renaissance and Reformation*, trans. James I. Porter (Philadelphia: Fortress Press, 1984); Thomas Kaufman, *Luther's Jews: A Journey into Anti-Semitism* (Oxford: Oxford University Press, 2017).

2 See Mark Greengrass, ed., *The Longman Companion to the European Reformation, c.1500–1618* (Harlow: Longman, 1998), 257–261.

3 See the special issue edited by Sophia Johnson and Marietta van der Tol, "Old Testament Imaginaries of the Nation in German, Dutch, and Anglo-American Political Thought", *Journal of the Bible and its Reception* 8, no. 2 (2021), especially therein Marietta van der Tol, "The 'Jew', the Nation and Assimilation: The Old Testament and the Fashioning of the 'Other' in German and Dutch Protestant Thought", 143–162.

4 See Michael Walzer, *Exodus and Revolution* (New York: Basic Books, 1985); John Coffey, *Exodus and Liberation: Deliverance Politics from John Calvin to Martin Luther King Jr* (New York: Oxford University Press, 2014), chapters 1–2.

5 See Jon Balserak, *John Calvin as Sixteenth-Century Prophet* (Oxford: Oxford University Press, 2014).

6 See Robert O. Smith, *More Desired than Our Owne Salvation: The Roots of Christian Zionism* (Oxford: Oxford University Press, 2013).

7 Diarmaid MacCulloch, *The Reformation: A History* (London: Penguin, 2003), 307–308.

8 W. Stanford Reid, "The Battle Hymns of the Lord: Calvinist Psalmody in the Sixteenth Century", *Sixteenth Century Journal* 2 (1971): 36–54.
9 See Eric Nelson, *The Hebrew Republic: Jewish Sources and the Transformation of European Political Thought* (Cambridge, MA: Harvard University Press, 2010).
10 G. Sujin Pak, *The Judaizing Calvin: Sixteenth-Century Debates over the Messianic Psalms* (Oxford: Oxford University Press, 2017).
11 On early modern 'Hebraic nationalism', see Philip Gorski, "The Mosaic Moment: An Early Modernist Critique of Modernist Theories of Nationalism", *American Journal of Sociology* 105 (2000): 1428–1468.
12 Michael Walzer, *Exodus and Revolution* (New York: Basic Books, 1985), 123.
13 David Nirenberg, *Anti-Judaism: The Western Tradition* (New York: W.W. Norton & Co, 2013), 253–255.
14 Luther and Calvin, *On Secular Authority*, ed. Harro Hopfl (Cambridge: Cambridge University Press, 1991), 3–43.
15 Stephen G. Burnett, "Lutheran Christian Hebraism at the Time of Solomon Glassius (1593–1656)", in *Hebraistik – Hermeneutik – Homiletik*, ed. Christoph Bultman and Lutz Danneberg (Berlin: De Gruyter, 2011), 441–467.
16 See Pasi Ilhainen, *Protestant Nations Redefined: Changing Perceptions of National Identity in the Rhetoric in the English, Dutch and Swedish Public Churches, 1685–1772* (Leiden: Brill, 2005).
17 Karl Marx, "The Eighteenth Brumaire of Louis Bonaparte" (1852).
18 Eric Nelson, *The Hebrew Republic: Jewish Sources and the Transformation of European Political Thought* (Cambridge, MA: Harvard University Press, 2010), 53.
19 John L. Thompson, *Reading the Bible with the Dead: What You Can Learn from the History of Exegesis that You Can't Learn from Exegesis Alone* (Grand Rapids, MI: Eerdmans, 2007).

8 Islam and Protestantism

Mehmet Karabela

From the beginning of the Reformation, Islam and Protestantism have had many significant interactions, varying from theological engagement to convenient political alliances. Protestant theologians soon embarked on an intellectual exploration to understand and interpret Islam in relation to their own beliefs and political context. Some translated authoritative Islamic sources and others wrote academic dissertations and disputations on theological, philosophical, and political thought. Protestant scholars examined Islamic thought extensively, often with a view to underscoring perceived similarities between Catholicism and Islam, not only to critique Catholicism but also to use as a means of reinforcing their own theological stance as the correct one – a shocking rhetorical move at the time. This chapter discusses Protestant perspectives on Islam, including the Protestant idea of Islam as a political religion, their perception of the Sunni-Shi'a schism, interactions between the Ottoman Empire and Protestants, as well as their view on Islamic religious tolerance, coercion, and conversion.

Islam and the life of Muhammad played a significant role in shaping religious thought in Europe in the early modern period. While Catholic theologians attempted to downplay religious movements that emerged from the Reformation (such as Socinianism and Unitarianism) by associating them with Islam, some Calvinist theologians praised Islam over Catholicism. Lutheran Pietists and members of the Calixtinian Syncretic movement saw Muslims as potential candidates for conversion, particularly after the Austrian Habsburg Empire regained control of Turkish Hungary through the Peace of Karlowitz (1699). On the contrary, some Protestants wielded comparisons between Muhammad and the pope as iterations of the anti-Christ. In a similar vein, Catholics sometimes used Islam and Muhammad to disparage Protestants by likening **Martin Luther** to Muhammad or equating Calvinist heresies with Islam. In response, Protestant scholars frequently drew parallels between Judaism and Islam to reinforce their own distinct religious identity.[1]

Among the Protestant denominations, Lutheran scholars emerged as the pre-eminent contributors to the study of Islam and Muslim culture. The geopolitical risks stemming from the Ottoman Empire were regularly cited as a reason not to extend toleration to Lutherans in the Habsburg Empire,

DOI: 10.4324/9781003247531-9

which Lutherans vehemently argued against from the early days of the Reformation. In the seventeenth and eighteenth centuries, the Lutherans wrote more scholarly writings and studied Islam more closely than other Christian groups, including the Roman Catholics, Socinians, Anglicans, Calvinists, Anabaptists, and Quakers.[2] The Ottoman Empire's expansion into Europe in the seventeenth century and the fragmentation of religious unity within Christianity during the Reformation and following the Thirty Years' War heightened the interest in Islam among Lutherans. Lutherans also used Islam to criticise intra-Protestant movements like Pietism, the Syncretic movement, and the Reformed Church.

Rationality, Religious Tolerance, Coercion, and Conversion

One way in which Protestants equated Muslims and Catholics was through the criticism of coercion and political power. They perceived Muslims as violent converters and Catholics as coercive converters through methods like the Inquisition. Their literary strategy would come to highlight the incompatibility of coercive actions carried out by the Catholic Church and the Ottoman Empire with the notion of rationality. According to the Lutheran perspective, both Muslims and Catholics were unable to persuade others through logical reasoning, but instead resorted to forceful methods of conversion – unlike the Protestants who would be guided by rational arguments. Lutherans presented themselves as advocates for a logical form of faith, drawing parallels between Christ and Logos to emphasise their association with rationality.

For example, Dutch Calvinist theologian **Peter Beutterich** (d.1587) criticised the Roman Catholic Church in his *Catholicism and Tyranny over the Conscience*, arguing that supporting it is worse than the tyranny imposed by the barbarians and Turks. He claimed that while the Turks only controlled physical bodies without interfering with one's conscience, the Church sought to control both the body and the mind. According to Lutheran theologian **Friedrich Ulrich Calixt** (d.1701), the pope's behaviour was more heinous than the Muslim Turks, as they had at least tried peaceful coexistence, while the pope had resorted to vicious attacks on non-Catholic Christians with swords and fire.[3] In Lutheran interpretation, Muslims and Catholics relied heavily on harsh means of persuasion due to their lack of ability to influence others rationally, while they deemed Protestantism as superior because it reflected Christ's essence as the Logos.

The argument of irrationality was also present in the work of Johann Michael Lange (d.1731), a Lutheran theologian and professor, who slammed the Catholic Church for destroying copies of the Qur'an upon its arrival in Europe. He argued that the Church's fear of Christian conversions to Islam was baseless, as anyone who read the Qur'an could easily identify its contradictions. Furthermore, Lange called out the hypocrisy of allowing publications of other non-Christian religious texts while attempting to eradicate the Qur'an. He urged an end to burning the Qur'an unless all pagan works were

62   Mehmet Karabela

also suppressed by the Church. Lange firmly believed that his religion was more rational due to Protestants' ability to critically analyse various religious texts and pointed out flaws in the context of 'rational' Protestant dogma. On the contrary, he thought Catholics were illogical when it came to examining their own doctrines, resorting to book burnings instead of openly addressing any potential doctrinal fallacies they might have had.[4]

This burning of the Qur'an sparked a division between Catholics and Protestants regarding their approaches towards other religions, with Protestants advocating for a more rational stance in dealing with non-Christian religions. It is important to note that not all Protestants considered Islam an irrational religion; on the contrary, some post-Reformation Protestant groups such as Anglicans, as well as deists and freethinkers, believed that Islam stood out as the most rational belief system among other religions.[5]

During the seventeenth century, the Calixtinians, a branch of ecumenical Protestantism, had a distinctive approach to Islam; they wanted to save Muslims from their current religious beliefs and bring them to Christianity. Unlike other Protestant groups, they perceived Islam not solely as a means to criticise Catholicism: rather, they saw Muslims as souls who could be saved with the spreading of universal Christian teachings. Their mission was to provide Muslims with a clear, simple, and precise interpretation of the scriptures. They argued that by presenting the Holy Bible in an uncomplicated and plain manner, Muslims would come to understand Jesus' divinity. To ease the conversion process for Muslims, Calixt suggested prioritising doctrines that all Christians generally agreed on, based on self-evident principles derived from scripture instead of intricate syllogisms and logical reasoning. He believed that this simplified version of Christianity was more suitable for new believers and that Lutheranism aligned more closely with this desired model.[6]

Islam as a Political Religion versus Non-political Christianity

Another strategy to criticise both Islam and Catholicism was to accuse them of being political religions. In the late sixteenth century, Protestant universities in Germany developed political science as a separate academic field, although it was closely connected to ethics, theology, and law. Seventeenth-century Lutheran scholars, including Johann Heinrich Boeckler (d.1672), Daniel Clasen (d.1678), and Daniel Georg Morhof (d.1691), developed a specialised subdiscipline known as *theologia politica* (political theology).[7] Their perspective on religious politics was more than just statecraft, seeing it instead as a way for Catholic Machiavellians and ruling elites to manipulate religious beliefs for political advantage, as opposed to their claim that Protestantism was non-political. They criticised Catholics who saw the ruler as the representative of God on earth and believed in the divine right of kings.

During the seventeenth century, many Lutherans viewed the development of political religion with alarm, as they thought that using religion for political gains was dangerous. According to their interpretation of theology, they contended that religion should only promote spiritual fulfilment, not worldly success. Some Lutherans questioned the predominant political stance of the Catholic Church that divine authority validated the deeds of rulers, and they framed Catholicism as idolatrous and unworthy of trust. The majority of Lutheran scholars advocated for the separation of religion from politics. German biblical scholarship, influenced by Luther's two-kingdoms doctrine, asserted that Christianity was fundamentally spiritual rather than political. From the 1600s onwards, this view that spiritual and temporal matters must not be merged prevailed among Lutherans. They believed early Christianity prioritised the quest for spirituality.[8]

Lutherans regarded both Catholicism and Islam as inherently political religions. In his analysis of Sunni and Shi'a groups, the orthodox Lutheran theologian August Pfeiffer (d.1698) drew comparisons between Muslim religious leaders and the Catholic pope. Like Catholics who mixed religion with politics triggering the Reformation, his argument was that the combination of politics and religion also led to Islam's division. Shi'a Muslims believed that Ali was rightfully chosen as the first Caliph, following Prophet Muhammad's death, while Sunni Muslims supported Abu Bakr in this position.[9] Additionally, Samuel Schelwig (d.1715), a proponent of Lutheran orthodoxy, believed there was a strong similarity between Turkish Sufi dervishes and Catholic Jesuits, which demonstrated the dangers associated with religious sects interfering in politics.[10]

Contributing to the political theology discourse, **Michael Wendeler** (d.1671), a theology professor at the University of Wittenberg, offered his own critical analysis of the political and religious similarities between Catholicism and Islam. He compared the 'little horn' from the Book of Daniel to the Turkish sultan, arguing that Turkish Muslims were led by a tyrant who used violence to expand his territories, taking advantage of the divisions among neighbouring Christian nations. Drawing on Aristotle's *Politics*, Wendeler characterised rulers who acted solely in their own self-interest as tyrants, implicating both Islamic and Catholic authorities in this flawed governance. Conversely, he praised the dependability of the Turkish sultan, arguing that the sultan was more reliable than the pope when it came to treaties and politics.[11]

Protestant Interpretations of the Sunni and Shi'a schism

In the aftermath of the **Thirty Years' War,** it became evident that the religious division between Catholics and Protestants would be permanent. Moreover, the proliferation of Protestant groups made the issue of toleration and coexistence more complex. It was within this historical context that Lutherans examined the schism in Islam to gain insights into their own experience of living with difference. Lutheran scholars analysed the Sunni-Shi'a divide by framing it as a conflict between the Sunni Ottoman Turks and the Shi'ite Safavid Persians. Their interest in this matter was driven by their preoccupation

64 Mehmet Karabela

with the Catholic and Protestant schism during the Reformation and the further splintering of the Protestant faith. Despite tackling questions about faith, Lutheran scholars' main aim was not primarily to gain a comprehensive understanding of Islam or its various emerging traditions. Instead, they leveraged the political and theological divide within Islam to affirm Protestantism as the only legitimate faith, while highlighting its difference from Catholicism.

While most Protestant scholars viewed Islam with disdain, several Lutheran theologians had studied Islam to the extent that they made a distinction between the Shi'a and Sunni, demonstrating a more comprehensive understanding of Islam compared to other Protestant scholars. It is noteworthy that these Lutheran authors held Persian Shi'a Muslims in higher regard than Turkish Sunnis, as the Shi'ite split from the Sunnis mirrored their split from Catholicism. Sebastian Kirchmaier (d.1700), a Lutheran theology professor at the University of Wittenberg, went so far as to write his *Oratio Persica* in Persian, focusing on the Sunni-Shi'a divide, a departure from the predominantly German or Latin Lutheran works of the time. The Rector of the Academy of Wittenberg, Johann Erich Ostermann (d.1668), praised Kirchmaier's work, which portrayed Persians as a noble and ancient people. In contrast, Ostermann expressed strong contempt towards the Turks, whom he described as 'foul and four-day-old swill'.[12] Previously, Luther had also extensively criticised the Turks in his *On War against the Turks* but refrained from doing so towards the Persians.[13]

Kirchmaier's contemporaries, Pfeiffer and Hieronymus Kromayer (d.1670), also wrote studies on the division between the Sunni and Shi'a division in Islam.[14] Their understanding of the schism not only reflects the orthodox Lutheran perspective of Islam during the seventeenth century, but also demonstrates how they utilised this to further their own religious identities. Protestant scholars rarely focused on the Sunni-Shi'a divide before the 1660s. Given Europe's ongoing conflict with the Ottoman Empire and its support for the Safavid Empire against the Turks – during which time these works by Kirchmaier, Pfeiffer, and Kromayer were written – it is understandable why they focused on this division within Islam. They were also concerned about divisions within Protestant Christianity, which led them to analyse this Islamic divide by portraying it as a mix of both political and theological conflicts between the Turks and Persians.

Some Lutherans viewed the Ottoman-Safavid conflict favourably since it aligned with their own political interests. Many thought that Turks resembled Arabs (Saracens) in their harshness and cruelty, while Persians were viewed as noble and non-threatening. Any favouritism towards Persians or Shi'ites could be explained by their greater fear of Ottoman Turks, whom they saw as enemies since the threat posed by the expansion of the Ottoman Empire in Europe played a significant role in shaping their perception of Sunni Muslims. The discovery of Christians held captive by the Ottomans intensified their concerns, particularly due to reports about some captives converting to Islam.[15] Due to this first-hand exposure to Turkish force, they preferred peaceful Shi'ite Persians over militaristic Sunni Turks.

The preference of Protestant scholars for Persians was not based on their appreciation of the Shi'ite faith, but rather on its utility for them to construct a specific historical narrative that aligned with their own theological beliefs, particularly *Sola Scriptura*. According to Protestant theologians, one of the main religious distinctions between Sunnis and Shi'ites was the differing value they placed on scripture and oral tradition. Both groups consider the Qur'an their holy text, but Sunnis also adhere to the *sunna* or 'oral law' compiled in the *ḥadīth* collections, which are believed to contain Muhammad's teachings, actions, and words. Because Sunnis follow these separate *ḥadīth* traditions along with the Qur'an, they are often referred to as traditionalists. On the contrary, Shi'ites are presented as scripturalists because they reject anything not found in the Qur'an alone – a belief that aligns with the Protestant doctrine of *Sola Scriptura*.

Pfeiffer also compared the differences between Sunnis and Shi'ites with various Jewish groups. He observed that just as the Sadducees rejected oral traditions, so did the Shi'ites. On the contrary, he noted that like the Pharisees, Sunnis followed not only written texts but also ancient traditions and oral laws. Pfeiffer emphasised how divisions within Islam were similar to those in Christianity due to differing interpretations of scripture, oral history, and tradition. He also drew parallels with conflicts within Judaism, interpreting animosity between Sunnis and Shi'ites as reminiscent of Rabbanite Jews' contempt for Karaite Jews who rejected Talmudic practices.

Interactions between the Ottoman Empire and Protestants

The Ottomans initially saw the Reformation as a theological issue, but soon, however, as a potential ally against the Habsburg Empire. For example, Süleyman the Magnificent (r.1520–1566), the Ottoman sultan, participated in an alliance that supported Protestants in their fight against King Charles V (r.1516–1556). He extended friendly gestures to Martin Luther and promised support to German Protestant princes, Calvinists in the Netherlands, and Calvinists in Hungary and Transylvania. Despite initial hesitations among Protestants regarding cooperation with the Ottomans, Süleyman employed his diplomatic skills along with Ottoman pressure on the Habsburgs to reinforce Protestant demands, leading Charles V to sign crucial peace agreements that recognised Protestantism in the Peace of Nuremberg (1532).[16]

The Habsburg Empire, under the rule of Charles V, struggled to suppress the spread of Lutheran ideas and maintain Catholic dominance. The pressure from the Ottoman Empire on the Habsburgs played a significant role in their decision to tolerate Lutherans in German lands. The refusal of religious toleration by the Habsburg Empire prompted Protestants to develop resistance

66   *Mehmet Karabela*

theories and form the **Schmalkaldic League** as direct responses to Ottoman influence. A crucial moment for Protestant Reformation took place at Speyer in 1529 when they named themselves 'Protestants' during an act of protest called **Protestation at Speyer**. With political backing from princes, German Lutheran theologians began to develop theological and legal frameworks for resistance against authority, as conveyed in **German Theologians on the Legal Grounds for Resistance** (1530). The German princes who supported Lutheranism gathered at the Imperial Diet in Speyer to protest the decision to rescind the previous religious freedoms granted to Lutherans at the **Diet of Augsburg** in 1530. This protestation united the Lutheran princes against the Catholic majority and laid the foundation for the formation of the **Schmalkaldic League** in 1531.

The Habsburg Empire's denial of religious toleration and subsequent development of Protestant resistance theory were closely linked to the presence of the Ottoman Empire on the borders of Europe. The Ottoman threat forced the Habsburgs to rethink their approach to religious dissent, as they recognised the need for unity and toleration in the face of external aggression. The Habsburg Empire was acutely aware of the dangers of religious division within its own domains as the Muslim influence on the borders of Europe served as a constant reminder of the need for unity and tolerance. The emergence of Protestantism would not have been as rapid without the ongoing conflict between the Ottoman Empire and the Habsburg monarchy.[17] The Ottomans served as a distraction for Catholic powers, diverting their attention from countering the spread of Protestant ideas.

The Ottoman Empire strategically supported and protected Lutherans and Calvinists against Catholicism to advance their own political agenda within Europe. The Ottoman Empire's imperial policy had a major impact on the consolidation, expansion, and validity of Lutheranism. The Turks demonstrated a preference for Protestants as long as it furthered their interests within Europe, while the Protestant groups fully capitalised on Ottoman incursions to strengthen their influence.[18] In the second half of the sixteenth century, the French Calvinists argued that the alliance with the Ottomans must be used against Catholic Spain. Both parties shared an objective: diminishing Habsburg control and subsequently weakening the power of the Catholic Church.

Many Protestants crossed confessional divides to ensure that power was properly balanced. **György I Rákóczi** (1593–1648), a Calvinist ruler of Transylvania, known for his pragmatism, navigated the complicated political landscape of seventeenth-century Europe. Rákóczi believed that it was necessary to confront other Christians, particularly Catholics, by aligning with the Ottomans, traditionally viewed as a threat to Christian Europe, to assert his authority and defy the Habsburgs (Catholics) in Upper Hungary.[19] In his *Reasons for Going to War* (1644), Rákóczi justified this decision by explaining his reasons for going to war against the Habsburgs and argued that it

Islam and Protestantism   67

was acceptable to engage in conflict with fellow Christians while receiving assistance from the Ottomans.

During the seventeenth century, Lutherans developed a growing fascination with eschatology due to the ongoing threat posed by the Ottoman Turks. They viewed the Turkish advance as a tangible manifestation of Gog and Magog – a clear indication that the long-awaited final battle between the faithful and the Antichrist was imminent. These theologians were also deeply troubled by Christian conversions to Islam, as such conversions played a crucial role in establishing Ottoman imperial identity and promoting Sunni Muslim orthodoxy against the Shi'ite Safavids. It is in this period of expansion that the term 'Turk' came to represent Muslims in the European mind. While other terms like Saracen, Persian, and Moor were available options, 'Turk' became widely accepted as the label for Muslims.

The Treaty of Karlowitz in 1699 marked the beginning of a decline in Ottoman expansion in Europe. Previously seen as an imminent danger, Islam's perceived threat to a religiously divided Europe diminished significantly after Turkish influence ceased instilling apocalyptic fears among Protestant theologians and scholars. The Turks were no longer viewed as symbolic figures representing the Antichrist besieging Christian Europe through Vienna; their fears were proven wrong as the Turkish threat gradually faded away and the apocalypse failed to arrive. The decline of Ottoman power in Europe also changed the prevalence of the 'Turk' as the Muslim, and under the influence of the Enlightenment ideas and the European interest in the Middle East, intellectual and political pursuits came to identify the 'Arab' as the Muslim.[20]

Notes

1 Mehmet Karabela, *Islamic Thought Through Protestant Eyes* (New York: Routledge, 2021).
2 Alastair Hamilton, "'To Rescue the Honour of the Germans': Qur'an Translations by Eighteenth-and Early Nineteenth-Century German Protestants", *Journal of the Warburg and Courtauld Institutes* 77 (2014): 173–209.
3 Friedrich Ulrich Calixt, *De religione muhammedana dissertatio* (Helmstedt, Hammius, 1687).
4 Johann Michael Lange, *Dissertatio historico-philologico-theologica de Alcorani prima inter Europaeos editione Arabica* (Altdorf: Literis Henrici Meyeri, Vniversitatis Typographi, 1703).
5 Noel Malcolm, "Islam as a 'Rational' Religion: Early Modern European Views", in *Scholarship between Europe and the Levant: Essays in Honour of Alastair Hamilton*, ed. Jan Loop and Jill Kraye (Leiden: Brill, 2020), 15–33; and Humberto Garcia, *Islam and the English Enlightenment, 1670–1840* (Baltimore, MD: Johns Hopkins University Press, 2012).
6 Friedrich Ulrich Calixt, *De religione muhammedana dissertatio* (Helmstedt: Hammius, 1687).
7 Daniel Clasen, *De religione politica* (Zerbst: Lüderwald, 1681); and Martin Mulsow, *Moderne aus dem Untergrund: Radikale Frühaufklärung in Deutschland 1680–1720* (Göttingen: Wallstein Verlag, 2018).

68   *Mehmet Karabela*

8 Christopher Rowland, "Scripture," in *The Cambridge Companion to Christian Political Theology*, ed. Craig Hovey and Elizabeth Phillips (Cambridge: Cambridge University Press, 2015), 157–175.

9 August Pfeiffer, *Dissertatio philologica quinta de Alishiis et Sunnitis, sive de praecipuis Persarum et Turcarum circa religionem dissidiis* (Wittenberg: J.W. Fincelius, 1670).

10 Samuel Schelwig, *De philosophia Turcica, oratio inauguralis* (Danzig: Gedani Rhetius, 1686).

11 Michael Wendeler, *Disputatio politica de republica Turcica* (Wittenberg: J.W. Fincelius, 1655).

12 Sebastian Kirchmaier, *Oratio Persica de differentia religionis Turcicae & Persicae* (Wittenberg: J.W. Fincelius, 1662).

13 Gregory Miller, "Luther on the Turks and Islam", *Lutheran Quarterly* 14 (2000): 79–97.

14 August Pfeiffer, *Dissertatio philologica quinta de Alishiis et Sunnitis, sive de praecipuis Persarum et Turcarum circa religionem dissidiis* (Wittenberg: J.W. Fincelius, 1670); and Hieronymus Kromayer, *Scrutinii religionum disputatio III, de Muhammetismo tum Turcarum tum Persarum* (Leipzig: Wittigau, 1668).

15 On the conversion to Islam in the post-Reformation period, see Marc David Baer, *Honored by the Glory of Islam: Conversion and Conquest in Ottoman Europe* (Oxford: Oxford University Press, 2007); and Tijana Krstić, *Contested Conversions to Islam Narratives of Religious Change in the Early Modern Ottoman Empire* (Stanford: Stanford University Press, 2011).

16 Stephen Fischer-Galaţi, *Ottoman Imperialism and German Protestantism 1521–1555* (Cambridge, MA: Harvard University Press, 1959); and Kenneth Setton, "Lutheranism and The Turkish Peril", *Balkan Studies* 3 (1962): 133–168.

17 Murat Iyigun, *War, Peace, and Prosperity in the Name of God: The Ottoman Role in Europe's Socioeconomic Evolution* (Chicago, IL: University of Chicago Press, 2015).

18 Daniel Goffman, *The Ottoman Empire and Early Modern Europe* (Cambridge: Cambridge University Press, 2004).

19 Gábor Kármán, *Tributaries and Peripheries of the Ottoman Empire* (Leiden: Brill, 2020).

20 Ivan Kalmar, *Early Orientalism: Imagined Islam and the Notion of Sublime Power* (New York: Routledge, 2011).

Part II

Sources

Note on Symbols in Titles

PEOPLES/GROUPS

Anabaptist, Antitrinitarian, Arminian, Asian Baptist, Calvinist, Church of England, Church of Ireland, Church of Sweden, Congregationalist, Dutch Reformed, Fifth Monarchist, Huguenot, Hutterite, Indigenous American, Interconfessional, Islam, Judaism, Labadists, Leveller, Lutheran, Mennonite, Moravian, Non-Christians, Presbyterian, Polish Brethren, Puritan, Quaker, Radical Reformation, Reformed, Roman Catholic Seeker, Separatist, Socinian, Spiritualist, Unitarian, Unity of Brethren, Waldensian, Zwinglian

NATIONS (MODERN BOUNDARIES)

Austria, Belgium, Belarus, Bermuda, Brazil, Czech Republic, Denmark, Dominican Republic, England, Estonia, Finland, France, Germany, Haiti, Hungary, India, Indonesia, Ireland, Italy, Japan, Latvia, Liechtenstein, Lithuania, Malaysia, Netherlands, Poland, Romania, Russia, Scotland, Spain, South Africa, Switzerland, Sweden, Turkey, Ukraine, United States, Wales

Africa, Americas, Asia, Global, Europe

KEYWORDS

Animals
Confession of Faith
Economics: Charity, Commerce, Common Good, Communal Living, Contract, Economics, Poverty, Property, Social Welfare, Trade
Education
Equality
Eschatology, Revelation
Evangelisation, Missions
Family
Freedom/Liberty: Academic Freedom, Freedom of Speech, Freedom of the Press, Freedom of Religion
Gender: Patriarchy, Women, Women's Rights (see also Marriage and Family)
Government: Absolutism, Authority, Balance of Powers, Church-State Relations, Common Good, Commonwealth, Democracy, Election, Government,

DOI: 10.4324/9781003247531-11

72 *Sources*

Intervention, Magistrates, Monarchy, Nation, Obedience, Patriotism, Parliament, Rebellion, Royal Supremacy, Submission, Tyranny
Irenicism
Language
Law: Antinomianism, Covenants, Divine Law, Duty, International Law, Law, Natural Law, Rights, Ten Commandments
Love
Marriage
Morality
Oath, Swearing
Petition
Place: Land, Colonisation, Paternalism
Religious Uniformity/Pluralism: Blasphemy, Censorship, Conscience, Heresy, Excommunication, Freedom of Religion, Liberty, Persecution, Pluralism, Toleration
Scripture: Hebrew Bible, New Testament
Sexuality
Supernatural: Revelation, Prophecy, Miracles, Witchcraft
Unfreedom: Serfdom, Servants, Slavery
Violence: Capital Crime, Coercion, Execution, Exile, Domestic Abuse, Murder, Non-violence, Peace, Punishment, Refugees, Violence, War

1 Martin Luther, *To the Christian Nobility of the German Nation* (1520)

Keywords: #Church-State Relations, #Authority, #Nation, #Law, #Commerce, #Morality, #Equality, #Poverty, #Marriage, #Sexuality, #Heresy
Region: #Germany
Group: #Lutheran | #Roman Catholic

Martin Luther's (1483–1546) *Ninety-Five Theses* (1517) marked a point of departure for many who would come to define themselves as Protestants. Luther had studied liberal arts and law at the University of Erfurt before embarking on the study of theology, and he became one of the towering figures of the Reformation, even as he did not originally set out to depart from the Roman Catholic Church. His political writings have impacted centuries of Christian and non-Christian political theorising – whether one is adopting, modifying, extending, or rejecting his arguments. These writings were usually occasional in nature, meaning they were not mere theoretical texts detached from pressing circumstances. In many works, he was quickly responding to the violence or counter-violence that came in the wake of the breakdown of civil and ecclesiastical unity. Luther's emphasis on the primacy of scripture and a believer's direct relationship with God challenged inherited notions of authority.[1]

In this following selection from *To the Christian Nobility of the German Nation Concerning the Reform of the Christian Estate* (1520), Luther's concern for order and hierarchy was evident in his attack on the first wall defending Romanism, the supposed privileges of those in the 'Spiritual Estate'. However, his assault on the Catholic fortress opened with a vision of all Christians standing in spiritual equality before God. It would only be a matter of time before those who wanted further Reformation would apply this spiritual levelling to temporal authority and societal distinctions. The second half of the excerpt contains Luther's recommendations to temporal powers about reforming all of society. The reform of the church should be done by the church, Luther argues. However, because the clergy were unwilling to do so, temporal powers must reform both church and state.

74   *Sources*

Martin Luther, "An Open Letter to the Christian Nobility" (1520) in *Works of Martin Luther*, trans. C.M. Jacobs and ed. Lane Hall (Philadelphia, PA: A. J. Holman, 1915) II:61–69, 99–162.

To the Esteemed and Reverend Master, Nicholas von Amsdorf

The time to keep silence has passed and the time to speak is come, as saith Ecclesiastes [3:7]. I have followed out our intention and brought together some matters touching the reform of the Christian Estate, to be laid before the Christian Nobility of the German Nation, in the hope that God may deign to help His Church through the efforts of the laity, since the clergy, to whom this task more properly belongs, have grown quite indifferent....

To His Most Illustrious and Mighty Majesty [Charles V],
and to the Christian Nobility of the German Nation

It is not out of sheer frowardness or rashness that I, a single, poor man, have undertaken to address your worships. The distress and oppression which weigh down all the Estates of Christendom, especially of Germany, and which move not me alone, but everyone to cry out time and again, and to pray for help, have forced me even now to cry aloud that God may inspire some one with His Spirit to lend this suffering nation a helping hand.

[*Previous attempts at reform have been thwarted by powerful popes because those reforming did not rely on God alone.*] That this may not so fare with us and our noble young Emperor Charles, we must be sure that in this matter we are dealing not with men, but with the princes of hell, who can fill the world with war and bloodshed, but whom war and bloodshed do not overcome. We must go at this work despairing of physical force and humbly trusting God.... Let us act wisely, therefore, and in the fear of God. The more force we use the greater our disaster if we do not act humbly and in God's fear. The popes and the Romans have hitherto been able, by the devil's help, to set kings at odds with one another, and they may be able to do it again, if we proceed by our own might and cunning, without God's help.

The Three Walls of the Romanists

The Romanists, with great adroitness, have built three walls about them, behind which they have hitherto defended themselves in such wise that no one has been able to reform them; and this has been the cause of terrible corruption throughout all Christendom.

First, when pressed by the temporal power, they have made decrees and said that the temporal power has no jurisdiction over them, but, on the other hand, that the spiritual power is above the temporal power. Second, when the attempt is made to reprove them out of the Scripture, they raise the objection that the interpretation of the Scriptures belongs to no one except the pope.

Sources 75

Third, if threatened with a council, they answer with the fable that no one can call a council but the pope....

Against the first wall we will direct our first attack. It is pure invention that pope, bishops, priests and monks are to be called the 'spiritual estate'; princes, lords, artisans, and farmers the 'temporal estate'. That is indeed a fine bit of lying hypocrisy. Yet no one should be frightened by it; and for this reason – viz., that all Christians are truly of the 'spiritual estate', and there is among them no difference at all but that of office, as Paul says in I Corinthians 12, We are all one body, yet every member has its work, whereby it serves every other [1 Cor. 12:12–27], all because we have one baptism, one Gospel, one faith [Eph. 4:5], and are all alike Christians; for baptism, Gospel and faith alone make us 'spiritual' and a Christian people....[*He then argues for the priesthood of all believers, including temporal magistrates.*]

Since, then, the temporal authorities are baptised with the same baptism and have the same faith and Gospel as we, we must grant that they are priests and bishops, and count their office one which has a proper and useful place in the Christian community. For whoever comes out of the water of baptism can boast that he is already consecrated priest, bishop and pope, though it is not seemly that everyone should exercise the office. Nay, just because we are all in like manner priests, no one must put himself forward and undertake, without our consent and election, to do what is in the power of all of us. For what is common to all, no one dare take upon himself without the will and the command of the community; and should it happen that one chosen for such an office were deposed for malfeasance, he would then be just as he was before he held office. Therefore a priest in Christendom is nothing else than an office-holder. While he is in office, he has precedence; when deposed, he is a peasant or a townsman like the rest. Beyond all doubt, then, a priest is no longer a priest when he is deposed. But now they have invented [the idea of an indelible mark], and prate that the deposed priest is nevertheless something different from a mere layman. They even dream, that a priest can never become a layman, or be anything else than a priest. All this is mere talk and man-made law.

From all this it follows that there is really no difference between laymen and priests, princes and bishops, 'spirituals' and 'temporals', as they call them, except that of office and work, but not of 'estate'; for they are all of the same estate....

Therefore, just as those who are not called 'spiritual' – priests, bishops or popes – are neither different from other Christians nor superior to them, except that they are charged with the administration of the Word of God and the sacraments, which is their work and office, so it is with the temporal authorities, – they bear the sword and rod with which to punish the evil and protect the good [Rom. 13:4]. A cobbler, a smith, a farmer, each has the work and office of his trade, and yet they are all alike consecrated priests and bishops, and everyone by means of his work or office must benefit and serve

76 *Sources*

every other, that in this way many kinds of work may be done for the bodily and spiritual welfare of the community, even as all the members of the body serve one another....

Proposals for Reform

1 Every prince, nobleman and city should boldly forbid their subjects to pay the annates to Rome and should abolish them entirely; for the pope has broken the compact, and made the annates a robbery, to the injury and shame of the whole German nation....

2–3 [*The power of Rome to make ecclesiastical appointments in the German nation should be withdrawn, and the consecration of Bishops by local Bishops or Archbishops restored.*]

4 It should be decreed that no temporal matter shall be taken to Rome, but that all such cases shall be left to the temporal authorities....

7 The Roman See should also do away with the *officia*, and diminish the swarm of vermin at Rome, so that the pope's household can be supported by the pope's own purse. The pope should not allow his court to surpass in pomp and extravagance the courts of all kings....

8 The hard and terrible oaths should be abolished, which the bishops are wrongfully compelled to render to the pope, and by which they are bound like servants....

9 The pope should have no authority over the emperor, except that he anoints and crowns him at the altar....

10 The pope should restrain himself, take his fingers out of the pie, and claim no title to the Kingdoms of Naples and Sicily. He has exactly as much right to that kingdom as I have, and yet he wishes to be its overlord. It is plunder got by violence, like all his other possessions....

11 The kissing of the pope's feet should take place no more....Compare the two – Christ and the pope! Christ washed his disciples' feet...; the pope, as though he were higher than Christ,...allows people to kiss his feet....

12 Pilgrimages to Rome should be abolished [in most instances]....

14....[P]riests should not be compelled to live without a wedded wife, but should be permitted to have one....

17 Certain of the penalties or punishments of the canon law should be abolished, especially the interdict, which is, beyond all doubt, an invention of the evil Spirit....The ban is to be used in no case except where the Scriptures prescribe its use, that is, against those who do not hold the true faith or live in open sin; it is not to be used for the sake of temporal possessions....

18 All festivals should be abolished, and Sunday alone retained....

21 One of our greatest necessities is the abolition of all begging throughout Christendom [particularly by the Mendicant order]....Every city could support its own poor, and if it were too small, the people in the surrounding villages also should be exhorted to contribute, since in any case they have to feed so many vagabonds and knaves in the guise of

mendicants. In this way, too, it could be known who were really poor and who not....

24 It is high time that we seriously and honestly consider the case of the Bohemians, and come into union with them so that the terrible slander, hatred and envy on both sides may cease. [*He mentions the mistreatment of Jan Hus and Jerome of Prague, particularly when they were promised safe passage and then captured and executed. Luther expresses sympathy for Hus' theology and objects to burning heretics.*] We should vanquish heretics with books, not with burning; for so the ancient fathers did. If it were a science [a branch of knowledge] to vanquish heretics with fire, then the hangmen would be the most learned doctors on earth; we should no longer need to study, but he who overcame another by force might burn him at the stake....

25 The universities also need a good, thorough reformation.... [*He discourses on the disciplines needing reform and why before mentioning the lamentable state of legal learning.*] The temporal law, – God help us! what a wilderness it has become! Though it is much better, wiser and more rational than the 'spiritual law' which has nothing good about it except the name, still there is far too much of it. Surely the Holy Scriptures and good rulers would be law enough; as St. Paul says in 1 Corinthians 6[:1], 'Is there no one among you who can judge his neighbour's cause, that ye must go to the law before the heathen courts?' It seems just to me that the territorial laws and territorial customs should take precedence over the general imperial laws, and the imperial laws be used only in case of necessity. Would to God that as every land has its own peculiar character, so it were ruled by its own brief laws, as the lands were ruled before these imperial laws were invented, and many lands are still ruled without them! These diffuse and far-fetched laws are only a burden to the people, and hinder causes more than they help them....

26 [*He argues that the pope unjustly took the Holy Roman Empire from the Greek emperor and gave it to the Germans.*] Because then, the empire has been given us without our fault, by the providence of God and the plotting of evil men, I would not advise that we give it up, but rather that we rule it wisely and in the fear of God, so long as it should please Him. For, as has been said, it matters not to Him where an empire comes from; it is His will that it should be ruled. Though the popes took it dishonestly from others, nevertheless we did not get it dishonestly. It is given us by the will of God through evil-minded men....

27 Enough has now been said about the failings of the clergy.... We would say something too about the failings of the temporal estate.

First. There is great need of a general law and decree of the German nation against the extravagance and excess in dress, by which so many nobles and rich men are impoverished....

Second. In like manner it is also necessary to restrict the spice-traffic which is another of the great ships in which money is carried out of

German lands. There grows among us, by God's grace, more to eat and drink than in any other land, and just as choice and good. Perhaps the proposals that I make may seem foolish and impossible and give the impression that I want to suppress the greatest of all trades, that of commerce; but I am doing what I can. If reforms are not generally introduced, then let every one who is willing reform himself. I do not see that many good customs have ever come to a land through commerce, and in ancient times God made His people of Israel dwell away from the sea on this account, and did not let them engage much in commerce.

Third. But the greatest misfortune of the German nation is certainly the traffic in annuities. [*In this way, laws against charging interest were circumvented and large corporations amassed wealth. Of the wealthy Fugger family, he says:*] I am not a mathematician, but I do not understand how a man with a hundred gulden can make a profit of twenty gulden in one year, nay, how with one gulden he can make another; and that, too, by another way than agriculture or cattle-raising, in which increase of wealth depends not on human wits, but on God's blessing.... This I know well, that it would be much more pleasing to God if we increased agriculture and diminished commerce....

Fourth. Next comes the abuse of eating and drinking which gives us Germans a bad reputation in foreign lands, as though it were our special vice. Preaching cannot stop it; it has become too common, and has got too firmly the upper hand. The waste of money which it causes would be a small thing, were it not followed by others sins, – murder, adultery, stealing, irreverence and all the vices. The temporal sword can do something to prevent it....

Fifth. Finally, is it not a pitiful thing that we Christians should maintain among us open and common houses of prostitution, though all of us are baptised unto chastity?...[S]hould not the temporal, Christian government consider that in this heathen way [allowing houses of prostitution] the evil is not to be controlled. If the people of Israel could exist without such an abomination, why could not Christian people do as much....

2 Philip Melanchthon, *Natural, Divine and Human Laws* (1521)

Keywords: #Law, #Natural Law, #Divine Law, #International Law, #Conscience, #Communal Living, #Crime, #Capital Crime, #Contract, #Punishment, #Violence, #Slavery, #Submission, #Magistrate, #Ten Commandments
Region: #Germany
Group: #Lutheran

Philip Melanchthon (1497–1560) was a German humanist who was educated at Pforzheim, Heidelberg, and Tübingen. His interest in theology grew while teaching Greek at Wittenberg alongside **Martin Luther**. During Luther's forced seclusion in the early 1520s, Melanchthon continued working in Wittenberg. The following extract comes from his influential *Loci Communes Theologici*, which first appeared in 1521 and was expanded multiple times. It was a groundbreaking theological text, offering the first systematic theology of the Reformation.[2] He was also the principle author of the **Augsburg Confession** (1530). Both documents set contours for Lutheran teaching and impacted the Protestant relationship with the state. The *Loci Communes* ('Common Places') is topically arranged and touches on politics at several points. The following excerpts relate to law, natural law, divine laws, human laws, and magistrates. In later editions of the *Loci Communes*, Melanchthon warned against closely linking the church or state with biblical Israel, citing the cautionary example of **Thomas Müntzer**.[3]

Philip Melanchthon, *Commonplaces: Loci Communes 1521*, trans. Christian Preus (Saint Louis, MO: Concordia Publishing House, 2014), n.p. Used with permission. cph.org.

LAW

…Now the Law is the judgement that demands good and forbids evil. 'Right' is the authority to act according to the Law. The ancients have said much both in favour of laws and against laws, and before long we will show from

80 *Sources*

what source their judgements have sprung. Some laws are natural, some divine, and some human.

NATURAL LAW

...But Paul does teach that there is a law of nature in us. He does so with a marvellously elegant and well-argued enthymeme in Romans 2, reasoning in the following way: the Gentiles have a conscience that either defends or accuses their actions [Rom. 2:15]. It is therefore a law. For what else is the conscience except a judgement over our actions that is derived from some law or common principle? And so natural law is a judgement common to all and suited to the formation of morals. To it, all men assent together. Thus God has engraved it upon everyone's mind. For as there are in the theoretical disciplines, like mathematics, certain common principles or [common understandings or preconceptions] (such as that the whole is greater than the parts), so are there in ethics certain common principles and a priori conclusions (for the sake of instruction, we need to use their terms), which serve as rules over all human actions. These you should properly call natural laws.

Marcus Cicero, in his books *On Laws*, copies Plato and derives the foundations of laws from human nature. And although I do not condemn this reasoning, I see it as more urbane than precise. Moreover, there are very many godless notions in Cicero's argument, as is generally the case when we follow the methods and devices of our reason rather than the precepts of Holy Scripture. For judgement based on human comprehension is generally deceptive because of our inborn blindness. As a result, although a certain moral blueprint has been engraved upon our minds, we still can hardly grasp it. And when I say that God has imprinted the laws of nature on human minds, I mean that the understanding of these laws is a certain concreated condition (to use their language). This knowledge is not a discovery made by our genius. Rather, it is a standard that God has placed in us for judging what is moral....

[T]he following seem to be the foundations of the laws that properly pertain to man.

I God must be worshiped.
II Because we are born into a certain society in life, nobody should be harmed.
III Human society requires that we possess all things in common.

We have taken the first law about worshiping God from Romans 1, where Paul unmistakably counts it among natural laws. For he says that God has declared his majesty to all men by the creation and governance of the whole universe [Rom. 1:19–20]....

The second law, which warns against harming anyone, is unmistakably derived from common necessity, since we are all born connected with one another and obligated to each other, as Scripture indicates when it says that it is not appropriate for a man to live alone, but that help must be given to

Sources 81

him for the betterment of his life [Gen. 2:18]. And so this law commands us not to harm anyone, that is, that we should all eagerly love each other so that by zealously doing our duty all may experience our kindness. Therefore, this law embraces the divine laws that we not kill anyone, steal others' property, and the like.

Perhaps you will ask: 'Why then do magistrates kill criminals?' My response is that after the fall of Adam [Gen. 3] imprinted the mark of sin on us all, it is the condition of human affairs that evil people often harm good people. And so the human race very often must depend on the protection of the law against harming others. Therefore, those who disturb the public peace and hurt innocent people must be coerced, restrained, and removed from the public so that by their removal more people can be protected. The law remains: harm no one. But if someone has been harmed already, the one who did the harming has to be removed so that more people are not harmed. It is more important to preserve the entire population than one individual or another. Therefore, he is removed who threatens harm to the entire population by the commission of one crime or another that shows his harmfulness. For this reason the state has magistrates, punishes criminals, and wages wars, all of which the lawyers assign to the right of nations.

The third law, which concerns sharing things, evidently arises from the nature of society among the human race. For if among a few friends the common adage should be valid...that all things should be shared among friends, why should the same proverb not be valid among all men? For all people should be in harmony with one another, just as brothers are in harmony with brothers, children with parents, and parents with children. The law against harming others demands this.

But because human greed does not permit us to enjoy all things in common, this law must be governed by a higher law, namely, the law against harming others. Things should be held in common only insofar as public peace and the safety of the populace allow....Therefore, contracts have been invented through which one may share his possessions with many others, so that there can be at least some sharing of things.

So much concerning the general outline of natural laws, which you can summarise in the following way

I   Worship God.
II   Since we are born into a common society in life, harm no one but be helpful and kind to everyone.
III If it cannot happen that absolutely no one is harmed, then it should be so arranged that the fewest are harmed. Those should be removed who disturb public tranquillity, and for this reason magistracies and punishments should be instituted to deal with criminals.
IV   Property must be divided for the sake of public peace. But let some alleviate the lack of others through contracts.

82 *Sources*

[*This is followed by a cursory discussion of the law of nations (ius gentium) and a reflection on the use of non-Christians authors in forming law, which leads into a discussion of slavery.*] Also in civil law, as they call it, there are many things that reflect human affections instead of natural laws. For what is more foreign to the law of nature than slavery? And in some contracts the details that matter most are unjustly concealed. But more on this elsewhere. A good man will fashion civil constitutions according to a just and good rule, that is, with both divine and natural laws. And whatever is instituted against these laws can be nothing but unjust....

DIVINE LAWS

Divine laws are those laws that God has decreed through the canonical Scriptures. They have been arranged under three categories: some are moral, some judicial, and some ceremonial. [*Melanchthon then discourses at length about the Ten Commandments, whether God's commands are recommended or required, and the applicability of Moses' Judicial and Ceremonial Laws.*]

HUMAN LAWS

Human laws are all the laws that men have established. And as human affairs stand right now, some human laws are civil and some pontifical. Civil laws are those laws that magistrates, princes, kings, and cities institute in their state. In Romans 13:[1–3], Paul teaches what should be thought concerning the authority of this sort of law, when he says,

> Let every soul be subject to the higher powers. For there is no power except from God. But what powers exist have been instituted by God, so that whoever resists the power, resists the institution of God. But those who resist acquire for themselves condemnation. For princes are not a terror to good works, but to evil.

Indeed, the purpose of magistrates and civil laws is none other than to punish and prevent injustices. Thus laws are enacted for the division of property, the forms of contracts, and the punishment of wrongdoers. For the magistrate is the minister of God, a wrathful avenger against him who does wrong. But it is not acceptable for a magistrate to legislate against divine law, nor should we obey anything contrary to divine law, as it is written in Acts [5:29], 'We ought to obey God rather than men'. And from this passage the prudent reader will easily be able to judge to what extent we are subject to human laws. But maybe we will speak more about magistrates later when we treat the condition of mankind.

[*He then discusses the extent to which pontifical laws should be heeded, and argues that concerning the*] faith, neither the priests nor the councils nor the Church catholic have the right to change or legislate anything. Rather, articles of faith should be examined simply, according to the rule of Holy

Scripture. Nor should anything be considered an article of faith that is handed down outside of Scripture. [*He then gives guidelines for testing law by the rule of scripture, arguing that those claiming to speak for God (whether ministers or councils) are prone to error. This leads to a consideration of the importance of tradition.*]

What then? How do human traditions bind consciences? Do they sin who violate human decrees? I answer that papal laws should be borne just as we bear any injury or tyranny, according to the passage in Matthew 5:[41], 'Whoever compels you to go a mile, walk with him also another two'. But they can be tolerated only insofar as the conscience remains untroubled by them: 'We ought to obey God rather than men' (Acts 5:[29]). Therefore when traditions obscure faith, when they are an occasion for sin, they should be violated....

MAGISTRATES

A section on magistrates seemed especially necessary. For pedagogical reasons, we will, to start out, follow the common division. Magistrates are divided into civil and ecclesiastical. The civil magistrate is one who wields the sword and protects civil peace. Paul approves of this kind of magistrate in Romans 13:[1–7]. The functions of the sword include civil laws, the civil ordinances of public courts, and the punishments of criminals. The duty of the sword includes administering laws against murder, against taking vengeance, etc. Therefore, the magistrate administers the sword with God's approval. The same can be said of lawyers if they issue opinions concerning the law or defend the oppressed. But people who go to court commit an especially grievous sin.

Now these are my thoughts on wielding the power of the sword. First of all, if princes command anything against God, they should not be obeyed, according to Acts 5:[29], 'We ought to obey God rather than men'. You have innumerable examples of this principle, perhaps the most beautiful of which is in Amos 7:[10–17]. Second, if they command what is in the public's best interest, they should be obeyed, according to Romans 13:[5], 'They should be obeyed not only because of wrath but because of conscience'. For love obligates us to all kinds of civil responsibilities. Finally, if they issue any tyrannical commands when nothing can be done about it short of a disturbance or sedition, we should also bear with this magistracy because of love. For this is what Christ says, 'If anyone strikes you on the right cheek, turn to him also the left' [Matt. 5:39]. But if you can disobey it without scandal and a public disturbance, do so. For example, if you have been thrown into prison undeservedly and you can break out without a public disturbance, nothing forbids you from escaping. This agrees with 1 Corinthians 7:[21], 'If you can be free, rather use it'.

Now for our thoughts on ecclesiastical magistrates: First, ministers are bishops, not rulers or magistrates. Second, bishops do not have the right to

84 *Sources*

establish laws, since they have been commanded to preach only the Word of God, not the word of men. We explained this above, and it is clear enough from Jeremiah 23:[16].

I In the first place, then, if they teach Scripture, they must be heard as if they were Christ....

II Second, if they have taught anything against Scripture, they should not be heard....

III Third, if they have issued anything outside of Scripture so as to bind consciences, they should not be heard....

IV In the fourth place, if you are not burdening the conscience with the law of the bishop but interpret it as an external obligation, as spiritual men do who understand that the conscience cannot be bound by any human law, you will be judging the law of the bishop as you would the tyranny of the civil magistrate.

3 Reports Concerning the Zwickau Prophets (1521)

Keywords: #Violence, #Revelation, #Prophecy
Region: #Germany
Group: #Radical Reformation, #Anabaptist

The boundaries of acceptable reform were soon tested by prophets in Zwickau (Saxony) who claimed to directly hear from God. These 'Zwickau Prophets', Nicholas Storch, Marcus Thomae Stübner, and Thomas Drechsel, were expelled from the city. **Philip Melanchthon** felt conflicted by these prophets. He wrote to Elector Frederick at the close of 1521 of how he sensed an extraordinary influence of the Holy Spirit in them that manifested in 'the clear voice of God' that sometimes reveals 'the future'. He also wrote to Georg Spalatin, saying 'they are doing things which, unless Luther intervenes, will end I know not where'. Luther, in a 13 January 1522 letter, chided Melanchthon for his balanced approach to these prophets. Scriptural prophets were attested by miracles, not a bare claim to have heard from God: 'Do not by any means receive them if they assert that they are called by mere revelation'.[4] The first excerpt comes from Nicholas Hausmann (c.1478–1538), a Lutheran Reformer based in Zwickau who served in the place of the recently expelled radical preacher, **Thomas Müntzer**. Hausmann wrote the following critical report about the Zwickau Prophets, and the excerpt claims to quote at length from one of the prophets named Nicholas Storch, a weaver by profession. The second selection comes from Heinrich Bullinger (1504–1575), a leader of the Reformation in Zürich.[5] Prophecy and direct revelation would long be associated with political rebellion, violence, and social instability, from the Zwickau Prophets to Thomas Müntzer to the **Münster Commune** to **Anne Hutchinson** and into the present.

Eric W. Gritsch, *Reformer Without a Church* (Philadelphia, PA: Fortress, 1967), 25–26; C. Henry Smith, *The Mennonites of America* (Scottsdale, AZ: Mennonite Publishing House, 1909), 25.

———

86 *Sources*

[Comments of Nicholas Hausmann]

[Quotation from the prophet, Nicholas Storch]: Those in authority live only in lust, consume the sweat and blood of their subjects, eat and drink night and day, hunt, run, and kill....Everyone therefore should arm himself and attack the priests in their fat nests, beating, killing, and strangling them, because once the bellwethers are removed, the sheep are easier to handle. Afterward the land-grabbers and noblemen should be attacked, their property confiscated, and their castles destroyed.... [*He then denounces the feudal system at length and critiques the 'tomfoolery' of priests.*]

You can receive the forgiveness of sins without all this nonsense, in your own quiet home or wherever you are, if you believe in the revelation of the Spirit....Don't you believe that God has another word which he will reveal to you through the Spirit? Why should God be chained to the creature?...He is absolutely free. He does what he wills. Thus the external, audible word of the priests is not the word of God but their own....[*He then denounces infant baptism.*]

[Comments of Heinrich Bullinger]

About the year 1521 or 1522 there arose in Saxony a number of restless spirits among whom Nicholas Storch was one of the most influential, who went about saying that God revealed himself to them through dreams and visions, that there must be a new world in which only righteousness shall prevail. Therefore all godless people must be destroyed from the earth and all godless princes and lords. They called all people godless who did not partake with them. At first they kept these matters secret. From this same school came Thomas Müntzer who also had his followers.... This Müntzer boasted that God had revealed Himself to him. All his conversation and writing was bitter against the preachers and also against the magistrates.

4 Social Welfare Legislation for the City of Wittenberg (1522)

Keywords: #Economics, #Poverty, #Charity, #Social Welfare, #Family, #Sexuality, #Education
Region: #Germany
Group: #Lutheran

Martin Luther's earlier works, like *To the Christian Nobility* (1520), called for financial reform of the church and state, partly to correct what he saw as financial abuses of the church. The following legislation from Wittenberg was instituted under **Andreas Karlstadt** (1486–1541) when Luther was in hiding. It ordered that financial support for monasteries would be diverted to social welfare, and established 'a common chest' from which support would be offered to vulnerable members of the local community. It makes provisions for those who are not able to work or secure their livelihood through marriage, and regulates access to loans and conditions of repayment.[6]

Carter Lindberg, *Beyond Charity: Reformation Initiatives for the Poor* (Minneapolis, MN: Fortress, 1993), 200–202.

———

1 It is unanimously resolved that all income from the churches, all of the brotherhoods, and the guilds shall be collected together and brought into a common chest....
3 Likewise, no beggars shall be tolerated in our city, rather one shall urge them to work or expel them from the city. But they who because of age or sickness or other misfortune have fallen into poverty shall be provided for from the common chest through the appropriate delegated manner.
   [*This was followed by stipulations against religious orders that wander or depend on charity, and against foreign students who would become a financial burden.*]
9 Likewise, loans shall be made from the common chest to poor artisans who without this are unable to support themselves daily by their trade... When they are established, however, they can repay the loan without

88 *Sources*

interest; but if they are unable to repay the loan, it shall be pardoned for God's sake.

10 Likewise, the common chest shall provide for poor orphans, the children of poor people, and maidens who shall be given an appropriate dowry for marriage.

[They then legislated about collecting money for good works, supporting priests, making sure priests do not benefit from wills, the simple adornment of churches and the proper order of church services].

15 We also will not permit unchaste persons to be supported by us; they should have recourse to marriage....

[They then make provisions for lessening the burden of high interest rates.]

17 Likewise, particular regard shall be given to the children of poor people [that they are educated or trained in a craft].

5   Andreas Karlstadt, *On the Abolition of Images and Poverty* (1522)

Keywords: #Violence, #Poverty, #Charity
Region: #Germany
Group: #Lutheran

Andreas Karlstadt (1486–1541) was born in Karlstadt am Main, studied at Erfurt and Cologne, and earned his doctorate in theology from Wittenberg in 1510. He was ordained and taught at the University of Wittenberg, where he worked alongside **Martin Luther**, whose ideas he initially opposed. Karlstadt played an important role in the debates between the Catholic theologian Johann Eck and Luther. Eck was a theology professor at the University of Ingolstadt who led the early phase of Catholic opposition to reforming ideas. While Luther was in hiding, Karlstadt worked towards the Reformation of Wittenberg. The speed of reform alarmed many, including Luther. Karlstadt was eventually censored and banished from Saxony, a move that brought him into the orbit of radical Reformers who published his works. Although he wanted to reform at a greater pace than Luther, he recoiled at **Thomas Müntzer**'s recourse to violence. After the **German Peasants' War**, the fugitive Karlstadt was both concealed and confined in Wittenberg. He eventually escaped and made his way to Zürich, where he worked with **Huldreich Zwingli** and took up a position at the University of Basel.

In the following excerpt, Karlstadt advocated the immediate destruction of idolatrous images, arguing at the same time for the care and reform of the poor. In *Whether One Should Proceed Slowly* (1524), he argued that just as one would not let a child handle a dangerous knife, so brotherly love required the forcible removal of the blade of heresy and idolatry: 'Where Christians rule, there they should consider no government, but rather freely on their own hew down and throw down what is contrary to God, even without preaching'.[7] Luther, in 1524, argued that Karlstadt and others were so eager to follow what they thought to be the 'living voice from heaven' that in their excitement, 'Christ is forgotten'.[8] In his *Letter to the Princes of Saxony* (July 1524) and *Against the Heavenly Prophets* (1525), Luther critiqued prophet-led iconoclasm. He worried that invoking the precedent of

90 *Sources*

Hebrew Bible, iconoclasm was risky because the text sanctioned both iconoclasm and the execution of idol-worshipping humans. Thomas Müntzer, Luther warned, had 'already progressed from images to people' and linked these
ideas with a justification of rebellion.[9]

Andreas Karlstadt, *On the Abolition of Images and that there should be No
Beggars Among Christians* (27 January 1522), trans. Carter Lindberg, in *The
European Reformations Sourcebook*, ed. Carter Lindberg (Malden, MA: Black-
well, 2000), 57. Reproduced with permission of the Licensor through PLSclear.

[Images]

See how God forbids all kinds of images,...God says you shall not worship
them, you shall not even honour them [Exod. 20:4–5]. Therefore, God forbids all veneration [of images] and breaks down the papist refuge which by
their agility always does violence to the Scriptures and makes black white
and evil good....

Now I will and shall say to the pious Christians that all of you who stand
in fear of an image have idols in your heart [e.g., Jer. 10:5; Ezek. 14:1–8]....

Thus shall you deal with them, says God (Deut. 7:5): You shall overturn and
overthrow their altars. You shall break their images to pieces. You shall hew
down their pillars and burn up their carved images. We have no godly altars
but rather heathen and human ones, as noted in Ex. 20:4. Therefore Christians
shall abolish them.... The highest authorities should also abolish images....

[O]ur magistrates should not wait until the priests of Baal purge out their
wooden vessels and required hinderances. For they will never begin to do it.
The highest civil authorities should command and do this....

I say to you that God has forbidden images no less nor with less purpose
than murder, stealing, robbery, adultery [Exod. 20]....

I have written too much and too little concerning idols, therefore I must
write the following more briefly. In short, I can say that I have a sure sign
when I come into a city that there are no Christians, or if there are, they are
discouraged and few, if I see men begging for a living.

There shall be no beggar among you because the Lord your God blessed
you in the earth which he gave you to possess (Deut. 15:14)....

If one of your brothers who dwells in the gate of your city comes to poverty, you shall not harden and shut your heart; you shall also not close your
hand but rather open it to the poor and lend him what he needs.... Thus
where one falls into poverty, everyone, and in particular the highest civil
authority, should have compassion upon the poor and no one should stop
the heart, but rather open his hands and lend the poor brother what he needs
[Deut 15:7–8]....

[*Money taken from Catholic endowments should be put into a common
chest for the good of the community.*]

6   Martin Luther, *Temporal Authority: To What Extent it Should Be Obeyed* (1523)

Keywords: #Freedom, #Submission, #Authority, #Church-State Relations, #Violence, #Heresy
Region: #Germany
Group: #Lutheran

'At Worms in 1521', writes J. M. Porter, 'Martin Luther was commanded by the highest temporal authority, the emperor, to recant his works, and he had refused'. Luther's books were ordered to be burned, and he was excommunicated. He defied authority and, unlike Jan Hus (c.1370–1415), lived to write and preach about it. The following selection comes from *Temporal Authority: To What Extent It Should Be Obeyed* (1523). In that work, Luther 'explains the nature of temporal authority, its limitations, and the responsibilities of the Christian subject and the Christian ruler'.[10] A hallmark of Luther's thought is the distinction between 'two kingdoms', secular and ecclesiastical, and the jurisdiction of each. This distinction developed around 1522 and 1523.[11] Secular authority and the church were independent entities, and yet, Luther called on Christian magistrates to work through church authorities to institute reforms.[12] In the following excerpt, Luther explored distinctions between the civil and ecclesiastical kingdoms, and some of the overlap between them. Crucially, this division undergirds his resistance to commands deemed unbiblical.

Martin Luther, *Temporal Authority: To What Extent it Should be Obeyed*, trans. J. J. Schindel and rev. Walther I. Brandt, in *Luther's Works*, ed. Walther I. Brandt (Philadelphia, PA: Muhlenberg, 1962) 45:111–114, 117–123, 125–126.

———

Thereby [St. Peter] clearly sets a limit to temporal authority [Acts 5:29], for if we had to do everything that the temporal authority wanted there would have been no point in saying, 'We must obey God rather than men'.

92 Sources

If your prince or temporal ruler commands you to side with the pope, to believe thus and so, or to get rid of certain books, you should say,

> It is not fitting that Lucifer should sit at the side of God. Gracious sir, I owe you obedience in body and property; command me within the limits of your authority on earth, and I will obey. But if you command me to believe or to get rid of certain books, I will not obey; for then you are a tyrant and overreach yourself, commanding where you have neither right nor authority....

You must know that since the beginning of the world a wise prince is a mighty rare bird, and an upright prince even rarer. They are generally the biggest fools or the worst scoundrels on earth; therefore one must constantly expect the worst from them and look for little good, especially in divine matters which concern the salvation of souls. They are God's executioners and hangmen; his divine wrath uses them to punish the wicked and to maintain outward peace [Rom. 13:1–5]....

Again, you will say, 'The temporal power is not forcing men to believe, it is simply seeing to it externally that no one deceives the people by false doctrine, how could heretics otherwise be restrained?' Answer: This the bishops should do; it is a function entrusted to them and not to the princes. Heresy can never be restrained by force. One will have to tackle the problem in some other way, for heresy must be opposed and dealt with otherwise than with the sword. Here God's word must do the fighting. If it does not succeed, certainly the temporal power will not succeed either, even if it were to drench the world in blood. Heresy is a spiritual matter which you cannot hack to pieces with iron, consume with fire, or drown with water....

But you might say, 'Since there is to be no temporal sword among Christians, how then are they to be ruled outwardly? There certainly must be authority even among Christians'. Answer: Among Christians there shall and can be no authority; rather all are alike subject to one another [Rom. 12; 1 Pet. 5:5; Luke 14:10].... Among Christians there is no superior but Christ himself, and him alone. What kind of authority can there be where all are equal and have the same right, power, possession, and honour, and where no one desires to be the other's superior, but each the other's subordinate? Where there are such people, one could not establish authority even if he wanted to, since in the nature of things it is impossible to have superiors where no one is willing to be a superior. Where there are no such people, however, there are no real Christians either.

What, then, are the priests and bishops? Answer: Their government is not a matter of authority or power, but a service and an office, for they are neither higher nor better than other Christians. Therefore, they should impose no law or decree on others without their will and consent....

Sources 93

Now that we know the limits of temporal authority; it is time to inquire also how a prince should use it. We do this for the sake of those very few who would also like very much to be Christian princes and lords, and who desire to enter into the life in heaven....

First. He must give consideration and attention to his subjects, and really devote himself to it. This he does when he directs his every thought to making himself useful and beneficial to them....

Second. He must beware of the high and mighty and of his counsellors, and so conduct himself towards them that he despises none, but also trusts none enough to leave everything to him....

Third. He must take care to deal justly with evildoers. Here he must be very wise and prudent, so he can inflict punishment without injury to others....

What if a prince is in the wrong [in going to war]? Are his people bound to follow him then too? Answer: No, for it is no one's duty to do wrong; we must obey God (who desires the right) rather than men [Acts 5:29]. What if the subjects do not know whether their prince is in the right or not? Answer: So long as they do not know, and cannot in all diligence find out, they may obey him without peril to their souls....

7 Argula von Grumbach, *Against Coercion in the University* (1523)

Keywords: #Academic Freedom, #Authority, #Women, #Coercion
Region: #Germany
Group: #Lutheran | #Roman Catholic

———

Argula von Grumbach (c.1492–c.1554), a well-connected Bavarian noblewoman, gained notoriety for her challenge of the faculty of Ingolstadt, which boasted Martin Luther's famous interlocutor Johann Eck. In 1523, the theological faculty of Ingolstadt arrested a young scholar, Arsacius Seehofer, on account of his sympathy for Luther. Seehofer eventually caved under pressure and renounced his Lutheran views, sparking protests among his supporters. The case was followed closely by Argula von Grumbach. She travelled to Nuremberg to discuss the matter with the Reformer **Andreas Osiander**, and soon wrote two letters that displayed her capacious grasp of scripture: the first to the university; the second to Duke Wilhelm IV (of Bavaria). Princes, she told Wilhelm, should not be 'led along like monkeys on a chain by these so-called spiritual rulers'.

Some of her letters made their way into print, and even became bestsellers in 1523 and 1524, and as many as 30,000 copies would come into circulation. The letters, eight in total, were addressed to audiences ranging from theologians to magistrates to commoners. She forcefully challenged ecclesiastical leaders by asserting the individual's right to interpret scripture. She wrote at a time of increasing anxiety over the destabilising nature of evangelical ideas, at a time when authorities tried unsuccessfully to coax heterodoxy back into Pandora's box.

Publication of these letters, she later claimed, took place without her knowledge, but 'now I see that God wishes to have it made public'. She then harnessed the printing press for her cause, and her first letter quickly went through 14 editions. One edition depicted her alone, holding scripture, instructing the teachers of canon law (their books lying on the ground). Although she wanted to debate the theological faculty, her 'Here I stand' moment before the faculty never happened. They would not engage her on

Sources 95

the level of ideas, and instead pressured her to keep silent. Her publications brought notoriety. Count Palatine Johann von Simmern invited Argula to speak in Nuremberg, while the imperial diet met in 1523. Some Reformers, like Luther, followed the events at Ingolstadt closely and admired her courage. Although she withdrew from the public eye, authorities imprisoned her in old age for beliefs and practices that undermined Catholic teachings.[13]

Argula von Grumbach, "To the University of Ingolstadt" (1523), in *Argula von Grumbach: A Woman's Voice in the Reformation*, ed. Peter Matheson (Edinburgh: T&T Clark, 1995), 72–93 (76, 79, 81–82, 84, 89–90). Used with kind permission of T&T Clark, an imprint of Bloomsbury Publishing Plc.

———

How in God's name can you and your university expect to prevail, when you deploy such foolish violence against the word of God; when you force someone to hold the holy Gospel in their hands for the very purpose of denying it, as you did in the case of Arsacius Seehofer? When you confront him with an oath and declaration such as this, and use imprisonment and even the threat of the stake to force him to deny Christ and his word?

Yes, when I reflect on this my heart and all my limbs tremble. What do Luther or Melanchthon teach you but the word of God? You condemn them without having refuted them. Did Christ teach you so, or his apostles, prophets or evangelists? Show me where this is written! You lofty experts, nowhere in the Bible do I find that Christ, or his apostles, or his prophets put people in prison, burnt or murdered them, or sent them into exile…. Don't you know that the Lord says in Matthew 10[:28]? 'Have no fear of him who can take your body but then his power is at an end. But fear him who has power to despatch soul and body into the depths of hell'.

One knows very well the importance of one's duty to obey the authorities. But where the word of God is concerned neither Pope, Emperor nor princes – as Acts 4[:19] and 5[:29] make so clear – have any jurisdiction….

[*She considered the objection that it was not a woman's place to correct the errors of a theological faculty. When she initially heard of what happened to Seehofer, she held her tongue.*] Because Paul says in 1 Timothy 2[:12]: 'The woman should keep silence, and should not speak in church'. But now that I cannot see any man who is up to it, who is either willing or able to speak, I am constrained by the saying: 'Whoever confesses me', as I said above. And I claim for myself Isaiah 3[:4, 12]: 'I will send children to be their princes; and women or those who are womanish, shall rule over them'. And Isaiah 29[:24]: 'Those who err will know knowledge in their spirit, and those who mutter will teach the law'….

My heart goes out to our princes, whom you have seduced and betrayed so deplorably. For I realise that they are ill informed about divine Scripture. If they could spare the time from other business, I believe they, too, would

96 Sources

discover the truth that no one has a right to exercise sovereignty over the word of God. Yes, no human being, whoever he be, can rule over it. For the word of God alone – without which nothing was made – should and must rule.

If one could enforce faith why weren't all unbelievers given instructions to believe long ago? The difficulty is that it is the word of God which has to teach us, not flesh and blood. You won't be able to gain any such fame with Arsacius Seehoffer, prettying him up with a coerced and dictated oath, calling him a Master of Arts. For you have forgotten one thing: that he is only 18 years old, and still a child….A disputation is easily won when one argues with force, not Scripture. As far as I can see that means that the hangman is accounted the most learned….

I do not flinch from appearing before you, from listening to you, from discussing with you. [*She expresses admiration for Martin Luther and his translation of scripture.*] And even if it came to pass – which God forfend – that Luther were to revoke his views, that would not worry me. I do not build on his, mine, or any person's understanding, but on the true rock, Christ himself, which the builders have rejected….

Jurisprudence cannot harm me; for it avails nothing here; I can detect no divine theology in it. Therefore I have no fears for myself, as long as you wish to instruct me by writing, and not by violence, prison or the stake.

I have no Latin; but you have German, being born and brought up in this tongue. What I have written to you is no woman's chit-chat, but the word of God; and (I write) as a member of the Christian Church, against which the gates of Hell cannot prevail. Against the Roman, however, they do prevail….

8 Huldreich Zwingli, *The Sixty-Seven Articles* (1523)

Keywords: #Confession of Faith, #Magistrate, #Authority, #Obedience
Region: #Switzerland
Group: #Reformed, #Zwinglian

Huldreich Zwingli (1484–1531) was born in the Alpine valley of Toggenburg and studied in Bern and at the universities of Vienna and Basel. He grew up in the Confederation of Swiss Cantons where decentralised government and political independence were highly prized. He was an early Swiss Reformer whose evangelical experience and push for reform coincided with that of **Martin Luther**. Zwingli is considered the founder of the Reformed branch of Protestantism, and **John Calvin** would become the primary exponent of this tradition. Although Zwingli and Luther's reforms overlapped, they could not iron out their disagreements. In particular, they fell out of communion over the issue of communion because they could not agree on how Christ was physically represented in the Eucharist. Generations of Protestants would follow suit. Like Luther, Zwingli worked to reform both the church and state. Under his influence, the government of Zürich passed orders that mandated or prohibited a wide range of beliefs or behaviours.

The following excerpt comes from the *Sixty-Seven Articles* (1523). 'With some justice', writes Mark Noll, 'this document can be considered the first Protestant confession'. Like Luther's *Ninety-Five Theses*, Zwingli drafted the articles for public disputation (29 January 1523). Zürich approved Zwingli's articles, placing the primacy of scripture at the heart of both church and state. These articles influenced subsequent Reformed confessions and set some of the contours for Reformed Protestantism into the present.[14]

Mark A. Noll, *Confessions and Catechisms of the Reformation* (Repr., Vancouver, BC: Regent College, 2001), 39–46 (43–44).

———

35 But secular authority does have the rightful power and is supported from the teaching and action of Christ....

98 *Sources*

37 To these authorities all Christians are obliged to be obedient, with no exceptions;
38 So long as the authorities do not command anything in opposition to God.
39 Therefore all secular laws should be conformed to the divine will, which is to say, that they should protect the oppressed, even if the oppressed make no complaint....
42 But if rulers act unfaithfully and not according to the guiding principles of Christ, they may be replaced by God.

9   Huldreich Zwingli, *Divine and Human Righteousness* (1523)

Keywords: #Law, #Divine Law, #Poverty, #Authority, #Obedience
Region: #Switzerland
Group: #Reformed, #Zwinglian

In 1523, **Martin Luther** and Huldreich Zwingli produced important documents on church-state relations. In contrast to the two-kingdoms framework in Luther's *On Temporal Authority*, Zwingli collapsed much of the distinction between the spheres. In *On Divine and Human Righteousness*, Zwingli argued for a return to scripture as the cornerstone of society. The immediate context was a controversy about the biblical nature of the tithe and property ownership. He assumed that the church and state could not be separated, much like the body and soul are entwined in human life. Individuals within Zürich fell under the jurisdiction of both church and state, but each had complementary roles in society. There were two forms of righteousness (inward and outward), and these corresponded to Christian and civil laws. The inward law raised the standard for behaviour, and the minister's preaching of the gospel fostered higher obedience. The state could not bring about inward righteousness, but it could play a subservient role by fostering conditions in which outward and inward righteousness flourished.[15]

J. J. Hottinger, *The Life and Times of Ulric Zwingli*, trans. T. C. Porter (Harrisburg, PA: Theo. F. Scheffer, 1856), 132–134.

———

There are two laws, as well as two kinds of righteousness; a human and a divine. One part of the law regards the inner man alone, for we must love God and our neighbour [Lev. 19:18; Mark 12:31]. But no one can fulfil this command; hence no one is righteous [Rom. 3:10], because God only and He by grace, the pledge of which is Christ, can make us righteous through faith [Rom. 3:22]. The other part of the law regards the external man alone, and hence we may be outwardly pious and righteous, and still none the less wicked within. For example: 'Thou shalt not steal', is a command for external life and piety. 'Thou shalt not covet the property of thy neighbour', is a command for inward, divine life and righteousness [Exod. 20:15, 17]; yet both have respect

100 Sources

to one thing, *taking*. So, if one only does not steal, he is pious in the eyes of men, but may at the same time be unjust before God; for he has a stronger desire and temptation perhaps to seize foreign property, than one who has stolen. He, who does not practise usury, is pious before men; for he may be restrained by force from doing it; but nevertheless he is not pious before God; for he must sell all his goods and give to the poor [Matt. 19:21]. Indeed, the rich man is bound to give to the poor, that is, to God [Prov. 19:17]. But, though no man can ever fully attain this divine righteousness, yet believers have special delight in conforming to it more and more, and the desire is greater in one than in another, according as God has kindled his fire in our hearts; for he works all things in us. Therefore, the divine righteousness ought to be made known and preached to all men without ceasing, else godliness will vanish, and all men content themselves with lame, human righteousness, and all righteousness be turned into an allegory; for then no one would respect God, but look out only as to how he might be shielded from punishment before men, as for some time back we have grieved to see happen in many cases.

We have now seen, as I hope, how widely the divine righteousness differs from what is merely human. Although this human righteousness is not worthy to be called a righteousness, yet we examine it in comparison with that which is divine; yet has God also commanded it, because he has seen in our fallen estate, that our temptations and desires could not follow or do his will. Christ tells us to be obedient to this human righteousness; for he says: Render unto Cæsar the things that are Cæsar's [Mark 12:17]. He does not mean to say that the whole world should obey Cæsar, but only that portion of mankind, which was subject to him. Had he found the Jewish nation under the king of Babylon, he would have spoken: Render unto the king of Babylon what is due to the king of Babylon. We must understand this of every several government. If you live under the king of France, then render to him what is due to him; and so on, through the whole catalogue....

In short [he concludes] the Divine Word ought to rule over all men, be set before them and truly made known; for we are bound to follow it. But in this, the grace of God through our Lord Jesus Christ alone can aid our weakness. For the more we discover our guilt, the more we discover the beauty and the almightiness of God, and the love and assurance of his grace, which makes us more pious than we can be in any other way. Besides, though some will be found, who do not release the ungodly and unbelievers from the duty of living according to God's Word, yet God has given us also as the lowest command, not that, living only therein, we may be pious, but that human society may be upheld and protected, and guardians appointed, who may earnestly look to it, that the last vestige of human righteousness also be not swept away. Such guardians are the powers that be, who are no other than they that bear the sword, whom we call worldly authorities. These authorities must not indeed trample on the Word of God; for they punish outward transgressions only [Rom. 13:1–7], but cannot make righteous or unrighteous inwardly; for that God alone does in the hearts of men.

10 Gustav Vasa, *Test Luther with Scripture* (1524)

Keywords: #Church-State Relations, #Censorship
Region: #Sweden
Group: #Church of Sweden

At the opening of the sixteenth century, Sweden was under the dominion of the Danish King, Christian II. Disputes over church appointments led Christian II to impose his will through force. In the Stockholm Bloodbath of 1520, many of Sweden's nobility were executed. The Danish-controlled church played an important role in marking out nobles for execution, and the parents of Gustav Vasa (1496–1560) were among the victims. He led the opposition to the union of Denmark and Sweden. Many in the Swedish church hierarchy supported his insurrection, and he was elected as the King of Sweden in 1523 (r.1523–1560). Over the previous years, he acquired a distaste for religious interference from outside the state. Although he did not break with Rome at this moment, the following letter from early in his reign shows openness to reforming ideas and an insistence that all teaching should be measured against the rule of scripture.[16]

Paul Barron Watson, *The Swedish Revolution Under Gustavus Vasa* (London: Sampson Low, Marston, Searle & Rivington, 1889), 160–161.

———

His Majesty desires that when you discover strange doctrines in the books of Luther or any other, you should not reject them without a fair examination. If then you find anything contrary to the truth, write a refutation of it based on Holy Writ. As soon as scholars have seen your answer and have determined what to accept and what reject, you can preach according to their judgement and not according to your individual caprice. I suspect, however, there will hardly be many among you able to refute these doctrines; for, though but little of the so-called Lutheran teaching has come to my knowledge, I am convinced that Luther is too great a man to be refuted by simple men like us, for the Scriptures get their strength from no man, but from God. Even if we have the truth on our side, 'tis folly for us who have no arms to attack those

102 *Sources*

who are well equipped, since we should thus do nothing but expose our own simplicity.... Prove all things; hold fast to that which is good [1 Thess. 5:21]. Search the spirit to see whether it be of God [I John 4:1]. I would urge every one to read the new doctrines. Those who persuade or command you otherwise, appear to me to act contrary to the Scriptures, and I suspect that they do not want the truth to come to light.... If there be any among you whom this letter offends, let him write to me, pointing out where I am wrong, and I will withdraw my statements.

11 Thomas Müntzer, *Sermon to the Princes* (1524)

Keywords: #Church-State Relations, #Magistrates, #Violence, #Execution, #Hebrew Bible, #Eschatology, #Prophecy
Region: #Germany
Group: #Radical Reformation, #Anabaptist

Thomas Müntzer (d.1525) was born in Stolberg in central Germany and educated at the universities of Leipzig and Frankfurt before his ordination in 1514. In the opening years of the Reformation, he was in Wittenberg, where he came into contact with **Andreas Karlstadt** and **Martin Luther**. He was drawn to the writings of the mystics and echoed their ideas when he attacked the Catholic Church. Luther vehemently disagreed with the direction of Müntzer's reforms. In 1520, Müntzer began ministering in Zwickau where the **Zwickau Prophets** claimed new revelations from God. After being expelled, he travelled through Bohemia and Prague, where his preaching was condemned. In his *Prague Manifesto* (1521), Müntzer claimed to hear the direct voice of God and warned his readers that 'If you refuse [to defend God's word] God will let you be struck down by the Turks in the coming year'. The following year, he chided **Philip Melanchthon** for adoring a 'dumb God'. In his 1524 *Vindication and Refutation*, he thought it ludicrous that Luther approved of 'spilling people's blood for the sake of their earthly good; something which God has never commanded or approved'.[17] Luther recoiled at the idea of killing or rebelling in God's name: 'leave the name Christian out of it', he reprimanded peasants in 1525.[18]

Carlos Eire aptly summarised Müntzer's distinct mixture of theology: he 'combined *sola scriptura* biblicism with elements of medieval mysticism and millennialism, and added on top of that a highly charged critique of social, political, and economic inequalities'.[19] Drawing on mysticism, he grounded controversial decisions in personal experience; drawing on millennialism, he saw his agitation as playing a significant role in ushering in a prophesied age. In 1524, Müntzer preached an infamous sermon on Daniel, the *Sermon to the Princes*. It was delivered at the castle at Allstedt on 13 July 1525 to an audience that included Duke John of Saxony and John Frederick, his son. They did

104   *Sources*

not respond warmly to the message. The sermon evidenced Müntzer's willingness to leverage the secular sword in God's cause. The godless only have a right to live if the godly grant it to them, he argues. He took a leading role in the **German Peasants' War**, viewing the conflict in apocalyptic terms. He hoped physical warfare might usher in the rule of the saints. He was captured at the May 1525 battle of Frankenhausen and was beheaded. Many Reformers recoiled at Müntzer's radicalism. However, his sympathy for the plight of poor workers, as evidenced in his **Letter to the People of Allstedt** (1525), earned him the veneration of advocates of socialism in later generations.[20]

G. H. Williams and A. M. Mergal, eds., *Spiritual and Anabaptist Writers* (Philadelphia, PA: The Westminster Press, 1957), 49–70 (64–70). Parenthetical notes inserted by translator. Paragraphs divided in keeping with the *Cambridge Texts* edition.

An Exposition of the Second Chapter of Daniel

Allstedt, July 13, 1524

[*The sermon begins by highlighting corruption within the church, noting how the field where the wheat of the pure gospel grows is a field where weeds masquerade as wheat. However, the weeds are taking over as the swine trample upon true Christianity. The strong arm of God is needed to protect the godly by separating them from the impious. The sermon also highlights the need to be led directly by God, discusses how to discern visions and revelations, and applies the prophecies of Daniel to events in his day.*]

Therefore, you esteemed princes of Saxony, step boldly on the Cornerstone [of Christ] as Saint Peter did (Matt. 16:18) and seek the perseverance [imparted] by the divine will. He will surely establish you upon the Rock (Ps. 40:2). Your ways will be right. Seek only straightway the righteousness of God and take up courageously the cause of the gospel! For God stands so close to you that you wouldn't believe it! Why do you want then to shudder before the spectre of a man (Ps. 118:6)?

Look at our text well [Dan. 2:13]. King Nebuchadnezzar wanted to kill the wise men because they could not interpret the dream for him. That was a deserved reward, for they wished to rule his whole kingdom with their cleverness and yet could not even do that for which they had been installed. Such is also the case of our clerics now, and I say this to you for a truth. If you could only as clearly recognise the harm being [done] to Christendom and rightly consider it, you would acquire just the same zeal as Jehu the king (2 Kings 9–10); and the same as that which the whole book of Revelation proclaims. And I know for a certainty that you would thereupon hold yourselves back only with great effort from [letting] the sword exert its power. For the pitiable corruption of holy Christendom has become so great that at the present time no tongue can tell it all.

Therefore a new Daniel must arise and interpret for you your vision and this [prophet], as Moses teaches (Deut. 20:2), must go in front of the army. He must reconcile the anger of the princes and the enraged people....

O beloved, yea, the great Stone there is about to fall and strike these schemes of [mere] reason and dash them to the ground, for he says (Matt. 10:34): I am not come to send peace but a sword. What should be done, however, with the same? Nothing different from [what is done with] the wicked who hinder the gospel: Get them out of the way and eliminate them, unless you want to be ministers of the devil rather than of God, as Paul calls you (Rom. 13:4). You need not doubt it. God will strike to pieces all your adversaries who undertake to persecute you, for his hand is by no means shortened, as Isaiah (59:1) says. Therefore he can still help you and wishes to, as he supported the elect King Josiah and others who defended the name of God. Thus you are angels, when you wish to do justly, as Peter says (2 Pet. 1:4). Christ commanded in deep gravity, saying (Luke 19:27): Take mine enemies and strangle them before mine eyes. Why? Ah! because they ruin Christ's government for him and in addition want to defend their rascality under the guise of Christian faith and ruin the whole world with their insidious subterfuge. Therefore Christ our Lord says (Matt. 18:6): Whosoever shall offend one of these little ones, it is better for him that a millstone be hung about his neck and that he be thrown in the depth of the sea....

Now if you want to be true governors, you must begin government at the roots, and, as Christ commanded, drive his enemies from the elect. For you are the means to this end. Beloved, don't give us any old jokes about how the power of God should do it without your application of the sword. Otherwise may it rust away for you in its scabbard! May God grant it, whatever any divine may say to you!

Christ says it sufficiently (Matt. 7:19; John 15:2, 6): Every tree that bringeth not forth good fruit is rooted out and cast into the fire. If you do away with the mask of the world, you will soon recognise it with a righteous judgement (John 7:24). Perform a righteous judgement at God's command! You have help enough for the purpose (Wis. 6), for Christ is your Master (Matt. 23:8). Therefore let not the evildoers live longer who make us turn away from God (Deut. 13:5). For the godless person has no right to live when he is in the way of the pious. In Exodus 22:18 God says: Thou shalt not suffer evildoers to live. Saint Paul also means this where he says of the sword of rulers that it is bestowed upon them for the retribution of the wicked as protection for the pious (Rom. 13:4)....

I suppose at this point our learned divines will bring out the goodness of Christ, which they in their hypocrisy apply by force. But over against this [goodness] they ought also to take note of the sternness of Christ (John 2:15–17; Ps. 69:9), when he turned over the roots of idolatry....

Therefore no justification is given us in the inadequacy and the negligence of the saints to let the godless have their way. Since they with us confess God's name they ought to choose between two alternatives: either to repudiate the Christian faith completely or put idolatry out of the way (Matt. 18:7–9)....

106 *Sources*

That this might now take place, however, in an orderly and proper fashion, our cherished fathers, the princes, should do it, who with us confess Christ. If, however, they do not do it, the sword will be taken from them (Dan. 7:26). For they confess him all right with words and deny him with the deed (Titus 1:16). They [the princes], accordingly, should proffer peace to the enemies (Deut. 2:26–30). If the latter wish to be spiritual [in the outmoded sense] and do not give testimony of the knowledge (*kunst*) of God (cf. 1 Pet. 3:9, 12), they should be gotten out of the way (1 Cor. 5:13). But I pray for them with the devout David where they are not against God's revelation. Where, however, they pursue the opposition, may they be slain without any mercy as Hezekiah (2 Kings 18:22), Josiah (23:5), Cyrus (2 Chron. 36:22), Daniel (6:27), Elijah (1 Kings 18:40) destroyed the priests of Baal, otherwise the Christian church cannot come back again to its origin. The weeds must be plucked out of the vineyard of God in the time of harvest. Then the beautiful red wheat will acquire substantial rootage and come up properly (Matt. 13:24–30). The angels [v. 39], however, who sharpen their sickles for this purpose are the serious servants of God who execute the wrath of the divine wisdom (Mal. 3:1–6)....

Therefore in order that the truth may be rightly brought to the light, you rulers – it makes no difference whether you want to or not – must conduct yourselves according to the conclusion of this chapter (Dan. 2:48), namely, that Nebuchadnezzar made the holy Daniel an officer in order that he might execute good, righteous decisions, as the Holy Spirit says (Ps. 58:10). For the godless have no right to live except as the elect wish to grant it to them, as it is written in Exodus 23:29–33....

12 *Conrad Grebel to Thomas Müntzer* on Separation and Violence (1524)

Keywords: #Excommunication, #Coercion, #Non-violence
Region: #Switzerland
Group: #Radical Reformation, #Anabaptist

Conrad Grebel (c.1498–1526) was one of the founders of the Swiss Brethren. He undertook some university training in Vienna and Paris but was unsuccessful as an academic. Changing course, he moved back to Zürich where he became involved in the reforms of **Huldrych Zwingli**. Like **Andreas Karlstadt** and others, he was frustrated by the slow pace of reform. He soon came into conflict with the Zürich council and with Zwingli by applying the logic of scriptural primacy to new areas of civic and ecclesiastical life. Grebel then aligned with Karlstadt and **Thomas Müntzer**. Grebel identified infant baptism as a cornerstone of a corrupt system of church and state. In January 1525, a group meeting in the house of Felix Mantz underwent adult baptism, with George Blaurock receiving the first baptism at Grebel's hands. Zürich's council soon made such acts illegal, and Grebel was imprisoned before escaping and dying of plague in 1526. That same year, Zürich issued an **Order to Drown Anabaptists**.[21]

Grebel and his colleagues wrote the following document. This warm letter to Thomas Müntzer expressed mutual affection in Christ for a fellow Reformer and hoped they could learn from each other and not split over disagreements. However, they offered some words of correction, particularly concerning singing in church. They also discussed the Lord's Supper at length before moving on to the relationship between Christianity, heresy, compulsion, and defending the gospel with the sword's power.[22]

Walter Rauschenbusch, "The Zurich Anabaptists and Thomas Münzer", *The American Journal of Theology* 9, no. 1 (1905): 91–106 (95, 97–98).

———

September 5, 1524

Go forward with the word and establish a Christian church with the help of Christ and his rule, as we find it instituted Matthew 18 and applied in the

108   *Sources*

epistles. Use determination and common prayer and decision according to faith and love, without command or compulsion, then God will help thee and thy little flock to all sincerity, and the singing and the tablets will cease. There is more than enough of wisdom and counsel in the Scripture, how all classes and all men may be taught, governed, instructed, and turned to piety. Whoever will not amend and believe, but resists the word and doings of God and thus persists, such a man, after Christ and his word and rule have been declared to him and he has been admonished in the presence of the three witnesses and the church, such a man we say, taught by God's word, shall not be killed, but regarded as a heathen and publican and let alone.

Moreover, the gospel and its adherents are not to be protected by the sword, nor are they thus to protect themselves, which, as we learn from our brother, is thy opinion and practice. True Christian believers are sheep among wolves [Matt. 10:16], sheep for the slaughter [Rom. 8:36]; they must be baptised in anguish and affliction, tribulation, persecution, suffering, and death [Rom. 6:4]; they must be tried with fire [1 Pet. 1:7], and must reach the fatherland of eternal rest [Heb. 4:1–11], not by killing their bodily, but by mortifying their spiritual enemies [Eph. 6:12]. Neither do they use worldly sword or war, since all killing has ceased with them; unless, indeed, we are still of the old law; and even there (much as we consider it) war was a misfortune after they had once conquered the Promised Land....

[*The letter closes by discussing Müntzer's acceptable teachings on baptism. Grebel returns to seeking and offering guidance on doctrinal and practical matters and offers wisdom on interacting with other antagonistic Reformers. The letter is followed by a postscript which directly responds to Müntzer's* Prague Protest (1521) *and his openly militaristic* Sermon to the Princes (1524).]

Dearly beloved Brother Thomas. When I had subscribed all our names in a hurry and had thought this messenger would not wait until we wrote to Luther, too, he had to bide and wait on account of rain. So I wrote to Luther, too, on behalf of my brethren and thine, and have exhorted him to cease from the false sparing of the weak, who are [really] themselves. Andreas Castelberg has written to Carlstadt. Meanwhile Hans Hujuff of Halle, our fellow-citizen here and brother, has arrived who recently visited thee, [and brings] a letter and shameful tract by Luther [*Letter to the Princes of Saxony, Concerning the Rebellious Spirit* (June 1524), written against Müntzer], which no man ought to write who wants to be a [leader] like the apostles. Paul teaches differently: *porro servum Domini* ['but the servant of the Lord'; 2 Tim. 2:24], etc. I see that he wants to have thee outlawed and deliver thee to the prince [Frederick of Saxony] to whom he has tied his gospel, even as Aaron had to hold Moses as his god [Exod. 7:1].

As for thy tracts and Protestations I find thee without guilt, unless thou doest reject baptism entirely, which I do not gather from them...The brother of Hujuff writes that thou hast preached against the princes, that they are

Sources 109

to be attacked with the fist. Is it true? If thou art willing to defend war, the tablets, singing, or other things which thou doest not find in express words of Scripture, as thou doest not find the points mentioned, then I admonish thee by the common salvation of us all that thou wilt cease therefrom and all notions of thine own now and hereafter, then wilt thou be completely pure, who in other points pleasest us better than anyone in this German and other countries. If thou fallest into the hands of Luther or the duke [George of Saxony], drop the points mentioned, and stand by the others like a hero and champion of God. Be strong. Thou hast the Bible (of which Luther has made Bible, Bubel, Babel) for defence against the idolatrous caution of Luther, which he and the learned shepherds in our parts have propagated in all the world; against the deceitful, weak-kneed faith, against their preaching, in which they do not teach Christ as they should, although they have just opened the gospel for all the world that people may or should read for themselves; but not many do it, for everybody follows their authority. With us there are not 20 who believe the word of God; they trust the persons, Zwingli, Leo [Jud], and others, who elsewhere are esteemed learned. And if thou must suffer for it, thou knowest well that it cannot be otherwise. Christ must suffer still more in his members [Col. 1:24]. But he will strengthen and keep them steadfast to the end [1 Cor. 1:8]. May God give grace to thee and us. For our shepherds also are so wroth and furious against us, rail at us as knaves from the pulpit in public, and call us *Satanas in angelo slucis conversos* ['Satans disguised as angels of light'; 2 Cor. 11:14]. We, too, shall in time see persecution come upon us through them. Therefore pray to God for us.

13 Peasants of Upper Swabia, *Twelve Articles* (1525)

Keywords: #Rebellion, #Serfdom, #Authority, #Submission
Region: #Germany
Group: #Radical Reformation

One of the consequences of the Black Death (1347–1351) was that the peasants who survived could demand higher wages and more rights from their landlords. By the beginning of the sixteenth century, the population had rapidly increased, the cost of living outpaced real wages, and churches and landlords demanded greater rents for land use. Many landlords clawed back the peasants' liberties and tried to reduce them to serfdom.[23] Martin Luther's call for spiritual reform resonated with peasants who wanted to see changes in the social sphere. The *Twelve Articles* originated in southern Germany's Swabian or Black Forest region in early 1525 and was one of the most important documents produced by the peasants. It was quickly reprinted dozens of times. These short articles detailed common grievances held by peasants across Germanic regions and, in the words of Peter Blickle, 'offered, with the gospel as legitimation, a new legal basis for the formation of the relationship between peasant and lord'.[24] They are thought to be the work of Sebastian Lotzer (1490?–1525?), a fur trader from Memmingen. In 1522, he converted and befriended **Christoph Schappeler** (1472?–1551), a minister who may have co-authored the articles.

Peasant armies adopted the *Twelve Articles* in their bid for greater rights, with some variations to accommodate regional interests. After the Swabian League suppressed the peasants, Lotzer became a wanted man who found refuge in St. Gall (Switzerland), leaving no further historical trace. In May 1525, **Martin Luther** responded to the *Twelve Articles*, arguing that the peasants placed too much emphasis on the physical and that serfdom accorded with scripture. Their teaching, he suggested, might even be contrary to the gospel.[25] Despite having considerable reservations about peasant agitation, Luther thought they had many just grievances against their rulers and that rulers should welcome reform. However, he was adamant that peasant rebels should stop invoking the name of Christ to sanctify their violent actions.[26]

James Harvey Robinson, *Readings in European History* (Boston, MA: Ginn & Company, 1906), II:94–99.[27]

Peace to the Christian reader and the grace of God through Christ

There are many evil writings put forth of late which take occasion, on account of the assembling of the peasants, to cast scorn upon the gospel, saying, 'Is this the fruit of the new teaching, that no one should obey but that all should everywhere rise in revolt, and rush together to reform, or perhaps destroy altogether, the authorities, both ecclesiastic and lay?' The articles below shall answer these godless and criminal fault-finders, and serve, in the first place, to remove the reproach from the word of God and, in the second place, to give a Christian excuse for the disobedience or even the revolt of the entire peasantry.

In the first place, the gospel is not the cause of revolt and disorder, since it is the message of Christ, the promised Messiah; the word of life, teaching only love, peace, patience, and concord. Thus all who believe in Christ should learn to be loving, peaceful, long-suffering, and harmonious. This is the foundation of all the articles of the peasants (as will be seen), who accept the gospel and live according to it. How then can the evil reports declare the gospel to be a cause of revolt and disobedience? That the authors of the evil reports and the enemies of the gospel oppose themselves to these demands is due, not to the gospel, but to the devil, the worst enemy of the gospel, who causes this opposition by raising doubts in the minds of his followers, and thus the word of God, which teaches love, peace, and concord, is overcome.

In the second place, it is clear that the peasants demand that this gospel be taught them as a guide in life, and they ought not to be called disobedient or disorderly (Rom. 11; Isa. 40, Rom. 8, Exod. 3, 14, Luke 18). Whether God grant the peasants (earnestly wishing to live according to his word) their requests or no, who shall find fault with the will of the Most High? Who shall meddle in his judgements or oppose his majesty? Did he not hear the children of Israel when they called upon him and save them out of the hands of Pharaoh [Exod. 3:7–9]? Can he not save his own to-day? Yea, he will save them and that speedily. Therefore, Christian reader, read the following articles with care and then judge. Here follow the articles:

[*Points 1 and 2 argue that pastors are to be chosen by the people and the tithe will support the pastor and the poor.*]

The Third Article. It has been the custom hitherto for men to hold us as their own property, which is pitiable enough, considering that Christ has delivered and redeemed us all, without exception, by the shedding of his precious blood, the lowly as well as the great. Accordingly it is consistent with Scripture that we should be free and should wish to be so (Isa. 53; 1 Pet. 1; 1 Cor. 7). Not that we would wish to be absolutely free and under no authority (Rom. 13; Wis. 6; 1 Pet. 2). God does not teach us that we should lead a

112   *Sources*

disorderly life in the lusts of the flesh (Deut. 6; Matt. 4), but that we should love the Lord our God and our neighbour [Lev. 19:18; Mark 12:31]. We would gladly observe all this as God has commanded us in the celebration of the communion (Luke 4, 6). He has not commanded us not to obey the authorities, but rather that we should be humble, not only towards those in authority, but towards every one (Matt. 7; John 13; Rom. 13). We are thus ready to yield obedience according to God's law to our elected and regular authorities in all proper things becoming to a Christian (Acts 5). We therefore take it for granted that you will release us from serfdom as true Christians, unless it should be shown us from the gospel that we are serfs.

[*Points 4–11 relate to natural resources, duties, taxes, and the proliferation of new laws.*]

Conclusion. In the twelfth place, it is our conclusion and final resolution that if any one or more of the articles here set forth should not be in agreement with the word of God, as we think they are, such article we will willingly retract if it is proved really to be against the word of God....

14 Thomas Müntzer, *Letter to the People of Allstedt* (1525)

Keywords: #War, #Violence, #Serfdom
Region: #Germany
Group: #Radical Reformation, #Anabaptist

From 1523 to 1524, Thomas Müntzer ministered in Allstedt (Saxony). With the city council's blessing, he began reforming church and state. He found supporters and courted controversy. His rift with **Martin Luther** widened and was exacerbated by Müntzer's heady mixture of prophecy and calls for apocalyptic violence. Many secular authorities in Allstedt and the surrounding area turned on Müntzer. In response, he formed a league held together by a covenant (*Bund*), and members included those sitting on the council of Allstedt. Duke John of Saxony – who had responded coldly to the *Sermon to the Princes* – now barred Müntzer from preaching and shut down his printing operation.

Martin Luther's *Letter to the Princes of Saxony Concerning the Rebellious Spirit* (June 1524) argued for the expulsion of insurrectionists. Müntzer fled and responded in *A Highly Provoked Defence and Reply to the Soft-Living Flesh at Wittenberg* (September 1524). Müntzer wrote the following letter to those in Allstedt (c.26 or 27 April, 1525). He reflected on the meaning of the ongoing **German Peasants' War**. Whereas his earlier *Sermon to the Princes* charged authorities with reform and threatened slackers, this letter took a similar approach to individual Christians. Müntzer was captured during the battle of Frankenhausen and executed one month later.[28]

Eric Lund, ed., *Documents from the History of Lutheranism*, 1517–1750 (Minneapolis, MN: Fortress, 2002), I:40–41.

———

May the pure fear of God prevail, dear brothers. How long will you sleep [Prov. 6:9]; how long will you go on without acknowledging the will of God, in your estimation, he has forsaken you? Alas, how many times have I told you how it must be, how God cannot reveal himself in any other way, and you must remain undisturbed? If you fail to do so, then your heart-breaking

114 Sources

sacrifice, your heart-wounding suffering is to no avail. You might then have to begin your suffering all over again. I will tell you this, that if you do not want to suffer according to God's will [1 Pet. 4:19], then you will have to be martyrs for the devil. So watch out, don't be faint-hearted or negligent and no longer the perverted fools, the godless evildoers. Get going and fight the fight of the Lord! It is high time. Keep your brothers all at it, so that they do not scorn the divine witness, or else they will all perish. The entire lands of Germany, France, and Italy are awake; the master wants to play the game and the evildoers must be in it too. At Fulda, during Easter week, four abbeys were laid waste; the peasants in the Klettgau and the Hegau in the Black Forest have risen, 3,000 strong, and the more time passes, the larger their number grow. My only worry is that the foolish people will consent to a false treaty....

Even if there are only three of you who submit to God and seek his name and honour alone, you need not fear a hundred thousand. So go onward, onward, onward! Now is the time since the evildoers have lost heart, like [scared] dogs! Arouse your brothers, so that they may come to peace and bear witness to their commitment. It is extremely urgent! Go onward, onward, onward! Show no pity, even if Esau offers kind words to you, Genesis 33. Pay no heed to the cries of the godless. They will plead with you so amicably, weeping and begging like children. Show them no pity, as God commanded through Moses, Deuteronomy 7[:1–5], and has revealed the same to us. Arouse the villages and towns and especially the mine-workers and other good comrades who can do us some good. We must sleep no longer....

15 Christoph Schappeler, *To the Assembly of the Common Peasantry* (1525)

Keywords: #Serfdom, #Rebellion, #Freedom
Region: #Germany
Group: #Radical Reformation

Novel ideas about politics and religion percolated during the **German Peasants' War,** including ideas about civil reform and army conduct. The *Field Ordinance of the Franconian Peasantry* (May 1525), for example, set standards for the morality of soldiers and tried to bring their actions into line with scripture while also floating the idea of a democratically elected military leadership. Christoph Schappeler (1472?–1551), a minister in Memmingen, may have had a hand in crafting the **Twelve Articles of the Peasants of Upper Swabia** (early 1525). He was likely responsible for the anonymously published tract, *To the Assembly of the Common Peasantry* (May 1525). Michael G. Baylor calls this tract 'the most thoroughly developed and forcefully presented justification for the Peasants' War'. The document was wide-ranging. Schappeler began by arguing that true Christians did not need authority because religious principles regulated them. He acknowledged that God instituted authority to curb human depravity while also arguing that God placed limits on temporal authority and even sanctioned rebellion against those who abused power. He preferred a republican government modelled on Switzerland instead of hereditary rule.[29]

Michael G. Baylor, *The German Reformation and the Peasants' War: A Brief History with Documents* (Boston, MA: Bedford/St. Martins, 2012), 121–122.

——

Chapter 7. Whether a Community May Depose Its Authorities or Not

Now to the heart of the matter! God wants it! Now the storm bells will be sounded! Now the truth must come out, in this time of grace, Luke 19[:11], even if the cliffs should speak [cf. Luke 19:40]. May the almighty lord and God, and also your pleas, protect me from the intentions of the lords, to say

116   *Sources*

nothing of their desire to do me in.... [*He then argues that the lords are the real robbers who commit injustice.*]

Now, to knock people such as Moab, Agag, Ahab, and Nero from their thrones is God's highest pleasure. Scripture does not call them servants of God, but instead snakes, dragons and wolves. Go to it!...

I will prove that a territory or community has the power to depose its pernicious lords by introducing...sayings drawn from the divine law....

And the first saying from divine law is this. Joshua 1[:7] commands the principle that no lord has the power to act according to his own will, but only on the basis of divine law. If he does not, simply get rid of him and leave him far behind. This is most pleasing to God. St. Paul provides us the second saying from divine law in 2 Corinthians 10[:8], where he says 'Power is given to build up and not to destroy'. And what does St. Paul intend with his punishing and mocking words other than that a harmful ruler should not be tolerated?...

Behold! Should a condemned Antichrist then rule the people of Christ, whom the lord of heaven and earth purchased so dearly with his bitter death? What a great need there is to reflect seriously on these words of the divine spirit!...

Thus, in any case, we Christians have sufficiently sound and sincere reasons [to depose our lords]. and we are also obliged to redeem ourselves from these godless lords out of this Babylonian captivity, as St. Peter says, Acts 5[:29], 'We must obey God rather than men'. And earlier the divine chancellor, Paul, says in 1 Corinthians 7[:21]. 'If you are a slave, you can make yourself free, so take the chance'.

16 Urbanus Rhegius, *Serfdom and the Kingdom of Christ* (1525)

Keywords: #Serfdom, #Rebellion, #Submission
Region: #Germany
Group: #Lutheran | #Radical Reformation

Urbanus Rhegius (1489–1541) was a leader of the Lutheran Reformation in Augsburg and Lower Saxony. As a student, he followed the Catholic scholar Johann Eck to the University of Ingolstadt. After his ordination in 1519, Rhegius preached in the cathedral at Augsburg. By 1521, he began espousing Lutheran ideas and left his post under pressure, returning upon invitation in 1523. While furthering reform in the city, he preached against peasants agitating for social change and Anabaptists pushing unwelcome theological reform.

Martin Luther was sympathetic to the plight of German peasants, and although he counselled that they should submit to the authorities, he urged princes to take their complaints seriously. However, Luther argued for swift and merciless punishment of peasants who took up arms. Rhegius preached the following sermon in response to the **German Peasants' War**. In the first part, excerpted below, he argued that all humans were naturally similar, and regeneration brought considerable spiritual equality. However, the gospel did not erase social distinctions. Bondage was compatible with freedom in Christ, and Christian serfs should embrace servitude as divine chastisement. He defended this argument from scripture. In the second part of this sermon, he addressed rulers and tried to temper the harshness of their authority with evangelical love.[30]

B. Ann Tlusty, *Augsburg During the Reformation Era: An Anthology of Sources* (Indianapolis, IN: Hacket, 2012), 17–18.

———

It is being asked in light of the Gospels if servitude or serfdom should be tolerated among Christians, who are all born of one earthly father and reborn of one Heavenly Father, and who are all made evangelically free through the

118 *Sources*

blood of Christ. To this question, I answer that the holy Scripture tells us what to say to Lords and servants....

We are all born of Adam as children of wrath, with no difference in our natural origins. We Christians are then born again in water and in spirit, and in this rebirth we become children of God.... Nonetheless, afterward there is a great difference in how the gifts of God, the Holy Spirit, are distributed among mankind. For one is given more than the other, as it pleases God. But only sweet faith sets apart the sons of the kingdom from the sons of damnation.

We are also all priests in Christ, and may appear before God by the power of this priesthood, pray for one another in the spirit of faith, proclaim the kingdom of heaven, and bring our offering of the cross and our praises. But our king's realm is not of this world. He reigns in matters of heaven and the spirit...so that the kingdom of the faithful is not a visible, temporal kingdom here on earth, rather a spiritual kingdom of faith....

Therefore a believer in Christ is completely free and Lord of all things, and can and should at the same time be a servant of all people and subject to everyone. For Christian freedom is of the spirit, and should not be a smokescreen for the flesh and unrestrained wickedness. For that reason, civic servitude or serfdom, through which a Christian is subject and bound to a physical person for taxes, tolls, rents, veneration, or whatever else such servitude may entail, may well stand beside evangelical freedom in our kingdom....

Thereby a pious Christian should consider that bondage and servitude were established because of sin, so that he may bear them as a scourge of God. For he professes to be a poor sinner, as he should, and therefore should accept his father's discipline as does an obedient child, and not flee from it.

17 Zürich, *Order to Drown Anabaptists* (1526)

Keywords: #Heresy, #Violence
Region: #Switzerland
Group: #Zwinglian, #Reformed | #Anabaptist

In early 1519, **Huldreich Zwingli** became the priest at Zürich's Grossmünster. The church's theological faculty was the first training centre for the Reformed faith and would become a powerhouse of the Reformation in Zürich and beyond. The reform was received differently in various parts of the Swiss Confederation owing to the regions' considerable political independence and diversity. Reforming efforts were challenged both by political threats emanating from nearby Catholic regions and by the destabilising effect of the rise of Anabaptism. Baptism was an entry point for full participation in the Christian community, and the baptism of adult believers would split the fabric of church and state. On 18 January 1525, the Zürich Council mandated infant baptism.[31] In the following year, Zürich made nonconformity a capital offence.[32] The same logic that led Catholics to persecute Zwinglians led Zwinglians to persecute Anabaptists, and as the Reformation progressed, differences became justifications for violence against fellow Protestants.[33] Similar orders to punish Anabaptists would be used against **Michael Sattler**, the author of *The Schleitheim Articles* (1527), and his wife, Margaretha. The punishment was tailored to the crime: partaking again in the waters of baptism merited execution by water.

Henry Gee and William John Hardy, eds., *Documents Illustrative of English Church History* (London: Macmillan, 1896), 212.

———

Whereas our Lords the Burgomaster, Council, and Great Council, have for some time past earnestly endeavoured to turn the misguided and erring Anabaptists from their errors; and yet several ... to the injury of the public authority and the magistrates as well as to the ruin of the common welfare and of right Christian living, have proved disobedient; and several of them, men, women, and girls, have been by our Lords sharply punished and put into

120 *Sources*

prison: Now therefore, by the earnest commandment, edict, and warning of our Lords aforesaid, it is ordered that no one in our town, country, or domains, whether man, woman, or girl, shall baptise another: and if any one hereafter shall baptise another, he will be seized by our Lords and, according to the decree now set forth, will be drowned without mercy. Wherefore everyone knows how to order himself, and to take care that he bring not his own death upon himself.

18 Martin Luther, *Whether Soldiers, Too, Can Be Saved* (1526)

Keywords: #War, #Violence, #Conscience, #Submission, #Authority, #Tyranny
Region: #Germany
Group: #Lutheran

Martin Luther viewed war as evil because of the destruction that accompanied it, in keeping with the Augustinian view of war. However, killing was not always wrong, provided the cause was just and defensive. He strongly objected to dragging God's name through the battlefields, as he charged **Thomas Müntzer** and the peasants with doing. Although he wanted some distance between war and worship, the following source evidences how deeply they were intertwined in Luther's thinking. Shortly after the **Peasants' War**, and in the context of increasing Catholic hostility, Luther penned *Whether Soldiers, Too, Can Be Saved* (1526). In this work, he summarised his view of the two kingdoms and his previous arguments on the nature, extent, and limitations of secular authority. He argued that taking life could sometimes be right and righteous. By applying a two-kingdoms framework to conflict, Luther turned obedience to the state into obedience to God. This reading used passages that seemed to limit military involvement to sanctify warfare. For example, Luther's exegesis of the Sermon on the Mount argued that individuals had one set of commands if they acted in a private Christian capacity and another if they possessed some form of authority in (or duty towards) the secular world.[34]

In *Whether Soldiers, Too, Can Be Saved*, Luther discussed various topics related to authority and violence. It was difficult, he argued, to craft just laws that could not be abused and that fit all the peculiarities of person, rank, and circumstance. He offered the example of the law that 'All rebels deserve death' after the **German Peasants' Revolt**, and showed how individuals rebelled for differing reasons and to different degrees. Those in power should try to discern these differences and moderate severe laws by applying them in a nuanced way to particular circumstances, recognising that some rebelled with good intentions. He then discussed who could declare war, how justice

122 Sources

served law, how treachery and vice could pervert the law, and how Christianity set higher ethical standards on violence than non-Christian polities. Aggrieved Christians, he argued, should choose suffering over rebellion. He discussed deposing a madman (permissible) or tyrant (impermissible) and warned that mobs could become tyrants in the name of removing tyranny. A tyrant's grasp on power was insecure, and they should fear divine wrath in this world and the next. In the meantime, Christians should wait on God and allow proper authorities to handle injustice, even if the ruler broke their own laws. His instructions applied to everyone under authority, not only to peasants. He also argued that war was only permissible for rulers to declare when driven to it by the violence of others. The holiness in the conflict derived from its justice, but it could be difficult to tell which side was just. If one knew for certain that a ruler's cause was unjust, one should not fight and be willing to bear the consequences. However, if one was unsure whether the cause was just, Christians could fight with a clean conscience.

Martin Luther, "Whether Soldiers, Too, Can be Saved", trans. Charles M. Jacobs, rev. Robert C. Schults, in *Luther's Works*, ed. Robert C. Schultz (Philadelphia, PA: Fortress, 1967) 46: 93–137 (93–97, 99–100). Used by permission.

———

[*Luther begins by noting how a friend's question prompted the following publication.*]

In the first place, we must distinguish between an occupation and the man who holds it, between a work and the man who does it. An occupation or a work can be good and right in itself and yet be bad and wrong if the man who does the work is evil or wrong or does not do his work properly....[W]ith the profession or work of the soldier; in itself it is right and godly, but we must see to it that the persons who are in this profession and who do the work are the right kind of persons, that is, godly and upright, as we shall hear.

In the second place, I want you to understand that here I am not speaking about the righteousness that makes men good in the sight of God. Only faith in Jesus Christ can do that; and it is granted and given us by the grace of God alone, without any works or merits of our own...Rather, I am speaking here about external righteousness which is to be sought in offices and works. In other words, to put it plainly, I am dealing here with such questions as these: whether the Christian faith, by which we are accounted righteous before God, is compatible with being a soldier, going to war, stabbing and killing, robbing and burning, as military law requires us to do to our enemies in wartime. Is this work sinful or unjust? Should it give us a bad conscience before God? Must a Christian only do good and love, and kill no one, nor do anyone any harm? I say that this office or work, even though it is godly and right, can nevertheless become evil and unjust if the person engaged in it is evil and unjust.

Sources   123

In the third place, it is not my intention to explain here at length how the occupation and work of a soldier is in itself right and godly because I have written quite enough about that in my book *Temporal Authority: To What Extent It Should Be Obeyed*. Indeed, I might boast here that not since the time of the apostles have the temporal sword and temporal government been so clearly described or so highly praised as by me....For the very fact that the sword has been instituted by God to punish the evil, protect the good, and preserve peace [Rom. 13:1–5; I Pet. 2:13–14] is powerful and sufficient proof that war and killing along with all the things that accompany wartime and martial law have been instituted by God....

Now slaying and robbing do not seem to be works of love. A simple man therefore does not think it is a Christian thing to do. In truth, however, even this is a work of love. [W]hen I think of a soldier fulfilling his office by punishing the wicked, killing the wicked, and creating so much misery, it seems an unChristian work completely contrary to Christian love. But when I think of how it protects the good and keeps and preserves wife and child, house and farm, property, and honour and peace, then I see how precious and godly this work is; and I observe that[, like a doctor,] it amputates a leg or a hand, so that the whole body may not perish....

[*The 'plague' of war must be understood in light of the 'plague' that war remedies: lawlessness and violence perpetrated by people who refuse to live at peace with others.*]

To sum it up, we must, in thinking about a soldier's office, not concentrate on the killing, burning, striking, hitting, seizing, etc. [We must see the office as] godly and as needful and useful to the world as eating and drinking or any other work. [*He goes on to illustrate, citing scripture at length, how the abuse of an office does not invalidate the office itself. Ruling that war is wrong would inevitably lead to the conclusion that punishing criminals is wrong.*]

As for the objection that Christians have not been commanded to fight and that these examples are not enough, especially because Christ teaches us not to resist evil but rather suffer all things [Matt. 5:39–42], I have already said all that needs to be said on this matter in my book *Temporal Authority*. Indeed, Christians do not fight and have no worldly rulers among them. Their government is a spiritual government, and, according to the Spirit, they are subjects of no one but Christ. Nevertheless, as far as body and property are concerned, they are subject to worldly rulers and owe them obedience. If worldly rulers call upon them to fight, then they ought to and must fight and be obedient, not as Christians, but as members of the state and obedient subjects. Christians therefore do not fight as individuals or for their own benefit, but as obedient servants of the authorities under whom they live. This is what St. Paul wrote to Titus when he said that Christians should obey the authorities [Titus 3:1]. You may read more about this in my book *Temporal Authority*.

That is the sum and substance of it. The office of the sword is in itself right and is a divine and useful ordinance, which God does not want us to

124 *Sources*

despise, but to fear, honour, and obey, under penalty of punishment, as St. Paul says in Romans 13[:1–5]. For God has established two kinds of government among men. The one is spiritual; it has no sword, but it has the word, by means of which men are to become good and righteous, so that with this righteousness they may attain eternal life. He administers this righteousness through the word, which he has committed to the preachers. The other kind is worldly government, which works through the sword so that those who do not want to be good and righteous to eternal life may be forced to become good and righteous in the eyes of the world. He administers this righteousness through the sword. And although God will not reward this kind of righteousness with eternal life, nonetheless, he still wishes peace to be maintained among men and rewards them with temporal blessings....

[*Luther closes with a model prayer for the soldier, instructing them in how to place their trust in God in the hour of need. They are to remember that obedience to their sovereign in lawful matters is obedience to God. Therefore, the soldier can have confidence that God will not consider their actions to be sinful, provided all their trust is placed in the life-saving blood of Christ.*]

19 Ordinance of the Diet of Odense (1527)

Keywords: #Toleration, #Conscience, #Marriage, #Church-State Relations
Region: #Denmark
Group: #Lutheran

Christian II of Denmark was ousted from his throne in 1523. His successor, Frederick I (r.1523–1533), feared his return. Frederick's personal religious commitments were complicated, but he weakened the power of the Roman Catholic Church in an attempt to strengthen his regime. He claimed neutrality on many issues but repeatedly showed sympathy for evangelicals. He allowed his son Duke Christian (future Christian III) to marry Dorothea, the daughter of an infamous convert to Lutheranism, Duke Magnus of Saxony-Lauenburg. Frederick also shed some overtly Catholic practices and did not stop Duke Christian from reforming his fiefdom. Christian turned Haderslev into a northern Wittenberg. Frederick also offered protection to evangelical ministers, an act that critics said violated his coronation oath. Scholars debate the timing, purpose, and extent of the toleration measures extended at Odense in 1527. They evidence Frederick I's willingness to make space for the spread of reforming ideas within this Catholic region.[35] In regions where magistrates officially backed the Reformation, authorities often did not extend the same toleration to Catholics.[36]

B.J. Kidd, ed., *Documents Illustrative of the Continental Reformation* (Oxford: Clarendon, 1911), 234.

——

1 Henceforth every man shall enjoy freedom of conscience. No one shall be at liberty to ask whether a man is Lutheran or Catholic. Every man shall answer for his own soul.
2 The King extends his protection to the Lutherans, who hitherto have not enjoyed such full security and safe-conduct as the Catholics.

126 *Sources*

3 The marriages of ecclesiastics, canons, monks, and other spiritual persons which for several centuries has been forbidden, is now allowed; and everyone is free to choose whether he will marry or remain celibate.
4 In future, bishops shall no more fetch the pall from Rome: but after they have been duly elected by the chapters possessed of the right, they shall seek confirmation from the Crown.

20 Michael Sattler, *The Schleitheim Articles* (1527)

Keywords: #War, #Magistrates, #Violence, #Excommunication, #Non-violence
Region: #Switzerland | #Germany
Group: #Anabaptist

Michael Sattler (c.1490–1527) was an early Anabaptist leader from the Black Forest region of Germany. He was a Benedictine monk but left the Black Forest monastery of St. Peter's, possibly because of his interest in the **German Peasants' War** and the grievances of those revolting. By 1525, he made his way to Zürich and established himself in Anabaptist circles there, only to be expelled. Zürich was in the process of making Anabaptism illegal, and in 1526, they issued an **Order to Drown Anabaptists**. Sattler took the lead in writing *The Schleitheim Articles* (1527) – named after the Swiss town where the brethren met. The *Articles* argued for separation from an evil world – a conviction that proscribed the resort to violence or holding office. Sattler then ministered in the town of Horb in Württemberg. He was tried, convicted, tortured, and executed for heresy in 1527, followed shortly by the drowning of his wife, Margaretha. Sattler has long been given credit as the guiding hand behind these articles. His greatest impact on Swiss Anabaptism came after his death. As Michael G. Baylor has noted, *The Schleitheim Articles* aimed to persuade 'fellow radicals who have not accepted the strategy of nonresisting separatism which is set forth in the body of this work'.[37] The articles also countered those who claimed the gospel freed them from moral and ethical duties.

The salutation warmly addressed believers and expressed hope for reconciliation with erring brothers and sisters, trusting that God would protect and guide his people. The *Articles* opened by praising God for concord among the brethren, but believers should separate from false teachers. The document contains seven articles: (1) believers should be baptised, not infants. (2) Excommunication should be biblically carried out and was for those who professed faith and obedience before falling away. (3) Communion involved holiness and union with Christ and was between fellow Christians; therefore, the church should selectively enter into communion. (4) There should be a

128 *Sources*

strict separation from all persons and activities that do not further union with Christ. (5) Pastors should be qualified, elected, and held accountable. (6) The use of the sword was forbidden (excerpted below). (7) The swearing of oaths was forbidden. The conclusion pleaded with erring brothers and sisters to cleave to the simplicity and purity of divine truth.

Thomas Armitage, *A History of the Baptists; Traced by their Vital Principles and Practices* (New York: Bryan, Taylor & Co., 1887), 949–952.

———

Sixthly, we were united concerning the sword, thus: The sword is an ordinance of God outside of the perfection of Christ, which punishes and slays the wicked and protects and guards the good. In law the sword is ordained over the wicked for punishment and death, and the civil power is ordained to use it [Rom. 13:1–5]. But in the perfection of Christ, excommunication is pronounced only for warning and for exclusion of him who has sinned, without death of the flesh, only by warning and the command not to sin again. It is asked by many who do not know the will of Christ respecting us, whether a Christian may or should use the sword against the wicked in order to protect and guard the good, or for [the sake of] love

The answer is unanimously revealed thus: Christ teaches and commands us that we should learn from him, for he is meek and lowly of heart, and so we will find rest for our souls. Now, Christ says to the heathen woman who was taken in adultery, not that they should stone her according to the law of his Father (yet he also said, 'as the Father gave me commandment, even so I do' [John 14:31]), but in mercy, and forgiveness, and warning to sin no more, and says, 'Go and sin no more' [John 8:11]. So should we also closely follow according to the law of excommunication.

Secondly, It is asked concerning the sword, whether a Christian should pronounce judgement in worldly disputes and quarrels which unbelievers have with one another? The only answer is: Christ was not willing to decide or judge between brothers concerning inheritance, but refused to do it [Luke 12:13–14]; so should we also do.

Thirdly, It is asked concerning the sword, Should one be a magistrate if he is elected thereto? To this the answer is: It was intended to make Christ a King [John 6:15], and he fled and did not regard [this position as] the ordinance of his Father. Thus should we do and follow him, and we shall not walk in darkness. For he himself says, 'Whosoever will come after me, let him deny himself and take up his cross and follow me' [Matt. 16:24]. Also, he himself forbids the power of the sword and says, 'The princes of the Gentiles exercise lordship', etc., 'but it shall not be so among you' [Matt. 20:25]. Further, Paul says, 'for whom he did foreknow he also did predestinate to be conformed to the image of his son' [Rom. 8:29–30]. Also, Peter says, 'Christ has suffered (not ruled), leaving us an ensample that ye should follow his steps' [1 Pet. 2:21].

Sources 129

Lastly, it is remarked that it does not become a Christian to be a magistrate for these reasons: The rule of the magistrate is according to the flesh, that of the Christian according to the Spirit [e.g., Rom. 8:5–8]; their houses and dwelling remain in this world, the Christian's is in heaven; their citizenship is in this world, the Christian's citizenship is in heaven [Phil. 3:20]; the weapons of their contest and war are carnal and only against the flesh, but the weapons of the Christian are spiritual, against the fortresses of the devil; the worldly are armed with steel and iron, but the Christians are armed with the armour of God, with truth, righteousness, peace, faith, salvation, and with the word of God [Eph. 6:10–20]. In short, as Christ our head was minded towards us, so should the members of the body of Christ through him be minded, that there be no schism in the body by which it be destroyed [1 Cor. 12:25; Col. 1:18]. For every kingdom divided against itself will be brought to destruction [Matt. 12:25]. Therefore, as Christ is, as it stands written of him, so must the members be, that his body be whole and one, to the edification of itself.

21 Hans Denck, *Concerning True Love* (1527)

Keywords: #Love, #Magistrate, #Coercion, #Violence, #Excommunication, #Family
Region: #Germany
Group: #Anabaptist, #Spiritualist, #Radical Reformation

Hans Denck (c.1500–1527) was a leader of the spiritualist strand of the Anabaptist movement in the south of Germany. He was influenced by medieval mysticism and the theology of **Andreas Karlstadt** and **Thomas Müntzer** and was expelled from Nuremberg in 1525 for heterodoxy. In his remaining years, he wandered to places like Augsburg, Strasbourg, and Worms before dying of the plague in 1527. Denck downplayed outward religious forms and located spiritual authority in the inner reaches of the soul. He came to advocate positions opposed to **Martin Luther,** particularly on the bondage and freedom of the will.[38] In the excerpt below, Denck expounded on the spiritual and societal implications of love (or 'charity'). Christian love knits a community together, provided a standard for godly teaching and heightened ethical obligations. Those who love desire the good of everyone, and when someone walked contrary to the gospel, Denck argued that love required rejection and excommunication.[39]

Hans Denck, "Concerning True Love" (1527), trans. Daniel Liechty, in *Early Anabaptists Spirituality: Selected Writings*, ed. Daniel Liechty (New York: Paulist, 1994), 112–121.

———

Love is a spiritual power. The lover desires to be united with the beloved. Where love is fulfilled, the lover does not objectify the beloved. The lover forgets himself, as if he were no more, and without shame he yearns for his beloved. The lover cannot be content until he has proven his love for the beloved in the most dangerous situations....

When love is true and plays no favourites, it reaches out in desire to unite with all people (that it, without causing divisions and instabilities.)

[*Human love is rooted in divine love, a delight and love that God has in himself. True love was made comprehensible through God's many demonstrations – most fully in the person and passion of Christ. It calls one to a higher standard than mere justice: if Moses were following the rule of love, he would have died for the Egyptian rather than killed him (Exod. 2:11–13). He then discourses at length on the superiority of the calling and practice brought into being by Christ. This new dispensation comes with heightened obligations, particularly those related to submission to God and separation from the world. Every Christian teaching must be measured by whether or not is accords with love. However, love and rejection can go together, as when one lovingly separates from the ungodly. He then discusses theological distinctives such as baptism, a renunciation of oaths and swearing.*]

No Christian who wants to bring honour to his Lord can use force or be a ruler. For the governance of our King consists only in teaching and in the power of the Spirit. Whoever truly acknowledges Christ as Lord should not act contrary to his commandments. And Christ has commanded his disciples to deal with evildoers in no way other than to teach and admonish them for their own improvement. If they will not listen, one should leave them alone and avoid them [e.g., 1 Thess. 5:14; 2 Thess. 3:6, 14–15]. Those who are outsiders (that is, unbelievers) do not concern the community of Christ, except that Christians hope to serve by teaching. Not that power is wrong in itself, in view of how wicked the world is. It can serve as God's wrath [Rom. 13:4]. But love teaches its children something better – that they should serve the grace of God.

It is in the nature of love never to desire the worst for anyone. Rather, love seeks to serve for improvement wherever that is possible. The head of a household should treat the household members as he himself would want God to treat him, that is, not contrary to love. And if it would be possible for a governor to do the same, he might also be a Christian in that position. But because the world would not tolerate this, a friend of God should not be a ruler. He should leave that position if he wants Christ as Lord and Master. One may love the Lord in any station in life. But he must not forget what is proper for one who loves the Lord – to forsake all violence for the Lord's sake and to be subject to others as unto the Lord....

22 *King Gustav Vasa Renounces the Crown* (1527)

Keywords: #Royal Supremacy, #Election
Region: #Sweden
Group: #Church of Sweden | #Lutheran

As reforming ideas entered Sweden, King Gustav Vasa recommended that his people **Test Luther With Scripture** (1524). The king was less sympathetic to more radical Reformers, and in 1526, he expelled Melchior Hoffman, an apocalyptically minded self-proclaimed prophet. The king's split with Catholicism became more open, motivated to a large extent by political and financial considerations. He had borrowed immense sums from the church to fund the insurrection that led to Swedish independence. The king's views of the church continued to evolve, as did his distaste for transferring funds from Sweden to Rome. As in Henry VIII's England, altering the relationship between the church and crown brought financial benefits. The church and many nobles opposed his Reformations, and some sought to dethrone him. In response, Gustav Vasa executed a few agitators and renounced the crown in 1527. This dramatic act worked its intended effect, and he was asked to remain in power. Having now been chosen twice as king, he was able to solidify his power, and the Estates supported him in his struggle against rebels. The subsequent **Diet of Västerås** (1527) wrote the new arrangement between king and church into law.[40]

Paul Barron Watson, *The Swedish Revolution Under Gustavus Vasa* (London: Sampson Low, Marston, Searle & Rivington, 1889), 250–251.

———

I have no further desire, then, to be your king. Verily I had not counted on such treatment at your hands. I now no longer wonder at the perversity of the people, since they have such men as you for their advisers. Have they no rain? They lay the blame on me. Have they no sun? Again they lay the blame on me. When hard times come, hunger, disease, or whatever it may be, they charge me with it, as if I were not man, but God. This is your gratitude to me for bringing rye and malt at great expense and trouble from foreign lands,

Sources 133

that the poor of Sweden might not starve. Yea, though I labour for you with my utmost power both in spiritual and in temporal affairs, you would gladly see the axe upon my neck; nay, you would be glad to strike the blow yourselves. I have borne more labour and trouble both at home and abroad than any of you can know or understand, – and all because I am your king. You would now set monks and priests and all the creatures of the pope above my head, though we have little need of these mighty bishops and their retinue. In a word, you all would lord it over me; and yet you elected me your king. Who under such circumstances would desire to govern you? Not the worst wretch in hell would wish the post, far less any man. Therefore I, too, refuse to be your king. I cast the honour from me, and leave you free to choose him whom you will. If you can find one who will continue ever to please you, I shall be glad. Be so considerate, however, as to let me leave the land. Pay me for my property in the kingdom, and return to me what I have expended in your service. Then I declare to you I will withdraw never to return to my degenerate, wretched, and thankless native land.

23 Diet of Västerås Elevated the Swedish King Above the Church (1527)

Keywords: #Church-State Relations, #Monarchy, #Authority
Region: #Sweden
Group: #Church of Sweden | #Lutheran

After Gustavus Vasa **renounced the crown** (1527) and was asked by the Estates to put it back on, the king enjoyed wider support for his reforming efforts. He insisted that he was not moving towards a new religion but was shedding some of the antiquated trappings that obscured true Christianity. The following excerpt comes from the Diet of Västerås (1527). The Diet did not focus on confessional matters. Instead, it detailed the relationship between the crown and the church. Although they did not openly break with Rome or establish a Protestant state, this document represents an important step in that direction. Further, it subjected the clergy to the same laws as the laity and placed the king in a position of authority over many aspects of an episcopal national church.[41] Many Reformers set great hope on a royal Reformation of the church and state. For example, John Calvin dedicated his *Commentary on Hosea* to his majesty (1559).

B.J. Kidd, ed., *Documents Illustrative of the Continental Reformation* (Oxford: Clarendon, 1911), 234–236.

———

1 Vacancies in the parish churches are to be filled up by the bishop of the diocese. If, however, he appoints murderers, drunkards, or persons who cannot or will not preach the Word of God, the King may expel them and appoint other persons who are more fit.
3 All bishops shall furnish the King with a schedule of their rents and income of every kind. From these schedules he shall determine the relative proportions for them to keep and to hand over to the crown.
9 Since it has been decreed that the King, and not the bishop, is to receive all fines imposed in cases within ecclesiastical jurisdiction, the provosts

may hereafter hold court as the bishops have done hitherto, and shall render an account of their doings to the King.

11 Priests shall be subject to temporal laws, and temporal counts, in all disputes of their own and of their churches, concerning property, torts, or contracts, and shall pay to the King the same penalties as laymen. But all complaints against the clergy for non-fulfilment of their priestly duties shall be laid before the bishop.

13 Since it has been found that mendicant friars spread lies and deceit about the country, the royal stewards are to see that they do not remain away from their monasteries more than five weeks every summer and five weeks every winter. Every friar must get a license from the steward or burgomaster before he goes out, and return it when he comes back.

15 When a priest dies the bishop is not to defraud the priest's heirs of their inheritance. Priests shall be bound, in regard to their wills, by the same law as other people.

18 The sacrament shall not be withheld from any one for debt or other reason. The church or priest has a remedy in court.

20 The Gospel shall hereafter be taught in every school.

21 Bishops shall consecrate no priests who is incompetent to preach the Word of God.

22 No one shall be made a prelate, canon, or prebendary unless he has been recommended by the King, and his name submitted to the King.

24 Balthasar Hubmaier, *On the Sword* (1527)

Keywords: #Violence, #Magistrate, #Authority, #Love, #Punishment, #Crime, #Capital Crime, #Submission
Region: #Czech Republic | #Germany, #Switzerland
Group: #Anabaptist

Balthasar Hubmaier (c.1484–1528) was a prominent Anabaptist theologian from Bavaria. He had studied under Johann Eck – a theologian famous for his disputations with **Martin Luther** – and became a pastor in Regensburg. Like Luther in *On the Jews and Their Lies* (1543), Hubmaier argued for the expulsion of local Jews and the destruction of their synagogue. A chapel was built over the ruins, and he ministered there until he took up a new post in Waldshut. From 1523, he openly supported the Reformation. He had come under the influence of **Huldreich Zwingli** in the early 1520s but ended up with the radical Anabaptists in Zürich and became a leading teacher and writer in the early Anabaptist movement. The breakdown of power due to the **Peasants' War** allowed space for Anabaptist ideas to grow. As Anabaptists came under significant pressure, he wrote a defensive treatise titled *On Heretics and Those Who Burn Them* (1524). His main argument concerned the ineffectiveness of violence in forcing one's conscience and maintained that one could not suppress the truth. He became an advocate for non-violent reform. He was baptised in 1525, then baptised several hundred adults, and explained his theological reasons for doing so in *On the Christian Baptism of Believers* (1525).

Fleeing from persecution instigated by Prince Ferdinand of Austria, he was arrested at the urging of Zwingli in Zürich later that year, where he was tortured into recanting. Although some governmental bodies were exploring a measure of heterodoxy, Zürich was less hospitable. A group of Anabaptists, including Hubmaier, left for Moravia (current Czech Republic), and Zürich would issue an **Order to Drown Anabaptists** (1526). In Moravia, he published *On the Sword* in 1527, extracts of which appear below. This piece offered an interesting take on Augustine's two kingdoms, in that he suggested

Sources 137

that those kingdoms are never fully separated in human experience, except in the person of Christ. He recognised the temporal authority of magistrates, in that they carried the sword to protect good and innocent subjects. The magistrate might punish evil but should never hate the evildoer. This high standard came with a specific consequence: a ruler who broke these conditions would, in his estimation, no longer represent God. And while unjust punishment might lead a subject to emigrate, his commitment to non-violent reform limited the options of victims of persecution to emigration or suffering. He paid the ultimate price: charged with rebellion by Ferdinand, he was extradited to Vienna and burned at the stake in 1528, followed shortly by the drowning of Elsbeth, his wife.[42]

Balthasar Hubmaier, *On the Sword* (1527), in *From Balthasar Hübmaier: The Leader of the Anabaptists*, ed. Henry C. Vedder (New York: Knickerbocker, 1905), 279–310 (279–282, 294–304).

———

On the sword. A Christian exposition of the Scriptures, earnestly announced by certain brothers as against magistracy (that is, that Christians should not sit in judgement, nor bear the sword).
[Dedication 'To the noble and Christian Lords, Arekleb of Bozkowitz and Tzerne-hor at Trebitz, Chancellor of the Margravate of Moravia']

The First Passage

Christ says to Pilate, 'My kingdom is not of this world; if it were of this world my servants would doubtless fight for me, that I should not be delivered to the Jews' – John 18:36.

From this Scripture many brothers say, 'A Christian may not bear the sword, since the kingdom of Christ is not of this world'. *Answer:* If these people use their eyes aright, they would say a very different thing, that our kingdom should not be of this world. But with sorrow we lament before God that it is of this world, as we testify when we offer the Lord's Prayer, 'Father, thy kingdom come' [Matt. 6:10; Luke 11:2]. For we are in the kingdom of the world, which is a kingdom of sin, death and hell [Rom. 5:18]. But, Father, help thou us out of this kingdom. We stick in it clear over our ears, and shall not be freed from it till the end; it clings to us even in death. Lord, forgive us this evil, and help us home into thy kingdom! Yet such brothers must see and confess the truth, that our kingdom is of this world, which should cause us heartfelt sorrow. But Christ alone could say with truth, 'My kingdom is not of this world', since he was conceived and born without sin, a lamb without blemish, in whom is no deceit, but without sin or any spot' [John 1:47; 1 Pet. 1:19]....

138 *Sources*

The Second Passage

Jesus says to Peter:

> Put up thy sword in its place, for he who taketh the sword shall perish
> by the sword. Or thinkest thou that I could not pray to my father, and
> he would send me more than twelve legions of angels? But how would
> Scripture be fulfilled, that it must be thus.
>
> Matt. 26:53–54

Mark here well, pious Christian, the word of Christ, so will you have an
answer to the accusations of the brothers. First Christ says, 'Put your sword
into its place', he does not forbid you to bear it. You are not in authority; it
is not your appointed place, not are you yet called or elected thereto. 'For
who takes the sword shall perish with the sword'. The sword means those
who act without election, disorderly, and of their own authority. But no
one should take the sword himself, except one who has been elected and
appointed thereto....Besides, do you hear this: Christ said to Peter, 'Put up
thy sword in its sheath'. He did not say, Put it away, throw it from thee. For
Christ blames him because he seeks it first, and not because he has it at his
side – otherwise he would have blamed him long before if that were wrong.

It follows further: 'Who takes the sword shall perish by the sword', that
is, he is brought under the judgement of the sword. Though he may not wish
it, he will always be judged by the sword for his fault. Do you mark here
how Christ sanctions the sword, that they shall punish with it, and suppress
self-constituted authority and wickedness? And that they shall do who are
elected for the purpose, whoever they are. Hence it is evident that if men are
pious, good and orderly, they will bear the sword for the protection of the
innocent, according to the will of God, and for a terror to evil-doers, according as God has appointed and ordained [Rom. 13:1–5]. [*Further, Peter was
obstructing the foreordained plan of God.*]

From that every Christian learns that one should not cease to protect and
guard all pious and innocent men, so long as he does not certainly know that
even now the hour of their death is here. But when the hour comes, whether
you know it or not, you can no longer protect and guard them. Therefore the
magistrate is bound by his soul's salvation to protect and guard all innocent
and peaceful men, until a certain voice of God comes and is heard to say,
Now shalt thou no longer protect this man – as Abraham also heard a voice
that he should slay his son [Gen. 22:2], contrary to the commandment, Thou
shalt not kill [Exod. 20:13]. Therefore the magistrate is also bound to rescue
and release all oppressed and persecuted men, widows, orphans, whether
known or strangers, without any respect of persons, according to the will and
most earnest command of God [Isa. 1:17; Jer. 21:12; 22:3; Rom. 13:1; and
many other passages] until they are called by God to something else, which

Sources 139

they will not need to wait for long. Therefore God has hung the sword at their side and given it to his disciples [Rom. 13:4].

[*In passage 3, Hubmaier considers Christ's rejection of fire from heaven against the insolent in Luke 9:51–56, and he argues that this does not imply that authorities cannot punish. He then affirms that Christians can be judges and use the courts (passage 4–6 relate to Luke 12:13, Matt. 5:40 and 1 Cor. 6:7 respectively). He differentiates the church's excommunication from the use of the sword by civil authority in passage 7 (Matt. 18:15–17). Both are ordained by God and compliment each other. He argues that righteous authorities are a gift of God and unrighteous ones a punishment for sin. In passage 8 he argues that Christ's command to turn the other cheek does not apply to authorities (Matt. 5:38; Luke 6:27–29). Passages 9 and 10 consider spiritual warfare, and a brief excerpt is included below.*]

Mark here, dear friends; if your hearts were right, you would say, There are two kinds of swords in the Scriptures; one spiritual, which we are to use against the wily assaults of the devil [Eph. 6:11], as Christ has commanded us against Satan [Matt. 4:1–11]. That is the word of God. Yes, of that sword Paul speaks here to the Ephesians and Corinthians [2 Cor. 10:3–6] what Christ himself says, 'I have not come to send peace but a sword' [Matt. 10:34]. Besides there is a temporal sword, which is borne for the protection of the pious, and for the frightening of the wicked here on earth. With that the magistrate is girded, that he may with it preserve the peace of the land, and it will also be called a spiritual sword when it is used according to the will of God. These two swords are not opposed to each other.

The Eleventh Passage

[*Hubmaier quotes at length Matthew 5:43–48 where Jesus commands the love of enemies.*]

Here the brothers once more cry out murder on the magistrate, and say, 'See there, the [Christian magistrate] does not smite the wicked with the sword, but has love for his enemy, does him good and prays for him'. *Answer:* Well now, let us take these words of Christ for ourselves and weigh them, and we shall not err. Christ says, 'You have heard that it hath been said, Thou shalt love thy neighbour and hate thine enemy' [Matt. 5:44]. Mark there precisely who is an enemy, namely, he whom one hates and envies. But now a Christian should hate or envy nobody, but should have love for all; therefore a Christian magistrate has no enemy, for he hates and envies no one. For what he does with the sword he does not perform out of hatred or envy, but according to the command of God. Therefore to punish the wicked is not to hate, envy or act the enemy. For in that case even God were moved by hatred, envy and enmity, which he is not, since when he wills to punish the wicked he does not do it out of envy or hate, but justice.

Therefore a just and Christian magistrate does not hate him whom he punishes; he is sorrowful of heart that he rules over people deserving of such

140 *Sources*

punishment. Yea, what he does he does according to the ordinance and earnest command of God, who has appointed him a servant and has hung the sword at his side for the administration of justice. Therefore at the last day he must give an exact account [Rom. 14:12] of how he has used the sword. For the sword is nothing else than a good rod and scourge of God, which he [the magistrate] is called to use against the wicked. Now what God calls good is good, and if he calls thee to slay thy son, it would be a good work [Gen. 22:2]. When therefore God wills to do many things through his creatures, as his instruments, which he might accomplish alone and without them, he yet wills so to use us as that we serve each other, and do not go idle, but each one fulfils his own duty to which God has called him. One shall preach, another shall protect him, a third shall till the field, a fourth shall do his work in some other way, so that we shall all eat our bread in the sweat of our faces. Verily, verily, he who rules in a just and Christian way has to sweat enough – he does not go idle.

Now we see again plainly how the above-mentioned word of Christ and the sword so completely agree; wherefore one dare not, for the sake of brotherly love, ungird the sword. Yea, and if I am a Christian and rightly disposed, if I fall into a sin I shall wish and pray that the magistrate may punish me quickly, that I may no more heap sin on sin [Sir. 3:25]. Whence it follows that the magistrate may and should punish, not alone from justice, but from the love that he bears to the evil-doer (not to his evil deed); for it is good and profitable to the sinner that a millstone be at once hanged about his neck, and he be drowned in the water [Matt. 18:6].

The Twelfth Passage

'Ye have heard that it was said to them of old, Thou shalt not kill, but he who kills shall be in danger of the judgement' – Matthew 5:21

Why is it now, dear brethren, that you cry out to Heaven and shout overloud, 'It stands written, 'Thou shalt not kill, Thou shalt not kill'. Now we have also in the Old Testament, plain and clear, that we nevertheless shall kill. Do you say, 'Yes, but God commanded them'? then I reply, God has also commanded that the magistrate shall kill and degrade the turbulent. He has for that girded them with the sword, and not in vain, as Paul writes to the Romans [13:1–5]. Do you now ask, pious Christian, how 'kill' and 'do not kill' agree with each other? *Answer:* completely. [*Hubmaier then gives many examples of tensions in scripture.*]

…Wherefore now the magistrate may kill the evil-doer, and in doing this he is guiltless according to the ordinance of God, and himself cannot be judged. And I, or any other required and summoned thereto, am guiltless in helping him; and who so withstands him withstands the ordinance of Christ and himself will incur the eternal judgement. Do not believe me here, dear brothers, but believe Paul, that you will find yourselves safe. Therefore those whom we call hangmen were in the Old Testament pious, honourable, and brave men, and were called prefects, that is, executors of the ordinance and law of God. Since it is honourable to the judge to condemn with the mouth the guilty, how can it be wrong to kill the same with the sword and fulfil the word of the judge, since the executor of the law strikes or kills with the sword none but whom the judge had not commanded him....Since neither the judge nor the executioner kill the evil-doer, but the law of God, therefore are the judge, magistrate and executioner called in the Scripture servants of God and not murderers. God judges, condemns and kills through them, and not they themselves. Whence it follows, they who would not kill the evil-doer but let him live, even murder and sin against the command, 'Thou shalt not kill'. For he who does not protect the pious kills him and is guilty of his death, as well as he who does not feed the hungry.

[*In the thirteenth passage, Hubmaier considers the proscription on Christians in positions of civil authority (Luke 22:25). He argues that this only applies to ministers of the gospel. In the fourteenth, he considers whether all vengeance should be left to God (Rom. 12:19), arguing that this does not apply to magistrates. In the fifteenth passage, he rejects the notion that union with Christ (Eph. 1, 4–5; Col. 1–2) – who did not fight – means that the magistrate cannot use the sword for righteous ends*].

The Last Passage a Sanction of Magistracy Among Christians

[*Hubmaier quotes at length Romans 13:1–7, where Paul expounds on the ordination of civil powers.*]

This passage alone, dear brothers, is enough to sanction the magistracy against all the gates of hell. When Paul says plainly, 'Let every one be submissive to the magistrate', whether he is a believer or unbeliever, you ought always to be submissive and obedient. He gives as a reason, 'For there is no power but of God'. Wherefore this obedience is the duty of all who are not against God, since God has not ordained the magistrate against himself. Now the magistrate will punish the wicked, as he is bound to do by his own soul's salvation; and if he is not able to do this alone, when he summons his subjects by bell or gun, by letter or any other way, they are bound by their soul's salvation also to stand by their prince and help him, so that according to the will of God the wicked may be slain and uprooted.

Nevertheless, the subjects should carefully test the spirit of their ruler, whether he is not incited by haughtiness, pride, intoxication, envy, hatred, or his own profit, rather than by love of the common weal and the peace of society. When that is the case, he does not bear the sword according to the ordinance of God. But if you know that the ruler is punishing the evil only, so that the pious may remain in peace and uninjured, then help, counsel, stand by him, as often and as stoutly as you are able; thus you fulfil the ordinance of God and do his work, and not a work of men.

But if a ruler should be childish or foolish, yea, even entirely unfit to rule, one may with reason then escape from him and choose another, since on

142 *Sources*

account of a wicked ruler God has often punished a whole land. But if it may not well be done, reasonably and peaceably and without great shame and rebellion, he should be suffered as one whom God has given us in his anger, and wills (since we are worthy of no better) thus to chastise us for our sins.

[*He closes by arguing again for authority and for the duty to obey God through obeying the magistrate in their pursuit of justice. He then calls erring brethren – those who deny the Christian use of the sword – to turn from error. This call is followed by a summary of the goodness of secular government and some of the limitations on it.*]

25 William Tyndale, *The Obedience of a Christian Man* (1528)

Keywords: #Authority, #Magistrate, #Liberty, #Conscience, #Family, #Obedience, #Submission, #Charity, #Violence, #Resistance
Region: #England
Group: #Church of England

William Tyndale (1494?–1536) is perhaps best known for translating the Bible into English, which became formative for the development of the English language. Indeed, his work played a significant role in introducing reforming ideas in England. Tyndale was educated at Oxford and possibly at Cambridge, where he became acquainted with early reformist ideas from **Martin Luther** and his circle. While vigorously promoting reform in England, he did so from continental Europe for safety reasons. He spent time in Wittenberg but disagreed with Luther on key issues like communion, oracular confession, and the importance of James' epistle. His activism led him into exile in the Low Countries, where he was nevertheless tracked down and burned at the stake. King Henry VIII would later issue his own Bible in English, heavily borrowing from Tyndale. **John Foxe** included him in his influential history of the Protestant martyrs, titled *Acts and Monuments*.

In the following extract from *The Obedience of a Christian Man* (1528), Tyndale showed a commitment to the office of the secular magistrate, which he subsumed in a stratification of authority and submission. This stratification of authority was held together in the one body of Christ and made every bearer of authority directly accountable to God. While this connection between the two kingdoms might resemble some of the structures of the late medieval *corpus christianum*, he concurrently began to draw boundaries to structures of authority and submission. Authority and submission would be limited by a measure of liberty, particularly the liberty of conscience. His logic draws on a conceptual connection between the family or household on the one hand and the political community as a whole on the other hand. This treatise informed a vigorous debate with Thomas More on authority and Christianity (1528).[43]

144 *Sources*

Tyndale was concerned with authority and submission in all its forms. He began with children and the obedience and love they owe to their elders. Children pleased God by pleasing their parents. He then grounded the wife's submission to her husband in several verses: The fall of humanity in Genesis 3; Peter's praise of Sarah's submission to Abraham, and his description of woman as the weaker vessel [1 Pet. 3:6–7]; Paul's commands concerning the household [Eph. 5:21–33]. The husband stood in the position of God to his wife: 'his commandments are God's commandments'. From there, he discussed servants and masters, subjects and princes, and the false authority of the pope. The following extract comes from his summary of the entire book.

William Tyndale, *The Obedience of a Christian Man and How Christian Rulers Ought to Govern* (Antwerp: [J. Hoochstraten], 1528), 151–155. Text modernised by the editors.

———

A compendious rehearsal of that which goeth before.

I have described the obedience of children, servants, wives and subjects. These four orders are of God's making and the rules thereof are God's word. He that keeps them shall be blessed: yes is blessed already and he that breaks them shall be cursed. If any impatient, stubborn or rebellious person withdraws himself from any of these commandments and puts himself under another order: let him not think he can avoid the vengeance of God by obeying the rules and traditions of man's imagination.... And be sure God is more jealous over his commandments than man is over his commandments or any man is over his wife.

Because we are blind, God has appointed in the scripture how we should serve him and please him. As pertaining unto his own person, God is abundantly pleased when we believe his promises and holy testament which he has made unto us in Christ, and for the mercy which he there showed us who love his commandments. All bodily service must be done to man in God's place. We must give obedience, honour, toll, tribute, custom and rent unto whom they belong. And you have more reason to bestow and give unto the poor who are left here in Christ's place that we show mercy to them. If we keep the commandments of love then we are sure that we fulfil the law in the sight of God and that our blessing shall be everlasting life. Now when we obey patiently and without grudging evil princes that oppress us and persecute us and are kind and merciful to them that are merciless to us and do the worst they can to us and so take all fortune patiently and kiss whatsoever cross God lays on our backs: then we are sure that we keep the commandment of love.

I declared that God has taken all vengeance in to his own hands and will himself avenge all that is not right [Rom. 12:19]: either by the powers or officers who are appointed thereto or else, if they are negligent, he will send his curses upon the transgressors and destroy them with his secret judgements. I showed also that whosoever avenges himself is damned for the act and falls into the hands of the temporal sword because he takes the office of God upon him and robs God of his most high honour in that he will not patiently abide his judgement. I showed you the authority of princes, how they are in God's place and how they may not be resisted even when they are evil, and they must be left unto the wrath of God. Never the later if they command us to do evil we must then disobey and say we are otherwise commanded by God: but not to rise against them. 'They will kill us then', you say. Therefore I say a Christian is called, to suffer even bitter death for his hope's sake and because he will do no evil. I showed also that kings and rulers, however evil they are, are yet a great gift from a good God and defend us from a thousand things that we do not see.

[*He then argues that all people – ministers of the gospel included – are subject to civil laws and punishment. Appealing to Genesis 9:6, he argues that no one is exempt. Christ's example shows how the high and powerful make themselves subject and poor out of love, and Christians are to follow this example. However, the humility should not be performed in a way that undermines civil and familial submission. Authority is given by God and is good, and Christians can even receive blessings under wicked rulers.*]

I declared how those whom God has made governors in the world ought to rule if they are Christian. They ought to remember that they are heads and arms [1 Cor. 12:12–27], to defend the body to minister peace, health and wealth and even to save the body, and that they have received their offices of God to minister and to do service unto their brethren. King, subject, Master, servant, are names in the world: but not in Christ [Gal. 3:28]. In Christ we are all one [Rom. 12:5] and even brethren. No man is his own but we are all Christ's servants bought with Christ's blood [1 Cor. 6:19–20]. Therefore no man ought to look out for himself or his own profit: but Christ's and his will. In Christ no man rules as a king does over his subjects or a master over his servants: but serves as one hand does to another and as the hands do to the feet and the feet to the hands [in 1 Cor. 13]. We also serve not as servants do unto masters: but as those who are bought with Christ's blood serve Christ himself. We are all servants unto Christ. For whatever we do to one another in Christ's name we it unto Christ [Matt. 25:40] and we shall receive the reward from Christ. The king counts his commons of Christ himself and therefore does them service willingly seeking no more of them than is sufficient to maintain peace and unite and to defend the Realm. And they obey again willingly and lovingly as unto Christ. And of Christ every man seeks his reward.

[*He argues that magistrates should not pry into people's conscience, and then advises the king to remove wicked and false subordinates. The king should also consider the high cost of continuing to follow the pope, and the meagre benefits received from the association. If the monarch should not act, then people should patiently wait under God's judgement.*]

26 *The Protestation at Speyer* (1529)

Keywords: #Church-State Relations, #Toleration, #Conscience
Region: #Germany
Group: #Lutheran | #Roman Catholic

The Diet of Speyer assembled in March 1529 upon the fall of large swaths of Hungarian lands to the Ottomans, whose empire soon set its eyes on Vienna, the capital of the Habsburg Empire. Meanwhile, internal religious divisions compromised the stability and unity of the Habsburg Empire. The military threat from the Ottoman Empire led the Diet to end the fragile *de facto* toleration that had been in place since 1526. The revocation of this toleration prompted immediate protest from a minority of princes with Lutheran sympathies. They pleaded for toleration, stating they would not enforce intolerance in their territories. Their inclination had been to offer this plea of toleration to Emperor Charles V in person, but he sent representatives in his stead.

The Protestation at Speyer was signed by princes, who bore civil authority, but it has become theologically and historically significant for several reasons. First, it is from this document that 'Protestants' derived their name. The Protestation also evidenced a growing belief that a Reformation within the Roman Catholic Church might be impossible and that Protestants might need to protect themselves to survive. With the political support of princes, Lutheran theologians began to develop theologies of resistance. Lastly, although the minority of princes were not yet militarily united, they later entered the **Schmalkaldic League** in 1531.[44]

B.J. Kidd, ed., *Documents Illustrative of the Continental Reformation* (Oxford: Clarendon, 1911), 243–244.

———

The Resolution of the Minority, 19–25 April 1529.

From the Protest of 19 April.

You, well-beloved, and you, dear Lords, Cousins, Uncles, Friends, and others, know what objections we caused to be raised, both orally and in writing, on the last day of the late Diet, against certain points in the article for the preservation of peace and unity in view of the religious division imminent in the Empire, pending the Council; and this, although (while holding that we then said nothing but what our conscience requires for God's honour and the hallowing of His Name) we were aware of the very great need in the Empire of the peace and unity aforesaid. You, Well-beloved, and you others should have sought means whereby we might have been able, with a good conscience and without objection, to come to an agreement with you for the interpretation of the late Recess of Speyer, where it might by difference of opinion be perverted; whereby, too, the late Recess (which hitherto was everywhere considered just, and that, so far, unanimously) should also remain in essence and substance as then. Further we, Duke John, Elector of Saxony, proposed a conciliatory amendment to the resolution adopted by the Grand Committee with reference to the perversion aforesaid and the maintenance of the said peace; and afterwards we again set it before the said Committee, and subsequently had it submitted to you, well-beloved, and you others, trusting that the same proposal would have been considered by you as a moderate and peaceful solution and would have been accepted.

But whereas we have found that you, well-beloved, and you others persist in the maintenance of your intention [namely, to revoke the toleration of 1526]; and whereas (for stated and weighty reasons and objections which we have now and at all times wished, declared, and repeated) both for conscience' sake and because you, Beloved, and you Excellencies, in view of the imminent religious division above-mentioned, have not reconciled yourselves to assist in the preservation of peace and unity pending the Council, we do not agree or consent herein; and whereas, from the form of procedure, and even before that, on account of the above-mentioned Recess of Speyer, we are not bound herein, especially without our consent, by reason of the following written, strongly binding clauses and words from the said late Recess made and sealed here at Speyer which, at the end of the same Recess, are, in due form, written as follows: 'Hereby so declare and promise We. Ferdinand, Prince and Infant of Spain, &c., and we Electors. Princes, Prelates, Counts and Lords', &c.

Now, therefore, we hold that, as regards the oft-mentioned objections, our great and urgent needs require us openly to protest against the said resolution of you, Well-beloved, and you others as being, in view of the said late Recess, null and void, and, so far as we ourselves and our people, one and all, are concerned, not binding. This we hereby presently do. We hereby protest to you, well-beloved, and you others, that we, for kindred reasons, know not how to, cannot, and may not, concur therein, but hold your resolution null and not binding; and we desire, in matters of religion (pending the said general and free Christian council or national assembly) by means of the godly help, power, and substance of the oft-mentioned late Recess of Speyer, so to live, govern, and carry ourselves, in our governments, as also with and among our subjects and kinsfolk, as we trust to answer it before God Almighty and his Roman Imperial Majesty, our most gracious Lord.

27 *The First Peace of Kappel (1529)*

Keywords: #War, #Peace, #Pluralism, #Coercion, #Toleration
Region: #Switzerland
Group: #Reformed, #Zwinglian | #Roman Catholic

As the Reformation gained ground in Switzerland, Protestant and Catholic cantons wrestled with toleration and coexistence within and between the cantons. From 1527, several Protestant regions in contemporary Switzerland participated in a political union called the *Christliches Burgrecht*. This alliance sought to protect and further reform in the area. Although no major outbreaks of violence occurred between Protestant and Catholic cantons, their fragile coexistence broke down when Jakob Kaiser, a reform-minded priest, was burned at the stake for heresy in the Catholic canton of Schwyz on 29 May 1529. **Huldreich Zwingli** urged an armed response. Zürich declared war, and troops were mustered from the Swiss Confederate states of Appenzell, Basel, Bern, and Schaffhausen. The First Peace of Kappel of 26 June 1529 prevented bloodshed, although this peace would not last.

This First Peace of Kappel is one of the earliest attempts to recognise the autonomy of the cantons in matters of religion. It enabled the recognition of entire regions as either Protestant or Catholic based on the formation of local majorities and the development of local practices of toleration. Moreover, it provides an account of arguments against religious violence and coercion. It thus shaped a Protestant alternative to the intolerance of the **Diet of Speyer**. But this balance implied that Catholic cantons were not to seek protection from the Habsburg Empire anymore. Two years later, Protestant and Catholic cantons engaged in war again, leaving Zwingli dead on the battlefield.[45]

B.J. Kidd, ed., *Documents Illustrative of the Continental Reformation* (Oxford: Clarendon, 1911), 470–471.

———

Sources 149

First Peace of Kappel

First, as concerns the Word of God. Inasmuch as no man ought to be forced in matters of faith, the Cantons and their domains shall not be put under compulsion therein: but as touching the subject districts and bailiwicks, which are under the lordship of either side – where they have abolished the Mass and burnt or done away with Images, they shall not be punished in person, honours, or goods: and where the Mass and other ceremonies are still retained, they shall not be punished in person, honours, or goods: and where the Mass and other ceremonies are still retained, they shall not be subjected to force, nor shall any preachers be sent, appointed, or assigned to them, so long as the majority objects; but whatsoever the majority of their parishioners shall resolve to admit or to abolish, such as meats which God has not forbidden to eat, so shall it remain during the pleasure of the parishioners, and neither side shall make war upon nor chastise the other for its faith.

Secondly, as concerning the alliance and Union with Ferdinand. Inasmuch as this was concluded solely for faith's sake, and it is now determined by the arbitrators that neither side shall for faith's sake force, fight, or hate the other, therefore, before any one moves from the field, the said Union shall be forthwith given up and surrendered into the hands of the arbitrators, its seals broken, its parchment pierced and slit, so that every one may see the pieces; and the same shall be dead and done with, and neither side shall hereafter make use of it or its like. As concerning the other Civic Alliances and leagues lately concluded, a conference shall be held as to how they shall be carried on. But the Christian Civic Alliance between the six cities of Zürich, Bern, Basel, St. Gall, Mühlhausen, Biel, and others, shall remain unbroken and inviolate....

28 Johannes Bugenhagen, *Whether One Can Wage War for the Sake of the Gospel* (1529)

Keywords: #Authority, #Magistrates, #Resistance, #Rebellion, #Law
Region: #Germany
Group: #Lutheran | #Islam

Johannes Bugenhagen (1485–1558) was ordained in 1509 and started reforming the church after independently adopting a humanist reading of scripture. He first came to Wittenberg in 1521 and ministered there in cooperation with **Martin Luther** and **Philip Melanchthon**. Bugenhagen was Luther's long-time pastor and counsellor and delivered the oration after Luther's funeral in 1546. Like Luther, his political writings were prompted by specific events and did not necessarily form a coherent mode of political thought. Nevertheless, he offered an early Lutheran justification for resistance that relied heavily on legal thought and theory, which drew heavily on canon law.[46]

The source below was written in response to the **Protestation at Speyer**. The minority of princes were contemplating the legality and legitimacy of using force to oppose a divinely ordained order. Dr Gregor Brück, the Saxon Chancellor, asked Bugenhagen to weigh in on the justice of fighting to defend the gospel, and this verdict was delivered in writing to Elector John, brother of Frederick the Wise. Bugenhagen thought one must distinguish between civil offices and their office bearers. Whereas it would not be permissible to rebel against the divinely ordained offices, he articulated a right to resist office bearers when they violated the conditions of their oath, for example, when they failed to protect their subjects. While this perhaps resonates with dimensions of social contract theory, these thoughts on resistance cannot be read as such, especially with the strong emphasis on the natural order as instated by God and the fact that his audience was lower civil authorities.

Johannes Bugenhagen, *Selected Writings*, ed. Kurt K. Hendel (Minneapolis, MN: Fortress, 2015), I:103–110. Used by permission.

———

The Question

Whether one can resist the Emperor with force when he intends to invade us with force for the sake of God's word.

Sources 151

My Answer

If he were our equal, or when princes fight with princes, or if those were fighting to whom we do not owe fealty, then this question would not be necessary. However, because he is a sovereign lord, I am not certain what should be concluded. However, I have my opinion in order to assist those who have better understanding.

1 The Emperor is not judge or a sovereign lord in this matter but God's word is.

2 In his imperial role we intend to obey him in all matters, even more than others and in accordance with Christ's teaching, 'Render to Caesar what belongs to Caesar' [Matt. 22:21; Mark 12:17; Luke 20:25].

3 However, in those matters that belong to God he is neither emperor nor a sovereign lord. He also should not desire to be, and he is also not accepted by us for such a purpose. No one has sworn allegiance to him in this matter. We are also not eager to inform him of this truth if he wants to hear us as a Christian lord, for Christ says concerning this, 'Give to God (not the Emperor) what belongs to God' [Matt. 22:21; Mark 12:17; Luke 20:25].

4 Therefore he should perceive himself to be an emperor, not a murderer; a Christian lord and not a persecutor of the gospel; a lord and father and not a tyrant, as Paul says in Romans 13[:1], where he writes thusly:

5 'All authority is from God'. Therefore, when authority wishes to go against God or against God's word, then it ceases to have authority, as Samuel also says plainly to Saul in [1 Sam. 15:23], 'Now, because you rejected the LORD's word, He has also rejected you so that you may not be king'.

6 However, we should also be obedient to godless lords in all matters in which they are our sovereigns if God has placed us under their authority, just as the Jews obeyed Saul there afterwards until God gave them David. Only Saul neglected God's command.

7 However, if Saul had proceeded and had wished to compel the people with force from God's word to idolatry and had, to this end, begun to strike and to murder, I think that Samuel would have stabbed him mortally himself and would have joined the people in armed opposition to him....

10 However, when the authority itself transcends its authority ordained by God and asserts another authority to judge God's word and to oppress it, to compel people away from God, to rob, to murder, etc., to the eternal corruption of its people and its descendants, in that case one should acknowledge publicly that it acts unjustly. In such matters one has no command from God to obey. We also do not recognise it as our government and have also not sworn allegiance to it when it acts in such a way. Whoever is a Christian should suffer such personal injustice. Therefore, Christian princes should also suffer when only their person is affected and not their people. They do so as Christians and not as princes.

152 *Sources*

[Bugenhagen discusses how subjects should seek remedy when wronged by their sovereign as well as the sovereign's duty to protect subjects from external aggressors.]

13 No lesser lord should act against his sovereign lords. I am not speaking about others. However, if they do not want to be sovereign lords according to the proper authority of God but violent murderers and Turks, it does not follow that the godly princes should also disregard their rightful authority commanded by God to protect their subjects rightfully. Rather, a godly prince may think this way:

Although someone else forsakes his proper, divine authority, I will not forsake it. I cannot justify this before GOD that I hand the sheep over to the wolf. If another person does not want to be my sovereign lord to whom I want to entrust dutifully body, property, land, and people with all obedience but wants to be a murderer and Turk against God's order and law, I still remain in the authority and in the power commanded to me by God and should protect my people from murderers and Turks. They do not want to hear our just cause. I know that my people are innocent, etc....

29 Johannes Brenz, *The Case for State-Established Lutheranism* (1529)

Keywords: #Church-State Relations, #Authority, #Magistrate, #Peace, #Violence
Region: #Germany
Group: #Lutheran

Johannes Brenz (1499–1570) was born in Swabia and studied at the University of Heidelberg, where he met **Martin Luther** in 1518. He became an active Lutheran Reformer, first in the city of Schwäbisch Hall, and then across the region of Württemberg. He served as a theological advisor to a range of German nobility, some of whom kept him out of the hands of the emperor and assisted in the establishment of the Lutheran Church throughout the Duchy of Württemberg. He took an interest in Reformation elsewhere, but stayed at a distance from **John Calvin**.

Brenz served as an advisor to Margrave George of Brandenburg-Ansbach, and Brenz may have written the following source for his instruction. In the document, he detailed the role of territorial magistrates in reforming the church. Brenz was more radical than **Martin Luther** in arguing that the Christian magistrate would have a robust and active role in rooting out false worship and in establishing orthodoxy. Firstly, because God had ordained the secular magistrate, they had an obligation to foster the church's flourishing. Secondly, he argued that the secular task of maintaining peace could only be accomplished after the removal of error and the establishment of truth. However, a theological debate soon erupted in Nürnberg where Reformers cited Bohemia as an example of how political stability might coexist with religious pluralism. Brenz abandoned this second line of argument in his later writings.[47]

James M. Estes, *Godly Magistrates and Church Order: Johannes Brenz and the Establishment of the Lutheran Territorial Church in Germany, 1524–1559* (Toronto, ON: Center for Reformation and Renaissance Studies, 2001), 95–98. Reproduced with permission from the Center for Reformation and Renaissance Studies, Victoria College, University of Toronto.

154　*Sources*

The Reason Why A Prince Should Cause Christian Worship to Be Established in His Jurisdiction and Territory (1529)

There is a great difference between a heathen prince, heedless of God, and a Christian God-fearing prince. For a prince who is heedless of God is, according to his own opinion (I should say: his lack of faith), enfeoffed with his principality by the secular emperor alone. Accordingly, he imagines that his office is adequately performed if he maintains external peace in his territory in accordance with secular, imperial law, letting things happen however they will between the word of God, peace and life. But a Christian prince has been instructed by God's word that he has been enfeoffed with his principality not merely by the secular emperor but, much more, from the heavenly Lord God and father [Dan. 4:25; John 19:11; Rom. 13:1]....Therefore, it behoves such a prince to rule and order the territory entrusted to him not merely according to secular, imperial law but, much more, according to the word, law, and command of the highest and supreme lord, our God and father.

But it is a supremely important commandment of our Lord God that all worship originating in human command and tradition should yield place to true divine worship founded on God's word, as our Lord Christ himself so well says in Matt. 15:[1–9]. Accordingly, a Christian uses all godly, orderly, and convenient means to ensure that this divine command of God is carried out in act and deed.

Moreover, every prince is, by reason of the authority entrusted to him, obligated to seek the peace of his territory....Now there is nothing that brings more peace and unity than proper, true, and godly worship. On the other hand, nothing causes more dissensions and disunity than idolatrous, perverse, human worship....

Thus far the words of Holy Scripture, from which it is to be well noted that hypocritical and idolatrous worship in the churches is the chief cause of all misfortune and strife in our lands. For although the event described happened to the Jews in the Old Testament, nevertheless our Lord desired to show by the example of his chosen people how he will behave towards every land that is burdened with false, ungodly worship. As St. Paul says, Scripture has been given to us for teaching and correction. Therefore, if a Christian prince desires to seek true, endurable, and divine peace for his territory (as he is responsible before God to do), he can do so by no more effective means than by rooting out ungodly worship, the ground and root of all misfortune and of all dissension and disunity, and replacing it with true divine worship. [*He recounts how God blessed biblical kings who violently rooted out idolatry.*] In this age of the gospel it would be well not to imitate Jehu's smiting and slaying [2 Kings 9–10], for these means were commanded at the time to his person alone. But one should imitate him in the abolition of ungodly worship by evangelical means, with the proclamation of the word of God and the establishment of true divine worship....

Sources 155

In addition to all this, a prince is also by virtue of his office duty-bound to maintain secular decency and piety in his territory. Now, ungodly worship in the church is certainly the cause of all worldly evil and indecency, while godly worship, on the other hand, is the source of all decent and upright life in the world [Rom. 1:21–24, 28–30]....From [these words] it is easy to perceive that ungodly worship is the origin and chief cause of all dishonourable life and behaviour. Accordingly, if a Christian prince desires to perform his office diligently and to preserve secular decency, as is proper, he can do this in no more effective way than by establishing and ordering true divine worship in the place of ungodly worship, so that true divine peace before God and piety in worship will overflow into every day civil life and lead both prince and subjects to God's grace, favour, and salvation. Amen.

30 Olaus Petri, *Rules for Judges* (c.1520–1540)

Keywords: #Law, #Economics, #Crime, #Poverty, #Equality
Region: #Sweden
Group: #Lutheran

Olaus Petri (1493–1552) is sometimes referred to as the 'Martin Luther of Sweden'. He was born in Örebro and became an early leading Reformer. He studied at Uppsala, Leipzig, and spent 1516–1518 in Wittenberg. Petri returned to Sweden and was ordained around the same time Philip Melanchthon came to Wittenberg. Petri supported Swedish independence from the Danish King Christian II and the Kalmar Union. Just after Christian's coronation in November 1520, authorities executed around 80 nobles and clergy on account of heresy. Petri recorded the massacre in *A Swedish Chronicle*. During the Swedish War of Liberation (1521–1523), Petri sided with Gustav Vasa, who would become the first Swedish king in 1523. Petri was appointed to Stockholm's Saint Nicholas' Church and supported the Diet of Västerås (1527), which elevated Vasa over the church. At Vasa's coronation in 1528, Petri preached a sermon on kingship and the common good, the *Krönungspredikan*. About a decade later, he fell from the king's grace upon an unproven charge of treason.[48]

The excerpts below come from *The Rules for Judges* (c.1520–1540), attributed to Petri. It reflects on wisdom in relation to procedural fairness, evidence, personal integrity, and the meaning of punishment. Petri not only had a high regard for judges but also believed that poor judging was a damnable offence. His perspective on the relationship between poverty and crime is noteworthy, as well as his argument that punishment should aim at the improvement of behaviour and not leave the accused in despair. *The Rules for Judges* reads as a charge to the legal profession and has become part of the Swedish legal canon.

Jarkko Tontti, "Olaus Petri and the Rules for Judges", *Associations: Journal for Social and Legal Theory* 4, no. 1 (2000): 113–128. Reproduced with the kind permission of the translator.

Sources 157

Some General Rules Which a Judge Should Abide by Closely

It behoves a judge to imagine himself first as a governor of God and the office he keeps as belonging to God and not to him; therefore, the judgement he pronounces is God's judgement, because it is delivered in God's office and for God's sake; it is indeed God's judgement and not man's. And it behoves a judge to be watchful lest he hand down a false judgement for God's sake, which by doing so condemns him to eternal damnation because he wreaks violence and falsehood out of God's judgement and command which God has set down as law. If a judge wishes to judge right and studies law with his best efforts, but because of a want of understanding falters, and thereby renders a false judgement, let it be said in his defence that he acted with no malice aforethought, but the judging went awry notwithstanding his design, and, should any penalty happen to be levied, then it is to be a civil fine....

2 A judge is further advised to remember that just as he is a governor of God, so too are the people which he judges God's own. It behoves him therefore to judge God's people and not his own, at God's behest not his own. For this reason, he ought to judge God's people in the same fashion as he himself would wish to answer to Him, whose people they are.

3 A judge would be wise to remember that the office of a judge is for the avail of the common people and not for the avail of the judge himself, and therefore he must mind it for the good of the common people and not for his own good, even though good will come to him when he tends to it well. Moreover, he ought to use his office to seek the common good, and not his own good. The judge is there for the common people and not the common people for the judge....

5 Whosoever chooses not to heed this, will surely learn for himself from experience. God will not suffer violence to go unpunished, especially when it is inflicted by those who, by virtue of their office, should thwart it. So let each lord take pains whom he chooses to dispatch as his governor or bailiff, and let the lord say to him: Go thou and be loyal and obedient to me, and let no unlawfully gotten monies or penalty fees come into my hands, otherwise you will wreak harm upon me. This pertains to those who corrupt the law to wrest penalty fees and wreak violence and injustice upon the poor; but this is not uttered to be understood as pertaining to lawfully and duly acquired penalty fees....

7 All laws must be such that they are for the common good and for that reason when a law begins to wreak harm it no longer is law but rather iniquity and falsehood and must be forsaken.....

9 What is not just and fair cannot be law either; for it is on account of the fairness which dwells in the law that the law is accepted.

10 All law is to be wielded with wisdom because the greatest right is the greatest wrong; and there must be mercy in justice as well....

158 Sources

21 Like crimes demand like chastening, and therefore no heed should be paid to whether one be prince or pauper, but the one must be chastened like the other when their crimes are like....

23 Let a judge, while sitting in court, not grow wrathful with respect to any party, for wrath will encumber him from making the right decision in the case....

25 There is nothing of greater worth to a judge than wisdom so that he knows when he must be harsh and when he must be mild for the sake of the law, because all chastening must be for the purpose of curing, and, if possible, chastisement must not hinder the one who is chastised from mending his ways. This is what happens to those who have stolen: they are sent to the block, their ears are cut off and they are banished from their village. If they flee to distant lands, where no one knows them and try to mend their ways and live decently, they will not be trusted; and so the chastening will encumber the one who is chastened and he will plunge into despair and will become more aggrieved than ever, and it would well nigh have been better had he lost his life in the first place. The same happens to harlots who are put in a pillory and ordered away from the village; when they only had carnal knowledge of one or two men, they will then turn into harlots for all men, which will not reform them, but a chastening of this kind will give them cause to worsen. Therefore, a judge must act in such matters wisely so that he does not cause wickedness to grow, but the law always demands the mending of ways and it must be used for that end....

35 Every judgement must be based upon clear grounds and evidence, and let the judge decide only according to the grounds and evidence....

38 Let no one be judged on the basis of a confession, which he has been prodded to make because of having been tortured and persecuted because such confessions tend to be false and it often occurs that because of torture, many confess something which has never been true and never took place.... [*He makes qualified exception for 'high treason and for capital crimes'*].

40 If a matter be unclear, then the judge ought to be more inclined to favour the accused than the accuser; let the one who has the risk receive the benefit and let the one who receives the benefit and the profit bear the risk.

31 Andreas Osiander, *Against Incredible Antisemitic Accusations* (1529)

Keywords: #Persecution, #Violence, #Murder, #Law
Region: #Germany | #Hungary
Group: #Lutheran | #Judaism

Andreas Osiander (c.1498–1552) was born near Nuremberg and spent much of his life ministering in that city. Before his ordination, he studied at the University Ingolstadt – the theological faculty that **Martin Luther** and **Argula von Grumbach** had clashed with. The young minister was an early supporter of Luther's reforms and furthered similar aims in Nuremberg. He was involved in many of the important events of the early German Reformation. Osiander's interests were capacious in keeping with his humanist education (e.g., publishing Nicolaus Copernicus' *On the Revolution of the Heavenly Spheres* in 1543), and he showed an independence of mind in theological matters. Notably, he disagreed with Luther and many Catholics about their attitudes towards Jews.

Osiander had a long-established relationship with members of the Jewish community. His treatise on blood libel accusations was prompted by events in Poesing (Hungary) where a 1529 trial for ritual murder ended in the death of 30 Jews. At the prompting of a nobleman, Osiander wrote an anonymous treatise against Christians who spread blood libel charges or killed on the basis of those accusations. During a 1540 trial for ritual murder, two Jews published Osiander's treatise and invoked his words in their defence. According to Joy Margaret Kammerling, 'Osiander's defence of the Jews against the charge of ritual murder offered the first rational Christian refutation of the time-honoured belief that the Jews killed small Christian children'.

Osiander presented the Christian reader with a difficult scenario: 'either the Jews murder Christian children most horrifically or ... Christians most shamefully murder innocent Jews'. His treatise undermined the first option, leaving Christians with the harder pill to swallow: they were the murderers. Osiander did share many of the biases of his time about Jews, but many Jews seemed to appreciate his more tolerant attitude. Catholic and Protestant theologians wrote treatises in response to Osiander (Johann Eck directly and

160 *Sources*

Martin Luther indirectly). Eck's response reiterated centuries of antisemitism, and he blamed Lutheranism for being too friendly to Jewish communities. Eck's accusations were one of the factors prompting Luther's antisemitic writings.[49]

Andrew L. Thomas, *The Apocalypse in Reformation Nuremberg: Jews and Turks in Andreas Osiander's World* (Ann Arbor: University of Michigan Press, 2022), 233–254 (234–235, 237, 252–253).

———

[*The Hebrew Bible forbade murder.*] So it is wrong on both accounts for a Christian to murder a Jew or a Jew to murder a Christian. Now it happens at any rate with certainty and nevertheless by all measure unjustly that either the Jews murder Christian children most horrifically or that the Christians most shamefully murder innocent Jews, a thing which Christians not only should not do, but also about which they should not remain quiet nor allow it if they see it from a different view or notice it....

Thus, it is clear [*from the law, writings and prophets*] that whoever sheds blood unlawfully is cursed by God and is guilty of death by the world and has all unhappiness to expect, primarily that God will demand the blood from his hand and not let it go unavenged. The Jews know this well for they read it every day and learn and practice it in their law most diligently, and experience all over the world that it happens like it was declared. That is why it is not believable that they would so wilfully go against God's commandment and that they would arrange and cause their own corruption of body and soul for the sake of obtaining innocent blood....

The third point is that the commandment stating that bloodshed is wrong and forbidden is not given alone to the Jews in writing but is also planted by nature into the hearts of all men. For one cannot find any people on the earth that are so blind that manslaughter is praised or allowed....

Think now, your honour, whether one does not stir up the severe wrath of God, who allows no shedding of innocent blood to go unavenged, whether it be the blood of Jews, Turks, heathens, or Christians, and whether it is not a great disgrace before the world. And where injustice happens to the Jews, as I for myself consider to be completely the case, I do not doubt whether it is also a great scandal where such hue and cry come from among the Turks and other unbelieving people, namely that the Christians are either so foolish a people that they believe such things, and if this is not true, and instead they know that it is not true, then they wrongly murder [Jews] under a false pretence. Therefore, it is no wonder if the Christian name is hated by the unbelievers [non-Christians]....

32 Anonymous, *Whether Secular Government Has the Right to Wield the Sword in Matters of Faith* (1530)

Keywords: #Violence, #Church-State Relations, #Toleration #Non-violence, #Hebrew Bible
Region: #Germany
Group: #Radical Reformation, #Anabaptist?

Several works on the righteous use of the sword appeared after the **German Peasants' War** and the revocation of toleration for Protestants after the 1529 **Diet of Speyer**. The following anonymous pamphlet of 1530 argued against violence and coercion by Catholics and Protestants alike. Its rejection of violence, focus on the New Testament, and disinterest in secular authority suggest someone with Anabaptist inclinations may have written the piece. This pamphlet first surfaced in Nuremberg in 1530. **Johannes Brenz** responded in *An Answer to the Memorandum That Deals with this Question: Whether Secular Government Has the Right to Wield the Sword in Matters of Faith* (8 May 1530).

This anonymous pamphlet argued against the use of the sword in matters of faith, making the case that potential sources of legitimation, such as Catholic canon law, the Hebrew Bible, and the teachings of Jesus, did not support this position. Notable is his assertion that Jewish law and the Hebrew Bible were no longer binding in the political context. This argument would be developed to a greater extent among German jurists of the seventeenth century. The separation of civil and spiritual authority was perhaps most strongly expressed in the statement that Christian or popish governments have the same authority as a Turkish or non-Christian government would. This pamphlet is a remarkable early statement of the theological and practical benefits of toleration, and people like **Roger Williams** would later wield similar arguments.[50]

James M. Estes, *Whether Secular Government Has the Right to Wield the Sword in Matters of Faith. A Controversy in Nürnberg over Freedom of Worship and the Authority in Spiritual Matters* (Toronto, ON: Center for Reformation and Renaissance Studies, 1994), 41–54. Reproduced with permission from the Center for Reformation and Renaissance Studies, Victoria College, University of Toronto.

162 Sources

There is simply no end to executions and banishments for reasons of faith. Lutheran governments will not tolerate Anabaptists or Sacramentarians [i.e., Zwinglians]. Zwinglian governments also refuse to tolerate Anabaptists. Then come the papists, who burn, hang, or banish evangelicals, Lutherans, Zwinglians, Anabaptists and everyone who is not of their faith....

But if you ask them to cite scripture [showing the state has power in spiritual matters], either no one is at home or else they refer us to the Old Testament record of the Jewish kings who supported true worship, abolished idolatrous worship, and destroyed idols. If you reply that the Old Testament and Jewish law are no longer binding, and that they should show where in the New Testament the secular government is commanded to be responsible for faith or to punish unbelievers with force or with the sword, then they are stuck....

But the New Testament speaks of two kingdoms on earth, namely the spiritual and the secular. The spiritual kingdom is the kingdom of Christ in which Christ is king. Similarly, the secular realm also has its king, namely the emperor and other authorities. Just as each kingdom has its own distinct king, so each has its own distinct sceptre, goal, and end. The sceptre of the spiritual realm is the word of God; the goal and end to which this sceptre should attract and move us is that men turn to God and after this life be saved. The sceptre of the secular realm, on the other hand, is the sword; the goal and end toward which it should drive and force men is that external peace be maintained....

Therefore, the sum and substance of the whole matter is this, that a government that wishes to discharge its office and not claim more than has been entrusted to it should and must leave it entirely to Christ the king to determine and judge, by means of the sceptre of his divine word, whether any teaching about faith, how man may come to God and be saved, be true or false. Just as one clearly sees that in his kingdom Christ does both things, namely, teaches the true faith and condemns the false, pours the holy spirit into the heart and drives the devil out, doing both through his sceptre, the word, and calls on no secular authority to assist. Hence it is not proper for secular authority to do this. Rather it should use its sceptre or sword in the secular realm against external misdeeds, so that no one may be harmed in his body or goods. In such matters the secular sword is effective and God has established it for that reason [Rom. 13:1–5]. But the sword is of no use in forcing people to adhere to this or that faith. In the final analysis, whether you hang or drown them, the choice must still be left to those who do not want to go to heaven to go down to hell to the devil or his mother instead.

But someone may object that this is too crudely put, and that while it might perhaps be appropriate for a Turkish or heathen government to ignore the spiritual welfare of its subjects, a Christian government must not allow its subjects to be led astray by false doctrine. Answer: we have already heard that Christ, the king in the spiritual realm, not only gives true faith and the

Sources 163

holy spirit but also drives out false faith and the devil. Now, just as it is neither right nor possible for the secular government, by means of its sceptre of the sword, to give anyone true faith or the holy spirit, so also it is neither right nor possible to drive out false faith, heresy, or the devil by means of the sword. Thus Turkish, heathen, Christian, and popish governments all have exactly the same authority. And both things, namely fighting for or against the true faith, the one as well as the other, constitute interference in Christ's kingdom and rebellion against it. If a government wishes to be Christian and further Christ's kingdom, it may do so as an individual person, but its office remains the same one way or the other. And if it is not proper for Turks and heathen to meddle in Christ's kingdom with the sword, it is even less so for a Christian government. But a Christian government can choose another course of action that is consistent with Christ's kingdom, namely by appointing good preachers who do battle by means of the word of God. Likewise, if it personally wishes to bring others from false faith to Christ, let it remain under the kingdom of Christ, use his sceptre, the word, and not have recourse to its sword in the secular kingdom.

33 *Copenhagen Confession* (1530)

Keywords: #Church-State Relations, #Confession of Faith
Region: #Denmark
Group: #Lutheran

The Lutheran-leaning King Frederick I (r.1523–1533) ousted his older and Catholic-leaning brother Christian II in 1523. He began to work towards the toleration of Lutherans as confirmed at the **Diet of Odense** in 1527. This new phase of toleration enabled Lutherans to organise themselves and develop a measure of confessional consistency. Around the same time as the **Augsburg Confession**, the *Copenhagen Confession (Confessio Hafniensis)* influenced the religious parameters for Lutheranism in Denmark. One of its main composers, Hans Tausen (1494–1561), studied under **Martin Luther** at Wittenberg. The drafters of the Confession presented the articles to the Danish National Assembly ahead of a religious disputation that would never materialise. Formal recognition of Lutheranism would follow under his son Christian III in 1536, who would continue to support Luther's family and to whom **Katharina von Bora Luther** would appeal upon her husband's death.[51] The following excerpt from the *Copenhagen Confession* relates to the relationship between church and crown.

"*Confessio Hafniensis* (The Confession of Copenhagen), 1530", trans. Eric Lund, in *A Documentary History of Lutheranism*, ed. Eric Lund (Minneapolis, MN: Fortress, 2017), I:485.

———

37 We also believe and teach that all people, both the religious, as they are called, and the secular, in whatever estate they are, must be subservient to the princes and secular authorities and honouring laws, customs and Christian decrees and privileges which are not contrary to God and are fruitful for the general welfare. Whoever opposes them we consider unchristian….

34 *Augsburg Confession* (1530)

Keywords: #Confession of Faith, #Church-State Relations, #War
Region: #Germany
Group: #Lutheran

The *Augsburg Confession* (1530) is one of the most important and
well-known documents of the Reformation. **Philip Melanchthon** drafted the
confession in preparation for the Diet of Augsburg (1530), which Emperor
Charles V ordered for the restoration of political unity within the empire.
The diet was particularly important to those princes who had participated in
the **Protestation at Speyer**. In the face of the revocation of toleration and the
interest of the emperor in unity on account of the ongoing threat from the
Ottoman Empire, Protestants needed to present a politically unified front.
Unity was impossible without a measure of religious uniformity. Melanchthon began drafting a document based on confessional material submitted
from the Protestant-leaning regions. The document set out the basic tenets
of Protestant theology. The excerpts below from the *Augsburg Confession*
discuss the relationship between civil authorities and Christianity. It affirms
a commitment to dividing ecclesial and civil powers and argues that ecclesial
power would have no divine mandate to engage in civil affairs. These points
were important for Protestant minorities seeking toleration, even as they implied a departure from the intricate unity of ecclesial and civil powers in
the context of the *corpus christianum*. Catholic theologians quickly issued a
rebuttal in the *Confutatio Confessionis Augustanae*, led by the German theologian Johann Eck. Melanchthon issued an apologetic response, the *Apology
of the Augsburg Confession*, which, together with the *Augsburg Confession*,
would later be included in the Lutheran canon.[52]

Philip Schaff, ed., *The Creeds of Christendom, Vol. III: The Evangelical
Protestant Creeds* (New York: Harper and Brothers, 1887), 3–73 (3, 16–17,
58–72).

———

Presented to the Invincible Emperor Charles V., Cæsar Augustus, at the Diet of Augsburg, Anno Domini MDXXX.

I will speak of thy testimonies also before kings, and will not be ashamed.
– Psalms 119:46

First Part

Chief Articles of Faith

Art. XVI. – *Of Civil Affairs.*

Concerning civil affairs, they teach that such civil ordinances as are lawful are good works of God; that Christians may lawfully bear civil office, sit in judgements, determine matters by the imperial laws, and other laws in present force, appoint just punishments, engage in just war, act as soldiers, make legal bargains and contracts, hold property, take an oath when the magistrates require it, marry a wife, or be given in marriage. They condemn the Anabaptists who forbid Christians these civil offices. They condemn also those that place the perfection of the Gospel, not in the fear of God and in faith, but in forsaking civil offices, inasmuch as the Gospel teacheth an everlasting righteousness of the heart. In the mean time, it doth not disallow order and government of commonwealths or families, but requireth especially the preservation and maintenance thereof, as of God's own ordinances, and that in such ordinances we should exercise love. Christians, therefore, must necessarily obey their magistrates and laws, save only when they command any sin; for then they must rather obey God than men (Acts 5:29).

Second Part

Articles in Which are Recounted the Abuses Which Have Been Corrected

Art. VII. – Of Ecclesiastical Power.

There have been great controversies touching the power of Bishops; in which many have incommodiously mingled together the Ecclesiastical power and the power of the sword.

And out of this confusion there have sprung very great wars and tumults, while that the Pontiffs, trusting in the power of the keys, have not only appointed new kinds of service, and burdened men's consciences by reserving of cases, and by violent excommunications; but have also endeavoured to transfer worldly kingdoms from one to another, and to despoil emperors of their power and authority.

These faults did godly and learned men long since reprehend in the Church; and for that cause our teachers were compelled, for the comfort of men's consciences, to show the difference between the ecclesiastical power and the power of the sword. And they have taught that both of them, because of God's commandment, are dutifully to be reverenced and honoured, as the chiefest blessings of God upon earth.

Now their judgement is this: that the power of the keys, or the power of the Bishops, by the rule of the Gospel, is a power or commandment from God, of preaching the Gospel, of remitting or retaining sins, and of administering the Sacraments....

This power is put in execution only by teaching or preaching the Word and administering the Sacraments, either to many or to single individuals, in accordance with their call....

Seeing, then, that the ecclesiastical power concerneth things eternal, and is exercised only by the ministry of the Word, it hindereth not the political government any more than the art of singing hinders political government. For the political administration is occupied about other matters than is the Gospel. The magistracy defends not the minds, but the bodies, and bodily things, against manifest injuries; and coerces men by the sword and corporal punishments, that it may uphold civil justice and peace.

Wherefore the ecclesiastical and civil powers are not to be confounded. The ecclesiastical power hath its own commandment to preach the Gospel and administer the Sacraments. Let it not by force enter into the office of another; let it not transfer worldly kingdoms; let it not abrogate the magistrates' laws; let it not withdraw from them lawful obedience; let it not hinder judgements touching any civil ordinances or contracts; let it not prescribe laws to the magistrate touching the form of the republic; as Christ saith, 'My kingdom is not of this world' (John 18:36). Again, 'Who made me a judge or a divider over you?' (Luke 12:14). And Paul saith, 'Our conversation [citizenship] is in heaven' (Phil. 3:20). 'The weapons of our warfare are not carnal, but mighty through God, casting down imaginations', etc. (2 Cor. 10:4). In this way do our teachers distinguish between the duties of each power one from the other, and do warn all men to honour both powers, and to acknowledge it both to be the [highest] gift and blessing of God.

If so be that the Bishops have any power of the sword, they have it not as Bishops by the commandment of the Gospel, but by man's law given unto them of kings and emperors, for the civil government of their goods. This, however, is a kind of function diverse from the ministry of the gospel.

[*There follows a lengthy critique of the rights claimed by Bishops to decide traditions and bind consciences.*]

35 German Theologians on the Legal Grounds for Resistance (1530)

Keywords: #Resistance, #Rebellion, #Law
Region: #Germany
Group: #Lutheran

The Elector of Saxony, Johann the Constant, had supported the **Protestation at Speyer**. Finding himself at odds with the emperor, he sought advice from legal scholars regarding his obligation to the emperor. **Martin Luther** had been hesitant about a right to resist, but his position was informed more by theology than law, and the experts in constitutional law made a different argument. The Saxon jurists argued that the relationship between the princes and the emperor was one of the mutual obligations. The question then concerned the consequence for violating obligations: was one freed from submission? Luther, who had studied law for only a couple of weeks, deferred to legal advice on this point.

The following document evidences the acceptance of the legal advice by the Wittenberg theologians. The changed direction was cleverly stated as a matter of law instead of theology and as a matter of positive law instead of principle, affirming that they had always taught that laws were to be obeyed. These theologians were still not convinced of the right of commoners to resist civil authority, although **Johannes Bugenhagen** developed some thoughts on resistance theory. A year later, the Elector would participate in the **Schmalkaldic League,** a political alliance of Protestant princes formed to defend civil and religious rights. No doubt, this alliance would have been more difficult had Luther persisted in his opinion that resistance was altogether forbidden.

It is often argued that German Reformers advocated submission to authority while Swiss Reformers sowed the seeds of armed resistance. However, many of the early German writings were composed at a time when reconciliation with the Roman Catholic Church was believed to be possible. Matters looked different after the revocation of concessions to the Protestants at the 1529 Diet of Speyer (prompting the **Protestation at Speyer**). Further, Johannes Bugenhagen showed how Wittenberg could also be a centre for the development of resistance theory. The following year, the **Augsburg Confession** was brought before the Diet of Augsburg and rejected. Cynthia Grant Bowman describes Luther's Reluctant Conversion in late 1530 to resistance against superior magistrates. In this process, a constitutional – not biblical – argument proved decisive. In certain circumstances, resistance thus became a way of expressing faithfulness to a higher law, the German constitution.[53]

Franklin Sherman, ed., *Luther's Works* (Philadelphia, PA: Fortress 1971) 47:8.

———

October 1530

We [Martin Luther, Justus Jonas, Philip Melanchthon, Georg Spalatin, and other theologians] are in receipt of a memorandum from which we learned that the doctors of law have come to an agreement on the question: In what situations may one resist the government? Since this possibility has now been established by these doctors and experts in the law, and since we certainly are in the kind of situation which, as they show, resistance to the government is permissible, and since, further, we have always taught that one should acknowledge civil laws, submit to them, and respect their authority, inasmuch as the gospel does not militate against civil laws, we cannot invalidate from Scripture the right of men to defend themselves even against the emperor in person, or anyone acting in his name. And now that the situation everywhere has become so dangerous that events may daily make it necessary for men to take immediate measures to protect themselves, not only on the basis of civil law but on the grounds of duty and distress of conscience, it is fitting for them to arm themselves and to be prepared to defend themselves against the use of force; and such may easily occur, to judge by the present pattern and course of events. For in previously teaching that resistance to governmental authorities is altogether forbidden, we were unaware that this right has been granted by the government's own laws, which we have diligently taught are to be obeyed at all times.

36 *Founding of the Schmalkaldic League* (1531)

Keywords: #War, #Coercion, #Church-State Relations
Region: #Germany
Group: #Lutheran

The Schmalkaldic League, an armed federation of Protestant princes, was established in 1531 at the initiative of Landgrave Philip of Hesse. The revocation of toleration in the **Diet of Speyer** (1529) prompted a collaborative plea for toleration by a number of Protestant princes in the **Protestation at Speyer**. In 1531, it became clear that Protestant princes in the Holy Roman Empire needed a defensive military pact. In practice, the league was limited to Lutheran princedoms as Swiss Protestants could not agree to the Lutheran-oriented terms. The league enjoyed mixed success in political and military affairs, most notably in the Peace of Nuremberg of 1532. In political-theological terms, the princes justified the league with the duty to protect Protestants from coercion and to sustain true religion – this was emphasised in the following letter to the emperor. At once, they were careful to stress the formation of this league would contribute to peace and prosperity in the Empire, rather than consolidating division.

The league, however, was plagued by internal divisions, most notably about Philip of Hesse's desire to take a second wife. He sought permission from the Reformers who considered his case in light of precedent in the Hebrew Bible. Philip used the carrot of financial assistance and the stick of turning to the pope. **Martin Luther, Philip Melanchthon, Martin Bucer** and others replied in 1539. After a lengthy argument against bigamy – on both scriptural and practical grounds – the Reformers concluded by permitting a second wife, provided the marriage remained a secret.[54] Philip's bigamy increased tensions within the league and with Catholics and contributed to the Schmalkaldic War (1546–1547). By the outbreak of war, the alliance was already showing signs of fragmentation. The league offered protection to Protestants, allowing the nascent evangelical movement to grow and spread.[55] The stout resistance to Catholicism also contributed to the later **Peace of**

Sources   171

Augsburg (1555) and the principle that regional princes could determine the religion in their region (*cuius regio, eius religio*).

"The First Agreement on the Founding of the Schmalkaldic League, February 27, 1531", *German History Documents and Images*, https://germanhistorydocs.ghi-dc.org/sub_document.cfm?document_id=4389 (retrieved 21 May 2021). Reproduced by permission.

———

We, by the grace of God … declare and inform everyone

Recent events have gone back and forth, rapidly and menacingly, in such ways that they seem to develop, signal, and portend that some intend to coerce those who, through God's grace and grant, have allowed the open, clear, pure, and unspotted Word of God to be preached and spread in their principalities, cities, lands, and regions, by means of which all sorts of abuses are reformed or abolished. The former intend to block with armed force the latter's Christian enterprise, even though every Christian ruler is obliged by his office not just to have the holy Word of God preached to his subjects, but also to employ every effort, firmness, and resource to assure that they are not coerced away from God's Word or even against it. For us, the highest duty and obligation of the ruler's office requires that if it should happen, now or in the future, that anyone should attempt to force us or our subjects to surrender the Word of God and the clear truth – which God may prevent, and which we expect from no one – and to return to the abolished and corrected abuses, we intend with all possible effort to see that such coercion is blocked and our ruin, body and soul, ruler and ruled, may be avoided. Therefore, we have formed a Christian brotherly agreement with and among one another. We make it for the praise of God Almighty, for the spread and growth of godly, free doctrine, and for the revival and promotion of a united, Christian body, and for the peace of the Holy Roman Empire of the German Nation and all that is honourable, also for the prosperity, welfare, benefit, and honour of all of our principalities, cities, and lands. We do this solely for the purpose of defence and self-preservation, which is accorded to everyone both by customary and written law....

This, our Christian League, is not intended to be against His Imperial Majesty, our most gracious lord, or anyone else, but only to sustain Christian truth and peace in the Holy Empire and the German Nation. It is meant, therefore, solely as a defence and protection for us, our subjects, and our relations against unjust coercion. Otherwise, each of us is willing to seek and accept the law's judgement....

37 Ambrosius Blaurer, *Memmingen Resolution Against Persecuting Anabaptists* (1531)

Keywords: #Coercion, #Persecution, #Toleration
Region: #Germany
Group: #Lutheran, #Zwinglian | #Anabaptist

Ambrosius Blaurer (1492–1564) studied at the University of Tübingen and entered the Benedictine monastic order before converting to the evangelical faith. He worked in Constance and several other South German cities and often found himself in the middle of conflict over doctrinal differences between the Lutheran and Swiss Reformers. Blaurer had befriended **Philipp Melanchthon**, while in Tübingen, and later in his ministry, he would correspond to German and Swiss Reformers. He often downplayed rigid forms of dogmatism, caring more for how doctrinal education changed one's behaviour. For this reason, he came into conflict with those who chose doctrinal rigidity over compromise.[56]

When the **Schmalkaldic League** was formed, Blaurer found himself in the middle of arguments among the Swiss over the Lutheran terms of the league. Membership was open to the other political communities who were sympathetic to the Protestant Reformation. The towns of Biberach, Constance, Isny, Lindau, Memmingen, and Ulm, all in South Germany, wanted to join. But some had reservations about the lack of protection for Anabaptists. Blaurer then composed the Memmingen Resolutions (March 1531). The extract below expresses dismay with the sanctions against Anabaptists propounded by those **Protesting at Speyer** in 1529. Blaurer's dismay was notable, as he was not an Anabaptist and was arguing for the protection of a community he did not himself belong to. He advanced arguments against coercion, referring to the anti-coercion language of the league. Moreover, he called Anabaptists 'harmless persons'. The latter argument would be compromised by the bloodshed following the rise and fall of the **Kingdom of Münster**, which contributed to radicalisation among Anabaptists and their persecutors.

George H. Williams, *The Radical Reformation* (Philadelphia, PA: Westminster, 1962), 190–191.

———

Sources 173

On account of the Anabaptists we wish very sincerely that they be treated as tolerantly as possible, so that our gospel be not blamed or impugned on their account. For we have hitherto seen very clearly that the much too severe and tyrannical treatment exercised toward them in some places contributes much more towards spreading them than toward checking their error, because many of them, some out of stubbornness of spirit and some out of pious, simple steadfastness, endured all dangers, even death itself, and suffered with patience that not only were their adherents strengthened, but also many of ours were moved to regard their cause as good and just.

Thus it is contrary to the right of Christian government to force faith upon the world with the sword and other violent compulsion and to uproot evil therein, which should be resisted alone through the mighty Word of God, and the person erring in faith shall not be suddenly knocked down, but should be tolerated in all Christian love as a harmless person.

38 Huldreich Zwingli, *A Short Exposition of the Christian Faith* (1531)

Keywords: #Government, #Church-State Relations, #Rebellion
Region: #Switzerland
Group: #Reformed, #Zwinglian

Huldreich Zwingli (1484–1531) studied at Vienna and Basel before he was appointed a priest in Zürich, where he would become one of the leading figures of the Swiss Reformation. After two disputations with the Catholic bishop in 1523, the city ceased observing the liturgical calendar and moved decisively in the direction of the Reformation. Zwingli contested the doctrine of transubstantiation and instead argued the Eucharist was but a memorial of the death of Christ, challenging the very heart of the Catholic liturgy. The growth of the Reformation in Switzerland exacerbated tensions between Protestant and Catholic cantons, leading to two rival alliances and the **Kappel Wars,** during which Zwingli would die. A Zürich statue fittingly depicts him with a Bible in one hand and a sword in the other.

Like many Reformers, Zwingli valued the primacy of scripture as the foundation of 'all human systems', as he wrote in *Of the Clarity and Certainty of the Word of God* (1522). This interest in foundations sprung from his training in the tradition of Renaissance humanism, which oriented itself on ancient classical and biblical sources. Zwingli was highly skilled in classical and biblical languages and referred to these in his theological writings. His skill is demonstrated in the following excerpt from *A Short and Clear Exposition of the Christian Faith* (1531). In it, Zwingli appealed to antiquity to argue for the importance of a properly organised civil government. The civil government, he argued, would facilitate the conditions in which religion would flourish. His sympathy for civil government was countered by the spiritualist-minded Anabaptists, and he often clashed sharply with them.[57]

Huldreich Zwingli, *A Short and Clear Exposition of the Christian Faith Preached by Huldreich Zwingli, Written By Zwingli Himself Before His Death to A Christian King (July 1531)*, in *The Latin Works of Huldreich Zwingli*, trans. Samuel Macauley Jackson, ed. William John Hinke, vol. 2 (Philadelphia, PA: Heidelberg, 1922), 235–293 (261–263).

Sources 175

7. Governments

The Greeks recognise these three kinds of governments with their three degenerate forms: Monarchy, which the Latins call '*regnum*, kingdom', where one man stands alone as the head of the state under the guidance of piety and justice. The opposite and degenerate form is a tyranny, which the Latins less fittingly call '*vis*' or '*violentia*', 'force' or 'violence', or rather, not having quite the proper word themselves, they generally use 'tyrannis', borrowing the word from the Greeks. This exists when piety is scorned, justice is trodden under foot, and all things are done by force, while the ruler holds that anything he pleases is lawful for him.

Secondly, they recognise an aristocracy, which the Latins call '*optimatium potentia*, the power of the best people', where the best men are at the head of things, observing justice and piety towards the people. When this form degenerates it passes into an oligarchy, which the Latins call literally '*paucorum potentia*, the power of the few'. Here a few of the nobles rise up and gain influence who, caring not for the general good but for private advantage, trample upon the public weal [i.e., the good of society] and serve their own ends.

Finally they recognise a democracy, which the Latins render by 'res publica, republic', a word of broader meaning than democracy, where affairs, that is, the supreme power, are in the hands of the people in general, the entire people; and all the civil offices, honours, and public functions are in the hands of the whole people. When this form degenerates, the Greeks call it σύστρεμμα ἡ σύστασις, that is, a state of sedition, conspiracy, and disturbance, where no man suffers himself to be held in check, and instead each one, asserting that he is a part and a member of the people, claims the power of the state as his own, and each one follows his own reckless desires. Hence there arise unrestrained conspiracies and factions, followed by bloodshed, plundering, injustice and all the other evils of treason and sedition.

These distinct forms of government of the Greeks I recognise with the following corrections: If a king or prince rules, I teach that he is to be honoured and obeyed, according to Christ's command, 'Render unto Caesar the things that are Caesar's and unto God the things that are God's' [Luke 20:25]. For by 'Caesar' I understand every ruler upon whom power has been conferred or bestowed, either by hereditary right and custom or by election. But if the king or prince becomes a tyrant, I correct his recklessness and inveigh against it in season and out of season. For thus saith the Lord to Jeremiah, 'See, I have ... set thee over the nations and over the kingdoms', etc. [Jer. 1:10]. If he listens to the warning, I have gained a father for the whole kingdom and fatherland, but if he becomes more rebelliously violent, I teach that even a wicked ruler is to be obeyed until the Lord shall remove him from his office and power or a means be found to enable those whose duty it is to deprive him of his functions and restore order.

In the same way we are watchful and on the alert, if an aristocracy begins to degenerate into an oligarchy or a democracy into a σύστρεμμα, mob. We have examples in Scripture, from which we learn what we teach and

176 Sources

demand, – Samuel endured Saul until the Lord deprived him of his kingdom along with his life [1 Sam. 15]. David returned to his senses at the rebuke of Nathan [2 Sam. 12], and remained on the throne under much trial and temptation. Ahab lost his life because he would not turn from wickedness when Elijah reproved him [1 Kgs 18:1–18]. John dauntlessly unbraided Herod when he felt no shame at his incestuous conduct [Luke 3:19]. But it would be a long task to bring forward all the examples in Scripture. The learned and pious know from what source we draw what we say.

To sum up, in the Church of Christ government is just as necessary as preaching, although this latter occupies the first place. For as a man cannot exist except as composed of both body and soul, however much the body is the humbler and lower part, so the Church cannot exist without the civil government, though the government attends to and looks after the more material things that have not to do with the spirit. Since, then two particularly bright lights of our faith, Jeremiah and Paul, bid us pray to the Lord for our rulers that they may permit us to lead a life worthy of God [Jer. 29:7; 1 Tim. 2:1–2], how much more ought all in whatever kingdom or people to bear and to do all things to guard the Christian peace! Hence we teach that tribute, taxes, dues, tithes, debts, loans, and all promises to pay of every kind should be paid and the laws of the state in general be obeyed in these things.

39 Michael Servetus, *Human Frailty and Religious Liberty* (c.1531)

Keywords: #Toleration, #Conscience, #Religious Liberty
Region: #Spain, #Switzerland
Group: #Antitrinitarian, #Radical Reformation

Michael Servetus (c.1509–1553) has become famous for his execution in Geneva, and **John Calvin**'s hand in it. He was born in Villanueva de Sijena (Spain) and studied and travelled across the continent, staying in Toulouse, Strasbourg, Basel, and Paris. He was a student of the medical sciences and is credited with first articulating pulmonary circulation in a theological piece of work. However, medicine had long been associated with unbelief and scepticism, perhaps to Servetus' disadvantage.[58] He also made contributions to higher biblical criticism and the study of geography. He was also an open and combative antitrinitarian whose work was accused of promoting gnostic and dualistic ideas. Servetus carried on a long correspondence with **John Calvin**, who seemed frustrated with Servetus' unwillingness to change his mind. Critics sometimes accused Calvin of antitrinitarian sympathies. After Servetus' arrest and escape from Vienne, he fled to Geneva, where he was again arrested and sentenced to death on account of heresy. Calvin received widespread praise for clamping down on heresy, but Servetus' execution also sparked a powerful call for toleration from **Sébastien Castellion**.

The following source comes from a letter that Servetus wrote to Johannes Oecolampadius when he was young (c.1531). After this publication of *On the Errors of the Trinity* (1531), he requested refuge in Basel, where he had been before for about a year. His argument for toleration was that humans were frail and fallible: even the apostles were sometimes in error. It would be disproportionate to punish error with death. The text suggested that Servetus applied this logic to his request for refuge: if Oecolampadius found errors in his thought, he did not want to be condemned. However, the argument of the possibility of error may also be applied to those who hold religious power: they may also err. Perhaps an undercurrent of the text would be that to punish heresy with death was an error in itself. He eventually escaped the Inquisition and continued to write under a pseudonym, Michel de Villeneuve.

178 *Sources*

Servetus' antitrinitarianism influenced the course of the Reformation in Poland, Lithuania, Transylvania, and beyond, where there was a greater openness to toleration, perhaps because of the practical necessity to live with persons of differing religious persuasions.[59]

Roland H. Bainton, *Hunted Heretic: The Life and Death of Michael Servetus, 1511–1553* (Boston, MA: Beacon, 1960), 62.

——

If you find me in error in one point [he wrote] you should not on that account condemn me in all, for according to this there is no mortal who would not be burned a thousand times, for we know in part [1 Cor. 13:9]. The greatest of the apostles were sometimes in error. Even though you see Luther erring egregiously at some points you do not condemn him in the rest.... Such is human frailty that we condemn the spirits of others as imposters and impious and except our own, for no one recognises his own errors.... I beg you, for God's sake, spare my name and fame.... You say that I want all to be robbers and that I will not suffer any to be punished and killed. I call Almighty God to witness that this is not my opinion and I detest it, but if ever I said anything it is that I consider it a serious matter to kill men because they are in error on some question of scriptural interpretation, when we know that even the elect may be led astray [Matt. 24:24].

40 Johannes Eisermann, *The Body of Christ and the Body Politic* (1533)

Keywords: #Common Good, #Government, #Law, #Natural Law, #Ten Commandments, #Charity
Region: #Germany
Group: #Lutheran

Johannes Eisermann (c.1485–1558) became a prominent Reformer from within the legal guild. He trained under **Philip Melanchthon**, founded the law school at the Evangelical University of Marburg, and advised Landgrave Philip of Hesse, a prominent Protestant prince. According to John Witte Jr., he wrote 'one of the very first detailed statements of Evangelical legal and political theory', which 'anticipated many of the more famous political formulations of Protestant writers in the later sixteenth and seventeenth centuries'. Eisermann wove arguments from natural law with ideas about human depravity and a deep appreciation for classical philosophers. These non-Christians exemplified common grace and the engraving of natural law on the human heart. Those outside Christ could possess civil righteousness. However, a Christian commonwealth would bring society to a higher level of righteousness and prepare the people for the kingdom of heaven.

Eisermann thought that ancient philosophers would lament the degeneration of Christendom, especially since Christians had access to greater revelations. This sense of decay then undergirded his call for civil and religious reform. Eisermann conceived of the commonwealth as a place where the eternal and the temporal met. The godly prince should see to it that civil law, divine law, and natural law are all in accord. The prince was to promote the Golden Rule, to enforce the Ten Commandments, to suppress idolatry, and to foster a society that nudged people towards godliness. This rightly ordered commonwealth, led by the godly, would draw the people into a truly blessed life. Within the commonwealth, each vocation – from the highest to the lowest – was of eternal significance, making the pursuit of the common good a personal matter with heavenly rewards. Each individual worked for the good of the entire commonwealth (*common weal*), and if done rightly, they would

180   *Sources*

store up treasures in heaven. The Christian body politic and the body of Christ thus shared the same *telos*.[60]

Johannes Eisermann, *A woorke of Ioannes Ferrarius Montanus, touchynge the good orderynge of a common weale* (London: 1559) I.IV, fol. 13–15. Text modernised by the editors.

———

The argument of Book 1 Chapter 4.

That common weals began when men first entered the society of life: and how we must behave ourselves therein, that it may be another framing house of blessedness, than the Philosophers teach.

But having now drawn out plainly, or rather slightly set forth, the form of a common weal, next of all it comes to hand, how therein one brings profit to another, whereby we do measure the weal, which we term Common, a word more used than understood, yea, among such as travail in the common weal. But for this point, we must first thoroughly know what appertains to a city before we meddle with the ordering of a common weal. Moreover, two things must principally be considered in a city: First of all, that a man seeks his own advantage honestly and without any wrong to others, which belongs unto private profit, which we may lawfully tender, so far further as we do not offend any law, or common ordinance of the city, seeing, according to the Stoics, and Marcus Tullius' [Cicero's] opinion, we do not account anything profitable, although it is greatly to our advantage, unless it is honest, that is, unless it is answerable to uprightness and goodness, and to knit up shortly, unless it agrees with the law, which reigns among men.

Secondly, we must show special regard for those things whereupon the common profit depends, and we term such things public or common, when we not only prefer honesty before profit, but also consent upon the common worship, and wealth of the whole city, with all study of mind, all endeavour to virtue. Which thing is done by no one, but a good citizen, whom notwithstanding, we do surely from a good man, who as one passing the reach of the common weal, for the love that he bears to virtue, well deserves of mankind.

For he is called a civil man, who is studious to keep the laws and judgements, which so far as he may, will commit nothing, either amiss or unadvisedly, who with his providence, religion, and fidelity, will see to the weal, both in common, and to each citizen, who will obey laws, defend his country, keep civil ordinances, and the league of mankind, and finally, is skilful to live well according to the civil virtues. And he is called a good man, who loves honesty without dread, who overcomes with no calamity, will yield to fortune, desires nothing, does nothing, but with great worship, according unto the appointment of equity and goodness, although he does not chiefly bend his mind, to the end of a common weal....

For I do not call every assembly of men, people, but such as are united together, by agreement of law, and participation of profit, which without

Sources 181

justice, the leader and rule of all virtues, will never come to pass. So that Saint Augustine himself allows the wealth, which belongs to a people, linked by the law of society, as public, albeit improperly, and not altogether usually: whereas true justice is not, but in that common weal whereof Christ, the fountain and original of all justice, is the founder and governor, which no man that is well in his wits, will deny. Let therefore all the Philosophers, all Lawmakers, all nations, however many they are, conceive the frame of a city, fashion it with ordinances, fence it with laws, deck it with judgements, if they do not seek in it, that Justice and only quickset, which is Christ, they shall have only the shadow of a city, like them that set a fair white colour upon a sepulchre, which outwardly seems gorgeous, but within it is full of rotten, and vile stinking carcasses [Matt. 23:27]. Whereupon it cometh to pass, that we may not arrogate to ourselves the name of any, either civil or Christian common weal, unless it is maintained by such, as are given to godliness, who worship and call upon God. As for the civil, if it were ever to be found, the Romans might have claimed that title themselves. But Tullie [Cicero] bewails it in his time, as bending to decay already, by reason of naughty conditions, in the first of his books of a common weal....

Hear what Tullie disliked in the Roman common weal in his day: what if he should see ours, which now decays and has for a long time grown to ruin? Wherein for the scarcity of men, good manners are utterly neglected: every place is full of sedition, sensuality, injustice, covetousness, and all manner of improper living. Would he not forthwith cry out that there were nothing less in our common weals thus abused, than any point of common weals? All which things do make, that the institution of a common weal, which is fitting the Christian people, is through forgetfulness, as it were worn out: for there is nowhere, any honesty of manners, any discipline, any obedience of laws, any reverence, any love of virtue, any defence of godliness, so that we cannot see so much, as the shadow of a common weal, much less of a perfect common weal, and that which may be fitting for the people of Christ.

Nevertheless, we must endeavour to amend and recover what has become corrupt and destroyed by our vicious and ungodly living. For the everlasting God, who does not will that man should die [2 Pet. 3:9], but live, stirs up good men, who love justice and religion, who gather companies of men together, and properly instruct them, and continue to preserve the same, in the love of godliness. That so the common weal, which is no more the people's, but God's, may be preserved although not in the whole multitude, which for the most part, used to walk in the beaten way, and that which leads to the left hand, yet in them, which God has elected as his own people, who have a tender regard for his commandments. Whereupon naughty men, although not all, yet some of them shall learn from the example of better living, and declining from iniquity, shall work good, and call upon the name of God, with a sincere heart: for God wills not the death of a sinner, but rather that he be converted and live. For to this end we are taught that denying ungodliness, and secular business, as Saint Paul says, we may live in this world soberly,

182 Sources

righteously, and godly, looking for a blessed hope, and the glorious coming of the great God and our saviour Jesus Christ, who gave himself for us, to redeem us from all iniquity, and to cleanse the people, which is acceptable to him, and a follower of good works [Tit. 2:12–14].

Whereby it appears that the people who are cleansed and redeemed by Christ are to be the followers of good works, and acceptable to God: who only can glorify his creator, and look for the blessed hope of everlasting life. And therefore, we live justly in this world and keep the community among men, coupled both by God's law, and man's, which is the true form and institution of a common weal and public estate. Which, therefore, it shall be convenient to our purpose to define, thus: An assembly and company of men lawfully gathered, to live well and blessedly, that being thereunto brought up in godliness, they may look for everlasting life. For so may it come to pass, that although there are many cities, and each of them using their own rights and manners, yet the form of the common weal is but one, not that, according to which, Aristotle appointed also one, after the form of a civil estate, whose drift and intent is only to his own end, but that which comes of that builder, master and author of all good life: who says, I am the way, the truth and life. No man comes unto the father, but by me [John 14:6]. In this common weal, as a shaping house of all virtue, we must be prepared for a better life, which is the heavenly, and appointed us from the beginning of the world, that from these visible things, we may be conveyed to the invisible, whereof the Philosophers can promise us nothing for all their vain pretended sale of the blessed life, wherein they do no less beguile the world, than such as make men believe that smoke is fire.

Therefore, as there is one master, one moderator of our common weal, and one head: so we call that properly one common weal, wherein, however many parts there are, however many citizens, every one of them has their due place: and one bears another's burden, and always goes forward to help him. So says Saint Paul, for as in one body we have many parts, and every part has a different office, so we being many, are but one body in Christ, and everyone has parts and members together, having diverse gifts, according to the grace given unto us [Rom. 12:3–5]. So those, who are in this common weal, think all one, every man content with his own office, he that can comfort the poor with his riches and goods, ought to do it cheerily. He that can teach, to teach, he that can work, to work, he that can govern, to do it carefully, he that can obey, to be obedient, and reverence the officer: in fine, to become all in all, that he may well apply his talent, and restore it again to the good man of the house with gain [Matt. 25:14–30], and all to this end, that we may be received into the communion of saints, and be entertained in the household of God. This thing must the smith at his anvil consider, the maiden while spinning wool, the ploughman at his plough-tail, the woman at her babe's cradle, and everyone in his vocation must weigh this, referring all his works to the glory of God his creator and redeemer, and have in special care, that this common weal whose beginning nature has almost wrought, may be the image of that, which is in heaven, that the passage and flight from this to that, may be the more readily had. Certainly, who so liveth in a common weal, unless he aims at this mark, and directs all his doings thereunto with a mind lightened upward, he is an unprofitable citizen: for he hath not charity, and if he shows anything in outward appearance good, because he does not place it well. It is all in vain and but a civil piece of work which shall receive his own honour and vanish away like the sounding brass, or tinkling cymbal [1 Cor. 13:1], even with the sound thereof.

41 Violence, Polygamy and Theocracy in the Anabaptist Kingdom of Münster (1534)

Keywords: #Apocalypticism, #Violence, #Church-State Relations, #Covenant, #Authority, #Obedience, #Blasphemy, #Family, #Women, #Sexuality, #Capital Crime, #Communal Goods
Region: #Germany
Group: #Anabaptist

The short-lived Anabaptist commune at Münster left an indelible mark on the mental landscape of the early modern world. The following sources relate to the commune's rise and decline. The story began with **Thomas Müntzer** and his disciple Hans Hut (c.1490–1527), who blended a close identification with biblical prophets with apocalyptic calls for theological and social reform. After Hut's death, Melchior Hoffman (1495?–1543) emerged as a new prophetic leader. He was an itinerant Lutheran preacher who, under the influence of various 'prophets' like Barbara Rebstock and Lienhard and Ursula Jost, embraced a prophetic role and adopted a distinct form of Anabaptism. He believed Christ would return in 1533 and establish the New Jerusalem in Strassburg. Although Strassburg did not want Anabaptists, he had to be there for the Second Coming of Christ – even if that meant courting a prolonged and harsh prison sentence. Christ did not return, and Hoffman died. His followers went in two directions: some espoused pacifist principles and joined **Menno Simons** and his followers; others reverted to violence to usher in the New Jerusalem.

Bernard Rothman (c.1495–1535), a converted Catholic priest, encouraged the city of Münster to convert to Lutheranism in 1532. He allowed Melchiorites (a version of Anabaptism) to preach in 1533, and Jan van Leiden (1509–1536) used the opportunity to spread apocalyptic messages. Rothman converted again by the end of the year and was baptised in 1534 by Jan Matthijs (d.1534). Mass baptisms followed. Riding on rising expectations, Jan Matthijs and Jan van Leiden gained control of the city. They amended Hoffman's prophecies and expected Christ to return in 1535 to the newly identified New Jerusalem: Münster. As this entailed a major challenge to public order, Catholics and Lutherans embarked on the violent repression of the Melchiorites at Münster. Rothmann detailed the spiral of violence as those inside the

Sources   185

city – and outside opponents – became more willing to use force against theological outsiders.[61] As hostile forces surrounded Münster and those dissenting from the Melchiorites fled, appeals were sent to sympathetic co-religionists to travel to the New Jerusalem to help usher in the return of Christ.[62]

1. Hans Hillerbrand, *The Reformation: A Narrative History Related by Contemporary Observers and Participants* (Grand Rapids, MI: Baker, 1972), 253–254; 2. Hillerbrand, *The Reformation*, 257–259; 3a. Hillerbrand, *The Reformation*, 259; 3b, Used by permission of Baker Books, a division of Baker Publishing Group. Lowell H. Zuck, *Christianity and Revolution: Radical Christian Testimonies, 1520–1650* (Philadelphia, PA: Temple, 1975), 98–101; 4. Zuck, *Christianity and Revolution*, 102–104.

———

1. Appeal to join Münster's New Jerusalem (c.1534).

[*The following appeal for Anabaptists to join Münster cites seemingly random verses from the Hebrew Bible and the New Testament, which do not necessarily systematically cohere or give evidence of sophisticated political thought. They demonstrate the themes that emerge as important when a community is under significant pressure, including references to the New Jerusalem and the equation of their opponents with evil, here through the dragon metaphor. It also impresses the urgency of individual support for the political cause of Münster, stressing impending judgement and offering redemption through taking up arms.*]

Dear friends, you are to know and recognise the work God has done among us so that everyone might arise to the New Jerusalem, the city of the saints, for God wants to punish the world. Let everyone watch lest he through carelessness fall under the judgement. Jan Bokelson, the prophet of Münster, has written to all his helpers in Christ that no one can remain free under the dragon of this world, but will suffer bodily or spiritual death. Therefore let no one neglect to come unless he wishes to tempt God....

Do not look after earthly goods.... Here are available sufficient goods for the saints. Therefore do not take anything along, except money and clothes and food for travel. Whoever has a knife, lance, or rifle should take it along. Whoever does not have such should buy himself such for the Lord will redeem us through his mighty hand and through his servants, Moses and Aaron....

———

2. Laws in Münster's New Jerusalem (mid-1534).

[*In 1534 the prophet Jan Matthijs died in battle. Jan van Leiden, assuming the role of a second David, was crowned as king of the New Jerusalem (Menno Simons vigorously disputed this claim). The civil government, Münster's council, was ousted and replaced by religious leaders who styled*

186 *Sources*

themselves as the 12 Elders, symbolically representing the 12 tribes of ancient biblical Israel. The excerpt below includes some of the core rules for private and public life. Although the aim may have been to establish a relatively egalitarian community, the rules indicate authoritarian structures and relationships, as well as isolationism. The supersessionist character of the community is underscored by the almost exclusive reliance on the Hebrew Bible, and there was little reference to the gospels and the New Testament.[63]]

Thirteen Statements of the Order of [Private] Life

The Scripture that those who are disobedient and unrepentant regarding several sins shall be punished with the sword

1   Whoever curses God and his holy Name or his Word shall be killed (Lev. 24).
2   No one shall curse governmental authority (Ex. 22, Deut. 17), on pain of death.
3   Whoever does not honour or obey his parents (Ex. 20, 21) shall die.
4   Servants must obey their masters, and masters be fair to their servants (Eph. 6).
5   Both parties who commit adultery shall die (Ex. 20, Lev. 20, Matt. 5).
6   Those who commit rape, incest, and other unclean sexual sins should die (Ex. 22, Lev. 20)....
13 Concerning slander, murmuring, and insurrection among God's people (Lev. 19): There shall be no slanderer or flatterer among the people....

Whoever disobeys these commandments and does not truly repent, shall be rooted out by the people of God, with ban and sword, through divinely ordained governmental authority.

"A Code for Public Behaviour" (mid-1534)

The elders of the congregation of Christ in the holy city of Münster...desire the following duties and articles be faithfully and firmly observed by every Israelite and member of the house of God.

1   What the Holy Scripture commands or prohibits is to be kept by every Israelite at the pain of punishment....
7   What the elders in common deliberation in this new Israel have found to be good is to be proclaimed and announced by the prophet John of Leiden as faithful servant of the Most High and the holy government to the congregation of Christ and the entire congregation of Israel.
8   Lest among the sincere and unblemished Israelites open transgression against the Word of God be tolerated, and in order that the evildoer and transgressor, if apprehended at an obvious transgression, meet his just punishment, the swordbearer...will punish him according to his deed....

Sources 187

29 When a stranger who does not adhere to our religion, be it brother, countryman, or relative, comes to this our holy city, he is to be referred to the swordbearer.... so that he can talk with him....

30 A baptised Christian is not to converse with any arriving person or pagan stranger and is not to eat with him, lest there arise the suspicion of treacherous consultation.

___

3. Polygamy Ordered in Münster (c.1534)

[*Marriage laws were vigorously debated during the Reformation. Many Reformers opposed restrictions on clerical marriage and decided to marry. Divorce remained a frequent topic, too, as when Philip Melancthon told Martin Bucer in 1531 that he couldn't approve of magistrates divorcing in cases 'where a marriage is not repugnant to the law of God'.[64] Philip, Landgrave of Hesse, wanted to take on a second wife, and the divorce of King Henry VIII from his wife also involved a divorce of the Church of England from papal authority.[65] The Münster commune is perhaps best known for the institution – they would have said 'restoration' – of polygamy. The following two excerpts discuss polygamy. Many men had fled when the Melchiorites took control of the city, leaving behind a high number of women. The first account is hostile to the community at Münster. The second excerpt, by Bernard Rothmann, is sympathetic to polygamy and relies on the precedent of the Hebrew Bible. These excerpts provide a window into gender relations in the besieged city.*]

[a. *Hostile account.*]

Thus Jan van Leiden – together with the bishop, the preachers and the 12 elders – proclaimed concerning the married estate that it was God's will that they should inhabit the earth. Everyone should take three or four wives, or as many as were desired. However, they should live with their wives in a divine manner. This pleased some men and not others....

Jan van Leiden was the first to take a second wife in addition to the one he had married in Münster. It was said that there was still another wife in Holland. Jan van Leiden continued to take more wives until he finally had 15. In similar fashion all the Dutchmen, Frisians and true Anabaptists had additional wives. Indeed, they compelled their first wives to go and obtain second wives for them. The devil laughed hard about this. Those who had old wives and wanted to take young ones had their way.... The Anabaptists in Münster, especially the leaders, such as Jan van Leiden and the 12 elders, were planning it well. They had done away with money, gold and silver, and had driven everyone from his property. They sat in the houses, held the property, and also wanted to have 10 or 12 wives. I presume they called this the 'right baptism'.

___

188   *Sources*

[b. *Sympathetic Account.*]

God has restored the true practice of holy matrimony amongst us. Marriage is the union of man and wife – 'one' has now been removed – for the honour of God and to fulfil his will, so that children might be brought up in the fear of God.

Freedom in marriage for the man consists in the possibility for him to have more than one wife.... This was true of the biblical fathers until the time of the apostles, nor has polygamy been forbidden by God....

But the husband should assume his lordship over the wife with manly feeling, and keep his marriage pure. Too often the wives are the lords, leading the husbands like bears, and all the world is in adultery, impurity, and whoredom. Nowadays, too many women seem to wear the trousers. The husband is the head of the wife, and as the husband is obedient to Christ, so also should the wife be obedient to her husband, without murmuring and contradiction [Eph. 5:22–23].

---

4. Bernard Rothmann, Concerning Revenge (December 1534)

[*It is hard to see how the Münster commune could have ended in anything but bloodshed. Catholics and Lutherans were in armed opposition to Münster's theological and legal innovations, and the presence of eschatologically-expectant prophets declaring a violent victory hardened resolve. Jan van Leiden was captured, tortured and executed. The bodies of the leaders were hung in cages from the tops of St. Lambert's Church, and the cages are still visible today. The following excerpt from Bernard Rothmann, written in December 1534, dates from right before the violent dénouement. He argued that Münster's new Israelites needed to imitate their warrior God.*]

Now God has risen in his wrath against his enemies [Ps. 68:1]. Whoever wishes to be God's servant, must arm himself in the same way and manner. That time is now here. The day of wrath has begun meaningfully in our midst, and will spread over the entire world....

Thus we, who are covenanted with the Lord, must be His instruments to root out the godless on the day which the Lord has prepared....

Our duke and prince [Jan van Leiden] has appeared and has already been established upon the throne of David.... God has awakened the promised David, armed together with his people, for revenge and punishment on Babylon [Rev. 17–18]. You have now heard what will happen, what rich reward awaits us, and how gloriously we shall be crowned, if only we fight bravely. Whether we live or die, we know that we cannot be lost (2 Tim. 2:5; 2 Cor. 6:9).

42 Menno Simons, *The Blasphemy of Münster's King David* (1535)

Keywords: #Non-Violence
Region: #Netherlands
Group: #Anabaptist, #Mennonite

Although Menno Simons became a Catholic priest in 1524, he soon felt drawn towards the radical Reformation, especially Anabaptism. After the fall of the **Kingdom of Münster**, the differences between militaristic and pacifist branches of Anabaptism became more pronounced. Simons became one of the exponents of the alternative pacifist tradition. He defended his position against violent Anabaptists and against Catholic, Lutheran, and Reformed opponents. He spent much of the rest of his life moving from region to region, often due to persecution. Contemporary Mennonites observe his pacifist teachings on violence and some of his distinctive theological and social teachings.[66]

The following excerpt stems from the time of his renunciation of Catholicism in 1535. He then identified with the peaceful wing of the Melchiorites. In this work, he thoroughly rejected the sacralisation of bloodshed. He relentlessly fixed his attention on the person and work of Christ, similar to **Roger Williams** in his argument for toleration. Simons' writing was eschatologically dense, but he argued that judgement was solely in the hands of God. He vigorously argued against the identification of modern-day rulers with the magistrates in the Hebrew Bible, especially the identification of Münster with Jerusalem and **John of Leiden** with King David. If there were a Christian prince, it would be Christ himself.

"Testimony Against John Van Leyden", in *The Complete Works of Menno Simon*, trans. John F. Funk (Elkhart, IN: John F. Funk and Brother, 1871), 427–440 (430–444).

———

As Christ is become our joy [John 15:11], so every one may judge for himself what an abomination it is in the sight of God, that a man would be that which our Saviour, Christ is. Is it not an abomination standing in the holy

190   *Sources*

place [Mark 24:15]? And what is worse yet, this John Van Leyden is not satisfied with passing himself for the joyous king of all, who is become the joy of the miserable; but he also claims to be the promised David of whom all the prophets testify; and does not admit that Christ is he who was promised.

Of such a mind are all false prophets and anti-Christs. That they have on their heads the names of blasphemy, and crowns like unto gold, by which is meant pride [Rev. 13:1], as may be seen by the Babylonian whore who was arrayed in scarlet colour, having a golden cup in her hand, full of abominations and filthiness of her fornications; for she saith in her heart, I sit a queen, and shall see no sorrow (Rev. 17:4; 18:7)....

It is incontrovertible that this king David can be none other than Christ Jesus, whom all must seek who want to be saved, as it is written, 'Seek the Lord and ye shall live' (Amos 5:4)....

Therefore this servant David is Christ; and he is the Prince of the Christians. And who else should be a prince of the church of Christ, but Christ, as Paul testifies that he alone is the Prince; and as the prophet says,

Thou Bethlehem Ephratah, though thou be not the least among the thousands of Judah, yet out of thee shall he come forth unto me that is to be ruler in Israel; whose goings forth have been from of old, from everlasting.

(Micah 5:2)

The Lord further speaks through the same prophet, 'So shall they be my people and I will be their God, and David my servant shall be King over them; and they all shall have one Shepherd' (Ezek. 37:24). We have heretofore clearly proven by the Scriptures that God the Father has placed no other king over Zion, than his Son Jesus Christ, and that he gave him an eternal kingdom....

By the grace of God we will also write a little about warfare, that Christians are not allowed to fight with the sword, that we may unanimously leave the armour of David to the carnal Israelites; and the sword of Zerubbabel to those who build the temple of Zerubbabel in Jerusalem, which was a figure of them and a shadow of things coming. For the body itself is in Christ as Paul says (Col. 2:9)

Now we should not understand that the figure of the Old Testament is so applied to the truth of the New Testament, that flesh is understood as referring to flesh; but the figure must answer the truth; the image, the being, and the letter, the Spirit.

If we take this view of it we shall easily understand with what kind of arms Christians should fight, namely, with the word of God, which is a two edged sword (Heb. 4:12; Eph. 6:17).

43 John Calvin, *Dedication to Francis I* (1536)

Keywords: #Government, #Authority, #Exile, #Magistrate
Region: #Switzerland, #France
Group: #Reformed, #Calvinist | #Roman Catholic

John Calvin (1509–1564) was born in Noyon (France) and studied in Paris, Orleans, and Bourges. Following the anti-mass 'Affair of the Placards', Calvin was forced to seek refuge outside France.[67] The King of France, Francis I, had earlier been more lenient towards Protestants and Calvin would strive to convince him to be tolerant again. Calvin first settled in Basel, where he published the first edition of his landmark work *Institutes of the Christian Religion*. The *Institutes* evolved over 20 years, and through its many expansions and revisions, 'Calvin was becoming Calvin', as Bruce Gordon notes.[68] Although the *Institutes* evolved, the dedication to Francis I appeared in all editions. The dedication gives a glimpse into Calvin's ambition to convince the French king to recognise the Reformed community as part of the historical apostolic church and to argue that Reformed communities were not like the **Münster** commune, would not threaten public order, and could be tolerated.[69] His explicit rejection of Anabaptism was vital to the development of his argument because by distancing himself from Anabaptist theology, he could also argue that he was distanced from their violence. Calvin's theological and political arguments show his legal training in that his arguments centre around the issue of legitimacy: the legitimacy of the substantive theology and the legitimacy of Protestants as trustworthy subjects. But despite his best efforts, he would live the rest of his life in exile. Only in 1598, with the Edict of Nantes, would Protestants receive a measure of toleration, but still, its wording did not recognise Protestants as a legitimate religion.

John Calvin, *The Institutes of the Christian Religion*, trans. Henry Beveridge (Edinburgh: Calvin Translation Society, 1846), 3–5.

———

192 *Sources*

Prefatory Address to His Most Christian Majesty,

The Most Mighty and Illustrious Monarch,

Francis, King of the French, His Sovereign

John Calvin Prays Peace and Salvation in Christ

Sire, – When I first engaged in this work, nothing was farther from my thoughts than to write what should afterwards be presented to your Majesty. My intention was only to furnish a kind of rudiments, by which those who feel some interest in religion might be trained to true godliness. And I toiled at the task chiefly for the sake of my countrymen the French, multitudes of whom I perceived to be hungering and thirsting after Christ, while very few seemed to have been duly imbued with even a slender knowledge of him. That this was the object which I had in view is apparent from the work itself, which is written in a simple and elementary form adapted for instruction. [*The Institutes, especially this short 1536 edition, were modelled as a catechism.*]

But when I perceived that the fury of certain bad men had risen to such a height in your realm, that there was no place in it for sound doctrine, I thought it might be of service if I were in the same work both to give instruction to my countrymen, and also lay before your Majesty a Confession, from which you may learn what the doctrine is that so inflames the rage of those madmen who are this day, with fire and sword, troubling your kingdom. For I fear not to declare, that what I have here given may be regarded as a summary of the very doctrine which, they vociferate, ought to be punished with confiscation, exile, imprisonment, and flames, as well as exterminated by land and sea.

I am aware, indeed, how, in order to render our cause as hateful to your Majesty as possible, they have filled your ears and mind with atrocious insinuations; but you will be pleased, of your clemency, to reflect, that neither in word nor deed could there be any innocence, were it sufficient merely to accuse. When any one, with the view of exciting prejudice, observes that this doctrine, of which I am endeavouring to give your Majesty an account, has been condemned by the suffrages of all the estates, and was long ago stabbed again and again by partial sentences of courts of law, he undoubtedly says nothing more than that it has sometimes been violently oppressed by the power and faction of adversaries, and sometimes fraudulently and insidiously overwhelmed by lies, cavils, and calumny. While a cause is unheard, it is violence to pass sanguinary sentences against it; it is fraud to charge it, contrary to its deserts, with sedition and mischief.

That no one may suppose we are unjust in thus complaining, you yourself, most illustrious Sovereign, can bear us witness with what lying calumnies it is daily traduced in your presence, as aiming at nothing else than to wrest the sceptres of kings out of their hands, to overturn all tribunals and seats of justice, to subvert all order and government, to disturb the peace and quiet of society, to abolish all laws, destroy the distinctions of rank and property, and, in short, turn all things upside down. And yet, that which you hear is but the smallest portion of what is said; for among the common people are disseminated certain horrible insinuations – insinuations which, if well founded, would justify the whole world in condemning the doctrine with its authors to a thousand fires and gibbets. Who can wonder that the popular hatred is inflamed against it, when credit is given to those most iniquitous accusations? See, why all ranks unite with one accord in condemning our persons and our doctrine!

Carried away by this feeling, those who sit in judgement merely give utterance to the prejudices which they have imbibed at home, and think they have duly performed their part if they do not order punishment to be inflicted on any one until convicted, either on his own confession, or on legal evidence. But of what crime convicted? 'Of that condemned doctrine', is the answer. But with what justice condemned? The very essence of the defence was, not to abjure the doctrine itself, but to maintain its truth. On this subject, however, not a whisper is allowed!

Justice, then, most invincible Sovereign, entitles me to demand that you will undertake a thorough investigation of this cause, which has hitherto been tossed about in any kind of way, and handled in the most irregular manner, without any order of law, and with passionate heat rather than judicial gravity.

Let it not be imagined that I am here framing my own private defence, with the view of obtaining a safe return to my native land. Though I cherish towards it the feelings which become me as a man, still, as matters now are, I can be absent from it without regret. The cause which I plead is the common cause of all the godly, and therefore the very cause of Christ – a cause which, throughout your realm, now lies, as it were, in despair, torn and trampled upon in all kinds of ways, and that more through the tyranny of certain Pharisees than any sanction from yourself. But it matters not to inquire how the thing is done; the fact that it is done cannot be denied. For so far have the wicked prevailed, that the truth of Christ, if not utterly routed and dispersed, lurks as if it were ignobly buried; while the poor Church, either wasted by cruel slaughter or driven into exile, or intimidated and terror-struck, scarcely ventures to breathe. Still her enemies press on with their wonted rage and fury over the ruins which they have made, strenuously assaulting the wall, which is already giving way. Meanwhile, no man comes forth to offer his protection against such furies. Any who would be thought most favourable to the truth, merely talk of pardoning the error and imprudence of ignorant men. For so those modest personages speak; giving the name of *error and imprudence* to that which they know to be the infallible truth of God, and of *ignorant men* to those whose intellect they see that Christ has not despised, seeing he has deigned to intrust them with the mysteries of his heavenly wisdom. Thus all are ashamed of the Gospel.

194   *Sources*

Your duty, most serene Prince, is, not to shut either your ears or mind against a cause involving such mighty interests as these: how the glory of God is to be maintained on the earth inviolate, how the truth of God is to preserve its dignity, how the kingdom of Christ is to continue amongst us compact and secure. The cause is worthy of your ear, worthy of your investigation, worthy of your throne.

The characteristic of a true sovereign is, to acknowledge that, in the administration of his kingdom, he is a minister of God. He who does not make his reign subservient to the divine glory, acts the part not of a king, but a robber, He, moreover, deceives himself who anticipates long prosperity to any kingdom which is not ruled by the sceptre of God, that is, by his divine word. For the heavenly oracle is infallible which has declared, that 'where there is no vision the people perish' (Prov. 29:18).

[*The rest of the dedication discusses doctrine, his condemnation of the Anabaptists, and why Protestants are faithful and reliable subjects.*]

44 Marie Dentière, *Defence of Women* (1539)

Keywords: #Women, #Violence, #Coercion, #Equality
Region: #Switzerland
Group: #Reformed

Marie Dentière (d.1561?) served as an Augustinian prioress in Belgium. Upon her encounter with **Martin Luther's** teaching, she became one of the earliest female voices of the Reformation and a staunch advocate for the role of women in church. She married the Reformed pastor Simon Robert, with whom she moved to Switzerland. After he died in the early 1530s, she married the Reformed pastor Antoine Froment, leading her to Geneva. There, she chronicled the early days of the Reformation, and her work provides important references to the rise of Guillaume Farel and **John Calvin**. She is the only woman whose name appears on Geneva's Reformation wall.

In 1539, Marguerite d'Angoulême, Queen of Navarre, requested information about the Reformation in Geneva, expressing her sympathy for the movement. In the following source, Dentière's *Epistle to Marguerite de Navarre* (1539), she explains why Farel and Calvin were expelled from the city. But her epistle offered much more. In the words of Irena Backus, it was 'the only "feminist" theological treatise to issue from Calvin's Reformation…[It] contains a passionate defence of Calvin and Farel as well as a plea for greater involvement of women in the church'. It was anonymously published that same year. Although Calvin did not have a good relationship with the Froment after his return to Geneva – after which Marie Dentière became less active – she may have penned the preface to his 1561 *Sermon on Female Apparel.*[70]

The first selection comes from her 'Defence of Women', in which she argues for the female duty to admonish one another in writing. She celebrated the influential women in scripture: Sarah, Rebecca, Moses' mother, Deborah, Ruth, the Queen of Sheba, Mary, Elizabeth, the Samaritan woman, and Mary Magdalene. Some of these women held authority, like she did as a prioress, others were particularly favoured or considered wise. Some even proclaimed messages about God. Her message is amplified by her ridicule of the flaws of men.

196   *Sources*

The second selection derives from the epistle, where she laid out Reformed doctrines and contrasted them with – as her subtitle indicates – 'The Turks, Jews, Infidels, False Christians, Anabaptists, and Lutherans'. Her primary concern, however, was with Catholicism. She critiqued superstitious rituals, warned against false prophets, rejected clerical celibacy, the Mass, confession, and penance, and denounced the corruption and hypocrisy of church leaders (including the pope). She also laid out her position on pressing theological matters like Christology, justification by faith, and her understanding of communion and baptism. In the Epistle, she was more explicit in what specific steps Marguerite and Francis should take. What stands out in her writing is her tendency to speak in the voice of Christ, as well as her apocalyptic tone.

Marie Dentière, *Epistle to Marguerite de Navarre and Preface to a Sermon by John Calvin*, ed. and trans. Mary B. McKinley (Chicago, IL: University of Chicago Press, 2004), 49–87. Scriptural citations have been altered or amended in the brackets.

———

To the most Christian princess Marguerite of France, Queen of Navarre...

Defence of Women

Not only will certain slanderers and adversaries of truth try to accuse us of excessive audacity and temerity, but so will certain of the faithful, saying that it is too bold for women to write to one another about matters of scripture. We may answer them by saying that all those women who have written and have been named in holy scripture should not be considered too bold....

Even though in all women there has been imperfection, men have not been exempt from it. Why is it necessary to criticise women so much, seeing that no woman ever sold or betrayed Jesus, but a man named Judas? Who are they, I pray you, who have invented and contrived so many ceremonies, heresies, and false doctrines on earth if not men? And the poor women have been seduced by them. Never was a woman found to be a false prophet, but women have been misled by them. While I do not wish to excuse the excessively great malice of some women that goes far beyond measure, neither is there any reason to make a general rule of it, without exception, as some do on a daily basis.... Therefore, if God has given grace to some good women, revealing to them by his holy scriptures something holy and good, should they hesitate to write, speak, and declare it to one another because of the defamers of truth? Ah, it would be too bold to try to stop them, and it would be too foolish for us to hide the talent that God has given us, God who will give us the grace to persevere to the end. Amen.

Epistle

[*Against the corrupt clergy and magistrates who listen to them*:]…Why don't you [defend scripture] without using so many swords, without so many wars, without so much persecuting, killing, murdering, burning innocents, good and faithful people whose blood will come upon you and cry out for vengeance against you before God [Matt. 23:33–36]. Or at the very least, since you cannot vanquish truth, which is invincible, we pray you, for the honour of God, kings, princes, and lords, to whom God has given the sword to punish the wicked and protect the good [Rom. 13:1–7], allow the truth to be preached in your lands and kingdoms, so that you and your poor people be led no longer by those miserable blind men. They are leading you to the slaughterhouse like poor, tied-up beasts. Do you have a nose made of wax, so that they can turn you about every which way? You seem to be completely emasculated, out of your senses, without fear of God….

[*She urges Marguerite to distance herself from such ministers. Later in the epistle, she asserts Christian equality in the face of those who use distinction – education, power, masculinity – to exclude some from interpreting scripture.*]

I ask, did not Jesus die as much for the poor ignorant people and the idiots as for my dear sirs the shaved, tonsured, and mitred? Did he preach and spread my Gospel so much only for my dear sirs the wise and important doctors? Isn't it for all of us? Do we have two Gospels, one for men and another for women? One for the wise and another for the fools? Are we not one in our Lord? In whose name are we baptised? By Paul or by Apollo, by the pope or by Luther? Is it not in the name of Christ? He is certainly not divided [I Cor. 1:10–17]. There is no distinction between the Jew and the Greek; before God, no person is an exception [Rom. 2:11, 10:12; Eph. 6:9]. We are all one in Jesus Christ. There is no male and female, nor servant nor free man [Gal. 3:28; I Cor. 12:13]. I am not talking about the body, for there is the father and the son, one to be honoured and the other to honour [Exod. 20:12]; the husband and the wife, she to love and the other to hold her in esteem [Eph. 6:1–9]; the master to command, the servant to serve and obey; the king, prince, and lord to rule and judge, the subject to obey, carry, tolerate, and pay tribute, taxes, charges, and rents, according to God's word. The person who resists, resists God [Rom. 13:2].

45 David Joris, *Plea for the End of Persecution in Holland* (1539)

Keywords: #Persecution, #Toleration
Region: #Netherlands
Group: #Anabaptist | #Roman Catholic, #Judaism, #Islam

By profession, David Joris (c.1501–1556) was a prosperous painter of glass, but he emerged as one of the most important Anabaptist leaders after the fall of the **Anabaptist Kingdom of Münster**. He had already been critical of violent Anabaptism and thought that spiritualising violent language could bring together the violent and non-violent wings of the movement. For example, he argued one could not map Christ's kingdom onto physical polities and that the warfare of the Christian was not against flesh and blood enemies. He also thought that physical violence required the supernatural participation of angels, which would only occur in the context of the apocalypse. At the end of 1536, he claimed he had apocalyptic visions about himself as a 'third David', who would found a new spiritual kingdom.

His followers (Davidjorists) were viewed as a threat to public peace and order and experienced persecution. In 1539, over 100 followers were killed. Joris fled to Antwerp. In relative safety, he continued the process of spiritualising his faith. He came into conflict with another Anabaptist leader, **Menno Simons,** over issues of doctrine and authority and eventually moved to Switzerland, where he lived under a pseudonym and wrote to his followers. After his death, his identity was made known, and he was posthumously burned at the stake for heresy.[71]

In the following 1539 letter to the Court of Holland at The Hague, Joris argued that his followers should be permitted to peacefully practise their faith, although the community was willing to continue suffering. He suggested that they should be treated like other tolerated religious groups and be made to wear a distinctive marker on their clothing so that they can be easily identified and examined.

David Joris, *Letter to the Court of Holland* (1539), in *Global Reformations Sourcebook: Convergence, Conversion, and Conflict in Early Modern Religious Encounters*, ed. Nicholas Terpstra (New York: Routledge, 2021), 123.

———

For the evil shall maintain the upper hand until the end..., all of which signifies for as long as it shall endure. So always work (if you have any affection for the understanding of the fear of God) and do so much for this until there is quiet and peace in the earth under you for us, and grant our poor ones of this world bread and water, that we had previously had freedom in. Yes, we would prefer to live on the fields as outcasts, so that we grow up as children in stillness and peace and might live our faith in Christ Jesus, until perhaps over time we die and perish, if it is so ordained. Thus allow or permit us little ones to be just like the dogs that wander among the people and give us a sign on our cloak, that people could know us thereby and speak to us to inspect our doctrine, so that you will have no concern over this, since holiness is so easy to have. The Jews and heathens have their free places or dwellings among the peoples. Turks, Saracens and other horrible folk are allowed in these lands, as well as our people among them, in their land, so that, contrary to here, anyone can live there, as each is allowed their own faith. It would be good were it so in these lands, but you cannot seem to understand that this is good, this I know well. Though I leave it here.

46 Peter Riedemann, *Account of our Religion, Doctrine and Faith* (1541)

Keywords: #Confession of Faith, #Non-violence, #Church-State Relations, #Government, #Authority, #War, #Economics,
Region: #Czech Republic, #Germany
Group: #Hutterite, #Anabaptist, | #Judaism

Peter Riedemann (1506–1556) was one of the first significant theologians who emerged from the Hutterite Brethren in Moravia. His main work was a lengthy *Confession of Faith*, which he wrote from 1540 to 1541 while imprisoned for his Anabaptist beliefs in Hesse. This confession reads as a systematic account of Hutterite convictions and one upon which the Hutterite tradition built its doctrinal identity (compare **Peter Walpot**). Characteristic for Riedemann's theology is his spiritual understanding of the Christian life, his distancing from politics and power, and his radical commitment to non-violence, all inspired by the life of Christ.

In the excerpts below on government, warfare, and taxation, he spoke of the kingdom of Christ as almost entirely separate from the world. In his argument, temporal government kept evil in check, whereas spiritual authorities disciplined Christians who did not need any temporal authority. He went so far as to argue that although temporal authority was necessary, it was not proper for Christians to serve in the government. Although Christians were to pay taxes, they were not to contribute to acts of violence or warfare. His work thus represents the strong dualist and pacifist language common in Anabaptist traditions, as well as a supersessionist orientation on the scriptures that ventures into theological anti-Judaism.[72]

Peter Riedemann's Hutterite Confession of Faith, trans. and ed. by John J. Friesen (Walden; NY: Plough Publishing House, 2019), 217–223, used with the kind permission of Plough Publishing House.

Whether Rulers Can Also Be Christians

Here beginneth a quite other kingdom and reign, therefore that which is old must stop and come to an end, as also the symbol of the Jewish royal house signifieth, which was there until Christ came, as the scriptures declare, 'The sceptre shall not depart from Judah until the hero, Christ, shall come'. Therefore it is ended, stopped and broken in Christ. He now sitteth upon the throne of his father, David, and hath become a king of all true Israelites. He also hath now begun a new regime that is not like the old one and is not supported by the temporal sword.

Now, since the regime of the Jews, who until then were God's people, came to an end in Christ, ceased and was taken from them, it is clear that it should be no more in Christ, but it is his desire to rule over Christians with his spiritual sword alone. That the power of the temporal sword was taken from the Jews and hath passed to the heathen signifieth that from henceforth the people of God ought no longer to use the temporal sword and rule therewith; but ought to be ruled and led by the one Spirit of Christ alone. And that it hath gone to the heathen signifieth that those who do not submit themselves to the Spirit of Christ – that is, all heathen and unbelievers – should be disciplined and punished therewith. Therefore hath governmental authority its place outside Christ, but not in Christ.

[*Riedemann continues to argue that the kingship of Christ stands in opposition to every form of temporal authority and that the way of Christ requires the laying down of earthly glory.*]

Now because in Christ our King is the full blessing of God – yea, he is himself the blessing – all that was given in wrath must come to an end and cease in him, and hath no part in him. But governmental authority was given in wrath, and so it can neither fit itself into nor belong to Christ. Thus no Christian is a ruler and no ruler is a Christian, for the child of blessing cannot be the servant of wrath. Thus, in Christ not the temporal, but the spiritual sword doth rule over men, and so ruleth that they [those who] deserve not the temporal sword, therefore also have no need of it.

If one were to say, however, 'It is necessary because of evil men', this we have already answered in saying that the power of the sword hath passed to the heathen, that they may therewith punish their evildoers. But that is no concern of ours....

Concerning Warfare

Now since Christ, the Prince of Peace, hath prepared and won for himself a kingdom, that is a Church, through his own blood; in this same kingdom all worldly warfare hath an end, as was promised aforetime,

> Out of Zion shall go forth the law, and the word of the Lord from Jerusalem, and shall judge among the heathen and shall draw many peoples, so that they shall beat their swords into ploughshares and their lances or spears into pruning hooks, sickles and scythes, for from thenceforth nation shall not lift up sword against nation, nor shall they learn war anymore.
>
> [Isa. 2:1–4; Mic. 4:1–4]

202 Sources

Therefore a Christian neither wages war nor wields the worldly sword to practice vengeance, as Paul also exhorteth us saying. 'Dear brothers, avenge not yourselves, but rather give place unto the wrath of God, for the Lord saith, Vengeance is mine; I will repay it' [Rom. 12:9]. Now if vengeance is God's and not ours, it ought to be left to him and not practised or exercised by ourselves. For since we are Christ's disciples, we must show forth the nature of him who, though he could, indeed, have done so, repaid not evil with evil. For he could, indeed, have protected himself against his enemies, the Jews, by striking down with a single word all who wanted to take him captive.

[He gives the example of Peter, who Jesus told to hold back his sword, and of Jesus, who taught his disciples to turn the other cheek.]

Concerning Taxation

Since governmental authority is ordained by God and hath its office from him, the payment of taxes for this purpose is likewise ordained and commanded, as Paul saith, 'Thus ye must also pay tribute' [Rom. 13:6]. For this reason we, likewise, willingly pay taxes, tribute or whatever men may term it, and in no way oppose it, for we have learned this from our master, Christ, who not only paid it himself, but also commanded others to do so, saying 'Render unto Caesar what is Caesar's, and to God what is God's' [Matt. 22:22]. Therefore we, as his disciples, desire with all diligence to follow and perform his command, and not to oppose the government in this.

But where taxes are demanded for the special purpose of going to war, massacring and shedding blood, we give nothing. This we do neither out of malice nor obstinacy but in the fear of God, that we make not ourselves partakers of other men's sins.

47 John Calvin, *Ecclesiastical Ordinances for Geneva* (1541)

Keywords: #Church-State Relations, #Law, #Authority, #Coercion, #Communion
Region: #Switzerland
Group: #Reformed, #Calvinist

Shortly after publishing the ***Institutes of the Christian Religion*** in 1536, Calvin left Basel and passed through Geneva on his way to Strasbourg. The Reformation in Geneva was already underway in the city when Guillaume Farel persuaded him to stay. Calvin was appointed as a lecturer and then as a pastor. However, he came into conflict with the Geneva city council, and they rejected the 1537 proposal of several pastors to change local ecclesiastical structures. Calvin's licence to preach was taken away. After he violated the order, he was banished in 1538, as **Marie Dentière** detailed in her writings. Calvin then partnered with **Martin Bucer** in Strasbourg. He ministered among a French-speaking congregation and married Idelette de Bure. He was invited back to Geneva in 1541. This time, Calvin undertook legal reform on the church's relationship with the state, working alongside city councillors and other pastors.

The source below reproduces Calvin's *Ecclesiastical Ordinance* for Geneva. This document showcases his legal training and interest in creating structures of accountability between ecclesial and civil powers. Calvin elaborated upon his plan for a 'consistory': a body composed of clergy and laity that was tasked with maintaining the church's health and overseeing the city's godliness. As Reformed churches spread, this ordinance shaped church-state relations elsewhere too. The document below shows the magistrate's additions in italics before the ordinance became law on 20 November 1541.[73] These additions evidence the magistrates' concern for a clear separation of power between the churches and the city council, and especially the consolidation of their role in contrast to the ecclesial powers.

J.K.S. Reid, *Calvin: Theological Treatises* (Philadelphia, PA: Westminster, 1954), 58–61, 63–64, 70–72.

———

204 Sources

There are four orders of office instituted by our Lord for the government of his Church.

First, pastors; then doctors; next elders; and fourth deacons.

[*The ordinance then explains the duty of pastors and how they are to be examined.*]

There follows, to whom it belongs to institute Pastors

It will be good in this connection to follow the order of the ancient Church, for it is the only practice which is shown us in Scripture. The order is that ministers first elect such as ought to hold office [having made it known to the Seigneury]; afterwards that he be presented to the Council; and if he is found worthy the Council receive and accept him [as he will see to be expedient]; giving him certification to produce finally to the people when he preaches, in order that he be received by the common consent of the company of the faithful. If he be found unworthy, and show this after due probation, it is necessary to proceed to a new election for the choosing of another....

When he is elected, he has to swear in front of the Seigneury. Of this oath there will be a prescribed form, suitable to what is required of a minister....

If there appear difference of doctrine, let the ministers come together to discuss the matter. Afterwards, if need be, let them call the elders [and the clerk at the Seigneury] to assist in composing the contention. Finally, if they are unable to come to friendly agreement because of the obstinacy of the parties, let the case be referred to the magistrate to be put in order.

To obviate all scandals of living, it will be proper that there be a form of correction [correction of ministers, as will be set forth] to which all submit themselves. It will also be the means by which the ministry may retain respect, and the Word of God be neither dishonoured nor scorned because of the ill repute of the ministers....

But first it should be noted that there are crimes which are quite intolerable in a minister, and there are faults which may on the other hand be endured while direct fraternal admonitions are offered.

Of the first sort are: heresy, schism, rebellion against ecclesiastical order, blasphemy open and meriting civil punishment, simony and all corruption in presentations, intrigue to occupy another's place, leaving one's Church without lawful leave or just calling, duplicity, perjury, lewdness, larceny, drunkenness, assault meriting punishment by law, usury, games forbidden by law and scandalous, dances and similar dissoluteness, crimes carrying with them loss of civil rights, crime giving rise to another separation from the Church.

Of the second sort are: strange methods of treating Scripture which turn to scandal, curiosity in investigating idle questions, advancing some doctrine or kind of practice not received in the Church, negligence in studying and reading the Scriptures, negligence in rebuking vice amounting to flattery, negligence in doing everything required by his office....

In the case of the crimes which cannot at all be tolerated, if some accusation and complaint arise, let the assembly of ministers and elders investigate it, in order to proceed reasonably and according to whatever is discovered in judging the case, and then report judgement to the magistrate in order that if required the delinquent be deposed....

[*The second order, doctors, teach the faithful and their appointment also involves the government. The Ordinance then establishes schools and colleges to train children for ecclesiastical and civil roles. Girls are also to be trained in their own schools*].

Concerning the third order which is that of Elders [who are to be sent or deputed by the Seigneury to the Consistory]

Their office is to have oversight of the life of everyone, to admonish amicably those whom they see to be erring or to be living a disordered life, and, where it is required, to enjoin fraternal corrections themselves and along with others....

The best way of electing them seems to be this, that the Little Council suggest the nomination of the best that can be found and the most suitable; and to do this, summon the ministers to confer with them; after this they should present those whom they would commend to the Council of Two Hundred which will approve them. If it find them worthy [after being approved], let them take the special oath, whose form will be readily drawn up [will be drawn up as for the ministers]. And at the end of the year, let them present themselves to the Seigneury for consideration whether they ought to be continued or changed. It is inexpedient that they be changed often without cause, so long as they discharge their duty faithfully.

[*The ordinance then discuss the two types of deacons: those who care for the poor and those more focused on the sick. They then stipulate concerning the proper regulation of hospitals and the care of the needy, as well as stipulations for the removal of beggars. It then discusses the administrations of the sacraments, ministering to prisoners and the Christian education of children in the catechism.*]

Of the Order which is to be observed in the case of those in authority, for the maintenance of supervision in the Church.

The elders, as already said, are to assemble once a week with the ministers, that is to say on Thursday morning, to see that there be no disorder in the Church and to discuss together remedies as they are required.

Because they have no compulsive authority or jurisdiction, may it please their Lordships [we have advised], to give them one of their [our officers] officials to summon those whom they wish to admonish.

If anyone refuse with contempt to comply, their office will be to inform their Lordships [the Council], in order that remedy be applied.

There follows the list of persons whom the elders ought to admonish, and how one is to proceed.

If there be anyone who dogmatises against the received doctrine, conference is to be held with him. If he listen to reason, he is to be dismissed without scandal or dishonour. If he be opinionative, he is to be admonished several times, until it is seen that measures of greater severity are needed. Then he is to be interdicted from the communion of the Supper and reported to the magistrate.

206 *Sources*

[*They describe steps that are to be taken for those who fail to attend church or show contempt for church authority. 'Secret vices' are to be treated in a private manner, but if the admonitions of a neighbour are not heeded, the church is to get involved. For 'notorious and public' sins, increasingly severe admonitions by church leaders are to be followed by exclusion from communion.*]

As for crimes which merit not merely remonstrances in words but correction by chastisement, should any fall into them, according to the needs of the case, he must be warned that he abstain for some time from the Supper, to humble himself before God and acknowledge his fault the better.

If any in contumacy or rebellion wish to intrude against the prohibition, the duty of the minister is to turn him back, since it is not permissible for him to be received at the Communion.

Yet all this should be done with such moderation, that there be no rigour by which anyone may be injured; for even the corrections are only medicines for bringing back sinners to our Lord. [All this is to take place in such a way that the ministers have no civil jurisdiction, nor use anything but the spiritual sword of the Word of God, as Paul commands them; nor is the Consistory to derogate from the authority of the Seigneury or ordinary justice. The civil power is to remain unimpaired. Even where there will be need to impose punishment or to constrain parties, the ministers with the Consistory having heard the parties and used such remonstrances and admonitions as are good, are to report the whole matter to the Council, which in their turn will advise sentence and judgement according to the needs of the case.]...

Form of Oath prescribed for Ministers, July 17, 1542

...I promise and swear that in the ministry to which I am called I will serve faithfully before God, setting forth purely his Word for the edification of this Church to which he has bound me; that I will in no way abuse his doctrine to serve my carnal affections nor to please any living man; but that I will employ it with pure conscience in the service of his glory and for the profit of his people to which I am debtor.

I promise also and swear to defend the Ecclesiastical Ordinances as they are approved by the Little, the Great and the General Councils of this City....

Thirdly, I swear and promise to guard and maintain the honour and welfare of the Seigneury and the City, to take pains, so far as possible for me, that the people continue in beneficial peace and unity under the government of the Seigneury, and to consent in no wise to those who would violate it.

Finally, I promise and swear to be subject to the polity and constitution of this City, to show a good example of obedience to all others, being for my part subject to the laws and the magistracy, so far as my office allows; that is to say without prejudice to the liberty which we must have to teach according what God commands us and to do the things which pertain to our office. And in conclusion, I promise to serve the Seigneury and the people in such wise, so long as I be not at all hindered from rendering to God the service which in my vocation I owe him.

48 Martin Luther, *On the Jews and Their Lies* (1543)

Keywords: #Violence, #Exile, #Blasphemy, #Economics, #Persecution
Region: #Germany
Group:#Lutheran, #Judaism

Luther's pronounced antisemitism was clearly represented in *On the Jews and Their Lies* (1543). It is a deeply troubling piece of writing, which reflects the gradual radicalisation of his understanding of Jewish communities. For example, earlier in 1523, he said,

> So long as we thus treat them [the Jews] like dogs, how can we expect to work any good among them? Again, when we forbid them to labour and do business and have any human fellowship with us, thereby forcing them into usury, how is that supposed to do them any good?[74]

But Luther increasingly lumped all of his enemies together, be they Jews, Catholics, Anabaptists, Muslims, or other persons who dared disagree with him.[75] From letters between Martin and **Katharina von Bora,** we glimpse the casual and common nature of antisemitism in the Luther household.[76] His opinion of Jewish communities worsened, and his last sermon shortly before his death again called for their harsh treatment.

The translation of *On the Jews and Their Lies* also has a dark history.[77] The translators claim it is the first English translation of this work (produced sometime before the Second World War). The openly antisemitic publisher claimed they were threatened by those not wanting Luther's true feelings about the Jews to come to light. They claimed this vast conspiracy to keep the Reformer's words secret was doomed to fail, and their translation would 'shake, shock and alert Christian America'.

The pre-WWII translation is itself problematic for what it altered or omitted. For example, it censored Luther's direct calls for violence against Jewish persons and property, creating a space for 'civilised antisemitism' or 'acceptable prejudice'. Moreover, the original translators added antisemitic remarks about the appearance of Jewish people. Whereas the pre-WWII translation

208   *Sources*

says, 'let them earn their bread in the sweat of their noses', the later scholarly edition translated this as 'sweat of their brow' (below, a more recent scholarly translation appears in brackets).

Martin Luther, *The Jews and Their Lies* (Boring, OR; CPA Book Publisher, n.d.), 39–46. For the scholarly edition, see Martin Luther, "On the Jews and their Lies", trans. Martin H. Bertram, in *Luther's Works*, ed. Franklin Sherman (Philadelphia, PA: Fortress 1971) 47:137–306 (268–271).

———

Now what are we going to do with these rejected, condemned, Jewish people?

We should not suffer it after they are among us and we know about such lying, blaspheming and cursing among them, lest we become partakers of their lies, cursing, and blaspheming. We cannot extinguish the unquenchable fire of God's wrath (as the prophets say), nor convert the Jews. We must practice great [*LW*: sharp] mercy with prayer and godliness that we might rescue a few from the flames and violent heat.

We are not permitted to take revenge. Revenge is around their neck a thousand times greater than we could wish them. I will give you my true counsel

First, that we avoid their synagogues and schools and warn people against them [*LW*: First, to set fire to their synagogues or schools and to bury and cover with dirt whatever will not burn, so that no man will ever again see a stone or cinder of them]. And such should be done to the glory of God and Christendom, that God may see that we are Christians and have not knowingly tolerated such lying, cursing and blaspheming His Son and His Christians. For what we so far have tolerated [we have done so in] ignorance.... Moses writes in Deuteronomy that where a city practiced idolatry, it should be entirely destroyed with fire and leave nothing. If he were living today he would be the first to put fire to the Jew schools and houses....

Secondly, that you also should refuse to let them own houses among us [*LW*: Second, I advise that their houses also be razed and destroyed]. For they practice the same thing in their houses as they do in their schools. Instead, you might place them under a roof, or a stable, like the Gypsies, to let them know that they are not lords in our country as they boast, but in exile as captives, like without ceasing they howl bloody murder and complain about us before God.

Thirdly, that you take away from them all of their prayer books and Talmuds wherein such lying, cursing, and blasphemy is taught.

Fourthly, that you prohibit their Rabbis to teach [*LW*: on pain of loss of life and limb]....

Fifthly, that protection for Jews on highways be revoked. For they have no right to be in the land, because they are not lords, nor officials. They should stay at home....

Sources 209

Sixthly, that their usury be prohibited, which was prohibited by Moses, where they are not lords in their own country over strange lands, and take away all the currency and silver and gold and put it away for safe-keeping. For this reason, everything they have they have stolen from us (as said above) and robbed through their usury, since they have no other income....

Finally: That young, strong Jews be given flail, axe, spade, spindle, and let them earn their bread in the sweat of their noses [*LW*: brow] as imposed upon Adam's children, Genesis 3:19....

Should we be concerned, however, that they might do bodily harm to us, to wife and children, servants, cattle, etc., when they serve us or should be compelled to work, because it is to be surmised that such noble lords of the world and poisonous, bitter worms, who are not accustomed to work, would be very remiss to humble themselves under the cursed Goyim; let us apply the ordinary wisdom of other nations like France, Spain, Bohemia, et al. who made them give an account of what they had taken from them by usury and divided it evenly; but expelled them from their country. For, as heard before, God's wrath is so great over them that through soft mercy they only become more wicked, through hard treatment [*LW*: sharp mercy], however, only a little better. Therefore, away with them!

49 Abraomas Kulvietis, *Confession Fidei* (1543)

Keywords: #Confession of Faith, #Heresy, #Persecution, #Magistrate, #Authority, #Marriage, #Common Good
Region: #Lithuania, #Russia
Group: #Lutheran

The Lithuanian humanist scholar Abraomas Kulvietis (c.1510–1545) became one of the early proponents of the Reformation in the Grand Duchy of Lithuania. He was born to rural nobility in Kulva and studied in Kraków, Louvain, Leipzig, Wittenberg, and Siena, where he earned his doctorate in canon law. At the time, Siena had become a centre for Protestant-leaning scholars. One of the city's leading families, the Sozzini's, would produce patrons of the radical Reformation in Poland and Lithuania, known as Socinianism. Kulvietis himself sympathised with the Lutheran Reformation and was probably influenced by **Bernardino Ochino**. Upon Kulvietis' return to Lithuania in 1541, he earned the favour of the Italian-born Queen Bona Sforza, who was familiar with Ochino. However, because of the King's disfavour of the Reformation, he fled to Königsberg with her help. He soon became the vice-rector of the Lutheran university at Königsberg on the recommendation of Duke Albrecht (1490–1568). He attempted to return to Lithuania in 1545, along with his friend Jurgis Zablockis, in order to reinvigorate the Reformation there, but he soon fell ill and died. He was denied the church rites, and his mother Elzbieta Kulvietienė, who suspected he was poisoned, buried him locally. Duke Albrecht ensured she received her son's personal possessions, including his personal library of about 80 books.

Kulvietis' fascinating life and work have long remained in obscurity, but the discovery of his *Confessio Fidei* and his biography *Oratio Funebris* (written by Johann Hoppe) in the library of Durham University has shed new light on his legacy. The Lithuanian scholar Dainora Pociūtė has produced a careful transcription of this work, and translated excerpts of his *Confessio Fidei* are produced below. The *Confessio Fidei*, which was addressed to Queen Bona Sforza, is the oldest surviving Protestant text from Lithuania. In the letter, he informs her of his potential appointment at the university and

Sources 211

expresses that he still wishes to work in Lithuania if possible. His dedication to the Lithuanian Reformation is further evidenced by the fact the letter was written in Latin, the language of choices for scholars in Lithuania.[78]

Dainora Pociūtė, ed., *Abraomas Kulvietis: Pirmasis Lietuvos reformacijos paminklas / The First Recorded Text of the Lithuanian Reformation.* Confessio fidei *by Abraomas Kulvietis and* Oratio funebris *by Johann Hoppe* (1547). Studija, faksimilė, komentuotas leidimas, vertimas į lietuvių kalbą / A Study, Facsimile, a New Edition with Commentaries and Translation into Lithuanian (*Monumenta Reformationis Lithuanicae,* t. 1) (Vilnius: Lietuvių literatūros ir tautosakos institutas, 2011). Translated by Odile Panetta.

———

Confession of faith of Abraham Kulvietis, written for the Most Serene Queen of Poland etc.

I send my greetings after most humbly recommending my services.

Although in a previous letter, Most Serene Queen and merciful Lady, I informed you about the state of my affairs, nonetheless my daily calamities spur me to write about the same matters again and again. Within our fathers' memory, most clement Lady, no one ever heard of someone being condemned when innocent and without a hearing. But my enemies not only condemned me, but even mark me with infamy, mock me, insult me, and offend me publicly every day in their speeches. Whence it has occurred that my friends are now hostile to me, while my enemies press me more insolently and petulantly. Indeed, my friends – those of my disciples whom I taught in Vilnius – with the exception of the Lord of Sandomir and a few others, rewarded me horribly. N. defrauded me of sixteen 60-groschen Lithuanian coins for the instruction and feeding of his son and of his nephew on his sister's side. Others imitated his example. I do not, however, regret the loss of the money, and the ingratitude returned for my labours. To this are added domestic offences, since my neighbours, taking advantage of my absence, each in competition, take as much as they can of my goods; the servants threaten flight, and therefore do not obey my mother, perform their farming tasks indolently, and agriculture is thereby neglected. And – what horribly afflicts me above all – my dearest mother, worn out in part by the recent mourning of my father, in part by the domestic offences, in part by my exile, painfully drags on her miserable life. Even a torturer could have felt pain for my sorrows; only my enemies cannot be satiated by my calamities.

But, they object, I suffer such things because of the crime of heresy. To them I reply: to raise objections against someone and not be able to provide proof is mere calumny and iniquity. I declare before God and all righteous people that I established the beliefs of my faith well, in fear of God and in discipline. No small number of my disciples, among whom is the son of Lord Paul Naruschovitz, will testify this of me before your Most Serene Majesty.

212 *Sources*

And, so that they might inspire trust in themselves and render me detested before your Majesties, they shrewdly pretend that they act out of zeal for faith. Yet in fact not zeal (*zelus*), but wickedness (*scoelus*); holy profit, the coffer (*fiscus*), not Christ (*Christus*), is the reason why they rage against me so furiously. Indeed, the Epicureans fear that their belly will be restrained; they fear, I say, that, since they are of no use in the commonwealth, they will be forced to the plough. In sum, they fear that their deceits and frauds, through which they deceived the commonwealth for so many centuries, will be openly revealed. Whence that holy zeal, for their God the belly; whence those calls, 'Crucify him, crucify him! Burn him, burn him! He blasphemed Christ, the divine virgin, the saints; he committed the crime of lèse-majesté; he denied the Catholic Church!' Such things they declaim in speeches [or: sermons], divulge in assemblies, exaggerate before your Majesties. Therefore neither am I surprised, nor do I take offence, if sometime your Majesties deal with me somewhat more harshly than I deserved.

Christ commands that we recognise the true teachers of the Church by the fruits of their labours [Matt. 7:20]. Come now, then, let us see those excellent fruits of theirs. Paul [Tit. 1:7–9; 1 Tim. 3:2–3] wants a teacher of the Church to be capable in doctrine, so that he might be able to teach the faithful and resist heretics, not greedy, not shamefully devoted to lucre, not violent, indeed so irreprehensible that public opinion might fear to lie about him. Now we see them more ignorant than uneducated monks, who are unsuited to being placed at the head of even a school for children, so far are they from being worthy of the title of teacher of the Church. What shall I say of their insatiable greed, of their arrogance, of their ambition, and the other innumerable disgraces in which they are steeped? And yet Christ calls them the salt of the earth, the light of the world [Matt. 5:13–14]. Assuredly, when the light itself is darkness, what shall we think of the inferiors, other than that they are external darkness? Therefore, since they are so ignorant of Scripture, so impious, and so cruel, that by their judgment not even Christ could be innocent; and since they are judges in their own cause, against the most just rule of law, which says that no one can be a judge in his own cause: I appeal to your Majesties, and pray in God's name, that your Majesties know of the conflict I have with my adversaries. If I obtain this, I hope in God that I will plainly reveal their deceptions, with which they assail the glory of God and consume the commonwealth. If your Majesties subject me to their jurisdiction, I shall appeal against them to the next general Council, as against the opposing party, which cannot be a judge in its own cause. I humbly beg that your Majesties concede this to me. Your Majesties should remember that all princes have been put in place by God so that they may punish the culpable and defend the innocent. If your Majesties were to disregard this and my adversaries were to spill my blood, I fear that God might demand from you an account of my fate. As for myself, if the glory of God requires as much, I am ready even to die.

Moreover, so that your Most Serene Majesty may learn of my faith from my own writing, rather than from my adversaries' accusation, I deemed it worthwhile to include a confession of my faith. To begin with, then, I swear by the ineffable and indivisible Holy Trinity that I am about to speak the truth. If I should say anything against my conscience, I invoke upon myself the wrath of God, the resentment of your Majesties, the loss of my goods, sudden death, and finally eternal damnation. First, I believe in all articles of faith that are contained in the Apostolic Creed. I likewise believe that the Sacraments are instituted in the Gospel, and all must practice them by divine command. I also believe that the ministry of the Gospel, the administration of the Sacraments, the keys of the Church are principally in the hands of the ministers of God's word or priests. In these aforementioned articles I agree with my adversaries; in those that follow, I disagree.

The first is this: I believe that we are saved by grace alone, because of Christ's passion, freely, due to no merits of our own. Good works are to be performed; but we are not to rely on them, for they are insignificant and impure, and, as Isaiah calls them, are filthy rags [Isa. 64:6]. Sins, on the other hand, are infinite. The righteous man falls seven times a day [Prov. 24:16]. Every day the holy Church prays, forgive us our debts. There is no proportion between the finite and the infinite. The first father Adam could not atone for a single sin, nor could all the angels, nor indeed the whole world. Christ's passion atoned for them.

The second article in which my adversaries do not agree with me is this: I believe that the venerable Sacrament of the Eucharist is to be administered in both kinds to the laypeople, according to Christ's prescription, and according to the custom of the Apostles and of the ancient Church. For one kind of Sacrament was denied to the laity not so long ago.

The third article: I declare that priests who cannot contain themselves are to marry. Nor is what they say, that the sacred order is polluted by marriage, of any weight. If marriage is an undertaking instituted by God, the sacred order cannot be polluted by it. The prophets, the saintly fathers, Chaeremon, Spyridon, and so forth were married. The ancient Canons likewise approve of it.

The fourth article: I assert that ecclesiastical goods are dissipated by the leaders of the Churches with great indignation of God and considerable damage to the commonwealth. For goods are donated to the Churches for the following reasons: first, that ministers of the Church live soberly and parsimoniously from them; then, that we provide for the interest of poor students; finally, that we assist the need of the commonwealth. If it were allowed, I could clearly prove that this is the case.

These four articles have been disputed over both in many previous councils and indeed in the recent council before His Imperial Majesty, the Estates and Orders of the Empire, and the Pope's Legate, and have generally been decided in favour of this view. If I, too, follow the judgment of such a venerable

214 *Sources*

gathering, I should not be incriminated for it. Regarding the divine virgin Mary I believe the following: she is the most chaste and holy virgin mother of God, to whom none of the holy virgins and mothers can be compared. I believe that we must honour the saints and praise their life and mores publicly in church; but I grant invocation and worship to God alone, in accordance with that saying, Thou shalt have no other gods before me [Exod. 20:3], and likewise, My glory I do not give to another [Isa. 42:8, 48:11].

But since my adversaries cry out that it is not my role to discuss such matters, I respond: in baptism I professed that I am a servant of God and a member of His Church. Further, when I received my doctorate, I was given the authority to interpret, discuss, and teach Scripture. I thus act rightfully if I defend the doctrine of my lord and creator. But I have said enough of this. If I shall seem to have written more vehemently and bitterly than was appropriate, I pray that this be attributed to my just affliction. For who does not cry out when he is struck?

I felt I must write these things publicly, by way of a confession, so that your Most Serene Majesty might clearly understand what I believe and teach. I pray the eternal father that He may long preserve your most serene Majesty unharmed. In the year 1543.

Many exceptionally learned Lithuanians are subjects of your holy Majesty, all of whom could have been useful to the commonwealth. But, frightened by my misfortune, they have chosen to live in Germany. Some support the most illustrious Duke of Prussia, others other princes. The same most illustrious Prince built a famous school at great expense, and called learned men from all over. He pays the professors some thousands of florins a year. He established free board for many poor students. He wants to place me at the head of this school. Therefore, should there be no place for me in Your Most Serene Majesty's domain, I will accept this appointment. But we all regret – God be with me – most merciful Lady, that while we hoped to benefit our own, now we benefit others.

Jan Weinreich printed this in the Königsberg Academy, in the month of June, in the year 1547.

50 Aonio Paleario, *Indictment Against the Roman Pontiffs* (1544)

Keywords: #Eschatology, #Pope, #Church-State, Relations, #Irenicism
Region: #Italy, #Switzerland
Group: #Reformed (close to)

A prominent member of the Italian Reform movement, Aonio Paleario (1503–1570) stands out for his decision to remain in the peninsula despite the onset of the Counter-Reformation. He was eventually executed in Rome for his Protestant sympathies. The following is a selection of extracts from his principal religious work, the *Indictment against the Roman pontiffs*. Paleario began to work on the *Indictment* as early as 1536, and greatly expanded the work in or around 1544, in preparation for the upcoming Council of Trent (1545–1563); he continued to revise it throughout his life, eventually entrusting it to the Swiss Reformed theologian Theodor Zwinger in Basel when the religious climate in Italy became too hostile. The work was only printed for the first time in 1600, through the efforts of the Italian Protestant exile Taddeo Duno.

The *Indictment* consists of 20 theses, each with an annexed commentary, in which Paleario lays out a sustained attack on the Papacy and discusses a number of themes, including, among others, purgatory, the Eucharist, and the value of oaths. Several features of the work make it an emblematic illustration of many key characteristics of Italian Protestantism: the belief in the fundamental unity of all Protestant churches; the peculiar emphasis placed on the Roman Church as the diabolical source of all corruption; the central role attributed to secular authorities in driving the Reformation. The work itself is a rallying call addressed to all 'Christian princes', whom Paleario charges with eliminating Catholic abuses and with overseeing the meeting of a universal council in which religious controversies may be decided through the word of God. The contrast between the free, open gathering proposed here and the Council of Trent, called and led by the papacy itself, would have been obvious to Paleario's readers. The extracts below expose some of the central elements of Paleario's broad view of Protestantism, of his conciliar vision, and of his stance towards civil authorities as agents of reform.[79]

216 *Sources*

Aonii Palearii Verulani, Iesu Christi martyris, Actio in Pontifices Romanos et eorum asseclas, ad Imp. Rom. reges et principes Christianae reipub. summos oecumenici concilii praesides conscripta, cum de Conc. Tridenti habendo deliberaretur ([Heidelberg]: Vögelin, [1600]), fols.):(5r–):(7v, a5v–a6v, 131–33. Translated by Odile Panetta. Available in modern edition in "Actio in pontifices romanos et eorum asseclas ad imperatorem romanum, reges et principes christianae reipublicae, summos oecumenici concilii praesides conscripta, cum de concilio Tridenti habendo deliberaretur", in *Opuscoli e lettere di Riformatori italiani del Cinquecento*, vol. 2, ed. Giuseppe Paladino (Bari: Laterza, 1927), 1–168 (see in particular 3–5, 15–17, 89–90).'

———

Preface

The letters I wrote in previous years to the Swiss and to the Germans – without prefacing them with my name – were able to express what my hope, my intent, my feelings are. God, the Father of our Lord Jesus Christ, is my witness that for some time it has been my desire that Christian princes, having summoned good and learned men, attend and preside over the gatherings that are to be held, so that in their presence I might give a firm and saintly testimony, and, if necessary, die for the glory of Christ. Since I harboured this desire for many years, and I saw that princes were occupied in other matters, and that the time of my end was approaching, I wrote my testimony, and from the testimony an indictment against the Roman pontiffs and their followers, so that if death, for which I am well prepared, were to catch me first, after death too I might be of service to my excellent brothers, whose evils I wanted to remedy by delivering this testimony in a council. I leave it, written sincerely, devotedly, and irreproachably, in the hands of saintly and faithful men, so that it may thereby be preserved until the time of a future council which – ecumenical, free, holy, solemn – will undoubtedly be held in due course (I pray the Father of our Lord Jesus Christ that this time come quickly).… For if that long-awaited day should come – when, out of a desire for public peace and concord of the Churches, the peoples that obey the Gospel might discuss among one another, and demand and obtain from the Emperor of the Romans, and from the Christian kings and princes, that a council be actually convened by the Roman pontiff, so that he might meet in some place with his cardinals and bishops and their followers in order to hold public and free gatherings of all the peoples and nations that invoke the name of our Lord Jesus Christ, in which all peoples might gladly and carefully be heard through speakers, who, with no danger, with no deception, with no fear may freely speak in the presence of the Emperor and of the kings and princes and delegates of cities, so that, if equity of judgement is established, through the sword of God's word abuses may be abolished, controversies in religion resolved, the Churches purged and healed so as to be joined in one body – when you see a council thus convened being prepared, then you will remember, O depositaries, and you will ensure that these writings of mine are delivered intact and sincere to the leaders of the Churches of Swiss and German believers and the defenders of the holy Gospel, whom, in the name of our Lord Jesus Christ and of the Holy Spirit, I make and establish true and legitimate custodians of this little book, once it leaves the hands of its depositaries.

To the leaders of the holy Churches of the Swiss and of the Germans

When this little book is brought to you, O leaders of the holy Churches of the Swiss and of the Germans, it will be your duty to either hold on to it or publish it in due time, so that, with your support and through public declarations, the testimony of a pious man – who, when dying, had no reason to lie to Christ – might be presented in that same ecumenical, free, holy, solemn council, so that this testimony, along with the indictment, may be as a sudden lightning bolt that might strike the Antichrist – to whom, O brothers, we must not grant space to reply for very long. That evil is to be suppressed through the word of God as soon as possible, in the council itself, before the face and eyes of great princes. As you well know, he has his sophists and illusionists, through whom, if space is given to them, he deceives kings and emperors; and therefore this little book is to be presented nowhere other than in the council. For if the experienced Roman fox were to raise hopes for a council, and, avoiding it herself, nonetheless send forward some bishops with the intent to deceive, as she has often already been wont to do, tempting the princes' soul and deceiving God's Church, hold back this little book, O brothers. For God, the Father of our Lord Jesus Christ, will concede that one day, with the peoples having been stirred up and gathering in flocks, the Pope will be forced by the kings to be there – he will be forced to be there, I say....

Bad habits, abuses, abominations are to be removed by public edict; for we have a sort of Bacchanalia, a sort of games, the abuse of simulacra. Indeed, just as once human weakness, upon Satan's instigation, placed gods and deities over illnesses, so among us, on the holy ground of Peter in Rome, there is a temple to fever in the name of Holy Mary; nor are brutes lacking the patronage of saints, with Roman pontiffs approving of this; it is licit to fornicate with impunity; everywhere there are public prostitutes, to the point that in Rome in previous years 10,000 public prostitutes have been counted; the pontiffs order that some portion of these prostitutes' profit be paid to them, and likewise from the Jews they demand the hundredth part of their earnings, in order to allow them to practice usury with impunity. Most bitter exactions indeed, most cruel despotisms, simony, fraud, sales and purchases of the Holy Spirit, and all other abominable things reign in Rome to such an extent, that those who have Christ's spirit clearly see written on the Roman curia's forehead: 'THE GREAT BABYLON, THE MOTHER OF FORNICATIONS AND ABOMINATIONS OF THE EARTH'.

Since the Roman pontiffs, their colleagues, and their followers introduced so many and such abominations, abuses, evils, offences, transgressions, when it comes to judging them, the Roman pontiffs, their colleagues, and their

218 *Sources*

followers should not act as judges. For who does not know that, if we were to follow the judgement of those by whom the Pope sits surrounded, whom he himself ordered to be by him, as members of his body, we would have such laws as those they have always approved of? For what else do you think these men wanted in the councils, and want today, other than that their decrees be ratified in the presence of a great number of peoples and princes, so that they might have ash to throw in the princes' eyes, and after a few years, mixing human and divine laws, rage against all those who dare to say a word? Do you believe that they came in such pomp to re-establish the Spirit? Having experienced for so long men burning with greed and enveloped in Satan's mud, do we not know what these whirling clouds bring? 'For the earth', says the man,

> which drinketh in the rain that cometh oft upon it, and bringeth forth herbs meet for them by whom it is dressed, receiveth blessing from God: But that which beareth thorns and briers *is* rejected, and *is* nigh unto cursing; whose end *is* to be burned [Heb 6:7–8].

When among the bishops and leaders of the Churches there is such corruption that we see abomination sitting in a holy place, we must flee into the mountains [Matt 24:16; Luke 21:21]. With your guidance, Christ, we must flee into the mountains, to the princes of your people. Thus, having given his testimony, a servant of Christ prays, begs, implores you, princes of the Christian commonwealth, towards whom the eyes of all peoples, all nations, are turned, for the coming of our Lord Jesus Christ, that you place all care and diligence in this work. The Lord Jesus shines in your hearts – he who is a trustworthy witness, who is the image of his father, in whom there is no darkness. Take on this care worthy of your souls, O princes. We have come to the end of the work. It is very easy for you to choose, from the cities and provinces that invoke the name of our Lord Jesus Christ, so that they might judge of such matters, men who fear God, whom the prophet Joel calls little ones and sucklings, that is to say, not those who want to be and be called prelates – 'gather the children', he says, 'and those that suck the breasts' [Joel 2:16] – not corrupt, not greedy, not arrogant men, not mindful of status, but whom God's holy people will testify to be of esteemed life and erudition in Scripture....

Thus great praise is to be attributed first of all to you, excellent and upright men, who, with the sound as if of some trumpet, extraordinarily raised peoples and nations; then I most ardently praise all you others, who have an opinion of Christ which is not fickle or vain but firm and stable, and, since you are most concerned with his glory and majesty, believe that any articles, inventions, and decrees of men that have been put forward or written are to be examined very diligently, lest they conflict with the Gospel or teach something else. Then, since, as is appropriate, you desire that the institutions of the most holy Apostles be re-established and rites in the Sacraments be

Sources 219

made as pure as possible, so that those brothers of ours who are not yet sufficiently firm in their faith – of whom we must take care in accordance with charity – may draw piety, not superstition from them; I thus exhort and beg you, for he who called you from darkness to his extraordinary light, that you remain in that opinion, nor should the violence or threats of anyone draw you from your deliberation, and – as in previous years I admonished the Germans through a letter – that you believe it necessary to turn to the Christian princes, so that by their work there be a selection, in France, Britain, Germany, Italy, Spain, and in all other Christian provinces, from those who, experts in divine matters, are far from all suspicion and Papal corruption; they should ensure that no damage touch the Christian commonwealth. For if some habit or custom has been accepted through councils, discipline, imprudence, or fraud, that conflicts with the precepts and institutions of Christ that have been divinely written down by Matthew, Mark, Luke, John, or that differs from those acts which are attributed to the Apostles, so that it does not take into account their example or admonishment or doctrine, or that is extraneous to that which Peter, Paul, Jacob, Judas, John taught through very famous letters, by these people's clear command it was null, inane, futile. The Christian commonwealth – if it could speak – ardently asks you again and again to obtain this from emperors, kings, and princes of cities through prayer, admonishment, plea.

51 *Anabaptist Appeal to Moravian Nobility* (1545)

Keywords: #Toleration, #Conscience, #War, #Coercion, #Magistrate, #Economics, #Tax
Region: #Liechtenstein, #Czech Republic
Group: #Anabaptist

Wherever Anabaptists spread, they could not shake the accusation that their beliefs would necessarily lead to anarchy and violence. Given the horrors of the short-lived and bloody attempt to usher in the **kingdom of God at Münster**, such suspicions were not unfounded. However, the fervour of the 1530s led the Anabaptists to split into violent and pacifist wings (**Menno Simons** represented the latter), with **David Joris'** spiritual violence as a *via media*. Peaceful Anabaptists felt they were being punished for the excesses of Münster and sought refuge elsewhere. At the far eastern edge of the Habsburg Empire, various Christian groups (Orthodox, Catholics, Protestants, etc.) and Muslims were in greater contact. This region was known for greater toleration, and some Anabaptists hoped there might be room for them and their beliefs.[80] But even there, Anabaptists could not shake their association with violence, and they were persecuted from 1535. Anabaptists produced the appeal in response to this persecution, pairing this document with a fuller articulation of the Anabaptist faith by **Peter Riedemann**, a leader of the Austrian Anabaptists.

"Appeal to the Lords of Lichtenstein", in *Baptist Confessions of Faith*, ed. William Joseph McGlothlin (Philadelphia, PA: American Baptist Publication Society, 1911), 19–23.

———

Sent to the Moravian Nobility, in the year 1545.

We, brethren and true followers of the Lord Jesus Christ, who from many and various places, especially of the German nation, have been called through great grace and mercy to the wonderful light of divine knowledge which has arisen in these times and shone to all men, and now assembled in his holy name: wish you the true knowledge of God and of his eternal truth and righteousness. Amen!

Beloved Lords of the Land of Moravia! It is well known to you in part how we have come out of various places and lands into the land of Moravia for no other reason than that we desire to serve [God] according to the known truth of God, piously and agreeably; which heretofore has not been permitted to us in many lands on account of the tyranny of the governments which have taken our possessions from us by force, have plunged us into misery and hunted us away, have held many of us in long and wearisome imprisonment and have strangled a good part.

But because the Lord God has spied out for his people especially this place and has so favoured them that they have assembled here, and we have received with thankfulness and have undertaken to serve him and walk before him blameless. Although we have been and are still diligent to do this, yet there has gone out from the fickle and especially from those who have gone out of our midst [and] have left the truth and made friends with the world, much evil report and much of such complaint has reached you, wherein we know ourselves to be blameless in all things.

Moreover because many of you are little acquainted with our doings or are in error on account of the slanders against us, we were moved to give you information concerning and justification of our doing, teaching and life, especially with regard to certain articles as for example, (a) magistracy, (b) taxes and (c) the assembly, which, we have been informed, are of special interest to you....

With regard to magistracy and the obedience which we are under obligation to render it we say, first, that of course there must be in the world governments, and also that they are ordained of God. Further, if any man opposes magistracy in equitable matters he opposes the ordinance of God [Rom. 13:2]. Yet we say with Peter that one should obey God rather than men [Acts 5:29], as also many of you yourselves know, and at first, when we came into the land, in fact showed that you feared to demand of us anything contrary to the conscience.

With regard to taxes we say that if any one objects to paying the government taxes, interest or rent so that the office can be carried on, he would be found to oppose the ordinance of God. Therefore we also, as the governments under which we have sojourned and lived must themselves testify, have never opposed due annual taxes or interest, rent, toll and just socage. But if anything which God has not ordained be demanded [of us] as war taxes and hangman's wages or other things which are not becoming to a Christian and have no ground in Scripture, these we can by no means approve.

But in that by many we are compared in all points with the [Anabaptists] of Münster and are accused of being of their kind [or spirit]; it is known to all men who are acquainted with us that nobody has less of the Münster kind [spirit] than we who hate the same most intensely and testify that it is a work of the devil....

52 Miles Coverdale, *Biblical Israel and the Righteous Use of the Sword* (1547)

Keywords: #Authority, #Violence, #Tyranny, #War, #Hebrew Bible
Region: #England
Group: #Church of England | #Anabaptist

Miles Coverdale (1488–1568) was part of a group of scholars, including Robert Barnes, **Thomas Cranmer, Hugh Latimer,** and **William Tyndale,** who met to discuss reforming the English church at the White Horse Tavern in Cambridge. Coverdale is best known for publishing the first complete Bible in English (1535), which he dedicated to Henry VIII. He adorned this edition of the Bible with a frontispiece that elevated the King's role in bringing the word of God to the people, reinforcing the idea that Reformation buttressed Christian kingship. This publication brought him patronage, and he then worked on an official version of scripture for the English church (the 1539 Great Bible). Coverdale was close to Thomas Cromwell (a driver of religious change at King Henry's court), and Cromwell's fall necessitated Coverdale's flight to the continent until 1548. Upon his return, he worked alongside Cranmer and contributed to the *Book of Common Prayer.* He was the bishop of Exeter from 1551 until 1553, but fled again to the continent when Mary I came to the throne. During this time, he worked on the landmark publication of the **Geneva Bible.** Although he returned to England under **Elizabeth I,** he was not restored to his ecclesiastical office.

The following extract is taken from *The Old Faith* (1547), a book that sought to trace stories of true faith since the foundation of the world. The eighth chapter discussed the wars, leadership and faith of Moses and Joshua, and how their efforts pointed to a greater ruler, Christ. Nestled in this overview of the Hebrew Bible is an articulation of the relationship between the Christian ruler and the temporal sword. He affirmed the use of violence on behalf of recognised authorities, including in war. In his opinion, contemporary kings could take inspiration from the Hebrew Bible. He thus criticised those who made sharper distinctions between power and polity in the context of the Hebrew Bible and that of early modern England. His reverence for the Hebrew Bible equally did not lead him to affirm rebellion or divinely approved tyrannicide, or any other expression of anarchy. It would have been the sort of message the new king, **Edward VI**, may have wanted to hear.[81]

Myles Coverdale, *The Old Faith* (1547), in *Writings and Translations of Myles Coverdale*, ed. George Pearson (Cambridge: Cambridge University Press, 1844), 50–53. Text modernised by the editors.

———

Chapter 8.

All Virtuous Kings, and the People of Israel, Trusted Christ, and Not the Law

Joshua and other judges, rulers, princes, and kings of Israel after him, undertook devastating warfare, fought many horrible battles, destroyed much land and people, and shed men's blood without measure; doing so as a chief head and as an instrument and vessel of God at the commandment of God who punished the idolatry and blasphemy of the ungodly whom God had long suffered and exhorted to amend their ways, but for all his patient abiding they would not convert. God rooted out these people through the sword of his beloved friends; sometime he delivered his people with the sword of the righteous, and saved them from the hand of their enemies. Other times he gave his people into the hand of their enemies because of their sins, to nurture and correct them with the rod: then the people of God fell and fled before their enemies and were subdued and oppressed by the ungodly, till they acknowledged their sins, called upon God and amended their ways, putting their trust in God only through the blessed Seed; worshipping him only, calling upon him, and honouring him according to his word, casting away false worship, the service of idols as well as shameful, blasphemous and ungodly living. Then God sent help and delivered them by his power, by the service of his appointed captains.

This warring, delivering and punishing was not a fleshly work done unfaithfully, a work that no man ought to follow, as is meant by those influenced by the wayward spirit of the Manichaeans and Anabaptists. For Paul clearly said:

> And what shall I say of Gideon, Barak, Samson and Jephthah, David and Samuel, and the prophets? which through faith subdued kingdoms, wrought righteousness, obtained the promises, stopped the mouths of lions, quenched the violence of fire, escaped the edge of the sword, of weak were made strong, became valiant in battle, turned to flight the armies of the aliens.
>
> (Heb. 11:32–33)

The holy apostle praises and commends all these works as excellent works of faith. Therefore, these are not works of the flesh; neither is it now contrary

224 *Sources*

to the holy faith, if Christian rulers deliver their innocent people, whom God has given to them as subjects, from wrongful violence, and defend their liberty, righteousness, house and land, or punish the shameful blasphemers, idolaters and persecutors of the holy faith, and not allow wrongdoers to enact their malicious will.

Nevertheless, this must be done by those to whom God has committed the sword. For thus says the Lord: 'Whoso taketh away the sword, shall perish through the sword' (Matt. 26:52). But especially in the battles of God's people and of the unfaithful, it comes to pass, and is expressly set before our eyes, that God said to the serpent at the beginning: 'I will put enmity between thy seed and the woman's seed' (Gen. 3:15). For the righteous are the seed of Christ, the unrighteous and unfaithful are the seed of the devil. We see great discord between them; but we also see that the faithful always tread the serpent on the head, though they are also be bitten on the heel. For faithful believers before the birth of Christ, in the time of the promise, had no less trouble and persecution, not only because of sin but also for righteousness and faith's sake, than the faithful after Christ's birth in the time of grace and perfectness. Therefore, it evidences little knowledge of the doings of the faithful when people say that the people of old were a victorious people who governed corporally, but that the people after Christ's coming are born to suffer and were not to know victory or governance.

53 Thomas Cranmer, *A Speech at the Coronation of Edward VI* (1547)

Keywords: #Church-State Relations, #Magistrate, #Submission, #Violence
Region: #England
Group: #Church of England

Thomas Cranmer (1489–1556) trained for ministry at Cambridge. However, he married and had to resign from his fellowship in 1516. Cranmer was allowed to return to his fellowship and ministerial training upon the death of his wife Joan and their child during labour. He became entangled in Henry VIII's efforts to change marriage partners, and the king was pleased with his treatise on marriage. He was then sent to Rome, became the royal chaplain, and encountered reforming ideas during his service there. He breached canon law by marrying again but was still consecrated as Archbishop of Canterbury in 1533. In his new position, he abetted Henry's marital ambitions, patronised Bible translations, and helped consolidate the king's authority over the church, including through the dissolution of English monasteries. There is much debate over Cranmer's Protestant sympathies during Henry's reign. It is clear, however, that once the king died, he began moving the church towards the Reformation.[82]

Cranmer wrote the coronation speech for the ascendancy of his nine-year-old godson **Edward VI**, which is excerpted below. It is significant for two reasons. First, the address projects the biblical precedent for boy kingship onto Edward VI. The concept of precedent is generally important to English law, but Cranmer goes further than that. He puts the English king in the lineage of the kings of the Hebrew Bible, thus assuming monarchical supersessionism. The argument of precedence would become important again to Elizabeth I, who strongly identified with biblical precedents for female leadership. Second, the speech is significant because the king was crowned without the blessing of the pope. To justify this deviancy, Cranmer crafted an argument around two structures of authority: civil and ecclesiastical. These two authorities independently traced their lineage directly to God. However, the speech left the question of ultimate authority open, laying the foundation for future conflicts between church and state.

226   *Sources*

John Edmund Cox, ed., *Miscellaneous Writings and Letters of Thomas Cranmer, Archbishop of Canterbury* (Cambridge: The Parker Society, 1846), 125–126. Text modernised by the editors.

———

Speech at the Coronation of Edward VI, February 20, 1547

Most dread and royal sovereign: The promises your highness has made here at your coronation, to forsake the devil and all his works, are not to be taken in the Bishop of Rome's sense, when you commit anything that is distasteful to that See, to hit your majesty in the teeth; as Pope Paul III, late bishop of Rome, sent to your royal father [Henry VIII], saying

> Didn't you promise, at our permission of your coronation, to forsake the devil and all his works, and do you now turn to heresy? For the breach of your promise, do you know that it is in our power to give thy sword and sceptre to whoever we please?

We, your majesty's clergy, do humbly conceive, that this promise to forsake the devil does not for your highness' sword, spiritual or temporal, or in the least at your highness' possession of the sceptre of your dominion, as you and your predecessors have been given them from God. Neither could your ancestors lawfully give over their crowns to the Bishop of Rome or to his legates, according to their ancient oaths then taken upon that ceremony.

The bishops of Canterbury, for the most part, have crowned your predecessors and anointed them kings of this land: yet it was not in their power to receive or reject them, neither did it give them authority to prescribe for them conditions to take or to leave their crowns; although the bishops of Rome would encroach upon your predecessors by his bishop's act and oil, that in the end, they might possess those bishops with an interest to dispose of their crowns at their pleasure. But the wiser sort will look at their claws and clip them.

The solemn rites of coronation have their ends and utility, yet neither direct force or necessity: they are good admonitions to help kings remember their duty to God, but it does not increase their dignity. For they are God's anointed, not because of the oil the bishop uses, but in consideration of their power which is ordained, of the sword which is authorised, of their persons which are elected by God, and endued with the gifts of his Spirit for the better ruling and guiding of his people. The oil, if added, is but a ceremony; if it is lacking the oil, the king is still a perfect monarch and God's anointed. Now for the person or bishop who anoints a king, it is proper to be done by the chief bishop; but if they cannot, or will not, any bishop may perform this ceremony.

The Bishop of Rome (or other bishops owning his supremacy) has no authority to place conditions upon monarchs during these ceremonies, but

Sources 227

he may faithfully declare what God requires at the hands of kings and rulers; that is, religion and virtue. Therefore not from the bishop of Rome, but as a messenger from my Saviour Jesus Christ, I shall most humbly admonish your royal majesty about the things your highness is to perform.

Your majesty is God's vice-regent and Christ's vicar within your own dominions, and with your predecessor Josiah you are to see God truly worshipped, idolatry destroyed, the tyranny of the bishops of Rome banished from your subjects, and images removed. These acts are signs of a second Josiah [2 Kings 23:1–27], who reformed the church of God in his days. You are to reward virtue, to revenge sin, to justify the innocent, to relieve the poor, to procure peace, to repress violence, and to execute justice throughout your realms. For precedents, on those kings who performed not these things, the old law [Hebrew Bible] shows how the Lord revenged his quarrel; and on those kings who fulfilled these things, he poured forth his blessings in abundance. For example, it is written of Josiah: 'Like unto him there was no king before him that turned to the Lord with all his heart, according to all the law of Moses, neither after him arose there any like him' [2 Kings 23:25]. This was to that prince of perpetual fame and dignity, to remain to the end of days.

Being bound by my function to lay these things before your royal highness, the one as a reward, if you fulfil; the other as a judgement from God, if you neglect them; yet I openly declare before the living God, and before these nobles of the land, that I have no commission to denounce your majesty deprived, if your highness miss in part or in whole, of these performances, much less to draw up indentures between God and your majesty, or to say you forfeit your crown with a clause, for the Bishop of Rome, as has been done by your majesty's predecessors, King John and his son Henry of this land. The Almighty God of his mercy let the light of his countenance shine upon your majesty, grant you a prosperous and happy reign, defend you and save you; and let your subjects say, Amen! God save the king.

54 Mikael Agricola, *On the Importance of a Finnish Translation of the New Testament* (1548)

Keywords: #Nation, #Language
Region: #Sweden, #Finland
Group: #Lutheran

Mikael Agricola (c.1510–1557) was born in a village in the southwest of contemporary Finland, then part of the Kingdom of Sweden. He studied Latin in Vyborg on the outer eastern border of the country. After serving as secretary to the bishop of Turku, he was sent to Wittenberg for further training under **Martin Luther** and **Johannes Bugenhagen,** and received financial support from the Swedish king. Agricola returned to Turku to teach at the cathedral school and was consecrated as bishop of Turku towards the end of his life. Although he was fairly quiet on politics, possibly due to his need for the King's favour, he made a significant contribution to the development of the Finnish language in his translation of the New Testament, published in the late 1540s.

Kaisa Häkkinen notes that Agricola may have had help from Martinus Teit and Simon Henrici Wiburgensis, who were his contemporaries at Wittenberg. It is in the preface to the second edition that Agricola expanded on the importance of the Finnish translation of the New Testament, recounted the founding myth of **Olaus Petri,** and commented on the process of translation. According to Häkkinen, the translation derived from a patchwork of texts in a variety of languages, which speaks to a need to work from different sources and the capacity to work with a high number of languages.[83] Agricola's work contains the first systematic use of written Finnish, even as he borrowed from other known languages and dialects. He is remembered by the Evangelical-Lutheran Church as one of the main Reformers, alongside Luther and **Philip Melanchthon.**

Mikael Agricola, *The New Testament,* 2nd ed. (1548), Preface, 17–21, https://www.doria.fi/bitstream/handle/10024/43367/p21-06_se_wsi_testamentti.pdf?sequence=1&isAllowed=y (accessed 9 October 2023), trans. Mika Vähäkangas.

Sources 229

To you, dear Christian reader, good Finn, Tavast, Karel, or whoever friend of Jesus Christ you may be, the books of the New Testament translated in the Finnish language. Parts of it are translated from Greek, Latin, German, and Swedish, through which Jesus Christ bestowed the gift of grace. Now before these times, the language of this country was rarely used in books or letters, so receive this gift as a favour from the Lord.

You should know that the New Testament was first written by the holy evangelists and apostles in the Greek language (except the Gospel of Matthew and Paul's letter to the Hebrews, which were probably written in Hebrew). But since the Christian faith spread throughout the Roman Empire, the New Testament was translated into the common language: Latin. The Christian faith and the church have grown in Germany, England, Denmark, Sweden, and also here, as well as to other provinces that have been under the remit of the Roman Church. Therefore, the Word of God, the Divine Service, the rites of the church, and canon law have been used in Latin across these countries, and thus also here – until now.

Every divine service has to be led in the common language of each province in which the faith has been received. In order for everyone to be set free in Christ and for the salvation of us all, it is crucial that his words will be taught publicly and understandably, and not hidden from anyone. This was the case until now, even with the greatest danger to our souls. As Paul writes in 1 Cor. 14, one should not speak in a manner that others cannot understand, for it is for the edification of our neighbour.

I believe it is better to speak few words in a language the congregation understands, than to use 10,000 words in a foreign language, such as has been the case with Latin until now. Because some of the priests who until now ruled the congregation had a varying capacity for Latin – if at all – they have taught very weakly and lazily, and do so even today. Some have seldom – if at all – studied the Word and taught the poor people to read the Lord's Prayer and the most important articles of faith, even though it should be the highest priority for priests to teach the Catechism and the Word of God....

[*Agricola offers more criticism of the priests' reluctance to study the Word, contrary to Jesus' command.*]

So that no priest can leverage the excuse that he does not know Latin or Swedish, and thus omits to teach properly, the New Testament has been translated as it is written, in Finnish....

[*He comments on the work of translation and its history.*]

Now, someone may object 'Ah, if I only knew how and when the people of Finland became Christians', this is how one should answer: 'In 1150 AD (original: anno Christi incarnati], (when the Finns became Christians) when the King of Sweden, St Erik was elected, he began supporting the growth of the Christian faith in Finland. He therefore went with a large army and St Henrik, whom the Bishop of Uppsala had appointed, to conquer the Finns. Thereafter, he took the Finns into grace, as friends, and ensured that the

230   *Sources*

Word of God was preached to them. When the King went home, he left St. Henrik (he was of English descent) as bishop and preacher, who was killed a few years later. Therefore, Latin has been used in this diocese until now, as well as in other churches and congregations.

In 1248, another King Erik came with a large army to Finland with his son-in-law Birger Jarl, who was the ruler of its people. He conquered the Tavasts, and converted them to Christianity. In 1293, Herr Torgil, the constable of Sweden, sent the army to Karelia to prevent the Karelians from ravaging the church in Tavastia and the Finnish speaking regions, and converted them thereby to faith.

It is believed that the Nyland [original: Uusimaa] coastal people, in the Borgå and Raseborg counties, as well as the people of the archipelago, the Kalantians and the people of Ostrobothnia who still speak Swedish today, have come from Sweden or Gollandista [Holland]. When the non-Christian Finns, who then were pagans and lived in the mainland, wanted to harm the archipelago and coastal population..., the Swedish-speaking coastal population asked for security and help from Sweden. Thus, the Swedish-speaking population had been Christian for a long time compared to the other tribes and peoples who also live in the Finnish diocese and country.

Finally, although there are many different languages or ways of speaking among these peoples, so that in each of the provinces there is a different dialect, anyhow the whole diocese is called the country of Finland which is like the mother of the other. They became Christians first in Turku, which is home to the mother church, the bishopric and the see. Because of this, Finnish is mainly used in these holy books of the New Testament. Since, however, the need is large, words have been included from other dialects as well.

It is not surprising that there are many dialects because even though it is one diocese, there are seven provinces here. Of which the first and foremost is Southern and Northern Finland; the second is upper and lower Satakunta; the third Tavastia; the fourth Karelia; the fifth Uusimaa; the sixth Raseborg; the seventh Ostrobothnia without Kaland. Different dialects are spoken in these provinces. Therefore, no reader should take offence if something sounds strange or terrible or new. Nam nihili simul inceptum et perfectum esse constat (For nothing is at the same time commenced and completed). If someone, friend of God, could do it better, they are free to try, as long as they are not overzealous. May everyone, Priest, Chaplain, Youth and all the people read God's words, ponder them, remember them, and live by them until eternal life, which Jesus Christ may give to all. AMEN.

55 Edward VI, *Act to Take Away All Positive Laws Against the Marriage of Priests* (1549)

Keywords: #Marriage, #Church-State Relations
Region: #England
Group: #Church of England

Edward VI (1537–1553) was the only son of Henry VIII and Jane Seymour. His brief reign from 1547 to 1553 saw the beginning of state-sponsored Protestantism, and his sudden death halted reforming efforts by the state. Edward was well educated, bright, and enjoyed religious discussions. However, for his entire reign he was a minor, and legal authority lay variously with counsellors and the church. Edward Seymour and John Dudley were two influential counsellors who worked alongside **Thomas Cranmer**. Seymour and Dudley possessed the authority to act in the king's name, and they moved the church towards Reformed Protestantism. The visual landscape of English Christianity was also transformed. Reformers demoted Catholic images and elevated the printed and preached word. Edward was often compared to another boy-king, Josiah, who instituted major religious reforms for the Kingdom of Judah. The following source details the state's role in introducing clerical marriage, something Luther and Cranmer had advocated for and which constituted a major reform. Upon her ascension to the throne, Mary I repealed the following Act: some wives were reclassified as concubines and clergy who remained married were deprived of their benefices.[84]

James Thomas Law, ed., *The Ecclesiastical Statutes at Large* (London: William Benning and Co, 1847), III:382–383.

Although it were not only better for the estimation of priests, and other ministers in the church of God, to live chaste, sole and separate from the company of women, and the bond of marriage, but also thereby they might the better intend to the administration of the gospel, and be less intricated and troubled with the charge of a household....

Yet forasmuch as the contrary hath rather been seen, and such uncleanness of living, and other great inconveniences, not meet to be rehearsed, have

232 *Sources*

followed of compelled chastity, and of such laws as have prohibited those (such persons) the godly use of marriage: it were better and rather to be suffered in the commonwealth, that those which could not contain, should after the counsel of scripture live in holy marriage, than feignedly abuse with worse enormity outward chastity or single life:

Be it therefore enacted by our sovereign lord the king, with the assent of the lords spiritual and temporal, and the commons, in this present parliament assembled, and by the authority of the same, that all and every law and laws positive, canons, constitutions and ordinance heretofore made by authority of man only, which do prohibit marriage to any ecclesiastical or spiritual person or persons ... which by God's law may lawfully marry ... shall be utterly void and of none effect.

56 Thomas Cranmer, *Notes on Rebellion* (1549)

Keywords: #Authority, #Rebellion, #Submission, #War, #Violence
Region: #England
Group: #Church of England | #Roman Catholic

Thomas Cranmer helped elevate Henry VIII over the Church of England, and his speech at the **coronation of Edward VI** indicated a high view of magistrates as God's anointed rulers. It is unsurprising, then, that Cranmer opposed rebellion. The following extract comes from the notes Cranmer prepared for a sermon, which is thought to be written in response to the Kett's Rebellion of 1549. The rebellion was centred in Norfolk, where people were angry about the enclosure of land by the wealthy. Cranmer viewed their concerns as illegitimate and pointed to the **Peasants' War** in Germany as a cautionary tale. He argued that scripture showed the violent end of rebels. The farmers should return to their fields, be content to humbly petition authorities regarding their interests, and be satisfied with their decision. His two New Testament examples of the justly deserved death of rebels are curious (Acts 5:35–37; 21:38). In his mind, Christians could not rebel, and those who rebelled would be punished. He also came close to identifying rebellion with apostasy. Later generations of English theologians would affirm that Christians could rebel and also that rebellion could be successful and even be blessed.[85]

John Edmund, ed., *Miscellaneous Writings and Letters of Thomas Cranmer, Archbishop of Canterbury* (Cambridge: The Parker Society, 1846), 188–189. Text modernised by the editors.

———

[*The notes begin with several Latin quotations (1 Cor. 3:3, 6:7, Jas 3:14–16, 4:1) to the effect that Christians should recognise the demonic nature of conflict, turn away from it and be willing to suffer injury.*]

How God has plagued sedition in the past.

234   *Sources*

Absalom, moving sedition against David, also miserably perished (2 Sam. 15 and 18).

Sheba for his sedition against David lost his head (2 Sam. 20).

Adonijah also for his sedition against Solomon was slain (1 Kgs 1–2).

Judas and Theudas for their sedition were justly slain (Acts 5:35–37).

An Egyptian likewise, who moved the people of Israel to sedition, received what he deserved (Acts 21:38)....

In one month in Germany about 200,000 were slain for their sedition.

God's word decrees that the sword does not belong to subjects, but only to magistrates.

Although the magistrates are evil, and are great tyrants against the commonwealth, and enemies to Christ's religion; yet the subject must obey in all worldly things, as the Christians do under the Turk, and ought so to do, so long as he does not command them to act against God.

How ungodly is it then for our subjects to take up the sword where a truly Christian prince reigns who desires to reform all griefs!

Subjects ought to make a humble suit to their prince for the reformation of all injuries, and not come with force.

Presently, the sword of the subject does not come of God, nor for the commonweal of the realm; but of the devil, and destroys the commonweal.

Firstly, it is against the word of God.

Secondly, they raise so many lies; whereof the devil is the author....

Thirdly, they spoil and rob men, and command every man to come to them, and to send to them what they please.

Fourthly, they let the harvest, which is the chief sustentation of our life, and God of his goodness has sent it abundantly; and they by their folly cause it to be lost and abandoned.

Fifthly, they are led by rage and fury, without reason; have no respect for the king's authority; nor for the papists in the west country; nor for our affairs in France, nor Scotland; which by their sedition is so much hindered, that there could not be imagined so great a damage to the realm.

Sixthly, they give commandments in the king's name, and upon pain of death, having no authority to do so.

The devil is always raising sedition against God.

As appears by the sedition of Dathan and Abiram; and all the murmurations of the children of Israel against Moses and Aaron [Num. 16].

Also, of the conspiracy against Zerubbabel in the re-edifying of the temple [Ezra 3–4].

Also, against Christ and his apostles, in various parts of the world.

Also in Germany lately, and now among us. For the devil cannot abide right reformation in religion.

Civil war is the greatest scourge there is, and it is a clear evidence of God's indignation against us for our ingratitude; that we either will not receive his true word, or that they who receive the same dishonour God in their living,

Sources 235

when they pretend to honour him with their mouths. God will certainly not bear with this ingratitude and insult coming at our hands.

The remedy to avert indignation is to receive his word, and to live according to it, returning unto God with prayer and penance. Or else surely more grievous affliction shall follow, if there is anything more grievous than civil war.

The chief authors of all these tumults are idle and naughty people, who have nothing and do little labour to have; they will riot in expending, but not labour in getting.

And these tumults first were excited by the papists and others who came from the western camp, to the intent, that by sowing divisions among ourselves we should not be able to impeach them.

57 Thomas Cranmer, *What Is Thy Duty towards Thy Neighbour?* (1549, rev. 1662)

Keywords: #Love, #Family
Region: #England
Group: #Church of England

Reforming efforts that began during the reign of Henry VIII accelerated under his openly Protestant son, **Edward VI** (r.1547–1553). The *Book of Common Prayer* is perhaps the most important document produced during Edward's Reformation. The prayer book was subsequently expanded with explanations and revised until 1661/1662. The version published in the United States (not included) modified the teachings on authority. The following excerpt comes from a short catechism produced by Thomas Cranmer, the Archbishop of Canterbury. It appears in the prayer book between the sections on baptism and confirmation. Under 'love of neighbour', Cranmer subsumed all of political and social life, from what one did with their hands to how they acted towards social superiors.[86]

The Creeds of Christendom, Vol. III: The Evangelical Protestant Creeds, ed. Philip Schaff (New York: Harper and Brothers, 1887), 517–522 (519–520).

———

Ques. What is thy duty towards thy neighbour?

Ans. My duty towards my neighbour is to love him as myself [Mark 12:31], and to do to all men as I would they should do unto me [Matt. 7:12]: to love, honour, and succour my father and mother [Exod. 20:12; Eph. 6:2]: to honour and obey the King (Queen) [1 Pet. 2:17], and all that are put in authority under him (her): to submit myself to all my governors, teachers, spiritual pastors and masters: to order myself lowly and reverently to all my betters: to hurt nobody by word nor deed: to be true and just in all my dealing: to bear no malice nor hatred in my heart: to keep my hands from picking and stealing, and my tongue from evil-speaking, lying, and slandering: to keep my body in temperance, soberness, and chastity: not to covet nor desire other men's goods; but to learn and labour truly to get mine own living, and to do my duty in that state of life unto which it shall please God to call me.

58 Martin Bucer, *On the Reign of Christ* (1550)

Keywords: #Church-State Relations, #Crime, #Toleration, #Violence, #Common Good, #Family, #Submission, #War, #Tyranny
Region: #England, #Germany
Group: #Interconfessional, #Lutheran, #Reformed, #Church of England

Martin Bucer (1491–1551) was born in the Alsace region of northern France. He entered the Dominican order and was sent to pursue doctoral studies in Heidelberg in 1517, where he was influenced by the ideas of Erasmus of Rotterdam and **Martin Luther**. His vision for reform drew on several Protestant Reformers, but he also branched out in idiosyncratic ways. Over his lifetime, he worked closely with several governments. His approach was ecumenical, striving to foster concord among the Reformers. Although his writings aimed to influence an audience across Europe, his greatest efforts were spent on the Reformation in Strassburg. **John Calvin**, during his exile from Geneva, ministered alongside Bucer. Towards the end of his life, **Thomas Cranmer** invited Bucer to England, where he took up a position at the University of Cambridge. He died in early 1551 and did not live to see whether or not the authorities enacted his reforms. Although **Edward VI's** successor, the Catholic Queen Mary I, ordered his body and books to be desecrated, **Elizabeth I** worked to restore Bucer's memory.

The following excerpt is taken from *De Regno Christi* (October 1550), which he composed for the boy king, Edward VI. Bucer's argument strengthened the church's position in society. In his estimation, the kingdom of Christ was built through discipleship, and to be fostered under the authority of the church, and not by the state. The role of the state was to support the church in its vocation, although Bucer distinguished between the reigning Christ and a Christian ruler. Rather than emphasising examples of Hebrew Bible kings, such as King David, he put Moses and Joshua forward as examples: in a Protestant interpretation, these figures combined the idea of the priesthood of all believers with the possibility of holding civil authority. This move allowed him to make a case for support for the church, which in his eyes was the means through which the reign of Christ would be built.[87]

238 *Sources*

Martin Bucer, *De Regno Christi*, in *Melanchthon and Bucer*, ed. Wilhelm Puck (Philadelphia, PA: Westminster, 1969), 153–394 (179–191).

———

What the Kingdom of Christ and the Kingdoms of the World Have in Common and What They Do Not

The first point of similarity between the kingdoms of the world and the kingdom of Christ is that one person exercises the supreme power of government. There is a difference, however, inasmuch as the kings of the world, since they cannot be everywhere present ... must establish in various places ... representatives, vice-regents, and other authorities....

But our heavenly King, Jesus Christ, is, according to his promise, with us everywhere and every day.... Therefore, he has no need of representatives to take his place. He does use ministers, and certain specific kinds of offices for his work of salvation....

Secondly, the governance of the kingdoms of this world and of Christ have this in common, that the kings of this world also ought to establish and promote the means of making their citizens devout and righteous who rightly acknowledge and worship their God and who are truly helpful towards their neighbours in all their action....

[However, earthly kings] are not able to purge the hearts of men of their innate impiety and unrighteousness nor endow them with true piety and righteousness. [*However, they can promote piety through good laws.*] But it cannot be expected that this field will bear the fruit of piety and righteousness until Christ our King has breathed his own increase upon the seed of the gospel....

Thirdly, it is common to the kingdoms of this world and to the Kingdom of Christ that they should tolerate the wicked while they lie hidden among the good; but when they have done their impious deeds openly, and will not change their ways when corrected, it is proper to remove them from the commonwealth.... For the Lord has commanded his people quite strictly that they are to drive criminals and incorrigible men from their midst, and to burn them with fire, and thus to wipe out their offensiveness as completely as possible (Deut. 13:5 ff.; 17:2–5; 19:11–21; 21:18–21; 22:13–28; and 24:7).

There is this difference, however, between the administration of the kingdoms of the world and the Kingdom of Christ, that the kings of the world, for the amendment of vice and the removal of unworthy citizens from the commonwealth, use, by God's command, beatings, whippings, prison, exile, and various forms of execution. 'For they do not bear the sword in vain' (Rom. 13:4). But in the Kingdom of Heaven and of Christ, those who have wandered from the way of salvation, if they are curable, are led back to it with the chains of repentance, under the impulse of only the word and the Spirit.... [*Although God often visits notorious sinners with spectacular judgement.*]

Sources   239

[*Fourthly, the kingdoms of the world and of Christ both desire that the people gather together and organise themselves in the proper way. Fifthly, in both kingdoms there is set up a care for life's necessities for the people. In the church, this involves putting others first, sharing temporal goods, and seeing that no poverty exists among Christians. Likewise the king also works to promote these same ends through the use of external power. Sixthly, both kingdoms are engaged in warfare, but one uses the carnal sword and the other the spiritual one.*]

Seventhly, there is this similarity between the kingdoms of the world and the Kingdom of Christ, that just as the kingdoms of the world are subordinated to the Kingdom of Christ, so also is the Kingdom of Christ in its own way subordinated to the kingdoms of this world. [*Christ, subject to no human, was willingly subject to earthly authority while on earth.*] [S]o he wills that his own also should obey from the heart not only the true kings and just princes of this world, but also very iniquitous lords and terrible tyrants to whom public power has been given (I Pet. 2:13–17), not only to pay legitimate taxes, but to observe their edicts with a patient spirit, acquiesce to their unjust judgements, and studiously meet all personal obligations to the State [*respublica*]. This is what the Holy Spirit commanded in the thirteenth chapter of the letter to the Romans....

Further, as the Kingdom of Christ subjects itself to the kingdom and powers of the world, so in turn every true kingdom of the world (I say kingdom, not tyranny) subjects itself to the Kingdom of Christ, and the kings themselves must be the first to do this, for they are eager to develop piety not for themselves alone, but they also seek to lead their subjects to it.... [*He then discourses upon the nature of 'true kings' (i.e., Christian kings) who heed 'true' ministers of God. Few people deserve these true kings, and God grants wicked ones.*]

But if our King, Christ, receives any people into his grace and favour, as of old he made the people of Israel a priestly kingdom, he sets over them princes and kings who, after the example of Moses and Joshua... are primarily concerned about instituting and promulgating religion and allow no one in the commonwealth to violate openly the covenant of the Lord, a covenant of faith and salvation....

It is the duty of all good princes to take every precaution to prevent any one of their subjects from doing injury to another, to prevent children from repudiating the guidance of their parents, slaves from escaping their masters or despising their commands, or anyone from neglecting his duty to any other man....

When pious kings are thus guarding against wrongs against God, the impiety of many is not indeed eliminated, but it is suppressed, lest it be an outrage before God or a stumbling block for the weak. God, the wise and good governor of mankind, has judged it good to have things this way, that the impious may be compelled to contain their impiety within themselves and to feign piety....

240 *Sources*

The Lord promised the people such kings through the prophets, on condition that they fully accept the Kingdom of his Son. But in order to show the secret and celestial power of his Son's kingdom, from the first revelation of his Kingdom to the Gentiles until Saint Constantine, he gave no king to his people; but he tried and proved them with cruel tyrants, even though he granted some respite of peace to them under impious tyrants....

59 *Magdeburg Pastors on Resistance to Authority* (1550)

Keywords: #Resistance, #Natural Law, #Submission, #Tyranny
Region: #Germany
Group: #Lutheran

After the defeat of the **Schmalkaldic League** in 1547, the city of Magdeburg continued to resist Emperor Charles V. Ministers sympathetic to the Reformation, including Nikolaus von Amsdorf, Matthias Flacius Illyricus, Erasmus Alber, and Nikolaus Gallus, justified their resistance. They put forward a doctrine of 'lesser magistrates' to argue for armed resistance to a superior power. Like many of the arguments for resistance in the Reformed tradition, the Magdeburg pastors appealed to scripture and natural law.[88]

Roland H. Bainton, *The Age of the Reformation* (Princeton, NJ: D. Van Nostrand, 1965), 172–173.

———

We will undertake to show that a Christian government may and should defend its subjects against a higher authority which should try to compel the people to deny God's word and practice idolatry. We scarcely expect to convince Catholics that subjects may resist their Lord and a lower magistrate may resist a higher if he seeks to uproot the Christian religion, for the Catholics do not admit that we have the Christian religion and consequently think they have the right to make war upon us. Our object is primarily to allay the scruples of those who adhere to the true Word of God. But first we would address ourselves to the Emperor and beg him not to let the Pope persecute the Lord, Christ [Acts 9:4]. But if your Majesty will not concede that Lutherans are Christians, bear in mind that Christ was considered a blasphemer [Matt. 26:57–67], and He has shown us one mark of the true Church, namely that it should not constrain anyone with the sword as the Roman Church does. Obedience to God and to Caesar are not incompatible, provided each stays within his own proper sphere [Mark 12:17]. Your Majesty has gone beyond your office and encroached upon the Kingdom of Christ....

242 Sources

We will show from Holy Scripture that if a higher magistrate undertakes by force to restore popish idolatry and to suppress or exterminate the pure teaching of the Holy Gospel, as in the present instance, then the lower god-fearing magistrate may defend himself and his subjects against such unjust force in order to preserve the true teaching, the worship of God together with body, life, goods, and honour. The powers that be are ordained of God to protect the good and punish the bad [Rom. 13], but if they start to persecute the good, they are no longer ordained of God. There are to be sure degrees of tyranny and if a magistrate makes unjust war upon his subjects contrary to his plighted oath, they may resist him, though they are not commanded to do so by God. But if a ruler is so demented as to attack God, then he is the very devil who employs mighty potentates in Church and State. When, for example, a prince or an emperor tampers with marriage against the dictates of natural law, then in the name of natural law and Scripture he may be resisted.

60 Katharina von Bora, *Appeal to the King of Denmark* (1550)

Keywords: #Family, #Charity, #Women
Region: #Germany, #Denmark
Group: #Lutheran

Katharina von Bora (1499–1552) was a well-educated nun who escaped her convent with other reform-minded women in 1523. They found refuge, and husbands, in Wittenberg. She married **Martin Luther** in July 1525. They enjoyed an affectionate marriage and brought up six children. The Luther home was both intimate and public. They frequently hosted Reformers from around Europe. She participated in Latin in many lively conversations over dinner, published as *Table Talk* – conversations that are still widely read.[89] Although she has left little direct written trace of her voice, scholars deem her impact on the Reformation to have been significant. Some evangelicals even decried how she influenced Luther. She wholeheartedly threw herself into spreading evangelical ideas. There was mutual respect and admiration between them, and Luther spoke of their equality in Christ.

The death of Martin in 1546 put strains on the strong and resourceful Katharina. Luther controversially desired that she be considered the head of the household after his death, and he left his estate to her, but the lawyers strongly challenged this arrangement. By order, some of her children were sent away, and she lost much of her autonomy and wealth. Geopolitical matters worsened the situation, as the Schmalkaldic War destabilised the region. By 1547, she was in dire financial straits and humbly and boldly appealed to a foreign king, Christian III, of Denmark (she even may have considered relocating there). She asked him to remember Martin's help and offer assistance in return. She appealed again in 1550 (translated below) and desperately a third time in early 1552. This final letter betrayed a sense of abandonment from the very people her family aided. **Philip Melanchthon, Johannes Bugenhagen**, Christian III, and others continued to support her, even when many others turned their backs on her. In an attempt to escape the 1552 plague in Wittenberg, she fell from a wagon and died in December of that year.[90]

244 *Sources*

Erik Pontoppidan, *Annales ecclesiae danicae diplomatici* (Copenhagen: A. Möllers Wittwe, 1741), Book 7, Chapter 3, 307–308. Translated by Mariëtta van der Tol.

———

Illustrious, noble and merciful King and Lord!

I humbly beseech His Royal Highness to mercifully receive my letter, considering, that I am a poor widow, and that my beloved husband, Doctor Martin Luther (blessed be his memory), faithfully served Christianity and in particular gracefully served His Royal Highness.

Now, His Royal Highness gracefully gifted my beloved husband 50 Thalers yearly for numerous years. For this, I humbly give thanks to His Royal Highness, and I constantly pray for His Royal Highness. But since I and my children have had little help and the unrest of this time brings many burdens, I beseech His Royal Highness to mercifully provide such help again.

Because I have no doubt that His Royal Highness has not forgotten the enormous burden and labour of my beloved husband. Moreover, His Royal Highness is the only king on earth, with whom we poor Christians may find refuge. And God will, without doubt, because of such kindness granted to the poor Christians pastors and their poor widows and children, grant special gifts and blessings to His Royal Highness – for which I will faithfully and earnestly intercede.

The almighty God may gracefully protect His Royal Highness, her royal highness the Queen, and the young Prince.

Datum Witteberg 6 October, Anno Domini 1550.

In humility to His Royal Highness,

Katharina, surviving widow of Doctor Martin Luther.

61 Menno Simons, *Magistrates, Marriage and Rebellion* (c.1552)

Keywords: #Magistrate, #Authority, #Submission, #Love, #Communal Living, #Property, #Charity, #Marriage, #Sexuality, #Non-violence
Region: #Netherlands, #Germany
Group: #Anabaptist, #Mennonite

In an earlier source, Menno Simons denounced the **Blasphemy of Münster's King David**. In it, he rejected the idea of the New Jerusalem in Münster and the self-identification of Jan van Leiden as the new King David. Simons thought the principle error at Munster was their close identification with the physical politics of the biblical Israelites under the law. His solution was to emphasise the New Testament and the creation narrative of Genesis. Nearly two decades later, Simons was still warding off accusations that he was sympathetic with the violent theopolitics of Münster and that his followers harboured a secret lust for world domination. In the following excerpt, he replied to slanderous accusations made against him and his co-religionists. By explaining their beliefs and practices, he hoped to end their persecution. He refuted the charge that they opposed the government, that they practised communal property ownership and polygamy, that their church discipline did not allow for post-baptism sin and repentance, and that they taught that perfection was possible. In the following excerpt, Simons addressed several of these issues and offered some guidelines for how Christianity should influence government. Whereas Simons was accused of disregarding the relationship between the magistrate and the Christian, he argued that the witness of scripture raised the bar for how a magistrate should act. By this higher standard, 'Christian' magistrates were shown to oppose Christ.[91]

"A Humble and Christian Defence", in *The Complete Works of Menno Simons* (Elkhart, IN: John F. Funk and Brother, 1871), 301–323 (301–310).

———

In the first place, they complain and accuse us of being Munsterites; and warn all people to beware of us and take example from those of Münster.

246   *Sources*

We do not like to reprove and judge those who are already reproved and judged of God and man; yet, as we are wrongly attacked and accused by our opponents, and that without truthfulness, therefore we would say in defence of us all that we consider the Munsterian doctrine and life, in regard to king, sword, rebellion, retaliation, revenge, polygamy and the temporal kingdom of Christ, as a new Jewism, and a misleading error, doctrine and abomination which is not at all in keeping with the Spirit, word and example of Christ. Behold, in Christ, we lie not....

I have never seen Munster nor have I ever been in their communion. And I trust that by the grace of the Lord, I shall never eat nor drink with such if there should yet be any, as the Scripture teaches me not to do; unless they sincerely acknowledge their abomination and truly repent, and follow the truth of the gospel in a becoming manner....

In short, we herewith, testify and confess before God, before you, before the whole world, that we, from our inmost hearts, detest the errors and abominations of the Munsterites....

In the second place they say that we will not obey the magistracy.

The writings which we have published during several years past abundantly prove that this accusation against us is wrong and untrue. We now publicly confess that the office of a magistrate is ordained of God, as we ever confessed since we serve, according to our small talent, the word of the Lord. And in the meantime, we have ever obeyed them when not contrary to the word of God, and we intend to do so all our lives; for we are not so stupid as not to know what the Lord's word commands in this respect. We render unto Caesar the things which are Caesar's as Christ teaches (Matt. 17:22); we pray for the imperial majesty, kings, lords, princes and all in authority, honour and obey them (1 Tim. 2:2; Rom. 13:1). And yet they cry that we will not be subject to and obey the powers that be, that they may disturb the hearts of those that have authority and excite bitterness against us, and that, thus, by their continual cries the bloody sword may be unmercifully used against us and never be sheathed (Rom. 13:7; Tit. 3:2; 1 Pet. 2:13).

[*Simons argues that so-called 'Christian' rulers and judges fail to take seriously God's word concerning magistrates. Moses commanded rulers to make copies of the law and practice the statutes. The king was to be humble, not covetous and not accumulate horses or wives (Deut. 17:16–20; Exod. 18:21). Judges are to impartially hear cases and refuse the bribe (Deut. 1:16–17; 2 Chron. 19:6–7). And rulers are to punish the wicked, not the good (Rom. 13:3–4). If these things are not practiced, and if the rulers will not submit to Christ, they 'cannot possibly avoid' divine judgement. They do not protect the good, provide for the needy, judge fairly or protect against violence, and indeed they promote the opposite. They obey the wicked magistrates of scripture, not the godly ones.*]

Inasmuch as the scale of justice is so very much out of balance; and as you are chosen and ordained of God to judge without respect to person and to deliver from the hands of the oppressor all the afflicted and oppressed strangers; therefore we pray you humbly, most beloved rulers and judges, for the sake of him who has called and chosen you to your offices, that you do not believe these cruel and envious men, who, according to Peter are born to corruption and torture; and who, ever publicly and privately, make us so obnoxious, by their cries, that we are not allowed a hearing and facing – so long as they, in our presence, do not prove (which, we are sure, they cannot do) against us that which they every day from their throne of pestilences and mockery, so shamefully proclaim to the world, to the shame and injury of great numbers of pious and godfearing children. Beloved rulers, we beseech you for Christ's sake, to fear and love God sincerely. Believe his true word and act accordingly (Isa. 1:23; Ps. 73:6).

In the third place, they say, That we are rebellious; that we would take cities and countries if we had the power.

This prophecy is false and will ever remain so....

The Scriptures teach that there are two opposing princes and two opposite kingdoms. The one is the Prince of peace; the other the prince of rebellion. Each of the princes has his particular kingdom and as the prince is, so is also the kingdom. The Prince of peace is Christ Jesus; his kingdom is the kingdom of peace, which is his church; his messengers are the messengers of peace; his word is the word of peace; and his body is the body of peace; his children are the seed of peace; and his inheritance and reward are the inheritance and reward of peace.... In short, with this King and in his kingdom and reign it is nothing but peace; everything that is seen, heard and done is peace (Rom. 10:15; Isa. 52:7; 9:6; Luke 2:7).

Peter was commanded to sheathe his sword. All Christians are commended to love their enemies; to do good unto those who abuse and persecute them; if any man shall smite thee on thy right cheek, turn to him the other, and if he take away thy coat, let him have thy cloak also. Say, beloved, how can a Christian, scripturally, retaliate, rebel, war, murder, slay, torture, steal, rob and burn cities and conquer countries (Matt. 5:12, 39, 40; 26:52; John 18:10)?...

Behold, reader, such a rebellion [against wicked spiritual powers] we seek and cause; but never, a rebellion of carnality. Not if we were as numerous as the spears of grass and the sand upon the sea shore....

In the fourth place, some of them charge that we have our property in common.

This charge is false and without truth. We do not teach and practice the doctrine of having goods in common. But we teach and maintain by the word of the Lord, that all truly believing Christians are members of one body and are baptised by one Spirit into one body (1 Cor. 12:13); they are partakers of one bread (1 Cor. 10:18); that they may have one Lord and one God (Eph. 4:4–6).

Inasmuch as they are thus one, therefore it is Christian and reasonable that they divinely love one another, and that the one member be solicitous for the

248 *Sources*

welfare of the other, for thus both the Scripture and nature teach. The whole Scriptures speak of mercifulness and love; and it is the only sign whereby a true Christian may be known, as the Lord says, 'By this shall all men know that ye are my disciples (that is, that ye are Christians), if ye have love one to another' (John 13:35).

Beloved reader, it is not customary that an intelligent person clothes and cares for one part of his body and leaves the rest destitute and naked. O, no. The intelligent person is solicitous for all his members. Thus it should be with those who are the Lord's church and body. All those who are born of God, who are gifted with the Spirit of the Lord, and who, according to the Scriptures, are called into one body of love in Christ Jesus, are prepared by such love, to serve their neighbours, not only with money and goods, but also after the example of their Lord and Head, Jesus Christ, in an evangelical manner, with life and blood. They show mercy and love, as much as they can; suffer no beggars amongst them; take to heart the needs of the saints; receive the miserable; take the stranger into their houses; console the afflicted; assist the needy; clothe the naked; do not turn their face from the poor, and do not despise their own flesh (Isa. 58:7–8; Rom. 12:13).

Behold such a community we teach. And not, that one should take and possess the land and property of the other, as many falsely charge....

In the fifth place some of them falsely charge, That we believe in polygamy; that we have our women in common....

As to polygamy we would say, The Scriptures show that before the law, some patriarchs had many wives. Yet they did not take the same liberty under the law and before the law....

As each period has had its particular liberty and usage according to the Scriptures; and as we now, under the New Testament, are not pointed by the Lord to the usage of the patriarchs before the law nor under the law, in the matter of marriage, but to the beginning of creation, to Adam and Eve (which word we sincerely desire to obey); therefore we teach, practice and consent to no other than the one which was in the beginning in Adam and Eve, namely, one husband and one wife, as the Lord's mouth has ordained (Matt. 19).

62 Hugh Latimer, *Obedience to God's Will Requires Submission* (1553)

Keywords: #Submission, #Authority, #Magistrate, #Rebellion
Region: #England
Group: #Church of England

Hugh Latimer (c.1485–1555) was born in Thurcaston (Leicestershire) and studied at Clare Hall (Cambridge), where he became a fellow. He defended Catholicism until around 1524, but became renowned for his preaching that pushed England towards Reformation. Latimer was animated not only by some of the ideas of **Martin Luther** but also by the much longer reforming tradition in England dating to John Wycliffe. Latimer cared about the day-to-day condition of the laity and criticised their economic exploitation. His work attracted positive attention from some in Henry VIII's mercurial court, and he frequently preached before **Edward VI**.

The following sermon was delivered in 1553, around the end of Edward's reign, and printed in 1562, a few years into the reign of the Protestant Queen, **Elizabeth I**. The sermon was delivered in the context of an uprising, and Latimer discussed the relationship between the will of God and the possibility of rebellion. According to him, limited disobedience was permissible when magistrates commanded what was ungodly. Rebellion, on the contrary, would never be the will of God. After England transitioned from Edward to the Catholic Mary, some English Protestants attempted to exclude Mary from the throne or else topple her regime once she was in power. Despite the risk of persecution, Latimer did not flee from or fight the reimposition of Catholicism, and he was burned at the stake in 1555.[92]

Hugh Latimer, *27 sermons preached by the ryght Reuerende father in God and constant matir* [sic] *of Iesus Christe, Maister Hugh Latimer* (London, 1562), Fol. 22–25. Text modernised by the editors.

———

250   *Sources*

The fourth Sermon of Mr. Latimer made upon the Lord's prayer.

Fiat voluntas tua, thy will be done....

Almighty God has revealed his will concerning magistrates, how he will have them honoured and obeyed. They [the rebels] were utterly bent against it, he revealed this will in many places of the Scripture: but especially by St. Peter where he says.... 'Be ye subject to all the common laws made by men of authority, by the king's majesty and his most honourable council, or by a common parliament, be subject unto them, obey them saith God' [1 Pet. 2:13–14]. And here is but one exception to this rule, that is, when obedience requires going against God. When laws are made against God and his word, then I ought to obey God rather than man [Acts 5: 29]. Then I may refuse to obey, with a good conscience: yet for all that, I may not rise up against the magistrates nor make any uproar. For if I do so, I sin damnably: I must be content to suffer whatsoever God shall lay upon me, yet I may not obey their laws. Men may only refuse to obey in this case; in all the other matters, we ought to obey. Whatever laws they make concerning outward things, we ought to obey and certainly not rebel, however hard, noisome and hurtful they are: our duty is to obey, and commit all the matters unto God, not doubting that God will punish them when they act contrary to their office and calling. Therefore wait till God correct them, we may not take it upon ourselves to reform them. For it is not part of our duty. If the rebels (I say) had considered this, do you think they would have preferred their own will before God's will?

[*Magistrates are also to be submissive to God's will by acting appropriately towards subjects. If they transgress divine and human law, God alone is the avenger.*] But magistrates must take heed that they go no further than God allows: If they do, they shall be personally punished. There are many examples in Scripture where it is demonstrated how God has grievously punished wicked magistrates.

63 Sébastien Castellion, *Concerning Heretics and Those Who Burn Them* (1554)

Keywords: #Heresy, #Coercion, #Violence, #Persecution, #Excommunication, #Love, #Censorship, #Toleration
Region: #France, #Switzerland
Group: #Reformed | #Lutheran, #Catholic, #Anabaptist, #Zwinglian, #Islam

Sébastien Castellion (1515–1563) was born in Saint-Martin-du-Fresne (France) and embraced Reformation principles while studying in Lyon. He moved to Strasbourg in 1540, during the period when **John Calvin** joined **Martin Bucer** in the Reformation of that city. However, he came into conflict with Calvin, lost his authority and permission to pastor, and moved to Basel in 1545. By 1553, he was professor of Greek at the university there. He edited several texts and completed the translation of the Bible into humanist Latin in 1551 and French in 1555. He dedicated the earlier translation to **Edward VI** and argued for religious toleration. Castellion continued to be a voice for toleration, and when religious conflict erupted in his home country, he wrote **Advice to a Desolate France** (1562). In that work, he urged Catholics and Protestants to eschew persecution and tone down their vitriolic rhetoric.

Castellion is best known for challenging the killing of heretics. The excerpt below was prompted by the execution of **Michael Servetus** in Geneva. It featured familiar arguments for toleration, such as the possibility of error or the disproportionality of a death sentence on account of heresy. Castellion seems to argue that ideas should never be opposed through violence, but rather with ideas and with proper arguments.[93]

Other Reformers, including **Theodore Beza** and Calvin, condemned Castellion's arguments in support of toleration. Castellion's source is structured as a dialogue between Calvin (via assertions drawn from his book) and Vaticanus (Castellion's pseudonym). The following excerpts reproduce only Castellion's reply, but the nature of Calvin's argument is apparent. Castellion showed a biting and barbed playfulness as he undermined Calvin's claims.

Sébastien Castellion, "Reply to Calvin's Book", in *Concerning Heretics: Whether They Are to be Persecuted and How They Are to be Treated: A Collection of the Opinions of Learned Men Both Ancient and Modern*, ed.

252   *Sources*

Roland H. Bainton (New York: Columbia, 1935), 265–287 (266–267, 269, 271, 276–277, 279–282). Reprinted with permission of Columbia University Press.

———

Vaticanus. You [Calvin] have only yourself to blame [for the spread of Servetus' ideas].... [N]ow that the man has been burned with his books, everybody is burning with a desire to read them....

Vaticanus. [Calvin] wishes to kill all heretics and wishes to hold as heretics all who disagree with him. His program would call for the extermination of all the Papists, Lutherans, Zwinglians, Anabaptists, and the rest. There would survive only Calvinists, Jews, and Turks, whom he excepts....

Vaticanus.... Before the coming of Christ there is no mention of heretics in the whole law.... I do not deny that there were heretics, but I do not find that the law prescribes any penalty for them. In the New Testament I find that they are to be avoided [e.g., Rom. 16:17]. So the penalty is not mitigated, but altered....

Vaticanus. He [Calvin] is wroth that anyone should declare the Scriptures obscure. He thinks them clear. He contradicts Zwingli who considers them obscure, and he contradicts himself who writes so many commentaries to explain what is so clear....

Vaticanus.... The true Church will be known by love which proceeds from faith, whose precept is certain [John 13:25] .... The doctrine of piety is to love your enemies, bless those that curse you, to hunger and thirst after righteousness, and endure persecution for righteousness' sake.... [Matt. 5] These and similar matters are certain, however dubious may be the obscure questions about the Trinity, predestination, election, and the rest on account of which men are regarded as heretics....

Vaticanus.... If Servetus had attacked you by arms, you had rightly been defended by the magistrate; but since he opposed you in writings, why did you oppose them with iron and flame? ...

Vaticanus.... To assert one's faith is not to burn a man, but rather to be burned....

Vaticanus.... Calvin boasts that he did not cut out Servetus's tongue. But he did cut off his life and burn his books.... Yet Calvin thinks that everyone should accept his judgement about Servetus and make no further inquiry after our master has made his pronouncement. Why did he burn the books [when the Qur'an and licentious classical authors are permitted in Geneva]?...

Vaticanus. When theft, rapine, adultery, and murder are punished they are not punished in order to establish the kingdom of Christ, to justify men, to save men, to generate a new creature, but to protect the bodies and possessions of the good....

Vaticanus. To kill a man is not to defend a doctrine, but to kill a man. When the Genevans killed Servetus they did not defend a doctrine; they killed a man.....

Sources 253

Vaticanus. 'No man can come to me, except the Father which hath sent me draw him [John 6:44]'. These persecutors wish the magistrate to draw men who are unwilling to be drawn by God, as if the magistrate could accomplish more than God....

Vaticanus.... Wolves come in sheep's clothing, but within they are ravening. By their fruits ye shall know them [Matt. 7:15–16]. The fruit of the wolf is to eat raw flesh. Hence, not those who are killed, but those who kill are wolves....

Vaticanus.... To kill a man is not to amputate a member.... When a man is killed as a heretic he is not amputated from the body of Christ [e.g., 1 Cor. 12:27], but from the life of the body. Otherwise, if the death of the body were amputation, all who die would be amputated from the Church...

Vaticanus. To root out the tares is to pronounce someone to be reprobate and cut off forever from the body of Christ. This should not be done before the day of the Lord [Matt. 13:24–30]....

Vaticanus.... You might as well argue: If ministers have authority over the souls of magistrates, how much more over their bodies? If with a word Peter struck Ananias [Acts 5:1–11], how much more Malchus with a sword [John 18:10]? If Elias was permitted to bring down fire from heaven to destroy the king's messengers [1 Kgs 18:36–40], how much more might the apostles burn the Samaritans [Luke 9:54]? If Moses might kill the Egyptian [Exod. 2:11–15], how much more might Christ? These are the fallacies devised by the sophists to impel men to shed blood....

Vaticanus. All sects hold their religion as established by the Word of God and call it certain. Therefore all sects are armed by Calvin's rule for mutual persecution. Calvin says he is certain, and they say the same. He says they are mistaken, and they say the same of him. Calvin wishes to be judge, and so do they. Who will be judge? Who made Calvin judge of all the sects, that he alone should kill? How can he prove that he alone knows? He has the Word of God, so have they. If the matter is so certain, to whom is it certain? To Calvin?...

64 Theodore Beza, *The Authority of the Magistrate in Punishing Heretics* (1554)

Keywords: #Heresy, #Blasphemy, #Crime, #Capital Crime, #Violence
Region: #France, #Switzerland
Group: #Reformed, #Calvinist

Theodore Beza (1516–1605) was born in Vézelay (France) and trained in law from a young age in Orléans. After practising law in Paris, he converted to Protestantism and moved to Geneva before teaching Greek at Lausanne. He was a poet and playwright, and he published the popular play *Abraham Sacrifiant* in 1550, shortly after his conversion. He made a significant contribution to the development of the Genevan Psalter, which is still in use in parts of the Reformed Church in and beyond Europe. After returning to Geneva at Calvin's request in 1557, he helped founding the Genevan Academy in 1559 and influenced a generation of Reformed ministers from across the continent. He was a prolific theologian who also contributed to several translations of scripture. After Calvin's death, he led the church in Geneva and the wider French Reformed movement. In 1586, he participated in the Colloquy of Montbéliard, yet another fruitless attempt to heal the rift between Lutherans and the Reformed, as well as to settle debates about who possessed regional authority in religious matters.

Beza dedicated a prayer book to **Elizabeth I**, and in 1562 (at the outbreak of the French Wars of Religion), he implored her aid on behalf of French Protestant refugees. In *Du droit des magistrats* (1574), he anonymously responded to the massacre on St. Bartholomew's Day (1572). Beza is typically identified as a Monarchomach – a term later given to Huguenots who theorised about the limits of the sovereign, the justice of resistance, and the possibility of tyrannicide. 'Bèze's thesis', writes Jill Raitt,

> was that all authority, including the authority of the French king, comes from God through election by the people. Kings remain responsible to the people, and if they abuse their authority by playing the tyrant, the people may rise up under the leadership of their elected magistrates.[94]

Sources 255

The massacre pushed theorists to articulate less-compromising resistance theories, and classic texts include **François Hotman's** *Francogallia* (1573), **Innocent Gentillet's** *Anti-Machiavel* (1576), and the anonymous *Vindiciæ Contra Tyrannos* (1579).

The following excerpt comes from a 1554 publication, *De haereticis a civili magistratu puniendis* – a pointed response to **Sebastian Castellio's** denunciation of the execution of **Michael Servetus**. In it, Beza acknowledged that Christian charity was the rule, but he denied that charity required allowing a heretic to spread their ideas. He framed heresy as an existential threat to the church of God, and even wounding God's majesty. If the punishment was measured by the status of the injured party, he argued, then executing a heretic was mild. Further, Beza argued that heretics denied what they knew to be true (they have been 'shown and convicted'). Beza rejected the possibility of genuine, scripturally derived differences of opinion on matters considered heresy, and a century later, John Cotton would make a similar argument when justifying the expulsion of **Roger Williams**.

Theodore Beza, *The Authority of the Magistrate in Punishing Heretics* (1544), trans. Michael W. Bruening, in *A Reformation Sourcebook: Documents from an Age of Debate*, ed. Michael W. Bruening (Toronto, ON: University of Toronto Press, 2017), 262–264. Reprinted with permission of the publisher.

———

Heretics are simply those who want to be considered Christians but who, after being duly shown and convicted of their error by the word of God, nevertheless prefer to follow their own judgement and obstinately and persistently support false articles of religion against the church.... Now such monstrous spirits are incredibly dangerous plagues in the church and are the true instruments of the devil for overturning the church....

As God created all things for himself, the chief end of human society is for God to be honoured by humans as he ought to be. Now the magistrate is established as the guard and governor of this society. It follows, then, that in its administration and conduct, the magistrate should have regard for the state of religion. And he cannot preserve and maintain religion unless he reprimand by the punishment of the sword those who obstinately hold religion in contempt and form sects....

There are certain crimes which are such that ... they are held, as by common right, for capitol crimes among all nations, ... such as parricide, premeditated homicide, sacrilege, blasphemy, impiety, or crime against the received religion of the land.... [A]s for the crime of blasphemy and impiety, I am amazed how some people call this into doubt. For everyone agrees that the enormity of the crime should be measured according to the quality of the victim.... And if this is true, it also follows, as I believe, that just as the glory

256 *Sources*

of God is more excellent than the honour of men, so also blasphemy and impiety are great and enormous crimes....

But if together with blasphemy and impiety there is also heresy, ... what crime could one find among humans that is greater and more outrageous? Certainly, if one wants to order a punishment according to the enormity of the crime, it seems to me that one could not even find a torment corresponding to the enormity of such a crime.... Indeed, anyone who attempts in the assembly and company of the church to corrupt the true service of God lights a fire which could spread, causing the eternal damnation of an infinite number of persons.... Therefore, whether the magistrate aims to maintain the glory of God or wants to preserve human society whole, there is no one whom he should punish with greater rigor and severity than heretics, blasphemers, and those who hold religion in contempt.

65 Heinrich Bullinger, *Obedience to Lawful Female Magistrates* (1554)

Keywords: #Authority, #Magistrate, #Women, #Submission, #Tyranny, #Rebellion, #Idolatry
Region: #Switzerland, #Scotland, #England
Group: #Reformed, #Zwinglian

Heinrich Bullinger (1504–1575) was the preeminent leader of the Reformation in Zürich after the death of Huldreich Zwingli on the battlefield. His theology emphasised the importance of biblical covenants and the ongoing authority of the Hebrew Bible for the church, although its meaning was mediated through the figure of Christ. Bullinger left a lasting impact on the Reformed tradition by contributing to the *First Helvetic Confession* (1536) and writing a personal confession, which became the *Second Helvetic Confession* (1562).[95]

Bullinger's influence on the English church was profound. He maintained an extensive correspondence with men and women in England, ministered to British refugees, and was widely read across the British Isles. His most influential work, *Sermonum Decades quinique*, was published in 1552 and translated into English in 1577. John Whitgift, Archbishop of Canterbury, required that every minister read the lengthy work.[96] In it, he argued that magistrates and ministers should be distinct but dependent on one another. The *Decades* contained lengthy reflections on the international use of the sword in matters of faith, leaving a lasting impact on discussions of just war. He also suggested that rebellion and removing a tyrant might be done at God's leading. Like his contemporaries, he described **Edward VI** as Josiah and argued that he should rule in a biblically informed way. This would include meting out punishment for civil and religious offences. In a section on why the New Testament did not advocate punishing heretics, Bullinger suggested that if Paul had written a letter to a magistrate, the apostle would have undoubtedly advocated using the sword.

Bullinger wrote the following letter in response to the queries of an unnamed Scotsman (presumed to be **John Knox**, but some have suggested it may have been **Christopher Goodman**). At the time, England was amidst

258   *Sources*

a sudden transition from Protestant to Catholic – and from male to female rule. This Scotsman was concerned about the Queen's lover, Philip of Spain. Parliament had to decide on the nature of the relationship between Philip and the kingdoms of England and Scotland. Bullinger maintained an interesting position. On the one hand, he did not support female rule, but on the other hand, he recognised that a woman could hold authority lawfully. This evidences how many in the Reformed tradition lived with the tension between convictions that may derive from scripture and practices in nature or law that may deviate from those convictions.

"Certain Questions Concerning Obedience to Lawful Magistrates, with Answers by Bullinger" (26 March 1554), in *The Works of John Knox* (Edinburgh: Johnstone and Hunter, 1854), ed. David Lang, III:221–226.

———

An answer given to a certain Scotsman, in reply to some Questions concerning the Kingdom of Scotland and England.

1. *Whether the Son of a King, upon his father's death, though unable by reason of his tender age to conduct the government of the kingdom, is nevertheless by right of inheritance to be regarded as a lawful magistrate, and as such to be obeyed as of divine right.*

     That person is, in my opinion, to be esteemed as a lawful King, who is ordained according to the just laws of the country. And thus it is clear that Edward VI of happy memory was ordained. For his father on his death-bed appointed him King, and so claimed for him the right of sovereignty, which they say is hereditary. The States of the kingdom acknowledged him, as they testified by his coronation. They provided him with councillors, endued as he was with the great gifts of God; nor was anything wanting to that kingdom, which is wont to be looked for in the most prosperous kingdom elsewhere. He was therefore a lawful Sovereign, and his laws and ordinances demanded obedience; and he ruled the kingdom after a more godly manner than the three most wise and prosperous kings of that country who immediately preceded him.

2. *Whether a Female can preside over, and rule a kingdom by divine right, and so transfer the right of sovereignty to her Husband?*

     The law of God ordains the woman to be in subjection, and not to rule; which is clear from the writings of both the Old and New Testament. But if a woman in compliance with, or in obedience to the laws and customs of the realm, is acknowledged as Queen, and, in maintenance of the hereditary right of government, is married to a Husband, or in the meantime holds the reins of government by means of her councillors, it is a hazardous thing for a godly person to set themselves in opposition to political regulations; especially as the gospel does not seem to unsettle or abrogate hereditary rights, and the political laws of kingdoms; nor do we read that Philip the eunuch [Acts 8:26–40], by right of the gospel, drove out Candace from the kingdom of Ethiopia. And if the reigning Sovereign be not a Deborah [Judg. 4], but an ungodly and tyrannous ruler of the kingdom, godly persons have an example and consolation in the case of Athaliah [2 Kings 11:1–12:16; 2 Chron. 22:10–12]. The Lord will in his own time destroy unjust governments by his own people, to whom he will supply proper qualifications for this purpose, as he formerly did to Jerubbaal [Gideon, Judg. 6:32], and the Maccabees, and Jehoiada [2 Chron. 23]. With respect, however, to her right of transferring the power of government to her Husband, those persons who are acquainted with the laws and customs of the realm can furnish the proper answer.

3. *Whether obedience is to be rendered to a Magistrate who enforces idolatry and condemns true religion; and whether those authorities, who are still in military occupation of towns and fortresses, are permitted to repel this ungodly violence from themselves and their friends.*

The history of Daniel, and the express command of God (Matt. 10:16–20), and the examples of the apostles in Acts 4 and 5, as also that of many of the martyrs in ecclesiastical history, teach us that we must not obey the king or magistrate when their commands are opposed to God and his lawful worship; but rather that we should expose our persons, and lives, and fortunes to danger. This power is the power of darkness, as the Lord saith in the gospel. And Eusebius records ... that the Armenians took arms against their lawful sovereigns, the Roman emperors, who desired to force them to idolatry. And this conduct is not reproved. Those very Armenians, many years after, by reason of the ungodliness of the kings of Persia, slew their ungodly commanders, and revolted to the Emperor Justinian.... For the Holy Scriptures not only permits, but even enjoins upon the magistrate a just and necessary defence.

But as other objects are often aimed at under the pretext of a just and necessary assertion or maintenance of right, and the worst characters mix themselves with the good, and the times too are full of danger; it is very difficult to pronounce upon every particular case. For an accurate knowledge of the circumstances is here of great importance; and as I do not possess such knowledge, it would be very foolish in me to recommend or determine anything specific upon the subject. For even Paul, we read, made use of the Roman soldiery against those who plotted against him [Acts 23], and was right in doing so: yet at another time, though under almost the same or similar circumstances, he is recorded to have only used the arms of patience, and none else. There is need, therefore, in cases of this kind, of much prayer, and much wisdom, lest by precipitancy and corrupt affections we should so act as to occasion mischief to many worthy persons. Meanwhile, however, death itself is far preferable to the admission of idolatry.

260 *Sources*

4. *To which party must Godly persons attach themselves, in the case of a religious Nobility resisting an idolatrous Sovereign?*

I leave this to be decided by the judgement of godly persons, who are well acquainted with all the circumstances, who look up in all things to the Word of God, who attempt nothing contrary to the laws of God, who obey the impulses of the Holy Ghost, and who are guided by circumstances of place, time, opportunity, and things, without making any rash attempt, and who can therefore be directed more safely by their own sense of duty than by the consciences of others. But I would advise them, above all things, that those causes may be removed, on account of which hypocrites are predominant: iniquities, I mean, that we may become reconciled to God by true repentance, and implore his counsel and assistance. He is the only and true deliverer; and, as we read in the books of Judges and Kings, and the Ecclesiastical histories, has never been wanting to his Church. Let us lift up our eyes to Him, waiting for his deliverance, abstaining in the meantime from all superstition and idolatry, and doing what he reveals to us in his Word.

66 *The Peace of Augsburg* (1555)

Keywords: #Treaty, #Toleration, #Pluralism, #Coercion, #Church-State Relations
Region: #Germany
Group: #Roman Catholic, #Lutheran

The unsettled relationship between Catholics and Lutherans in the Holy Roman Empire contributed to ongoing tensions and violent conflict. The Peace of Augsburg, negotiated by the Diet of the Holy Roman Empire between 1554 and 1555, provided a trans-regional legal framework for religious toleration. The treaty is famous for the principle of *cuius regio eius religio,* which would play a significant role again in the Peace of Westphalia (1648). This principle allowed princes to determine whether their territory would be Catholic or Lutheran. Some places, like Imperial Cities, remained bi-confessional. However, the Peace of Augsburg was not intended as a permanent arrangement: it depended on the expectation that religious differences would eventually be resolved and religious unity be restored. Although the Peace of Augsburg is known as a toleration settlement, its aim was not to secure toleration; it was intended to secure 'the peace of the land', to which toleration at the time was believed to be instrumental. Moreover, this toleration was conditional upon the respect for public order and peace, the breach of which came with a threat of punishment on behalf of the entire Diet.

The Peace of Augsburg only applied to Lutherans (those of the *Augsburg Confession*) and not to other and ever-increasing branches of Protestantism. This means that it did not protect Anabaptist and Reformed minorities. It allowed for freedom of movement, relative freedom of worship, and property for those covered by the arrangement. The listing of types of property suggests that the priority of the parties was with the position of the princes themselves, rather than with their subjects. Other clauses related to confiscated church lands, ecclesiastical jurisdiction, and the renunciation of private wars. Although the Peace was only meant as a temporary measure, it remained in place until the Thirty Years' War (1618–1648). At the conclusion of this war, the 1648 Treaty of Westphalia reaffirmed many of these specific provisions.

262   *Sources*

The papacy strongly objected to the religious clauses that were brokered in 1555 and 1648, particularly as more rulers throughout northern Europe moved towards the Reformation. In response, Pope Paul IV issued the bull *Cum ex Apostolatus officio* in 1559, arguing for the general deposition of heretical rulers. Pious V would issue *Regnans in Excelsis* (1570) specifically against England's **Elizabeth I.**

Emil Reich, *Selected Documents Illustrating Mediæval and Modern History* (London: P.S. King, 1905), 230–232. Section 14 from James Harvey Robinson, *Readings in European History* (Boston, MA: Ginn & Company, 1906), II:116.

———

14 But since in many free and imperial cities both religions – namely, our old religion and that of the Augsburg Confession – have hitherto come into existence and practice, the same shall remain hereafter and be held in the same cities; and citizens and inhabitants of the said free and imperial cities, whether spiritual or secular in rank, shall peacefully and quietly dwell with one another; and no party shall venture to abolish the religion, church customs, or ceremonies of the other, or persecute them thereof.

15 In order to bring peace into the holy Empire of the Germanic Nation between the Roman Imperial Majesty and the Electors, Princes and Estates: let neither his Imperial Majesty nor the Electors, Princes &c. do any violence or harm to any estate of the empire on account of the Augsburg Confession, but let them enjoy their religious belief, liturgy and ceremonies as well as their estates and other rights and privileges in peace; and complete religious peace shall be obtained only by Christian means of amity, or under threat of the punishment of the imperial ban.

16 Likewise the Estates espousing the Augsburg Confession shall let all the Estates and Princes who cling to the old religion live in absolute peace and in the enjoyment of all their estates, rights and privileges.

17 However all such as do not belong to the two above named religions shall not be included in the present peace but be totally excluded from it....

20 The ecclesiastical jurisdiction over the Augsburg Confession, dogma, Appointment of Ministers, Church ordinances, and Ministries hitherto practised (but apart from all the rights of the Electors, Princes and Estates Colleges and Monasteries to taxes in money or tithes), shall, from now cease and the Augsburg Confession shall be left to the free and untrammelled enjoyment of their religion, ceremonies, appointment of ministers, as is stated in a subsequent separate article, until the final transaction of religion will take place.

23 No estate shall try to persuade the subjects of other estates to abandon their religion nor protect them against their own magistrates. Such as

had from olden times the rights of patronage are not included in the present article.

24 In case our subjects whether belonging to the old religion or the Augsburg Confession should intend leaving their homes with their wives and children in order to settle in another place, they shall be hindered neither in the sale of their estates after due payment of the local taxes nor injured in their honour.

67 John Calvin, *International Relations and National Boundaries* (1555)

Keywords: #Land, #International Relations, #War, #Equity, #Love
Region: #Switzerland
Group: #Reformed, #Calvinist

The following excerpt by John Calvin reads as a theology of international relations. Calvin fronts the importance of shared humanity, based on the Imago Dei: all people are made in the image of God, are fundamentally related to each other, and therefore ought not to be arbitrarily harmed. It leads Calvin to conclude that unjust violence is a breach of the natural order and an act of rebellion against God. He builds this argument on his understanding of Deuteronomy 2:4–5, in which Israelites are told not to harm their 'cousins', the children of Esau, when they pass through their territory on the way to Canaan. However, Calvin is realistic enough to understand that wars and violence do happen and that boundaries can change due to sinful desires. Namely, if a ruler unjustly attacks a neighbour, the victim may understand this as a sign that God will depose this ruler on account of his unjust behaviour. The victim may even have a right to their neighbour's land. In a later sermon, he argued that God's presence in war depended on the presence of justice, and he placed higher restrictions on conduct in war. What stands out is his explicit affirmation that enemies, too, are made in the image and likeness of God.[97]

John Calvin, *The sermons of M. John Calvin upon the fifth booke of Moses called Deuteronomie*, trans. Arthur Golding (London, 1583), 62–64. Text modernised by the editors.

———

The Eleventh Sermon on Chapter 2 (25 April 1555)

[Deuteronomy 2:1–7]

Another point is, *That God gave Mount Seir in possession to Esau*: it was his lot. When he had excluded him from the land of Canaan, he gave him the other country for himself and his successors. Forasmuch then as it was assigned him of God: it was not for men to attempt to deprive or bereave him thereof.

Now as touching this brotherhood, God will have it to move us [Calvin's audience], and to be as a certain bond to knit us together, so as nature may persuade us to be kind-hearted one to another, and restrain us from doing wrong or harm to any man. True it is that there is not fleshly kindred between all men, to make them so near of blood that they might call one another cousins, and name themselves by any lineage whereof both were descended: but yet there is a certain common kindred in general, which is, that all men ought to think how they are fashioned after God's image, and that there is one nature common among them all. Even the heathen men knew that very well. So then, whereas we have some discretion to maintain peace and concord, and to yield every man his right without taking away any man's goods, and without committing any extortion or outrage: and we pervert the order of nature and are worse than the wild beasts which make countenance one to another when they are all of one kind. For the wolves are not at such variance among themselves as men are.

And therefore let us learn that although there is not any near kindred among us, yet notwithstanding inasmuch as we are men, there ought to be some common bond between us and a certain brotherly love. But there is yet another consideration among Christians: for God has adopted them into his household: and that ought to avail more than all the kindred on the earth.

[*He then reflects on the failure of Christians to maintain brotherly love and on the fallen nature of humanity in general. Few are concerned with the good of their neighbour. He then argues from providence that God gives his beloved people their habitations while at the same time arguing that all peoples receive their homelands from God.*]

But yet for all that, this rule shall hold forever: that is, that look what lands, what kingdom, what Lordship, what principality, what state, or whatever free city there is: we may assure ourselves that this distribution is done by God: and that whosoever wages battle against them, seeks to break the bounds which God has set. I mean here, such wars as are undertaken through ambition, or covetousness, or pride. Otherwise, we see here that the children of Israel [are told in this text that they] ought to make war: for God avows their doing, because he had ordained them to be owners of the land [of Canaan], and will have the former inhabitants driven out as they deserved.

But are wars made nowadays by the authority of God? Have men an eye to a thing that is lawful? Yes, or do they delay till they have a commandment from God? No, they go to war in despite of God, the devil drives them forward. [Although many realms have historically been invaded and conquered,] yet for all that, it is not for men to remove bounds. Although they have been confounded: yet it is not for us to enterprise anything. For our Lord hath not given us commission to do so: he has reserved that to himself.

But let us mark likewise that when men have once altered the order that God has set, he must overthrow them. And that is the reason why there happens to be so many changes [to boundaries], and it is a marvel that there are not a hundred times more changes. Surely if God did not have a special

266 *Sources*

regard to the preservation of mankind: no doubt but we should see alterations of kingdoms every day, so that within two or three days, he that is now a king should be but as one that were dressed in a player's apparel, to play an interlude upon a stage.

But yet for all that we must mark well, that the alterations of kingdoms serve to punish the changes that were made before, when men removed their bounds at the beginning, and would needs pervert the order that God had set. Nevertheless, however, the case stands, let us bear this lesson in mind that God has limited realms and countries: and that whereas it is his will that there should be principalities established everywhere, forasmuch as the same comes of his providence: it is our duty to hold ourselves contented and not to alter anything, unless we have good warrant that he [God] opens the gate and arms us. As for example, if violence is offered unto us, then is it certain that if God gives victory to the one that was wrongfully assailed so that he overcomes his enemy and puts him to flight: that is a change [of boundaries] that comes of God. But for those who assail [unprovoked:] that (as I said before) is not to fight against creatures, but against the living God....

To be short, the war shall not spring on their own side [i.e., it shall not be caused by the godly]. Therefore we must conclude that when a people puts forth themselves, or when a prince attempts a foolish enterprise and meddles here and there: we may perceive it is God's doing, for the purpose of overthrowing him and bereaving him of the country that he had given him. So much the more then ought we to pray God to maintain us and to make us mild and peaceable, that we may not follow those whom we see that have their heads full of unquietness.

68 *Philip Melanchthon to King Sigismund II Augustus of Poland* (1556)

Keywords: #Government, #Magistrate, #Idolatry, #Church-State Relations, #Authority
Region: #Germany, #Poland
Group: #Lutheran | #Roman Catholic, #Islam

Throughout the 1540s and 1550s, the Reformation was introduced in Poland, Bohemia, and Hungary, with varying levels of success and official support. There was considerable religious diversity within Poland, writes George Huntston Williams:

> Thus for more than three quarters of the century of the Reformation the land now thought of as most tenaciously Catholic [Poland] was confessionally and remarkably pluralistic.... In no country in Europe were Christians faced with so many plausible options for reformation (and restoration) in church and society as in the Polish-Lithuanian Commonwealth, not even in multi-ethnic Transylvania.[98]

Sigismund II's attitudes towards reform were complex. For example, in 1550 he declared that he would uphold the 'Holy Roman Church' and 'drive from our Realm not only Gentiles (*Ethnicos*), but also heretics who under the cover of the Christian name and by a false use of the Word of God wholly overthrow all Christian teaching'.[99] Such proclamations were not well received by the nobles. Also, the king would not establish a national Protestant church as called for by **John Łaski**, a Polish Calvinist Reformer. However, his humanism and extension of toleration led to conditions under which the Reformation might flourish.

The following letter, from Philip Melanchthon (1497–1560) to Sigismund II, was carried by Łaski after his flight from England. Reformers frequently corresponded with distant rulers who were, or might become, sympathetic towards reform. For example, in 1554 and 1555, **John Calvin** and **Heinrich Bullinger** wrote letters to Sigismund II Augustus of Poland (r.1548–1572) reiterating his God-given duty to care for the church's health.[100] Calvin even

268   *Sources*

dedicated a 1539 work to Sigismund II, then heir to the throne. In the following letter, Melanchthon urged Sigismund to further the Reformation within his realms. He reminded Sigismund of the abuses of the Roman Catholic Church while also undermining the legitimacy of the government of the Ottoman Empire. Melanchthon argued that Poland had been protecting an ungrateful Europe from the advances of the Turks for 500 years. The letter is an important reminder that the Reformation, from its earliest days, was undertaken against the backdrop of an expanding Ottoman Empire. In the previous quarter century, Hungary, another 'bulwark' of Christendom, had been largely subdued by the Ottomans. It was frequently argued that Protestants benefited from Ottoman advances, either because the Ottomans distracted Catholic powers or they allowed considerable latitude for Protestant ideas.[101]

Stanislas Lubieniecki, *History of the Polish Reformation*, trans. and ed. George Huntston Williams (Minneapolis, MN: Fortress, 1995), 154–155. Used with permission. Text modernised by the editors.

———

Illustrious King and Most Gracious Lord,

There is no doubt that the society of the human race, so far as it is preserved, is preserved by God, and that by the wisdom of God, monarchies and other governments have been established with a view to the service that they render to the human race. Thus the realm of the Turks is a desolation of the world and only a horrible punishment, not a government. With regard to such great concerns as these, God's counsel must be considered, and for serviceable governments, thanks ought to be given to God.

The Kingdom of Poland has been of special service indeed to the rest of Europe for 500 years now, for it has been our bulwark against the Tartars, and has waged no wars against us. The other kingdoms of Germany and France have neglected their duty towards the general welfare, while fighting each other for the possession of Italy. Since, therefore, peculiar gratitude is due to the Kingdom of Poland, deserving so well of all of Europe, I pray God to preserve your Kingdom and your Majesty.

I also wish, since serviceable kingdoms are the work of God, and the knowledge of God should be especially apparent in them, that in our Kingdom, too, God may be rightly acknowledged and worshiped. Nor can it indeed be denied that in the churches there are great abuses, which God has commanded to be reformed by the wisdom of kings, saying: 'And now, ye kings, understand' [Wisdom of Solomon 6:1]. Wherefore, in undertaking this office, your Royal Majesty is acting piously. No sacrifice could be more pleasing to God than that some kings, setting up a consultation of pious and learned men, should undertake to make clear the truth, to destroy idols, and to establish pious harmony.

Sources 269

We have read the writings of [Stanisław] Hosius [the bishop of Ermland] and certain others who undertake by their devious intention to extinguish the rising light of truth, and establish idols. But it becomes your Royal Majesty's wisdom to inquire into the sources. What we profess, is shown by the [1530 *Augsburg Confession*]....

Given at Wittenberg 18 October 1556

Your Royal Majesty's most humble servant, Philip Melanchthon.

69 *John Łaski to King Sigismund II Augustus of Poland* (1556)

Keywords: #Idolatry, #Authority, #Government, #Magistrate
Region: #Poland
Group: #Reformed, #Lutheran | #Roman Catholic

John Łaski (1499–1560) was born in central Poland to a family of warlords and clerics. He was a learned theologian who was expected to make a career in the Catholic Church: he took up a titular role as bishop of Veszprém (Hungary) and, in 1538, became an archdeacon. However, his interest in Renaissance humanism and his international connections with figures like **Erasmus of Rotterdam** and **Huldreich Zwingli** made him open to the Reformation. He left to study in the Low Countries in 1539 and broke his vows when he married in 1540, after which he ministered in Emden. Due to Lutheran intolerance, he fled to England. At the invitation of **Thomas Cranmer** and by appointment of King **Edward VI**, he ministered at the Dutch Church.[102] As such, he made a lasting impression upon the Protestant Reformation. The ascension of Queen Mary I, however, then made England unsafe. By 1556, King Sigismund II of Poland seemed open to the Reformation, and Łaski contemplated a return to Poland. When he failed to persuade Sigismund II to form a national church, he established a Calvinist church in Minor Poland. He died a few years later of poor health.[103]

Łaski wrote the following letter in December 1556 upon returning to Poland, which he passed on to the king along with **Phillip Melanchthon**'s letter. In his letter, Łaski explained why he had returned and sought to show his alignment with the **Augsburg Confession**. He described himself as a defender of the king's dignity, both abroad and now at home. He urged wisdom when weighing the words of those who slandered Łaski and the church and expressed a willingness to be corrected if his errors could be demonstrated. He denied the accusation that the teaching of the Reformers contributed to the ruin of kingdoms. This letter was an explicit order to the king to put away the foreign gods, that is, the papal church to which he was openly hostile. The letter then closed with prayers for the king, declarations of respect, and the assertion of the 'supreme power of God in this Kingdom'.

Sources 271

"John Łaski to Sigismund II" (2 Dec 1556), in Stanislas Lubieniecki, *History of the Polish Reformation*, trans. and ed. George Huntston Williams (Minneapolis, MN: Fortress, 1995), 144–154 (152). Used with permission.

———

...According to this counsel, then, proceeding from the Spirit of God himself, if you also, Most Serene King, fear for yourself and your Kingdom, you must first return not with a half, but with your whole heart. And as proof that you are doing this truly and without hypocrisy, do what you see that the Prophet here directs....

Do therefore, most excellent King, with your leading men, what the Lord has commanded. Put away the foreign gods from your Kingdom, but especially the guardian god of the papal kingdom which anyway our ancestors, that is, the Prophets and the Apostles, never knew: I mean the tonsured god MAYZIM [Dan. 11:38] in which alone resides all the strength and protection of the Antichristian impiety, and serve God alone in the *restitutio* of the true and perfect worship of God. Then and only then the Lord will indubitably deliver both you and your Kingdom from all the Philistines of this world.

But if you do not do this, beware, lest from the source whence you may be promising yourself deliverance you instead bring ruin upon yourself and your Kingdom. There is no counsel against the Lord. And, outside Christ alone, it is a wretched thing to seek refuge from the judgement of God. For who is there who hideth himself from his wrath?

70 John Ponet, *On Deposing or Killing a Tyrant* (1556)

Keywords: #Authority, #Tyranny, #Rebellion, #Natural Rights, #Magistrate, #Family, #Common Good, #Natural Law
Region: #England
Group: #Church of England

John Ponet (c.1514–1556) was born in England and studied at Cambridge. He became a priest and served in several academic and ministerial roles – including as chaplain to **Thomas Cranmer** and to Henry VIII. He rose to the bishoprics of Rochester and Winchester under **Edward VI**. His role in the Edwardian Reformation and support for Wyatt's Rebellion (1544) made him a target of Mary I, and he fled to Strasbourg. In *A Short Treatise of Political Power* (1556), he advocated resistance to a ruler who overturned religion and abused power, and even entertained the possibility of tyrannicide. Events on the continent were causing others to advocate armed resistance to such tyrants. For example, the recent violence in Flanders led Christopher Mont – a German Lutheran diplomat – to write to **Heinrich Bullinger**:

> What if a lawful sovereign should degenerate into a tyrant, can he be said to be the minister of God? Peace must be cultivated, and obedience rendered; but at the same time the natural rights, laws, and customs of kingdoms, dominions, and powers, are to be maintained, and especially the things which are God's are to be given to God.[104]

In the following selection, Ponet argues that power derived from the people and was to be used for the benefit of the people. When a legitimate monarch used power for personal gain and against the people, they became a tyrant. The same arguments for deposing a tyrant could also be deployed to justify killing one. The people could withdraw their support for a ruler at will, and even more so if a ruler was unjust. This right was natural, internally written on the hearts of all people.

John Ponet, *A short treatise of political power and of the true obedience which subjects owe to kings and other civil governors* (Strasbourg: W. Köpfel, 1556). Text modernised by the editors.

———

Whether it be lawful to depose an evil governor, and kill a tyrant.

As there is no better nor happier common wealth nor no greater blessing of God, than where a good, just and godly man rules: so there is none worse nor none more miserable, nor a greater plague of God, than where one rules who is evil, unjust and ungodly. A good man knowing that he was called to such office for his virtue, to see the whole state well governed and the people defended from injuries: neglects utterly his own pleasure and profit and bestows all his study and labour to see his office well discharged. And as a good physician earnestly seeks the health of his patient and a Shipmaster the wealth and safety of those in his ship, so does a good governor seek the wealth of those he rules. And therefore, the people feeling the benefit coming through good governours, formerly called such good governors 'fathers': and gave them no less honour than children owe to their parents.

An evil person coming to the government of any state, either by usurpation, election or succession, utterly neglecting the reason why kings, princes and other governours in common wealths are made (that is, the wealth of the people) seeks only or chiefly his own profit and pleasure. And as a sow coming into a fair garden roots up all the fair and sweet flowers, leaving nothing behind but her own filthy dirt: so does an evil governor subvert the laws and orders or make them to be wrenched or racked to serve his affections, that they can no longer do their office. [*He bankrupts his people with pleasant words and spends all on pleasure and vainglory. He also takes away the people's ability to defend themselves and, like a hunter, makes sport of them – a game that the people can neither win nor absent themselves from. This magistrates also enlists the church in devouring the people.*] Such evil governors are properly called Tyrants.

Now forasmuch as there is no express positive law for the punishment of a Tyrant among Christian men, the question is whether it is lawful to kill such a monster and cruel beast covered with the shape of a man.

And first, for the better and more plain proof of this matter, the manifold and continual examples across time of the deposing of kings, and killing of tyrants, do most certainly confirm it to be most true, just and consonant to God's judgement. The history of kings in the Old Testament is full of it. [*He cites examples of Christians deposing monarchs in England, Denmark, Hungary and Portugal.*]

But here you see, the body of every state may (if it will), yes and ought to, redress and correct the vices of their governors. And forasmuch as you have already seen, whereof political power and government grows, and the purpose whereunto it was ordained: and seeing it is before manifestly and

274 Sources

sufficiently proved, that kings and princes do not have absolute power over their subjects: that they are and ought to be subject to the law of God, and the wholesome, positive laws of their country: and that they may not lawfully take or use their subject's goods at their pleasure: the reasons, arguments and laws that serve for the deposing and displacing of an evil governor, will do as much for the proof, that it is lawful to kill a tyrant. As God hath ordained Magistrates to hear and determine private men's matters, and to punish their vices: so also [God wills], that the magistrate's doings are called to account and reckoned with, and their vices corrected and punished by the body of the whole congregation or common wealth....

Kings, Princes and governors have their authority from the people, as all laws, usages and policies declare and testify. [*This is true, even though the political structures differ from region to region.*] All laws agree that men may revoke their proxies and letters of Attorney when it pleases them: much more when they see their proctors and attorneys abuse them.

But now, to prove the latter part of this question affirmatively, that it is lawful to kill a tyrant: no man can deny it....

For it is no private law to a few or certain people, but common to all: not written in books, but grafted in the hearts of men: not made by man, but ordained of God: which we have not learned, received or read, but have taken, sucked, and drawn it out of nature: whereunto we are not taught, but made: not instructed, but seasoned: and (as *Saint Paul* says) man's conscience bearing witness of it [Rom. 2:15].

This law testifies to every man's conscience that it is natural to cut away an incurable member, which would destroy the whole body.

Kings, Princes and other governors, albeit they are the heads of a political body, yet they are not the whole body. And though they are the chief members, yet they are but members: neither are the people ordained for them, but they are ordained for the people.

71 Christopher Goodman, *The People May Disobey, Resist and Dethrone Magistrates* (1558)

Keywords: #Rebellion, #Authority, #Magistrate, #Idolatry, #Tyranny, #Submission
Region: #England, #Switzerland
Group: #Reformed, #Calvinist

Christopher Goodman (c.1521–1603) was educated at Oxford and became part of a circle surrounding **Peter Martyr Vermigli,** a leading scholar who pushed for the reform of the Church of England. He was appointed Lady Margaret Professor of Divinity at Oxford in the late 1540s, but fled after the accession of Mary I, and ministered among English refugees in Geneva alongside **John Knox.** Their congregation greatly influenced Scottish Presbyterian worship and produced the *Geneva Bible* (1560) – a translation supplemented with commentary encouraging resistance to authority. Goodman's treatise, *How Superior Powers Ought to be Obeyed*, was published around the time of Knox's controversial *First Blast of the Trumpet against the Monstrous Regiment of Women* (1558). Like Knox, Goodman encouraged resistance to ungodly authority, especially if the ruler was female. Such arguments earned him the contempt of **Elizabeth I.** He returned to minister in Scotland and Ireland, eventually moving to England, where he was known for nonconformity. Among other contributions, his work influenced resistance to Charles I in the next century.

In the following work, Goodman was incensed by Englishmen who insufficiently resisted the reimposition of Catholicism. Such complicity made the people ripe for divine judgement. It was never permissible, he argued, for anyone to make peace with idolatry. Indeed, much of his radical argument for deposing or killing magistrates rested on his interpretation of commands and examples from the Hebrew Bible. According to him, every Israelite was charged with rooting out idolatry, a crime that required death. Christians, likewise, were to be vigilant against idolatry, especially when political leaders were the chief idolaters. Love of God, he argued, required removing those who did not love God. When the ruler refused the headship of God, the

276 Sources

people were transferred under the headship of God and derived their authority directly from him.[105]

How superior powers oght to be obeyd of their subiects and wherin they may lawfully by Gods Worde be disobeyed and resisted (Geneva: 1558), 175–191. Text modernised by the editors.

———

Forsake with speed the unlawful obedience of flesh and blood, and learn to give honour in time to the living Lord, that he may stay his hand, and draw to him again his stretched out arm, that you may find mercy, and that the bottom of your cup may not be turned upward.

Alas, say you, what is this we hear? Are not the people of themselves as sheep without a pastor? If the Magistrates and other officers regard with contempt their duty to defend God's glory and the Laws committed to their charge, does it lie in our power to remedy it? Shall subjects take the sword in our hands? ... [There is] no excuse for you, seeing, the evil done by others (whether they are Lords, Dukes, Barons, knights or any inferior officers), may not excuse you in evil. And though you had no powerful persons upon your side: yet, it is a sufficient assurance for you, to have the warrant of God's word upon your side (Deut. 4–6), and God himself to be your Captain who wills not only that the Magistrates and officers root out evil from amongst them (be the evil, idolatry, blasphemy or open injury), but the whole multitude are therewith charged also, to whom a portion of the sword of justice is committed, to execute the judgements which the Magistrates lawfully command. And therefore if the Magistrates would wholly despise and betray the justice and Laws of God, you who are subjects with them shall be condemned except you maintain and defend the same Laws against them [the evil magistrates], and all others to the uttermost of your powers, that is, with all your strength, with all your heart and with all your soul [Deut. 6:5], for God has required this of you, and you have not promised this unto him under condition (if it is the will of the Ruler) but without all exceptions to do whatsoever your Lord and God shall command you (Exod. 17).

[*He then argued at length from scripture that all people, individually and collectively, are charged with discovering and rooting out idolatry, wherever it manifests.*]

Next, no person is exempted by any Law of God from this punishment [for idolatry], be they King, Queen or Emperor (anyone openly or privately known to be an idolater, however dear they are unto us, they must die the death). For God has not placed them above others to transgress his Laws, but they are subject unto them just as those over whom they govern are also subject. And if they are subject unto God's Laws, they must also be subject to the punishment when they are found disobedient transgressors: yea, so much the more as their example is more dangerous. For look what wickedness reigns in the Magistrates, and subjects commonly take encouragement by this and imitate the same, as we see in the examples of Jeroboam (1 Kgs 14, 21)....

And although it appears at first sight a great disorder (if the people should take unto themselves the punishment of transgression), yet, when the Magistrates and other officers cease to do their duty, the people are as it were, without officers, yea, worse than if they had none at all, and then God gives the sword into the people's hand, and he himself [God] becomes immediately their head (If they will seek the accomplishment of his Laws) and has promised to defend them and bless them (Lev. 26; Deut. 27, 30).

[*He reflects on Joshua 22 and punishment for improper worship.*] Wherefore this zeal to defend God's Laws and precepts, wherewith all sorts of men are charged, it is not only praiseworthy in all, but required of all, not only in abstaining from the transgression of the said Laws, but also to see the judgements thereof executed upon all manner of persons without exception. And that if it is not done by the consent and aid of the Superiors, it is lawful for the people, yea it is their duty to do it themselves, as well upon their own rulers and Magistrate, as upon their other brethren, having the word of God for their warrant, to which all are subject, and by the same charged to cast forth all evil from them and to cut off every rotten member, for fear of infecting the whole body, how dear or precious soever it be. If death is deserved, death: if other punishments, to see them executed.

For this cause have you promised obedience to your Superiors (Rom. 13), that they might herein help you: and for the same intent have they taken it upon themselves. If they will so do, and keep their promise with you according to their office, then you owe unto them all humble obedience: If not, you are discharged, and no obedience belongs to them: because they are not obedient to God.... And therefore your study, in this case, ought to be to seek how you may dispose and punish according to the Laws, such rebels against God, and oppressors of yourselves and your country: and not how to please them, obey them, and flatter them as you do in their impiety. Which is not the way to obtain peace and quietness, but to fall into the hands of the almighty God and to be subject to his fearful plagues and punishments.

72 John Knox, *Letter to the Commonality of Scotland* (1558)

Keywords: #Authority, #Resistance, #Idolatry, #Tyranny, #Equality
Region: #Scotland, #Switzerland
Group: #Reformed, #Calvinist, #Presbyterian

John Knox (1513–1572) was born in Haddington, Scotland, studied at the University of Saint Andrews, and worked briefly as a lawyer before his ordination in the Catholic Church in 1536. Little is known about when or why he embraced the Reformation. After a controversial sermon against the papacy in 1547, he was sentenced to the galleys for two years. He then ministered in Scotland and later became a royal chaplain to **Edward VI**. He fled after the accession of Mary I and ministered to English Protestants in Frankfurt and Geneva.

The following selection presents Knox's direct appeal to the people of Scotland, his *Letter to the Commonality*. Printed in Geneva, this address to commoners was paired with the *Appellation of John Knox*, in which he urged the nobility to take up the cause of reform and defend him against condemnations of the Scottish clergy. The *Appellation* also described the godly prince and put forward the argument that lesser magistrates, the nobility, had a duty to act contrary to their sovereign in promoting reform and protecting Reformers like Knox. They also had an obligation – as divinely ordained authorities – to oppose other divinely ordained authority when that authority opposed God. Knox worked these ideas out more fully in his later writings.[106]

The *Letter to the Commonality* addressed many of the same themes but applied them to ordinary people who were not in a position of authority. Some claim this *Letter* argued for a popular right to resistance – perhaps similar to the argument of **Christopher Goodman**. Although Knox stopped short of clearly arguing for armed confrontation, the *Letter* insisted that the people were in some sense responsible for the idolatry in their land. God would judge them if they did not act to bring reform (through acts of defiance like refusing to pay taxes) or separate from the ungodly. However, as shown in the following excerpt, Knox emphasised one's duty to resist an idolatrous ruler to secure one's personal salvation. When faced with a choice between

Sources 279

punishment from God and punishment from a ruler, the subject should obey God and accept punishment from their ruler.

John Knox, *Letter to the Commonality of Scotland* in *The Works of John Knox*, ed. David Lang (Edinburgh: Johnstone and Hunter, 1855), IV:523–538 (526–528, 33–35). Text modernised by the editors.

———

Geneva, 14 July 1558

To his beloved brethren, the Commonality [common people] of Scotland, John Knox wishes Grace, Mercy, and Peace, with the spirit of Righteous judgement.

What I have required of the Queen Regent, Estates, and Nobility, as of the chief heads (for this present) of the realm, I cannot cease to require of you, dearly beloved Brethren, which are the Commonalty and body of the same....

I wish that you were certainly persuaded that a corrupt religion defiles the whole life of man, however holy it appears. Nor would I want you to esteem the Reformation and the care of Religion to appertain less to you because you are not Kings, Rulers, Judges, Nobles, nor in authority. Beloved Brethren, you are God's creatures, created and formed to his own image and similitude, for whose redemption was shed the most precious blood of the only beloved Son of God, to whom he has commanded his gospel and glad-tidings to be preached, and for whom he has prepared the heavenly inheritance.... For the gospel and glad-tidings of the kingdom truly preached, is the power of God to the salvation of every believer [Rom. 1], which to credit and receive, you the Commonalty, are no less due then are your Rulers and Princes. For although God has put and ordained distinction and difference between the King and subjects, between the Rulers and the common people (in the regiment and administration of Civil policies), yet in the hope of the life to come, he has made all equal. For as in Christ Jesus, the Jew has no greater prerogative than the Gentile, the man than the woman, the learned than the unlearned, the Lord than the servant, but all are one in him (Gal. 3: 28), so there is only one way and means to attain to the participation of his benefits and spiritual graces, which is a lively faith working by charity.

Therefore, I say that it no less appertains to you, beloved Brethren, to be assured that your faith and religion are grounded and established upon the true and undoubted Word of God than to your Princes or Rulers. For as your bodies cannot escape corporal death if you eat or drink deadly poison with your Princes (although it is done in ignorance or negligence), so you shall not escape everlasting death if you profess a corrupt religion along with them....

But to return to our former purpose, I say it is no less required of the subject to believe in Christ and profess his true religion, than of the Prince and King. And therefore I affirm that in God's presence, it shall not excuse you to

280 *Sources*

allege that you were not chief rulers, and therefore that the care and reformation of Religion did not appertain unto you....

I think you still doubt what you ought and may do in this weighty matter. In a few words, I will declare my conscience in the one and the other. You ought to prefer the glory of God, the promoting of Christ's Evangel, and the salvation of your souls, to all earthly things: and although you are only subjects, you may lawfully require of your superiors (be it of your King, Lords, rulers, and powers) that they provide true Preachers, and that they expel such as, under the name of Pastors, devour and destroy the flock, not feeding the same as Christ Jesus has commanded. And if, in this point, your superiors are negligent or claim the right to maintain tyrants in their tyranny, you may justly provide true teachers for yourselves, whether in your cities, towns, or villages: you may maintain them and defend against all that shall persecute them (and by that means seek to defraud you of the gospel). You may, moreover, withhold the fruits and profits your false Bishops and Clergy most unjustly receive of you until they are compelled to faithfully do their charge and duties, namely to truly preach Christ Jesus unto you.... [*God will hold the common people accountable and without excuse, and he will bless or judge accordingly. The godly must either agitate for reform or separate from the ungodly system, which is doomed to destruction. He closes by warning them not to become complicit in the rule of the ungodly through their direct support or winking at the magistrate's injustice.*]

73 John Knox, *Outline for the Second Blast of the Trumpet* (1558)

Keywords: #Women, #Authority, #Idolatry, #Tyranny, #Rebellion, #Election
Region: #Scotland, #Switzerland, #England
Group: #Reformed, #Calvinist, #Presbyterian

Many of John Knox's most controversial political writings were published around the end of Mary I's life: *The First Blast of the Trumpet against the Monstrous Regiment of Women* (1558), *The Letter to the Regent* (1558), *The Appellation to the Nobility and Estates* (1558), **The Letter to the Commonality** (1558), and the *Proposed Second Blast* (1558). Knox did not know the future, and it seemed possible that England would long remain a Catholic country. In this context, Knox encouraged resistance to ungodly authority in general and to female authority in particular.

Although the *First Blast* (1558) was written against a female Catholic monarch, it was published around the time **Elizabeth I** ascended to the throne. Knox defended himself in a 20 July 1559 letter to the Queen, professing loyalty and admiration for her just rule, but she was not swayed.[107] Her fury at Knox extended to **John Calvin** and all things Genevan, even though Calvin protested that Knox did not speak for the wider Reformed churches. It was neither the first nor last time that Knox made matters worse for fellow Protestants.[108] Having angered Elizabeth I, Knox chose to return to his work of reforming Scotland. Although his tactics often put him at odds with other Protestants, he became the leading figure of the Scottish Reformation and wrote the *History of the Reformation in Scotland*. The following excerpt comes from a proposed outline for the *Second Blast*, a work he never wrote.[109]

John Knox, "Contents of the Second Blast", in *John Knox: The First Blast of the Trumpet against the Monstrous Regiment of Women (1558)*, ed. Edward Arber (Westminster: Archibald Constable and Co., 1895), 57–60.

---

282 *Sources*

To the Christian Reader

Because many are offended at the *First Blast of the Trumpet*, in which I affirm, that to promote a woman to bear rule or empire above any realm, nation, or city, is repugnant to nature, contumely [insolent] to God, and a thing most contrary to his revealed and approved ordinance; and because also, that some have promised (as I understand) a confutation of the same, I have delayed the second blast till such time as their reasons appear, by the which I either may be reformed in opinion, or else shall have further occasion more simply and plainly to utter my judgement. Yet in the mean time, for the discharge of my conscience, and for avoiding suspicion, which might be engendered by reason of my silence, I could not cease to notify these subsequent propositions, which, by God's grace, I purpose to treat in the second blast promised.

1 It is not birth only, nor propinquity [nearness] of blood, that makes a king lawfully to reign above a people professing Christ Jesus and his eternal verity; but in his election must the ordinance, which God has established in the election of inferior judges, be observed.
2 No manifest idolater, nor notorious transgressor of God's holy precepts, ought to be promoted to any public regiment, honour, or dignity, in any realm, province, or city that has subjected itself to his blessed gospel.
3 Neither can oath nor promise, bind any such people to obey and maintain tyrants against God and against his truth known.
4 But if either rashly they have promoted any manifestly wicked person, or yet ignorantly have chosen such a one, as after declares himself unworthy of regiment above the people of God, (and such be all idolaters and cruel persecutors), most justly may the same men depose and punish him that unadvisedly before they did nominate, appoint, and elect.

Matthew 6:22

'If the eye be single, the whole body shall be clear'

74 Elizabeth I, *Proclamation Forbidding Preaching* (1558)

Keywords: #Church-State Relations, #Censorship, #Ten Commandments, #Women
Region: #England
Group: #Church of England | #Reformed, #Roman Catholic

Elizabeth Tudor (1533–1603) ascended the throne (r.1558–1603) around the time **John Knox** wrote against female authority and **Christopher Goodman** put forward theories of resistance. Although Elizabeth I was a Protestant queen, she was not necessarily sympathetic to its Calvinist branches. Her ascension encouraged English Protestants to come out of hiding and return from exile, and she restored the reforms of **Edward VI**. However, many of her subjects wanted to bring the English church into greater alignment with the Reformed movement on the continent, but she resolutely thwarted such efforts throughout her reign. Those agitating for further reform would later be described pejoratively as 'Puritans' because they wanted to purify the Church of England of the remnants of Catholicism.

Elizabeth tried to contain the risk that emanated from discontented preachers, be they Protestant or Catholic. The following excerpt comes from a temporary prohibition on preaching about politically sensitive topics. It ordered preachers to observe the limits of the official church's liturgy and teaching. The monarch, in the interest of public order and peace, assumed jurisdiction over the content of preaching. The subsequent *Act of Uniformity* (1559) restored Protestantism, reaffirmed the 1552 *Book of Common Prayer*, and secured Elizabeth's authority over the church. It also checked the aspirations of those wanting further Reformation and asked them to conform.[110]

Henry Gee and William John Hardy, eds., *Documents Illustrative of English Church History* (London: Macmillan, 1896), 416–417. Text modernised by the editors.

———

The Queen's Majesty, understanding that there are certain persons who formerly ministered in the Church and now intend to resume their former office of preaching and ministry, and have partly started doing to, assembling great

284 *Sources*

numbers of people in various places, particularly in the city of London, and upon such occasions commoners not only engage in unfruitful disputes in matters of religion, but also are contentious and break the peace, has therefore, according to the authority committed to her Highness for the quiet governance of all manner of her subjects, thought it necessary to charge and command, as by this her Highness does charge and command, all manner of her subjects, both those who are called to ministry in the Church as well as all others, that they do not preach, teach or listen to any doctrine or preaching other than the Gospels and Epistles, commonly called the Gospel and Epistle of the day, and to the Ten Commandments in the vernacular language, without adding any exposition or interpretation; or to use any other public prayer, rite, or ceremony in the Church, but that which is already used and by law received; or the common Litany presently used in Her Majesty's own chapel, and the Lord's Prayer, and the Creed in English; until there is a consultation by Parliament, Her Majesty and her three estates of this realm, for the better, conciliation and accord of such causes, as at this present are put forward in religious matters and ceremonies.

The true promotion of the rightful honour of Almighty God and the increase of virtue and godliness, along with universal charity and concord amongst her people, Her Majesty greatly desires and intends to bring about by all possible means, to procure and to restore to this her realm. As Her Majesty immediately requires all her good, faithful, and loving subjects to assent and abide by this with due obedience, so if any shall disobediently break these commands, Her Majesty must and will see them rightly punished, both because of the nature of the offence and as an example to all others about neglecting Her Majesty's reasonable commandment.

Given at her Highness's palace of Westminster the 27th day of December, the first year of Her Majesty's reign.

God save the Queen.

75 *John Calvin to William Cecil on Female Authority* (1559)

Keywords: #Women, #Authority, #Church-State Relations
Region: #Switzerland, #England
Group: #Reformed, #Calvinist | #Church of England

As **Elizabeth I** ascended the throne in 1558, several controversial works were produced by Genevan publishers, most notably by **John Knox** and **Christopher Goodman**. Although written during the reign of Mary I, the texts entered a world where a new Protestant Queen endeavoured to secure her authority. Her fury at Knox reflected on **John Calvin** and, in her mind, discredited the Reformed churches on the continent. In the following letter, Calvin wrote to Elizabeth's chief minister, **William Cecil**. He was a committed Protestant, but like Elizabeth, he had little sympathy for the more zealous Reformers. In this letter, Calvin tried to control the damage caused by Knox and Goodman, arguing that female authority could be a judgement by God, as well as a blessing from him.[111]

"John Calvin to Sir William Cecil" (after 29 January 1559), in *The Zurich Letters*, ed. Hastings Robinson (Cambridge: Cambridge University Press, 1845), II:168–170 (169).

John Calvin to Sir William Cecil

Geneva (after 29 January 1559)

The messenger to whom I gave in charge my commentaries upon Isaiah to be presented to the most serene queen [Elizabeth I], brought me word that my homage was not kindly received by her majesty, because she had been offended with me by reason of some writings published in this place [by John Knox and Christopher Goodman]. He also repeated to me, most illustrious sir, the substance of a conversation held by you, in which you seem to me more severe than was consistent with your courtesy, especially when you had been already assured by my letter, how much I promised myself from your regard towards me. But though sufficient reasons prevent me from vindicating

286   *Sources*

myself by a serious discussion, yet lest I should seem by my silence to confess in some measure the consciousness of having done wrong, I have thought it right to state, in few words, how the matter stands.

Two years ago John Knox asked of me, in a private conversation, what I thought about the government of women. I candidly replied, that as it was a deviation from the original and proper order of nature, it was to be ranked, no less than slavery, among the punishments consequent upon the fall of man; but that there were occasionally women so endowed, that the singular good qualities which shone forth in them, made it evident that they were raised up by divine authority; either that God designed by such examples to condemn the inactivity of men, or for the better setting forth his own glory. I brought forward Huldah [2 Chron. 34:22] and Deborah [Judg. 4]; and added, that God did not vainly promise by the mouth of Isaiah, that queens should be the nursing mothers of the church [Isa. 49:23]; by which prerogative it is very evident that they are distinguished from females in private life.

I came at length to this conclusion, that since both by custom and public consent and long practice it has been established, that realms and principalities may descend to females by hereditary right, it did not appear to me necessary to move the question, not only because the thing would be invidious, but because in my opinion it would not be lawful to unsettle governments which are ordained by the peculiar providence of God. I had no suspicion of the book [against female rule], and for a whole year was ignorant of its publication. When I was informed of it by certain parties, I sufficiently shewed my displeasure that such paradoxes should be published; but as the remedy was too late, I thought that the evil which could not now be corrected, should rather be buried in oblivion than made a matter of agitation. Inquire also of your father-in-law [Sir Antony Cook], what my reply was when he informed me of the circumstance through Beza. And [the Catholic Queen] Mary was still living, so that I could not be suspected of flattery. What the books contain, I cannot tell; but Knox himself will allow that my conversation with him was no other than what I have now stated. But although I was moved by the complaints of some godly men, yet, as I had not been informed in time, I did not dare to make any decided opposition, lest greater confusion should ensue. If my easiness has occasioned any offence, I think there would have been just reason to fear, lest if the subject had been brought under consideration, by reason of the thoughtless arrogance of one individual, the wretched crowd of exiles would have been driven away not only from this city, but even from almost the whole world; especially since the mischief could not now be remedied, otherwise than by applying a mitigation.

I am indeed exceedingly and undeservedly grieved, in proportion to my surprise, that the ravings of others, as if on a studied pretext, should be charged upon me, to prevent my book from being accepted. If the offered present were not acceptable to the queen, she might have rejected it by a single word, and it would have been more candid to have done so. This certainly would have been more agreeable to myself, than to be burdened with false accusations, in addition to the ignominy of a repulse. However, I shall always reverence both the most serene queen, and shall not cease, most illustrious sir, to love and respect yourself also, for your most excellent disposition and your other virtues, although I have found you less friendly to me than I had hoped, and though you say nothing about mutual good-will for the time to come. From this however, I am unwilling to draw any unfavourable conclusion. Farewell, most accomplished and esteemed sir. May the Lord evermore be present with you, guide, protect, and enrich you with his gifts.

76 *Elizabeth I as Deborah* (1559)

Keywords: #Women, #Authority
Region: #England
Group: #Church of England

When **Elizabeth I** paraded through London shortly before her coronation in early 1559, the city staged elaborate spectacles that celebrated her ascension to the throne. The performances illustrated the difference between godly and wicked rule. Although the pageantry was performed for Elizabeth, she knew she was part of the spectacle and that her actions were closely scrutinised. It was during her procession that a child famously handed her a Bible, whereupon she 'received the book, kissed it, and with both her hands held up the same, and so laid it upon her breast with great thanks to the City thereof'. The act was taken as indicative of her high regard for scripture and her genuine adherence to Protestantism. In contrast, two years later, Mary Queen of Scots entered Edinburgh to much pageantry. However, the pageants there were barbed, as was her cold reaction to their unwelcome displays of Protestant sympathy.

The following selection comes from an account of Elizabeth's triumphant entry into London. During one pageant, she was portrayed as Deborah [Judg. 4], who fought against the Canaanites. A child rehearsed the following lines for her majesty. Whereas preachers like **John Knox** mined scripture for negative portrayals of female leadership, Elizabeth welcomed the association with the heroic and godly leaders in sacred writ.[112]

A. F. Pollard, ed., *Tudor Tracts, 1532–1588* (Westminster: Archibald and Co., 1903), 387.

———

Jaban, of Canaan King, had long, by force of arms,
Oppressed the Israelites; which for God's people went:
But God minding, at last, for to redress their harms;
The worthy Deborah as judge, among them sent.

Sources 289

In war, She, through God's aid, did set her foes to flight,
And with the dint of sword the band of bondage brast [burst].
In peace, She, through God's aid, did always maintain right
And judged Israel, till forty years were passed.

A worthy precedent, O worthy queen! thou hast!
A worthy woman, Judge! a woman sent for stay!
And that the like to us endure, alway thou may'st;
Thy loving subjects will, with true hearts and tongues, pray.

77 The French Confession of Faith (1559)

Keywords: #Confession of Faith, #Submission, #Violence, #Church-State Relations, #Law, #Magistrates, #Economics, #Communal Living, #Ten Commandments
Region: #France
Group: #Reformed

As the French Reformed moved out from Switzerland, they needed to relate to different theological and political dynamics, and this engendered new confessional writing. Such was the case for Huguenots who settled France Antarctique in the mid-1550s in Guanabara Bay (modern Rio de Janeiro in Brazil). After one of the leaders, Nicholas Durand de Villegaignon, wrote **John Calvin** in 1557 and explained the grounds for the colony and asked for Reformed clergy, two ministers were sent with the expedition. The Guanabara Confession of 1558 was the first Protestant writing to come out of the Americas. Its writers, Jean du Bourdel, Matthieu Verneuil, Pierre Bourdon, and André la Fon, were executed the day after committing their beliefs to paper. The confession did not speak of magistrates, authority, or submission. Villegaignon, who had since converted to Catholicism, ordered their execution. Huguenots also settled Fort Caroline in Florida between 1562 and 1565, and the destruction of the colony by the Spanish, coupled with religious warfare in France, deepened mistrust of Catholics at home and abroad.[113] To keep Protestants out of the region, the Spanish had established St. Augustine, Florida – the oldest European settlement in the United States.

The Reformed were also embattled – to varying degrees – within France. The French *Confession of Faith*, writes Matthew J. Tuininga, was the product of the 'first national synod of the French Reformed Church, meeting in Paris in 1559'. Calvin's theology, ecclesiology, and views of church and state influenced the document they produced. The preface to the king, reproduced below, argued that the king had real, but limited, authority. There were two distinct kingdoms, and the magistrate had no authority over the soul or over one's conscience. However, the Reformed asserted that they must submit to legitimate authority, even if the one in authority would be an unbeliever.[114]

The Creeds of Christendom, vol. III: The Evangelical Protestant Creeds, ed. Philip Schaff (New York: Harper and Brothers, 1887), 356–382 (356–359, 376–377, 381–382).

———

The French Subjects who wish to live in the purity of the gospel of our Lord Jesus Christ.

To the King.

Sire, we thank God that hitherto having had no access to your Majesty to make known the rigor of the persecutions that we have suffered, and suffer daily, for wishing to live in the purity of the Gospel and in peace with our own consciences, he now permits us to see that you wish to know the worthiness of our cause, as is shown by the last Edict given at Amboise in the month of March of this present year, 1559, which it has pleased your Majesty to cause to be published. This emboldens us to speak, which we have been prevented from doing hitherto through the injustice and violence of some of your officers, incited rather by hatred of us than by love of your service. And to the end, Sire, that we may fully inform your Majesty of what concerns this cause, we humbly beseech that you will see and hear our Confession of Faith, which we present to you, hoping that it will prove a sufficient answer to the blame and opprobrium unjustly laid upon us by those who have always made a point of condemning us without having any knowledge of our cause. In the which, Sire, we can affirm that there is nothing contrary to the Word of God, or to the homage which we owe to you....

May it please your Majesty, then, instead of the fire and sword which have been used hitherto, to have our Confession of Faith decided by the Word of God: giving permission and security for this. And we hope that you yourself will be the judge of our innocence, knowing that there is in us no rebellion or heresy whatsoever, but that our only endeavour is to live in peace of conscience, serving God according to his commandments, and honouring your Majesty by all obedience and submission....

And if it should not please you, Sire, to listen to our voice, may it please you to listen to that of the Son of God, who, having given you power over our property, our bodies, and even our lives, demands that the control and dominion of our souls and consciences, which he purchased with his own blood, be reserved to him.

Confession of Faith

29 As to the true Church, we believe that it should be governed according to the order established by our Lord Jesus Christ. That there should be pastors, overseers, and deacons, so that true doctrine may have its course, that errors may be corrected and suppressed, and the poor and all who are in affliction may be helped in their necessities; and that assemblies may be held in the name of God, so that great and small may be edified.

292 *Sources*

39 We believe that God wishes to have the world governed by laws and magistrates, so that some restraint may be put upon its disordered appetites. And as he has established kingdoms, republics, and all sorts of principalities, either hereditary or otherwise, and all that belongs to a just government, and wishes to be considered as their Author, so he has put the sword into the hands of magistrates to suppress crimes against the first as well as against the second table of the Commandments of God. We must therefore, on his account, not only submit to them as superiors, but honour and hold them in, all reverence as his lieutenants and officers, whom he has commissioned to exercise a legitimate and holy authority.

40 We hold, then, that we must obey their laws and statutes, pay customs, taxes, and other dues, and bear the yoke of subjection with a good and free will, even if they are unbelievers, provided that the sovereign empire of God remain intact. Therefore we detest all those who would like to reject authority, to establish community and confusion of property, and overthrow the order of justice.

78 Geneva Bible, *Dedication to Elizabeth I and Notes on Tyranny* (1560)

Keywords: #Tyranny, #Authority, #Women, #Submission, #Resistance
Region: #Switzerland, #England
Group: #Reformed, #Calvinist | #Church of England

Exiles who fled to Geneva during Mary I's reign produced a translation of the Bible that had an enduring impact on the history of the Reformation in England, Scotland, and colonial America. The Geneva Bible (or sometimes Breeches Bible) drew on earlier English translations, like that produced by **William Tyndale**, but it went back to the Hebrew and Greek, following Renaissance humanist methods. It 'became the most popular translation for at least 80 years, going through at least 140 complete or partial editions up to 1644', writes David Norton.

> It gave people what they wanted: a relatively cheap, exceptionally well-presented Bible, with every possible aid to understanding except a concordance. The reader could feel he understood everything and that he was being placed in the position of a scholar.

This effect was achieved through the introduction of verse divisions and marginal notes. Both changed the reader's experience of scripture itself. The translation profoundly impacted England and Scotland, and the young **James VI** of Scotland (who had not yet become **James I** of England) even ordered the book printed with his royal imprimatur. However, after James ascended the English throne, he ordered a new translation, the Authorised (or King James) Bible of 1611. He took particular issue with the Geneva Bible's notes on tyranny and disobedience to authority, which is excerpted below. 'Tyrant', 'tyranny', or 'tyrannous' appear nowhere in his new note-free translation.[115]

The Geneva Bible featured a woodcut of the Red Sea moment of the Exodus on the cover, and this same image appeared in the book of Exodus and before the New Testament. The repeated use of this image emphasised the importance of the biblical Exodus to the self-understanding of Protestants. Two verses framed the woodcut:

294 *Sources*

Horizontal: 'Feare ye not. Stand stil, and beholde the salvation of the Lord, which he wil shewe to you this day. The Lord shal fight for you: Therefore holde you your peace'.

(Exod. 14:13–14)

Vertical: 'Great are the troubles of the righteous: but the Lord delivereth them out of all'.

(Ps. 34:19)

Because the godly were righteous (Ps. 34:19), they could expect God to fight for them (Exod. 14:13–14).[116]

A similar theme appeared in the dedication to **Elizabeth I,** which is also excerpted below. Such a dedication might seem to sit awkwardly with some of the controversial scriptural glosses in the Bible itself. However, the lengthy dedication made it clear that the queen was the hoped-for 'Zerubbabel' who would build the temple, but she was also to be instructed by clergy as to what godly government would mean. By implication, if she remained unteachable, she would have ceased to heed the voice of God.

The Bible and Holy Scriptures Conteyned in the Olde and Newe Testament (Geneva: Rouland Hall, 1560). Text modernised by the editors.

———

To the most virtuous and noble Queen Elizabeth....
Your humble subjects of the English Church at Geneva, wish grace and peace
from God the Father through Christ Jesus our Lord

...Which thing when we rightly weigh, and consider earnestly how much greater charge God hath laid upon you [the Queen] in making you a builder of his spiritual Temple, we cannot but partly fear, knowing the craft and force of Satan our spiritual enemy, and the weakness and inability of this our nature: and partly be fervent in our prayers toward God that he would bring to perfection this noble work which he hath begun by you: and therefore we endeavour ourselves by all means to aid and to bestow our whole force under your grace's standard, whom God hath made as our Zerubbabel for the erecting of this most excellent Temple [Zech. 4:9], and to plant and maintain his holy word to the advancement of his glory, for your own honour and the salvation of your soul, and for the singular comfort of that great flock which Christ Jesus the great shepherd has bought with his precious blood, and committed unto your charge to be fed both in body and soul.

———

Sources 295

[Textual notes in the Geneva Bible]
Genesis 6:4 (cf. 10:9)

There were giants* in the earth in those days; yes, and after that the sons of God came unto the daughters of men, and they had born them children, these were the mighty men, which in old time were men of renown.**

* *Or tyrants*
** Which usurped authority over others and did degenerate from the simplicity, wherein their fathers lived.
Exodus 1:16–17

[Pharaoh's command to the midwives.] When you do the office of a midwife of the Hebrews and see them on their stools,* if it is a son, then you shall kill him: but if it is a daughter, then let her live. Notwithstanding the midwives feared God, and did not do as the King of Egypt commanded them, but preserved alive the male children.

*Their disobedience herein was lawful, but their dissembling evil. [Pharaoh is also described as a tyrant in the notes].
Deuteronomy 17:20

[Commands for Israel's future king.] That his heart be not lifted up above his brethren,* and that he turn not from the commandment, to the right hand or to the left...

*Whereby is meant, that Kings ought so to love their subjects as nature binds one brother to love another.
Judges 9:54

Then Abimelech called hastily his page who bare his harness, and said unto him, Draw thy sword and slay me, that men say not of me, A woman slew him. And his page* thrust him through, and he died.

*Thus God by such miserable death takes vengeance on tyrants even in this life.
1 Samuel 26:9

And David said to Abishai, Destroy him [King Saul] not: for who can lay his hand* on the Lord's anointed, and be guiltless?

*Specifically, in his own private cause: for Jehu slew two Kings at God's appointment.

296   *Sources*

1 Kings 9:33

And he [Jehu] said, Cast her [Jezabel] down: and they cast her down*

> *This he did by the motion of the Spirit of God, that her blood should be shed, that had shed the blood of innocents, to be a spectacle and example of God's judgements to all tyrants.

79 *The Scottish Confession of Faith* (1560)

Keywords: #Confession of Faith, #Authority, #Magistrate, #Violence, #Church-State Relations, #Idolatry, #Resistance, #Submission
Region: #Scotland
Group: #Reformed, #Presbyterians

As Reformed confessions sprung up across Europe in the second half of the sixteenth century, the *Scottish Confession* (1560) emerged as a particularly important one. It was supplemented by the *Aberdeen Confession* (1616) and remained the official doctrinal statement of the Church of Scotland until the adoption of the **Westminster Confession** in 1647. Like Westminster, the following document emerged from political struggle. It was produced shortly after the downfall of Catholic power in Scotland and as Reformers gained the upper hand in church and state. The document was quickly written and is thought to be the work of **John Knox**, John Winram, John Spottiswoode, John Willock, John Douglas, and John Row. After Mary Stuart (Queen of Scots) was deposed, the confession was ratified by Parliament in 1567 under the reign of the infant **James VI** (the future James I of England).[117] The following extract comes from the section on the civil magistrate.

The Creeds of Christendom, Vol. III: The Evangelical Protestant Creeds, ed. Philip Schaff (New York: Harper and Brothers, 1887), 437–479 (474–476). Text modernised by the editors.

———

Article 24: Of the Civil Magistrate

We confess and acknowledge Empires, Kingdoms, Dominions, and Cities to be distinct and ordained by God; the powers and authority in the same, be it of Emperors in their Empires, of Kings in their Realms, Dukes and Princes in their Dominions, and of other Magistrates in the Cities, to be God's holy ordinance, ordained for the manifestation of his own glory, and for the singular profit and commodity of mankind: So that whosoever goes about to take away, or to confound the whole state of Civil policies, now long established;

298   *Sources*

we affirm the same men not only to be enemies to mankind but also wickedly to fight against God's expressed will. We further confess and acknowledge that such persons as are placed in authority are to be loved, honoured, feared, and held in most reverent estimation; because they are the Lieutenants of God, in whose Sessions God himself does sit and judge: Yea, even the Judges and Princes themselves, to whom by God is given the sword, to the praise and defence of good men, and to revenge and punish all open malefactors [Rom. 13:1–5]. Moreover, to Kings, Princes, Rulers and Magistrates, we affirm that the conservation and purgation of the Religion chiefly and most principally appertains; so that not only are they appointed for Civil policy but also for the maintenance of the true Religion, and for suppressing of Idolatry and Superstition whatsoever: As in David, Jehoshaphat, Hezekiah, Josiah, and others highly commended for their zeal in that case, may be discerned.

And therefore we confess and avow, that such as resist the supreme power, doing that thing which appertains to his charge, do resist God's ordinance; and therefore cannot be guiltless. And further, we affirm that whosoever denies unto them aid, their counsel and comfort, while the Princes and Rulers vigilantly travel in the execution of their office, that the same men deny their help, support and counsel to God, who, by the presence of his Lieutenant, does demand it of them.

80 Erik XIV, *Edict Concerning Religious Refugees* (1561)

Keywords: #Exile, #Refugee, #Pluralism, #Toleration, #Heresy, #Censorship
Region: #Sweden
Group: #Lutheran | #Reformed

Erik XIV (1533–1577) ascended Sweden's throne after the death of his father, Gustavus Vasa. His reign (1560–1568) was relatively short, and he likely experienced some cognitive challenges. His reign was marked by familial conflict and intense suspicion. When he decided to marry a commoner, his brothers opposed him, leading to his resignation and imprisonment until he died in 1577. Like his father, Erik supported the Reformation, but tried to avoid doctrinal disputes. Religious strife in other kingdoms might present an opportunity for Sweden. Many Reformed refugees had skills and money that might benefit any kingdom, and Gustavus Vasa and Erik sought to make Sweden attractive for religious exiles. Although Lutheranism was dominant, Erik showed considerable sympathy for the Reformed, extending toleration to them. In the first edict, reproduced below, Erik expressed distress at the plight of Protestants in France and offered his nation as a place of refuge. In the second edict, he required loyalty from these refugees and limited the public profession of their non-Lutheran version of Protestantism. A meagre number of refugees settled in Sweden as a result of such policies.[118]

Frank Puaux, *Histoire de L'établissement des protestants français en Suède* (Stockholm: Emile Giron, 1891), 11–12. Translated by Mariëtta van der Tol.

———

Edict of 5 February 1561

Touched with compassion for the persecuted, said he, wanting to facilitate the means for their salvation, [wanting] to relieve them in their affliction, and desiring to give them consolation and refuge, he permitted them to establish themselves in his kingdom, there wherever they desired.

300 *Sources*

Edict of 18 February 1561

They should also not sow any sect or heresy, nor despise or slander the religion which the King and the kingdom profess. If there were any doubts, they are obliged to go to the bishops in order to humbly reason with them. All religious propaganda was prohibited and above all, they were not to teach anything that was contrary to the Word of God.

81 Casiodoro de Reina, *Confessio Hispanica* (1560/1561)

Keywords: #Confession of Faith, #Authority, #Magistrate, #Church-State Relations, #Submission, #Violence
Region: #Spain, #England, #Switzerland
Group: #Lutheran, #Calvinist

Casiodoro de Reina (c.1520–1594) is one of the lesser known Protestants of the sixteenth century. He was part of a small circle of Protestant-leaning scholars in Sevilla, which dispersed under the pressure of the Spanish Inquisition. He lived in exile, moving between French, Swiss, German, Dutch, and English towns for the rest of his life. He produced two particularly notable works: a Spanish confession of faith as well as a Spanish translation of the Bible, which he completed while in Basel in 1569, and which is known as the *Biblia del Oso*.

The *Confessio Hispanica* stirred controversy by arguing that infant baptism was unscriptural. Further, both Lutherans and Calvinists would have been delighted and dismayed by aspects of his discussion of communion. Spain was associated with antitrinitarianism because of **Michael Servetus**, and Reina was accused of similar views. Even though this confession was orthodox on the Trinity, he was likely sympathetic to antitrinitarian arguments, and he openly critiqued Servetus' execution. Reina's theological allegiance was ill-defined, sometimes claiming this confession supported Calvinism and other times that it supported Lutheranism (he spent the latter part of his life as a Lutheran minister). In 1563, Reina fled to England after being accused of crimes ranging from heresy to sodomy, fearing that he would be executed after an unfair trial.

Reina produced the *Confessio Hispanica* as part of the process of establishing a separate strangers' church for the Spanish Protestant exiles in London. Bishop **Edmund Grindal** was satisfied with the confession. The following section on magistrates reads fairly deferentially, especially concerning the idea of the Christian magistrate. The text affirmed the distinct duties of civil and ecclesial authorities, but it maintains that the Christian magistrate could be the head of the church, holding together the distinct orders into the one jurisdiction of Christ.[119]

302 *Sources*

A. Gordon Kinder, ed., *Confessión de Fe Christiana* (Exeter: University of Exeter Press, 1988), 27–28. Reproduced with permission of the Licensor through PLSclear. Translated by Joshua Rowley.

———

13. Concerning the ministry of the word and the authority of ministers

1 We likewise consider the external ministry of the word to belong to the same category as the outward means of our justification. We confess that this ministry has been instituted by the Lord with the goal that his elect, who are spread throughout the world, will be called into his flock with the voice of his Gospel, and having been called, they would be justified by it. In this way the purpose and intent of God who chose them will be completed.

2 We believe that it is the office of the Lord himself – the Lord of the harvest – to call, authorise, and equip ministers of the New Testament with his gifts and Spirit, and to send them out to call his Church. Once the Church is called, the minister shall gather her together with a bond of faith and charity, grazing her upon the grass of God's word, and by his word, shall keep her in Christian unity and discipline.

3 Since all the authority of the apostleship or ministry of the word resides entirely (Lat: *in solidum*) in the one apostle who is the minister and master of our faith – the Christ – and since these ministers are sent out in his name, as has already been said, we confess that they are owed respect and obedience to the word that they administer. Because of this, those who obey or disobey them will actually be obeying or disobeying the Lord himself, since they are his ambassadors. We understand that this is the legitimate call of ministers; to teach no other Gospel than the one which the Lord taught and commanded to be preached among all people, and to avoid holding this teaching in a tyrannical way over the consciences of the people they are meant to serve by being the kingdom and inheritance of the Lord.

15. Concerning church discipline

1 Although we are not justified by the use of church discipline, there is good reason to consider it to be one of the external means of justification. First, it is used to keep the faithful who are gathered in a local body living righteous and pure lives. Second, it maintains the unity of faith and the knowledge of the doctrines that the catholic church professes.

2 We confess that all the faithful should submit to this doctrine of church discipline as governed by God's Spirit and his Divine Word, within the boundaries that Christian liberty permits and brotherly love demands.

Sources 303

3 We also submit ourselves to this doctrine with good will, both desiring and asking to be lovingly taught by those who better understand it, and to be corrected by the word in those areas that we also, as humans, find ourselves failing.

16. Concerning the political magistrate

1 We consider the political magistrate to be in the same category as church discipline, since we understand that they are ordained by God and by him given the sword to maintain the state (*la república*) in peace and rest, while defending it from enemies, punishing evildoers, and honouring and rewarding the virtuous. All this is done for the advancement of Christ's kingdom and glory.
2 Because of this, the magistrate is owed respect, tribute, and obedience by all people, no matter their condition in life, so long as he commands nothing in defiance of God's will and his word; This responsibility to submit is owed to him even if he is unfaithful.
3 Although we recognise that in the Christian church the offices of magistrate and minister of the word are different, just as the governance of a civil society is different to that of a church, still since the church gathered in a given place is not entirely distinct from a Christian state (*una Christiana república*), or its civil government, we understand that as long as the magistrate is faithful, he is the head of church discipline and has supreme authority to put into practice anything necessary for the Kingdom of the Lord and the advancement of his glory. This is true not only in matters of civil government, but also and most importantly in matters touching on the worship of God. In reality, we do not understand there to be more than one single jurisdiction within the faithful Church, having as its laws the Word of God and other laws that conform to it, and having the Christian magistrate as its supreme earthly judge.

82 Peter Martyr Vermigli, *Gideon and the Godly Commonwealth* (1561)

Keywords: #Magistrate, #Authority, #Submission, #Commonwealth, #Election, #Common Good, #Tyrant
Region: #Italy, #Switzerland
Group: #Reformed

Peter Martyr Vermigli (1499–1562) was born in Florence to a family of shoemakers. He entered a monastery before earning his doctorate at the University of Padua. After his ordination in 1525, he preached and lectured in philosophy. A Jewish doctor taught him Hebrew, and an interest in the Hebrew language, scripture, and political thought remained throughout his career. At various points in his ministry, he came under the suspicion of the Catholic hierarchy, although allies sometimes shielded him from penalties. However, he fled to Italy in 1542 to escape from the Inquisition. He made his way to Basel before **Martin Bucer** invited him to Strasbourg, where he lectured on the Hebrew Bible.

From 1548, he taught at Oxford at the invitation of **Thomas Cranmer**, participated in several important disputations, and helped produce the *Book of Common Prayer* (1552). Like many prominent Protestants, he left England upon the death of **Edward VI** (1553), and he lectured for a while to exiles in Strasbourg on the book of Judges. Pressure to conform to Lutheranism led him to relocate to Zürich in 1556. He made frequent trips at John Calvin's invitation to nearby Geneva. Vermigli's life was marked by persecution and exile, and, unsurprisingly, political theology infused much of his writings. He wrote on 'the authority of princes and magistrates, civil and ecclesiastical jurisdiction, exile and banishment, treason, sedition, tyranny, rebellion, and war'. Political theory commonly appears throughout his commentaries on biblical books, particularly in his expositions of Judges, the Books of Samuel, and the Books of Kings.

The following selection comes from his commentary on the eighth chapter of Judges (published in 1561). In the text, God raised up Gideon for the purpose of bringing Israel back to God and defeating Midianite enemies. After victory, the people tried to change Gideon's vocation from a judge to

Sources 305

a king, but Gideon refused the crown. Vermigli used this narrative to discourse on how God establishes godly rule, if the people are allowed to alter a God-ordained political arrangement, and what the people should do if they find themselves living under ungodly rulers. The text shows his oscillation between the political situation of the ancient Israelites, the errors he perceives in present church-state relations, and the proper ordering of the godly commonwealth. Vermigli argues that those wanting to govern in the sixteenth century must heed lessons from Israel's history. Over the next century, the Hebrew commonwealth, Hebrew republicanism, and the Talmud would grow in importance for Protestant political thought.[120]

Peter Martyr Vermigli, *Most Fruitfull [and] Learned Co[m]mentaries of Doctor Peter Martir Vermil Florentine* (London: John Day, 1564), 147–150. Text modernised by the editors.

———

Judges 8:22–23: Then the men of Israel said unto Gideon: Reign thou over us, both thou and thy son and thy son's son, because thou hast delivered us out of the hand of Midian. And Gideon answered them: I will not reign over you, neither shall my child reign over you, the Lord shall reign over you.

The people, receiving a benefit at Gideon's hand, would have made him king, in order that they might not be considered ungrateful. But seeing gratitude is a virtue, it ought to have no unjust thing joined with it: which these men observed not. For they appointed not their kingdom by the law of God. In Deuteronomy 27, it is written that the one whom God had chosen should be king. It is also not the people's role to appoint as king whoever they would. They do not freely give what is their own, but give what is another man's. The right to appoint a king belonged to God, and not unto men: which thing also Gideon wisely saw. Christ knew authority was God's to give: when the people who were filled with bread came unto him to create him a king, Christ refused the kingdom offered unto him.

[*Christ and the Hebrew Bible taught the same thing: people should not undertake to change an authority structure that was God ordained. Vermigli then discourses at great length on what he sees as a foundational error of the Roman Catholic Church. In his reading, they departed from the standard established by God in the New Testament and practised in the early church and by early bishops. They did so by arrogating spiritual authority to themselves. Gideon and Christ witness against Roman Catholicism. With Gideon, the people themselves sought to change the God-ordained order.*]

We must not trust unto the inconstancy of the common people, which is always moveable: now they will have Gideon to reign, a little afterwards you shall see that they were most ungrateful: for (as the history declares) they slew his children. Gideon did not refuse the principality because he did not want to labour for the public wealth [common good], but because he

306   *Sources*

understood that it was not a lawful vocation (Popes ought to regard this example). Gideon had before his eyes the law in Deuteronomy. The Pope ought also to look upon the words of Christ: Kings of the nations (saith the Lord) bear rule over their subjects: but you shall not do so: and being asked who should be greatest, he answered that the greatest was the lowest, the one who more served others [Luke 22:25–26]. This is what it means to govern the church: not to command but to serve. Peter also taught ministers not to bear dominion over their flock [1 Pet. 5:2–3]. And Paul hath written that Christ is the head of the church, and not men [Col. 1:18]: [*even as those who are preeminent servants of the church should be highly honoured*]. If we more highly honour such men in the church above others (not as lords, not as universal bishops, not as heads of the church, but as excellent ministers thereof), the authority and obedience of the word of God should not thereby be diminished.

[*Vermigli again jumps from the book of Judges into a lengthy discussion of the errors of the papacy and how that has influenced church-state relations. But Judges 8:23 raises another problem: Gideon seems to imply that human rule and divine rule were mutually exclusive.*]

Here is another question: is the rule and government of God excluded because the government of a public wealth, Aristocracy or kingdom is given unto a man? The question arises because when the people said unto Gideon, 'Thou shalt reign over us', he answered, 'I will not reign over you, but the Lord shall reign over you. It is not hard to dissolve this question: God's government of public wealths does not hinder the Magistrate, who is his Vicar and Minister. And God surely reigned together with David and Josiah: and the Israelites at that time had a certain Magistrate, and one of their own, with whom God himself also governed. Wherefore the words of Gideon do not teach that God cannot reign there, when there is a lawful king. But this is what Gideon had in mind: that the present state of things, which was instituted by God [in Deuteronomy 27], ought not to be altered without God's permission. At that point in Israel's history, there was a public wealth: they had Senators, and in all places, Judges were appointed. Therefore the form of the public wealth could not be changed by men without great offence. If this is the case thou will ask, when does God govern and rule in other Magistrates? I answer: Then, when this only is provided for, that Citizens may live virtuously. And forasmuch as piety is of all virtues the most excellent, the Lord doth then reign, when all things are referred unto it. Further, as concerning civil actions, when to every man is rendered his own, and Magistrates govern not for their own benefit, but for the public utility....

But when Princes are corrupt, what is to be done? We must obey, to the extent that religion allows. May private men take upon themselves to alter a corrupt Prince? They may do so by admonishing, by giving counsel and reproving, but not by force of weapons.... In the public wealth of the Hebrews, which flourished in the time of Gideon, God certainly governed. It was (as

I have said) an Aristocracy, where Elders were chosen by common voices, to do justice: in which office, if they did not rightly behave themselves, they were both punished and put out of their room. However, if a difficult war occurred, God himself raised up Judges who were not chosen by the people (neither did children succeed Parents in that office). God governed the Hebrews in this manner. The words of Gideon sufficiently declare that the Judges exercised not the office of an ordinary Magistrate. It was the Lord's prerogative to raise up for the time whom he would, therefore the Lord said unto Samuel: They have not rejected thee, but me, that I should not reign over them [1 Sam. 8:7].

By this example, we learn that when anything is offered to us, we must always weigh if it is good in itself, whether it is lawfully given, and may lawfully be used. If it is not, let us put the offered thing away from us, just as Christ rejected Satan when he promised him all the kingdoms of the world [Matt. 4:8–10]. He also refused the kingdom when it was offered by the people [John 6:15]. The Pope does not consider this point, rather he continually wars to protect his unlawful Supremacy or tyranny.

83 John Calvin's Letters to Jeanne III (1561–1563)

Keywords: #Women, #Authority, #Idolatry, #Coercion, #Church-State Relations
Region: #Switzerland, #France
Group: #Reformed, #Calvinist

John Calvin kept up correspondence not only with magistrates, but interestingly also with a number of aristocratic women.[121] Knowing how important support from the nobility was for the success of the Reformation, he often urged these women to draw their husbands towards the Reformation. **Jeanne III** (1528–1572) was such a woman: married to Antoine the Bourbon and daughter of Marguerite de Navarre, she became the Queen of Navarre in 1555. Jeanne III would publicly declare her conversion to Calvinism in 1560 and would actively foster Huguenot activities in her lands. Her husband was more ambivalent in his support for the Reformation, not least because of his political opportunism and political pressure. This ambivalence and his sexual affairs put their marriage under strain. Jeanne's growing estrangement from her husband provides the background for the following series of letters from John Calvin.[122] The letters show something of Calvin's opportunism in furthering the Reformation in France, the affirmation of the role of aristocratic women, and his willingness to mix pastoral support with political strategy.

In the first letter (16 January 1561), Calvin rejoiced in her conversion and encouraged her to influence her husband, Antoine, to remain sympathetic to Protestantism. By the second letter (24 December 1561), Calvin urged her to try to get her husband to take a more definitive stand for the evangelical faith. The tenor shifted in the third letter (22 March 1562): her husband thwarted the Reformation and threatened Jeanne. Antoine blamed Jeanne for publicly supporting Protestantism and especially for siding with Reformed rebels. Her husband died later that year in battle, having supported the Catholics (although it was claimed he died a Lutheran). Calvin dispatched another letter (20 January 1563) to the queen, along with a Reformed minister, to help her bring her realm into the fold of the Reformation. The letters evidence the precarious situation of a Protestant noblewoman whose conscience led her to take a vocal and active role in aligning her realms with her faith commitments.

Jules Bonnet, *Letters of John Calvin*, trans. Marcus Robert Gilchrist (Philadelphia, PA: Presbyterian Board of Publication, 1858), IV:163–165, 245–246, 266–267, 90–93.

———

Geneva, 16 January 1561

Madame: – I cannot adequately express my joy at the letter you were pleased to write to my brother Monsieur de Chatlonné [pseudonym for Theodore Beza], seeing how powerfully God had wrought in you in a few hours. For though already long ago he had sown in you some good seed, you know at present that it was almost choked out by the thorns of this world....

[*He encourages her to devote herself to the faith out of gratitude to God and not* 'swim between two currents'.] Having then received so great and inestimable a benefit, you have reason to be so much more zealous to dedicate yourself (as you do) entirely to Him, who has bound you so closely to himself. And whereas kings and princes would often wish to be exempted from subjection to Jesus Christ, and are accustomed to make a buckler of their privileges under pretence of their greatness, being ashamed even to belong to the fold of this great Shepherd, do you, Madame, bethink you that the dignity and grandeur in which this God of goodness has brought you up, should be in your esteem a double tie to bind you to obedience to him, seeing that it is from him that you hold everything, and that according to the measure which each one has received, he shall have to render a stricter account [Jas 3:1]. But since I see how the Spirit of God governs you, I have more reason to render him thanks than to exhort you as if you needed to be goaded forward. When, besides, I doubt not but you apply all your zeal to that end, as is indeed very requisite, when we reflect on the coldness, weakness, and frailty that is within us.

Long ago we had already essayed to discharge our duty with respect to the king your husband, and even more than once to the end that he might quit himself manfully. But you will see once more, Madame, by the copy of the letter which we have sent to him, what effects your admonition has produced....

Geneva, 24 December 1561

...[W]e have wherewith to bless God for having wrought so efficaciously in you, Madame, and caused you to surmount everything that might have turned you aside from the right path. It were much to be wished that the king, your husband, once for all, form a firm resolution not to swim any longer between two currents. I know, Madame, how much you are labouring to bring that about. But I entreat you, if you do not succeed so soon as we should wish, that the delay does not exhaust your patience, nor cool your zeal. For the rest, Madame, whatever happen, you know how carefully

310 *Sources*

we should beware of withdrawing ourselves from God to gratify mortal creatures, which ought to give you courage zealously to persevere, aiming at the end which is proposed to you, whatever winds blow from opposite directions....

Geneva, 22 March 1562

Madame: – My compassion for your sorrows makes me feel, in part, how severe they must be to you, and how bitter to support. But be they what they will, assuredly it is infinitely better to be sorrowful for such a cause than to live in contented indifference to the perdition of your soul.... You have been taught, Madame, that we cannot serve him [God] without fighting. The kinds of combats are diverse, but in whatever way it shall please God to exercise us, we ought to be prepared for it. If the assaults you have to sustain are rude and terrible, God has long ago furnished you with an opportunity of meditating on them beforehand.... Not only has he [her husband, the king] allowed himself to be cast down by them [ungodly teachers], but, of his own accord, he arms himself against God and God's children. I speak as of a thing that is notorious. I know, Madame, that the first batteries are directed against you. But though the difficulties should be a hundred times greater, the courage comes from on high, when we have recourse to it, will be victorious....

Geneva, 20 January 1563

Madame: – Since it has pleased God, in removing from this world the late king, your husband, to put into your hands the entire charge of your country and subjects, you do well to think of acquitting yourself of your duty, as having to render an account to a Master and Sovereign Prince, who desires that his right should be maintained. For in commanding that he himself should be feared and kings honoured, thus doing you the honour of associating you with himself, it is every way reasonable that you should strive to do him homage and show him gratitude for the state and dignity which you hold from him; and just as you would not suffer the superiority which belongs to you to be taken from you by your officers, so you are bound, if you desire to be maintained under the protection of God, to take measures as far as it shall be in your power to have him served and honoured, showing to others the example. And in fact Madame, it is only in subjecting your majesty to him that your reign will be established before him. You know that every knee should bend under the empire of our Lord Jesus Christ, but kings are specially commanded to pay him this mark of homage, for the purpose of showing better how much more they are held to cast down the loftiness which has been bestowed on them, and exalt him who is the chief of the angels of paradise and consequently of the great ones of this world. Wherefore, Madame, since the government is now come into your hands, know that God wishes to prove more and more the zeal and solicitude you have to acquit yourself faithfully in giving the pre-eminence to the true service which he demands. There are several reasons which prevent me from pushing this argument any farther.

For all who have any dominion are also enjoined to purge their territories of every kind of idolatry and corruption, by which the purity of true religion is defiled. And when St. Paul commands to pray for kings and all who are in authority, it is not without cause that he adds this reason, 'In order that we may live under them in all godliness and honesty' [1 Tim. 2:2]. Before speaking of civil virtues, he enjoins the fear of God, by which he signifies that the office of princes is to see that God be adored with purity. I take into consideration the difficulties which may retard you, the fears and doubts which may debilitate your courage, and I am persuaded that the numerous councillors you shall have around you, if they think only of the world, will endeavour to stay your hand in this good work. But it is certain that all fear of men which will divert us from paying to God the homage he deserves, and induce us to deprive him of his due, proves that we do not fear him in good earnest, and make but small account of his invincible power, by which he has promised to protect us. Wherefore, Madame, in order to surmount all difficulties, lean upon the assurance which is given you from on high, after complying with all that God requires.

These are the two points on which it behoves you to have your eyes constantly fixed, which should serve you even as wings to raise you above all the obstacles of the world: namely, to know what God commands you to do, and that he will never fail so to strengthen your hands that you will succeed in all you shall attempt in obedience to him. I know indeed the arguments that several bring forward to prove that princes ought not to compel their subjects to live in a Christian manner. But it is a dispensation far too profane – that which permits the man who will give up nothing that belongs to himself, to defraud his superior of his rights. If God's command does not move us, this threat should cause us to tremble; every kingdom that will not be subservient to that of Jesus Christ shall come to nought. For that refers properly to the state of the Christian Church. Thus whatever fine excuses the persons produce who wish to colour over their own cowardice, I entreat you, Madame, to reflect seriously with yourself, and judge whether the empire of God should not be preferred to the honour which he has bestowed on you, and you will be able speedily to resolve this point.

[*As a second point of concern, Calvin urges the queen to trust that God will preserve her kingdom against hostile neighbours. Along with the letter, he sent a minister, Raymond Merlin, to give her more detailed instructions about governing well. He closes by urging her to quickly reach out to the Protestant princes of Germany.*]

84 Sébastien Castellion, *Advice to a Desolate France* (1562)

Keywords: #Pluralism, #Irenicism, #Violence, #Toleration, #Conscience
Region: #France
Group: #Reformed | #Roman Catholic

The French theologian Sébastien Castellion (1515–1563) moved in the circles of the Genevan Reformers, but he took a different position on religious toleration. He was propelled into the spotlight by **Concerning Heretics and Those Who Burn Them** (1554) – a work that condemned **John Calvin** for justifying the execution of **Michael Servetus** on account of heresy. Another major work is his *Advice to a Desolate France* (1562), which he wrote in response to the eruption of religious tension and violence in France. In this work, he urged Catholics and Protestants to eschew persecution and tone down their vitriolic rhetoric. These works have in common that they leverage a very powerful critique of Protestants who engage in forms of violence, clearly speaking from within the Reformed tradition, previously to Calvin and here against the Reformed in France.

His *Advice to a Desolate France* followed on the heels of three important events: the 1650 Conspiracy of Amboise, which was a failed attempt to bring Henri II towards Protestantism resulting in the execution of conspirators; the 1652 January Edict, which allowed for limited Protestant toleration and worship; and the 1662 Wassay Massacre, which entailed an attack on Protestant worshipers by Duke François de Guise. The excerpts below show his plea with the magistrates, clergy, and people of France to de-escalate the situation by following the example of Christ. He argued that fighting between Catholics and Protestants had already cost tens of thousands of lives, and this scourge of God (war) might be followed by God's two other weapons – plague and famine. Everyone could see the malady, but their solutions – violence and religious coercion – only made matters worse. Castellio identified the 'principle and effective cause of your malady' to be 'the forcing of consciences'. His work aimed to be non-partisan, referring to the two sides as Evangelics (instead of Huguenots) and Catholics (instead of Papists). His critique and advice, similarly, aimed to be even-handed. The following selection comes from his opening address and demonstrates his admonishing tone to both sides of the violent conflict.[123]

Sebastian Castellio, *Advice to a Desolate France*, trans. Wouter Valkhoff (Grand Rapids, MI: Acton Institute, 2016), 7–14. Reproduced with permission.

———

To the Catholics

First of all I want to talk to you, O Catholics, who claim to have the ancient, true and catholic faith and religion.... Remember how you have hitherto treated the Evangelics. You know well that you have persecuted them.... And for what crime? Because they did not want to believe in the Pope, or mass, or purgatory and such other things, all of which so completely lack any foundation in the Scriptures, that even their names are nowhere to be found in them. Is that not a beautiful and just reason for burning people alive? You call yourselves Catholics and make it your business to uphold the Catholic faith, as contained in the Holy Scriptures, but you nevertheless hold for heretics, and burn alive, those who only want to believe that which is contained in the Scriptures?

[*Consider this question that you will*] be asked on the Day of Judgement. Would you yourselves like to be treated in this manner? Would you like to be persecuted, imprisoned, locked in subterranean cellars, given as food to lice and fleas, to rot in mud pits, to be kept in hideous dark places and under the shadow of death and, finally, to be roasted alive on a small fire, for not having believed in or confessed to something which was against your conscience? What do you answer? But what need is there for an answer; it is well known that your conscience says no, so emphatically indeed that even the most impudent amongst you would not dare to deny it.

[*God will judge those who have done evil in forcing consciences.*] And this is proof that to force a person's conscience is worse than to deprive him cruelly of his life, for a God-fearing person prefers to have himself cruelly deprived of his life rather than to let his conscience be forced. [*He acknowledges how Evangelics try to force Catholics to attend church. Catholics who know what it is like to have their conscience violated should not violate consciences.*]

To the Evangelics

Now I am coming to you, Evangelics. In the past you peaceably suffered persecution for the sake of the Gospel, loved your enemies and rendered good for evil. You blessed those who cursed you, resisting them in no other way than by fleeing, if necessary, and all this you did in accordance with the commandment of the Lord. From where, now, comes such a great change in some of you? ... Has the Lord changed His commandment, and have you received a new revelation telling you to do exactly the opposite of what you did before? You began well in spirit, but how did you manage to succeed in the flesh?

314 *Sources*

He who formerly commanded you to endure, and to render right for wrong, and whom you then obeyed in enduring, and in rendering right for wrong, has He now commanded you to render wrong for wrong, and to persecute others, instead of enduring persecution? Or have you now turned your back on His commandment, and do you henceforth want to shake His yoke off your shoulders and live as it pleases you, by following the world, your minds and your enemies? For what else can one think, when you exchange all your possessions and even those of the poor, for halberds and harquebuses, when you kill and massacre your enemies and put them to the point of the sword, when you fill and besmirch the paths and streets, and even the houses and temples, with the blood of those for whom, like for yourselves, Christ has died, and who, like you, have been baptised in His name?

What more can I say but that you are forcing them against their consciences to attend your sermons and, what is worse, that you are forcing some to take up arms against their own brothers and those of their own religion....

[*Protestants might justify coercion on the grounds that their doctrine is in the right and the Catholics are in the wrong, but this same logic would license Catholics in their suppression of Protestantism. He then argues that all the prayer and fasting will not avert God's ire if Protestants continue disobeying God through their mistreatment of Catholics. Protestant killers should take warning from David's example. He was not allowed the build a physical temple because of bloodshed and Protestant killers are unqualified builders of a spiritual temple.*]

85 John Foxe, *To the Persecutors* (1563)

Keywords: #Persecution, #Law, #Violence, #Church-State Relations, #Heresy
Region: #England
Group: #Church of England | #Roman Catholic

The English historian and theologian John Foxe (1517–1587) is known for writing one of the most influential and widely read books in Christian history, *The Acts and Monuments of John Foxe* (better known as *Foxe's Book of Martyrs*). His mixture of historical detail and dialogue – coupled with visually appealing illustrations – contributed to the proliferation of this work across all classes of English society. It profoundly shaped English Protestant identity and Protestant history more broadly. Like many others, he sought refuge from Mary I. Persecution was a personal matter for him.

Acts and Monuments detailed the lives of those killed by unjust rulers. However, in places where Protestants gained power, Protestant magistrates would use the sophistry Foxe denounced to put to death those deemed guilty of heresy. The ambivalent relationship between power, persecution, and orthodoxy is evident in the dedication of the *Acts and Monuments* to **Elizabeth I**. Catholics and some 'Puritan' Protestants came to view Elizabeth as the persecutor of the faithful. The following extract is taken from the preface to the *Acts and Monuments*: 'To the Persecutors of God's Truth', which has strongly anti-Catholic overtones. In the following excerpt, Foxe argued that individual Catholics were guilty of complicity in the shedding of the blood of Christians. He argued that Catholics could not hide behind divine or human law.[124]

John Foxe, *The Acts and Monuments of John Foxe*, ed. Rev. George Townsend (London: Seeley, Burnside and Seeley, 1843), I:xiv.

———

Perhaps you will excuse yourselves, and say, that you did but the law [when you persecuted Protestants]; and if the law did pass upon them, you could not do otherwise. But here I will ask, what law do you mean? The law of God, or the law of man? If ye mean the law of God, where do you find in all

316 *Sources*

the law of God, to put them to death, which, holding the articles of the creed, never blasphemed his name, but glorified it, both in life, and in their death? If you answer, by the law of man, I know the law ('ex officio' or rather ex *homicidio*) which you mean and follow. But who brought that law in first, in the time of king Henry IVth, but you? Who revived the same again in queen Mary's days, but you? Further, who kept them in prison before the law, till, by the law, you had made a rope to hang them withal? And think you by charging the law, to discharge yourselves? But you will use here some translation of the fact perchance; alleging that you burnt them not, but only committed them to the secular power, by whom, you will say, they were burnt, and not by you. It will be hard to play the sophister before the Lord. For so it may be said to you again, that the fire burned them, and not the secular power. But I pray you, who put them in? But they were heretics, you will say, and Lutherans, and therefore we burnt them, thinking thereby to do God good service, etc. Of such service-doers Christ spake before, saying, that such should come, who, putting his servants to death, should think to do good service to God.

86 *Heidelberg Catechism* (1563)

Keywords: #Family, #Authority, #Submission, #Oath, #Crime, #Violence, #Communion, #Love
Region: #Germany
Group: #Reformed

The *Heidelberg Catechism*, as one of the *Three Forms of Unity*, is among the most important documents in the continental Reformed tradition. Designed for the religious instruction of ordinary Protestants, it condensed some of the core doctrines of the Reformed tradition, especially on the doctrine of covenant.[125] It was Frederick III, Elector of the Palatinate, who ordered its production under the leadership of **Zacharias Ursinus** (1534–1583) and Caspar Olevianus (1536–1587). Ursinus also wrote a *Commentary on the Heidelberg Catechism*. The catechism would contribute to the standardisation of basic systematic theology in the Reformed tradition, which served the interests of religious unity and provided a theological defence against the emerging Counter-Reformation stemming from the Council of Trent.[126]

The *Heidelberg Catechism* contains few references to political authority or political theology in general, although there are some important cues. For example, the section on the Ten Commandments extended the obedience due to one's parents to all forms of authority. This suggests an understanding of the political community as a large family, under the leadership of a father-like monarch, who was to be revered. Another cue was the condemnation of the Catholic Mass as 'cursed'. This raises significant questions about the understanding of political order, especially as the Eucharist had been a gatekeeper in the political imaginary of the *corpus christianum*. It appears as if the existing political order within the Palatinate was taken for granted, and that within those parameters, ordinary Christians were simply expected to be faithful to Christ, loyal to the Prince, and obedient to the magistrates as sanctioned through oath-taking as expedient.

The Creeds of Christendom, Vol. III: The Evangelical Protestant Creeds, ed. Philip Schaff (New York: Harper and Brothers, 1887), 307–355 (335–336, 344–347).

———

318   *Sources*

Question 80.

What difference is there between the Lord's Supper and the Popish Mass?

Answer: The Lord's Supper testifies to us that we have full forgiveness of all our sins by the one sacrifice of Jesus Christ, which he himself has once accomplished on the cross; [and that by the Holy Ghost we are ingrafted into Christ, who with his true body is now in heaven at the right hand of the Father, and is to be there worshiped]. But the Mass teaches that the living and the dead have not forgiveness of sins through the sufferings of Christ unless Christ is still daily offered for them by the priests; [and that Christ is bodily under the form of bread and wine, and is therefore to be worshiped in them]. And thus the Mass at bottom is nothing else than a denial of the one sacrifice and passion of Jesus Christ [and an accursed idolatry].)

Question 101.

But may we not swear by the name of God in a religious manner?

Answer: Yes; when the magistrate requires it, or it may be needful otherwise to maintain and promote fidelity and truth, to the glory of God and our neighbour's good. For such swearing is grounded in God's Word, and therefore was rightly used by the saints in the Old and New Testament.

Question 104.

What does God require in the fifth commandment?

Answer: That I show all honour, love, and faithfulness to my father and mother, and to all in authority over me; submit myself with due obedience to all their good instruction and correction, and also bear patiently with their infirmities, since it is God's will to govern us by their hand.

Question 105.

What does God require in the sixth commandment?

Answer: That I neither in thought, nor in word or look, much less in deed, revile, hate, insult, or kill my neighbour, whether by myself or by another; but lay aside all desire of revenge: moreover, that I harm not myself, nor wilfully run into any danger. Wherefore, also, to restrain murder, the magistrate is armed with the sword.

Question 107.

Is it, then, enough that we do not kill our neighbour in any such way?

Answer: No; for in condemning envy, hatred, and anger, God requires us to love our neighbour as ourselves, to show patience, peace, meekness, mercy, and kindness towards him, and, so far as we have power, to prevent his hurt; also, to do good even unto our enemies.

Question 110.

What does God forbid in the eighth commandment?

Answer: Not only such theft and robbery as are punished by the magistrate, but God views as theft also all wicked tricks and devices whereby we seek to draw to ourselves our neighbour's goods, whether by force or with show of right, such as unjust weights, ells, measures, wares, coins, usury, or any means forbidden of God; so, moreover, all covetousness, and all useless waste of his gifts.

87 Bernardino Ochino, *On the Toleration of Heretics* (1563)

Keywords: #Heresy, #Persecution, #Violence, #Pluralism, #Toleration
Region: #Italy, #Switzerland
Group: #Antitrinitarian (close to)

Bernardino Ochino (1487–1564/1565) was one of the most important and controversial figures of the Italian Reformation. Formerly vicar-general of the Capuchin order, his defection to Protestantism and flight from the Italian Peninsula in 1542, alongside **Peter Martyr Vermigli**, sent shockwaves across the Roman establishment. He subsequently pursued his preaching activities as he travelled across Europe, from Geneva, to Augsburg, to England, eventually settling in Zurich as the minister of the local Italian refugee congregation. His anti-Catholic polemical works were immensely successful, and saw translations into Latin, French, English, German, Dutch, Danish, and Polish. His career took an unexpected turn in the early 1560s, however: the publication of a number of increasingly radical works of his culminated in his expulsion from Zurich following the scandal caused by his *Thirty Dialogues* (1563), in which, under the veil of ambiguity provided by the dialogue form, he put forward heterodox views on a number of contentious theological issues, including the Trinity, polygamy, and the nature of true doctrine.

The following is an extract from Dialogue 28, where the two interlocutors, Pope Pius IV and the reform-minded cardinal Giovanni Morone, discuss the question of whether or not heretics should be punished. The ideas put forward by 'Moronus', the clear winner in the debate, are very close to those espoused by Ochino's close friend and collaborator **Sebastian Castellio** (1515–1563), perhaps the most prominent theorist of religious toleration of the sixteenth century. Castellio himself was responsible for the translation of Ochino's *Dialogues* from Italian into Latin. Although the two speakers in the dialogue are Catholic, the text is in fact also intended as a not-so-veiled critique of the stance on the coercion of heretics adopted by the Reformed churches in which Ochino operated: the arguments adopted by Pius often echo those of **Theodore Beza**'s *That heretics should be punished by the civil magistrate* (1554). Ochino's dialogue is thus to be read as a contribution to the debate over the toleration of heretics that had been raging in Reformed

Switzerland since the burning at the stake of the antitrinitarian heretic **Michael Servetus** in Geneva in 1553.[127]

Bernardini Ochini Senensis Dialogorum liber secundus, cum aliis de rebus variis, tum potissimum de Trinitate, vol. 2 (Basel: [Perna], 1563), 379–387. Translated by Odile Panetta.

——

[Pius]:   While many and most serious burdens weigh on our shoulders, what is most vexing is this: that not only in Italy, but also in other parts of Europe, heretics are tormented most cruelly, and deprived of their goods and honour, and thrown into prison; and finally, having endured all iniquities, they are burned; and all these things are done under the appearance of religion and care for justice, and by our authority. And since by experience we know that the more they have been tormented, the more they have proliferated – which makes it seem like God favours them – we have begun to suspect that to rage against them in this way is something which is unwelcome to God, and we have learned to avoid that serious punishment which our predecessor, a most cruel enemy of theirs, and his intimate and dearest friends incurred. Therefore we want what our duty towards them is to be properly stated.

[Moronus]:   If someone takes up the defence of a thief, or a murderer, or a bandit, he is not therefore considered similar to the person he defends; but in the case of a heretic, he is. I think the reason for this is the following: that it generally occurs that heretics are both many in number and held to be among the powerful and authoritative, and to be Evangelicals, when in fact true, sincere, and saintly Christians are both few in number, and deemed to be heretics. And since the former cannot refute the latter, who hold the truth through reasoning and authority, they deploy fraud and force; and in order to ensure that no one take on the defence of the heretics' cause, when someone does so, they declare him a heretic, expose him to ridicule, and punish him as such. Indeed, if I deservedly take on the defence of their cause, I do not want to incur your suspicion. On the other hand, God, through Solomon's voice, commands that I speak and defend the cause of the mute [Prov. 31:8]. I call mute he who either does not know how to defend his cause or cannot defend it.

[Pius]:   Speak freely now: for we will not judge you to be different from what you are. Certainly, if knowledge of the truth could constrain our power, I would order you to keep quiet; but this

322   Sources

power has always been, and is, and will be for as long as it lasts, free, unbound, and higher than all equity.

[Moronus]: So that we might find the truth in this case, it must be known that sometimes he is called a heretic who chooses some thing for himself to believe and follow, believing it to be good and true. Thus if this thing is true and good, he is a good heretic; and for this reason true and good Christians are rightly called heretics (*haeretici*), since they firmly adhere (*adhaerescunt*) to Evangelical truth [Acts 24:14]. And certainly such people are to be defended and received with approval, not tormented. I admit that generally the name 'heretic' is interpreted as a fault, and is attributed to those who both err and adhere obstinately to their error. But here one must consider whether they err in a matter which is necessary to salvation or not. For if they err in a matter which is not necessary to salvation, they must not be burned, nor held as enemies of God. Indeed, not only do Scholastic doctors hold many conflicting opinions – of which sort comes to mind that of the virgin Mary's conception, with some contending that she was conceived in original sin, others the opposite – but even Canonists disagree among one another on many matters; nor did our ancient scholars never disagree among one another, and yet, however, they did not deserve to be burned, excommunicated, execrated, since they did not err in matters necessary to salvation.

[Pius]: If the Apostles' Creed contains all things which are necessary to salvation, as is to be believed, and all those who within about forty years have been tormented, defamed, vexed under the name of heresy believed and professed (as indeed we've heard) whatever is contained in the Apostles' Creed, it follows that they were tormented for matters which are irrelevant and unnecessary for salvation; and perhaps, since they did not believe some things which, had they believed them, would have made them most terrible heretics, they should not have been tormented. If this is the case, the Popes that killed them, and likewise their ministers, were most cruel and wicked tyrants and torturers. Truly you have stung us.

[Moronus]: You commanded me to say what I think, so you cannot deservedly complain about me, if I obey you.

[Pius]: Please, continue.

[Moronus]: Further, if the heretic errs in the fundamentals of faith and out of ignorance, being willing to embrace the truth and to abandon his error if he knew it, he should not be burned. For not only nature, but even Moses' law decrees that if you see an ox, or an ass, or a lamb belonging to, I won't say a brother, but a

Sources 323

stranger, and even an enemy of yours, in danger, you should not kill it, but on the contrary bring it back to the right path as far as is possible [Deut. 22:4]. All the more should the same be done to man, to the extent that he is both more noble and dearer to God than beasts, and his salvation or destruction is of greater importance than that of other animals. The law of charity commands this; and when it is done, he who errs out of imprudence and does not lack reason, if the right way is shown to him, will certainly embrace it, having abandoned the false one, and will thank the person who showed it to him.

[Pius]: Our Inquisitors do not assess the matter in such detail; indeed, if someone errs, they burn him, lest he cause revulsion.

[Moronus]: But Scripture relays that God commanded that if someone errs in matters necessary to salvation he should be instructed, not that he should be burned. And if in Rome there were some mad nephew of yours, you would ensure not that he be burned, but that he be locked up and restrained in some room, so that he could not harm either himself or others; and further, you would arrange for doctors, if they can, to heal him. Likewise, since heresy is nothing other than some madness that possesses men, you should see to it that heretics be detained in some place where they cannot harm others; and further, ensure that learned men instruct them. This pertains to Christian piety.

God never established that he who erred unknowingly should be killed, even if he killed a man; indeed, so as to care for the life of murderers of this kind, he established refuges [Lev. 4; 5:14–16; 16]. And the Jews' high priest did not kill those who had erred unknowingly, but performed sacrifices and prayed for their imprudence, as is relayed in Scripture [Heb. 9:7]. Abimelech said to God: 'Will you kill even the innocent?' Where he numbers himself among the innocent, since he had unknowingly taken for himself another's wife, namely Sara [Gen. 20:2–7]. Christ himself, speaking of the Jews, said: 'If I had not come, and spoken to them, they would not have been in sin; now they have no excuse for their sin' [John 15:22]. Thus if Christ himself had come, but had not revealed himself to be the Messiah, the Jews would have been excusable for not holding him to be the Messiah. Indeed, even though Jesus did reveal himself to them so clearly and in so many ways, and nonetheless was not received by them, still not only did he not kill them, but even prayed for them while dying on the cross, and excused them. 'They know not', he said, 'what they do' [Luke 23:34]. And we burn men if they do not accept, I won't say Christ, but our decrees?

324 *Sources*

I will add another point: it is not licit for the magistrate to kill a man suddenly and without having given him space to repent [...]. For if he were to kill him having given him no space for repentance, he might perhaps cause him to perish eternally, when maybe he would have repented, had he been warned in advance of his death; or, if, having been warned, he had not repented, this would not have depended on the magistrate. Likewise, it is not licit for the magistrate to kill a heretic, if he is a heretic in matters which are necessary to salvation, but out of ignorance. For he will not repent if he is killed, since he does not believe he is in error, and not even if he is given space for repentance; indeed, he will strive to be all the firmer in his error. Thus he who believed himself to be a martyr of Christ would be condemned to eternal suffering, and this at the fault of the magistrate, who should have instructed him, not burned him. Consequently, if the magistrate were to kill a heretic who errs knowingly and out of a corrupt will, and in matters which are necessary to salvation, he would err less than if he were to kill someone who does err, but out of ignorance, in matters likewise necessary to salvation. For there is hope for the repentance and salvation of the former, but not for that of the latter – although in this case, the fear of death can sometimes lead to lying, namely, to his saying that he believes what in fact he does not believe.

Therefore the true and only remedy for those who err out of ignorance is this: that they be instructed in the truth, and that we pray for them. For heresy is some error in men's minds, and thus a spiritual and indivisible matter, which cannot be eradicated from the soul with chisels, nor with pikes, and not even with fire, but only with the light of God's word, which, as soon as it has illuminated the mind, causes all darkness of error to vanish. For this reason, Paul says,

> The weapons of our warfare are not carnal, but divinely powerful, for the demolition of strongholds, with which weapons we cast down imaginations, and every high thing exalted against the knowledge of God, and we compel every mind to obey Christ [2 Cor. 10:4–5].

Further, if we seek to coerce heretics, we immediately make ourselves suspicious in their eyes. For they reason to themselves thus: 'If these people could have convinced us with arguments or with God's word, they would never have used force; therefore they are utterly iniquitous'. Thus they hold us as frauds and enemies, and therefore become more resolute and resist; whereas if we had used charity and God's word against them, they would have given themselves over to us, and perhaps we might have converted them.

It wholly pertains to our duty to eradicate their heresy, which is corrupt, in such a way as to save the heretic, who is good, since he is God's creature. But heresy is defeated, like all other bad things, through its opposite, as fire is extinguished with water. Moreover, if the heretic errs out of ignorance, it is our duty to instruct him; if he errs out of malice, it is our duty, according to Paul's doctrine, to defeat him with favours. At present the opposite occurs,

Sources 325

when, by being burned, God's creature is damned, not healed, and even sent to hell in its heresy.

Moreover, heresies arise not from the study of Scripture, but from Satan and the flesh, of which they are fruits, as Paul writes [Gal. 5:20]. Thus if they arise from Satan, Satan must be driven away from the heretic. But Satan fears neither sword, as Job says [Job 41:26–30], nor fire, nor our forces; but he fears God's word, and is reduced to nothing by it, as Isaiah and Paul wrote [2 Thess. 2:8–12]. If they arise from the flesh, the heretic should not be burned, but be regenerated, and from carnal made spiritual, which is done by faith, which, as Paul writes, comes from the word of God [Rom. 10:17]. If we could obtain through promises or threats, or gifts or torments, or even death itself, that the heretic abandon his error, it would be licit for us to use such devices, provided they not be contrary to God's word. But these things are not conducive to dissuading heretics from their opinion, but rather to ensuring that they lie, and say, against their own conscience, either that they believe what they do not truly believe, or that they do not believe what they do believe; and this because they do not want to be punished.

Thus there is no true remedy by which they may be drawn from their error, other than the light of divine doctrine and prayers, accompanied by an honest life. These are the remedies we must use. If it were in our power to give heretics that infused, supernatural, living, true faith, and they were to reject it from us when we offer it, their error would be great, and deserving of grave punishment, especially if they recognised that it is true. But to either give it to them, or even deny it, is not in our power. Nay, even if heretics tried with great effort to obtain living faith, still they would not elicit it from God; for, as Paul wrote, it is a gift of God [Eph. 2:8], and does not depend on our works, but on His grace alone, which only enlightens, and concedes living faith to, those whom He wants, and when He wants, not according to our will. God called some to cultivate His vineyard early in the morning, others at the third hour, others at the sixth, others at the ninth, others at the eleventh [Matt. 20:1–16]; nor should we establish limits on His mercy, as Judith says [Jdt. 8:16], or fix a time for Him to help us. Thus it is our duty, not to burn heretics, but to pray God, that He gift them living faith; and moreover, with regard to voluntary faith, to instruct them through Scripture, remitting the outcome to God.

88 Jacopo Aconcio, *Satan's Strategy of Persecution* (1565)

Keywords: #Persecution, #Toleration, #Censorship, #Heresy, #Violence
Region: #Italy, #Poland, #Czech Republic
Group: #Antitrinitarian

Jacopo Aconcio (c.1520–c.1566) was born in or near Trento, Italy. He studied law and worked for several prominent individuals in church and state. As his sympathies for the Reformation grew, he anticipated a moment when he would no longer be safe in Italy. Thus, he sought skills, like military engineering, that might be of use in exile. He fled to Basel in 1556 and likely met Italian Reformers like **Bernardino Ochino**. While there, he began publishing on theology, religious disagreement, and how one arrives at the belief that a proposition is true. He eventually went to England, where he hoped to work as a military engineer. While there, he pursued a number of patents for inventions and worked to drain some of England's wetlands. His interest in religious conflict remained, particularly when he witnessed first-hand disagreements among foreign Protestants who sought refuge in England. He fled England with many other Protestants upon the accession of Mary I. He spent time in Switzerland, Poland, and Moravia, and he was frequently forced to relocate on account of his beliefs.

His most important theological text is excerpted below. *Stratagematum Satanae* (1565) seems to have been written in a context of intra-Protestant dispute. As with previous works, he was concerned with how one arrived at truth and how self-interest influenced what arguments an individual found persuasive. Before directly addressing how the use of the sword related to doctrinal differences, he laid the groundwork for toleration in human fallibility.[128] He approached the topic by discussing what doctrines were necessary for eternal salvation, and he argued that far fewer doctrines needed to be considered essential. The disciples, for example, received communion before they knew important truths about Christ and his kingdom. He then argued that suppressing the ability to proclaim unorthodox ideas had disastrous unforeseen consequences. For example, suppression drove heterodox ideas underground, where they flourished undetected and were harder to counter. His greatest contribution is the central theme of the book. Satan's strategy was twofold: he not only seduced persons into holding incorrect beliefs (heresy), but he also seduced persecutors by convincing them that persecution was godly.[129]

Giacomo Aconcio, *Satans stratagems, or The Devils cabinet-councel discovered* (London: John Macock, 1648). Text modernised by the editors.

—

Hence it must be concluded that all things Christ taught were not so necessary to salvation, such that if a man were ignorant of some part of them, he could not be saved. It is worth observing that Christ gave the disciples the figures of his body and blood when they did not yet understand that Christ's Kingdom was spiritual or that the Gentiles were, in a special manner, sharers in the purchased salvation.

Not every Truth of God is of similar condition and rank. Some truths must necessarily be known and perfectly understood; some may remain unknown to an individual without them risking inevitable damnation. We need some way to mark this distinction between one type of belief and the other. Or we must only consider those points of Christian doctrine as necessary to be known if there is a special and particular testimony from Scripture about the necessity of this knowledge....

[*He discourses at length on essential doctrines for salvation before turning to faith and the use of the sword.*]

Wherever it has become common to decide controversies in religion by the sword, whatever doctrine is considered orthodox at that particular time, whoever opposes that doctrine (be the doctrine actually right or wrong), will be considered a heretic. Whatever texts of Scripture or arguments this person might appeal to while defending himself, the hangman will be the only man to answer him. In the passage of time, measures that looked like a just severity will later be viewed as a monstrous and horrible cruelty. Imagine that you lived in a time when it was unlawful to hold the convictions that you currently consider to be true; a time when to believe differently was to risk the sword, the gallows or having fire lick your heels. There would be nowhere to plead your cause. You might come to think that such great tyranny stemmed from punishing those considered heretics. Indeed, you would rather wish that no heretic had ever been punished than that such tyranny should be practiced.

We should also consider how ineffective killing a heretic is, and those who practice such things are often disappointed with the results. When a man knows that he cannot safely proclaim his opinion, he will not openly say what he believes to everyone he meets. He will start by discreetly sharing his beliefs and seeing how people respond to them. Then, little by little he will insinuate himself. If these people recoil at his beliefs, he will try to do the same thing with another group. He will start small, and if they favourably

328 *Sources*

accept his opinions, he will progress with them until the whole group comes to think like him. He will then do the same with another group, and more people will be companions in his error. These converts will become partners in spreading the message abroad, corrupting others and propagating the sect. As a result of being forced into secrecy, before the magistrate is even aware that one person was seduced into error, a great part of his people have been led astray, and the wound will be incurable. Because of the private spread of error, the church is unable to remedy the problem through the word of God. Ministers might hear rumours of these private beliefs, yet they cannot grasp what the seducer is doing or what doctrines they are spreading.

Pastors who hope to defend their doctrine and resist heretics by the sword will neglect learning and become addicted to idleness. As a result, general ignorance follows, making it easier for Satan to spread superstition and error. Also, we must not forget that it is commonly the lot of godly persons to suffer persecution, reproach and affliction for the sake of religion. The common people look favourably upon those who courageously and cheerfully suffer persecution, and they view those inflicting the punishment as unjust and cruel tyrants. Through harsh measures towards dissenters, people are confirmed in their error, and the situation becomes incurable....

It is certain that the Old Law commanded that seducers were to be punished with death, and any City drawn from the proper worship of God and into idolatry was to be destroyed and burnt, never to be rebuilt. However, some argue that this Law was only applicable until Christ and that it does not apply under the New Testament. As a ground for this position, they argue that the Israelite nation was a type of the Christian Church. Israel had promises of sensible earthly things, things that were useful in this life, and their sacrifices and worship were of a similar manner. These things signified invisible things related to eternal life. Those taking this position argue that corporal punishment was a type of eternal damnation; and therefore, this Law, like many others that foreshadowed things to come, ended with the coming of Christ. This interpretation seems so probable that it would be difficult to offer an argument against it. One could note that the reason given for this Law was that all Israel may fear God and not commit idolatry in the future, and it remains in force that people should do these things. So someone could argue that even though the Law itself expired, the magistrate has as much power to make another law about worshipping God as he has about making laws against murder, adultery and other crimes.

However, our Lord seems to argue the contrary position when he propounds the parable of the tares [Matt. 13:28–29]. For to the servants asking whether they should go to the fields and pluck up the tares, the householder is said to have answered that they should not go. In ripping out the tares, they might also pluck up the wheat. Some interpret this parable one way and some another, showing the difference between those who search the Scriptures for

Sources 329

things that confirm a previously held opinion and those who use the Scripture to arrive at the truth.

This is the way to find the truth: when you find an exposition of Scripture which seems to strengthen your previous opinion, you should imagine a person of the dissenting party and consider how they might argue against your interpretation. If you do this, those who dissent might not always dissent and those in error might change their mind and agree with those who judge rightly. However, most people care more for victory than for truth. Whenever the solution to a debated problem seems to depend entirely on the exposition of a text, we must be cautious again and again lest interest blind our eyes.

89 George Buchanan, *Romans 13 and the Limits of Lawfull Magistracy* (1567)

Keywords: #Obedience, #Submission, #Magistrate, #Resistance, #Liberty, #Tyranny
Region: #Scotland
Group: #Presbyterian

The Scottish historian George Buchanan (c.1506–1582) was educated at St Andrews and in Paris in the humanist tradition. He became tutor to Mary Queen of Scots, as well as the young **James VI** (future **James I** of England). Buchanan was an early resistance theorist, grounding limited sovereignty in a strong sense that power derived from subjects and must be exercised in accord with a contract. Buchanan's history of Scotland, *Rerum Scoticarum Historia* (1582), and his political philosophy, *De Jure Regni* (1579, written a decade earlier), reinforced each other and served the Reformation of church and state. He was a leading theorist of limited sovereignty, armed resistance, and the possibility of tyrannicide (later called a Monarchomach).[130]

Buchanan played an important role in the development of Scottish resistance theory and would be highly esteemed by the **Covenanters**. However, his writings differed from the likes of **John Knox, Samuel Rutherford,** and other Scottish Reformed writers, as John Coffey notes:

> In the Scottish Reformed tradition, of course, intensive mining of the Old Testament went back to Knox himself. The Covenanters inherited his conviction that the Bible – specifically the Old Testament – was the definitive sourcebook for Protestant politics. It is here that the contrast with Buchanan is sharpest. Buchanan, who had spent only a small portion of his life in Calvinist circles, who was steeped in the classics, who was addressing an audience both Protestant and Catholic, devoted relatively little space to Scripture, and placed significantly less weight on it than other Calvinist writers. He showed no interest in amassing biblical examples to back up his argument, and concentrated on neutralizing biblical texts quoted against resistance (I Samuel 8 and Romans 13).[131]

Sources 331

The following excerpt comes from Buchanan's discussion of Romans 13 in *De Jure Regni*, a treatise written in the form of a humanist dialogue. An English translation of this work was suppressed in 1664 (after the Restoration of the Stuarts), and it was published in 1680. In this excerpt, Buchanan's interlocutor raised the question of the apostle Paul's teaching on authority. In reply, Buchanan argued that these verses did not apply in the sense that they were commonly understood.

De jure regni apud Scotos, or, A dialogue, concerning the due priviledge of government in the kingdom of Scotland, betwixt George Buchanan and Thomas Maitland by the said George Buchanan; and translated out of the original Latine into English by Philalethes (1680), 91–95. Text modernised by the editors.

———

That you [the interlocutor] put so much weight on the authority of Paul, so that one sentence of his has more weight with you than the writings of all philosophers and lawyers, I think you do well: but see that you fully consider his judgement or meaning: for you must not examine the words only, but in what time, to whom, and why he wrote. First, let us see what Paul wrote. For he writes to Titus in chapter 3[:1]: Put them in mind to be subject to principalities and powers, and to be ready to every good work. I suppose, you see, what the appointed end of obedience and subjection is. He likewise wrote to Timothy in chapter 2[:1–2] that we should pray for all men, even for kings, and other magistrates, that, said he, we may live a peaceable life in all godliness and honesty. And here you see the appointed end of praying: namely, not for the king's safety, but the church's tranquillity, from which it will not be difficult to conceive also the form of prayer. Now in his epistle to the Romans [13:1–5], he defines a king with a subtle logic: he is a minister to whom the sword is given by God for punishing the wicked and for cherishing and relieving the good. For, said Chrysostom, Paul did not write these things of a tyrant, but of a true and lawful magistrate, who is the vicegerent of the true God on earth, and whoever resists, certainly resists the ordinance of God.

Now although we ought to pray for wicked princes, we should not conclude from this that their vices should go unpunished: nor does it follow that we should not punish the plundering of robbers, for whom we are also commanded to pray. And if we should obey a good prince, it does not therefore follow that we should not resist a wicked prince. But if you consider the reason that moved Paul to write these things, the argument could be used against you. For he wrote this to chastise the rashness of some who denied that the authority of magistrates was necessary for Christians. For since the power of magistrates is ordained against wicked men, that we may all live righteously and that an example of divine justice might remain among men, they affirmed that there was no use thereof among men who greatly abhor the contagion of vices, as they are a law to themselves.

332 *Sources*

Paul does not therefore speak of those who bear rule as magistrates, but of magistracy itself, that is, of the function and office of those who rule: neither does he speak of one or the other kind of magistracy, but of every form of a lawful magistracy. Nor does he debate with those who think that wicked magistrates should be restrained, but with those men who completely deny the authority of magistrates, who absurdly interpreting Christian liberty, affirmed it to be an indignity for those that were made free by the Son of God and ruled by the Spirit of God, to be under the power of any man. That Paul might refute their error, he showed that magistracy is not only a good thing, but also sacred, namely an ordinance of God, and for that end instituted, that the assemblies and incorporations of men might be so continued, that they might acknowledge God's benefits towards them, and might stop wronging one another. God commanded those who were appointed to a dignified office to be keepers of his laws.

Now if we confess that laws are good (as indeed they are) and the keepers thereof are worthy of honour, we will be forced to confess that the office of the keepers is a good and profitable thing. But magistracy provokes terror, but to whom? To the good, or bad? To the good it is not a terror, it is their defence from injury. But to wicked men it is a terror: it is not so to you who are ruled by the Spirit of God.

But you will say to me, what need do I then have to be subject to magistracy, if I am the Lord's freeman? Yea, in order that you may prove you are the Lord's freeman, obey his Laws: for the Spirit of the Lord, by whom you boast to be led and governed, is both the lawgiver and the approver of magistrates, and also the author of obedience to magistrates. We, therefore, will easily agree in this, that there is need for magistracy even in the best common-wealths, and that we should fully honour them. But if any man thinks otherwise, we account him mad, infamous and worthy of all punishment. For he plainly contravenes the will of God revealed to us in the Scriptures.

But as for Caligula, Nero, Domitian and other tyrants, Paul does not say anything here about why they should not be punished as breakers of divine and human Law. He discussed the power of magistrates, but not of those who wickedly administer that power, nor will they be really magistrates, if you examine this kind of tyrants according to Paul's rule. [*He then discusses the objection that wicked magistrates are also ordained by God.*]

90 *Edict of Torda* (1568)

Keywords: #Toleration, #Coercion, #Pluralism, #Violence
Region: #Hungary, #Romania
Group: #Interconfessional, #Reformed, #Lutheran, #Unitarian, #Roman Catholic

The Edict of Torda (1568) is among the earliest edicts of toleration in Europe, establishing multi-confessionalism in Transylvania, then a quasi-autonomous part of the Ottoman Empire. Reformed, Catholic, Lutheran, and Unitarian communities already coexisted in the region, with relatively flexible boundaries between them. The nearby Ottoman Empire also provided alternative models for religious difference: non-Muslims were tolerated, albeit as second-class subjects. The main architect of the Edict of Torda, the Hungarian Dávid Ferenc (1510–1579), was a native of Transylvania who, over the course of his life, would belong to all four confessions. He was educated at Wittenberg and initially became a Lutheran minister in Kolozsvár (Cluj-Napoca), where he was born. His religious views continued to evolve even as he became the court preacher to John Sigismund Zápolya, who also belonged to each of the four confessions at some point in his life. The edict was issued within a few years of the execution of Michael Servetus in Geneva, during the Inquisition in the Netherlands, and shortly before the St. Bartholomew's Day massacre in France. As George Huntston Williams argues in his *History of the Polish Reformation*, confessional strife in Western Europe sometimes led Central and Eastern Europeans to choose a more irenic path.[132] A similar document was produced by the General Assembly of the Realm (**Confederation of Warsaw**, 1573), whereby differences of religion were not to lead to political instability or the shedding of blood.[133]

Joseph Henry Crooker, *The Winning of Religious Liberty* (Boston, MA: Pilgrim, 1918), 34.

———

334   *Sources*

The Edict of Torda, Transylvania

January 6, 1568

His Royal Highness, as in former Diets, so in this now present, confirms that ministers of the Gospel may everywhere preach and explain it, each according to his own understanding; and the community may accept or reject the teaching as it thinks good. No force may be used to compel acceptance against conviction. Congregations are allowed to have each the preacher they wish. Preachers shall not be molested, not any one persecuted, on account of religion; no one is permitted to remove from office, or to imprison, any one because of his teaching. Faith being the gift of God, which comes by hearing, and hearing by the word of God [Rom. 10:17].

91 Iwie Synod, *On Christians Holding Slaves* (1568)

Keywords: #Slavery, #Serfdom, #Submission, #Freedom
Region: #Belarus, #Poland, #Lithuania
Group: #Unitarian | #Non-Christian

The debates over slavery at Iwie Synod of 1568 are relatively unknown. However, as 'arguably the first substantive Christian debate on slavery',[134] they carry great significance for the contemporary student of Protestant political thought. Located in the Grand Duchy of Poland-Lithuania (contemporary Belarus), this discussion was not so much about race-based slavery as about both slavery and serfdom as two forms of unfree labour that had been common across the European continent and continued to be important in early modern Eastern Europe. Slavery and serfdom implied ownership, which rendered those in bondage property in relation to their master. This relationship is precisely at stake in the debate over slaveholding, especially when other Christians must first be considered 'brothers' and 'sisters'. The interlocutors were members of an antitrinitarian group (Minor Reformed Church) that had recently separated from the Trinitarian Major Reformed Church. Minutes of the debate are recorded by Simon Budny, a proponent of slavery who won this particular debate. His opponent, Jacob Kalinowski, departed from Lithuania shortly thereafter.[135]

From Donald J. Ziegler, *Great Debates of the Reformation* (New York: Random House, 1969), 243–279 (248–251, 257–259, 260, 267–270).

———

Jacob Kalinowski:	You, Brother Simon, claim that there may be male and female slaves. Tell me, therefore, who may these slaves be – of the faithful, or nonbelievers? Christians or non-Christians?
Simon Budney:	Believers or nonbelievers may be slaves of Christians.
Jacob:	That cannot be so by any standard. First of all, a Christian cannot have or keep a nonbeliever in bondage, for the apostle has written that Christ cannot be in accord

336 *Sources*

Simon: with Belial [2 Cor. 6:15], nor a believer with a nonbeliever. If, therefore, there cannot be agreement of believer with a nonbeliever, how then can the believer keep a nonbeliever in bondage? Regarding a member of the faith, it cannot by any means be that a Christian would have one of these in bondage. The apostle plainly states that with Christ there is neither Jew, nor Greek, there is neither slave, and so on [Gal. 3:28].

Simon: ...who could be so simple as not to understand that the apostle is not speaking here of bondage, but rather that being a Jew will not be of special benefit before God to anyone; neither will it be of help if one is free, not in bondage, nor will it hurt if one be a slave....

As to your claim that a Christian may not have a pagan as a slave because the apostle wrote that there is no accord between Christ and Belial, nor between a believer and a nonbeliever, in this too the apostle does not speak of Christians not being in bondage to a pagan, or a pagan to a Christian. Rather that Christians are not to be of assistance to pagans in doing evil; to the contrary, that they are to live differently from the pagans, that they have no part of evil or uncleanliness. For a Christian can be in bondage to a pagan and a pagan to a Christian.

This I will prove by the Scriptures. The apostle Paul wrote to Timothy: 'Let all who are under the yoke of slavery regard their masters worthy of all honour, so that the name of God and the teaching may not be defamed' [1 Tim. 6:1]. Here the apostle, speaking of the slaves who are also Christians and have pagans as masters, tells Timothy to teach them that they should hold their masters in respectful regard, even though they are pagans, so that they would not defame the teachings of Christ. I say that these were slaves who were Christians and had masters who were nonbelievers....

Jacob: I cannot understand what type of Christian would have slaves – ruling, commanding, and a brother at that.

Simon: Well, now, I will show you, for nothing could be more simply proved, especially with the use of the letter of St. Paul to Philemon....

[*They debate the terminology of scripture with reference to words like servant and slave. Jacob accuses Simon of sanctioning error through linguistic sophistry, a charge that Simon reverses. They continue their discussion of language, also turning to the Hebrew Bible to discuss the language of servitude and the many biblical characters who held slaves. They then discuss*] *the ministry and poverty of Christ, and Simon argues that Christians are not called to imitate every aspect of Jesus' life.*]

Jacob: You have talked a long time, brother, but if you had talked ten times as long, you could not have convinced me that it is proper for a Christian to have servants, less so slaves. The Lord Christ does not wish to have his followers gain property by working people like animals, but rather that they should sell properties already in their possessions, denying themselves everything to take up the cross and follow him.

Simon: Denial and renunciation do not mean discarding or selling everything. Rather they mean being ready and willing to give up all possessions, wealth, honours, position, friends, even life itself for Christ and his teaching, permitting them to be taken, but not allowing him to be torn away from you, nor you frightened away from him....

Since it is plain from the Scriptures that former Christians had possessions, homes, farms, land, slaves, and so on, therefore they may also have them today. However, they are to use these differently from pagans and nonconverted people. They may have subjects, but not abuse them, so that these would not weep because of them but rather praise God for such masters. They may have male slaves and female slaves, but be merciful to them and not only forgive them some threatened punishment, but, as the apostle writes, to some who served well, honestly, and faithfully, grant them their freedom.... [*He then urges caution with freeing enslaved persons since some are ready for freedom and will use it responsibly and others are not. He also asks that God would lead the lords and gentry to properly rule over enslaved persons*].

92 *The Protestation of Louis de Bourbon, Prince of Condé* (1568)

Keywords: #Authority, #Resistance, #Conscience, #Freedom of Religion
Region: #France
Group: #Reformed, #Huguenot

In 1560, the young Francis II died, and the Queen Regent, Catherine de Medici, governed on behalf of Charles IX. The French monarchy was already weak, and tensions between Catholics and Huguenots threatened to tear the country apart. In early 1562, Protestants were massacred in Wassay during a worship service. Louis de Bourbon, prince of Condé (1530–1569), responded with the force of arms. **Sébastien Castellion** urged both sides to de-escalate, but the war quickly spread, and atrocities multiplied. A series of wars raged for the next 36 years. When there was not open violence, France experienced high levels of civil unrest.[136] Some embraced violence as a means to settle religious disagreements. Others sought some form of reconciliation and a lasting peace settlement that accepted some form of religious diversity.

After a short-lived peace, a third round of hostilities began in August 1568. The Protestant minority found protection in La Rochelle, where **Jeanne III** assumed leadership and furthered the Reformation. From La Rochelle in September 1568, the Prince of Condé (Jeanne's brother-in-law) protested against the treatment of Protestants. Those who were willing to fight swore allegiance to him (see document below). He protested his loyalty to the king and argued that he had defensively taken up arms and to protect the freedom of conscience and religion. In response to Protestant re-armament, the Ordinance of Saint-Maur (Sept 1568) revoked toleration. The Prince of Condé was captured in 1569 and executed.[137]

David Potter, ed., *The French Wars of Religion: Selected Documents* (London: Macmillan, 1997), 110.

———

We ... protest before God ... that, as declared in the remonstrances sent by us to our lord the King, we have no intention of taking arms to attempt anything to the prejudice of His majesty or his state. Rather, we recognise him as

Sources 339

our King and sovereign lord ordained by God and declare that what we do is only for the preservation of our liberty of conscience and the exercise of the Reformed Religion, to guarantee our lives, honour and goods from tyranny and oppression that the cardinal of Lorraine, and other enemies and disturbers of the good and the public peace of the realm, have constantly exercised against those of the Religion, contrary to the will of His majesty both by his edicts and by various express declarations and dispatches made to us. To this end and to preserve the lives, honour and liberty of conscience both of us and of the lords, gentlemen and other subjects of this realm who profess the Reformed Religion, we declare ourselves ready to employ our person, life and all other means that it may please God to give us.

[*Followed by an oath to follow the prince and obey his orders, and then an ordinance on military discipline*].

93 *Jeanne III to Catherine De Medici on Religious Toleration (1568)*

Keywords: #Toleration, #Pluralism, #Conscience, #Women
Region: #France
Group: #Reformed, #Huguenot

Jeanne III (1528–1572), Queen of Navarre, became a figurehead for the Reformed faith, and she was supported in this role by Protestants within and beyond France. **John Calvin** kept a lively correspondence with her, urging her to publicly support the Reformed even though this action drove a wedge into the strained relationship with her husband, Antoine de Bourbon. After Antoine's death, she sought to further the reform of church and society within her realm. In 1568, with the outbreak of another war, she fled to the Protestant stronghold of La Rochelle. While there, she engaged in military affairs and also led a propaganda war for the Protestant cause. She worked to reform La Rochelle and even established a seminary there. Jeanne III had long been at odds with Catherine De Medici, who was the Queen of France. Jeanne's son, the future King Henri IV, would marry Catherine's daughter Marguerite and return to Catholicism. Jeanne died shortly before their wedding in 1572, a celebration that was followed by the infamous St. Bartholomew's Day Massacre. The following letter dates to 1568, at the opening of the third war of religion. Jeanne appealed to Catherine, pleading that she would establish peace on the foundation of toleration. Pluralism and respect for conscience, she argued, was the only path to stability.[138]

Martha Walker Freer, *The Life of Jeanne D'Albret, Queen of Navarre* (London: Hurst and Blackett, 1855), II:153–155.

———

Jeanne, Queen of Navarre, to Catherine De Medici, Queen of France

Madame,

It has pleased your majesty to receive and listen to the sieurs de Renty and la Chassetière with so much condescension and favour, that I should fail in my obligation if I omitted to return you my humble thanks. Nevertheless, madame, as it has pleased you to return us no answer to the things we craved of your majesty's goodness – such as, that it would please the king to grant us liberty of conscience, the public exercise of our faith, with the restitution of our estates, honours and dignities, we cannot proceed with this negotiation.... I can scarcely persuade myself, having once had the honour to know your majesty's sentiments intimately, that you would wish to see us reduced to such an extremity as to profess ourselves of no religion whatever, which must be the case if we are denied the public exercise of our own ritual.

As you, moreover, assured them, madame, that you sincerely desired peace, I will state to you the only way to obtain this blessing: it is, madame, to be achieved only by allaying the feuds and animosities which now exist amongst all classes in the realm: and to satisfy your humble subjects, of whatever degree and faith, who desire nothing so much as permission to worship God according to their conscience in obedience to their king. Madame, with tears in my eyes, and actuated by sentiments of affection and loyalty towards you, I solemnly assure your majesty, that if it will not please the king and you to condescend to our sorrowful demands, I see that nothing can result from this negotiation but a truce, to be followed by disastrous civil conflicts. We have come to the determination to die all of us rather than to abandon our God, and our religion, the which we cannot maintain unless permitted to worship publicly.... I pray you, therefore, madame, take gracious heed of my fervent, and humble supplications, and grant us peace, with tranquillity, to this realm. I have indicated to you the sole method of achieving this purpose; consider, moreover, madame, the torrents of blood which must flow; the iniquities certain to be committed during this cruel war, which one word from your royal lips can arrest.

You may, perhaps, suspect, madame, that we ask much at first, in order to obtain concessions the more readily on diverse points. Believe, madame, however, that the affairs of the immortal soul, admit not of the same latitude as temporal concerns: there is only one road to obtain eternal salvation: therefore, what we propose for your majesty's acceptance, is all that we can concede, and neither more nor less. I can, therefore, but implore for it, your majesty's earnest attention. I know well, that if it pleases you, you can grant our demands to the full: the age of the King, and the maturity of his sense, and judgement having confirmed his sense of duty as a son towards his mother, of which legitimate influence and authority, if your majesty makes the use we trust in, all will doubtless be well....

Written at La Rochelle, this 27th day of December.

94 Thomas Erastus, *State Power and Excommunication* (1568)

Keywords: #Church-State Relations, #Excommunication, #Authority, #Violence, #Magistrate, #Toleration
Region: #Switzerland, #Germany
Group: #Reformed, #Zwinglian

Thomas Erastus (1524–1583) was born in Baden, Switzerland, and studied theology and medicine. He was a committed Zwinglian who spent much of his life in the German lands. During his life, his medical acumen brought him fame. He worked closely with Elector Otto Heinrich of the Palatinate as his trusted physician who also gave counsel and theological advice. Although he worked to bring the Palatinate towards Reformed theology, in the late 1560s, he opposed efforts to install a Geneva-style system of church government and discipline. He argued that the church did not have the power to withhold communion from anyone who wanted it. This argument struck at a central pillar of church discipline – excommunication. Since society still needed discipline against transgressors, Erastus argued that the power to punish sins resided in the state. Those in favour of excommunication prevailed, and Erastus was briefly excommunicated for heterodox views on the Trinity. He taught medicine at the University of Heidelberg before losing the post for opposing Lutheranism, teaching medicine and ethics at the University of Basel from 1580.

Scholars continue to debate the relationship between Erastus and the later 'Erastian' position. In 1568, Erastus detailed his positions on church-state relations in 100 theses written against excommunication (later refined into 75 theses). They were posthumously published in 1589. 'Erastianism' likely emerged as a term of abuse in the 1640s, at a time when Presbyterians, Puritans, and supporters of the Church of England intensely debated church government and the limits of communion. Although so-called 'Erastians' were diverse in their ideal church-state relations, Eric Nelson argues that a common feature was that they 'regarded the civil magistrate as the only potential source of valid religious law. That is, they insisted that for a religious practice or observance to become law, it must be promulgated as such by the civil sovereign'.

Sources 343

Erastus' views on church-state relations were closely aligned with **Huldrych Zwingli,** and he did not give the state unlimited power over the church. In Erastus' work on excommunication, excerpted below, he leaned heavily on the idea of a Jewish Republic. The Sanhedrin possessed authority over religious and civil matters, even under Roman occupation. They issued laws and commanded armed forces but did not debar people from worshipping at the temple. As a corollary, Christian magistrates held power over religion – and even over punishing sinful acts as in biblical Israel. However, just as Jesus was censured by the Sanhedrin but not debarred from the temple, so the Christian magistrate might punish sin, but the church could not bar anyone who desired it from communion. These arguments were also linked with Erastus' call for limited toleration. In the Hebrew Commonwealth, he argued, Israel did not persecute people for erroneous doctrines or opinions, provided religious disagreement did not upset the peace and order of the state. Thus, by giving the magistrate power over religious matters, Erastus carved out a limited space for toleration.[139]

Thomas Erastus, *Theses of Erastus on Excommunication*, trans. Robert Lee (Edinburgh: Myles Macphail, 1844), 40–42, 53, 55–57, 62, 66–67, 73, 99, 101, 130, 152, 160–165.

———

17.

I answer, 1*stly*, that it is very improbable indeed, that God should command something in plain words, and yet, at the same time, should, in a figurative way, forbid the same thing. He enjoins plainly, by an ordinance sundry times repeated, that every male should celebrate the Passover, except those who were unclean, or detained on a journey. He could not, therefore, intend, by the figure of the leaven [in the bread], to deter any other but these. There were bad men in abundance who were present at those celebrations, so that there was no need of typifying them by leaven; for the wicked were as visible as the leaven was. Seeing, then, types are not adopted of things which are present, and equally perceptible by the senses as the types, much less, if the things typified are much more open and common than the types themselves, it is vain to fancy that here the leaven was a type of the wicked. 2*dly*, Moses does not appoint, that he who had eaten of leaven should be debarred from partaking of the Passover, but that he should be put to death. Wherefore it would follow, that profligate persons should not be excluded from the Lord's Supper, but executed – a consequence which I should admit without difficulty, and which I even desire. For nothing do I more wish, than that a most rigorous discipline of manners should be maintained in the Christian Church; – only let it be that which God has appointed, not that which men have devised....

344 *Sources*

22.

There remains to be considered only that *casting out of the synagogue*, with which some marvellously please themselves, alleging in defence of excommunication what is written on this subject in the 9th, 12th, and 16th chapters of John's Gospel. But here, also, an abundance of solid answers are at hand.

The name, *synagogue*, sometimes signifies a *place*, as when Jesus is said to have entered into a synagogue, and there to have taught; and sometimes an *assembly*, or *congregation*, whether convened in the place called a synagogue or elsewhere; as when the Pharisees are spoken of as desiring the highest seats at feasts, and the first places in the *synagogues*....

From comparing these passages with each other, it most distinctly appears that our Lord and his Apostles, in these last quoted passages, understood nothing else by the word *council* or *synagogue*, but the law-courts of the Jews, which were composed of several members; as the courts of the Gentiles are denoted by the words 'power', 'authority', 'rulers', 'kings'. In these, one person almost always presided, or if more than one administered justice, they did it in the name of one. In these meetings or synagogues, those who were pronounced guilty were punished corporally (Matt. 10, 22; Acts 17, 26; 2 Cor. 11:24) a passage, which anyone who peruses Deuteronomy 25 will easily understand. The casting out any one of such a synagogue as this, was thus a kind of political disgrace and punishment, and so a sort of banishment from the locality; as we may infer from what is said (Luke 4:29). This kind of casting out cannot be transferred to the sacraments, which were celebrated only in the temple (and there was but one temple) and at Jerusalem....

Wherefore, there is a very wide difference between exclusion from the synagogue, and exclusion from the sacraments and institutions appointed by God – as evidently appears from all that has been said....

23.

This, then, remains firm and immovable that, in the Old Testament, none was debarred from the sacraments on account of the immorality of his conduct: but, on the contrary, the pious priests, prophets, judges, kings, and finally that most illustrious and holy forerunner of our Lord, John the Baptist, instead of debarring, rather invited all the people to the celebration of the sacrament, as the law required them to do....

25.

For, as we properly urge against the Anabaptists this very valid argument, that, because baptism has come in the place of circumcision, and Christ nowhere forbade the baptising of infants, therefore we are no less permitted to baptise our infants than the Jews were to circumcise theirs: So, in the case before us, we may reason no less conclusively in this manner. The Lord's Supper has come in the room of the Passover. But men's sins were not punished by denying them the Passover, nor was anyone kept back from it on account of his sins; but, on the contrary, all the people, especially males, were, by the law of Moses, invited to join in the celebration of it. And seeing we nowhere read that this principle has been superseded, or abolished, therefore the people's sins are not to be punished now by refusing them the Lord's Supper, neither is any one for that reason to be kept back....

26.

Our Lord and Saviour, Jesus Christ, in like manner, is never spoken of as having forbidden any one to partake of the sacraments....

31.

It is not the will of Christ that his kingdom in these lands (I speak of that which is outward) should be circumscribed within narrower limits than he appointed for it anciently among the Jews. Wherefore, as God required all that were outwardly circumcised to partake in the same sacraments and ceremonies, but appointed that they who were guilty of crimes should be restrained and punished with the sword and other such penalties; so among us now, it is the will of Christ that all baptised persons, or Christians, who hold the pure doctrines of the Gospel, should unite in the same ceremonies and sacraments, but that the immoral should be visited by the magistrate with death, banishment, imprisonment, and the like. To this the parables of the Net, the Marriage-supper, and the Tares, seem to point.

34.

Further, in the same passage (1 Cor. 10) Paul thus reasons: As God spared not those of old who lusted after evil things, – idolaters, fornicators, tempters of Christ, murmurers, although they had been baptised with the same baptism as all the rest, and had eaten the same spiritual bread, and had drank the same spiritual drink, – so neither will he spare you, as many of you as defile yourselves with the like iniquities, although you all eat of the same bread, and drink of the same cup, of which all the children of God partake. From these expressions we may clearly see, 1*stly*, That our sacraments, and those of the ancient Church, are the same, so far as the substance which is internal, or heavenly, is concerned: – otherwise the Apostle's reasoning would be of no force. 2*dly*, It is evident that, in both cases, many wicked persons, very and even publicly known to be such, were admitted. 3*dly*, This is also plain, that no one was ordered to abstain from the sacraments in the way excommunicated persons are ordered to abstain: for the Apostle does not say that such characters as those ought to be debarred, but he foretells that God will punish them in the same manner in which the ancient Israelites had been punished. Some of these Moses killed by the Levites (Exod. 32); others God destroyed by fire, by serpents, by the sword, and by the earth cleaving asunder. So it happened also to the Corinthians, many of whom the Apostle

346 *Sources*

affirms to have been afflicted with diseases, and many even to have been punished with death....

39.

Thus far have we unquestionably proved that neither Christ nor his Apostles spoke a single word, or gave any example, of this method of correcting, or rather restraining vicious persons. Wherefore, since neither the Old nor the New Testament requires this method of punishing transgressors, but a different method is spoken of in both, we feel warranted in concluding that excommunication (so far forth as it is a driving of men from the sacraments on account of the sins of their life and conversation) is rather a human invention than any law of God....

48.

[*He discussed cases of discipline where Christ told followers to bring the matter before the church.*] Seeing, then, they who preside in that manner are nothing but a Senate or Sanhedrim, it is again rendered evident that the command of our Lord is – that the matter be told, not to the multitude, but to the Sanhedrim. But the people, in the time of Christ, possessed not the power of electing magistrates and princes for themselves. Wherefore, by 'the Church', we must needs understand the Jewish Senate or Sanhedrim – which also the disciples must have understood by the expression, as the foregoing observations prove. Therefore, if by 'the Church' we understand the multitude itself, the Church to which we tell the matter, must have the power of choosing for itself such a council as was the Jewish Sanhedrim. But our churches have not the power to choose such a council as the Sanhedrim was; yea, even among the Jews themselves, the people had no such power in the days of our Saviour, as I have just said....

49.

But it is evident, from the sacred Scriptures and from history, that the Sanhedrim was a lawful magistracy, and, even in the time of Christ, it still held and exercised the power of the sword. Proof of this is found [in their prosecutions of Christ and Stephen, and in their authorising Saul (later Paul) to pursue followers of Christ].

52.

It has now been most firmly established, that *tell it to the Church*, means nothing else but, tell it to the magistrate of thy own people (or who professes the same religion with thee) before engaging in a litigation with thy brother in a heathen court of law; as Paul most excellently explains (1 Cor. 6), where, for this very reason, he instructs them to appoint arbiters from among themselves. But who can doubt, that such an expedient would have no place where God grants us a Christian government?...

59.

[*He discussed what delivering someone over to Satan meant, and other verses about handing people over.*] Do not these passages shew that the persons spoken of were delivered to be afflicted, killed, condemned? To express the matter in one word, no one will ever be able to shew that such a phrase is used as an equivalent for exclusion from the sacraments, unless *the destruction of the flesh*, and *the prohibition of the sacraments* are the same things....

70.

Concerning the origin of this excommunication I am not able at present to produce anything certain, except that a little before the year 200 of our era, I find some such thing to have been first done or attempted.... But, however that may be, this at least is sufficiently evident, that the design with which excommunication was introduced into the Church was, that it might serve in it as some restraint on wickedness, and as a punishment. Afterwards, when the Church had now obtained the power of the sword, in other words, when the civil rulers had become Christian, that same power remained, nevertheless, in the hands of the bishops; partly because it was believed to be a divine ordinance, and partly because they felt it hard to lay down this spiritual sword, which rendered them formidable to the greatest princes. For they easily persuaded others, as they too easily and willingly themselves believed, that this practice had the authority of Jesus Christ. Superstition, by ascribing salvation to the sacraments, strengthened that notion.... [*He discussed how the pope used fear of excommunication to accumulate power and control kings.*]

73.

I see no reason why the Christian magistrate at the present day should not possess the same power, which God commanded the magistrate to exercise in the Jewish commonwealth. Do we imagine that we are able to contrive a better constitution of Church and State than that? We read in the 4th chapter of the Book of Deuteronomy that, on account of the statutes and judgements which the Lord gave to them, all nations would admire and praise the Jews as a wise and understanding people. But they had no such excommunication as that now in debate: and the power to coerce the impure and criminal lay with the magistrate, to whom it pertained not only to punish, according to the law of God, such characters as these, but even to order the whole external part of religion. For this latter duty was committed, by the command of God, not to Aaron, but to Moses.... And, indeed, it was lawful for the High Priests, under the Old Testament, to govern also the state, because they bore the type of Jesus Christ, who is at once King and Priest. But our clergy have been directed not to do so (1 Pet 5:3).

348   *Sources*

74.

...If, then, the Christian magistrate possesses not only authority to settle religion according to the directions given in holy Scripture, and to arrange the ministries and offices thereof – for which reason Moses requires him who should be elected king to transcribe with his own hand the Book of the Law, or writings of Moses, and to exercise himself in the study of these continually – but also, in like manner, to punish crimes; in vain do some among us now meditate the setting up a new kind of tribunal, which would bring down the magistrate himself to the rank of a subject of other men. I allow, indeed, the magistrate ought to consult, where *doctrine* is concerned, those who have particularly studied it; but that there should be any such ecclesiastical tribunal to take cognisance of men's conduct, we find no such thing anywhere appointed in the holy Scriptures.

75.

But in those churches, the members of which live under an ungodly government (for example, Popish or Mohammedan) grave and pious men should be chosen, according to the precept of the Apostle, to settle disputes by arbitration, compose quarrels, and do other offices of that sort. These men ought also, in conjunction with the ministers, to admonish and reprove them who live unholy and impure lives; and if they do not succeed, they may also punish, or rather recall them to virtue, either by refusing to hold private intercourse with them, or by a public rebuke, or by any other such mark of disapprobation. But from the sacraments which God has instituted, they may not debar any who desire to partake....

95 Niels Hemmingsen, *On Obeying Idolatrous Princes* (1569)

Keywords: #Idolatry, #Tyranny, #Submission, #Resistance, #Obedience, #Rebellion, #Ten Commandments, #Natural Law
Region: #Sweden, #Denmark
Group: #Lutheran

Niels Hemmingsen (1513–1600) was a humanist and theologian educated at Roskilde, Lund, and Wittenberg, where he came under the close influence of Philip Melanchthon. He became a renowned professor at the University of Copenhagen (1542–1579), and his writings on many topics, including natural law and ethics, were widely read outside of Denmark. Hemmingsen would often analyse matters from several angles, sometimes emphasising reason and at other times revelation. This approach has led some scholars to argue that he divorced reason from revelation in his works on law, but this dichotomy does not do justice to the depth of his thought.

The selection below is taken from a lengthy work on Psalm 84. Hemmingsen took the opportunity to discuss a wide array of topics, focusing in particular on the nature of the church. The work decried the errors of the Jews, Turks, Anabaptists, and Catholics, and argued that Christ was the defender of the true church. He also touched on how Christians should conduct themselves when their faith was allowed to flourish and when they experienced persecution. The following excerpt relates to obedience to tyrannous and idolatrous princes. His arguments about resisting tyranny were mostly based on biblical interpretation. However, when he discussed armed resistance by lesser magistrates, like Calvin, his examples came from classical antiquity.[140]

Niels Hemmingsen, *The faith of the church militant moste effectualie described in this exposition of the 84*, trans. Thomas Rogers (London: H. Middleton, 1581), 430–433. Text modernised by the editors.

———

Some wonder if it is lawful for any man to set himself against tyrants who maintain idolatry, especially seeing that Christians are commanded to obey

350 *Sources*

even the cruel: For so Peter said: *Be subject to your Masters with all fear, not only to the good and courteous, but also to those who are harsh* [1 Pet. 2:18.]. This commandment of the Apostle, whereby we are commanded to obey even those who are harsh does not mean that we should obey them in matters against our salvation. Rather they are to be followed so long as they command either such things as are honest or things against our rights (provided they only make our bodies miserable and do not make our souls ungodly). Therefore Polycarp said: *That honour is to be given to the Magistrate, which is not contrary to religion.*

Therefore, if he commands thee to do something against religion, answer with Peter, *we ought rather to obey God than man* [Acts 5:29.]. For we obey the Magistrate because God has commanded that we should. And therefore, if he commands what God has forbidden, subjects are excused by the commandment of a superior, namely God; and delivered from obedience to the inferior, which is man, notwithstanding the mighty authority of the Magistrate.

Tyrants are to be resisted in two ways. Subjects may respond to wicked decrees like those three young men of whom Daniel speaks. They refused to adore the image erected by the tyrant and chose to be cast into the burning furnace rather than obey the wicked commandment of the Tyrant [Dan. 3: 12–18.]. For this commandment, *Fly from idolatry* [1 Cor. 10:14], binds all men, no matter what position of authority they are in. The other way to resist a tyrant is for subjects to resort to their weapons, whereby they remove wicked commandments.

Some ask whether it is lawful to resist tyrants in order to maintain religion or to use the sword to hinder wicked and ungodly decrees? I distinguish between the types of people who are under subjection to the chief head (a King, Emperor or other Monarch).

Some people are simply subjects. Others are Magistrates under chief Magistrates (they are called popular magistrates). Consider the ancient example of the Ephors at Lacedemonia or the Demarchs at Athens or the Tribunes at Rome or the chief Senators under Kings in every Realm. They are placed in such positions by God, first to be the keepers of the first and second tables, that is, to see that true religion is professed and that honest discipline is used. They are also placed there to moderate, and if need requires, to bridle the raging desires of kings and monarchs when they decree anything against the laws and religion, these persons may, and indeed are bound to, set themselves against tyrants; and by their wisdom stop their foolish enterprises. But if tyrants do not heed their wise counsel, then they are bound, even with weapons, to defend godly subjects, remove idolatry and restore true religion: if they do not do this, they are not being faithful in their duties.

Sources   351

Although the Church does not increase through war: yet outward violence, which is directed at religion by tyrants, may be forcefully repelled by the magistrate (by the ones who stands between the chief head and private men). Such an action is taught by nature, is confirmed by the office of the popular magistrate and is exemplified by holy men: therefore let the magistrates, and moderators of the chief head, have this saying of the Lord before their eyes: *Give unto Caesar, the things which are Caesar's, and give unto God, those things which are God's* [Matt. 22:21].

96 Protestant Peace Terms in the French Wars of Religion (1569)

Keywords: #Treaty, #Peace, #Pluralism, #Toleration, #Freedom of Religion
Region: #France
Group: #Reformed, #Huguenot | #Roman Catholic

Towards the end of 1569, warring Protestants and Catholics in France considered peace talks. The following document outlines the Protestant terms for peace, dating from November 1569. **Jeanne III** was responsible for negotiating these terms with Catherine de Medici when talks began in February 1570. The proposals provide a window on what it was like to be a Protestant in France during a time of religious hostility. They also show creative attempts to keep religious differences from spilling over into violence. The excerpt below lists some of the practical solutions. However, fighting resumed during the initial negotiations, and Protestant victories forced the king back to the bargaining table. This victory resulted in the Edict of Pacification of Saint-Germain (8 August 1570), an edict that was declared to extend in perpetuity. A marriage alliance was to cement bonds between Protestants and Catholics. The future Henri IV (Jeanne's son) married Marguerite (Catherine's daughter). However, their 1572 wedding was the occasion for one of the worst massacres in French history, known as the St. Bartholomew's Day Massacre. These events prompted some of the most thorough calls for resistance to authority, most notably **François Hotman's** *Francogallia* (1573) and the anonymous *Vindiciæ contra tyrannos* (1579).[141]

David Potter, ed., *The French Wars of Religion: Selected Documents* (London: Macmillan, 1997), 115–117 (115–116).

———

That the Reformed Religion may be exercised in all towns, villages, castles and other places in this kingdom without exception where any of the inhabitants wish it in general or private and all persons may attend without distinction, subjects or non-subjects, native or foreign. For this exercise, the evangelicals may be able to build for their use temples and other places as they need without restriction of numbers....

That all ministers, native or foreign, may exercise their ministry in this kingdom.

That, for the exercise of that Religion and observation of church discipline, synods, colloquies and consistories may be permitted them in places and at times that they think fit....

That, to avoid both the multiplicity of religions and impiety and atheism, all natives shall be required to declare themselves of one of the two religions: that is, the Reformed, according to the confession approved in it, or the Roman, also according to its confession, without liberty to choose a third or declare neutrality. Nor shall this article remove the liberty of those who have so declared themselves afterwards to join the other or attend preaching or other practice. Also, ministers and prelates shall not be prevented from the use of ecclesiastical censures against recalcitrants....

[*They argue that his majesty should appoint learned Protestants to the Privy Council, and that Protestants should serve in the court system.*]

97 Synod of Sandomierz, *Consensus of Sandomierz* (1570)

Keywords: #Pluralism, #Toleration
Region: #Poland, #Lithuania, #Belarus, #Ukraine, #Russia, #Latvia, #Estonia
Group: #Reformed, #Lutheran, #Moravian | #Socinian, #Unitarian, #Anabaptist, #Roman Catholic

In 1569, the Union of Lublin knit together the Kingdom of Poland and the Grand Duchy of Lithuania, creating one of the most populous and powerful political entities in Europe, the Polish-Lithuanian Commonwealth. The lesser known Polish-Lithuanian Reformation took place almost a generation later than elsewhere in Europe, not least because of the intolerance of its King and Grand Duke Sigismund I. His wife Bona Sforza (1494–1557) and son Sigismund Augustus had been open to the Reformation, and upon his death, the Reformation took off in the Polish-Lithuanian Commonwealth. Notable figures spread Protestant ideas through the Protestant hotbed of Königsberg, such as the humanist scholar **Abraomas Kulvietis**, who was influenced by **Bernadino Ochino** during his legal training in Siena. Along with Lutheran and Calvinist reforms came antitrinitarian ideas, not least through the lively connections with Italian Protestants. The Synod of Sandomierz brought together three Polish-Lithuanian Protestant groups: the Reformed, the Lutherans, and the Brethren. In the wake of the increasing influence of Socinian theology and the pressure mounted from the Catholic Church, these Protestant communities resolved to move forward in harmony.

Although no confessional agreement was reached at Sandomierz, the delegates reached consensus on how to live with those differences. Crucially, these churches recognised each other as part of the one body of Christ, in contrast to antitrinitarian sects or indeed the Roman Catholic Church. In practice, this meant that they regarded their differences as part of the *adiaphora*, the things one could have different opinions about. They agreed that churches could exchange their pastors and that communion was open between these communities. As such, it shows something of the fluidity of the Protestant Reformation in Eastern Europe, not unlike the **Edict of Torda** in Transylvania. George Huntston Williams notes how confessional pluralism was first established at

Kutná Hora (Kuttenberg) in 1485 and strengthened by subsequent edicts: 'Religious Toleration in Poland and Transylvania owed much to this Bohemian precedent' at Kutná Hora. He continues: 'The Bohemian model for ritual and then confessional pluralism was thus extended on Polish soil during the pan-Commonwealth interdenominational Federation and Concensus of Sandomierz (in Little Poland) in 1570'. Nevertheless, tensions increased with the Lutherans, and the agreements would not hold beyond 1595.[142]

Edmund De Schweinitz, *The History of the Church Known as the Unitas Fratrum* (Bethlehem, PA: Moravian Publication Council, 1901), 354–357.

———

Consensus in the chief Articles of the Christian Religion between the Churches of Great and Little Poland, Russia, Lithuania and Samogitia, which, in view of the Augsburg Confession, the Confession of the Bohemian Brethren and the Helvetic Confession, have in some measure appeared to differ from each other. Adopted at the Synod of Sendomir, in the year of our Lord 1570, on the fourteenth of April....

After long and frequent disputes with the sectarian Tritheists, Ebionites [Unitarian] and Anabaptists, and after having at last been delivered, by the grace of God, from such great and lamentable controversies, the Polish reformed and orthodox churches, which, according to the assertions of the enemies of the Truth and of the Gospel, seemed not to agree in some points and formulas of doctrine, have thought proper, induced by love and peace and concord, to convene a Synod and to testify to a complete and mutual agreement. We have, therefore, held a friendly and Christian conference and have established, with united hearts, the following points:

First, Not only we [the Reformed] who have presented our Confession of Faith to this Synod, but also the Bohemian Brethren have always believed, that the adherents of the Augsburg Confession teach nothing but pious and orthodox doctrines with regard to God, the Holy Trinity, the incarnation of the Son of God, justification and other fundamental articles of faith. In the same way the followers of the Augsburg Confession have honestly testified, that they do not find in the Confession of our churches, or in that of the Bohemian Brethren, whom some ignorant men call Waldenses, any doctrine with regard to God, the Holy Trinity, the incarnation of the Son of God, justification and other fundamental articles of faith, at variance with orthodox truth and the pure word of God. We have, therefore, mutually and solemnly promised each other, that we will, with united strength and according to the dictates of the Divine Word, defend this our *Consensus*, embracing as it does the pure and true Christian faith, against Papists, Sectaries and all other enemies of the Gospel and of the Truth.

[*Although there were differences on communion and baptism, the document emphasises points of agreement.*]

356 *Sources*

We have also thought that it would serve to establish this our mutual and holy *Consensus*, if, even as the (Lutheran brethren) have pronounced us and our churches and our Confession, communicated at this Synod, as also the Confession of the Bohemian Brethren, orthodox, we, on our part, show their (Lutheran) churches the same Christian love and pronounce them orthodox. We will put an end to and bury in perpetual silence all those controversies, strifes and differences by which the progress of the Gospel has been hindered, grave offence given to many pious souls, and an opportunity to our enemies grievously to malign us and oppose our true peace and public tranquillity, to show love to another, and with united hearts, agreeably to our fraternal union, to strive to build up the church....

We have mutually pledged each other the right hand of fellowship and solemnly promised to live at peace, to further peace more and more, to avoid all occasions for strife. And now, finally, we covenant together not to seek our own interests, but as becometh true servants of God, to promote the glory of our Saviour Jesus Christ alone, and both by precept and by works, to spread the truth of the Gospel....

'*Behold how good and pleasant it is for brethren to dwell together in unity!*' (Ps. 133:1)

98 A Defence and True Declaration of the Things Lately Done in the Low Country (1570)

Keywords: #Persecution, #Rebellion, #Freedom of Religion, #Rights, #Violence, #War
Region: #Netherlands, #Spain | #Germany
Group: #Dutch Reformed | #Roman Catholic, #Islam, #Judaism

The Dutch Revolt was a complex and evolving series of political, religious, and military struggles that date from around 1566 until 1648 when Spain recognised the independence of the Dutch Republic at the Peace of Münster (part of the **Peace of Westphalia** in 1648). From the middle of the sixteenth century, the Burgundian-Habsburgs sought to centralise their power and subordinate the Low Countries, laying the groundwork for popular dissatisfaction. Philip II frequently clashed with the provinces, especially as he tried to govern without the States General in which they exercised their rights and privileges. *Super Universas*, a papal bull from 1559, reorganised the church structure and granted Philip II the rights to make ecclesiastical appointments. Tension grew with the nobility of the Low Countries, particularly in the circle of William of Orange. The increased efforts of the Inquisition angered the growing and increasingly vocal Protestant population, as well as many non-Protestants who were uncomfortable with this encroachment of power and persecution. A wave of iconoclasm started in 1566. Protestant armies were defeated later that year, and in the following year, the Duke of Alba was appointed as Governor-General. William of Orange, Stadholder of Holland, Zeeland, and Utrecht, went into exile only to return militarily in 1568 and lead a series of campaigns.

The following extract comes from *Libellus supplex Imperatoriae Majestati* (published in English as *A defence and true declaration of the thinges lately done in the lowe countrey*). This work was anonymously published in October 1670 and has been traditionally attributed to Petrus Dathenus and, more recently, to Philip Marnix van St. Aldegonde – both advocates of the Reformation. The intrusion of the Inquisition and its manifold abuses occupy an important place in *A defence*. The Duke of Alva, the *bête noire* of Dutch Protestantism, is singled out for his tyrannous religious persecution. Pleas

358   *Sources*

for help went out to other princes. The following selection comes from *A defence,* which appealed to the German Reichstag meeting at Speyer.[143]

A defence and true declaration of the thinges lately done in the lowe countrey (London: John Day, 1671), n.p. Text modernised by the editors.

The same tempest [the Spanish Inquisition], most victorious Emperor and most noble Princes [of the German Reichstag], which has troubled several parts of Europe for almost a 100 years, has now also at this time by most cruel tyranny led to us being deprived of our goods, chased out of our native countries, oppressed with slander by our adversaries, and tossed with all kind of calamities, to flee and humbly ask for you clemency and help.

[*They recount a history whereby members of the Inquisition became close to the nobility and gained power by manipulating religion and using their power to manipulate kings, challenge ancient liberties, drive a wedge between the king and his people and inflame conflict.*]

If any province in Europe has ever felt this, surely our county, namely that part of base Germany that is subject to the king of Spain, has suffered destruction. Through slanderous, corrupt and crafty means of the Spanish Inquisitors, this country has been accused of heresy and impiety, and been made displeasurable to Emperor Charles V of happy memory and his son King Philip of Spain and Lord of base Germany, and oppressed with most heinous Edicts about religion procured by guile and slanderous reports, and the people have been obedient to their sovereign Lords more than 50 years while enduring with the Inquisitors' cruel yoke with incredible patience, and because matters in other nearby countries are well settled to peace and quietness, and the truth of the cause is commonly disclosed, we hoped to find some relief from so great a calamity: it has now come to pass that the adversaries being grieved to see them aspire to such liberty of religion as by this time flourished not only in Germany but also in France and many other places, have in a strange manner and with most earnest endeavour laboured, not only to frustrate the hope of the inhabitants, but also to strip them of the remainder of their right and liberty by bringing in a far more grievous tyranny: and so to rob the wealthy of their goods, and the noble and mighty of their lives.

Therefore joining with the Bishop of Rome, and having obtained his Bull [*Super Universas*, 1559], they used slander and extreme harassment to wrest from the King an Edict against all the Privileges of the country, against their laws, ordinances, and ancient liberties, namely, for the precise observing of the decrees of the Counsel of Trent, and for bringing in new Bishops, that should put in execution throughout the whole land a new form of Inquisition, far more cruel than the very Spanish Inquisition which was first invented against Jewish and Mohammedan Apostates [Conversos and Moriscos], and so they will quickly reduce a flourishing and free Province to the most dishonourable service of strangers, and villainous and abominable persons will torment at their pleasure the most honest and best men ... and they will utterly destroy with most exquisite torments, murdering and rooting up all those who refused to obey the Roman Bishop's power; those who would have their consciences subjected only to the word of God as contained in the books of the Old and New Testament.

[*They argue that opponents poisoned relations between the people and the king: they spread the lie that Protestants were seditious; they thwarted the king's attempt to personally search into the truth; they convinced the king to send a representative, the Duke of Alba.*]

Alba covers his malicious intentions with the glorious appearance of zeal to restore the Roman religion and to chastise Rebels, it is incredible to tell of the great and outrageous cruelty he has everywhere executed upon the poor inhabitants of the Low Country, without respect or difference: by how many and how strange devises he has robbed all men's goods: how he has spoiled the whole Province of all their ornaments, disarmed them of their defences, deprived them of their liberties, and stripped them out of their laws and privileges: how he has condemned every honest man by private warrant without a judicial order, how he has shed every innocent man's blood, how he has vilely shamed every virtuous person, how he has violated all laws of God and man, how he has broken the bands of marriage, how he has polluted the Sacrament of Baptism, how he has overthrown all order of charity and friendly society; finally how he has done every imaginable cruelty. And yet, at the same time, he throws upon us the blame of his heinous deeds, and by proclamations published and by infamous libels, he has accused us in print of the most grievous crimes to all princes and states, all this only because when we were fleeing we gave place to his furry, and by God's protection have escaped his blood-thirsty sword.

[*They argue that they would remain silent while suffering injustice, knowing God willed these hardships, but they made their complaints known so that their cause could be fairly weighed and so the gospel would not suffer disrepute.*]

Wherefore we have utterly determined that we cannot, with good peace of conscience, keep silence any longer. But [they make this plea because] we know that the order of these usual assemblies of the states of the sacred Empire has for their chief purpose this end, that such as are oppressed by force and injury may present their complaints to the chief throne of Justice in Christendom....

[*They plead again for justice, mercy and aid for the innocent, and they urge the emperor and princes to read the history of the conflict, which they annexed to this plea.*]

99 Zacharias Ursinus, *Commentary on the Heidelberg Catechism* (c.1570)

Keywords: #Church-State Relations, #Ten Commandments, #Law, #Natural Law, #Conscience, #War, #Punishment, #Magistrate, #Authority
Region: #Poland, #Germany
Group: #Reformed

Zacharias Ursinus (1534–1583) was born in Silesia (Poland) and studied at Wittenberg, where he became close with **Philip Melanchthon**. He travelled through many of the Reformation centres of Europe and was often caught up in debates between the Reformed and Lutherans on the nature of communion. He became the principal of a college in Heidelberg in 1561 and led the drafting of the anti-Catholic **Heidelberg Catechism** (1563) as the Palatinate moved in the direction of Calvinism. As a professor, he expounded on the Catechism over the course of each year, a practice that was echoed in weekly sermons on the Catechism in parts of the continental Reformed tradition. After his death, some students published these lectures, and they were compiled into an authoritative edition. Although Ursinus acquired fame in his time, he is largely unknown in the anglophone world today.[144]

In the following selection, Ursinus expanded on the nature of the law, which shows depth to his political thought. Like many of his contemporaries, he distinguished between divine and human laws. Divine law, as chiefly expressed in moral law, can be known from doctrine and, to some extent, from nature, and the summary of which is given through the Decalogue. He wrote that obedience to the moral law would not be a matter of outward compliance but of inward obedience. He distinguished moral laws from human laws, including civil or ecclesiastical laws, which may reflect moral law. Yet insofar as they represent exclusively human laws, they do not require one's inner commitment. Moreover, insofar as human laws conflict with moral laws, one has an obligation not to comply. Thus, he introduced an interesting nuance: although church and state are necessary for the protection of order, neither is infallible with respect to the moral law, which is spiritually superior to either.

Zacharias Ursinus, *The Commentary of Dr. Zacharias Ursinus on the Heidelberg Catechism*, trans. G. W. Williard, 4th ed. (Cincinnati, OH: Elm

Sources 361

Street, 1888), 449–456, 490–492, 520–521, 586–587. Text modernised by the editors.

———

What Are the Parts of the Law, and What Their Differences?

Laws are divine and human. *Human laws* are such as are instituted by men, and which bind certain persons to certain external duties concerning which there is no express divine precept or prohibition with a promise of reward and threatening of punishment, corporal and temporal. Human laws are either civil or ecclesiastical. *Civil* are such positive laws as are instituted by magistrates, or by some corporation, or state, in reference to a certain order or class of actions to be observed in the state in contracts, trials, punishments, etc. *Ecclesiastical* or ceremonial laws are those which the church institutes in reference to the order which is to be observed in the ministry of the church, and which lay down certain prescriptions in reference to those things which contribute to the divine law.

Divine laws are those which God has instituted, which belong partly to angels, partly to men, and partly to certain classes of men. These do not only require external actions or obedience, but they also require internal qualities, actions and motives: nor do they merely propose temporal rewards and punishments; but also such as are spiritual and eternal. They are also the ends for which human laws are instituted. Of *divine laws* there are some that are eternal and unchangeable; whilst there are others that are changeable; yet only by God himself, who has instituted them.

The divine law is ordinarily divided or considered as consisting of three parts; the moral, the ceremonial and the judicial.

The *moral law* is a doctrine harmonising with the eternal and unchangeable wisdom and justice of God, distinguishing right from wrong, known by nature, graven upon the hearts of creatures endowed with reason in their creation, and afterwards often repeated and declared by the voice of God through his servants, the prophets; teaching what God is and what he requires, binding all intelligent creatures to perfect obedience and conformity to the law, internal and external, promising the of God and eternal life to all those who render perfect obedience, and at the same time denouncing the wrath of God and everlasting punishment upon all those who do not render this obedience, unless remission of sins and reconciliation with God is secured for the sake of Christ the mediator.

Harmonising with the eternal and unchangeable wisdom of God: That the law is eternal is evident from this, that it remains one and the same from the beginning to the end of the world. We were also created and have been redeemed by Christ and regenerated by the Holy Spirit, that we might keep this law, or love God and our neighbour as it requires, both in this and in the life to come. 'I write no new commandment unto you, but an old commandment which ye had from the beginning' (John 2:7).

362　*Sources*

Afterwards often repeated: God repeated the law of nature which was graven upon the mind of man: (1) Because it was obscured and weakened by the fall. (2) Because many things were entirely obliterated and lost. (3) That what was still left in the mind of man might not be regarded as a mere opinion or notion and so at length is lost.

Ceremonial laws were those which God gave through Moses in reference to ceremonies or the external solemn ordinances which were to be observed in the public worship of God, with a proper attention to the circumstances which had been prescribed; binding the Jewish nation to the coming of the Messiah, and at the same time distinguishing them from all other nations; and that they might also be signs, symbols, types and shadows of spiritual things to be fulfilled in the New Testament by Christ. *Ceremonies* are external solemn actions which are often to be repeated in the same manner and with the same circumstance, and which have been instituted by God or by men to be observed in the external worship of God for the sake of order, propriety and signification. The ceremonies which have been instituted by God constitute divine worship absolutely; whilst those which have been instituted by men, if they are good, merely contribute to divine worship.

The judicial laws were those which had respect to the civil order or government and the maintenance of external propriety among the Jewish people according to both tables of the Decalogue; or it may be said that they had respect to the order and duties of magistrates, the courts of justice, contracts, punishments, fixing the limits of kingdoms, etc. These laws God delivered through Moses for the establishment and preservation of the Jewish commonwealth, binding all the posterity of Abraham, and distinguishing them from the rest of mankind until the coming of the Messiah; and that they might also serve as a bond for the preservation and government of the Mosaic polity, until the manifestation of the Son of God in the flesh, that they might be certain marks by which the nation which was bound by them, might be distinguished from all other nations, and might at the same time be the means of preserving proper discipline and order, that so they might be types of the order which should be established in the kingdom of Christ.

All good laws, which alone deserve the name of laws, are to be traced *to the moral law* as their source, which agrees in every respect with the Decalogue and may also, by necessary consequence, be deduced from it, so that he who violates the one, violates the other likewise. As it respects *ceremonial and judicial laws*, however, whether they are divine or human, if they are only good, they do, indeed, agree with the Decalogue, but cannot be deduced from it by necessary consequence, as the moral law, but are subservient to it, as certain specifications of circumstances. From this, we may easily perceive the difference which exists between these laws: for it is one thing to flow out of the Decalogue necessarily, and another thing to agree with it, and contribute to its observance. Yet this difference varies because the government of the church and the state is not the same; nor do these have the same end, nor are they abrogated in the same way.

But the chief difference between these laws lies in their obligation, manifestation, duration and use. *The moral law* is known naturally, binds all men, and that perpetually; it is different, however, with the ceremonial and judicial law. *The moral law* requires obedience which is both internal and external; the others merely require that which is external. The precepts of the *moral law* are general, having respect to all men, whoever they may be; the others are special and do not thus apply to all men. The *precepts of the moral law* are the ends of the others; whilst they again are subservient to those which are moral. The ceremonial and civil laws were also types and figures of other things for which they were instituted; it is different, however, with the moral law. The moral law does not give place to the ceremonial; it, on the other hand, gives place to the moral.

We must also observe, in passing, the difference which exists between the moral law, the natural law, and the Decalogue. *The Decalogue* contains the sum of the moral laws which are scattered throughout the Scriptures of the Old and New Testaments. *The natural and moral law* were the same in man before the fall, when his nature was pure and holy. Since the fall, however, which resulted in the corruption and depravity of our nature, a considerable part of the natural law has become obscured and lost by reason of sin so that there is only a small portion concerning the obedience which we owe to God still left in the human mind. It is for this reason that God repeated and declared to the church the entire doctrine and true sense of his law, as contained in the Decalogue. The Decalogue is, therefore, the renewal and re-enforcing of the natural law, which is only a part of the Decalogue. This distinction, therefore, which we have made between the several parts of the divine law must be retained, both on account of the difference itself, that so the force and true sense of these laws may be understood, and that we may also have a correct knowledge and understanding of the abrogation and use of the law [, a topic that he then discussed at length.]

Can magistrates bind the conscience in civil matters?

Secondly, there are civil ordinances prescribed by men, which include the arrangement or fixing of those circumstances which are necessary and useful for securing the observance of the moral precepts of the second table. Such are the positive laws of magistrates, parents, teachers, masters, and all those who are placed in positions of authority. Obedience is *the worship of God* in as far as it has respect to the general, which is moral and commanded by God, and includes obedience to the magistrate and others in authority; but not in as far as it pertains to that which is special in regard to the action, or to the circumstances connected with it – in this respect it is not the worship of God because only those works constitute divine worship, which it is necessary to do on account of the commandment of God, even though no creature

364 *Sources*

had given any precept respecting them; but these, were it not that the magistrate commands them, might be done or omitted without any offence to God. But yet, these civil ordinances prescribed by magistrates and others bind the conscience; that is, they must necessarily be complied with and cannot be disregarded without offence to God, even though it might be done without being connected with any public scandal, if we would keep our obedience pure, and unspoiled. So to bear, or not to bear arms, is not the worship of God; but when the magistrate commands, or prohibits it, the obedience which is then rendered constitutes divine worship: and he who acts contrary to this command, or prohibition, sins against God, even though he might so conceal it, as to offend no man; because the general, viz. obedience to the magistrate, which is the worship of God, is then violated. Yet these actions do not in themselves, constitute the worship of God; it is only by accident, on account of the command of the magistrate. If this were not to intervene, obedience would not be violated. The following passages of Scripture are here in point; 'Let every soul be subject unto the higher powers'. 'Whosoever resisteth the power, resisteth the ordinance of God'. 'Wherefore ye must needs be subject not only for wrath, but also for conscience sake'. 'Put them in mind to be subject to principalities, and powers, to obey magistrates, &c' (Rom. 13:1, 3, 5; Titus 3:1; Eph. 6:1; Col. 3:22–23).

[*This argument raises the objection that some magistrates command evil.*]

Fourthly, there are human enactments which are in opposition to the commands of God. These God forbids us to comply with, whether they be enjoined by the civil magistrate, or by the church and her ministry, according as it is said: 'We ought to obey God rather than men'. 'Why do ye transgress the commandment of God by your tradition' (Acts 5:29; Matt. 15:3).

From what has now been said, we may easily answer the following objections: Objection 1. God commands us to yield obedience to the enactments of men. Answer. God require us to comply with: (1) Such as are good and not opposed to his word; (2) Such as he himself has commanded by men, that worship may be thus paid unto him; (3) Such civil enactments as depend upon the authority of men, to which we render obedience not for the sake of divine worship, but for conscience sake; (4) Such ecclesiastical ordinances as those which we observe, not for the sake of worship, nor for conscience sake, but that we may avoid giving any offence....

How Does the Power of the Keys Differ from Civil Power?

The points of difference are many, and such as are apparent:

1 Ecclesiastical discipline is exercised by the church; civil power by the judge or magistrate.
2 In the state, judgement is passed according to civil and positive laws; in the church, according to the divine law or word of God.

3 The power of the keys committed to the church depends upon the word of God, and the church exercises her power by the word, denouncing the wrath of God upon the impenitent; punishes the obstinate with the word of God alone, yet in such a way that this punishment takes hold even upon the conscience: civil power employs the sword, and compels the refractory to submit to its authority by temporal punishment alone.

4 The church has different steps of admonition, and if the offender is brought to acknowledge his sin and repents of it, it does not proceed to execute punishment in his case; the magistrate punishes the offender even though he repent.

5 The church, in the exercise of discipline, looks to the reformation and salvation of the offender; the magistrate to the execution of justice and the public peace....

[He then answers several objections to the church's authority.]

Objection 3. Christ says in the parable of the wheat and tares, 'Let both grow together until the harvest' (Matt. 13:30). Therefore, none ought to be excluded [from the church]. Answer (1) Christ here speaks of hypocrites, who cannot always be discerned from those who are truly pious. Therefore the meaning is that hypocrites ought not to be cut off and separated from the church when we do not certainly know them to be such; for the angels will do this at the last day. (2) Christ here distinguishes the office of ministers from that of the magistrate. *Let them grow*, that is, do not put to death those that are estranged from the church; for the minister must not use temporal power against any man, as the magistrate does. If this difference is properly considered, the difference which exists between the church and the kingdom of the devil will still remain....

Objection 8. *[Israelites brought religious matters before a civil council, and Jesus referred people to these councils.]* The question now is, did Christ command to tell it to the council as to its civil or ecclesiastical character? We hold that it was in its ecclesiastical character, and prove it from the text itself: because we are commanded, in the first place, to regard the excommunicated person as a heathen man and publican; that is, as an alien from the kingdom of God. But to declare a man a publican, and an alien from the kingdom of God, does not belong to the civil magistrate, but to the church; because a publican may be a member of the state, but not of the church of Christ....

[He also counters the argument that civil penalties were added to excommunication with the advent of the Christian magistrate.]

What Virtues Contribute to Human Safety?

V. Communicative Justice in Punishing is a virtue which preserves equality between offences and punishments, inflicting either equal punishments or less in view of just and satisfactory causes, having a proper regard to the circumstances which should ever be taken into consideration in civil courts, for the

366 *Sources*

sake of maintaining the glory of God, and the preservation of human society. For when God forbids the infliction of any wrong upon society and wills that the magistrate be the defender and preserver of order according to the whole Decalogue, he also designs that those who manifestly and grossly violate this order be restrained and kept within proper bounds by just punishments. The magistrate, therefore, may be guilty of doing wrong not only in being cruel and unjustly severe but also in being too lenient and in granting permission to certain persons to injure others....

Objection. It is here said, *Thou shalt not kill*. Therefore no one must be put to death – consequently, this justice is not comprehended in this commandment in as much as it cannot be maintained without putting many to death. Answer. *Thou shalt not kill*, that is, not thou who art merely a private person, according to thy judgement and desire, when I do not command thee and give thee any warrant from this law. But this does not do away with the office of the magistrate; 'for he is the minister of God and does not bear the sword in vain' (Rom. 13:4). Hence when the magistrate puts wicked transgressors to death, it is not man, but God who is the executioner of the deed. We may also reply to this objection by reversing the argument thus: Therefore, some are to be put to death, lest human society be destroyed by thieves and robbers.

The opposite of this virtue is: (1) Cruelty, or too great severity; (2) Private revenge; (3) Lenity, when those are not punished who ought to be punished; (4) Partiality. Or, to express it more briefly, we may say that the opposite of commutative justice is injustice, which either does not punish at all or else punishes unjustly.

100 *A Homily Against Disobedience and Wilful Rebellion* (1570)

Keywords: #Submission, #Rebellion, #Servants, #Authority, #Magistrates
Region: #England
Group: #Church of England

As England turned towards the Reformation, it took considerable time to address the problem of untrained clergy. Towards the end of Henry VIII's lifetime, **Thomas Cranmer** began thinking through ways of instructing the people in the word of God, even in the absence of a qualified minister. In 1547, he published the *Book of Homilies*, a compilation of 12 sermons written by several persons on fundamental theological issues. All parishes were ordered to purchase a copy and use the homilies in weekly services.[145] The following source relates a second compilation of homilies published under **Elizabeth I**, which deals with the question of rebellion and obedience. Through the *Homily*, the state dictated what the church should say about the obedience of subjects, and the average parishioner would have listened to this sermon many times during their lifetime.

The wider context to this source is a revolt in the north of England, which was prompted by Mary Queen of Scots' flight from rebels to England. The rebellion was supported by the pope, who issued the papal bull *Regnas in excelsis,* in which he excommunicated **Elizabeth I** and absolved her subjects from their duty of obedience. The northern rebellion was easily crushed, but the idea that the pope freed subjects from obedience to her majesty was much harder to suppress. From Zürich, **Heinrich Bullinger** quickly published a refutation of the papal bull (1571, trans. 1572). English authorities tried to undercut rebellion by publishing a *Homily Against Disobedience and Wilful Rebellion* (1570). The *Homily* shows traces of being partly written during the rebellion, but it seems to have taken final form after the rebellion was suppressed and before the papal bull reached England. It was originally intended for the rebellious northern provinces, but it quickly made its way into a second collection of homilies and thus became a regular part of the Church of England.[146]

368   *Sources*

A Homily Against Disobedience and Wilful Rebellion: Printed for the Society for Promoting Christian Knowledge (London: Gilbert & Rivington, 1837), 1–14 (4–5, 7–9). Text modernised by the editors.

———

[*The opening of the 'First Part of this Homily' roots government in the divine order with God as the king. Humanity rebelled against God in the garden at the behest of the original rebel, Lucifer.*]

As in reading of the Holy Scriptures we shall find in very many and almost infinite places, as well of the Old Testament as of the New, that kings and princes, as well the evil as the good, do reign by God's ordinance, and that subjects are bound to obey them, that God gives princes wisdom, great power, and authority: that God defends them against their enemies, and destroys their enemies horribly, that the anger and displeasure of the prince is as the roaring of a lion, and the very messenger of death; and the subject, that provokes him to displeasure, sins against his own soul; with many other things concerning both the authority of princes and the duty of subjects. But here, let us rehearse two special places out of the New Testament, which may stand instead of all other, Romans 13 and 1 Peter 2. [*He cites Paul at length about God-ordained authority and Peter's words about submission, punishment and the limits of liberty.*]

By these two places of the Holy Scriptures, it is most evident that kings, queens, and other princes (for he speaks of authority and power, be it in men or women) are ordained of God, are to be obeyed and honoured by their subjects; that such subjects as are disobedient or rebellious against their princes, disobey God, and procure their own damnation; that the government of princes is a great blessing of God, given for the commonwealth, especially of the good and godly; for the comfort and cherishing of whom, God gives and establishes princes; and, on the contrary part, to the fear and for the punishment of the evil and wicked. Finally, that if servants ought to obey their masters, not only being gentle, but also those who are more disagreeable; as well, and much more, ought subjects to be obedient, not only to their good and courteous princes but also to their sharp and rigorous ones. It comes, therefore, neither by chance and fortune (as they term it) nor by the ambition of mortal men and women, climbing up of their own accord to dominion, that there are kings, queens, princes, and other governors over men who are their subjects: but all kings, queens, and other governors are specially appointed by the ordinance of God. [*There is a resemblance between the rule of God and the rule of princes, especially when earthly princes rule in godly and just ways. The people are blessed through the rule of the just and cursed through the rule of the unjust.*]

What shall subjects do then? Shall they obey valiant, stout, wise, and good princes, and show contempt towards, disobey, and rebel against children who are their princes or against indiscreet and evil governors? God forbid:

Sources 369

for first, what a perilous thing it would be to commit unto the subjects the judgement, which prince is wise and godly, and his government good, and which is otherwise; as though the foot must judge of the head: an enterprise very heinous, and must needs breed rebellion.

But whereas indeed a rebel is worse than the worst prince, and rebellion worse than the worst government of the worst prince that hitherto hath been; both are rebels unsuitable ministers, and rebellion an unfit and unwholesome medicine to reform what is lacking in a prince, or to cure any little griefs in government, such lewd remedies being far worse than any other maladies and disorders that can be in the body of a commonwealth. But whatsoever the prince is, or his government, it is evident that for the most part those princes, whom some subjects do think to be very godly, and under whose government they rejoice to live, some other subjects do take the same to be evil and ungodly, and do wish for a change. If, therefore, all subjects who dislike their prince should rebel, no realm should ever be without rebellion. It were more fitting that rebels should hear the advice of wise men and give place unto their judgement, and follow the example of obedient subjects, as reason is, that they whose understanding is blinded with so evil an affection should give place to them that are of sound judgement, and that the worst should give place to the better; and so might realms continue in long obedience, peace, and quietness.

[*Even if the prince openly rebels against God, the people are not absolved from obedience. Indeed, their disobedience to God might be the reason they deserve an unjust prince. Righteous and wicked rulers are given by God, and the people should endeavour to move God to give righteous rulers through their godly submission to authority. The Homily then calls rebellious subjects to repent, knowing that they deserve judgement from earthly and heavenly powers. It ends by directing subjects into prayers for such a gracious Queen who rules justly and righteously.*]

101 Jeanne III, *The Magistrate's Duty to Further Christ's Rule* (1571)

Keywords: #Church-State Relations, #Magistrate, #Authority, #Submission, #Women, #Confession of Faith
Region: #France
Group: #Reformed, #Huguenot

In the last year of her life, **Jeanne III** (1528–1572) continued to work towards reforming the church, protecting Protestantism, amending poor laws, and establishing a seminary. She fashioned herself into a Protestant leader similar to **Elizabeth I** of England. Like Elizabeth, she freely discoursed upon the prerogatives of the magistrate over religious matters, as the following source demonstrates. She claimed responsibility for the spiritual health of her kingdom even as she described herself as responding to the earnest desire of the people to root out idolatry and establish pure worship.[147]

Nancy Lyman Roelker, *Queen of Navarre: Jeanne d'Albret, 1528–1572* (Cambridge, MA: Harvard University Press, 1968), 430–432.

———

Ecclesiastical Ordinances of Jeanne d'Albret, November 1571

There is no monarch alive who is not obligated to use his full powers to place his subjects under the rule of Jesus Christ, since the Eternal Father has given Him all power in Heaven and earth and commanded all his creatures to seek Him above all things. How much greater is the obligation of princes who He has saved from sin and death by his grace and goodness alone to procure the complete establishment and advancement of [Christ's] kingdom. If it be their duty to conserve the public peace, which affects only their estates, how much greater [is their duty] to establish piety so that the administration will not fail to destroy anything by which God is not purely served according to his word. Who then can doubt that princes who do not follow the examples of Josiah, Ezekiel, and Theodosius will fall under the wrath of God in the end? These [princes] … were moved by the spirit of God to eject all idolatry and superstition from their domains and to enthrone instead the true religion….

Sources 371

The punishment [of princes who do not follow such examples] would be all the more justified if, their subjects being ready to embrace the Gospel (as in the case of our own) they failed in any degree to assure the eternal salvation of those from whom they shall have to answer of they neglect to do so....

[*In order to further this reformation, Jeanne III publishes the Confession of La Rochelle that was formulated in April 1571.*]

Article 1

The clergy ... shall be subject not only to the magistrates and to our laws, but to all points established by our authority in consultation with the national synod of the said country ... and if anyone attempts to exercise a ministry without an authorised vocation ... he shall bow to the discipline of the church and be punished and chastised by our magistrates by banishment from our said country for two years....

Article 11

Those who are legitimately called to the consistory ... before exercising their charge in any manner whatever, ... shall take an oath before the magistrates of their place of residence ... to eliminate all idolatry, superstitions, and everything contrary to God's commandments....

Article 25

Since all civil jurisdiction belongs originally to princes and their magistrates ... all degrees of judicial authority ... are hereby removed from ecclesiastics [who formerly exercised them] and reunited in our hands and those of our magistrates....

102 *The Thirty-Nine Articles of Religion of the Church of England* (1571/1801)

Keywords: #Confession of Faith, #Authority, #Magistrate, #Violence, #Capital Crime, #War
Region: #England
Group: #Church of England | #Roman Catholic

After the northern rebellion of 1569, **Elizabeth I** became less tolerant of theological dissent. Her government controlled what could be said from the pulpit about authority and submission when they published *A Homily Against Disobedience and Wilful Rebellion* (1570). The people were regularly reminded of the contents of this sermon. Her government also tightened the doctrines imposed on the clergy, who were required to affirm the *Thirty-Nine Articles* of 1571. This document built on and modified earlier collections of articles, which date to 1553 (the *Forty-Two Articles*) and 1563 (the *Thirty-Eight Articles*). The *Thirty-Nine Articles* are a foundational part of the theology of the Church of England, although aspects of it have been reinterpreted, challenged, or ignored. Included below is Article 37 of the *Thirty-Nine Articles* from 1571, which explicitly affirms the authority of the queen over the church. After the American Revolution, the Episcopal Church in the United States modified the article so that it applied to the American nation, omitting any references to royal supremacy.[148]

The Creeds of Christendom, vol. III: The Evangelical Protestant Creeds, ed. Philip Schaff (New York: Harper and Brothers, 1887), 486–516 (512–513). Text modernised by the editors.

—

37. Of the civil Magistrates.

The Queen's Majesty has the chief power in this Realm of England, and her other dominions, unto whom the chief government of all estates of this Realm, whether they be Ecclesiastical or Civil, in all causes does appertain, and is not, nor ought to be subject to any foreign jurisdiction.

Where we attribute to the Queen's Majesty the chief government, by which titles we understand the minds of some slanderous folks to be offended: we give not to our Princes the ministering either of God's word or of Sacraments, a position that the injunctions lately set forth by Elizabeth our Queen plainly demonstrate: But that only prerogative which we see to have always been given to all godly Princes in holy Scriptures by God himself, that is, that they should rule all estates and degrees committed to their charge by God, whether they be Ecclesiastical or Temporal, and restrain with the civil sword the stubborn and evil-doers.

The bishop of Rome hath no jurisdiction in this Realm of England.

The laws of the Realm may punish Christian men with death, for heinous and grievous offences.

It is lawful for Christian men, at the commandment of the Magistrate to wear weapons, and serve in the wars.

103 Confederation of Warsaw, *Pax Dissidentium* (1573)

Keywords: #Toleration, #Pluralism, #Peace
Region: #Poland, #Lithuania, #Belarus, #Ukraine, #Russia, #Latvia, #Estonia
Group: #Interconfessional

Polish-Lithuanian multi-confessionalism had flourished under King Sigismund II Augustus (see also the **Consensus of Sandomierz**), making the Polish-Lithuanian Commonwealth a relatively hospitable place for a variety of religious groups, including Protestants, Jews, and Tatars. The Polish Parliament needed to elect a new king upon his childless death. One of the contenders was Henry Valois, son of the French Queen Catherine de' Medici (who opposed **Jeanne III**) and who had participated in the St. Bartholomew's massacre. Anxious for their future, Protestants insisted on protections for their liberties. Morse Wilbur writes that the Protestant nobility would only allow the election once sufficient assurances were provided. Parliament approved the *Confederation of Warsaw*, the foundational document for the election. It required the king to uphold religious liberty, and the document included a promise to rise up against a king who disrespected Polish-Lithuanian multi-confessionalism. Henry Valois accepted this statement as part of the conditions of his kingship, as did his successor, the Catholic Stephen Báthory of Transylvania, when Henry abdicated in favour of the French throne upon the death of his brother. The section on religious liberty and the accompanying oath are known as the *Pax Dissidentium* of 1573.[149]

Earl Morse Wilbur, *A History of Unitarianism, Socinianism and Its Antecedent* (Boston, MA: Beacon Press, 1945), 363–364.

———

Since there is in our Republic no little disagreement on the subject of religion, in order to prevent any such hurtful strife from beginning among our people on this account as we plainly see in other realms, we mutually promise for ourselves and our successors forever, under the bond of our oath, faith, honour, and conscience, that we who differ with regard to religion (*dissidentes de religione*) will keep the peace with one another, and will not for a different

Sources 375

faith or a change of churches shed blood nor punish one another by confiscation of property, infamy, imprisonment, or banishment, and will not in any way assist any magistrate or office in such an act.

[*Rulers, conforming to this article, were to swear the following at their coronation.*]

I promise and solemnly swear by almighty God that ... I will preserve and maintain peace and quiet among those that differ with regard to religion (*dissidentes de religione*), and will not in any way, whether by our jurisdiction or by authority of any of our officers and institutions whatsoever, suffer any one to be influenced or oppressed by reason of his religion, nor will I myself influence or oppress him.

104 François Hotman, *Francogallia* (1573)

Keywords: #Tyranny, #Absolutism, #Common Good, #Liberty, #Consent, #International Law
Region: #France
Group: #Reformed, #Huguenot | #Islam

François Hotman (1524–1590) was born in Paris to an aristocratic family. He was a humanist and legal scholar who was educated at the Universities of Paris and Orléans. He lectured at several universities across Europe throughout his lifetime. His father played an important role in the violent suppression of Protestantism: he sat on the 'Chambre Ardente', the 'burning chamber', formed in 1547 to persecute and trial heretics. François himself converted to the Reformed faith around this time. He befriended **Théodore de Bèze** and spent considerable time in Geneva as a secretary to **John Calvin**. Hotman vigorously defended the Reformation, and his contribution to the cause entailed focusing on the nature, history, and response to tyranny. The St. Bartholomew's Day Massacre (1572) hardened his opposition to Catholicism.

Francogallia (1573) was his most thorough and sustained argument that the people should root out all forms of civil and ecclesiastical tyranny. He attacked, in particular, theories of royal absolutism that hindered the reform of the church. The work was rich with argumentation from classical antiquity, European (particularly French) history, and citations from scripture.[150] In the following selection, Hotman elevated the importance of the people and the duty of the king to their welfare: when monarchs failed to govern for the good of the people, they effectively descended into tyranny. Hotman's argument expanded ideas about who government was instituted for, and who should develop state policies. Popular government had limits, and a later chapter painted an unflattering picture of feminine rule.[151]

Ralph E. Giesey, ed., and J.H.M. Salmon, trans., *Francogallia by Fraçois Hotman* (Cambridge: Cambridge University Press, 1972), 297–298, 317.

Sources 377

'LET THE WELFARE OF THE PEOPLE BE THE SUPREME LAW'. The wisdom and utility of this practice is very apparent in three respects. First, the large number of men of prudence ensure that there would be an amplitude of advice, and advice of the kind to procure the welfare of the people.... Next, because it is an attribute of liberty that those at whose peril a thing is done should have some say and authority in arranging it, or, as it is customarily and commonly said, what touches all should be approved by all. Lastly, those who have great influence with the king, and are foremost in great affairs of government, should, in the performance of their office, be held in fear of this council, in which the requests of the provinces are freely heard. When certain kingdoms are governed by the will and pleasure of a single king – as today the Turks are ruled – their government would lack the advice of free men and enlightened opinion and would be like that of the cattle and beasts, as Aristotle rightly observes in his *Politics*....

In the same way a multitude of men ought not to be ruled and governed by one of their own number, who, peradventure, sees less than others do when taken together, but rather by proven men of excellence, selected with the consent of all, who act by combined advice as if they possessed one mind composed from many....

[*He appeals at length to antiquity and to European history to argue that a multitude of counsellors leads to civil flourishing. There is also a long precedent for opposing rulers who bring their people harm rather than good.*]

Since this is the way things are, and since, as I say, there has always been this common law among all peoples and nations who practice regal rather than tyrannical government, namely, that 'THE WELFARE OF THE PEOPLE WAS THE SUPREME LAW', it is obvious not only that this celebrated liberty of holding a common council is a part of the law of nations but also that kings who oppress that sacred liberty with their evil arts, as if they were violators of this international law and beings set apart from human society, should not be regarded as kings but rather as tyrants.

105 Edmund Grindal, *Preaching, Rebellion and the Limits of Royal Authority* (1576)

Keywords: #Resistance, #Censorship, #Church-State Relations, #Obedience
Region: #England
Group: #Church of England | #Puritan

Edmund Grindal (c.1519–1583) was born to impoverished farmers in the northwest of England, yet he went on to serve in some of the most important ecclesiastical posts in the land: master of Pembroke Hall (Cambridge), Bishop of London, Archbishop of York, and Archbishop of Canterbury. His ministry spanned from Henry VIII to **Elizabeth I**. His appreciation for the Reformed tradition grew during his time in exile under Mary I. His theological leanings, however, were more moderate, which was apparent from his willingness to compromise on matters of secondary importance. As he rose through the ranks, it became apparent that he would not satisfy the desires of those wanting to substantially reform the church, but neither did he side with the religious policies of **Elizabeth I**. His middle position is demonstrated in the following source where Grindal refused to intervene in the Puritan 'prophesyings'. To the queen, these practices were a potential source of disorder, which needed to be suppressed; to Grindal, they merely needed to be regulated.

The state of preaching in England was relatively poor: the **Book of Homilies** tried to fill the need by offering basic theological sermons that ministers could read to parishioners. Another way of bettering the ministry was through 'prophesyings'. At these regular events, ministers learned skilful exegesis and compelling preaching. At 'prophesyings', several ministers might preach on the same day. Parishioners often enjoyed judging and ranking the skills of the preachers, then carrying on the debate at the local tavern. Many of the ministers involved in prophesying wanted to see greater alignment with the continental Reformation, and they would become derisively known as 'Puritans'. From early on, prophesying was controversial, especially since the crown had little ability to control what was being said from the pulpit and then debated in the taverns and streets. These fears seemed confirmed when rumours spread in 1574 of a supposed Presbyterian plot to kill bishops

Sources 379

and the queen. Persecution ensued, but the fraudulent nature of the rumours was quickly discovered.

In this context, Edmund Grindal became the next Archbishop of Canterbury. He disappointed Puritans because of how far he had moved from the continental Reformed tradition. However, this coolness towards Puritanism did not mean that Grindal sided with Elizabeth I on all matters. She ordered him to end the prophesyings, controversially saying that she preferred few preachers to an abundance of unregulated ones. In the following source from 1576, Grindal refused to comply with the queen's order. Although he wanted prophesyings to be regulated, he generally saw them as a positive indication of the people's thirst for God's word. Viewed in this light, suppressing the prophesyings was depriving the people of the gospel. In response to this letter, **Elizabeth I** placed Grindal under house arrest and restricted his ministerial capacity until his death several years later. **Elizabeth I** moved ahead with the suppression of prophesyings on her own authority.[152]

From William Nicholson, ed., *The Remains of Archbishop Grindal* (Cambridge: Parker Society, 1843), 376–390. Text modernised by the editors.

———

Archbishop Edmund Grindal to Queen Elizabeth I (1576)

...The prophet Ezekiel calls ministers of the church 'speculators' [watchmen] and not 'adulatores' [flatterers] (Ezek. 33:7). If we see the sword coming upon the land for any offence towards God, we must of necessity give warning, or else the blood of those that perish will be required at our hands. I beseech your Majesty thus to think of me, that I do not conceive any evil opinion of you, although I cannot assent to those two articles [commanding him to suppress 'prophesyings']. With the rest of all your good subjects, I acknowledge that we have received from your government many excellent benefits, among them freedom of conscience, suppression of idolatry, sincere preaching of the gospel, along with public peace and tranquillity. I am also persuaded that even in these matters, which you seem now to urge, your zeal and intent is for the best....

Public and continual preaching of God's word is the ordinary means and instrument for the salvation of mankind. St Paul calls it the *ministry of reconciliation* of man unto God [2 Cor. 5:18]. Through the preaching of God's word, the glory of God is enlarged, faith is nourished, and charity increased. By it, the ignorant are instructed, the negligent are exhorted and called to action, the stubborn are rebuked, the weak in conscience are comforted, and to all those that sin of malicious wickedness, the wrath of God is threatened. By preaching, also, due obedience to Christian princes and magistrates is planted in the hearts of subjects: for obedience proceeds from conscience; conscience is grounded upon the word of God; the word of God works his

380   *Sources*

effect by preaching. Generally speaking, where preaching is insufficient, obedience fails....

I am forced, with all humility, and yet plainly, to profess that I cannot, with safe conscience and without the offence of the majesty of God, give my assent to the suppressing of the said exercises: much less can I send out any injunction for the utter and universal subversion of the same. I say with St Paul, 'I have no power to destroy, but to only edify [2 Cor. 10:8];' and with the same apostle, 'I can do nothing against the truth, but for the truth [2 Cor. 13:8]'.

If it is your Majesty's pleasure, for this or any other cause, to remove me from this place, I will with all humility yield thereunto, and render again to your Majesty what I received of the same. I consider with myself, *Quod horrendum est incidere in manus Dei viventis* [Heb. 10:31; That it is a fearful thing to fall into the hands of the living God].... 'And what should I win, if I gained' (I will not say a bishopric, but) 'the whole world, and lose mine own soul [Matt. 16:26]!'

Bear with me, I beseech you, Madam, if I choose rather to offend your earthly majesty, than to offend the heavenly majesty of God. And now, being sorry that I have been so long and tedious to your Majesty, I will draw to an end, most humbly praying the same well to consider these two short petitions following.

The first is that you would refer all these ecclesiastical matters which touch religion or the doctrine and discipline of the church unto the bishops and divines of your realm; according to the example of all godly Christian emperors and princes of all ages.... The second petition I have to make to your Majesty is this: that, when you deal in matters of faith and religion, or matters that touch the church of Christ, which is his spouse, bought with so dear a price, you would not pronounce so resolutely and peremptorily, *quasi ex auctoritate* [as if from authority], as you may do in civil and external matters; but always remember, that in God's causes the will of God, and not the will of any earthly creature, is to take place....

106 Innocent Gentillet, *Against Machiavelli's Amoral Politics* (1576)

Keywords: #Authority, #Magistrate, #Violence, #War, #Submission, #Liberty
Region: #France
Group: #Reformed, #Huguenot | #Roman Catholic, #Non-Christian

Niccolò Machiavelli's (1469–1527) life intertwined with power struggles in and beyond Florence. His best-known works, *The Prince* (1513; pub. 1532) and *Discourses on Livy* (pub. 1531), had little to say about religion, but what they included alarmed many. In his *Discourses*, he argued that Christianity was effeminate because followers of Christ could not fight. Further, Christians valued suffering in this life and were too focused on other-worldly gain. He preferred religions that inculcated military virtue: classical antiquity, Judaism, and Islam. Machiavelli argued that religion was useful for a prince so long as it helped him establish or maintain power, and the prince should try to appear pious. He should also encourage religion among his subjects because it fostered a stable and submissive society. But the prince should be ready to dispense with ethical norms when it was practical to do so. In the sixteenth century, Protestants and Catholics accused each other of being Machiavellian atheists: Protestants shared his distaste for the papacy; Catholics seemed to embrace duplicity.

The arguments of *The Prince* shocked many across Europe, and the book prompted several critical responses. Innocent Gentillet (c.1532–1588) was a Huguenot jurisconsult and leader of Protestants in Dauphiné, and he spent considerable time as a refugee in Geneva. He penned an important response to the Florentine statesman, *Anti-Machiavel* (1576). It was written during spiralling tensions between French Protestants and Catholics. The 1572 massacre of Protestants on Saint Bartholomew's Day was still a fresh memory. *Anti-Machiavel* refuted amoral politics while targeting Catherine de Médicis 'Machiavellian' policies. He surveyed Machiavelli's central arguments only to refute them, countering the use of faith as a cloak for ambition or instrument for power. If Machiavelli was a prophet of pragmatic, amoral politics, Gentillet casts a prophetic gaze deeper into the future: expedient, unholy, and unjust policies would ultimately destabilise a regime. Further, risking divine judgement was never pragmatic.[153]

382 *Sources*

Even as a Protestant, Gentillet wrote positively of Catholics and negatively of those who wrongly attacked them. Much united 'Christians', a term he applied equally to 'Catholic, and Evangelical, and Reformed'. Although the differences were real, 'the one and the other acknowledges Christ, which is the foundation; and hold the articles of the faith of the Apostles Symbol; approve the Trinity, and the Sacraments of Baptism, and the holy Supper'.[154] His irenicism evidenced a concern that Machiavelli's ideas had poisoned relations between Catholics and Protestants, with disastrous consequences for all of Europe.

Innocent Gentillet, *A Discourse ... Against Nicholas Machiavell the Florentine*, trans. Simon Patrick (London: Adam Islip, 1602), 92–93, 97, 107–110, 216–217. Text modernised by the editors.

—

Part II: Religion. First Maxim.

Epigraph: A prince above all things ought to wish and desire to be esteemed devout, though he is not so indeed.

The world (says *Machiavell*) looks but to the exterior, and to that which is in appearance; and judges all actions not by the causes, but by the issue and end: So that it suffices, if the prince seem outwardly religious and devout, although he is not so at all. For let it be so that some, who most narrowly frequent his company, discover that feigned devotion, yet he or they dare not challenge the multitude, who believe, the prince is truly devout.

This Maxim is a precept whereby this Atheist *Machiavell* teaches the prince to have contempt for God and religion, and only to make a show and outward appearance before the world, to be esteemed religious and devout, although he is not. *Machiavell* does not fear divine punishment for such hypocrisy and concealment, because he does not believe there is a God; but thinks that the course of the Sun, Moon and Stars, the distinction of the Spring, Summer, Autumn and Winter, the political government of men, the earth's production of fruits, plants and living creatures, that all this comes by chance and fortune: following the doctrine of *Epicurus* (the doctor of Atheists, and master of Ignorance) who esteems, that all things are done and come to pass by Fortune, and the meeting and encountering of atoms. But if *Machiavell* believed that those things came by the disposition and establishment of a sovereign cause (as common sense constrained *Plato, Aristotle, Theophrastus*, and all the other Philosophers who have had any knowledge to confess) he would believe there is one God, who rules and governs the world, and all things within it. And if he believed there is one God, he would also believe that men ought to honour him as the sovereign governor; and that he will not be mocked by his creatures: And he, therefore, would not advise people to make a show of being devout while not being so. For what is it to mock God, if that is not? ... Many Atheists, with a brutish boldness, have made a mockery of God: but they always felt the punishment and vengeance of their audacious impiety, as hereafter we will show by examples. Yet we have great cause to deplore the misery and calamity of our current time, which is so infected with Atheists and those with contempt for God and all religion, ... and those who studied their *Machiavell* well ... make no scruple nor have pangs of conscience about anything. Command them to slay and massacre, they slay and massacre; command them to rob and spoil good Catholics, and Clergymen, they rob and spoil all. They hold ecclesiastical office and wear soldier's garments, yet practice no religion, nor care about it unless they can gain by it. Command them to betray or poison this or that person, they do not hesitate: yes, they themselves contrive and devise wickedness and impiety, inventing new ways to financially burden the poor people, whom they destroy and kill with hunger, without having any commiseration or compassion upon them, no more than upon brute beasts....

A prince then must take another manner of resolution than that whereof *Machiavell* speaks; namely, That he resolves to fear God and to serve him with a pure heart free of disguise, according to his holy commandments, in practicing the true and pure religion of God, which is the Christian: if he does this, God will bless him, and make him prosper in his affairs....

Part II: Religion. *Third Maxim.*

Epigraph: The pagan religion holds and lifts up their hearts, and so makes them bold to undertake great things; but the Christian religion, persuading to humility, humbles and overly weakens their minds, and so makes them more ready to be injured and preyed upon....

True, our Christian religion teaches us humility towards God. For we ought to acknowledge before his face that we are poor sinners, and to demand pardon of him, as criminal persons do, who fall on their knees before a prince, begging grace and pardon. We ought also to acknowledge that the graces we have proceed from God, and that we ought not to be proud of any good thing in us. Moreover, we ought to be modest and gentle towards our neighbour and to detest all fierceness and cruelty. But do those things debase and make the hearts of good men unable to perform and execute their duties of fortitude and valiantness in war? Does this Christian humility diminish their generosity? ... If what he says were true, it should follow that no Christian prince could stand against Pagan and Infidel princes: but does not all ancient and modern history show us the contrary? The emperor *Constantine* the Great was a very humble Christian prince ... yet he vanquished *Licinius*, who was a Pagan emperor with him, and made him forsake the empire, and besides overcame many Pagan nations, as we have said in another place. The emperor *Theodosius* was so humble that being reprehended for a certain fault he had committed by *Saint Ambrose*, bishop of *Milan*, he debased himself so much to acknowledge his sin as he went trailing himself upon the ground upon his four feet, from the Church door, unto the place where *Saint Ambrose* administered the Sacrament, and by that means was received to the Communion: yet although he was so humble, he had very great and good

384 *Sources*

victories against the Barbarians and Infidels, and against other enemies of the Roman empire. The emperor *Valentinian*, who was a Christian, vanquished the Goths in Gall: and the emperor *Justinian* overcame them in Italy and in Africa. *Charlemagne*, and many other kings of France, who were both Christians and very humble, have notwithstanding gained and obtained notable victories against the Pagans, as we have elsewhere said. The emperor *Charles V* of late memory, also obtained notable victories in Africa against the Turk....

Touching his claim; That the Christian religion disposes men to receive blows rather than to vengeance. I confess that it is true that our religion forbids us to take vengeance for our own enmities and particular quarrels by our own authority; but the way and course of justice is not denied us. And if it were lawful for everyone to use vengeance; that would introduce confusion and disorder into the commonwealth, and to challenge the right that belongs to the magistrate, unto whom God has given the sword, to do right to everyone, and to punish the guilty, according to their merits: but what is all this to purpose, touching the generosity of heart that men should have in war? For although a man should not be quarrelsome nor vindictive, to find quarrels for needless points, yet he will not cease to perform his duty in warfare, for the service of his prince; yet is there one point in Christians, more than in Pagans, that is; That a Christian being well resolved in his conscience, that he bears arms for a good and just cause, as for the good of his prince, or of his country, or a similar good cause, he will value his life less, and will more willingly hazard it, than a Pagan or an Infidel will: because he has a firm trust and belief, that he shall enjoy the eternal life after this frail life....

Part III: Policy. *Ninth Maxim.*

Epigraph: It is better for a prince to be feared than loved.

Men (says our Florentine) do love as it please them, and do fear as it pleases the prince: Therefore the prince (if he is wise) ought to establish himself, and to lean that way which depends upon himself, and not that way which depends upon another. If the prince can have both together, to be feared and loved, that is the best: but because it is very difficult to have both, it is more assured to be feared than loved.

This Maxim is a saying or proverb that our elders have attributed to tyrants.... But it seems he made an evil match in coupling hatred with approbation: for that which a man hates, he does not willingly allow; and that which a man allows, he does not also hate. Moreover, all such sayings and proverbs (Let them hate, so they fear, and Let them hate, so they allow) are but tyrant's devices and our forefathers have so esteemed them, and tyrants have always practised them....

As for that which *Machiavell* says, That the prince is feared as he will, and as it pleases him: If this were true, all should go well for him: for he would always be so feared, as none should oppose themselves against his designs and commandments, but that everyone should come under the yoke, and obey him purely and simply: But experience shows us the contrary, and makes us see and know, That a prince cannot long be obeyed, if that which he commands is disagreeable and found unjust by those who should obey: at the first occasion that presents itself, they will unyoke themselves, and their obedience endures no longer than force and necessity endures: And because no force nor necessity can actually long endure: (because no violent thing naturally lasts) therefore it follows, that disagreeable commandments cannot long be observed; and that obedience, founded upon fear, is immediately broken: For the equity and justice of a commandment is the sinew thereof: And as the body cannot move without sinews, unless only for a leap like a stone; so a commandment, which for want of equity displeases those obeying, shall never be well put in action and practised, unless it is for a small time, and at the beginning.

And as for that which *Machiavell* says, That it is very hard for a prince to be feared and loved together, it is clean contrary: For there is nothing more easy for a prince, than to obtain them both, as reason shows: Because it is certain, that a prince who keeps his subjects in good peace, keeps them from oppressions, punishing all those who would oppress them, and who will maintain their liberties, and punish those who break them, and who will observe a good policy in his country, that there may be a free and assured commerce, without imposition of tributes or burdens, and he that shall cause good justice to be administered to everyone, it is certain, that such a prince shall be greatly beloved by his subjects, yes, and feared thus: When men understand, that the prince administers good justice in every place, without support, favour, or corruption, not leaving punishable faults unpunished, and is not prodigal in granting favours and pardons, unless they have a good foundation upon reason and equity, it is certain, that he shall be revered and feared, not only in his own country, but in strange countries also.... And how should they not be beloved by their subjects, being good kings as they were, seeing Frenchmen are of that nature, that they can never hate their king, however vicious he be, but always impute vices and faults to some of his governors and Counsellors, rather than to him? Truly, if princes always had good men about them, they could never be vicious, at the least to the detriment of the Commonwealth: Therefore, by good right, men impute the evil government of a country, rather to a prince's Counsellors, than to himself, as we have proved in another place.

107 Peter Walpot, *Non-Violence in the Gospels* (1577)

Keywords: #Non-Violence, #War, #Excommunication, #Magistrate, Church-State Relations
Region: #Czech Republic
Group: #Hutterite, #Anabaptist | #Lutheran, #Zwinglian, #Roman Catholic

Peter Walpot (1521–1578) was a significant figure in the community of Hutterian Brethren in Moravia, where the Anabaptist community thrived. Characteristic for this community was its radical commitment to pacifism, much like its historic leader, the Austrian Anabaptist Jacob Hutter (c.1500–1536). Hutterite convictions had been expounded more fully by **Peter Riedemann** (1506–1556) in his *Account of Our Religion, Doctrine and Faith*. Walpot represents a new generation of Brethren, building on the distinctives of adult baptism, the sharing of communal goods, the rejection of marriage with unbelievers, and the shunning of the sword. For Walpot, the entire canon, from Genesis to the Book of Revelations, revealed that non-violence was always God's ideal: according to him, it would be impermissible to take a human's life in any circumstance. Although his argument was not aimed against authority in general, he posited a radical discontinuity between the kingdom of the world and the kingdom of God, implying that Anabaptists could not serve in government or bear arms.[155]

Peter Walpot, "Non-Violence in the Gospels", in Peter Walpot, *The Christian and the Sword*, trans. Elizabeth Bender et al., ed. Art Wiser and Leonard Gross (Robertsbridge: Plough, 2011), 13–31, Used with kind permission of Plough Publishing House.

———

26 ... From [Matt. 5:5–10] it follows that the arrogant and surly are unchristian and unblessed, the unmerciful are unblessed, the war makers and those who quarrel are unblessed, those who cause persecution are unblessed. For that reason, whoever exercises the office of the sword cannot be in Christ. Whoever carries the sword at his side is not a peacemaker but a combat maker.

Sources 387

27 ... Now, if a Christian is not to be angry with his brother nor call him a fool without deserving eternal fire [Matt. 5:21–22], how would it be possible for him to wield the sword, even to kill him, or attack anyone in body or soul or help another to do so? No Christian may do this....

28 ... But someone may say, If all of us put away our swords and did what you do and say, who would resist the Turks and enemies? Answer: If everyone were Christian, it would be God who would resist the enemy. For he alone is the protection of his little church....

29 ... Thus the office of government and the power of the sword is in itself in all matters the contrary and opposite of the words and statements of Christ [in Matt. 5:43–44]. Consequently, there can be no Christian government nor can a Christian hold such an office. For it is impossible for two mutually contradictory things to be reconciled. But in the world, which does not live according to God's will, government is as necessary as daily bread. So we should hold it in honour, and be subject to it in all that is good.

36 ... The power of the keys, the Christian ban, removes from the church what is evil (1 Cor. 5:5). The worldly sword removes completely from the earth. The Christian punishment is love, indeed, a brotherly reproof; the punishment of the sword is wrath and ruthlessness. After the ban of Christians one can repent; but after the sword or worldly justice, penitence and reform are forever cut off. The ministers of the keys are the vessels of mercy, the ministers of the worldly sword are the vessels of wrath (Rom. 9:16–18; Hos. 13:11)....

37 ... Christ [delivered the parable of the tares (Matt. 13:28–29)] because he wanted to prevent wars and bloodshed among his people.... He does not forbid removing the evildoers and tares from his church by the power of the keys, but removing them with the sword. Killing and executing them is what he forbids, lest the tares that might still be transformed into good grain be thereby cut off.

38 Christ says to his disciples: 'If any man would come after me, let him deny himself and take up his cross and follow me' (Matt. 16:24). He does not say 'take up the sword', for the sword has absolutely no place next to the cross, and Christ cannot agree with Belial.... To bear the cross is to accept suffering and sorrow, and even persecution, with patience. The sword does not suffer anything, but terminates everything in its path. Christians are counted as sheep for the slaughter (Ps. 44:23; Rom. 8:36; 2 Cor. 4:11). The sword is what kills them.

43 Christ calls worldly government and force the gates of hell (Matt. 16:18). For just as Christ is the door and gate to God's kingdom (John 10:7, 9), they are called the gates of hell. As one can see, if the king, prince or authority is papist, then his subjects must also be papist; if he becomes Lutheran, they must also become Lutheran; if he is Zwinglian, they must also be Zwinglian; and what the government believes, its land and people must also believe....

45　... Therefore it is Christ's will that his people, in subjection to worldly authority, give and offer its dues – what belongs to it – for the sake of its office and God's order. We may give it its due, and what belongs to God we are to give to God [Matt. 22:21]....

46　... It does no good to say, David was a king and many pious men have exercised the power of the sword and gone to war. When the disciples cited Elijah as an example [Luke 9:51–56], Christ rebuked them, refusing to allow it, and said: 'Do you not know what manner of spirit you are of?'...

53　The Holy Spirit came in the form of a dove (Matt. 3:16 and elsewhere), sent upon the believers (Acts 2:4) not in the form of a griffon or other beast of prey. A dove (which has no gall or bitterness) does not fall upon a falcon or hawk or eagle, nor does it attack any other bird....

108 Peter Beutterich, *Catholicism and Tyranny over the Conscience* (1578)

Keywords: #Tyranny, #Conscience, #Persecution, #Violence, #Freedom of Religion, #Slavery
Region: #Netherlands | #Spain
Group: #Dutch Reformed | #Roman Catholic, #Islam

The Low Countries were under the dominion of the Spanish crown when Calvinism began to take root (see also the **Belgic Confession** and the **Heidelberg Catechism**). The King of Spain, who ruled through representatives from afar, sought to curtail the spread of the Reformation, resorting to coercion and violence. The heavy hand of the Spanish king's representative frequently provoked the ire of Protestants and nobles (see the **Union of Utrecht**). Like elsewhere, the Reformation was often attractive to nobles who tried to consolidate their power. From 1566, nobles pushed for greater rights for the Protestant church. A surge of popular iconoclasm was followed by heavy suppression thereof. The king's representative, the infamous Duke of Alba, forced the defeated Protestants to submit, flee, or risk execution. Alba's violence galvanised the Calvinist cause, imprinting memories of martyrdom in Dutch Protestantism.

Fierce debates erupted over the toleration of Catholics during the Dutch Revolt. William of Orange, whose vision had been to unite the Provinces on the basis of religious toleration, was structurally opposed by the radical Calvinist Peter Beutterich (1538–1587). Beutterich was one of the main advisors to Count Johann Casimir of the Palatinate, who supplied troops for the defence of the Low Countries and who was involved in procuring further military support from England. The following excerpt details his attitude towards the potential toleration of Catholics. To him, it would be impossible for Protestants to coexist with Catholics, as he associated the latter with violence and repression. As William of Orange pushed for greater toleration, he engaged in personal attacks on his religious integrity, which came to a climax in Ghent in 1578, where he accused him of atheism.[156]

William G. Naphy, ed., *Documents on the Continental Reformation* (London: MacMillan, 1996), 88–89.

———

390 *Sources*

[P]reserving the Roman Catholic Church and preserving tyranny amount to the same thing here. I will say it again, preserving the Roman Catholic Church here is the same thing as preserving a tyranny which is worse than the one inflicted by the barbarians and Turks. At least the Turks, who are dictators over the body leave the conscience alone. The supporters of the Roman Catholic Church want to be tyrants over the body and the mind.

Keeping the Roman Catholic Church means bringing back banishments and confiscations, burning people at the stake again, re-building the gallows throughout the provinces, bringing back the Inquisition, and, dredging up from Hell those vile, accursed laws. Remembering those laws fills every true patriot with dread and disgust. They recall the pouring of so much South Netherlandish [Belgian] blood from so many martyrs and that for one sole reason: the one and only Roman Catholic Church....

Maintaining real freedom and the Roman Catholic Church are mutually exclusive. Keeping the Roman Catholic religion means nothing less than restoring the Spanish tyranny. The goals of the Spanish and the Roman Catholics are identical. The Spanish want the Roman religion established, so do the Catholics. The Catholics want the king to be accepted and given his due, so do the Spanish. We accept, rather than deny, that the king should receive his due as sovereign lord. However, there is a vast difference between what is lawfully due to a king, and what the supporters of the Roman Catholic religion have in mind. They do not mean that one should obey the King in law, justice and fairness by keeping to the old customs and traditions. Rather, they mean that one should do everything the tyrant commands without a word of complaint, without challenge, without resistance. In sum, it means being a serf and slave.

This then is the goal of these tin-pot dictators, the supporters of the Roman Catholic religion, have in mind; this has always been the goal of the Spanish.

109 *Union of Utrecht* (1579)

Keywords: #Toleration, #War
Region: #Netherlands
Group: #Dutch Reformed | #Roman Catholic

The Union of Utrecht, along with the Pacification of Ghent (1576), was one of the formational documents in the history of the Low Countries and the later Kingdom of the Netherlands. The attempted repression of the Dutch Revolt (1568–1648) by the Spanish crown prompted greater collaboration between the seven northern provinces and a number of cities in the south of the Low Counties. The allies agreed on military and financial cooperation, and included agreements on free movement, trade, and monetary exchange. The Union would later inspire confederalism in America. Although the Low Countries and the later Dutch Republic have commonly been associated with idealistic toleration, the Union of Utrecht shows that toleration initially served economic and geopolitical interests. Religion was only covered in Article 13, which imposed the duty to tolerate Catholics on all provinces, except on the two richest: Holland and Zealand, whose leadership was fiercely anti-Catholic. William of Orange (1533–1584) was profoundly dissatisfied with this exemption and never signed the treaty.[157]

Herbert H. Rowen, ed. and trans., *The Low Countries in Early Modern Times: A Documentary History* (New York: Harper & Row, 1972), 69–74. Text modernised by the editors.

———

Whereas, since the Pacification made at Ghent, by which almost all the provinces of these Netherlands bound themselves to help each other with their lives and goods in order to drive out the Spaniards and other foreign nations, together with their adherents, we have discovered that these same Spaniards under Don John of Austria and their other chiefs and captains have endeavoured and still daily endeavour to bring these provinces as a group and individually under their subjection, tyrannical government, and slavery and to

392 *Sources*

divide and dismember these same provinces by arms and wily practices and to destroy and subvert the Union created by this aforesaid Pacification....

Therefore, the members for the Duchy of Gelderland and County of Zutphen, the counties and lands of Holland, Zeeland, Utrecht, Friesland, and the districts between Eems and Lauwers have found it wise to unite and bind each other more closely....

III.

That the aforesaid provinces shall also be bound to assist each other in the same way and to help each other against all foreign and domestic lords, princes, lands, provinces, cities or members thereof, who seek to do them, as a group or individually, any harm or injustice, or wage war upon them....

XI.

It is agreed that if any neighbouring princes, lords, lands, or cities desire to join with the aforesaid provinces and enter this Confederation, they may be accepted only by common advice and consent of these provinces....

XIII.

As for the matter of religion, the States of Holland and Zeeland shall act according to their own pleasure, and the other Provinces of this Union shall follow the rules set down in the religious peace drafted by Archduke Matthias, governor and captain-general of these countries, with the advice of the Council of State and the States General, or shall establish such general or special regulations in this matter as they shall find good and most fitting for the repose and welfare of the provinces, cities, and individual Members thereof, and the preservation of the property and rights of each individual, whether churchman or layman, and no other Province shall be permitted to interfere or make difficulties, provided that each person shall remain free in his religion and that no one shall be investigated or persecuted because of his religion, as is provided in the Pacification of Ghent...

110 *Vindiciæ Contra Tyrannos* (1579)

Keywords: #Tyranny, #Rebellion, #Covenants, #Authority, #Obedience
Region: #France
Group: #Reformed, #Huguenot

Vindiciæ Contra Tyrannos (1579) is one of the most important statements of Protestant resistance theory. It was written in the wake of the St. Bartholomew's Day Massacre (1572). The treatise's authorship has been a matter of speculation since its publication. Some argue it was penned by Hubert Languet (1518–1581), a doctor of law who was educated at Padua. He read Melanchthon's theology, moved to Wittenberg, and converted to Protestantism. He was nearly killed on St. Bartholomew's Day. He travelled widely throughout Europe and became a valued diplomat for Augustus I, Elector of Saxony. The other candidate is Philippe Duplessis Mornay (1549–1623) who was born to Protestants in Normandy and became a prominent defender of the Reformation. He wrote several political works, advised Henry of Navarre, and served as a diplomat to England and Flanders. In 1589, he became Governor of Saumur and founded an academy for the education of Protestants. He fell out of favour with Henry after the king's conversion to Catholicism. There is also the possibility that the work was a collaboration between the two men. The arguments in the *Vindiciæ* about resistance to authority have proved influential at many critical moments in political history. For example, a Dutch edition appeared in 1588, an English edition appeared in 1648 before the execution of Charles I, and another English edition appeared in 1689 after the 'Glorious Revolution'.

The treatise is important for many reasons. It distilled many prior arguments in favour of resistance. What was a Christian to do when obedience to their sovereign conflicted with obedience to God? *Vindiciæ Contra Tyrannos* approached this common dilemma through the lens of covenants and contracts (from the Reformed emphasis on covenants and the Roman and Medieval arguments about contracts). This work reached back to the Hebrew Bible, Roman law, and natural law to argue for political covenants in a way that construed tyranny as a crime. Drawing on biblical examples, he

394   *Sources*

argued that God made a double contract or covenant (*foedus*) with the king and the people. Either party could violate the covenant. If the king or the people turned from God and their covenant obligations, the covenant was no longer in force. God was also party to a second covenant, this one between the king and the people. Drawing on the Hebrew Bible, he argued that legitimate kings ruled by consent, and the people submitted so long as the king's rule was marked by justice. Where either party violated the arrangement, the agreement would be nullified. If the king was the transgressor, the people would be restored to their natural right of liberty. As the selection below shows, the right of rebellion and tyrannicide that was argued for in a later part of the treatise was built on a simple theological principle: God held absolute and indivisible sovereignty.[158]

Vindiciæ contra tyrannos: a defence of liberty against tyrants (London: Matthew Simmons and Robert Ibbitson, 1648), 1–16. Text modernised by the editors. George Garnett's scholarly edition provided helpful clarifications (*Brutus: Vindiciae, contra tyrannos, Or, Concerning the Legitimate Power of a Prince over the People, and of the People over a Prince* [Cambridge: Cambridge University Press, 2010], 14–34).

———

The first question: Whether subjects are bound and ought to obey princes, if they command what is against the Law of God.

…Princes should want to know how far they may extend their authority, and subjects should want to know when they may obey them, lest kings encroach on that jurisdiction which does not belong to them, and subjects obey someone who commands what he has no right to command. They will both be chastised when they shall give an account of their actions before another judge. Scripture will give the resolution to the following question. Are subjects bound to obey kings when they command that which is against the Law of God: that is to say, who must we obey (God or the king)? When the question is resolved concerning the king, to whom is attributed absolute power, that same conclusion will apply to other magistrates.

First, the Holy Scripture teaches that God reigns by his own authority, and Kings rule by derivation: God rules from himself and Kings from God; God has jurisdiction in himself, kings are his delegates. It follows then that the jurisdiction of God has no limits, that of kings is bounded; the power of God is infinite, that of Kings confined; the Kingdom of God extends itself to all places, that of kings is restrained within the confines of certain countries…. All the inhabitants of the earth hold all they have from him and are his tenants and farmers; all the princes and governors of the world are his stipendiaries and vassals and are bound to take and acknowledge their investitures from him. Briefly, God alone is the owner and Lord, and all men of any degree or rank are his servants, farmers, officers, and vassals and owe account and acknowledgement to him….

For the same reason, the people are always called the Lord's people and the Lord's inheritance, and kings are governors of this inheritance and conductors or leaders of the people of God – which is the title given to David, to Solomon, to Hezekiah, and to other good Princes. When the covenant [*foedus*] is ratified between God and the king, there is a condition: that the people be, and always remain, the people of God. This was done to show that God will not deprive himself of his property and possession when he gives to kings the government of the people....

Today at the inauguration of kings and Christian princes, they are called the servants of God, destined to govern his people. Since kings are only the lieutenants of God, made so in the throne of God by the Lord God himself, and the people are the people of God. The honour which is given to these lieutenants is owing to the one who sent them to perform this service: it necessarily follows that kings must be obeyed for the sake of God and not contrary to God.... God never divests himself of his power. He holds a sceptre in one hand to repress and quell the audacious boldness of those princes who mutiny against him. In the other hand, he holds a scale to see who equitably distributes right....

The vassal receives his fief from his lord with right of justice, and is charged to serve him in his wars. The king is established by the Lord God, the King of Kings, in order that they should administer justice to his people and defend them against all their enemies. The vassal receives laws and conditions from his sovereign: God commands the king to observe his laws and to have them always before his eyes.... The vassal is deprived of his fief if he commits a felony and by law forfeits all his privileges. Similarly, the king is deprived of his right – and many times his realm – if he despises God, if he sides with his enemies, and if he commits a felony against that Royal Majesty.

This is abundantly clear when considering the covenant [*foedus*] which is contracted between God and the king, for God honours his servants by calling them confederates. Now we read of a twofold covenant at the inauguration of kings: the first between God, the king and the people, that the people might be the people of God; The second between the king and the people, that the people shall obey faithfully, and the king command justly. We will discuss the second later, and now speak of the first....

It appears by [the inaugurations of Joash and Josiah] that the king and the people are jointly bound by promise and did oblige themselves by solemn oath to serve God above all things. After they had sworn the covenant, Josiah and Joash ruined the idolatry of Baal and re-established the pure service of God. The principal points of the covenants were these: that the king and all the people should carefully honour and serve God according to his scripture-revealed will, which if they performed, God would assist and preserve their estates; and if they did the contrary, he would abandon and exterminate them, which plainly appears by consulting several Scripture passages. [*He offers a lengthy history of the Hebrew Bible, focusing on Moses, Joshua, David and the later return of exiles from Babylon.*]

396 Sources

Now although the form of the church and the Jewish kingdom are changed – for that which was before enclosed within the narrow bounds of Judea is now dilated throughout the whole world. Despite these changes, the same things may be said of Christian kings, the Gospel has succeeded the Law, and Christian princes have replaced kings of the Jews: There is the same agreement [*pactum*], the same conditions, the same punishments, and if they fail, there is the same Almighty revenger of all perfidious disloyalty; as the former were bound to keep the Law, so the others are obliged to adhere to the doctrine of the Gospel, and at their anointing Kings promise to employ their utmost towards this end. [*He then gives examples from the New Testament, early Church history and European history to illustrate how kings who spurn God are brought to ruin. These kings might not be anointed with sacred oil like in scripture, but their authority is still derived from an avenging God.*]

[*God is the creator of the body and the soul, and the king is given limited authority over the former and none over the latter.*] But if a prince usurps the right of God [over the soul], he becomes like a giant trying to scale the heavens. He is guilty of high treason to his Sovereign and commits a felony, just as if one of his vassals should seize the rights of his crown....

In sum, God invests kings with their kingdoms almost in the same manner that vassals are invested into their fiefs by their sovereign. We must conclude that kings are the vassals of God and deserve to be deprived of the benefit they receive from their Lord if they commit a felony, in the same way that rebellious vassals lose their estates. Our question may now be easily resolved; for if God holds the place of sovereign lord, and the king as vassal, who would deny that we must obey the sovereign over the vassal? If God commands one thing and the king commands the contrary, who would be so arrogant to call the one who disobeys the king a 'rebel' when obedience to the king would be disobedience to God. Rather the true 'rebel' deserving condemnation fails to obey God or obeys the king's command to not give obedience to God.

111 Fausto Sozzini, *On Pacifism and the Love of Country* (1581)

Keywords: #Non-violence, #Patriotism, #Land, #Love
Region: #Italy, #Poland
Group: #Unitarian, #Socinian

Fausto Sozzini (1539–1604) was born in Siena, Italy, to a family of prominent lawyers who had a deep interest in theology. One of his relatives, Lelio Sozzini, explored antitrinitarian ideas and had to flee north, where he interacted with several prominent Reformers. Under pressure from the Inquisition, Fausto Sozzini later fled to France in 1561 and then went to Zürich to acquire Lelio's manuscripts after his death. He was deeply influenced by Lelio and by **Sébastien Castellion**. In 1579, he moved to Krakow, Poland, where antitrinitarians enjoyed a measure of toleration. He had close relations with the antitrinitarian Minor Church, although he was not initially accepted on grounds of doctrinal disagreements. He nevertheless became a prominent leader within the Church, and the Synod of Lublin (1598) adopted many of his positions. In 1591, he was burned in effigy by the Inquisition as a heretic, and in 1598, Catholic students intended to kill him, but only ended up destroying his manuscripts and books. Sozzini's teachings influenced European Protestantism long after his death, known as Socinianism.

Fausto's pacifism is not as well known as his antitrinitarianism. He wrote the following selection about the use of force shortly after he moved to Krakow. In it, he defended Racovians (Polish antitrinitarian Anabaptists who eschewed force) against another antitrinitarian theologian, Jacobus Palaeologus. His non-violence was informed by a sharp distinction between the Hebrew Bible and New Testament. In the work reproduced below, he also discussed whether a Christian should feel any attachment to their own country or give it preferential treatment. Towards the end of his life, he retreated from his arguments about non-resistance, but this retraction was not widely known until centuries later.[159]

Peter Brock, "Faustus Socinus Against War: From the First Chapter of the Third Part of His Reply to Jacobus Palaeologus (1581)", *The Mennonite Quarterly Review* 70 (1996): 419–430 (426–430). Used with permission.

———

398 *Sources*

[*Pacifism, Patriotism and Treason*]

We must consider as false your [Palaeologus] view that all Christians, evil as well as good, form the people of God in the same way as did once the people of Israel.... Certainly among those who are regarded as Christians such belong to the people of God as are obedient to, and trust in, Christ (and on this account they are not bad Christians). Indeed they are truly Christians, whereas the others are Christians only in name. The apostle Peter in 1 Peter 2:10 calls those to whom he is writing the people of God. But he shows he is writing not to the bad but to the good Christians when he says they love Christ and believe in him. To prove that some other people can justly wage war to defend their boundaries by the example of the people of Israel having done so, it is not sufficient to show that the former are a people of God. But it is necessary, besides, to demonstrate that the territory, whose boundaries are to be defended and preserved against outsiders, has been bestowed on this people by God and given as their property, as was the land of Canaan to the people of Israel. The people of Christ, on the other hand, possess here on earth no land of their own entrusted to them by God. But they are perpetual wanderers living on alien soil. How, then, can anyone claim that such a people must or can take up arms to protect their boundaries – a people that possesses no territory here? This people seeks heaven as once the people of Israel desired possession of the land of Canaan. Heaven, therefore, is the possession which God has allotted them. That is what they must strive to attain. Its undivided possession is something they must fight for, and any who, for whatever reason, try to snatch it from them must be stoutly resisted. But, as we have already said elsewhere, such [enemies] are not men to be fought with carnal weapons but demons and evil desires that can be overcome and suppressed only by spiritual weapons....

You [Palaeologus] are being quite ridiculous when you go on to say that he who is a friend [to his country] in good times should not desert it in evil times.... For all that we have said above proves that a Christian in a private capacity should never engage in war.... And how do you reconcile God's commandment to love one's neighbour as oneself with waging war and killing enemies? ... If, then, we are to believe you, we should kill our neighbour in order to carry out the commandment to love one's neighbour! Is there really anyone so foolish as not to acknowledge that these two things are plainly inconsistent with each other?...

You rail...against those who refuse to take up arms and repel the enemy as they leap to the attack, and ... you call them wicked people, traitors, deserters, infidels, as if they were among the worst of men.... Look how you do not hesitate to accuse of disgraceful deeds men entirely blameless, who would rather die themselves than inflict injury on others and who willingly expose themselves, like sheep or lambs, to the wolf's attack so as to remain obedient to God....

We must observe, what indeed has already been said, that the Christian insofar as he owns no property on this earth in reality possesses no country of his own. As the holy writer tells us, 'For here we have no enduring city, but we seek one to come' (Hebrews 13:14). Therefore, love of country does not affect a Christian in the least. Were we [Christians] truly to possess an earthly country of our own, then we might perhaps concede that, when the safety of the fatherland is at stake, we can violate a law in any manner whatsoever and that for the preservation of our country there is nothing that we should not do. [The Christian's] duty, though, is to do for the fatherland all things not contravening in any way the laws of Christ – the source of all that is right. True, no distinction whatsoever is to be drawn between one's own country and other lands; yet, although in general all are on an equality it is nevertheless permissible to place the former a trifle in front of the latter. But it may very easily happen [also] that a Christian must prefer another country to his own; in comparison to it he has sometimes to esteem his fatherland lightly. All this, though, applies scarcely if at all to the political man who holds nothing higher than love of country.

112 *The Declaration of the States General of the United Provinces* (1581)

Keywords: #Liberty, #Authority, #Tyranny, #Natural Law
Region: #Netherlands
Group: #Dutch Reformed

Many movements that ended in political independence began as a struggle to see abuses reformed and liberties restored. The Dutch struggle took nearly a century, from around 1566 until the Peace of Münster in 1646 (as part of the **Peace of Westphalia**), where Spain recognised the independence of the Dutch Republic. Negotiations in the late 1570s might have kept Catholic and Protestant regions of the Low Countries together; however, they failed, and the region split into a largely Protestant North and largely Catholic South. Many Protestants came to argue that reconciliation with Philip II was neither possible nor desirable. The Protestant regions formed the **Union of Utrecht** (1579) and pivoted towards independence in 1581 when they formally abjured the authority of Spain. The following official document argues that Philip II lost his right to govern the United Provinces because he violated God's purposes for kingship and the ancient privileges of the people.[160]

Oliver J. Thatcher, *The Library of Original Sources* (New York: University Research Extension, 1907), V:190.

———

The Declaration of the States General of the United Provinces; setting forth that Philip II had forfeited his Right of Sovereignty over the said Provinces.

At the Hague, 26 July 1581.

The States General of the *United Provinces* of the *Low Countries*, to all whom it may concern, do by these Presents send greeting:

As 'tis apparent to all, that a Prince is constituted by God to be ruler of a people, to defend them from oppression and violence, as the shepherd his sheep; and whereas God did not create the people slaves to their prince, to obey his commands, whether right or wrong, but rather the prince for the

Sources 401

sake of the subjects (without which he could be no prince), to govern them according to equity, to love and support them as a father his children, or a shepherd his flock, and even at the hazard of life to defend and preserve them. And when he does not behave thus, but, on the contrary, oppresses them, seeking opportunities to infringe their ancient customs and privileges, exacting from them slavish compliance, then he is no longer a prince, but a tyrant, and the subjects are to consider him in no other view. And particularly when this is done deliberately, and authorised by the states, they may not only disallow his authority, but legally proceed to the choice of another prince for their defence. This is the only method left for subjects, whose humble petitions and remonstrances could never soften their prince, or dissuade him from his tyrannical proceedings; and this is what the law of nature dictates for the defence of liberty, which we ought to transmit to posterity, even at the hazard of our lives. And this we have seen done frequently in several countries upon the like occasion, whereof there are notorious instances, and more justifiable in our land, which has been always governed according to their ancient privileges, which are expressed in the oath taken by the prince at his admission to the government; for most of the Provinces receive their prince upon certain conditions, which he swears to maintain; which if the prince violates, he is no longer sovereign....

113 William Cecil, *The Execution of Justice in England* (1583)

Keywords: #Execution, #Persecution, #Church-State Relations
Region: #England
Group: #Church of England | #Roman Catholicism

William Cecil (1520–1598) was one of the most powerful Protestants in sixteenth-century England. He studied at Cambridge when early ideas about the Reformation were debated. He rose to become secretary of state during the reign of **Edward VI**, retired to private life during the reign of Mary I, and was again secretary of state under Elizabeth I in 1558. Over the next 40 years, he would continue to rise through the ranks and become Elizabeth's most trusted adviser (created Lord Burghley in 1571). Cecil helped implement the Elizabethan settlement that placed the state over the church, carving out a middle space between Catholicism and Puritanism.[161]

The following extract comes from *The Execution of Justice in England* (1583). In it, Cecil engaged official proclamations from the papacy that touched on the legitimacy of **Elizabeth I**. In *Cum ex Apostolatus officio* (1559), Pope Paul IV argued that heretical rulers could be deposed. In *Regnans in Excelsis* (1570), Pope Pious V released English subjects from obedience to **Elizabeth I**. Such statements made it difficult to view religious dissenters in England as politically loyal. In fact, it made them vulnerable to persecution. Although Protestants painted the short reign of Mary as 'Bloody', Elizabeth also executed numerous religious dissenters. In this publication, Cecil explained why Catholic missionaries were being put to death. In case the reader missed the main argument of the tract, the running header read 'Execution for Treason, and not for Religion'. In theory and in practice, it was difficult to separate a crime against the state from a crime against the church.

William Cecil, *The Execution of Iustice in England for Maintenaunce of Publique and Christian Peace, Against Certeine Stirrers of Sedition, and Adherents to the Traytors and Enemies of the Realme* (London: Christopher Barker, 1583), n.p. Text modernised by the editors.

———

...There were and are many others, laymen of good possessions and lands, men of good repute, who have lately been seduced towards the Pope's authority, and yet none of these people have been impeached, charged with treason or lost their life or inheritance. This shows that it is not, and has not been, for contrary religious opinions or believing in the Pope's authority (as adversaries boldly and falsely claim) that any persons have suffered death during Her Majesty's reign. It is well known that some of these people believe the Pope should be the head of the church and rule in Ecclesiastical causes, and that the Queen does not have a right to govern over her subjects who are of the clergy. These opinions are doubtless punishable by law, and yet persons have not been prosecuted with treason or jeopardised their life for believing them.

What, then, are people being put to death for? As answered before, no one is impeached for treason or risks losing their life except those who obstinately defend the Pope's Bull. This document claimed that Her Majesty is not the lawful Queen of England (the first and highest point of treason), that all her subjects are discharged from their oaths of obedience (another point of treason) and that they may disobey her laws (a third and very large point of treason). Fourthly, these persons do not stand against the Pope's open war against Her Majesty in Ireland.

It is abundantly clear that this Bull provides the groundwork for rebellion in England and Ireland. Those who defend the Bull are sowing seeds of sedition. These persons are justly condemned for treason and lawfully executed by the ancient laws of the realm. They are condemned for conspiring abroad and at home against the Queen and her realm. They defend the Pope's authority and his Bull that was published to deprive Her Majesty of her crown. They draw subjects away from the natural allegiance they owe to Her Majesty and their country, thus moving them towards sedition. These are the religious causes and questions for which persons are condemned. The condemned claim they are being punished for their religious beliefs, but in reality they are being punished for instigating wars and rebellions against Her Majesty and her realm.

114 Richard Hakluyt, *A Discourse Concerning Western Planting* (1584)

Keywords: #Colonisation, #Evangelisation, #Intervention, #Missions
Region: #England
Group: #Church of England | #Indigenous American

Richard Hakluyt (c.1552–1616) was educated at Oxford, ministered in Bristol, and served as the chaplain to the English ambassador in Paris from 1583 to 1588. He then ministered in several places, including as an honorary cannon at Westminster Abbey. Hakluyt's name is famous for his two dozen travel books. He collected and popularised accounts of ancient and modern ventures around the world, and these were published at a time when European powers were rapidly expanding. His works on geography greatly influenced England's overseas expansion and shaped perceptions of what geographically distant peoples were like. Lesser known is his writing on 'plantings', in which he articulated a duty to colonise. The following source dates from 1584 and was written at the behest of Walter Raleigh. This alleged duty to colonise stemmed from his anti-Iberian and anti-Catholic sentiments. Spanish colonialists, he argued, abused their power: they not only engaged in trade, but they were also cruel to Indigenous peoples and forced Englishmen captured on the seas to renounce their faith and forsake their sovereign.

Hakluyt argued that it was the duty of **Elizabeth I** to sponsor colonies. As the 'defender of the faith', she was also charged with the duty to spread the gospel. Notably, Hakluyt did not ground his call for colonies in the conquest narratives of the Hebrew Bible. Rather, he argued from evangelical verses (Matt. 6:33; Acts 16:6–10; Rom. 10:13–15) that the English had an obligation to expand into the Americas. Hence, ministers must be sent, and colonies must be established to promote the work of ministers. In light of Spanish crimes in the Americas, Hakluyt made one of the earliest Protestant calls for humanitarian intervention through colonisation. These colonies were to be carefully thought through so that the English did not imitate Catholic practices. In this source, and throughout his writings, religious rationales sat alongside political, economic, and social arguments in favour of colonisation. Unlike his popular travel works, this discourse had little impact at the

Sources 405

time. English colonies were primarily undertaken by private persons, and it was not until the middle of the next century that the government took a more active role in planting and ruling colonies.[162]

Richard Hakluyt, *A Discourse Concerning Western Planting, Written in the Year 1584*, ed. Charles Deane (Cambridge: John Wilson and Son, 1877), 1–5, 71–72. Text modernised by the editors.

———

[HEADS OF CHAPTERS.]

1 That this western discovery will be greatly beneficial for the enlargement of the gospel of Christ, something that the princes of the reformed religion are bound to undertake (and Her Majesty is the principal leader).
2 That all other English trades have become impoverished or dangerous, especially in all the King of Spain's dominions, where our men are driven to fling their Bibles and prayer books into the sea, and to renounce their religion and conscience and thus to renounce their obedience to Her Majesty.
3 That this western voyage will yield unto us all the commodities of Europe, Africa, and Asia, as far as we desire to travel, and supply everything needed for our decayed trades....
11 That the Spaniards have committed outrageous and more-than-Turkish cruelties in the West Indies, making themselves odious to inhabitants who would join with us and shake off the intolerable yoke, something they have already begun to do in several places.
18 That the Queen of England's title to all the West Indies, or at least to as much as is from FLORIDA to the arctic, is more lawful and right than the title of the Spaniard's or any other Christian Prince.
19 An answer to the Bull of the Donation [*Inter Caetera* and *Dudum Siquidem* of 1493] of all the West Indies granted to the Kings of Spain by Pope Alexander VI who was himself Spaniard born....

Chapter 11

So many and so monstrous have been the Spanish cruelties, such strange slaughters and murders of those peaceable, lowly, mild, and gentle people, together with the spoils of towns, provinces, and kingdoms, which have been perpetrated in the West Indies in a most ungodly manner, in addition to many other terrible matters, that to describe the least part of them would require more than one chapter, especially where there are whole books in print, not only written by strangers, but also by their own countrymen (as evidenced by Bartolomé de las Casas, a bishop in New Spain)....

Nevertheless, I will repeat a few examples of atrocities drawn from a mighty mass and huge heap of massacres, that by these examples you may

406 *Sources*

estimate the rest, and consider the reasons why a small remainder of those most afflicted Indians have revolted from their obedience to the Spaniards, and shaken from their shoulders the most intolerable and insupportable yoke of Spain, which in many places they have already begun to do for themselves, without the help of any Christian prince.

This being so, I leave it to the deep consideration of the wise, what great matters may be brought about by our nation, if Her Majesty (being a mighty prince at sea) would help in that enterprise, and assist the Indians who are revolting....

115 *Elizabeth I to the King of Poland on Religious Refugees (1591)*

Keywords: #Toleration, #Refugees, #Women
Region: #England | #Poland
Group: #Church of England | #Roman Catholicism

Sixteenth-century Poland was notable for its confessional diversity, especially compared to Western Europe. To many Protestants and most Catholics, that diversity was a temporary necessity until one confession gained the upper hand. From 1545 to 1563, the Council of Trent debated how the Catholic Church should respond to the Reformation. This Counter-Reformation, or Catholic Reformation, addressed some clerical abuses and reaffirmed traditional Catholic teachings. They also set about the task of coaxing Protestant regions back towards Catholicism. The newly founded Jesuits (Society of Jesus) and other religious orders helped bring about the gradual catholicisation of the Polish state. From time to time, popular violence against Protestants and their sites of worship flared up (as suffered by **Fausto Sozzini**), and it was difficult for the monarch to prevent or contain such acts. By the first half of the seventeenth century, few Protestants were represented in the government, and far fewer Protestant churches dotted the landscape.[163]

The following source is a 1591 letter from Elizabeth I of England to Sigismund III Vasa (1566–1632). As his name suggests, Sigismund's lineage traced to Polish and Swedish royal lines. As King of Sweden (r.1592–1599), he unsuccessfully tried to bring that country back into the fold of Catholicism and was deposed. His reign in Poland (1587–1632) was longer and more successful, and he presided over Poland in the crucial decades in which Protestantism receded from public life.[164] The notoriety of Poland as a haven for religious dissenters forms the background to this 1591 letter. It was written in the context of Spain's war on the continent and with England (this was written only a few years after the failure of the 1588 Spanish Armada). The war in the Low Countries displaced many Protestant communities. Foreigners now populated Sigismund's cities, and they brought with them religious commitments that were different from his own, ones that might destabilise

408   *Sources*

the church and state. Elizabeth urged him to distinguish between normal dissenters who could be good subjects and a minority of radical Protestants.

Hastings Robinson, ed., *The Zurich Letters* (Cambridge: Cambridge University Press, 1845), II:321–322.

———

Queen Elizabeth I to the King of Poland

Greenwich, *April* 16, 1591.

Elizabeth, by the grace of God, of England, France, and Ireland, queen, defender of the faith, etc. To the most serene Prince and Lord Sigismund, by the grace of God, king of Poland, Grand Duke of Lithuania, our very dear brother and cousin.

We do not doubt but that your serene highness, and all other princes of Christendom, well understand in what manner we have been induced to succour the states of Lower Germany, now almost entirely overwhelmed by the tyranny of the Spaniards; since we were previously unable by our frequent embassies and intercessions both with Spain and the governors of the Low Countries to obtain for them any equitable conditions of peace. And there are three motives which have especially induced us to do this: first, the cause of the more pure religion which they professed in common with ourselves; next, the ancient rights of commerce and alliance with a neighbouring nation; and lastly, the numerous and manifest tokens which shewed that the same enemies would turn their arms against us and other princes professing the same religion, that they might extend the bounds of a monarchy which they unjustly claim.

It has thus come to pass that many inhabitants of those regions have been compelled to migrate into different provinces, and, among the rest, into some of the cities in Prussia, subject to your serene highness; in which many of them are now afraid, lest by reason of some difference in certain articles of religion, they may not be allowed the enjoyment of such immunity and free exercise of their religion as shall be suitable to their language and the former rites in which they have heretofore been instructed. And since we are informed that these Flemish, who are dwelling either in the city of Dantzig or in other sea-ports of Prussia, are not of that class of men who seek to overturn the lawful government and introduce anarchy, or who profess any heretical or impious error; we could not but, with our wonted affection towards the whole nation, commend them to your serene highness; entreating your serene highness, that, as it is plainly a royal act to deserve well of those who have been driven into exile from causes so honourable, your serene highness will exercise your authority in interceding with the magistrates of Dantzig, and others, if need be, that those parties who have migrated thither from Flanders may continue among them, without any difficulty or danger of this kind, the assemblies of the reformed religion, as they have been accustomed to do in their own country, and as they were for some time allowed in those cities; and that you will not suffer any injury to be done them, so long as they shall conduct themselves properly. For it cannot be either useful or honourable to your serene highness, nor to the cities themselves, to drive away strangers, and deny them the rights of hospitality, by reason of the evil disposition of certain individuals.

Wherefore we earnestly request your serene highness to confer this benefit upon them for our sake, which we shall accept as a mark of the greatest kindness on the part of your serene highness, which we will repay in our turn to those who may be commended to us by your serene highness, whenever any opportunity shall present itself; and so we pray God for every happiness to your serene highness and your kingdom.

From our court at Greenwich, April 16, 1591.

116 Richard Hooker, *Of the Laws of Ecclesiastical Polity* (c.1593)

Keywords: #Church-State Relations, #Hebrew Bible
Region: #England
Group: #Church of England

Richard Hooker (1554–1600) was an Oxford-educated theologian and philosopher. His magnum opus, *Of the Laws of Ecclesiastical Polity*, was foundational to the political theology of the Church of England after the Elizabethan Settlement of 1559, and his arguments have been variously received and applied over the centuries. As the title suggests, his concern for law – in its various sources and forms – was preeminent. Hooker challenged the political theology of Calvinists, Anabaptists, and other dissenting groups, even as he downplayed differences with Catholicism. He tried to show that his formulation of the relationship between church and state was more biblical and stable – supporting the vitality of both church and state. The work wrestled with and responded to the religious and political upheavals during his life and ministry. It is not surprising, then, that much of the work discussed issues of church government, conformity, and the relationship between the Church of England and Rome. As a staunch defender of the Elizabethan Settlement, Hooker's ideas occupy a privileged place in the history of Anglican identity. This prominence also attracted responses from those who disagreed with the Settlement. The book was published piecemeal: books 1–4 (1593), 5 (1597), 6 and 8 (1648), and book 7 shortly after the 1660 Restoration of the Stuarts. The most controversial parts of the treatise emerged at the height of the British Civil Wars (books 6 and 8) or during the Restoration.

He argued that societies had a right to decide the laws they would be governed by and that those laws became binding for all the members and for successive generations. Thus, many different consent-based forms of government might foster stability and godliness. His book explored the form of government established in England and argued for the ongoing nature of the inherited relationship between church and state. In his interpretation, this meant the supreme magistrate was responsible for religious matters, but this did not imply that they had the right to alter laws at a whim. The magistrate was to seek the consent of Parliament or advice from the clergy, and the ancient laws and the laws of the church constrained them. Ideally, the monarch guided the commonwealth even as the law guided the monarch. Although rulers were often less than ideal, subjects did not possess the right to armed resistance if the authority turned tyrannical. In the following extract, Hooker challenged opponents who argued that there was a separation between church and state. Reaching back to the pattern of the Hebrew Bible, he argued that no separation existed.[165]

Richard Hooker, *The Works of that Learned and Judicious Divine Mr. Richard Hooker*, ed. Isaac Walton (Oxford: Clarendon, 1820), III:285–289. Text modernised by the editors.

———

Of the Laws of Ecclesiastical Polity

Book VIII

Containing the Seventh Assertion: That a Civil Prince or Governor may be given the power of Ecclesiastical Dominion, as by the Laws of this Land belongs unto the Supreme Regent thereof.

We come now to the last thing whereof there is controversy, namely, *The power of supreme jurisdiction*, which for the sake of distinction, we call *The power of Ecclesiastical dominion*. It was not thought fitting in the Jewish commonwealth, that the exercise of Ecclesiastical supremacy should be denied unto him who held chief Civil power; and therefore their kings were invested with both. [*He offers examples of how power over religious matters was given to Israel's magistrates and how the piety (or lack thereof) of a magistrate altered the nature of worship.*]

Following this pattern, similar power in Ecclesiastical causes is legally given to the Crown in this realm; there are some who imagine that Kings are mere lay persons and that when they have Ecclesiastical power they exceed the lawful bounds of their calling; these people make a perpetual and personal separation between the Church and the Common-Wealth. Secondly, they tie all Ecclesiastical power to the church, as if the right only belonged to those who are by proper spiritual functions termed Church-governors, and that such rights do not pertain to Christian princes.

To hide under shifting ambiguities and equivocations of words in matter of such great importance is childish. A Church and a Commonwealth, we grant, are naturally distinguished from each other: a Common-wealth is defined one way; and a Church another way. In their opinions the Church and Commonwealth are corporations, not only distinguished in nature and definition, but in substance perpetually severed; so that those who belong to the one, can neither appoint nor execute, in whole nor in part, the duties which belong to those who belong to the other, without openly breaching the Law of God which divides them and requires that being so divided they should

412 *Sources*

distinctly or separately work, both depending upon God, and not hanging upon the approbation of the other for what it does.

We say that the care of Religion is common to all politic societies, such societies as embrace the true Religion have the name of the Church given unto them for distinction from the rest; so that every body politic has some Religion, but the Church has the only true Religion. Truth of Religion is the proper difference whereby a Church is distinguished from other politic societies of men; we here mean true Religion in gross, and not according to every particular: for those who in some particular points of Religion do depart from the truth, may nevertheless truly (if we compare them to men of a Heathen Religion) be said to hold and profess that Religion which is true. For although from of old there were so many politic societies established throughout the world, only the Commonwealth of Israel had the truth of Religion and was in that respect the Church of God: and the Church of Jesus Christ is every such politic society of men as holds in Religion to the truth which is proper to Christianity. As a politic society it maintains Religion, as a Church that Religion which God has revealed by Jesus Christ.

With us, therefore, the name of a Church means only a society of men, first united into some public form of Regiment, and secondly distinguished from other societies by the exercise of Religion. With them on the other side the name of the Church in this present question means not only a multitude of men so united, and so distinguished, but also the same divided necessarily and perpetually from the body of the Commonwealth; so that even in such a politic society as consists of none but Christians, yet the Church and Commonwealth are two corporations, independently subsisting by themselves.

We hold that there is no man of the Church of England who is not also a member of the Commonwealth, nor any member of the Commonwealth who is not also of the Church of England. Therefore as in the figure of a triangle, the base differs from the sides, and yet the same line is both a base and also a side; a side simply, a base if it happens to be the bottom and under the rest: so although properties and actions of one do cause the name of a Commonwealth to be given, qualities and functions of another sort cause the name of the Church to be given to a multitude, the same multitude may be in both. No, it is so with us, that no person belonging to the one can also be denied to be of the other: rather, unless they argue that the Church and the Commonwealth are two distinct and separate societies; and that persons belonging to the one do not belong to the other, they could draw the conclusion from the difference between the Church and the Commonwealth, namely, that the Bishops may not meddle with the affairs of the Commonwealth because they are governors of another Corporation, the Church; nor could kings make laws for the Church because their government, the Commonwealth, is another corporation, divided from it; and the walls of separation between these two must forever be upheld: they hold the necessity of personal separation which completely rules out the power of one man to deal with both; we of natural, but that one and the same person may influence both.

117 *The Decree of Uppsala* (1593)

Keywords: #Church-State Relations, #Trade
Region: #Sweden
Group: #Church of Sweden, #Lutheran

Sweden incrementally distanced itself from the Roman Catholic Church since the 1520s; however, the confessional anchoring of the Swedish church remained ambivalent. When King John III of Sweden died in 1592, the crown went to Sigismund III Vasa (r.1592–1599), who already possessed the Polish throne (r.1587–1632) through his mother, Queen Catherine Jagiellon. Sigismund was raised Catholic and made it clear that he intended to remain within the Catholic Church. Whereas the union of Sweden and Poland seemed advantageous in the struggle against Russia, the religious differences between these states led to political tensions. Swedes disliked being governed from a distance, but they also increasingly worried about the king's Catholic leanings. Meanwhile, the Vatican expected that Sigismund would bring Sweden into the Catholic fold, but he did not fulfil these expectations.

In the absence of Sigismund III, and before his coronation, the Swedish Council plotted to appoint Sigismund III's uncle, Duke Charles, as the head of the interim government. With Charles' approval, the council called the Church of Sweden to decide on some crucial doctrinal matters in a national assembly. The resulting 1593 Decree of Uppsala, excerpted below, formally adopted the **Augsburg Confession** and outlawed other religious services. After his coronation, Sigismund III derogated these stipulations and again ruled Sweden from a distance. Sweden's attempt to enforce the Decree of Uppsala led Sigismund III to invade in 1598, but this effort was in vain. The king was deposed in 1599.[166]

"The Decree of Uppsala (1593)", in *A Documentary History of Lutheranism*, ed. Eric Lund, trans. Eric Lund (Minneapolis, MN: Fortress, 2017) I:496.

———

414   *Sources*

...[S]ince there has been, as is well known, much strife and disagreement in our fatherland, Sweden, during the past years concerning matters of religion, and thereby great dissension and disgrace has occurred, and as we have learned from example and experiences in foreign countries and otherwise that nothing is to a kingdom more injurious than strife and discord, and nothing more beneficial and wholesome, more binding the heart together, than unity and agreement, especially in religion; ... it was by our unanimous desire and consent decided that there should be here in Uppsala, a general gathering of the principal estates of the kingdom, high and low, learned and lay ... for the purpose of establishing an agreement in matters of Christian doctrine, church ceremonies, church discipline, a legal election of archbishops and other bishops, and several other points considered necessary and useful....

First, that we all unanimously abide by the pure and saving Word of God, found in the writings of the holy prophets, evangelists and apostles....

[*They then denounce the Catholic liturgy.*]

Neither shall we receive or approve any other Popish doctrines or heresies, whatever they may be called, but reject them all together as human devices, contrived for worldly honour, dominion, power and riches, through which men are often misled. Likewise, we reject entirely the heresies of the Sacramentarians, Zwinglians, Calvinists and Anabaptists, and all other heresies, whatever be their name, which we at no time will approve or agree to....

And although it should not be tolerated or allowed that such should settle in the kingdom who hold false doctrines and are not one in faith with us, in order that they may not lead others astray, yet that trade and commerce may not be hindered, we agree that those who have any heretical doctrines shall not be allowed or permitted to hold any public meetings in houses or otherwise; and in case any should be found guilty of that or of speaking evil of our religion, that shall be duly punished....

118 Alberico Gentili, *International Laws of War* (1598)

Keywords: #Natural Law, #Divine Law, #International Law, #War, #Land, #Intervention, #Colonisation, #Refugees, #Slavery, #Trade, #Love
Region: #Italy, #England | #Global
Group: #Church of England

Alberico Gentili (1552–1608) was born in San Ginesio, Italy, and graduated with a doctorate in law from the University of Perugia in 1572. He served in municipal roles and practised law before turning to scholarly pursuits. In 1578, he left Italy with some of his family after the Inquisition suspected them of Protestant sympathies. The Earl of Leicester helped him secure a place at the University of Oxford in 1581, where he remained for much of his life. He was appointed Regius Professor of Civil Law in 1587 and soon published lectures on war and peace. In 1598, his more mature thoughts on war appeared in print (*De iure belli libri tres*, excerpted below), followed by publications weighing the justice of warfare in the Roman Empire. He practised law in 1600 after becoming a member at the Honourable Society of Gray's Inn. In 1603, his works appeared on the Index of Prohibited Books. Along with Francisco de Vitoria and **Hugo Grotius**, Gentili is considered as one of the founders of international law. His ideas built on the law of nature and divine law, and he argued for the protection of basic rights.[167]

De iure belli libri tres is an important work in the history of just war theory. His tripartite division of justice before, during, and after war (*ius ad bellum, ius in bello,* and *ius post bellum*) still informs discussions of legitimate warfare.[168] In the following excerpts, Gentili considered the relationship of warfare to international law, arguing that it was possible to speak of a law of nations because all humans knew certain things were right (1.1). Warfare on religious grounds was illegitimate since one could not coerce faith, and another person's errant beliefs could not harm one's relationship with God (1.8–9). He argued warfare was not grounded in nature, for every natural war would be just (1.12). Gentili then rooted humanitarian intervention in the fundamental unity of all humanity (1.15), and one could go to war over grave violations of the laws of nature (1.19). Here, Gentili discussed the right

416 *Sources*

of overseas explorers to trade with distant peoples and the refusal to allow trade constituted a breach of the law of nations.

Much of Gentili's scholarship and advocacy revolved around England's strained relationship with Spain. He challenged papal-backed Iberian claims to own the seas or Indigenous lands in the Americas. He critiqued a century of Iberian colonisation while adopting key aspects of their arguments for colonial expansion. At the time, Protestant nations were only beginning overseas exploration and colonisation. He argued not only that Indigenous persons 'possessed' land that Spaniards claimed to discover (1.19), but also that vacant land was available to those who first occupied and used it. There might be vacant land overseas, but he noted how much of Europe was depopulated and could be revitalised by an influx of exiles. Further, he argued that those fleeing dire circumstances had a right to find refuge, and they might even have a just cause to make war on those who would not take them in (1.27).

Although he defended Indigenous rights, he also argued that they violated fundamental laws of humanity by practising things like human sacrifice, and even though they were fully human by nature, they suppressed their humanity by killing innocents and could be punished (1.25). Gentili acknowledged the common proscription on Christians enslaving Christians but argued that this was allowed in the New Testament. He did not believe, contra Aristotle, that some people were natural slaves. Rather, humans were fundamentally alike, but some could be reduced to slavery due to circumstances. Being enslaved by the Turks was also a concern and a frightening reality for many Europeans (3.9).

Alberico Gentili, *De Iure Belli Libri Tres*, trans. John C. Rolfe (Oxford: The Clarendon Press; 1933), 3, 7–10, 36–41, 54–57, 67–69, 87–90, 122–125, 329–333.

———

1.1 International Law Applied to War

...Neither is it the part of the political philosopher to set forth the Law of War, since this relates, not to a single community, but to all. It is for this reason that Aristotle separates from political philosophy the part which has to do with the pursuit of arms and with military training. This philosophy of war belongs to that great community formed by the entire world and the whole human race....

And although international law is a portion of the divine law, which God left with us after our sin, yet we behold that light amid great darkness; and hence through error, bad habits, obstinacy, and other affections due to darkness we often cannot recognise it.... But truth exists, even though it be hidden in a well, and when it is diligently and faithfully sought, it can be brought forth and as a rule is brought forth. Abundant light is afforded us by the definitions which the authors and founders of our laws are unanimous in giving to this law of nations which we are investigating. For they say that the law of nations is that which is in use among all the nations of men, which native reason has established among all human beings, and which is equally observed by all mankind. Such a law is natural law. 'The agreement of all nations about a matter must be regarded as a law of nature'....

But there is another more elegant definition of the law of nations and it is to the same purport as that which Xenophon has handed down, namely, that there are everywhere certain unwritten laws, not enacted by men (since men could not all assemble in one place, nor were they all of one speech), but given to them by God. For example, the one which takes first place with all men, that one should worship God; and the second, that one should honour father and mother: Such laws are not written, but inborn; we have not learned, received, and read them, but we have wrested, drawn, and forced them out of nature herself. We have not received them through instruction, but have acquired them at birth; we have gained them, not by training, but by instinct.

Nevertheless, this definition also permits us to ask the question, what this natural reason is, or how it is made manifest. To this question the following reply must be made: that natural reason is evident of itself and therefore those who rely upon it are content merely to say: 'This is perfectly clear from nature itself', 'It is evident from natural reason', 'He has a knowledge derived from nature', 'Nature shows'; and there are many remarks of the same kind. So also 'Just by nature', 'Nothing is so completely in harmony with natural justice', 'It is contrary to nature', 'Nature does not allow', and hundreds of other phrases. Moreover, Aristotle says: 'By nature all men desire knowledge', 'All men seek the good', etc.

These things are so well known, that if you should try to prove them, you would render them obscure. At any rate, it would be useless to prove what is already manifest. Thus all the interpreters of the law say that things which are well known ought to be stated, but not demonstrated....

The words which are written in the Sacred Books of God will properly be given special weight; since it is evident that they were uttered not merely for the Hebrews, but for all men, for all nations and for all times. For that these words are of a true nature, that is to say, one which is blameless and just, is most certain.

> These testimonies are forthwith divine; they do not need the successive steps which the rest require. They are as simple as they are true, as widespread as they are as simple, as popular as they are widespread, as natural as they are popular, as divine as they are natural.
>
> [Tertullian, *De testimonio animae*]

1.8 Of Divine Causes for Making War

Divine causes for making war are such as we can attribute to God, as if He Himself had ordered the war; for example, when the Jews ascribed to God the cause of the war against the Canaanites. God also threatened the

418   *Sources*

Amalekites with a truceless war and enjoined upon his people unending hostility against them.

> That kind of war is unquestionably just which is commanded by God, in whom there is no injustice and who knows what ought to be done to each one. In such a war the army must be regarded not so much as the author of the war as the servant of God,

writes Augustine. And in another connexion he says:

> This command cannot be decided to be unjust, for it is the mandate of God, Who was not to be questioned, but obeyed. For He knows how just His command was, and it is the part of His servant to do obediently what He has ordered....

To these examples from Holy Writ add also that of the Ethiopians whose custom it was to undertake any war whatsoever, when bidden by the oracle of Jupiter; and of the Spartans, who because they were directed by oracles proceeded to war even against the powerful Argives.... The Turks too always have this reason for their wars, that it is the command of Mahomet to make war upon men of different religion from their own. And thus they themselves and the Persians, each heretics in the eyes of the other, are said to wage an almost ceaseless strife in behalf of their religion. So too the Turk is fired with hatred against the Persians and against the Christians because of religion. Moreover, Soliman is said to have been advised to make war rather against the Christians, since the Persians were only heretics. On the contrary, in the council of Portugal the last king Sebastian was ordered to war against heretics rather than against infidels.

Is not this the attitude of Spain? That decree by which Philip lately repudiated his debts and proved false to his pledges declares that he has irreconcilable wars with infidels and heretics, and others testify to this cause for Philip's wars; the whole earth, both East and West, testifies to it. But our decision is, that the Jews most justly waged war with the Canaanites, as was also said before. The others are upheld, not, it is true, by divine and genuine justice, but by human justice and the principles laid down by religious sects. For that is a general truth which is cited by one of our greatest medical writers [Galen], that decisions ought not to be criticised which are rendered according to the belief of the sect of the one who makes them. Accordingly, the acts of those men cannot be criticised, if they are in harmony with their own religion. 'If Gradivus bid a leader take up arms, it is as righteous to trust him as it would be unrighteous to hesitate. Mortal beings crave guidance. Perform with certainty the commands of God'. Such are the words of those men, and 'Who would take up arms against the Gods?' What has been said in another connexion applies also here. But we must go to the root of things and consider whether their religious feeling in these instances is correct.

Sources   419

1.9 Whether it is Just to Wage War for the Sake of Religion

Now if religion is of such a nature that it ought to be forced upon no one against his will, and if a propaganda which exacts faith by blows is called a strange and unheard of thing, it follows that force in connexion with religion is unjust. [*He then weighs the opinions of authorities from antiquity to early modernity.*]

But all this is another problem, namely that of [wars of] defence, which I shall investigate later. Now the question before us is, whether it is lawful to wage war with religion as the sole motive. This I deny and I give as my reason the following: since the laws of religion do not properly exist between man and man, therefore no man's rights are violated by a difference in religion, nor is it lawful to make war because of religion. Religion is a relationship with God. Its laws are divine, that is between God and man; they are not human, namely, between man and man. Therefore a man cannot complain of being wronged because others differ from him in religion....

But those who separate themselves from the rest of the body politic and arouse one part of the state against the other are disturbers of the public peace, and an injury to the rest of the citizens.... But if men in another state live in a manner different from that which we follow in our own state, they surely do us no wrong. Therefore, since war against them will be either vindictive or punitive, it can in neither event be just; for we have not been injured.... To punish a guilty person whom you have no right to punish is equivalent to chastising an innocent person.

[*In chapter 10, he argues that where there was an established religion, religious difference should be tolerated so long as the dissenters pose no threat to princely authority. In the next chapter, he argued from the golden rule that rulers should not force subjects in religious matters and the people should not force rulers, precisely because both would not want to be coerced. Those in a public position may defend themselves against coerced religion; private citizens can only flee.*]

1.12 Whether there are Natural Causes for Making War

[*He cites authors from antiquity that argued that some peoples were naturally at war with others. Greeks, endowed with wisdom, were said to be natural enemies of barbarians whose intellect resembled the beasts. On this basis, Aristotle argued that some people were naturally born for slavery, and superior peoples could make war on inferiors for the purpose of reducing them to slavery. Others said that Palestinians were natural enemies of Jewish people, or Saracens of Christians, and thus war between them would remain.*]

But I do not think this view correct. For, on the contrary, we are by nature all akin. But it is through the fault of the human race that dissensions arise, since mankind is uneasy and untamed, and always engaged in a struggle for freedom or glory or dominion, as Sallust says. And the cause is not the course or rotation of the stars, as is said elsewhere, or even fate, but the ambition

420 *Sources*

and injustice of men, as Agathias declares, a writer of the highest authority. Hence there is no natural repugnance between man and man....

If the causes for war were really due to nature, every war arising from them would also be just. But the causes are not of that kind. Men are not foes of one another by nature. But our acts and our customs, whether these be like or unlike, cause harmony or discord among us. They say that men are not friends by nature, a statement which I do not accept....

This, however, is the point which we are trying to establish, namely, to realise that no war is natural. Yet it is almost natural for us to war with the Turks, just as it was for the Greeks to contend with the barbarians. With the Saracens (who are Turks) we have an irreconcilable war. With other foreign peoples we have commercial relations, but certainly not war.

War is not waged on account of religion, and war is not natural either with others or even with the Turks. But we have war with the Turks because they act as our enemies, plot against us, and threaten us. With the greatest treachery they always seize our possessions, whenever they can. Thus we constantly have a legitimate reason for war against the Turks. We ought not to break with them; no! We ought not to make war upon them when they are quiet and keeping the peace, and have no designs upon us; no! But when do the Turks act thus? Let the theologians keep silence about a matter which is outside of their province.

1.15 Of Defence for the Sake of Honour

It remains to speak of defence for honour's sake, which is undertaken without any fear of danger to ourselves, through no need of our own, with no eye to our advantage, but merely for the sake of others. And it rests upon the fundamental principle, that nature has established among men kinship, love, kindliness, and a bond of fellowship (as Marcus Tallius says); and that the law of nations is based upon this association of the human race. It is precisely for that reason that the law of nations is called by Cicero 'civil'. In fact, the Stoics maintained that the whole world formed one state, and that all men were fellow citizens and fellow townsmen, like a single herd feeding in a common pasture. All this universe which you see, in which things divine and human are included, is one, and we are members of a great body. And in truth the world is one body. Moreover, nature has made us all kindred, since we have the same origin and the same abode. She has implanted in us love for one another and made us inclined to union. And this union of ours is like to an arch of stones, which will fall, unless the stones push against one another and hold one another up, to use Seneca's admirable comparison. Or, as Gellius has it, it stands as it were by mutual opposition and supported by its strain. This is what Horace calls 'the discordant harmony of things', of which we have spoken before.

Now you have heard that the whole world is one body, that all men are members of that body, that the world is their home, and that it forms a state.

Listen to these words once more, for they are beautiful. Varro calls the world 'the great home'. 'Since man is a social being and born for fellowship, he looks upon the world as one home', says Seneca in another passage. Lactantius calls the world a commonwealth.... So, too, Augustine recognises three social ties: first, that of the family; second, that of the city; third, that of the world; and he declares that the nations of the earth are united through this human society.

What then is that society and union? Good men have towards the good, as it were by necessity, a kindly feeling, which has been implanted by nature as the source of friendship; but that same kindliness also extends to the multitude. For virtue is not inhuman, savage, and haughty, or unwilling to have regard for all peoples, writes Cicero. And Ambrose declares: 'A law of nature constrains us to universal charity, that we may conduct ourselves towards one another as members of one body'. Therefore Baldus also declares that we are born not only for our own people, but for foreigners, because of the bond of charity. 'Those who say that we should have regard to our fellow citizens, but not to strangers, destroy the community and the fellowship of the human race', says Cicero again, a statement which Lactantius has quoted with approval.

Cicero also says: 'Shameful is the attitude of mind of those who look at everything from the standpoint of their own advantage'. And he is right in calling it 'shameful', for man was born for fellowship, and it is his duty to aid others, not to live for himself alone. And Cicero condemned the philosophers because, while they are free from one species of injustice and fulfil the most important function of equity (as another holier man writes), namely, to do no harm and not to attack another, they yet abandon the fellowship of life, and neglect the other principle of justice, which is to render aid when you can. 'Do you not see how the world itself, the fairest of works, is bound together by love?' We are bound by a natural law (so say the interpreters of the law) to aid one another. And they also declare that the defence of one's own people and of strangers is equally necessary, but in particular that of our allies, from whom harm must be kept; and they say that such defence is prescribed both by divine and by human law. Plato even believes that one who does not try to avert a wrong offered to another is deserving of punishment.

Now what Plato and those expounders of the law say of private citizens we feel justified in applying to sovereigns and nations, since the rule which governs a private citizen in his own state ought to govern a public citizen, that is to say a sovereign or a sovereign people, in this public and universal state formed by the world.... And since we are one body, just as the other members would aid the one that was injured, if one member should desire to harm another, since it is for the interest of the whole body, even of the offending member, that each of the members be preserved: exactly so men will aid one another, since society cannot be maintained except by the love and protection of those who compose it.

422 *Sources*

[*Having established the propriety of intervention because humans were fundamentally connected and similar, Gentili discusses whether one nation has a duty to intervene in other nations, especially when grave injustice is being perpetrated on the people by rulers. The ties of kinship and common religion heighten the duty to intervene on a neighbour's behalf (see also 1.16 On Defending the Subjects of Another against their Sovereign).*]

1.19 Of Natural Reasons for Making War

In this connexion a war will be called natural, if it is undertaken because of some privilege of nature which is denied us by man. For example, if a right of way is refused us, or if we are excluded from harbours or kept from provisions, commerce, or trade. ...

But if there is no reason why a passage should be refused, and it is nevertheless denied, this constitutes a just reason for war. To pass through another's territory is lawful. To enter the estate of another for the purpose of hunting is also allowed by the law of nations, and any who cross without asking permission will neither be regarded as doing wrong nor will they be prohibited. The law gives the owner of an estate the right to forbid the entrance of a hunter; a fact which is opposed to our present decision....

Indeed, one who takes away such privileges inflicts a wound on human society. For in harbours, navigation, communication, and accommodation is the strongest bond of human interdependence.... Everyone must realise that no blessing has been bestowed by divine Providence upon anyone for his sole enjoyment. But if nature had given everything equally to all men, the reasons for loving one another would readily be destroyed; for it is through this inequality that we ask and give in turn without ceasing. This is the law of friendship and its strongest bond. Thus it is an advantage to the earth that men sail the sea....

No one doubts to-day that what we call the New World is joined to our own and has always been known to the remote Indi. And that is one reason why the warfare of the Spaniards in that part of the world seems to be justified, because the inhabitants prohibited other men from commerce with them [as argued by the Spanish jurist and theologian, Francisco de Vitoria]; and it would be an adequate defence, if the statement were true. For commerce is in accordance with the law of nations, and a law is not changed by opposition to it. But the Spaniards were aiming there, not at commerce, but at dominion. And they regarded it as beyond dispute that it was lawful to take possession of those lands which were not previously known to us; just as if to be known to none of us were the same thing as to be possessed by no one....

I believe that it is a common characteristic of all uncivilised peoples to drive away strangers. But commerce cannot be said to be prohibited, as soon as some one phase of it is forbidden, but only when all trade is prohibited. For what if the importation of something is forbidden which seems to the natives harmful....

Again, what if traders are forbidden access to the interior parts of a country, and are admitted only as far as the frontiers? This, we learn, was a custom of the Britons in ancient days, and it is practised by the Chinese to-day. In such cases it does not seem to me that commerce is forbidden; for a guest is not said to be rejected when he is not admitted to every part of a house. It is lawful to keep the secrets of a kingdom concealed and to hold aloof all who come to spy into them or who might do so. It also seems proper sometimes to prohibit the exportation of certain commodities, such as gold and silver, in order that the provinces may not be exhausted and that wares may be exchanged for other wares....

But enough of commerce; I shall now speak about the sea. This is by nature open to all men and its use is common to all, like that of the air. It cannot therefore be shut off by anyone. Its shores, too, are by nature accessible to all, as well as the banks of rivers and rivers themselves, that is to say, running waters....

1.25 Of An Honourable Reason For Waging War

There remains now the one question concerning an honourable cause for waging war, which we further restrict to a war which is undertaken for no private reason of our own, but for the common interest and in behalf of others. Look, you, if men clearly sin against the laws of nature and of mankind, I believe that any one whatsoever may check such men by force of arm....

Therefore, I approve the more decidedly of the opinion of those who say that the cause of the Spaniards is just when they make war upon the Indians, who practised abominable lewdness even with beasts, and who ate human flesh, slaying men for that purpose. For such sins are contrary to human nature, and the same is true of other sins recognised as such by all except haply by brutes and brutish men. And against such men, as Isocrates says, war is made as against brutes. This in a state any one whatever is allowed to accuse and offender against the community, even one who is not a member of the state, when an action is defended which is not peculiar to the state but of interest to all men....

But the law of nature is not annulled by human sins. And we contend that to make war upon such men was, and is, lawful. The custom which the Carthaginians had of offering sacrifices with human blood was gloriously ended by Gelon, who would not grant them peace until they had renounced so abominable a practice. Even the king of Persia sent an embassy asking the Carthaginians not to sacrifice human victims and obtain his request. And the pretext of religion cannot be admitted in this case, when a right of humanity is violated at the same time. And therefore our commentators declare that war is lawful against idolaters, if idolatry is joined with the slaughter of innocent victims; for the innocent must be protected. And so war was justly made upon the Canaanites, where such sacrifices, etc. [Lev. 18:21; 20:2–3; Deut. 12:31; 18:10].

424 *Sources*

One reason I do not accept, although it is approved by others among the causes of the war waged by the Spaniards against the Indians; namely, that it was lawful to make war upon them because they refused to hear the preaching of the Gospel. For this is only a pretext of religion. And although it is said: 'Go, preach the Gospel to every creature' [Mark 16:15], it does not therefore follow that any creature which refuses to hear must be forced to do so by war and arms. Those are foolish arguments. I cannot approve Innocent nor Paul de Castro, who follows Innocent, when they say that love of God is a just cause of war against the infidels. Yet I do not condemn Dagobert, Charles the Great, Saint Louis, who imposed the necessity of hearing the divine word upon the Frisians, Saracens, and Africans. For they imposed it upon peoples already conquered, but did not make war for that purpose....

It is right to make war upon pirates [since pirates remove themselves from the company of humanity and violate the rights of everyone.]

Therefore, since we may also be injured as individuals by those violators of nature, war will be made against them by individuals. And no rights will be due to these men who have broken all human and divine laws and who, though joined with us by similarity of nature, have disgraced this union with abominable stains. In other words, not only is the civil law an agreement and a bond of union among citizens, but the same is true of the law of nations as regards nations, and the law of nature as regards mankind. The founders of our laws are not to be censured for defining natural law as that which nature teaches to all living things, even though there is no law, that is, no unity, between man and the lower animals. For to say nothing of the law which is common to us with the brutes, of our dominion over them, surely we cannot deny that what is natural to me is common to all men. Marriage, the begetting of children, and education belong to this law which they have violated, and they deprive all men, whose kindred and associates they are, of their natural rights....

Idolatry and religious infidelity do not give cause for divorce, but adultery does; as I argue elsewhere. Moreover, as has previously been shown, the law of religion is not the same as other laws. Faith is a special gift of God and Jesus Christ is foolishness among the heathen; but natural things are known naturally to all. Some kind of religion is natural, and therefore if there should be any who are atheists, destitute of any religious belief, either good or bad, it would seem just to war upon them as we would upon brutes. For they do not deserve to be called men, who divest themselves of human nature, and themselves do not desire the name of men. And such a war is a war of vengeance, to avenge our common nature.

[*He then discusses honourable reasons to take up arms. Subordinates should obey orders to fight, unless the cause is manifestly unjust and the war is offensive. Although subjects may defend themselves against their lord, subjects cannot make war on the lord.*]

Sources 425

1.27 Those Who Make War of Necessity

A second variety of this necessary warfare will be found in the case of those who, because they are driven from their own country or are compelled to leave it through some emergency and to seek another home, from necessity make war upon others, in order that they may make themselves masters of the latter's possessions. For some, the destruction of their cities has driven into the lands of others, since they were despoiled of their own territory; others the excessive growth of their population has sent forth, in order to relieve their own cities; still others a pestilence, or frequent earthquakes, or other intolerable defects of an unfavourable location, have banished....

The Ansibarii well said, when they had been driven out by the Chauci and, since they were bereft of their own homes, were asking for a safe place of exile:

> As heaven was given to the gods, so the earth was given to mortal men; whatever lands are vacant are public property. The sun and the other constellations have no inclination to look down upon vacant soil. Rather would they whelm in the sea the robbers of the land.

True indeed, 'God did not create the world to be empty' (Genesis 1; Isaiah 45:18). And therefore the seizure of vacant places is regarded as a law of nature....

The ruling of our jurists with regard to unoccupied land is, that those who take it have a right to it, since it is the property of no one. And even though such lands belong to the sovereign of that territory, as others maintain, yet because of that law of nature which abhors a vacuum, they will fall to the lot of those who take them. So be it, but let the sovereign retain jurisdiction over them....

But are there to-day no unoccupied lands on the earth? Is it not, pray, being reduced more and more to the wilderness of primeval times, or in this its decrepit old age is it more fruitful than ever before? What is Greece to-day, and the whole of Turkey? What is Africa? What of Spain? It is the most populous country of all; yet under the rule of Spain is not almost all of the New World unoccupied? Why should I name thee, Italy, in this connexion, and the country about Aquileia, Pisa, and Rome itself, unkempt and unwholesome because of the small number of its inhabitants? But of this I shall perhaps speak at another time.

Those lands which are not vacant ought not to be taken; for it is not right that one should neglect oneself through love for another [i.e., by hurting oneself when giving land to others].... Yet I think that in this case a slight loss ought to be endured; otherwise there will be hardly any reply which can be made to the exiles. And the slight loss should be put up with, since it is made good by a greater advantage, in the form of an increase in the number

426 *Sources*

of the citizens. For of course the newcomers ought to do what is most just and submit to the rule of him who is lord of the land....

But in some instances exiles are not made subject to the government; for example, if their number is so great as to be perilous to the commonwealth.... Again, if such fugitives brought war with them, because they had been conquered and were demanded by their conquerors, so that a refusal to give them up would be the cause of a new war against those who offered them asylum, that is a valid reason for not receiving exiles, and there are others of the same kind.

Yet even so you will perhaps not condemn the fugitives if, fleeing from extreme ills, they now make war upon those who, however lawfully, refuse to take them in. For what else could they do? If they provide that the numbers of the exiles should not be dangerous to the country to which they come, they are in the right.

3.9 Of Slaves

A state of slavery exists when there is no hope of freedom. Moreover, slavery is among the greatest ills which befall surrendered or captured soldiers, since by it one is subjected to another's domination and reduced to the condition of a beast. One is deprived of one's nature and becomes chattel instead of a person. Therefore those who were slaves were commonly called 'bodies' by the Greeks. Slavery is all but death.

With regard to slavery I have three questions to raise. First when we have slavery. Secondly, whether it is a just condition. Thirdly, what laws regulate the intercourse of master and slave.

As regards the first question, it is generally believed that in the wars of the Christians there was no slavery. For those wars are more than civil, since all men are brothers in Christ, since we are members of the one body of which Christ is the head, and since it is commonly believed that there is one Church of Christ and a single Christendom. From this it follows that an enemy may not be held captive perpetually, that he must not be sold, and so with the other things which have been mentioned. Whereas on the other hand, if a slave is captured by another enemy [i.e., a non-Christian enemy], he would remain a slave continually, even when the war was ended, if there was no provision about him [and his release] in the terms of peace....

[*He then discusses at length whether prisoners of war have a right to attempt escape.*]

But just as prisoners of war do not have the right of *postliminium* [returning to their previous rights] in time of peace, unless it is provided in the terms of peace that they shall have the right, so those who are taken in time of peace have the right of *postliminium* in time of peace, unless it has been stipulated that they shall not have it. This same distinction must be observed in captivity among Christians; namely, that one who has been taken in time of war may not run away when peace is made. For captivity among the Christians must be regulated after the patterns of the slavery of the ancients, unless there is some reason to the contrary.

There is no true condition of slavery among the Christians, whatever I hear said to the contrary by some, who therefore regard the will of our prisoners as null and void; for the rule has been established by invariable custom that there shall be no slaves....

There was no condition of slavery among the Jews, except a kind of a temporary one....

With regard to the second [question], I have no hesitation in saying that the condition of slavery is a just one. For it is a provision of the law of nations. But the objection is made, that natural reason, which is the basis of the law of nations, could not introduce slavery if we are all free by nature; therefore slavery is said to be contrary to nature and to owe its origin to the cruelty of the enemy. But there are many answers to this objection. I agree with Thomas Aquinas that slavery is really in harmony with nature; not indeed according to her first intent, by which we were all created free, but according to a second desire of hers, that sinners should be punished.

This opinion is also approved by some of our jurists who are most learned in that law. Accordingly they add that liberty is according to nature, but only for good men. With this view also a disquisition of Aristotle on the natural origin of slavery is in harmony. For although the philosopher is speaking of those who have servile dispositions, yet his arguments also apply to those who become slaves because of their wickedness and sins....

Add to this that the law of nations about making slaves provides that prisoners be slaves, if those who have captured them so desire. For example, the Christians and some others do not wish to introduce a condition of slavery. And although the law asserts that what is taken from the enemy at once becomes the property of the captors, it is not understood to mean that it becomes theirs even if they do not wish it....

[*He discusses various authors on whether slavery departs from natural law.*] But concerning the question before us, we reply that we are not created free by nature so absolutely that very many of us may not be made slaves; and besides, that fact that anything seems to all men to be true is an argument for its truth, as Seneca also says. Aristotle, too, declares that what always happens does not happen by fortune or by chance, and that a thing is natural which is wont to happen always and everywhere....

Therefore slavery belongs to the law of nations, and to-day is common to Christians with all infidels. Our countrymen who were captured by the Turks are slaves of the Turks, as others have well and truly noted. Some authorities wrongly question this on the ground that the cause of the Turks, who hunt us down and seize our goods, cannot be just. But this has been discussed before and exception made of pirates; and the same thing has been said of others with whom we have no friendship. Hence a threefold inquiry may be made

428 *Sources*

about the Turks: when they wage war, when they practice piracy, and when they seize us in other ways than in warfare.

Further as to the laws of slavery (which is our third point) this is my opinion: that one should not so strictly follow the letter of the law as not to make allowance for what is usually done among good men. According to the common, but false, belief there is nothing which a master is not allowed to do to a slave, exactly as there is nothing which a painter may not paint.... Plato also is wrong when he writes that slaves must be severely dealt with, and Aristotle is right in declaring that they should be mercifully treated. So, too, Marcus Cicero is right, when he says: 'We should remember that justice should be observed even towards the weak'...

[*He then argues that it would not make sense to treat humans with more cruelty than beasts. Masters were legally restrained in what they could do to their slaves, and slaves must be treated with some respect. Slaves cannot be killed by their masters, and they are not obligated to carry out immoral orders.*]

119 Ministers of England, *The Millenary Petition* (1603)

Keywords: #Church-State Relations
Region: #England
Group: #Church of England, #Puritan

The hotter sort of Protestants (known derisively as the 'Puritans' and positively as 'the godly') chafed under what they saw as the stalled Reformation of **Elizabeth I**. Not only did she refuse appeals for further Reformation, she also tried to pressure the Archbishop of Canterbury, **Edmund Grindal**, to shut down 'prophesyings' – meetings where preachers tried to learn the art of 'godly preaching'. Anti-Puritan measures continued throughout Elizabeth's reign. Upon her death, **James VI** of Scotland became **James I** of England. He was forcibly separated from his Catholic mother at a young age, educated by zealous Presbyterians, and developed a distaste for the Reformed tradition throughout much of his life. Puritans wanted to see the Church of England adopt many of the principles already enacted by the Church of Scotland, but James did not want to turn his new kingdom into his old kingdom. England afforded the king far more authority over the church, and he liked it that way.

The following document, the so-called 'Millenary' petition because of its claimed 1,000 Puritan signatories, was presented to the king as he made his way from Scotland to London in April 1603. The petitioners adopted a posture of humble submission to their new sovereign; however, they made it clear that they had many grievances with the previous administration. They registered their dislike of the use of the oath *Ex Officio*. Through the use of this oath, authorities in the Star Chamber would leverage the fear of eternal damnation in order to get individuals to self-incriminate. When Puritans grew in power later in the century, outlawing this oath was high on their agenda. In response to this petition, James convened the Hampton Court Conference (1604), but the results were not favourable to the Puritans.[169]

Henry Gee and William John Hardy, eds., *Documents Illustrative of English Church History* (London: Macmillan, 1896), 508–511.

———

430 *Sources*

Most gracious and dread sovereign, – Seeing it has pleased the Divine majesty, to the great comfort of all good Christians, to advance your highness, according to your just title, to the peaceable government of this Church and Commonwealth of England, we, the ministers of the gospel in this land, neither as factious men affecting a popular parity in the Church, nor as schismatics aiming at the dissolution of the State ecclesiastical, but as the faithful servants of Christ and loyal subjects to your majesty, desiring and longing for the redress of [several] abuses of the Church, could do no less in our obedience to God, service to your majesty, love to His Church, than acquaint your princely majesty with our particular griefs; for as your princely pen writeth, 'the king, as a good physician, must first know what [ailment] his patient naturally is most subject unto, before he can begin his cure;' and although [several] of us that sue for reformation have formerly, in respect of the times, subscribed to the [prayer] book – some upon protestation, some upon exposition given them, some with condition rather than the Church should have been deprived of their labour and ministry – yet now we, to the number of more than a thousand of your majesty's subjects and ministers, all groaning as under a common burden of human rites and ceremonies, do with one joint consent humble ourselves at your majesty's feet, to be eased and relieved in this behalf. Our humble suit, then, unto your majesty is that these offences following, some may be removed, some amended, some qualified: [*The points of contention were fourfold: reform of 'human' aspects of the church service; education of parish clergy; correction of clerical abuses; and the removal of hindrances to a Reformed church discipline.*]

These, with such other abuses yet remaining and practised in the Church of England, we are able to show not to be agreeable to the Scriptures, if it shall please your highness further to hear us, or more at large by writing to be informed, or by conference among the learned to be resolved; and yet we doubt not but that, without any further process, your majesty (of whose Christian judgement we have received so good a taste already) is able of yourself to judge of the equity of this cause. God, we trust, has appointed your highness our physician to heal these diseases; and we say with Mordecai to Esther, 'Who knoweth whether you are come to the kingdom for such a time [Esther 4:14]?' Thus your majesty shall do that which we are persuaded shall be acceptable to God, honourable to your majesty in all succeeding ages, profitable to His Church, which shall be thereby increased, comfortable to your ministers, which shall be no more suspended, silenced, disgraced, imprisoned for men's traditions, and prejudicial to none but to those that seek their own quiet, credit and profit in the world.

Thus, with all dutiful submission, referring ourselves to your majesty's pleasure for your gracious answer, as God shall direct you, we most humbly recommend your highness to the Divine majesty, whom we beseech, for Christ His sake, to dispose your royal heart to do herein what shall be to His glory, the good of His Church, and your endless comfort.

Your majesty's most humble subjects, the ministers of the Gospel that desire not a disorderly innovation, but a due and godly reformation.

120 *Regulating the Dutch Reformed Faith in Asia (1607–1642)*

Keywords: #Colonisation, #Trade, #Treaty
Region: #Netherlands, #Indonesia, #Malaysia, #Japan, #Asia
Group: #Dutch Reformed | #Asian, #Islam

The Papal Bull, *Inter Caetera* (1493), and the Treaty of Tordesillas (1494) split the Atlantic world between the Spanish and the Portuguese, while the Treaty of Saragossa (1529) divided the Pacific. Long before Protestants ventured into Southeast Asia, Muslims and Catholics competed for power and converts, while China (Qing dynasty) and India (Mughal Empire) remained the dominant powers in the region well into the 1700s.[170] When the Pacific was divided, the Low Countries were under Spanish control. However, during the Eighty Years' War (1568–1648) the Dutch asserted independence (**Declaration of the States General of the United Provinces**, 1581), and Spain was eventually forced to accept these claims. In the mid-1590s, the Protestant Dutch first sailed to the East Indies, and in 1602, they formed the Dutch East India Company (DEIC), challenging the dominance of Iberian Catholicism in the Pacific.

In 1605, Admiral Cornelis Matelieff (c.1570–1632) led a fleet of DEIC ships into Southeast Asia. He set up a school on the newly acquired Amboina (an island in Indonesia), 'the first Dutch school outside of Europe'. Similar schools appeared throughout the Dutch East Indies, and in 1638, **Godfried Udemans** referred to these schools as 'a second Reformation'. Matelieff made a treaty with Johar (Malaysia) in 1606 and fought with the Portuguese several times in the latter half of that year. In May of 1607, as the second source below indicates, he established a fort at Malayo and signed a Treaty with Ternate (island in Indonesia), returning to the Dutch Republic in 1608. The treaty of 26 May 1607 is interesting for several reasons. First, from an economic perspective, the treaty guaranteed exclusive rights to the clove trade, and this was perhaps the first monopoly secured by the DEIC. Monopolies like this contributed to the financial growth of the Dutch Republic. Second, it promised military assistance and stipulated what to do in cases of injustice between the two peoples. It can be compared to other documents in the long

432   *Sources*

history of colonisation. Third, it demonstrates how Protestants had a long history of allying with Muslims (often the Ottomans) against Catholic powers. In this case, the Dutch allied with the Sultan of Ternate, the adolescent Modafar, against the Spanish and Portuguese. Finally, the treaty minimised religion and emphasised a mutually beneficial commercial relationship.

Charles H. Parker notes the pertinence of the stereotype that Dutch traders placed paramount importance on commerce rather than conversion. However, he emphasises how most did not see proselytising as incompatible with profit. In keeping with the **Treaty of Utrecht** (1579), the DEIC promoted freedom of conscience. They were often preferred to Catholic regimes since the latter often aggressively pursued conversion. In this treaty, the DEIC even promised to return those who abandoned the Muslim faith to the sultan of Ternate. Dutch ministers complained about the obstacles Christian powers placed in the way of spreading the gospel. Ecclesiastical authorities in the Netherlands considered contextualising the faith for distant peoples. In the second source, they argue that the same theological rigour should be applied to all potential members of the church, whether Dutch by birth or not. On the question of worship in the church, they tried to prevent distant churches from adopting dissimilar practices. The final source reproduces the religious provisions of the 1642 Dutch East India Company charter.[171]

(1) Peter Borshberg, ed., *Journal, Memorials and Letters of Cornelis Matelieff de Jonge: Security, Diplomacy and Commerce in 17th-century Southeast Asia* (Singapore: NUS Press, 2015), 422–424; (2) Hugh Hastings, ed., *Ecclesiastical Records: State of New York* (Albany, NY: James B. Lyon, 1901), I:77–78; (3) V. Perniola, ed., *The Catholic Church in Sri Lanka. Vol 1: The Dutch Period* (Colombo-Dehiwala: Tisara Prakasakayo, 1983), 17.

———

1. Treaty with Sultan Modafar of Ternate (1607)

Agreement between Admiral Cornelis Matelieff de Jonge in the name of the Gentlemen States General of the United Provinces of the Netherlands on the one hand, and the king of Ternate and his Council on the other hand, this May 26 of the year 1607, off Malayo.

1 First, the Admiral, who brought us here to Ternate again, shall remain here with his entire fleet, until the fortress on the waterfront of this town of Malayo, which he has begun to fortify, is fully defendable.
2 Upon his departure, he shall leave four ships here….
3 He shall provide the fortress with sufficient artillery….
5 The Admiral shall be obliged to recommend Ternate's cause most highly to the Gentlemen States General upon his arrival in Holland, so that the States may send people to chase the Castilians from Ternate. The Ternatans hereby give full mandate to further their cause in their name.

Sources 433

6 In return, the Ternatans shall accept and acknowledge the Most Mighty Gentlemen States General as their protector, and they shall swear an oath to this if the High Gentlemen so desire.

7 The expenses which have been made and might still be made in the war shall be paid by the Ternatans....

10 They shall not be allowed to sell cloves, regardless to which community or people, but exclusively to the agent for the Gentlemen States General who shall live in Ternate, as such a price as shall be ordained by the Gentlemen States General and agreed with the king.

11 No one from either party shall do injustice to the other; but if one of the Dutch do injustice to the Ternatans, he shall be accused and punished by the authorities under which he comes, and the same for the Ternatans.

12 In matters of religion, no one shall ridicule or hinder another, but each shall live as he wants to answer to God for.

13 Should any of the Dutch defect to the Ternatans, he shall be handed over again by the Ternatans; likewise, should any one of the Ternatans come to the Dutch, he shall be handed over by them as well.

14 Without consent from both parties, no one shall make peace with the Spanish, nor with the Tidorese.

———

2. Synod of North Holland (20 Aug 1629)

Church Regulations for the East and West Indies

First: The question was asked, whether it were advisable, and whether it could be understood as approved, in the case of children whom they do not as yet find fit for baptism and whose parents are heathen, that a blessing and confirmation might be used, with the laying on of hands, instead of baptism. It was learned from the Acts handed in that this had already been done. This Synod having given heed, in the fear of God, to this matter, it was decided and understood, that what was proposed, ought not to be done. Such a practice was not Christian, and was not in conformity with the Word of God. It should not be done, especially because of its effect. [*They later add that such laying on of hands might be interpreted superstitiously.*] Adoption into the Christian Church in such a way, would produce evil consequences, and could in no sense be justified by the example of Christ's laying his hands upon the children of the Jews; inasmuch as those children were partakers of the covenant. Therefore, instead of such a confirmation and blessing, the children should be diligently instructed in the fundamental doctrines of Christianity.

In the second place, at the suggestion of the delegates from the Classis of Amsterdam, the question was taken up, whether the English mode of responsive reading and singing, could be permitted, as edifying, to the Church in the East Indies, where worship is conducted in the Malay-Japanese. This point,

434 *Sources*

having been maturely considered by the Synod, the Synod is of the opinion, that the following is most expedient in reference to the particular matter: Inasmuch as the Church of the East Indies is altogether one with the churches of our land, they should conform themselves to the Church of this land. Because not even where it is conducted in the Malay and Japanese languages, a marked difference is offensive....

3. Charter of the Dutch East India Company (1642)

1. Within the territories of the Dutch East Indian Company no other religion will be exercised, much less taught or propagated, either secretly or publicly, than the Reformed Christian Religion as it is taught in the public churches of the United Provinces. Whoever will be found holding any other religious services, whether Christian or heathen, will have his possessions confiscated and will be put in chains and expelled from the country; or he will, according to the circumstances, receive a punishment involving limb and life....

121 *Forming the Protestant Union (1608)*

Keywords: #Church-State Relations, #War, #Peace, #Pluralism
Region: #Germany
Group: #Reformed, #Lutheran | #Roman Catholic

In 1555, the **Peace of Augsburg** enacted the principle of *cuius regio, eius religio*, which afforded princes the right to determine the religious allegiance of their jurisdiction. Although intended to settle Catholic-Protestant controversies over religious establishment, new conflicts emerged over the recognition of territories that had ceased to be Catholic. By the first decade of the seventeenth century, several territories had become Protestant. Sometimes, Catholic powers used force to prevent a region from converting to Protestantism or to roll back Protestant gains, triggering a backlash. In 1608, when the Imperial Diet met in Regensburg, Protestant princes sought the recognition of the lands that had turned Protestant since 1555. When their appeal was rejected, Calvinist and Lutheran princes formed a union, drawing in about half of the Protestant princes (Catholic princes followed suit in 1609). Those entering the union claimed the pact was primarily defensive and formed out of a desire to strengthen the Empire. The signatories were also concerned with the effects of the polemical theological language that Protestants used against each other. However, while trying to tone down the rhetoric, they allowed theologians freedom to argue for their interpretation of scripture. The failure to arrive at a mutually satisfactory agreement was symptomatic of the rising tensions and contributed to the Thirty Years' War.[172]

Gerhard Benecke, ed., *Germany in the Thirty Years War* (New York: Bedford/St. Martin's, 1979), 9–10.

———

In view of the urgent necessity, we, the undersigned Electors and Estates of the Holy Empire, much less to damage but much more to strengthen and uphold peace and unity in the Holy Empire, as dedicated and obedient Estates of the Empire of the German Nation, our beloved fatherland, in order to advance common well-being, our land, and people, and those Estates who will

436 *Sources*

in the future join us to further the peace, order, and protection in the name of God the Almighty, have one and all reached the present amicable and confidential agreement that we acknowledge by virtue of this letter, as follows

1 That each member shall keep good faith with the other and their heirs, land, and people, and that no one shall enter any other alliances; also that no Estate, jurisdiction, territory, or subject shall damage, fight, or in any way harm another Estate, nor break the laws of the Imperial constitution, nor give aid in any manner if such a break should occur....

4 It is our wish that in matters concerning the liberties and high jurisdiction of the German Electors and Estates, as also of the Protestant (*Evangelische*) Estates' grievances as presented at the last Imperial assembly concerning infringements of those selfsame rights, freedoms, and laws of the Empire, these shall all be presented and pressed at the subsequent Imperial and Imperial Circle assemblies, and not merely left to secret correspondence with each other. We also agree to try to influence other Protestant Estates (that is, Saxony) toward an understanding with us.

5 We also agree that this secret union shall not affect our disagreement on several points of religion, but that notwithstanding these, we have agreed to support each other. No member is to allow an attack on any other in books or through the pulpit, nor give any cause for any breach of the peace, while at the same time leaving untouched the theologian's right of disputation to affirm the Word of God.

6 If one or the other of us is attacked ... the remaining members of the Union shall immediately come to his aid with all the resources of the Union, as necessity may demand, and as set out in the detailed agreement....

122 William Perkins, *A Discourse of the Damned Art of Witchcraft* (1608)

Keywords: #Witchcraft, #Law, #Hebrew Bible, #Ten Commandments, #Rebellion, #Capital Crime, #Covenant, #Women
Region: #England
Group: #Church of England, #Puritan

The tragic fate of those deemed witches, usually women, shows how superstitions could lead to the use of brute force, both in Catholic and Protestant contexts. Heinrich Kramer's infamous *Malleus maleficarum* (1486) had instigated a greater prosecution of witchcraft, often carried out by the Inquisition. The renowned political theorist Jean Bodin gave his hearty approval to the aggressive prosecution of 'witches' in *Démonomanie des sorciers* (1580). Even though Protestants commonly believed in malignant supernatural powers and feared witches, there was also a significant strain of scepticism about the alleged phenomenon. For example, the English Calvinist Reginald Scott linked witch-hunting with Catholic superstition in *The Discoverie of Witchcraft* (1584). Scott's antidote was a robust confidence in Providence and a proper Protestant interpretation of scripture, not the discovery and destruction of witches. Theoretical and theological attacks on the reality of witchcraft grew over the course of the seventeenth century, including by **Thomas Hobbes** (1651), **Robert Filmer** (1652), Baruch Spinoza (1661, 1675), John Webster (1677), and Balthasar Bekker (1695).

One of the most important Protestant treatises that justified executions on account of 'witchcraft' came from William Perkins (1558–1602). He was educated at Cambridge and became a leading Puritan during the reign of **Elizabeth I.** He shaped Puritan covenantal theology, which in turn deeply informed European pietist movements. Perkins' first work, published in 1584, was a treatise against astrology and almanacs. Ironically, many later Puritans would consult astrologers during the British Civil Wars. The following selection is drawn from Perkins' conclusion to *A Discourse of the Damned Art of Witchcraft* (1608). It was dedicated to **Edward Coke**, England's premier legal mind. Perkins argued that witchcraft should be a capital crime. Other Protestants would assert this argument, like **Richard Bernard** (1630) in England

438   *Sources*

and **Cotton Mather** (1692) in New England. Compared to continental Europe, English witch trials were rare and restrained, mostly flaring up during the Civil Wars and in New England during the Salem Witch Trials of the early 1690s. Notably, **Samuel Sewall**, one of the judges involved in the Salem Witch Trials, publicly stated his regret for his actions in 1697.

Perkins' treatise is notable for several reasons. First, he provided witch-hunting with a structural Protestant rationale. Second, Perkins asserted that both men and women could be witches, even though he believed the common trope that women would be more susceptible to it (see **James VI and I's** *Daemonologie*, 1597). Third, his work argued for execution based on divine law, natural law, and the laws of England. While doing so, Perkins articulated his understanding of the relationship between the Hebrew Bible and Christian scriptures. Intriguingly, in his final paragraph, he argued that the witch and the thief were both justly condemned to death – even though Moses' law (and later Puritans) did not sanction the death penalty for theft. Fourth, Perkins collapsed the difference between good and bad witches, shifting the perception of their crime from what they did (heal or harm), to who they derived their powers from. The central offence for Perkins, given his emphasis on covenant, was the act of allegedly entering into a covenant with Satan.[173]

William Perkins, *A Discourse of the Damned Art of Witchcraft* (Cambridge, 1610), 246–256. Text modernised by the editors.

———

Whether the Witches of our age are to be punished with death, and that by virtue of this law of Moses?

I doubt not, but in this last age of the world, and among us also, this sin of Witchcraft ought as sharply to be punished as in former times; and all Witches being thoroughly convicted by the Magistrate, ought according to the Law of *Moses* to be put to death. For proof hereof, consider these reasons.

First, this Law of Moses flatly enjoins all men, in all ages, without limitation of circumstances, not to suffer the Witch to live, and hereupon I gather, that it must stand the same, both now and forever, to the world's end.

Patrons of Witches [hold] that it was a Judicial law, which continued but for a time, and concerned only the Nation of the Jews, and is now ceased. But I take the contrary to be the truth, and that upon these grounds.

I Those Judicial Laws, whose penalty is death because they have in them a perpetual equity, and do serve to maintain some moral precept, are perpetual. The Jews indeed had some Laws of this kind, whose punishments were temporal, and they lasted only for a certain time: but the penalty of Witchcraft, being Death by God's appointment, and the inflicting of that punishment, serving to maintain the equity of the three first moral precepts of the first Table, which cannot be kept, unless this Law be put

Sources 439

in execution: it must necessarily follow, that it is in that regard moral, and binds us, and shall in like sort bind all men in all ages, as well as the Jews themselves, to whom it was at that time personally directed.

II Every Judicial law that has in it the equity of the law of nature, is perpetual; and the Law of punishing the Witch by death, is such. For it is a principle of the law of nature, held for a grounded truth in all countries and kingdoms, among all people in every age; that the traitor, who is an enemy to the State, and rebels against his lawful Prince, should be put to death: now the most notorious traitor and rebel that can be, is the Witch. For she renounces God himself, the King of kings, she leaves the society of his Church and people, she binds herself in league with the Devil: and therefore if any offender among men ought to suffer death for this, much more ought she, and that of due desert.

The second reason for the proof of the point in hand, is this; According to Moses' law every Idolater was to be stoned to death (Deut. 17:3–5).... Now this is the very case of a Witch, she renounces the true God, and chooses to serve the Devil, therefore, she is a gross Idolater and her punishment must be suitable....

The third reason. Every seducer in the Church, whose practice was to draw men from the true God to the worship of Idols, though it were a man's own son or daughter, wife or friend, by the peremptory degree and commandment of God, was not to be spared or pitied by anyone, but the hand of the witness first, and then the hands of all the people must be upon him, to kill him (Deut. 13:6–9). If this is so, no convicted Witches ought to escape the sword of the Magistrate: for they are the most notorious seducers of all. Once they become entangled in the Devil's league, they labour to draw their dearest friends and posterity into their cursed and abominable practices; that they may be the more easily drawn into the same confederacy, wherewith they themselves are united to Satan.... Notwithstanding all that hath been said, many things are brought in defence of them, by such as are their friends and well-willers.

[Objection] First, it is said that the hurt comes not from the Witch but from the devil: he deserves the blame because it is his work, and she is not to die for his sin. [Answer] Let it be granted that the Witch is not the author of the evil that is done, yet she is a confederate and partner with the Devil, and so the law takes hold on her.... In the working of wonders, and in all mischievous practises, he or she is partaker with the devil by consent of covenant....

[Objection] Convicted Witches either repent or do not: If they repent, then God pardons their sin, and why should not the Magistrate as well save their bodies and let them live, as God doth their souls. If they do not repent, then it is a dangerous thing for the Magistrate to put them to death: for by this means he kills the body and casts the soul to hell. [Answer] All Witches, judicially and lawfully convicted, ought to have space for repentance granted

440 *Sources*

unto them, wherein they may be instructed and exhorted, and then afterwards executed.... [*He cites passages from the Hebrew Bible where people were executed as a warning to others.*]

[*Objection*] But there are some Witches who cannot be convicted of killing any: what shall become of them? [*Answer*] As the killing Witch must die by another Law [i.e., the law against murder], though he were no Witch: so the healing and harmless Witch must die by this Law, though he kill not, simply for the covenant made with Satan. For this must always be remembered, as a conclusion, that by Witches we understand not those only which kill and torment: but all Diviners, Charmers, Jugglers [illusionists], all Wizards, commonly called wise men and wise women; yea, whosoever does anything (knowing what they do).... All these come under this sentence of Moses, because they deny God, and are confederates with Satan. By the laws of England, the thief is executed for stealing, and we think it just and profitable: but it were a thousand times better for the land, if all Witches, but especially the blessing Witch [i.e., 'good witch'] might suffer death. For the thief by his stealing, and the hurtful Enchanter by charming, hinder and hurt bodies and goods of many, but these are the right hand of the devil, by which he takes and destroys the souls of men. Men commonly hate and spit at the damnifying Sorcerer, as unworthy to live among them; whereas the other is so dear unto them, that they hold themselves and their country blessed that have him among them, they fly unto him in their necessity, they depend upon him as their God, and by this means, thousands are carried away to their final confusion. Death, therefore, is the just and deserved portion of the good Witch.

123 Edward Coke, *The Abrogation of Infidel Laws* (1608)

Keywords: #Law, #Colonisation, #War, #Non-Christians, #Divine Law, #Natural Law, #Ten Commandments
Region: #England
Group: #Church of England | #Non-Christians

Edward Coke was one of the preeminent legal minds of the sixteenth and seventeenth centuries, and his writings are still important legal texts. He filled high-ranking legal positions under several English monarchs, but he was often in conflict with them over his defence of the prerogatives of Parliament and deference to ancient liberties. He was a drafter of the 1628 Petition of Right, a document that appealed to the *Magna Carta* and other historic precedents to assert that taxation required consent and that imprisonment required a cause. Moreover, it challenged the billeting of soldiers and the application of martial law. The following excerpt comes from 'Calvin's Case' (1608). This famous case considered the rights of subjects between different realms (a pressing topic after **James VI** of Scotland became **James I** of England). The case addressed the rights of the Scotland-born Robert Calvin in England, a case that would become important to discussions in the United States over citizenship by birthright. Coke used the occasion to discourse on what happens to 'infidel' laws when the lands of unbelievers are conquered by a Christian king: Do the laws of unbelievers (here termed 'infidels') have to be respected by Christian conquerors?

In this excerpt, Coke not only argued that it might be permissible for Christian princes to conquer the lands of both Christians and unbelievers, but also he argued that there was a perpetual state of war between believers and unbelievers. Further, he reasoned that the laws of unbelievers were inherently illegitimate and did not need to be respected by Christian conquerors. Coke also impacted the laws in colonial America through his influence on **Roger Williams,** who was the founder of Rhode Island. From a young age, Williams served as Coke's apprentice, a position that brought Williams into close proximity with many prominent persons in England. It is notable, however, that Williams became an early and eloquent defender of the rights of

442   *Sources*

American Indians, even those who remained unbelievers. **Jacobus Arminius**, writing around the same time, similarly argued that the laws and governments of unbelievers were legitimate, even though they would fall short of the standards of Christian godliness.[174]

Edward Coke, *The Reports of Sir Edward Coke*, New ed. (London: Joseph Buttersworth and Sons, 1826), IV:29–30.

———

Every man is either *alienigena*, an alien born, or *subditus*, a subject born. Every alien is either a friend that is in league, etc. or an enemy that is in open war, etc. Every alien enemy is either *pro tempore*, temporary for a time, or *perpetuus*, perpetual, or *specialiter permissus*, permitted especially. Every subject is either *natus*, born, or *datus*, given or made. [*He then discussed several relations between a foreigner and an enemy, leading to a discussion of unbelievers and their laws.*] All infidels are in law *perpetui inimici*, perpetual enemies (for the law presumes not that they will be converted, that being *remota potentia*, a remote possibility) for between them, as with the devils, whose subjects they be, and the Christian, there is perpetual hostility, and can be no peace; for as the Apostle said in 2 Corinthians 6:15 [that Christ and Belial cannot have concord]...

And upon this ground there is a diversity between a conquest of a kingdom of a Christian King, and the conquest of a kingdom of an infidel; for if a King come to a Christian kingdom by conquest, seeing that he hath *vitæ et necis potestatem* [power over life and death], he may at his pleasure alter and change the laws of that kingdom; but until he doth make an alteration of those laws the ancient laws of that kingdom remain. But if a Christian King should conquer a kingdom of an infidel, and bring them under his subjection, there *ipso facto* the laws of the infidel are abrogated, for that they be not only against Christianity, but against the law of God and of nature, contained in the Decalogue; and in that case, until certain laws be established amongst them, the King by himself, and such judges as he shall appoint, shall judge them and their causes according to natural equity, in such sort as Kings in ancient time did with their kingdoms, before any certain municipal laws were given, as before hath been said.

124 Hugo Grotius, *On the Freedom of the Seas* (1609)

Keywords: #Commerce, #International Relations, #Law, #Law of Nations, #Natural Law, #War, #Property, #Conscience, #Land, #Slavery
Region: #Netherlands | #Portugal, #Spain, #Asia, #Global
Group: #Reformed | #Roman Catholic, #Non-Christians

Hugo Grotius (1583–1645) was a Dutch-born humanist who was educated at the University of Leiden. Throughout his entire life, the Dutch struggled for independence from the Spanish crown (the Eighty Years' War, 1568–1648). During this rebellion, fierce internal disagreement arose over the nature of this independence, for example, over the role of the old nobility and the provinces' assemblies, as well as the issue of centralisation, and the role of religion. A reprieve in the war, the Twelve Years' Truce from 1609 to 1621, afforded the opportunity to address the Arminian Controversy within the Reformed community. Grotius sympathised with the Remonstrants and was a proponent of a more tolerant, less dogmatic faith. When the international Synod of Dort (1618–1619) rejected Arminian teachings about predestination and free will, he fled the United Provinces after a famous prison escape, and remained in exile for most of his life.[175]

Grotius is known for his articulation of the principles of international law, particularly the laws of the sea (*Mare liberum*, 1609) and his work on rights, natural law, sovereignty, and just war theory (***De iure belli ac pacis libri tres,*** 1625). The following excerpt comes from *Mare liberum* (Free Sea). He wrote it when Iberian powers claimed jurisdiction over most of the world, grounding their claims in the doctrine of discovery and in the donation of these lands by the pope. The Dutch challenged the authority of Spain, and Dutch Protestants did not accept papal authority. Grotius provided a Protestant rationale that undermined Iberian and Catholic claims to global hegemony and argued from natural law and the law of nations that the oceans could not be possessed. Notably, he forcefully argued that the theological error of non-Christians could not be used to justify land dispossession. The English Protestant jurist and Hebraist, John Selden (1584–1654), countered some of Grotius' claims in 1631 in *Mare Clausum* (Closed Sea), arguing that England owned the waters adjacent to its borders.

444 *Sources*

Grotius argued that the Dutch had a right to venture into the seas and that they should also think carefully about distant religions. He wrote *The Truth of the Christian Religion* (various iterations from 1622 to 1640) for sailors encountering a greater variety of 'religions', a term with an expanding semantic range that Grotius used to describe Christian and non-Christian beliefs. Sailors would meet

> *Pagans* as in *China* or *Guinae*; or *Mahometans*, as in the *Turkish* and *Persian* Empires, and in the Kingdoms of *Fez* and *Morocco*; and also with *Jews* who are the professed Enemies of Christianity, and are dispersed over the greater part of the world.

The book was an apology for the Christian faith and a missionary aid since Grotius argued that Christian sailors should use spiritual weapons to draw those who err towards the truth. He believed that Christianity was superior in its proximity to truth, but Christians also followed a loftier ethical code that did not permit injustice against theological outsiders. Grotius emphasised core tenets shared by Christians and defended the reliability of scripture in the face of non-Christian outsiders, and his book was relatively well received by Protestants and Catholics alike.[176] This work made 'the case for an ethics-based, nondogmatic, and unifying Christianity at home and abroad'.[177]

Hugo Grotius, *The Freedom of the Seas*, trans. Ralph van Deman Magoffin, ed. James Brown Scott (New York: Oxford University Press, 1916), 1–17.

———

To the Rulers and to the Free and Independent Nations of Christendom

The delusion is as old as it is detestable with which many men, especially those who by their wealth and power exercise the greatest influence, persuade themselves, or as I rather believe, try to persuade themselves, that justice and injustice are distinguished the one from the other not by their own nature, but in some fashion merely by the opinion and the custom of mankind. Those men therefore think that both the laws and the semblance of equity were devised for the sole purpose of repressing the dissensions and rebellions of those persons born in a subordinate position, affirming meanwhile that they themselves, being placed in a high position, ought to dispense all justice in accordance with their own good pleasure, and that their pleasure ought to be bounded only by their own view of what is expedient. This opinion, absurd and unnatural as it clearly is, has gained considerable currency; but this should by no means occasion surprise, inasmuch as there has to be taken into consideration not only the common frailty of the human race by which we pursue not only vices and their purveyors, but also the arts of flatterers, to whom power is always exposed.

Sources   445

But, on the other hand, there have stood forth in every age independent and wise and devout men able to root out this false doctrine from the minds of the simple, and to convict its advocates of shamelessness. For they showed that God was the founder and ruler of the universe, and especially that being the Father of all mankind, He had not separated human beings, as He had the rest of living things, into different species and various divisions, but had willed them to be of one race and to be known by one name; that furthermore He had given them the same origin, the same structural organism, the ability to look each other in the face, language too, and other means of communication, in order that they all might recognise their natural social bond and kinship. They showed too that He is the supreme Lord and Father of this family; and that for the household or the state which He had thus founded, He had drawn up certain laws not graven on tablets of bronze or stone but written in the minds and on the hearts of every individual, where even the unwilling and the refractory must read them. That these laws were binding on great and small alike; that kings have no more power against them than have the common people against the decrees of the magistrates, than have the magistrates against the edicts of the governors, than have the governors against the ordinances of the kings themselves; nay more, that those very laws themselves of each and every nation and city flow from that Divine source, and from that source receive their sanctity and their majesty.

Now, as there are some things which every man enjoys in common with all other men, and as there are other things which are distinctly his and belong to no one else, just so has nature willed that some of the things which she has created for the use of mankind remain common to all, and that others through the industry and labour of each man become his own. Laws moreover were given to cover both cases so that all men might use common property without prejudice to anyone else, and in respect to other things so that each man being content with what he himself owns might refrain from laying his hands on the property of others.

Now since no man can be ignorant of these facts unless he ceases to be a man, and since races blind to all truth except what they receive from the light of nature, have recognised their force, what, O Christian Kings and Nations, ought you to think, and what ought you to do?

If anyone thinks it hard that those things are demanded of him which the profession of a religion so sacred requires, the very least obligation of which is to refrain from injustice, certainly everyone can know what his own duty is from the very demands he makes of others. There is not one of you who does not openly proclaim that every man is entitled to manage and dispose of his own property; there is not one of you who does not insist that all citizens have equal and indiscriminate right to use rivers and public places; not one of you who does not defend with all his might the freedom of travel and of trade.

446   *Sources*

If it be thought that the small society which we call a state cannot exist without the application of these principles (and certainly it cannot), why will not those same principles be necessary to uphold the social structure of the whole human race and to maintain the harmony thereof? If any one rebels against these principles of law and order you are justly indignant, and you even decree punishments in proportion to the magnitude of the offence, for no other reason than that a government cannot be tranquil where trespasses of that sort are allowed. If king act unjustly and violently against king, and nation against nation, such action involves a disturbance of the peace of that universal state, and constitutes a trespass against the supreme Ruler, does it not? There is however this difference: just as the lesser magistrates judge the common people, and as you judge the magistrates, so the King of the universe has laid upon you the command to take cognisance of the trespasses of all other men, and to punish them; but He has reserved for Himself the punishment of your own trespasses. But although He reserves to himself the final punishment, slow and unseen but none the less inevitable, yet He appoints to intervene in human affairs two judges whom the luckiest of sinners does not escape, namely, Conscience, or the innate estimation of oneself, and Public Opinion, or the estimation of others. These two tribunals are open to those who are debarred from all others; to these the powerless appeal; in them are defeated those who are wont to win by might, those who put no bounds to their presumption, those who consider cheap anything bought at the price of human blood, those who defend injustice by injustice, men whose wickedness is so manifest that they must needs be condemned by the unanimous judgement of the good, and cannot be cleared before the bar of their own souls.

To this double tribunal we bring a new case. It is in very truth no petty case such as private citizens are wont to bring against their neighbours about dripping eaves or party walls; nor is it a case such as nations frequently bring against one another about boundary lines or the possession of a river or an island. No! It is a case which concerns practically the entire expanse of the high seas, the right of navigation, the freedom of trade! Between us and the Spaniards the following points are in dispute: Can the vast, the boundless sea be the appanage of one kingdom alone, and it not the greatest? Can any one nation have the right to prevent other nations which so desire, from selling to one another, from bartering with one another, actually from communicating with one another? Can any nation give away what it never owned, or discover what already belonged to someone else? Does a manifest injustice of long standing create a specific right?

In this controversy we appeal to those jurists among the Spanish themselves who are especially skilled both in divine and human law; we actually invoke the very laws of Spain itself. If that is of no avail, and those whom reason clearly convicts of wrong are induced by greed to maintain that stand, we invoke your majesty, ye Princes, your good faith, ye Peoples, whoever and wherever ye may be.

It is not an involved, it is not an intricate question that I am raising. It is not a question of ambiguous points of those of you who are our nearer neighbours has always been so far as we are concerned. Caution us, we will obey. Verily, if we have done any wrong in this our cause, we will not deprecate your wrath, nor even the hatred of the human race. But if we are right, we leave to your sense of righteousness and of fairness what you ought to think about this matter and what course of action you ought to pursue....

If today the custom held of considering that everything pertaining to mankind pertained also to one's self, we should surely live in a much more peaceable world. For the presumptuousness of many would abate, and those who now neglect justice on the pretext of expediency would unlearn the lesson of injustice at their own expense....

Chapter 1

By the Law of Nations navigation is free to all persons whatsoever

My intention is to demonstrate briefly and clearly that the Dutch – that is to say, the subjects of the United Netherlands – have the right to sail to the East Indies, as they are now doing, and to engage in trade with the people there. I shall base my argument on the following most specific and unimpeachable axiom of the Law of Nations, called a primary rule or first principle, the spirit of which is self-evident and immutable, to wit: Every nation is free to travel to every other nation, and to trade with it.

God Himself says this speaking through the voice of nature; and inasmuch as it is not His will to have Nature supply every place with all the necessaries of life, He ordains that some nations excel in one art and others in another. Why is this His will, except it be that He wished human friendships to be engendered by mutual needs and resources, lest individuals deeming themselves entirely sufficient unto themselves should for that very reason be rendered unsociable? So by the decree of divine justice it was brought about that one people should supply the needs of another.... Those therefore who deny this law, destroy this most praiseworthy bond of human fellowship, remove the opportunities for doing mutual service, in a word do violence to Nature herself. For do not the ocean, navigable in every direction with which God has encompassed all the earth, and the regular and the occasional winds which blow now from one quarter and now from another, offer sufficient proof that Nature has given to all peoples a right of access to all other peoples?...

Again, [Francisco de] Victoria holds that the Spaniards could have shown just reasons for making war upon the Aztecs and the Indians in America, more plausible reasons certainly than were alleged, if they really were prevented from traveling or sojourning among those peoples, and were denied the right to share in those things which by the Law of Nations or by Custom are common to all, and finally if they were debarred from trade.

We read of a similar case in the history of Moses [Num. 21:21–26], which we find mentioned also in the writings of Augustine, where the Israelites

448 *Sources*

justly smote with the edge of the sword the Amorites because they had denied the Israelites an innocent passage through their territory, a right which according to the Law of Human Society ought in all justice to have been allowed.... When in days gone by the Christians made crusades against the Saracens, no other pretext was so welcome or so plausible as that they were denied by the infidels free access to the Holy Land.

It follows therefore that the Portuguese, even if they had been sovereigns in those parts to which the Dutch make voyages, would nevertheless be doing them an injury if they should forbid them access to those places and from trading there.

Is it not then an incalculably greater injury for nations which desire reciprocal commercial relations to be debarred therefrom by the acts of those who are sovereigns neither of the nations interested, nor of the element over which their connecting high road runs? Is not that the very cause which for the most part prompts us to execrate robbers and pirates, namely, that they beset and infest our trade routes?

Chapter 2

The Portuguese have no right by title of discovery to sovereignty over the East Indies to which the Dutch make voyages

The Portuguese are not sovereigns of those parts of the East Indies to which the Dutch sail, that is to say, Java, Ceylon, and many of the Moluccas. This I prove by the incontrovertible argument that no one is sovereign of a thing which he himself has never possessed, and which no one else has ever held in his name. These islands of which we speak, now have and always have had their own kings, their own government, their own laws, and their own legal systems. The inhabitants allow the Portuguese to trade with them, just as they allow other nations the same privilege. Therefore, inasmuch as the Portuguese pay tolls, and obtain leave to trade from the rulers there, they thereby give sufficient proof that they do not go there as sovereigns but as foreigners. Indeed they only reside there on sufferance. And although the title to sovereignty is not sufficient, inasmuch as possession is a prerequisite – for having a thing is quite different from having the right to acquire it – nevertheless I affirm that in those places the Portuguese have no title at all to sovereignty which is not denied them by the opinion of learned men, even of the Spaniards.

First of all, if they say that those lands have come under their jurisdiction as the reward of discovery, THEY LIE, both in law and in fact. For to discover a thing is not only to seize it with the eyes but to take real possession thereof.... No such claim can be established in the present case, because the Portuguese maintain no garrisons in those regions. Neither can the Portuguese by any possible means claim to have discovered India, a country which was famous centuries and centuries ago!

But in addition to all this, discovery *per se* gives no legal rights over things unless before the alleged discovery they were *res nullius* [no one's property]. Now these Indians of the East, on the arrival of the Portuguese, although some of them were idolators, and some Mohammedans, and therefore sunk in grievous sin, had none the less perfect public and private ownership of their goods and possessions, from which they could not be dispossessed without just cause. The Spanish writer Victoria, following other writers of the highest authority, has the most certain warrant for his conclusion that Christians, whether of the laity or of the clergy, cannot deprive infidels of their civil power and sovereignty merely on the ground that they are infidels, unless some other wrong has been done by them.

For religious belief, as Thomas Aquinas rightly observes, does not do away with either natural or human law from which sovereignty is derived. Surely it is a heresy to believe that infidels are not masters of their own property; consequently, to take from them their possessions on account of their religious belief is no less theft and robbery than it would be in the case of Christians.

Victoria then is right in saying that the Spaniards have no more legal right over the East Indians because of their religion, than the East Indians would have had over the Spaniards if they had happened to be the first foreigners to come to Spain. Nor are the East Indians stupid and unthinking; on the contrary they are intelligent and shrewd, so that a pretext for subduing them on the ground of their character could not be sustained. Such a pretext on its very face is an injustice. Plutarch said long ago that it was greed that furnished the pretext for conquering barbarous countries, and it is not unsuspected that greedy longing for the property of another often hid itself behind a pretext of civilising barbarians. And now that well-known pretext of forcing nations into a higher state of civilisation against their will, the pretext once monopolised by the Greeks and by Alexander the Great, is considered by all theologians, especially those of Spain, to be unjust and unholy.

Chapter III

The Portuguese have no right of sovereignty over the East Indies by virtue of title based on the Papal Donation

Next, if the partition made by the Pope Alexander VI is to be used by the Portuguese as authority for jurisdiction in the East Indies, then before all things else two points must be taken into consideration.

First, did the Pope merely desire to settle the disputes between the Portuguese and the Spaniards?

This was clearly within his power, inasmuch as he had been chosen to arbitrate between them, and in fact the kings of both countries had previously concluded certain treaties with each other on this very matter. Now if this be the case, seeing that the question concerns only the Portuguese and

450 *Sources*

Spaniards, the decision of the Pope will of course not affect the other peoples of the world.

Second, did the Pope intend to give to two nations, each one third of the whole world?

But even if the Pope had intended and had had the power to make such a gift, still it would not have made the Portuguese sovereigns of those places. For it is not a donation that makes a sovereign, it is the consequent delivery of a thing and the subsequent possession thereof. Now, if any one will scrutinise either divine or human law, not merely with a view to his own interests, he will easily apprehend that a donation of this kind, dealing with the property of others, is of no effect. I shall not enter here upon any discussion as to the power of the Pope, that is the Bishop of the Roman Church, nor shall I advance anything but a hypothesis which is accepted by men of the greatest erudition, who lay the greatest stress on the power of the Pope, especially the Spaniards, who with their perspicacity easily see that our Lord Jesus Christ when he said 'My kingdom is not of this world' [John 18:36] thereby renounced all earthly power, and that while He was on earth as a man, He certainly did not have dominion over the whole world, and if He had had such dominion, still by no arguments could such a right be transferred to Peter, or be transmitted to the Roman Church by authority of the 'Vicar of Christ'; indeed, inasmuch as Christ had many things to which the Pope did not succeed, it has been boldly affirmed – and I shall use the very words of the writers – that the Pope is neither civil nor temporal Lord of the whole world. On the contrary, even if the Pope did have any such power on earth, still he would not be right in using it, because he ought to be satisfied with his own spiritual jurisdiction, and be utterly unable to grant that power to temporal princes. So then, if the Pope has any power at all, he has it, as they say, in the spiritual realm only. Therefore he has no authority over infidel nations, for they do not belong to the Church.

It follows therefore according to the opinions of Cajetan and Victoria and the more authoritative of the Theologians and writers on Canon Law, that there is no clear title against the East Indians, based either on the ground that the Pope made an absolute grant of those provinces as if he were their sovereign, or on the pretext that the East Indians do not recognise his sovereignty. Indeed, and in truth, it may be affirmed that no such pretext as that was ever invoked to despoil even the Saracens.

[*The remaining chapters undermine Iberian claims to sovereignty of the seas based on war, occupation, papal donation or custom. He asserts, on the basis of the law of nations, the right of all to trade on the seas. Thus, the Dutch can circumvent Iberian claims, peacefully trade, make treaties with the peoples of the East Indies and defend their right to trade by war if necessary.*]

125 Jacobus Arminius, *On Magistracy* (1603–1609)

Keywords: #Authority, #Government, #Church-State Relations, #Obedience, #Ten Commandments
Region: #Netherlands
Group: #Dutch Reformed, #Arminian

Jacobus Arminius (1559–1609) was a Dutch theologian and minister who tested the bounds of Reformed orthodoxy, culminating in the Arminian controversy. He studied at the universities of Leiden, Geneva, and Padua before ministering at a Reformed Church in Amsterdam from 1588. From 1603, he taught at the University of Leiden. He courted controversy for his theological views already while in Geneva, but the theology he espoused from the pulpit in Amsterdam brought him notoriety. In particular, other Reformed ministers took issue with his understanding of sin, predestination, and free will, accusing him of Pelagianism and Socinianism. His colleague, Franciscus Gomarus, emerged as a vocal opponent. Shortly before his death, Arminius formulated a 'Declaration of Sentiments', which his successor, Johannes Uytenbogaert, used to formulate the Remonstrant position that was debated at the Synod of Dort (1618–1619). The Synod decided against Arminius' positions, for both theological and geopolitical reasons. The following source comes from a disputation held while he taught at Leiden (1603–1609). Arminius describes the purpose of Christian Government and the subordination of the church to the state.[178]

Jacobus Arminius, *The Works of James Arminius*, trans. James Nichols (Auburn: Derby, Miller and Orton, 1853) I:663–669.

———

452   *Sources*

Disputation 25: On Magistracy

Respondent, John Le Chantre

II   We therefore define magistracy, in the abstract, as a power pre-eminent and administrative, or a function with a pre-eminent power, instituted and preserved by God for this purpose, that men may, in the society of their fellow-men, 'lead a quiet and peaceable life, in all godliness and honesty', in true piety and righteousness, for their own salvation and to the glory of God (Rom. 13:1–3; 1 Tim. 2:2; 1 Pet. 2:13; Prov. 29:4; Psalm 62; Isa. 45:22–23)....

V   The end of the institution of magistracy, is the good of the whole, and of each individual of which it is composed, both an *animal* [or natural] good, 'that they may lead quiet and peaceable lives' (1 Tim. 2:2); and a *spiritual* good, that they may live in this world, to God, and may in heaven enjoy that good, to the glory of God who is its author (Rom. 13:4). For since man, according to his two-fold life (that is, the animal and the spiritual) stands in need of each kind of good (Num. 11:12–13) and is, by nature of the image of God, capable of both kinds (Gen. 1:26; Col. 3:10); since two collateral powers cannot stand (Matt. 6:24; 1 Cor. 14:33) and since animal good is directed to that which is spiritual (Matt. 6:33) and animal life is subordinate to that which is spiritual (Gal. 2:20; 1 Cor. 15:32), it is unlawful to divide those two benefits, and to separate their joint superintendence, either in reality or by the administration of the supreme authority; for, if the animal life and its good becomes the only objects of solicitude, such an administration is that of cattle. But if human society be brought to such a condition that the spiritual life, only, prevails, then this power [of magistracy] is no longer necessary. (1 Cor. 15:24.)

VI   The matter, of which this administration consists, are the acts necessary to produce that end. These actions, we comprehend in the three following classes: (1) The first is Legislation, under which we also comprise the care of the moral law, according to both tables, and the enacting of subordinate laws with respect to places, times and persons, by which laws, provision may be the better made for the observance of that immovable law, and the various societies, being restricted to certain relations, may be the more correctly governed; that is, ecclesiastical, civil, scholastic and domestic associations (Exod. 18:18–20; 2 Chron. 19:6–8; 2 Kings 13:4–5). (2) The second contains the vocation to delegated offices or duties, and the oversight of all actions and things which are necessary to the whole society (Deut. 1:13, 15–16; Exod. 18:21–22; 1 Pet. 2:14; 2 Chron. 19:2, 8–11; Num. 11:13–17). (3) The third is either the eradication of all evils out of the society, if they be internal, or the warding of them off, if they be external, even with war, if that be necessary, and the safety of society should require it (Prov. 20:26, 28; Ps. 101:8; 1 Tim. 2:2).

Sources   453

VII   The form is the power itself, according to which these functions them-selves are discharged, with an authority that is subject to God alone, and pre-eminently above whatever is human; (Rom. 13:1; Ps. 82:1, 6; Lam. 4:20) for this inspires spirit and life, and gives efficacy to these functions. It is enunciated 'power by right of the sword', by which the good may be defended, and the bad terrified, restrained and punished, and all men compelled to perform their prescribed duties (Rom. 13:4–5). To this power, as supreme, belongs the authority of demanding, from those under subjection, tribute, custom, and other burdens. These resemble the sinews, by which the authority and power necessary for these functions, are held together and established (Rom. 13:6)....

VIII   [*He argues that this power did not originate with the entrance of sin into the world, and indeed predated it.*]

IX   But this power is always the same according to the nature of its function and the prerogative of its authority; and it suffers no variation, either from the difference in number of those to whom this power is confided in a monarchy, an aristocracy, or a democracy, or from the difference of the manner in which this power is given, whether it be derived imme-diately from God, or it be obtained by human right and custom through succession, inheritance and election. Under all these circumstances, it remains the same, unless a limitation, restricted to certain conditions, be added by God, or by those who possess the right of conferring such a power (1 Tim. 2:2; 1 Pet. 2:13; Judg. 20; 1 Sam. 16:12; 2 Sam. 1; 1 Kgs 11:11–12; 14:8–10). And this limitation is equally binding on both parties; nor is it lawful for him who has accepted of this authority, by rescinding the conditions, to assume a greater power to himself, under the pretext that those conditions are opposed to his conscience or to his condition, and that they are even injurious to the society itself.

X   Since the end of this power is the good of the whole, or of the entire association of men, who belong to the same country or state, it fol-lows that the prince of this state is less than the state itself, and that its benefit is not only to be preferred to his own, but that it is also to be purchased with his detriment, nay, at the expense of life itself (Ezek. 34:2–4; 1 Sam. 12:2–3; 8:20). Though, in return, every member of the state is bound to defend, with all his powers, yet in a lawful manner, the life, safety and dignity of the prince, as the father of his country (2 Sam. 16:3).

XI   From the circumstance, also, of this power having been instituted by God and restricted within certain laws, we conclude that it is not lawful for him who possesses it, to lift up himself against God, to enact laws contrary to the divine laws, and either to compel the people who are committed to his care to the perpetration of acts which are forbidden by God, or to prevent them from performing such acts as he has com-manded. If he acts thus, let him assuredly know, that he must render an account to God, and that the people are bound to obey the Almighty

454   *Sources*

in preference to him (Deut. 17:18–19; 1 Kgs 12:28–30; 13:2; 22:5). Yet, on this point, the people ought to observe two cautions: (1) To distinguish actions which are to be performed, from burdens which are to be borne. (2) To be perfectly sure that the orders of the prince are in opposition to the divine commands. Without a due observance of these cautions, they will, by a precipitate judgement, commit an act of disobedience against the prince, to whom, in that matter, they are able, in an orderly manner, under God, to be obedient.

XII   The functions which we have described as essential to this power, are not subject to the arbitrary will of the prince, whether he may neglect either the whole of them, or one of the three. If he act thus, he renders himself unworthy of the name of 'prince;' and it would be a better course for him to resign the dignity of his office, than to be a trifling loiterer in the discharge of its functions (Ps. 82:1–8; Ezek. 11:1–13). But here, also, a two-fold distinction must be used: (1) Between a degree of idleness accruing from the function, and vice coming into it. (2) Between loitering, and hindering these duties from being performed in the commonwealth; for the latter of these faults (hindrance) would bring speedy destruction to the society, while the commonwealth can consist with the former, (laziness,) provided other persons be permitted to perform those duties.

XIII   We conclude further, from the author of the institution from the end and the use of the office – from the functions which pertain to it, and from the pre-eminent power itself, when they are all compared with the nature of Christianity, that a Christian man can, with a good conscience, accept of the office and perform the duties of magistracy; nay, that no one is more suitable than he for discharging the duties of this office, and, which is still more, that no person can legitimately and perfectly fulfil all its duties except a Christian. Yet, by this affirmation, we do not mean to deny that a legitimate magistracy exists among other nations than those which are Christian (Acts 10:31, 48; Exod. 18:20–23).

XIV   Lastly. Because this power is pre-eminent, we assert that every soul is subject to it by divine right, whether he be a layman or a clergyman, a deacon, priest, or bishop, an archbishop, cardinal, or patriarch, or even the Roman pontiff himself; so that it is the duty of every one to obey the commands of the magistrate, to acknowledge his tribunal, to await the sentence, and to submit to the punishment which he may award. From such obedience and subjection the prince himself cannot grant any man immunity and exemption; although in apportioning those burdens which are to be borne, he can yield his prerogative to some persons (Rom. 13:1, 5; 1 Pet. 2:13; 5:1; John 19:10–11; Acts 25:1, 10; 1 Kgs 1:26–27).

126 James I, *Speech on Divine Right Kingship* (1609)

Keywords: #Authority, #Submission, #Absolutism
Region: #England
Group: #Church of England | #Puritan

James VI of Scotland was tutored by Presbyterians who believed that monarchy was limited by law and subordinated to the church. He pushed back against this teaching as he matured and eventually countered these arguments in print. For example, in *The True Law of Free Monarchies* (1598) and *Basilikon Doron* (1598), he insisted that the right to rule derived from God directly, and therefore, monarchs were only accountable to God. *The True Law* responded to Reformed theorists, like his tutor **George Buchanan**, who advocated for limited powers and the possibility of legitimate resistance. He wrote *Basilikon Doron* for his son as a manual for kingship. When he ascended England's throne in 1603 as James I, many Reformers in England were worried about the implications of his treatises. After a Catholic attempted to blow up the king and Parliament (the 1605 Gunpowder Plot), James required that Catholic subjects swear an 'Oath of Allegiance' that declared the supreme authority of the king and abjured the authority of the pope. The following selection comes from a 1609 speech James VI and I made to the Lords and Commons. In it, he compared himself at length with God, and from this elevated position, he advised Parliament to observe the limits of their authority.[179]

James I, "A Speech to the Lords and Commons of the Parliament at White-Hall" (21 March 1609), in *Readings in European History*, ed. James Harvey Robinson (Boston, MA: Ginn & Company, 1906), II:218–221.

———

The state of monarchy is the supremest thing upon earth; for kings are not only God's lieutenants upon earth, and sit upon God's throne, but even by God himself they are called gods. There be three principal similitudes that illustrate the state of monarchy: one taken out of the word of God; and the two other out of the grounds of policy and philosophy. In the Scriptures

456 *Sources*

kings are called gods [Ps. 82:1], and so their power after a certain relation compared to the divine power. Kings are also compared to fathers of families; for a king is truly *parens patriae*, the political father of his people. And lastly, kings are compared to the head of this microcosm of the body of man.

Kings are justly called gods, for that they exercise a manner or resemblance of divine power upon earth; for if you will consider the attributes to God, you shall see how to give a plausible answer; for it is an undutiful part in subjects to press their king, wherein they know beforehand he will refuse them.

127 Lubbert Gerritsz and Hans de Ries, *Mennonite Confession of Faith* (c.1610)

Keywords: #Confession of Faith, #War, #Non-Violence, #Authority, #Government
Region: #Netherlands
Group: #Mennonite, #Anabaptist

The apocalyptic violence of the **Münster commune** cast a long shadow over the radical Reformation. For centuries, Mennonites and those drawn to the more radical end of the Reformation had to counter the charge that their pacificism veiled subversive tendencies and even a lust for dominion. The following source is one of the earliest Mennonite confessions defending the rejection of violence, penned by Lubbert Gerritsz (d.1612) and Hans de Ries (1553–1638). Their argument was based on an association of violence with biblical Israel and a reliance on the New Testament. The document, also known as the *Waterland Confession*, was intended to effect unity within the Mennonite community in Holland, and, indeed, with like-minded Christians from around Europe. The unity brought about by the confession did not last long and barely survived the death of Lubbert, and the Waterlanders soon united with the congregation of the exiled Englishman, **John Smyth** (Brownists).[180]

John de Rys and Lubbert Gerrits, "A Brief Confession of the Principal Articles of the Christian Faith", in *Baptist Confessions of Faith*, ed. William Joseph McGlothlin (Philadelphia, PA: American Baptist Publication Society, 1911), 31, 45–46.

———

A Brief Confession of the Principal Articles of the Christian Faith

Prepared by John de Rys and Lubbert Gerrits, Ministers of
the Divine Word among the Protestants who, in the
Belgian Confederacy, are called Mennonites.

458 *Sources*

Article 10

Of the Abrogation of the Law and Legal Things

The intolerable burden of the Mosaic law (Acts 15:10; 2 Cor. 3:11, 14), with all its shadows and types, was brought to an end in Christ (Col. 2:16–17) and removed from the midst of his people; namely, the sacerdotal office (Heb. 8:4–5; 10:1) together with temple, altar, sacrifices and whatever was typically connected with the sacerdotal office; and then the royal office (Luke 1:28–29; John 18:33; Matt. 20:25–27; Mark 10:43–45) and whatever adhered to that office, as kingdom (Isa. 2:4; Mic. 4:3), sword (Matt. 5:38), punishment agreeable to the law (Zech. 9:10), war, and, in one word, all that which typically looked to Christ's person, function or office and was a shadow and figure of him.

Article 37

Of the Office of Civil Magistrate

Government or the civil Magistrate is a necessary ordinance of God (Rom. 13:1–6), instituted for the government of common human society and the preservation of natural life and civil good, for the defence of the good and the punishment of evil. We acknowledge, the word of God obliging us, that it is our duty to reverence magistracy (Tit. 3:1; 1 Pet. 2:13, 17) and to show to it honour and obedience in all things which are not contrary to the word of God (Acts 4:19). It is our duty to pray to the omnipotent God for them (Jer. 29:7; 1 Tim. 2:1–2), and to give thanks to him for good and just magistrates and without murmuring to pay just tribute and customs (Matt. 22:17; Rom. 13:7). This civil government the Lord Jesus did not institute in his spiritual kingdom, the church of the New Testament, nor did he join it to the offices of his church (1 Cor. 12:28; Eph. 4:11): nor did he call his disciples or followers to royal, ducal or other power; nor did he teach that they should seize it and rule in a lordly manner; much less did he give to the members of his church the law (Matt. 20:25–28; Luke 22:25–27), agreeable to such office or dominion: but everywhere they are called away from it – which voice heard from heaven (Matt. 17:5) ought to be heeded – to the imitation of his harmless life (John 8:12; 10:27) and his footsteps bearing the cross (Heb. 12:2–3; 1 Pet. 2:21–23), and in which nothing is less in evidence than an earthly kingdom, power and sword. When all these things are carefully weighed (and moreover not a few things are joined with the office of civil magistracy, as waging war, depriving enemies of goods and life, etc., which [do not agree with] the lives of Christians who ought to be dead to the world), they agree either badly or plainly not at all, hence we withdraw ourselves from such offices and administrations. And yet we do not wish that just and moderate power should in any manner be despised or condemned, but that it should be truly esteemed, as in the words of Paul (Rom. 13:1–3), the Holy Spirit dictating, it ought to be esteemed.

128 Thomas Helwys, *A Call for Toleration* (1611–1612)

Keywords: #Magistrate, #Authority, #Toleration, #Church-State Relations, #Heresy, #Confession of Faith
Region: #Netherlands, #England
Group: #Baptist, #Mennonite | #Roman Catholic, #Judaism, #Islam, #Non-Christians

Thomas Helwys (c.1550–c.1616) was born to a gentry family, trained in law, and entered the Honourable Society of Gray's Inn in 1593. His theological convictions evolved such that he separated from the Church of England and joined a separatist congregation in Holland. He was rebaptised in 1609 and then connected with Mennonites. He believed there was still a role for a godly magistrate, a position that would have put him in opposition to some Anabaptists on the continent. The *Declaration of Faith* (1611) – of which sections 24 and 25 are reproduced below – was published in the context of rising tensions with separatists who were led by **John Smyth**.[181] Helwys' writings were deeply influenced by his ideas about the end times. A second excerpt is taken from the *Mystery of Iniquity* (1612), in which he critiqued King James I's usurpation of religious authority. He made an early appeal for toleration, reflecting on church-state relations and the treatment of heretics, unbelievers, and Jewish communities. Although he forcefully argued that Jewish persons should not be persecuted for their rejection of Christ, his arguments were still decidedly anti-Jewish.[182]

[Thomas Helwys], *A Declaration [of] Faith of Englis[h] People Remaining at Amsterdam in Holland* [Amsterdam], 1611; Thomas Helwys, *A Shorte Declaration of the Mistery of Iniquity* (Amsterdam, 1612), 66–79. Text modernised by the editors.

———

460   *Sources*

[Confession of Faith, 1611]

24.

That Magistracy is a Holy ordinance of God, that every soul ought to be subject to it not for fear only, but for the sake of conscience. Magistrates are the ministers of God for our wealth [good], they do not bear the sword in vain. They are the ministers of God to take vengeance on them that do evil (Rom. 13). That it is a fearful sin to speak evil of them that are in authority or to despise Government (2 Pet. 2:10). We ought to pay tribute, custom and all other duties. That we are to pray for them, for God would have them saved and come to the knowledge of his truth (1 Tim. 2:1–4). And therefore, they may be members of the Church of Christ, retaining their Magistracy, for no Holy Ordinance of God debars any from being a member of Christ's Church. They bear the sword of God, which sword in all Lawful administrations is to be defended and supported by the servants of God that are under their Government with their lives and all that they have in accordance with the first Institution of that Holy Ordinance. And whosoever holds otherwise must hold (if they understand themselves) that they are the ministers of the devil, and therefore are not to be prayed for nor approved in any of their administrations, seeing all things they do (such as punishing offenders and defending their countries, state, and persons by the sword) are unlawful.

25.

That it is Lawful in a just cause for the deciding of strife to take an oath by the Name of the Lord (Heb. 6:16; 2 Cor. 1:23; Phil. 1:8).

[Plea for Toleration, 1612]

And now we beseech the Creator of hearts to give our lord the King [James VI and I] a new heart to consider all the exalted abomination of desolation [Dan. 12:11] executed and practiced by this Hierarchy of Arch Bishops and Lord Bishops. Let our lord the King know that it concerns the King to consider the matter because these cruelties are executed by the King's power. In this way, unrighteous ecclesiastical authorities make our lord the King guilty of all the imprisonment, banishment and persecution, which by the King's power, they impose upon all the faithful subjects of the King who withstand their abominations [*Helwys then discusses the supposed kingly prerogative to appoint bishops and how the bishops draw the king away from the truth. This leads to a critique of Roman Catholicism and a defence of the ability of Roman Catholics to be good subjects.*]

We still pray our lord the King that we may be free from suspicion for having any thoughts of provoking evil against those who are of the Romish religion on account of their profession of faith; if they are true and faithful subjects to the King. Our lord the King has no more power over their

Sources 461

consciences then over ours (in other words, he has no power at all): for our lord the King is but an earthly King and he has no authority as a King but in earthly causes. If the King's people are obedient and true subjects, obeying all human laws made by the King, our lord the King can require no more: for men's religion is between God and themselves (the King shall not be accountable for their faith, neither may the King judge between God and man). Let them be heretics, Turks, Jews, etc., it is not the role of the earthly power to punish them in the least measure. This is made evident to our lord the King by the scriptures.

[*If legitimate authority had a right to demand religious obedience, he argues, then Jesus himself would have had to acquiesce in matters of religion.*]

Then let our lord the King judge by what warrant from God's word the King claims spiritual power and sets up a Hierarchy of Arch Bishop and Lord Bishop and gives authority to them to make laws and Canons of Religion, granting them power to compel men unto the obedience thereof; by such severe measure they have taken....

Here may our lord the King see a true pattern of how the people of God are persecuted when the Civil power judged their faith. [*It might be objected that unbelieving rulers persecuted Christians and have no right to decide matters of religion, but Christian rulers do have this right.*] However, if the king professes to be a disciple of Christ, that gives the King no power to imprison, banish or execute. Those powers belong only to his earthly Kingdom: for Christ and the Apostles had no such power given them. They did not teach anyone to take upon themselves any such power, or to execute that power against those contrary-minded. Rather they were taught *to instruct with meekness*, and by preaching the word to seek conversion, with all long-suffering, and not to destroy by severe punishments. Truly, the disciples of Christ must wait and labour for *the grafting in again of the Jews*, according to the prophecies of the scriptures (Rom. 11:24–27). Therefore the King knows they may not be destroyed, even though they are the greatest enemies of Christ upon the earth, and have in the past and still do cast the greatest reproach and contempt upon Christ with words that are most dreadful to utter. Even so, the disciples of Christ must wait for their conversion and not work their destruction. And let our lord the King call to mind, how the Apostle Paul teaches all the disciples of Christ act towards infidels (Rom. 1:14–15) where he says: *I am debtor both to the Grecian and to the Barbarian both to the wise and to the unwise.* And the same Apostle (1 Cor. 9:20–22) said: *To the Jews I become as a Jew....* All these instructions and directions are given for our lord the King to direct the King in how he should act in holiness and all meekness before his people so as to win them to Christ. He is not to set up a Cruel Hierarchy to make havoc of the King's people (as Saul did), pulling men and women out of their houses: casting them into prisons: forcing them to flee the land, and persecuting them with all cruelty....

462 *Sources*

Therefore our lord the King, cannot as a King, have any power over this kingdom, Temple, Tabernacle, house and People of God with respect to the Religion of God because our lord the King's kingdom is an earthly kingdom. Our lord the King is only owed earthly obedience, service and duty (which ought to suffice any earthly man). May the God of all Grace give our lord the King a gracious heart so that he is fully satisfied and contented with that great honour, power and dignity that belongs unto the King and to give glory and honour to God for it, that it may go well with the King and his posterity forever. May the God of heaven deliver the King from all such enchanters of Egypt who try to persuade the King to take upon himself the power of the Kings of Israel over the Church of Christ, only for the setting up and supporting of their *High Priesthood* with *Urim and Thummim*, with *Pompe and power* and with the *Levitical revenues of Israel* – things they hold as appertaining to Kings, forcing the King's people by cruelty to obey them, as if these people were in sole possession of the oracles of God.

129 Virginia Colony, *Laws Divine, Moral and Martial* (1612)

Keywords: #Colonisation, #Morality, #Blasphemy, #Sexuality, #Trade, #Violence
Region: #United States
Group: #Church of England | #Indigenous American

The English had a long history of venturing into the Atlantic that predated the voyages of Christopher Columbus. However, for a long time, such endeavours mostly involved trading and fishing, as well as piracy in Iberian-claimed waters. During the reign of **Elizabeth I, Richard Hakluyt** argued that the crown should take an active role in establishing colonies. The crown placed its imprimatur on patents to settle colonies, but these were initially established by private corporations. In 1606, **James VI and I** granted a charter for the colony of Virginia, which stretched across much of the eastern seaboard of what is now the United States. The living conditions in this colony were often dire as a result of economic instability, the spread of new diseases, and external threats. The colony at Jamestown barely survived, and its leaders desperately tried to enforce religious conformity to ward off the wrath of God. One of their measures was a strict enforcement of moral codes that aimed at raising the standard of behaviour.

The *Lawes Divine, Morall and Martiall* (known as 'Dale's Code') are excerpted below. This code included additions to previous laws made by Sir Thomas Dale, one of the leaders of the colony. The codes are notable for many reasons. First, they are often compared with the later laws in the 'Puritan' colonies of New England. However, Virginia legislated a more thorough union of church and state, as well as far more draconian punishments for religious crimes than were ever passed or practised in Puritan New England. Second, the laws aimed to protect Indigenous Algonquians from being assaulted or unfairly treated economically. They also made it a capital offence to rape any woman – English or Algonquian. Further, the oft-repeated threats of whippings and punishments for religious infractions reveal how difficult it was to bring the people into religious conformity within colonial Virginia.[183]

464 *Sources*

FOR The Colony in Virginea BRITANNIA. Lawes Divine, Morall and Martiall, &c. (London: Walter Burre, 1612), 1–19. Text modernised by the editors.

———

1 Since we owe our highest and supreme duty, our greatest, and all our allegiance to him from whom all power and authority is derived and flows as from the first and only fountain, and being special soldiers pressed in this sacred cause, we must only expect our success from him, who alone is the blesser of all good attempts, the King of kings, the commander of commanders, and Lord of Hosts. I do strictly command and charge all Captains and Officers, of whatever quality or nature...to take care that the Almighty God is duly and daily served and that they call upon their people to hear Sermons, as that also they diligently frequent Morning and Evening prayer themselves and by their own example of life and duty herein, encouraging others thereunto, and that such who shall often and wilfully absent themselves, be duly punished according to the martial law in that case provided.

2 That no man speak impiously or maliciously against the holy and blessed Trinity, or any of the three persons...or against the known Articles of the Christian faith, upon pain of death.

3 That no man blaspheme God's holy name upon pain of death....

4 No man shall use any traitorous words against His Majesty's Person or royal authority upon pain of death.

5 No man shall speak any word, or do any act, which may tend to the derision or despising of God's holy word upon pain of death: Nor shall any man unworthily act towards any Preacher or Minister of the same, but generally hold them in all reverent regard...otherwise the offender shall be openly whipped three times and ask public forgiveness in the assembly of the congregation over the course of three Sabbath days.

6 Twice a working day, every man and woman, upon the first tolling of the Bell, shall go to the Church to hear divine Service upon pain of losing his or her day's allowance for the first omission, for the second to be whipped, and for the third to be condemned to the Galleys for six Months. Likewise, no man or woman shall dare to violate or break the Sabbath by any gaming – public or private, abroad or at home – but duly sanctify and observe the Sabbath.... On that day, every man and woman shall go in the morning to the divine service... and in the afternoon to divine service and Catechising, upon pain for the first fault to lose their provision and allowance for the whole week following, for the second to lose the said allowance and also to be whipped, and for the third to suffer death.

Sources   465

7   [*On the duties of ministers to preach and diligently and attentively care for their people.*]

9   No man shall commit the horrible and detestable sins of Sodomy upon pain of death; and he or she that can be lawfully convicted of Adultery shall be punished with death. No man shall ravish or force any woman, maid or Indian, or other, upon pain of death, and let it be known that he or she that shall commit fornication (upon evident proof), for their first fault they shall be whipped, for their second they shall be whipped, and for their third they shall be whipped three times a week for one month and made to ask public forgiveness in the Assembly of the Congregation.

10   [*Law against stealing from the church or violating in some way things devoted to worship.*]

11   He that shall falsely take an oath or bear false witness in any cause, or against any man whatsoever, shall be punished with death.

12–13   [*Laws against slandering magistrates and other persons in authority, their judgements or their published declarations, grounding these stipulations in sacred writ.*]

14   No man shall give any disgraceful words or commit any act to the disgrace of any person in this Colony, or any part thereof, upon pain of being tied head and feet together, upon the guard every night for the space of one month, and he shall be publicly disgraced himself and be made incapable ever after to possess any place or execute any office in this employment.

15   No man of any condition shall barter, truck, or trade with the Indians, except he is thereunto appointed by lawful authority, upon pain of death.

16   No man shall rifle or despoil, by force or violence, take away anything from any Indian coming to trade, or otherwise, upon pain of death.

17–28   [*More economic sanctions related to merchants, inheritors, farmers, overseers and soldiers, with very grave penalties.*]

29   No man or woman (upon pain of death) shall run away from the Colony to Powhatan or any savage Weroance whatsoever [i.e., Indigenous Algonquians near the colony].

30–32   [*Further laws concerning obedience to authority, theft and exploration.*]

33   [*The minister is to warmly and lovingly encourage the people to visit him, recount their faith, and receive personal religious instruction, and the people had a duty to comply.*] If they shall refuse to go unto him…the Governor shall cause the offender for his first time of refusal to be whipped, for the second time to be whipped twice, and to acknowledge his fault upon the Sabbath day in the assembly of the congregation, and for the third time to be whipped every day until he has made the same acknowledgement and asked forgiveness for the

466   *Sources*

same, and this individual shall then go unto the Minister to be further instructed as aforesaid: and upon the Sabbath when the Minister shall catechise, and of him ask any question concerning his faith and knowledge, and this individual shall not refuse to answer upon peril of the aforementioned punishment.

[*Additional laws concerning deceit, trade and the repayment of debts.*]

Every Sabbath day before Catechising, every Minister or Preacher shall read all these laws and ordinances publicly in the assembly of the congregation upon pain of being deprived of his entertainment allowance for that week.

130 John Smyth, *Magistrates Should Leave Christian Religion Free* (c.1612)

Keywords: #Authority, #Submission, #Church-State Relations, #Law, #Freedom of Religion, #Confession of Faith
Region: #Netherlands, #England
Group: #Mennonite, #Baptist

Early on in **James VI and I**'s reign in England, the king ordered all ministers in the Church of England to use the Church's *Book of Common Prayer*. Even though some ministers were dismissed on account of their non-conformist stances, the church hierarchy generally hesitated to expel moderate Puritans. They also encouraged reform-minded ministers to stay within the Church of England. The king's approach to non-conformists was less lenient, and many separatist ministers and congregants fled to the Netherlands.[184] John Smyth (d.1612), a Cambridge-educated theologian, argued that magistrates should refrain from administering punishments on the grounds of doctrinal matters. He had fled to Amsterdam in 1606, along with other prominent non-conformists like **Thomas Helwys** (Smyth and Helwys soon fell out). Many Independents who would eventually settle in colonial New England moved to the Low Countries around this time. Smyth pastored in Amsterdam and came under the influence of the Mennonites. The following confession was put together by those in Smyth's church shortly after his 1612 death.[185]

"Propositions and Conclusions concerning True Christian Religion, containing a Confession of Faith of certain English people, living in Amsterdam", in *Baptist Confessions of Faith*, ed. William Joseph McGlothlin (Philadelphia, PA: American Baptist Publication Society, 1911), 66–84 (81–82).

———

Propositions and Conclusions concerning True Christian Religion, containing a Confession of Faith of certain English people, living in Amsterdam

82 That Christ hath set in his outward church the vocation of master and servant, parents and children, husband and wife (Eph. 5:22–25; 6:1–9), and hath commanded every soul to be subject to the higher powers (Rom.

468 *Sources*

13:1), not because of wrath only, but for conscience sake (13:5) that we are to give them their duty, as tribute, and custom, honour, and fear, not speaking evil of them that are in authority, but praying and giving thanks for them (1 Tim. 2:1–2), for that is acceptable in the sight of God, even our Saviour.

83 That the office of the magistrate, is a disposition or permissive ordinance of God for the good of mankind: that one man like the brute beasts devour not another (Rom. 13), and that justice and civility, may be preserved among men: and that a magistrate may so please God in his calling, in doing that which is righteous and just in the eyes of the Lord, that he may bring an outward blessing upon himself, his posterity and subjects (2 Kings 10:30–31).

84 That the magistrate is not by virtue of his office to meddle with religion, or matters of conscience, to force or compel men to this or that form of religion, or doctrine: but to leave Christian religion free, to every man's conscience, and to handle only civil transgressions (Rom. 13), injuries and wrongs of man against man, in murder, adultery, theft, etc., for Christ only is the king, and law-giver of the church and conscience (Jas 4:12).

85 That if the magistrate will follow Christ, and be His disciple, he must deny himself, take up his cross, and follow Christ; he must love his enemies and not kill them, he must pray for them, and not punish them, he must feed them and give them drink, not imprison them, banish them, dismember them, and spoil their goods; he must suffer persecution and affliction with Christ, and be slandered, reviled, blasphemed, scourged, buffeted, spit upon, imprisoned and killed with Christ; and that by the authority of magistrates, which things he cannot possibly do, and retain the revenge of the sword.

86 That the Disciples of Christ, the members of the outward church, are to judge all their causes of difference, among themselves, and they are not to go to law, before the magistrates (1 Cor. 6:1, 7), and that all their differences must be ended by (yea) and (nay) without an oath (Matt. 5:33–37; Jas 5:12).

131 Leonard Busher, *Certain Reasons Against Persecution* (1614)

Keywords: #Persecution, #Conscience, #Toleration, #New Testament
Region: #England, #Netherlands
Group: #Anabaptist | #Judaism, #Islam

Leonard Busher wrote one of the earliest calls for comprehensive religious toleration. He was baptised in Gloucestershire in 1573 and died sometime after 1651. He emigrated to the Netherlands in 1606, where he wrote *Religion's Peace, or, A Reconciliation, between Princes & Peoples, & Nations* in 1614. His work was addressed to the English king and the Parliament. Busher remained in the Netherlands and continued to advocate toleration into the period of the **British Civil Wars**. The following excerpt is taken from the middle part of *Religion's Peace*, a work that strongly relied on references to the New Testament. He maintained that persecution was detrimental to the larger religious and political community and that it seldomly accomplished what persecutors intended. Moreover, intolerance towards Turks and Jews would make their conversion impossible. His call for toleration reflects some of the envy that Protestant dissenters had for the toleration that the Turks extended to non-Muslims. He also called for the readmission of Jewish communities and argued that their conscience should not be forced, even as his agenda was still shaped by their anticipated conversion.[186]

Reprinted in Edward Bean Underhill, ed., *Tracts on Liberty of Conscience and Persecution, 1614–1661* (London: Hanserd Knollys Society, 1846), 27–38.

———

Certain Reasons for Persecution

1 Because Christ hath not commanded any king, bishop, or minister to persecute the people for difference of judgement in matters of religion.
2 Because Christ hath commanded his bishops and ministers to persuade prince and people to hear and believe the gospel, by his word and Spirit, and, as ambassadors for him, to beseech both prince and

470 *Sources*

people to be reconciled unto God; and not, as tyrants, to force and constrain them by persecution [2 Cor. 5:20].

3 Because through persecution it will come to pass, that the ambassadors of the only spiritual Lord and King, Jesus, may be persecuted and imprisoned, burned, hanged, or banished, for delivering the message of their gracious Lord, sincerely and often, both to prince and people. Which to do, is a more heinous fact, than to persecute the ambassadors of the greatest king and prince in the world. For instead of heretics, they shall, as they have already, burn, banish, and hang the ambassadors of the Lord Jesus Christ, who doth choose out whom he pleaseth, to bear his name before kings and rulers, for a testimonial to them [Mark 13:9].

4 Because then we cannot say we have the liberty of the gospel in our land; seeing where that is, there is no persecution for any difference in religion, nor [any] forcing of the conscience to believe the gospel, except by the word and Spirit of God only, the which do wound and kill the errors of men, and not their persons [2 Cor. 10:4].

5 Because *Christ came into the world to save sinners* [1 Tim. 1:15], and not to destroy them, though they be blasphemers; seeing the Lord may convert them as he did Saul, after called Paul. And though they have difference in religion, or will not hear nor believe in Christ that they may be converted, yet ought you not to persecute them, seeing, Christ rebuketh such [Luke 9:53–55]; and his Father *sent him not into the world to condemn the world, but to save it* [John 3:17]. Be ye, therefore, followers of Christ, and not of antichrist, in gathering people to the faith.

6 Because then you shall not *walk wisely towards them that are without* [Col. 4:5], as the scripture teacheth; but shall offend also the Jews [1 Cor. 10:32], and all other strangers, who account it tyranny to have their consciences forced to religion by persecution.

7 Because if persecution be not laid down, and liberty of conscience set up, then cannot the Jews, nor any strangers, nor others contrary-minded, be ever converted in our land. For so long as they know aforehand, that they shall be forced to believe against their consciences, they will never seek to inhabit there. By which means you keep them from the apostolic faith, if the apostolic faith be only taught where persecution is.

8–11 [*Persecution drives godly, faithful and productive subjects from the land. Those who remain might not be trustworthy. Since most people are willing to outwardly conform, persecution teaches people to hide or lie about their true beliefs. Further, persecution forces the ungodly (who have no intention of growing in godliness) into the church, thus making the church body impure. Further, persecutors are likely to target true Christians in their quest to root out the unorthodox.*]

12 [*Persecution should cease because unbelieving countries are watching and will learn from Christian kings that it is permissible and*

praiseworthy to persecute for the cause of religion.] And the king and parliament may please to permit all sorts of Christians; yea, Jews, Turks, and pagans, so long as they are peaceable, and no malefactors, as is above mentioned; which, if they be found to be, under two or three witnesses, let them be punished according to God's word. Also, if any be found to be willing liars, false accusers, false allegers and quoters of the scriptures, or other men's writings – as some men willingly do – let them be punished according to right and justice; it is due desert, and no persecution....

13 Because persecution for religion is to force the conscience; and to force and constrain men and women's consciences to a religion against their wills, is to tyrannise over the soul, as well as over the body. And herein the bishops commit a greater sin, than if they force the bodies of women and maids against their wills [2 Cor. 11:2]. Yea, herein they are more cruel and greater tyrants than the Turks, who, though they force the bodies of strangers to slavery and bondage, yet they let the consciences go free, yea, to Christians that are so contrary to them in religion. [*He then argues that false bishops create spiritual fornicators and align themselves with antichrist.*]

15 Because his majesty and parliament would not willingly themselves be forced against their consciences, by the persecution of the bishop of Rome and his princes. So, I beseech them, according to the law Christ hath enjoined Christians [Luke 6:31], not by persecution to force other men's consciences against their wills, by the irritation of the bishops of our land.

16 Because persecutions do cause men and women to make shipwreck of faith and good consciences, by forcing a religion upon them even against their minds and consciences: and also do send them quick to the devil in their errors, if that be heresy for which they are hanged and burned. Which to do, is a most unchristian, unnatural, cruel, and tyrannous deed; and I am sure you would not be content to be so dealt with yourselves....

132 Johannes Althusius, *Politics, Community and Covenant* (1614)

Keywords: #Divine Law, #Natural Law, #Covenant, #Commonwealth, #Authority, #Family
Region: #Germany, #Netherlands
Group: #Reformed

Johannes Althusius (c.1557–1638) was a German Calvinist jurist and philosopher. He studied law, philosophy, and theology at Marburg, Cologne, and Basel, where he obtained his doctorate in law. He spent the second half of his life as an eminent citizen of the city of Emden in Friesland, which became a centre for Calvinist thought during the Dutch Revolt, and where he held significant civil and ecclesial positions. His *Politica Methodice Digesta* presented a comprehensive vision of the organisation of public life, revolving around covenanted communities: families, corporations, cities, provinces; a logic that explains his understanding of Reformed ecclesiology as well. With its focus on local autonomy and a political organisation *from below*, his work contained the seeds of confederalism, the principle of subsidiarity, and the notion of political sovereignty. His theory interacted explicitly with Bodin's theory of sovereignty, which he found unconvincing: according to Althusius, political sovereignty was not eternal and certainly bound by divine and natural laws. Moreover, his Calvinist colours came through in his rejection of popular revolt to overturn tyranny. This, according to him, was the responsibility of minor public associations or, in the language of Calvin, the lower magistrates.[187]

The *Politica*, excerpts of which are produced below, needs to be read in conjunction with his *Dicaeologica* (On Law and Power), in which he elaborated upon his theory of law, and, in particular, the relationship between positive law and timeless laws and principles as laid down in divine and natural laws. Both of these works show a profound concern over order, whether in law, in politics, or in social life. Combining insights from law, philosophy, and theology, his work thus presents an unusually robust and interdisciplinary engagement with theories of the state. Although he understood these as distinct disciplines, he argued that they were 'in their use and practice ... often united, indeed, I should have said always united'.[188] The *Politica* was

Sources   473

first published in 1603 and updated in 1610 and 1614 as it attracted significant interest in his time. Althusius' work, however, was much less known by later generations. Even so, his influence can be felt in the work of Protestants such as **Friedrich Julius Stahl, Guillaume Groen van Prinsterer,** and **Abraham Kuyper**. With the renewed interest in Abraham Kuyper in North American neo-Calvinist circles, Althusius' ideas continue to shape debates on religion and politics in the United States of America, even if indirectly.

Johannes Althusius, *Politica Methodice Digesta*, in *The Politics of Johannes Althusius*, trans. and ed. Frederick S. Carney (London: Eyre & Spottiswoode, 1964), 12–14, 61–66. Used by the kind permission of Liberty Fund.

———

Politics is the art of associating (*consociandi*) men for the purpose of establishing, cultivating, and conserving social life among them. Whence it is called 'symbiotics'. The subject matter of politics is therefore association (*consociatio*), in which the symbiotes (those living together) pledge themselves each to the other, by explicit or tacit agreement, to mutual communication of whatever is useful and necessary for the harmonious exercise of social life.

The end of political 'symbiotic' man is holy, just, comfortable, and happy symbiosis (living together), a life lacking nothing either necessary or useful. Truly in this life no man is self-sufficient, or adequately endowed by nature.

[*Althusius argues that men are born in complete dependence and that even in adulthood, people remain dependent on one another.*]

Therefore, as long as he remains isolated and does not mingle in the society of men, he cannot live at all comfortably and well while lacking so many necessary and useful things.

This mutual communication, or common enterprise, involves (1) things, (2) services, and (3) common rights by which the numerous and various needs of each and every symbiote are supplied, the self-sufficiency and mutuality of life and human society are achieved, and social life is established and conserved.... By this communication, advantages and responsibilities are assumed and maintained according to the nature of each particular association.

[*Althusius understands associations as covenanted communities: from the family to political communities.*]

Now that we have discussed particular and minor public associations, we turn to the universal (inclusive of all other associations) and major public association. In this association many cities and provinces obligate themselves to hold, organise, use, and defend through their common energies and expenditures, the right of the realm in the mutual communication of things and services. For without these supports, and the right of communication, a pious and just life cannot be established, fostered, and preserved in universal social life.

Whence this mixed society, constituted partly from private, natural, necessary, and voluntary societies, partly from public societies, is called a universal association. It is a polity in the fullest sense, an imperium, realm,

474 Sources

commonwealth, and people united in one body by the agreement of many symbiotic associations and particular bodied, and brought together under one right. For families, cities, and provinces existed by nature prior to realms, and gave birth to them.

[*Althusius argues that the realm is constituted by public associations, such as cities, villages and provinces. Private associations, such as families are members of these minor public associations, but they are not direct members of the realm. He then goes on to discuss the competences of the realm.*]

Its right is the means by which the members, in order to establish good order and the supplying of provisions throughout the territory of the realm, are associated and bound to each other as one people in one body and under one head. This right of the realm is also called the right of sovereignty. It is, in other words, the right of a major state or power as contrasted with the right that is attributed to a city of a province ....

What we call this right of the realm has as its purpose good order, proper discipline, and the supplying of provisions in the universal association. Towards these purposes it directs the actions of each and all of its members, and prescribes appropriate duties for them. Therefore, the universal power of the ruling is called that which recognises no ally, nor any superior or equal to itself. And this supreme right of universal jurisdiction is the form and substantial essence of sovereignty or, as we have called it, of a major state. When this right is taken away, sovereignty perishes.

The people, or the associated members of the realm, have the power of establishing this right of the realm and of binding themselves to it.... And in this power of disposing, prescribing, ordaining, administering, and constituting everything necessary and useful for the universal association is contained the bond, soul, and vital spirit of the realm, and its autonomy, greatness, size, and authority. Without this power no realm or universal symbiotic life can exist....

This right of the realm, or right of sovereignty, does not belong to individual members, but to all members joined together and to the entire associated body of the realm....

Bodin disagrees with our judgement by which supreme power is attributed to the realm or universal association. He says that the right of sovereignty, which we have called the right of the realm, is a supreme and perpetual power limited neither by law nor by time. I recognise neither of these two attributes of the right of sovereignty, in the sense Bodin intends them, as genuine. For this right of sovereignty is not the supreme power; neither is it perpetual or above law. It is not supreme because all human power acknowledges divine and natural law as superior.

133 *The Irish Articles of Religion (1615)*

Keywords: #Church-State Relations, #Confession, #Punishment, #War, #Marriage, #Property, #Charity, #Capital Crime, #Love
Region: #Ireland
Group: #Church of Ireland | #Anabaptists, #Roman Catholic, #Non-Christians

English power over the diverse peoples of Ireland predated the Reformation by several centuries. Even though there were religious differences within Ireland and between Ireland and England before the Reformation, both were often united in their deference to the pope. The 1560 Act of Uniformity had imposed Protestantism on Ireland. Protestantism came slowly to Ireland, nevertheless, partially because of the language barrier and limited interest in translation. The exception was Dublin, where English settlers resided who were in communion with the Church of England, as well as the north, where colonists tended to be Scottish and Presbyterian.

The following document comes from James Ussher (1581–1656), the Archbishop of Armagh, who had a strong international reputation for his theological writings. He crafted the *Irish Articles* (1615), the first Protestant statement of faith for the Church of Ireland. The articles adopted some of the reforms advocated by the Puritans, moving beyond the official doctrines of the Church of England. It has been suggested that these differences amounted to a claim of independence from the Church of England. Even with a Protestant college (Trinity College, Dublin) and the *Irish Articles* of 1615, the Reformation made little headway in most of Ireland. The articles were revoked in 1634 and replaced with the *Thirty-Nine Articles* that governed the Church of England. Even as the Stuarts made efforts to appease the Irish and Catholic population, tensions continued to rise. The Irish Rebellion of 1641 pitted Catholics against Protestants in spiralling rounds of popular and military violence, lasting more than a decade.[189]

The Creeds of Christendom, Vol. III: The Evangelical Protestant Creeds, ed. Philip Schaff (New York: Harper and Brothers, 1887), 526–544 (536–538).

---

476 *Sources*

Of the Civil Magistrate

57 The King's majesty under God hath the sovereign and chief power within his realms and dominions, over all manner of persons, of what estate, either ecclesiastical or civil, soever they be; so as no other foreign power hath, or ought to have, any superiority over them.

58 We do profess that the supreme government of all estates within the said realms and dominions, in all cases, as well ecclesiastical as temporal, doth of right appertain to the King's highness. Neither do we give unto him hereby the administration of the Word and Sacraments, or the power of the Keys, but that prerogative only which we see to have been always given unto all godly princes in holy Scripture by God himself; that is, that he should contain all estates and degree committed to his charge by God, whether they be ecclesiastical or civil, within their duty, and restrain the stubborn and evildoers with the power of the civil sword.

59 The Pope, neither of himself, nor by any authority of the Church or See of Rome, or by any other means with any other, hath any power or authority to depose the King, or dispose any of his kingdoms or dominions; or to authorise any other prince to invade or annoy him or his countries; or to discharge any of his subjects of their allegiance and obedience to his Majesty; or to give license or leave to any of them to bear arms, raise tumult, or to offer any violence or hurt to his royal person, state, or government, or to any of his subjects within his Majesty's dominions.

60 That princes which be excommunicated or deprived by the Pope may be deposed or murdered by their subjects, or any other whatsoever, is impious doctrine.

61 The laws of the realm may punish Christian men with death for heinous and grievous offences.

62 It is lawful for Christian men, at the commandment of the magistrate, to bear arms and to serve in just wars.

Of Our Duty Towards Our Neighbours

63 Our duty towards our neighbours is, to love them as ourselves, and to do to all men as we would they should do to us; to honour and obey our superiors; to preserve the safety of men's persons, as also their chastity, goods, and good names; to bear no malice nor hatred in our hearts; to keep our bodies in temperance, soberness, and chastity; to be true and just in all our doings; not to covet other men's goods, but labour truly to get our own living, and to do our duty in that estate of life unto which it pleaseth God to call us.

64 For the preservation of the chastity of men's persons, wedlock is commanded unto all men that stand in need thereof. Neither is there any prohibition by the Word of God but that the ministers of the Church may enter into the state of matrimony: they being nowhere commanded

Sources 477

by God's law either to vow the estate of single life or to abstain from marriage. Therefore it is lawful also for them, as well as for all other Christian men, to marry at their own discretion, as they shall judge the same to serve better to godliness.

65 The riches and goods of Christians are not common, as touching the right, title, and possession of the same: as certain Anabaptists falsely affirm. Notwithstanding every man ought of such things as he possesseth liberally to give alms to the poor, according to his ability.

66 Faith given, is to be kept, even with heretics and infidels.

67 The Popish doctrine of Equivocation and Mental Reservation is ungodly, and tendeth plainly to the subversion of all human society.

134 People of Zizers, *Local Religious Co-Existence* (1616)

Keywords: #Toleration, #Pluralism, #Land
Region: #Switzerland
Group: #Reformed, #Roman Catholic

Coexistence was not always a matter of grand geopolitical settlements, such as the **Peace of Augsburg** or **The Peace of Westphalia**. Practices of toleration also arose from (begrudged) local compromises, such as in the Swiss village of Zizers. In the Graubünden in southeastern Switzerland, many local groups enjoyed relative autonomy in parish matters. A patchwork of policies towards the Reformation emerged, ranging from establishing one tradition to allowing parishioners to walk to a neighbouring congregation. In the mid-1610s, the Reformed community of Zizers sought to seize control of a Catholic church. Local Catholics responded with legal protests and riots, and tensions grew. Local leaders forged a solution that sanctioned a pattern of coexistence. Parts of the agreement are reproduced below and, interestingly, make some provision for the religious preferences of women.[190]

Randolph C. Head, trans., "A Swiss Village's Religious Settlement: Zizers in Graubünden, 1616", in *A Sourcebook of Early Modern European History: Life, Death, and Everything in Between*, ed. Ute Lotz-Heumann (London: Routledge, 2019), 99–100.

———

An agreement of the people of Zizers concerning religion and the church there.

We, the Evangelical and Catholic parties of the commune and parish of Zizers, make known and proclaim publicly and to everyone with this letter:

After experiencing some years of division among us and some interference in our parish on account of religion, which has not only resulted in mistrust, envy, and hatred among us, but also, notably, in considerable costs and damage (so that we must be concerned that further and greater inconveniences await us unless God, as the originator of peace, should grant us by his grace the spirit of peace and love). Therefore, we from both parties collectively and

Sources 479

separately, for ourselves and for our descendants, have come to agreement and united on the following articles, and we promise one another faithfully and without deceit to hold and keep to them for each other, and to live with and alongside one another according to their provisions henceforth, as befits honourable communal citizens and neighbours.

First, the two above-named religions shall be free in our entire parish, and neither party shall harass the other in the exercise of their religion, nor in offices, in the courts, or in communal benefits. And we shall behave not as two parties or communes, but as one commune, and we will hold our assembly henceforth also in the *Ballhütte* [a currently unknown structure] after services, without deceit, as in old times.

And he who earnestly tries to convince another to stand with his party, and tries to persuade him in this or that matter, shall be obliged to pay the other party a fine of 5 pounds for each instance, without reduction of the penalty.

[*They offer rules for dividing and sharing the church building and graveyard.*]

Marriages shall be held according to whichever religion the groom, or the bride, request.

[*They then discuss financial matters, and even try to think through what would happen if the entire parish became Evangelical or Catholic. They spell out penalties for disregarding this agreement and make certified copies of the document so both sides can retain a copy for future consultation.*]

Given at Zizers on St. Martin's Day [11 November], 1616.

135 David Pareus, *The Politics of Opposing the Antichrist* (1618)

Keywords: #Authority, #Tyranny, #Rebellion, #Church-State Relations, #Eschatology, #Ten Commandments
Region: #Germany | #Poland
Group: #Reformed | #Roman Catholic

David Pareus (1548–1622) was born in Silesia and trained for ministry at a seminary in Heidelberg. He was ordained in 1571, entered ministry, and joined the theological faculty at Heidelberg in 1598. He initially taught the Hebrew Bible but soon transitioned to the study of the New Testament. He became known for his skills in biblical exegesis. As the selection below shows, he grew alarmed by the growing threat of Catholic Habsburgs and the Jesuits. He leveraged ecumenical efforts to unite like-minded principalities, most notably England and Denmark, but these efforts were unsuccessful. In his *Commentary on Romans* (1609), Pareus interpreted Romans 13 in a way that tried to chart a course between Anabaptists and Catholics, emphasising order, hierarchy, and submission to authority. For this reason, he was often cited in favour of royal power. However, other statements in the commentary made him one of the most cited resistance theorists, particularly during the contest between the Puritans and the Stuarts in the mid-1600s.

According to him, princes had a duty to guard both tables of the Mosaic law and to serve the natural, moral, civil, and spiritual good of the people. However, that authority did not necessarily imply submission in religious matters. The overreach of civil power could amount to tyranny. Those who abused God-given power forfeited their right to wield it. Therefore, magistrates had spiritual incentives to remain within circumscribed limits. If they punished the good and rewarded evil, they would become the enemies of God. In a controversial discussion of submission and resistance, the *Explicatio Dubiorum*, he argued for government based on consensus; one where lesser magistrates could have a divine commission to use force against a tyrant. His argument even went as far as to suggest that *private persons*, should lesser magistrates fail, could violently resist their prince. In 1622, a fellow at Oxford defended the right to take up arms against a prince, citing Pareus. This led to the collection and destruction of Pareus' works there.[191]

Sources 481

Anti-papism undergirded Pareus' political works, including his teachings on tyranny. He argued that the papal usurpation of the 'double-sword' (spiritual and civil) exemplified the overreach of power that made one a tyrant, corrupting both church and state. Why had the papacy flourished so long if it was corrupt? In short, prophecy foretold how kings must follow the Antichrist before they *convert* (being 'conquered' by Christ) and war against the Antichrist. This schema was drawn from the Book of Revelation's comments about the downfall of the 'whore' (ch. 17). His anti-papism employed bestial, gendered, and apocalyptic language in describing his enemies. In the following excerpt from the preface to his *Commentary on Revelation* (1618), Pareus highlighted the importance of the civil and spiritual conversion of kings before the great fight that would bring an end to the tyranny of the 'whore'. Before this final battle, kingly former allies of the pope would heed the gospel and transform their kingdoms. Armed opposition to the popish Antichrist had to be undertaken by the supreme magistrate in any given kingdom. The following selection is drawn from the English edition that was printed during the upheavals of the **British Civil Wars,** a time of great violence and apocalyptic expectation.

David Pareus, *A Commentary upon the Divine Revelation,* trans. Elias Arnold (Amsterdam, 1644), 1–3. Text modernised by the editors.

———

The Author's Advertisement Touching the Publishing of this Commentary

...I am not the first to have explained the *Beast.* What do I speak of myself? Neither was the Apostle John the first who showed the Antichrist was at *Rome*: for before him *Paul* testified, that the *Son of perdition should sit in the Temple of God as God* [2 Thess. 2:4], that is, claim the *principality* in the Church....

[Since antiquity, church leaders] have demonstrated Rome to be the seat of Antichrist, and the Pope with his *double-sword* is the Antichrist. Wherefore it is not said in ignorance, but in malice, *that by us Protestants the Pope first began to be Antichrist....* [The fact that] *Antichrist now reigns at Rome, can scandalize none but evil-minded men.* Wherefore thou, O *Pope,* hear this truth and repent, before the Heavenly Conqueror gets his hands on you and casts you into the Lake of Fire and Brimstone....

And you, O unwise Kings: when will you understand whom to serve and what you should do? When will God put it into your hearts to do his will, that is, to make *Rome* the whorish woman desolate? *Oh serve the Lord with fear and trembling, kiss the Son lest he be angry, and you perish in the way* [Ps. 2:12]: let the *Lamb* conquer you, not unto destruction, in the manner the *Beast* overcomes, but unto conversion: do it (O kings) quickly, before it is too late. For God will not be mocked. He has begun to put it into the hearts of various good Kings to willingly do this: He will also put it into the hearts of others when it shall please him, according to the oracle of the Angel....

482 *Sources*

Those who cease to do this shall not be partakers of Salvation. Those who do it seriously, verily they are overcome by the Lamb unto their Salvation, and they make the whore desolate: late indeed, yet not too late. But let no man tempt God: for you do not know how soon you may be taken away. Therefore, while it is time, walk in the light, lest the darkness come upon you.

[*There is then the objection that the majority of political powers are in allegiance to the Antichrist. Pareus locates these Antichrist-aligned Christ-professing kings within prophecy. Crucially, he argues, Revelation shows that these kings will first fight against God before converting. These converted kingdoms will then be instrumental in the downfall of the 'whore'.*]

For the *Kings, who shall give their power to the Beast and fight against the Lamb,* shall be the same people whose hearts God leads *to hate the whore and make her desolate.* Now this argues that they shall not be Pagan but Christian kings, who before being deceived through ignorance, shall sin in fact: but at length being overcome by the *Lamb,* that is, brought to repentance; they shall, forsaking their error, turn their hearts and power against the *whore....*

136 *The Belgic Confession* (1561, rev. 1619)

Keywords: #Government, #Authority, #Obedience, #Property, #Confession of Faith
Region: #Belgium, #Netherlands
Group: #Dutch Reformed | #Anabaptist

The *Belgic Confession* is one of the earliest comprehensive statements of faith on behalf of emerging Calvinist communities in the Low Countries. It initially appeared in France in 1561, after it was completed under the leadership of Guido de Brès and in consultation with leading Reformed figures such as **Theodore Beza** and Petrus Dathenus. Such confessions played a meaningful role in uniting scattered Protestant communities, and this was especially pertinent in the context of the Spanish repression. This unity came under pressure as a result of the Arminian controversy, which pitted two major theologians against each other: **Jacobus Arminius** and Franciscus Gomarus. Central themes of the controversy were free will, predestination, and the role of the magistrate, which were debated at large during a 12-year cease-fire. The Synod of Dort (1618–1619) decided in favour of Gomarus for both theological and geopolitical reasons. The *Belgic Confession* would become one of the central documents of continental Calvinism and still is observed as one of the *Three Forms of Unity*.[192]

The following excerpt discusses the role of the magistrates, which Dutch Calvinists enlisted as protectors of the true faith and the adversary of false religion. Although civil and ecclesiastical authorities had distinct roles, they were believed to complement each other in preserving the common (Calvinist) good. A similar article was initially inserted in the **Westminster Confession,** but abandoned by American Presbyterians, to whom this article contradicted the principle of the separation of church and state. This particular article came under scrutiny in the Netherlands in the nineteenth century as well, when **Abraham Kuyper** and **Philippus Hoedemaker** would clash over its potential revision. Kuyper would argue that this article was not compatible with a nation-state and that the Reformed religion should not be imposed on others. Hoedemaker, on the contrary, argued for its continued importance

484 *Sources*

on the basis of supersessionist arguments. In all of this, the status and significance of the Hebrew Bible determined the orientation of Dutch Calvinism to the state.[193]

The Creeds of Christendom, Vol. III: The Evangelical Protestant Creeds, ed. Philip Schaff (New York: Harper and Brothers, 1887), 383–436 (432–433).

———

Art. 36: Of Magistrates

We believe that our gracious God, because of the depravity of mankind, hath appointed kings, princes, and magistrates, willing that the world should be governed by certain laws and policies; to the end that the dissoluteness of men might be restrained, and all things carried on among them with good order and decency. For this purpose he hath invested the magistracy with the sword, *for the punishment of evil doers, and for the praise of them that do well.* And their office is, not only to have regard unto and watch for the welfare of the civil state, but also that they protect the sacred ministry, and thus may remove and prevent all idolatry and false worship; that the kingdom of antichrist may be thus destroyed, and the kingdom of Christ promoted. They must, therefore, countenance the preaching of the word of the gospel everywhere, that God may be honoured and worshiped by everyone, as he commands in his Word.

Moreover, it is the bounden duty of every one, of what state, quality, or condition soever he may be, to subject himself to the magistrates; to pay tribute, to show due honour and respect to them, and to obey them in all things which are not repugnant to the Word of God; to supplicate for them in their prayers, that God may rule and guide them in all their ways, and that we may lead a quiet and peaceable life in all godliness and honesty.

Wherefore we detest the error of the Anabaptists and other seditious people, and in general all those who reject the higher powers and magistrates, and would subvert justice, introduce a community of goods, and confound that decency and good order which God hath established among men.

137 Sacred and Mundane Politics in Plymouth Colony (1620–1622)

Keywords: #Government, #Authority, #Submission, #Colonisation, #Covenant, #Law, #Land, #Love, #Hebrew Bible
Region: #United States | #England, #Netherlands
Group: #Separatist | #Indigenous American

In the early 1600s, pressure to conform to the Church of England led many English dissenters to seek refuge elsewhere. Advocates of toleration, like **Thomas Helwys, John Smyth,** and **Leonard Busher,** spent considerable time in the Netherlands. A group of dissenters wished to establish their own, more religiously pure community, which was further catalysed by new military activity from Spain. In 1620, the *Mayflower* set off for New England.[194] At the time, English colonies became increasingly common, and a group of English Separatists, mostly living in Leiden, received permission to start a colony in the northern part of Virginia – then a vast area that spanned much of the eastern seaboard of what is now the United States. In order to gain this patent, the Leiden Separatists emphasised their obedience to the English crown, in all godly commands, and downplayed the extent to which they viewed themselves as outside the Church of England. They left their ageing minister, **John Robinson,** in the Netherlands, and the pilgrims went without a minister for a decade.

Difficulties and setbacks characterised the Separatists' endeavours from the beginning, and a high percentage of the colonists did not survive the first year. They landed off the coast of Cape Cod in November 1620, far to the north of the received patent. Some worried that previously established laws would not apply. The *Mayflower* carried many who relocated for religious reasons ('the godly'), but there were also those with mundane reasons for sailing ('the strangers'). They needed to legally knit these communities together, preferably before people disembarked. The subsequent 'Mayflower Compact', the first source reproduced below, is important because the people themselves decided how they would be governed in Plymouth Colony. They entered a 'covenant' to create a 'civil body politic', one that could establish its own legally binding 'just and equal laws'. Signed by 41 men, this

486   *Sources*

document expanded political participation; for example, they could have crafted a document where only 'the godly', or only the wealthy, had a political voice. However, women were not included in the formal process.[195] Memories of this group of settlers continue to play an important role in narratives about the United States, and many claim that America's identity traces back to them. Although this document is often taken as a foundational text of the United States, those crafting it were simply trying to solve a practical problem that arose from accidentally landing outside of their patented lands.

The second source was written by Robert Cushman (c.1577–1625), a deacon in the Leiden congregation who was an early settler of Plymouth Colony. His work reflected on the right of the Separatists to occupy 'heathen' lands. Although he would have argued that the Separatists were beloved of God and that any property they enjoyed was a gift from God, he argued that God did not give Plymouth Colony to the Separatists like God gave Canaan to the children of Abraham. Israel was fundamentally dissimilar to Plymouth, and no land on earth was a promised land. Cushman grounded property rights in several ways: discovery, grant from the British king, evangelical intent, relative emptiness of the land, and the consent of Indigenous Sachems (whom he calls kings and emperors). He placed great weight on the argument that the Indigenous population did not use most of the land and that the Sachems welcomed their presence. He wrote it at a time of optimism about Anglo-Algonquian relations, and both groups had strategic reasons to ally.

1. William Mason West, *A Source Book in American History, to 1787* (Boston, MA: Allyn and Bacon, 1913), 116–117; 2. *A Relation or Journal of the Beginning and Proceedings of the English Plantation Settled at Plimoth in New England* (London: John Bellamie, 1622), 65–69. Texts modernised by the editors.

———

1. The Mayflower Compact (1620)

In the name of God, Amen. We whose names are written below, the loyal subjects of our dread sovereign Lord, King James, by the grace of God, King of Great Britain, France, and Ireland, defender of the faith, etc., having undertaken, for the glory of God, and advancement of the Christian faith, and honour of our king and country, a voyage to plant the first colony in the Northern parts of Virginia, do by these presents solemnly and mutually in the presence of God, and one of another, covenant and combine ourselves together into a civil body politic, for our better ordering and preservation and furtherance of the ends aforesaid; and by virtue of this to enact, constitute, and frame such just and equal laws, ordinances, acts, constitutions, and offices, from time to time, as shall be thought most fitting and convenient for the general good of the Colony, unto which we promise all due submission and obedience. In witness whereof we have hereunder subscribed our names....

———

Sources   487

2. Robert Cushman, *Reason and Considerations Touching the Lawfulness of Removing Out of England into the Parts of America* (1622)

Forasmuch as many exceptions are made daily against going into and inhabiting foreign desert places, to the hindrance of plantations abroad, and the increase of distractions at home....

And being studious of brevity, we must first consider that whereas God of old did call and summon our Fathers (Gen. 12:1–2; 35:1) by predictions, dreams, visions, and certain illuminations to go from their countries, places and habitations, to reside and dwell here or there, and to wander up and down from city to city, and land to land, according to his will and pleasure (Matt. 2:19; Ps. 105:13). Now no such calling is to be expected for any matter whatsoever, neither must any so much as imagine that there will now be any such thing (Heb. 1:1–2). God did once so train up his people, but now he does not, but speaks in another manner, and so we must apply ourselves to God's present dealing, and not to his wanted dealing: and as the miracle of giving Manna ceased when the fruit of the land became plentiful (Josh. 5:12), so God having such a plentiful storehouse of directions in his holy word, no extraordinary revelations must now be expected.

But now, the ordinary examples and precepts of the Scriptures, reasonably and rightly understood and applied, must be the voice and word that must call, press, and direct us in every action.

Neither is there any land or possession now, like unto the possession which the Jews had in Canaan (Gen. 17:8), being legally holy and appropriated unto a holy people the seed of Abraham, in which they dwelt securely, and had their days prolonged, it being by an immediate voice said, that he (the Lord) gave it them as a land of rest after their weary travels, and a type of Eternal rest in heaven, but now there is no land of that Sanctimony, no land so appropriated; none typical: much less any that can be said to be given of God to any nation as was Canaan, which they and their seed must dwell in, till God sends upon them sword or captivity: but now we are all in all places strangers and Pilgrims, travellers and sojourners, most appropriately, having no dwelling but in this earthen Tabernacle; our dwelling is but a wandering, and our abiding but as a fleeting, and in a word our home is nowhere, but in the heavens: in that house not made with hands, whose maker and builder is God (2 Cor. 5:1–3), and to which all ascend who love the coming of our Lord Jesus.

Though then, there may be reasons to persuade a man to live in this or that land, yet there cannot be the same reasons which the Jews had, but now as natural, civil and Religious bands tie men, so they must be bound, and as good reasons for things terrene and heavenly appear, so they must be led. And so here falls in our question, how a man that is here born and bred, and has lived some years, may remove himself into another country.

I answer, a man must not desire only to live and do good to himself, but he should see where he can live to do most good to others: for as one says, he whose living is but for himself, it is time he were dead....

488 *Sources*

[*He argues that many lazy and unprofitable people would benefit from the opportunities abroad and benefit humanity by their productivity.*]

But some will say, what right have I to go live in the heathen's country?

[*He chooses not to base his argument principally on 'discovery' and the right of English monarchs to the lands.*]

And first, seeing we pray daily for the conversion of the heathens, we must consider ordinary means and actions for us to convert them or whether prayer for them is only referred to God's extraordinary work from heaven. Now it seems unto me that we ought also to endeavour and use means to convert them, and means cannot be used unless we go to them or they come to us: they cannot come to us, our land is full; we may go to them, their land is empty.

This, then, is a sufficient reason to prove our going there to live lawfully: their land is spacious and void, and there are few who but run over the grass, as do also the foxes and wild beasts: they are not industrious, neither have art, science, skill or faculty to use either the land or the commodities of it, but all spoils, rots, and is marred for want of manuring, gathering, ordering, etc. As the ancient Patriarchs moved from tight places into more roomy ones, where the land lay idle and wasted, and none used it, though there dwelt inhabitants nearby (Gen. 13:6, 11, 12; 34:21; 41:20), so is it lawful now to take land which no one uses, and make use of it.

And as it is a common land or unused, and undressed country; so we have it by common consent, composition and agreement, which agreement is double: First the Imperial Governor Massasoit, whose circuits in likelihood are larger than England and Scotland, has acknowledged the King's Majesty of England to be his Master and Commander, and that once in my hearing, yea, and in writing, under his hand to Captain Standish, both he and many other Kings which are under him, as Paomet, Nauset, Cummaquid, Narraganset, Nemasket, etc. with divers others that dwell about the bays of Patuxet and Massachusetts: neither has this been accomplished by threats and blows, or shaking of sword, and sound of trumpet, for as our faculty that way is small, and our strength less: so our warring with them is after another manner, namely by friendly usage, love, peace, honest and just carriages, good counsel, etc. that so we and they may not only live in peace in that land (Ps. 110:3; 48:3), and they yield subjection to an earthly Prince, but that as voluntaries they may be persuaded at length to embrace the Prince of peace Christ Jesus, and rest in peace with him for ever.

Secondly, this composition is also more particular and applicable, as touching ourselves there inhabiting: the Emperor, by a joint consent, has promised and appointed us to live at peace, where we will in all his dominions, taking what place we will, and as much land as we will, and bringing as many people as we will, and that for these two causes. First, because we are the servants of King James of England, whose the land (as he confesses) is, and second because he has found us just, honest, kind and peaceable, and

Sources 489

so loves our company, yea, and that in these things there is no dissimulation on his part, nor fear of breach (except our security engenders in them some unthought of treachery, or our incivility provoke them to anger) is most plain in other Relations, which shows that the things they did were more out of love then out of fear.

Firstly, it is a vast and empty Chaos. Secondly acknowledged the right of our Sovereign King. Thirdly, by a peaceable composition in part possessed of divers of his loving subjects, I see not who can doubt or call in question the lawfulness of inhabiting or dwelling there....

138 Gustav II Adolf, *Letters Patent to the Newly Established Swedish South Company* (1622)

Keywords: #Colonisation, #Land, #Trade
Region: #Sweden, #United States
Group: #Lutheran | #Non-Christians

Patents and charters provide an excellent window into early Protestant ideas about interactions with foreign peoples in colonised lands. *The Avalon Project* at Yale Law School has compiled dozens of such documents.[196] The following extract comes from the opening of the Letters Patent granted by Gustav II Adolf to the Swedish South Company in 1622. Like other European monarchs, he assumed a right to explore and colonise distant lands.[197] This document reveals the entwinement of religion, commerce, and colonisation, and the ambivalence with which Indigenous peoples were approached. There was little doubt that Europeans thought they were superior, both culturally and religiously. However, their views of outsiders were multi-layered. For example, the text described some as 'effeminate people', echoing a history of describing Indigenous peoples as untainted by European vices and cruelties. It then described them as 'heathens and savages', echoing a long history of describing Indigenous persons as theological and civilisational outsiders. Further, evangelisation was explicitly stated as a motivation for colonisation. In European thought, there was often a debate about whether Indigenous persons needed to be 'civilised' before they could be evangelised, or vice versa.

B. Fernow, *Documents Relating to the History of the Dutch and Swedish Settlements on the Delaware River* (Albany, NY: Argus, 1877), 7–15.

Gustav II Adolf, Letters Patent to the Newly Established Swedish South Company (1622)

We, Gustavus Adolphus, by the grace of God, King of Sweden, Gothland, and the Wendes, Grand Duke of Finland, Duke in Estonia and Carelia, Lord of Ingermanland, etc.

Know ye, that whereas we find that it will considerably add to the welfare of Our Kingdom and of Our subjects and that it is necessary, that the

Sources 491

commerce, trades, and navigation in Our lands and territories should grow, be increased, and improved by all suitable means and whereas by the reports of experienced and trustworthy men We have received reliable and certain intelligence that there are in Africa, America, and Magellanica, or terra Australis many rich countries and islands, of which some are inhabited by quiet and rather effeminate people, some by heathens and savages, some uninhabited, and some as yet only imperfectly explored: with which said countries it will not only be possible to carry on an extraordinary large commerce from Our Kingdom, but it is also most likely, that the said people may likewise be made more civilised and taught morality and the Christian religion by the mutual intercourse and trade, therefore We have maturely considered and as far as in Our power concluded, that the advantages, profits and welfare of Our Kingdom and faithful subjects, besides the further propagation of the holy Gospel, will be much improved and increased by the discovery of new commercial relations and navigation.

We have been so much more induced thereto, as We understand, that Our faithful subjects, many merchants as well as others are willing to promote it and ready to make large advances of money for it. In consideration thereof, after much deliberation and for weighty causes and reasons, which have made Us well disposed towards this useful and praiseworthy undertaking, We have resolved, desired and demanded, that the commerce and navigation to the countries of Africa, Asia, America and Magellanica shall be begun and carried on, subject to the formerly stated conditions and rules by a powerful combination of inhabitants of Our lands and territories and others, who may desire to take part in it and join. For this purpose a General Company shall be established, which by special favours We will firmly maintain and strengthen with our help and assistance, granting it the proper permission and the following privileges.

139 James I, *Directions Concerning Preachers* (1622)

Keywords: #Authority, #Church-State Relations, #Censorship, #Ten Commandments
Region: #England
Group: #Church of England, #Puritan

The reign of James VI and I in England was marked by controversy from the beginning. Those who hoped for further reform submitted the **Millenary Petition** in 1603, but their hopes were dashed after the Hampton Court Conference of 1604 made it clear that James was not sympathetic to their views of church and state. Further, James mandated that ministers subscribe to the *Book of Common Prayer*, which led some dissenters to flee abroad. These measures did little, however, to quell theological disagreements. James, an eminently educated king, was unafraid to wade into controversial waters. His strong views on divine-right kingship meant that he thought his opinion carried the greatest weight. The following source, presumed to be written by James on 8 August 1622, ordered that certain controversial doctrines were not to be preached or debated. These included 'the deep points of predestination, election, reprobation or of the universality, efficacity, resistibility or irresistibility of God's grace'. Preachers were also not to meddle in matters of church and state or speak on limitations to monarchical power. They were also commanded to moderate the speech they used against theological opponents.[198]

Henry Gee and William John Hardy, eds., *Documents Illustrative of English Church History* (London: Macmillan, 1896), 516–518.

———

1 That no preacher under the degree and calling of a bishop, or dean of a cathedral or collegiate church ... do take occasion, by the expounding of any text whatsoever, to fall into any set discourse, or commonplace (otherwise than by opening the coherence and division of his text), which shall not be comprehended and warranted in essence, substance, effect or natural

Sources 493

inference within some one of the Articles of Religion set forth in 1562, or in some of the homilies set forth by authority in the Church of England....

2 That no parson, vicar, curate, or lecturer shall preach any sermon ... but upon some part of the catechism, or some text taken out of the Creed, Ten Commandments, or the Lord's Prayer....

3 That no preacher of what title soever under the degree of a bishop, or dean at the least, do from henceforth presume to preach in any popular auditory the deep points of predestination, election, reprobation or of the universality, efficacity, resistibility or irresistibility of God's grace; but leave those themes to be handled by learned men, and that moderately and modestly by way of use and application, rather than by way of positive doctrine, as being fitter for the schools and universities, than for simple auditories.

4 That no preacher of what title or denomination soever, shall presume from henceforth in any auditory within this kingdom to declare, limit, or bound out, by way of positive doctrine, in any lecture or sermon, the power, prerogative, jurisdiction, authority, or duty of sovereign princes, or otherwise meddle with these matters of state and the references betwixt princes and the people, than as they are instructed and presidented in the homily of obedience, and in the rest of the homilies and Articles of Religion, set forth (as before is mentioned) by public authority; but rather confine themselves wholly to those two heads of faith and good life, which are all the subject of the ancient sermons and homilies.

5 That no preacher of what title or denomination soever, shall causelessly and without invitation from the text, fall into bitter invectives, and indecent railing speeches against the persons of either papists or puritans; but modestly and gravely (when they are occasioned thereunto by the text of Scripture) free both the doctrine and discipline of the Church of England from the assertions of either adversary, especially when the auditory is suspected to be tainted with one or the other infection.

6 Lastly, that the archbishops and bishops of the kingdom, whom his majesty hath good cause to blame for this former remissness, be more wary and choice in the licensing of preachers....

140 William Ames, *The Duty Towards Our Neighbour* (1623)

Keywords: #Authority, #Submission, #Duty, #Marriage, #Family, #Servants, #Property, #Animals, #Murder, #Crime, #Punishment, #War
Region: #Netherlands | #England
Group: #Reformed, #Puritan

William Ames (1576–1633) was born in Ipswich in a community that was sympathetic to the further reform of the Church of England. He attended Cambridge, already a hotbed of Puritanism, and was deeply influenced by **William Perkins** (1558–1602). He sought refuge in the Netherlands in 1610 and lived there until his death in 1633. He served in several capacities: he ministered to local congregations of exiles, advised the Synod of Dort (1618–1619), accompanied troops onto the battlefield, and taught theology at the Frisian University of Franeker. Through his teachings and writings, he became an important defender of Calvinist theology and deeply influenced Puritanism on both sides of the Atlantic. The following selection comes from one of Ames' most popular works, *The marrow of sacred divinity* (1623). In the first selection, he detailed his understanding of the relationship between religious and political authority, repeatedly framing submission to authorities through the lens of relationships within the Christian family, order, and lawfulness. The second selection comes from Ames' discussion of the Christian's duty towards their neighbour, and engages the relationship between spiritual and corporal well-being.

William Ames, *The Marrow of Sacred Divinity Drawne Out of the Holy Scriptures* (London: Printed by Edward Griffin for Henry Overton, 1642), 359–361, 363–368. Text modernised by the editors.

———

2.17: Of the Honour of our Neighbour

44 Those who are in higher power ought to provide for the good of the souls of those who are under them, that they may have means of salvation (Eph. 6:4). With respect to their bodies, that they may have food, clothing, and fit dwelling.

Sources 495

45 And these higher powers are either private or public persons.
46 Private, are the husband in respect of the wife, parents in respect of children, and master in respect of servants: where the power of the husband is moderated with a certain equality: the power of the master is merely commanding: but the paternal power is as it were mixed.
47 They that are in public authority are either ministers or magistrates.
48 But there is this difference between magistrates and ministers of the church

    a Magistracy ... is an ordinance from man: but the ordinance of ministers is from God, which is declared in the Scriptures, when the power of magistracy although it is ordained by God (Rom. 13:1). Yet it is called a human creature (1 Pet. 2:13), which name does not at all agree to the lawful ministers of the church.
    b Magistracy is an ordinance of God the Creator, and so belongs to all kinds of men: but the Ecclesiastical ministry is a gift and ordinance of Christ the Mediator, and so only properly and ordinarily pertains to those who are of the church of Christ.
    c A magistrate has jurisdiction joined to his government, and so (if he is the supreme magistrate) upon just cause he may make and abolish laws, and commit jurisdiction to others: but the ministers of the church (considered in themselves) are merely mandated, meaning they have nothing of their own, but whatever they do lawfully, they do it as in the place of Christ who commands them, and so can neither make laws, nor give the power they received to others.
    d It is the responsibility of magistrates to procure the spiritual and corporal common good for all those who are committed to their jurisdiction, by political means and a coercive power (1 Tim. 2:2): but it is the duty of the minister to procure the spiritual good of those who are committed to them by ecclesiastical means (Acts 20:28; Heb. 13:17).

49 But magistrates and ministers cannot be perfectly distinguished: for there is no thing, person, or cause so ecclesiastical, that it does not pertain in some respect to the jurisdiction of the magistrate; neither is there any action so secular (if it is done by a member of the church), so far as it respects obedience to God, that the church will not take notice of it.
50 Therefore, the exempting of ecclesiastical men (as they are called) from the jurisdiction of the civil magistrate, as also the unloosing them from obedience due to magistrates, and parents, brought in by papists under a pretence of religion and perfection, is altogether contrary to the perfect law of God.
51 With respect to this ruling which comes from the power of superiors, subjection and obedience is due from inferiors (Heb. 13:17). Obey your leaders, and submit yourselves.
52 Subjection is an acknowledgement of their authority (1 Pet. 2:18; Eph. 5:22).

496　*Sources*

53　Obedience is the performance of those things that are prescribed (Eph. 6:1–5).
54　This obedience ought always to be limited according to the limits of power, which the superior commander has.
55　Hence we must not obey men in those things which are against the command of God, for we must obey in the Lord (Eph. 6:1). And in the fear of God (Col. 3:22). Or also against the command of those superior persons who have greater authority than they do.
56　Hence also obedience must not be blind, or without examination of the precept: but an inferior ought to enquire as far as is necessary for the matter in hand, whether the precept is lawful, convenient and binding (Acts 4:19).
57　But if the precept is not lawful, then enduring wrongfully inflicted punishment has the place and force of obedience (1 Pet. 2:19–20)....

2.18: Of Humanity toward Our Neighbour

1　That justice which respects the condition of our neighbour absolutely considered, either respects the person of our neighbour or his outward commodities.
2　That which respects his person either respects his life or his purity.
3　That which respects his life is humanity, and it is commanded in the sixth Commandment. For seeing here man's life is properly provided for, or as the Scripture speaks (Gen. 9:5–6). The soul of man and the blood of man; all that duty which is here handled is rightly set forth under the man: of humanity.
4　This Commandment does not properly consider the life of the brute creatures, because they are in man's power (Gen. 9:2–3). They also do not have common society with man: yet because a fit disposition toward the life of man implies some respect to another image of his which is found in other living creatures: and cruelty against them reveals a certain inhumane disposition, or by little and little accustomed to it: therefore clemency and inclemency towards the brute creatures, also pertains by inference.
5　Humanity is a virtue whereby we are inclined to preserve the life of our neighbour, and the peace thereof by lawful means.
6　But this is performed two ways, namely by supplying things helpful and hindering things hurtful.
7　But seeing the life of man which ought to be preserved is twofold, spiritual, and corporal, hence the duties of humanity are sometimes spiritual and sometimes corporal.
8　The spiritual duty is to do all things according to our power, which may further the edification of our neighbour....
13　Also, it is required of superiors that have power and authority, that they study to further the salvation of inferiors by their authority.

Sources 497

14 There are various degrees of our duty toward the corporal life of our neighbour, that it may be kept quiet and safe.
15 The first degree hereof is, in those virtues which keep us away from hurting our neighbour.
16 Of this kind are Meekness, Patience, Long-suffering, and placableness, or pardoning of wrong....
25 The second degree of this duty is in those virtues, which cherish society of life, as, concord, and benevolence which hath joined with it, courtesy, affability, and equanimity....
29 A third degree of this duty is in those endeavours whereby the life itself of our neighbour, is defended, furthered, and cherished.
30 An endeavour to defend, promote, and cherish the life of our neighbour, contains all those duties that conserve the life of man (Prov. 24:10).
31 Unto these are opposed all those sins, whereby the life of man is hurt, such as fierceness, cruelty and the like (Prov. 20:10).
32 All these are contained under the name of homicide.
33 Homicide is the unjust killing of a man.
34 Now that killing and hurting is also unjust, which not done by a just authority, that is a public authority; or not upon a just cause, or not in due order, or upon an intention that is not just; for those four conditions ought always to concur in a just killing; if one of them is wanting, homicide is committed.
35 Also, rash anger must be referred to homicide, so far as it tends to lead to the hurting of the life of our neighbour (Matt. 5:22). Whosoever is angry with his brother unadvisedly.
36 But those words mean that not all anger is condemned, for only rash anger is reproved, that is, anger that has no just cause or observes no just measure. Otherwise, the force of anger, as zeal of God, is often commended (Gen. 30:2; Exod. 11:8, 16:20; Num. 16:15, 31:14; 2 Kings 13:19). And hatred itself (Ps. 139:21–22).
37 This, for the most part, peculiarly belongs to the sixth precept, that those things which are forbidden may sometime (in another consideration) not be inappropriate and sometime might be rightly done in obedience toward God.
38 So he that kills another upon mere accident, to whom he gave no cause, while he is about a lawful work when and where it is lawful, fit diligence being used, does not sin (Deut. 19:5).
39 Such also is the reason people can defend themselves upon necessity, so long as the desire for revenge is lacking. For this is a blameless defence granted to everyone.
40 Also, sometimes God is obeyed by killing (Deut. 13:9). Namely when it is done by authority and commanded by God (1 Sam. 15:18–19).
41 No man has power from God, by common law to purposely kill a man he knows is innocent.

498 *Sources*

42 Nor does man possess power sufficient to give authority to any subject to slay someone whom he knows to be innocent and not deserving of death.

43 Therefore, a war can never be just on both sides because there cannot be cause of death on both sides.

44 Neither is it lawful in any war to target those who are not in some way partakers in the cause.

45 But if there is a lawful cause, together with a just authority and intention, and a just manner is used, the war itself, or warfare, is not against religion, justice, or charity (Num. 31:3; 1 Sam. 18:16, 25:28; 1 Chron. 5:22; Luke 3:14; Rom. 13:4; 1 Pet. 2:14).

46 Also, if the same conditions are observed, it is lawful for those who have skill with weapons (1 Chron. 5:18; Ps. 144:1) to offer and apply their help to lawful captains; to make war (Luke 3:14; 1 Cor. 9:7).

47 No law of God permits anyone to kill himself.

48 Yet it is sometimes lawful and just for one to endanger themselves.

49 There is sometimes a case where one may and ought to offer himself to death (Jonah 1:12).

141 John Robinson, *On Killing American Indians* (1623)

Keywords: #War, #Colonisation, #Non-Christians, #Violence
Region: #Netherlands, #United States
Group: #Separatist

The first winter for the separatist colonists at Plymouth was disastrous, and those who survived were desperate. Indigenous communities were also devastated by waves of disease that decimated the Algonquian populations – 'Algonquian' being a term used to describe the linguistic family of diverse and competing Indigenous sachemships along the eastern seaboard. Thus, there were reasons why both communities might cooperate with the other. The Wampanoag reached out first, and their efforts resulted in a harvest festival, which features in the origin stories of the 'First Thanksgiving'. The English, however, were quickly drawn into rivalries between Indigenous groups. In one such instance, the English were led to believe, and perhaps believed too willingly, that a neighbouring sachemship conspired to slaughter the English. The English used deception to lure the Massachusett close, and then, they killed seven of them. The English severed their heads and, in European fashion, mounted one on the wall of their fort. The violence was a public relations disaster for the fledgling colony, and they published an account of the event that downplayed the severity of what they had done, emphasising the pervasive nature of Indigenous plots.[199]

John Robinson, the former pastor of many of the Pilgrims in Leiden, wrote a stinging rebuke of the Wessagusset Massacre of 1623. The following letter, written by a self-described 'unfeigned wellwiller of your happy success', offered a seven-fold critique of their actions: *Practical*: it will be harder to contain violence after blood is first shed; *imitation*: other Englishmen might see this killing as a precedent; *equity*: other colonists had provoked the Indigenous populations; *jurisdiction*: Englishmen had no legal authority over Algonquians; *proportion*: the punishment did not fit the crime; *leadership*: a hot-headed military commander did not value people made in God's image; *theology*: killing Algonquians prevented their conversion to Christianity. The underlying assumption of the rebuke was that these American Indians, too,

500   *Sources*

were made in the image of God, and that the violence inflicted on them was a violation of the sanctity of life.[200]

"John Robinson to the Governor of Plymouth" (19 Dec 1623), in William Bradford, *History of Plymouth Plantation*, ed. Charles Deane (Boston, MA: Privately Published, 1856), 163–165. Text modernised by the editors.

———

Letter to the Governor of Plymouth

My loving and much beloved-friend, whom God has so far preserved, preserve and keep you still to his glory, and the good of many; that his blessing may make your godly and wise endeavours answerable to the evaluation....

Concerning the killing of those poor Indians, of which we heard at first by report, and since by more certain relation: Oh! how happy a thing it would have been if you had converted some before you had killed any. Besides, where blood has begun to be shed, it is seldom restricted for a long time after. You will say they deserved it. I grant it; but upon what provocations by those heathen Christians? [i.e., unchristian Englishmen who provoked Algonquians to act unjustly.] Besides, you, not being magistrates over them, were not to consider what they deserved but what you were required to inflict. I do not see the necessity of this, especially of killing so many (and they would have killed more if they could). Killing one or two principal wrongdoers should have been enough, according to that approved rule: the punishment to the few and the fear to many. Upon this occasion, let me boldly exhort you to seriously consider the disposition of your Captain [Myles Standish], whom I love. I am persuaded that the Lord mercifully sent him to you for your good, if you employ him rightly. He is humble and meek amongst you and towards all people in ordinary course. But if we consider humanity of spirit, there is cause to fear by this occasion; he may be lacking a fitting tenderness towards the life of man (made after God's image). It is more glorious in men's eyes, than pleasing in God's eyes, for Christians to be a terror to poor barbarous people. Indeed I am afraid lest, by these occasions, others should be drawn to act in a similar way. I do not doubt that you will consider these things and make use of them as you need....

Yours truly loving,
John Robinson
Leiden, 19 December 1623

142 Hugo Grotius, *Warfare and the Law of Nations* (1625)

Keywords: #Ten Commandments, #Natural Law, #Intervention, #War, #International Relations
Region: #Netherlands
Group: #Reformed

Hugo Grotius' (1583–1645) two main works on international relations related to the laws of the sea (*Mare liberum,* 1609) and the laws of war (*De iure belli ac pacis libri tres,* 1625). After receiving a life sentence for dissident political activity, Grotius escaped prison and spent most of the rest of his life abroad. He continued his writing while in exile and wrote *De iure belli* while in France. Grotius' thought shaped, and was shaped by, the political events of his time. Not only were the Dutch engaged in a protracted struggle for independence from the Spanish crown (the Eighty Years' War, 1568–1648), but much of Europe was also engaged in hostilities (such as the Thirty Years' War, 1618–1648). The Dutch were also expanding overseas, and in the following decades, they would become a major player in international trade, including in the transatlantic slave trade.

In *De iure belli,* Grotius articulated a theory of just warfare and argued that some matters of right could be established even if one did not believe in God's existence, a possibility he recoiled at. This statement has often led to the mistaken notion that Grotius divorced scripture and theology from politics and war. Modern editions sometimes contribute to this misunderstanding.[201] Grotius argued that scripture need not *construct* laws about politics and war, but for the Christian, these laws must *correspond* to scripture and theology.[202]

To him, the principles of natural law ultimately derived from God, and international law rested on precepts that were implanted in all humanity. Despite some overlaps concerning ethical principles, people were too quick to resort to war and too relaxed in their conduct in war, and Grotius argued for greater restraint. However, Grotius was not a pacifist, and he argued that any war must meet certain criteria related to justice. In the following selection, he discussed how natural law related to warfare, the applicability of the

502   *Sources*

Hebrew Bible and Christian scriptures to warfare, the punishment of those perpetuating injustice in other nations, and the propriety of warring against theological outsiders.

Hugo Grotius, ***The Rights of War and Peace, in Three Books***, trans. and ed. J. Barbeyrac (London: W. Innys and R. Manby, 1738), xix–xxvi, xxxii–xxxiii, 9–17, 21–23, 436–438, 440–449, 602–604, 607–608.

———

Preliminary Discourse

11   And indeed, all we have now said [concerning the principles of natural justice] would take place, though we should even grant, what without the greatest Wickedness cannot be granted, that there is no God, or that he takes no Care of human Affairs. The contrary of which appearing to us, partly from Reason, partly from a perpetual Tradition, which many Arguments and Miracles, attested by all Ages, fully confirm; it hence follows, that God, as being our Creator, and to whom we owe our Being, and all that we have, ought to be obeyed by us in all Things without Exception, especially since he has so many Ways shown his infinite Goodness and Almighty Power; whence we have Room to conclude that he is able to bestow, upon those that obey him, the greatest Rewards, and those eternal too, since he himself is eternal; and that he is willing so to do ought even to be believed, especially if he has in express Words promised it; as we Christians, convinced by undoubted Testimonies, believe he has.
12   And this now is another Original of Right, besides that of Nature, being that which proceeds from the free Will of God, to which our Understanding infallibly assures us, we ought to be subject: And even the Law of Nature itself, whether it be that which consists in the Maintenance of Society, or that which in a looser Sense is so called, though it flows from the internal Principles of Man, may notwithstanding be justly ascribed to God, because it was his Pleasure that these Principles should be in us....
14   Add to this, that sacred History, besides the Precepts it contains to this Purpose, affords no inconsiderable Motive to social Affection, since it teaches us that all Men are descended from the same first Parents. So that in this Respect also may be truly affirmed, what *Florentinus* said in another Sense, That Nature has made us all akin: Whence it follows, that it is a Crime for one Man to act to the Prejudice of another....

[*From this foundation of a divinely implanted natural sense of right, Grotius describes the origins of society, government and law. His work considers a wider law that transcends natural boundaries, the law of nations.*]

18   But as the Laws of each State respect the Benefit of that State; so amongst all or most States there might be, and in Fact there are, some Laws agreed

on by common Consent, which respect the Advantage not of one Body in particular, but of all in general. And this is what is called the Law of Nations, when used in Distinction to the Law of Nature....

26 But so far must we be from admitting the Conceit of some, that the Obligation of all Right ceases in War; that on the contrary, no War ought to be so much as undertaken but for the obtaining of Right; nor when undertaken, ought it to be carried on beyond the Bounds of Justice and Fidelity. *Demosthenes* said well, that War is made against those who cannot be restrained in a judicial Way. For judicial Proceedings are of Force against those who are sensible of their Inability to oppose them; but against those who are or think themselves of equal Strength, Wars are undertaken; but yet certainly, to render Wars just, they are to be waged with no less Care and Integrity, than judicial Proceedings are usually carried on....

29 Now for my Part, being fully assured, by the Reasons I have already given, that there is some Right common to all Nations, which takes Place both in the Preparations and in the Course of War, I had many and weighty Reasons inducing me to write a Treatise upon it. I observed throughout the Christian World a Licentiousness in regard to War, which even barbarous Nations ought to be ashamed of: a Running to Arms upon very frivolous or rather no Occasions; which being once taken up, there remained no longer any Reverence for Right, either Divine or Human, just as if from that Time Men were authorised and firmly resolved to commit all manner of Crimes without Restraint.

30 The Spectacle of which monstrous Barbarity worked many, and those in no wise bad Men, up into an Opinion, that a Christian, whose Duty consists principally in loving all Men without Exception, ought not at all to bear Arms; with whom seem to agree sometimes *Johannes Ferus* and our Countryman *Erasmus*, Men that were great Lovers of Peace both Ecclesiastical and Civil; but, I suppose, they had the same View, as those have who in order to make Things that are crooked straight, usually bend them as much the other Way. But this very Endeavour of inclining too much to the opposite Extreme, is so far from doing Good, that it often does Hurt, because Men readily discovering Things that are urged too far by them, are apt to slight their Authority in other Matters, which perhaps are more reasonable. A Cure therefore was to be applied to both these, as well to prevent believing that Nothing, as that all Things are lawful.

31 At the same Time I was likewise willing to promote, by my private Studies, the Profession of Law, which I formerly practised in publick Employments with all possible Integrity; this being the only Thing that was left for me to do, being unworthily banished from my Native Country, which I have honoured with so many of my Labours. Many have before this designed to reduce it into a System; but none has accomplished it; nor indeed can it be done, unless those things (which has not been yet

504 *Sources*

sufficiently taken Care of,) that are established by the Will of Men, be duly distinguished from those which are founded on Nature. For the Laws of Nature being always the same, may be easily collected into an Art; but those which proceed from Human Institution being often changed, and different in different Places, are no more susceptible of a methodical System, than other Ideas of particular Things are....

34 For in the first Book, after premising some Things concerning the Origin of Right, we have examined the general Question, whether any War is just; afterwards to discover the Difference between a publick and private War, our Business was to explain the Extent of the Supreme Power, what People, what Kings have it in full, who in part, who with a Power of alienating it, and who have it without that Power. And then we were to speak of the Duty of Subjects to their Sovereigns.

35 The second Book, undertaken to explain all the Causes from whence a War may arise, shows at large, what Things are common, what proper, what Right one Person may have over another, what Obligation arises from the Property of Goods, what is the Rule of Regal Succession, what Right arises from Covenant or Contract, what the Force and Interpretation of Treaties and Alliances, what of an Oath both publick and private, what may be due for a Damage done, what the Privileges of Embassadors, what the Right of burying the Dead, what the Nature of Punishments.

36 The third Book treats first of what is lawful in War; and then, having distinguished that which is done with bare Impunity, or which is even defended as lawful among foreign Nations, from that which is really blameless, descends to the several Kinds of Peace, and all Agreements made in war....

49 The Authority of those Books which Men inspired by God, either writ or approved of, I often use, but with a Difference of the Old and New Law. Some there are who urge the Old Law for the very Law of Nature, but they are undoubtedly in the wrong: For many Things in it proceed from the Free Will of God, which yet is never repugnant to the Law of Nature itself; and so far an Argument may be rightly drawn from it, provided we carefully distinguish the Rights of God, which God sometimes exercises by the Ministry of Men, from the Rights of Men among themselves. We have therefore avoided, as much as we could, both this Error, and also another contrary to it, *viz.* that since the Promulgation of the New Testament the Old one is of no Use. We are of a contrary Opinion, both upon Account of what we have said already, and also because the Nature of the *New Testament* is such, that whatever are the moral Precepts in the *Old Testament*, the same, or more perfect, are enjoined by the New also: And in this Manner we see the Testimonies of the *Old Testament* made Use of by the Writers among the Primitive Christians....

Sources 505

51 The *New Testament* I use for this Purpose, that I may show, what cannot be elsewhere learned, what is lawful for Christians to do; which Thing itself, I have notwithstanding, contrary to what most do, distinguished from the Law of Nature; as being fully assured, that in that most holy Law a greater Sanctity is enjoined us, than the mere Law of Nature in itself requires. Nor have I for all that omitted observing, what Things in it are rather recommended to us than commanded, to the Intent we may know, that as to transgress the Commands is a Crime that renders us liable to be punished; so to aim at the highest Perfection, in what is but barely recommended, is the Part of a generous Mind, and that will not fail of a proportionable Reward....

BOOK I

Chapter 1: What *War* is, and what *Right* is

Section 10: The *Law of Nature* defined, divided, and distinguished from such as are not properly called so.

1 *Natural Right* is the Rule and Dictate of *Right Reason*, showing the Moral Deformity or Moral Necessity there is in any Act, according to its Suitableness or Unsuitableness to a reasonable Nature, and consequently, that such an Act is either forbid or commanded by GOD, the Author of Nature.
2 The Actions upon which such a Dictate is given, are in themselves either Obligatory or Unlawful, and must, consequently, be understood to be either com manded or forbid by God himself; and this makes the Law of Nature differ not only from Human Right, but from a Voluntary Divine Right; for that does not command or forbid such Things as are in themselves, or in their own Nature, Obligatory and Unlawful; but by forbidding, it renders the one Unlawful, and by commanding, the other Obligatory....
5 As for the Rest, the Law of Nature is so unalterable, that God himself cannot change it. For tho' the Power of God be infinite, yet we may say, that there are some Things to which this infinite Power does not extend, because they cannot be expressed by Propositions that contain any Sense, but manifestly imply a Contradiction. For Instance then, as God himself cannot effect, that twice two should not be four; so neither can he, that what is intrinsically Evil should not be Evil.... For as the Being and Essence of Things after they exist, depend not upon any other, so neither do the Properties which necessarily follow that Being and Essence. Now such is the Evil of some Actions, compared with a Nature guided by right Reason. Therefore God suffers himself to be judged of according to this Rule (Gen. 18: 25; Isa. 5:3; Ezek. 18:25; Jer. 2:9; Mic. 6:2; Rom. 2:6, 3:6)....

506   *Sources*

Section 12. How the *Law of Nature* may be proved.

Now that any Thing is or is not by the Law of Nature, is generally proved either *à priori*, that is, by Arguments drawn from the very Nature of the Thing; or *à posteriori*, that is, by Reasons taken from something external. The former Way of Reasoning is more subtle and abstracted; the latter more popular. The Proof by the former is by showing the necessary Fitness or Unfitness of any Thing, with a reasonable and sociable Nature. But the Proof by the latter is, when we cannot with absolute Certainty, yet with very great Probability, conclude that to be by the Law of Nature, which is generally believed to be so by all, or at least, the most civilised, Nations. For, an universal Effect requires an universal Cause. And there cannot well be any other Cause assigned for this general Opinion, than what is called Common Sense....

Section 13: *Voluntary Right* divided into *human* and *divine*.

The other kind of Right, we told you, is the *Voluntary Right*, as being derived from the *Will*, and is either *Human* or *Divine*.

Section 14. *Human Right* divided into a *Civil Right*, a *less extensive Right than the Civil*, and a *more extensive Right*, or the *Law of Nations*: This explained and proved.

We will begin with the Human, as more generally known; and this is either a *Civil*, a *less extensive*, or a *more extensive Right than the Civil*. The *Civil* Right is that which results from the Civil Power. The Civil Power is that which governs the *State*. The State is a compleat Body of free Persons, associated together to enjoy peaceably their Rights, and for their common Benefit. The *less extensive* Right, and which is not derived from the Civil Power, though subject to it, is various, including in it the Commands of a Father to his Child, of a Master to his Servant, and the like. But the *more extensive* Right, is the *Right of Nations*, which derives its Authority from the Will of all, or at least of many, Nations. I say *of many*, because there is scarce any Right found, except that of Nature, which is also called the Right of Nations, common to all Nations. Nay, that which is reputed the Right or Law of Nations in one Part of the World, is not so in another, as we shall show hereafter, when we come to treat of *Prisoners of War*, and *Postliminy* or the *Right of Returning*. Now the Proofs on which the Law of Nations is founded, are the same with those of the unwritten Civil Law, namely continual Use, and the Testimony of Men skilled in the Laws....

Section 15: The *Divine Law* divided into that which is *universal*, and that which is *peculiar* to one Nation.

The *Divine voluntary Law* (as may be understood from the very Name) is that which is derived only from the Will of GOD himself; whereby it is distinguished from the Natural Law, which in some Sense, as we have said above, may be called Divine also. And here may take Place that which *Anaxarchus* said, as *Plutarch* relates in the Life of *Alexander*, (but too generally) that GOD does not *will* a Thing because it is just; but it is just, that is, it lays one

Sources   507

under an indispensible Obligation, because GOD *wills* it. And this Law was given either to all Man-kind, or to one People only: We find that GOD gave it to all Mankind at three different Times. First, Immediately after the Creation of Man. Secondly, Upon the Restoration of Mankind after the Flood. And thirdly, Under the Gospel, in that more perfect re-establishment by CHRIST. These three Laws do certainly oblige all Mankind, as soon as they are sufficiently made known to them....

[*He discoursed at length on God's unique relationship with Israel, and throughout the work he argued that Israel's laws regarding war and peace should be cautiously invoked since many of them were not intended for direct imitation by non-Israelites.*]

XVII. What Arguments *Christians* may fetch from the *Judaical* Law, and how.

Since then the *Mosaick* Law cannot directly oblige us (as I have already showed) let us see of what other Use it may be to us, as well in regard to the *Right of War*, which we are to treat of, as in other like Cases. For the Knowledge of it may be necessary in many Points.

First then, the Law of the antient *Hebrews* serves to assure us, that nothing is enjoined there contrary to the Law of Nature; for since the Law of Nature (as I said before) is perpetual and unchangeable, nothing could be commanded by GOD, who can never be unjust, contrary to this Law. Besides, the Law of Moses is called pure and right (Ps. 19:8) and by the Apostle St. Paul, holy, just, and good (Rom. 7:12)....

The next Observation is not unlike this, *viz.* That Christian Princes may now make Laws of the same Import with those given by *Moses*, unless they be such Laws as wholly related either to the Time of the expected *Messias*, and the Gospel, not then published; or that CHRIST himself has either in general, or in particular commanded the contrary: For, excepting these three Reasons, no other can be imagined, why that which the Law of *Moses* formerly established, should now be unlawful.

The third Observation may be this; whatsoever was enjoined by the Law of *Moses*, which relates to those Virtues that CHRIST requires of his Disciples, ought now as much, if not more, to be observed by us Christians. The Ground of this Observation is, because what Virtues are required of Christians, as Humility, Patience, Charity, &c. are to be practised in a more eminent Degree, than under the State of the *Hebrew* Law, and that with good Reason too; because the Promises of Heaven are more clearly proposed to us in the Gospel....

[*Chapter 2 countered the argument that warfare was proscribed by the law of nature, the law of nations, the Hebrew Bible or the Christian scriptures, although he acknowledged that divine law restricted when Israelites and Christians could go to war and how they should conduct themselves in war. Chapter 3 considered what constituted supreme authority and power, and how this supremacy related to submission. Chapter 4 argued that warfare*]

508   *Sources*

by subjects against sovereigns was proscribed by the Law of Nature, Hebrew Law, the Gospel and the witness of early Christianity. However, in kingdoms the people possessed liberties and rights, and in these cases, the people might have a right of resistance. Chapter 5 then outlined who may lawfully make war.]

BOOK II

Chapter 20: Of *Punishments*

Section 40. Whether it be *lawful* for *Kings* and *States* to make *War* upon *such* as *violate* the *Law of Nature*, tho' they have committed *nothing* against *them* or their *Subjects*; this explained, and the *Opinion* that would have Jurisdiction naturally *necessary* towards *punishing*, rejected.

1. We must also know, that Kings, and those who are invested with a Power equal to that of Kings, have a Right to exact Punishments, not only for Injuries committed against themselves, or their Subjects, but likewise, for those which do not peculiarly concern them, but which are, in any Persons whatsoever, grievous Violations of the Law of Nature or Nations. For the Liberty of consulting the Benefit of human Society, by Punishments, which at first, as we have said, was in every particular Person, does now, since Civil Societies, and Courts of Justice, have been instituted, reside in those who are possessed of the supreme Power, and that properly, not as they have an Authority over others, but as they are in Subjection to none. For, as for others, their Subjection has taken from them this Right. Nay, it is so much more honourable, to revenge other Peoples Injuries rather than their own, by as much as it is more to be feared, lest out of a Sense of their own Sufferings, they either exceed the just Measure of Punishment, or, at least, prosecute their Revenge with Malice....

[3. *He discusses intervening in regions that practice brutish behaviour.*] For of such Barbarians, and rather Beasts than Men, may be fitly said what *Aristotle* spoke out of Prejudice concerning the *Persians*, who were indeed nothing worse than the *Greeks*; that War against such is natural; and as *Isocrates* said in his *Panathenaic*, the justest War is that which is undertaken against wild rapacious Beasts, and next to it is that against Men who are like Beasts.

4. And so far we follow the Opinion of *Innocentius*, and others, who hold that War is lawful against those who offend against Nature; which is contrary to the Opinion of *Victoria*, *Vasquez*, *Azorius*, *Molina*, and others, who seem to require, towards making a War just, that he who undertakes it be injured in himself, or in his State, or that he has some Jurisdiction over the Person against whom the War is made. For they assert, that the Power of Punishing is properly an Effect of Civil Jurisdiction; whereas our Opinion is, that it proceeds from the Law of Nature, concerning which Point we said something in the Beginning of the first Book....

Sources 509

Section 44. Whether *War* may be made for *Offences* against *GOD* only.

1 The Order of our Discourse has now brought us to consider, those Offences that are committed against GOD. For the Question is, Whether for the revenging of these a War may be undertaken? [He argues at length that impiety is ruinous for a nation.]

6 Now the Usefulness of Religion is even greater in that great Society of Mankind in general, than in any particular Civil Society; for in a Civil State it is partly supplied by the Laws, and the easy Execution of the Laws; whereas, on the contrary, in the universal Society of Mankind, the Execution of Right is very difficult, as being to be performed no other Way than by Force of Arms, and the Laws are very few, which themselves, moreover, derive their Force chiefly from the Fear of a Deity; from whence those who offend against the Law of Nations, are every where said to violate the Law of GOD. It was not amiss therefore, that the Emperors asserted, that The Corruption of Religion was an Injury to all the World.

Section 45. Which are the most *common Notions* of a *GOD*, and how they are *contained* in the first Precepts of the *Decalogue*.

1. To take a closer View of the whole Matter, we must observe, that the true Religion, which has been common to all Ages, is built upon four fundamental Principles; of which the *first* is, that *There is a GOD, and but one GOD only*. The *second*, that *GOD is not any of those Things we see, but something more sublime than them*. The *third*, that *GOD takes Care of human Affairs, and judges them with the strictest Equity*. The *fourth*, that *The same GOD is the Creator of all Things but himself*. These four are expressed in so many Commandments of the Decalogue....

Section 46. That *those* who *first* violate these *Notions* are *punishable*.

1 And therefore those Men are not entirely blameless, who, tho' they are too stupid to find out, or comprehend, the Arguments that serve to demonstrate these Notions, do yet reject them, since these Truths lead to Virtue; and besides, the contrary Opinion has not Arguments to support it. But because we are here discoursing of Punishments, and those such Punishments as relate to Men, we must distinguish between the Notions themselves, and the Manner of rejecting them. That there is a Deity, (one or more I shall not now consider) and that this Deity has the Care of human Affairs, are Notions universally received, and are absolutely necessary to the Essence of any Religion, whether true or false. *He that cometh to GOD*, (that is, he who has any Religion, for Religion, by the Hebrews, is termed *A Coming to GOD*) *must believe that he is, and that he is a Rewarder of them that diligently seek him* (Heb. 9:6)....

510 *Sources*

4 It is my Judgement therefore, that those who first attempt to destroy these Notions, ought, on the Account of human Society in general, which they thus, without any just Grounds, injure, to be restrained, as in all well-governed Communities has been usual....

Section 47. But not *others*; which is shown by an Argument drawn from the *Mosaick* Law.

1 Other general Notions, as that *There is but one GOD*, that *No Object of our Sight is GOD*, not the World, not the Heavens, not the Sun, nor the Air; that *The World is not eternal, nor its compound Matter, but that it was created by GOD*, have not the same Degrees of Evidence as the former, and therefore the Knowledge of them in some Nations, through Length of Time, we find effaced, and almost extinguished; to this did contribute the Remissness of the Laws, which made but little Provision for them, because not deemed so absolutely necessary, but that without them some Sort of Religion might be kept up.....

4 As then they are excusable, and certainly do not deserve human Punishment, who having received no revealed Law, worship the Powers and Qualities of the Stars, or other natural Beings, or Spirits, either in Images, Animals, or any other Objects, or even the departed Souls of Men eminent for their Virtues, and useful in their Generations, or other spiritual Substances, especially if they were not themselves the Inventers of this Worship, and therefore do not forsake the Service of the true GOD: So, on the other Hand, those are not to be looked upon as People pardonably ignorant and mistaken, but as impious and perversely wicked, who pay divine Honours to evil Spirits under the Notion of such, to the Names of Vices, or to Men infamous for flagitious Lives.

5 Of the same Stamp are they likewise, who honour their false Deities with human Sacrifices.... [who after being told this is wrong, are forthwith to stop the practice.]

Section 48. That *War* cannot be *justly* made upon *those* who *refuse* to embrace the *Christian* Religion.

1 But how shall we determine of that War which is brought against a Nation, for no other Reason but because they reject the Laws of Christianity, when proposed unto them. I shall not here stand to enquire whether it be such, or after such a Manner propounded, as it ought: But taking them both for granted, there are two Things which occur observable. The *first* is, that the Truth of the Christian Religion, in those Particulars which are additional to natural and primitive Religion, cannot be evidenced by mere natural Arguments, but depends upon the History we have of CHRIST's Resurrection, and the Miracles performed by him and his Apostles, which

have been confirmed by unexceptionable Testimonies, but many Ages since, so that the Question now is of Matters of Fact, and those of a very antient Date; for which Reason this Doctrine cannot so easily gain Belief, and procure Men's Assent upon the first Promulgation of it, without the inward Assistance of GOD's Grace, in the Distribution of which his Methods are unsearchable; when he affords it plentifully, Merit in us is not the Motive, and when he withholds it, or dispenses it but sparingly, it is for Reasons not unjust, but concealed from Men, and therefore not punishable by any human Judicature. To this Effect is that Canon of the Council of *Toledo*, which forbids the Use of compulsive Means, in gaining Converts to Christianity, for *On whom he will have Mercy he will have Mercy; and whom he will he hardeneth*. It being the Practice of the inspired Writers to ascribe those Effects, whereof human Reason cannot discover the Cause, to the Divine Will....

Section 49. *War* may *justly* be made against *those* who persecute *Christians* only for their *being so.*

1 But they who punish Men, because they preach or profess Christianity, do, no Doubt of it, act against the Dictates of Reason; for the Christian Religion (considered untainted with Mixture, and in its primitive Purity) is so far from doing any Thing destructive to human Society, that in every Particular it tends to the Advantage of it. The Nature of it declares thus much, and those of a different Religion are forced to acknowledge the same....

2 They, therefore, who persecute Christians, as such, do make themselves justly obnoxious to Punishment. This is the Opinion of *Thomas Aquinas* (Summ. Theol. ii.2. *Quaest.* 103). It was for this Reason that *Constantine* commenced a War against *Licinius*, and other Emperors, against the *Persians*; which Wars however relate rather to an innocent self Defence, of which we shall treat hereafter, than to a Punishment properly so called.

Section 50. But *not* against those who are mistaken in the *Interpretation* of the *divine Law*; this illustrated by Authorities and Examples.

1 But as for those who use professed Christians with Rigour, because they are doubtful, or erroneous as to some Points either not delivered in Sacred Writ, or not so clearly but to be capable of various Acceptations, and which have been differently interpreted by the primitive Christians, they are undoubtedly very unjust....

2 But suppose the Error be more palpable, and such as one may be easily convicted of before equitable Judges, from the holy Scriptures, and from the concurrent Opinions of the primitive Fathers; even in this Case it is requisite to consider how prevalent the Force of a long standing Opinion

512 *Sources*

is, and how much the Attachment every Man has to his own Sect, perverts his Judgement, and destroys the Freedom of it; an Evil, according to *Galen*, more incurable than a Leprosy.... Besides, to determine how criminal this is, it is requisite to be acquainted with the Degrees of Men's Understanding, and other inward Dispositions of Mind, which it is impossible for Men to find out.

BOOK III

Chapter 7: Of the Right over Prisoners

Section 1. All Prisoners in a Solemn War are, by the Law of Nations, Slaves.

1 There is no Man by Nature Slave to another, that is, in his primitive State considered, independently of any human Fact, as I have said in another Place; in which Sense we may take the Lawyers, when they say that Slavery is against Nature; but it is not repugnant to natural Justice, that Men should become Slaves by a human Fact, that is, by Virtue of some Agreement, or in consequence of some Crime, as we have also said already.

2 But by the Law of Nations, which I am now treating of, Slavery is of a more large Extent, both as to Persons and Effects. For if we consider the Persons, not only they who surrender themselves, or submit by Promise to Slavery, are reputed Slaves; but all Persons whatsoever taken in a solemn War, as soon as they shall be brought into a Place whereof the enemy is Master....

Section 2. And their Posterity.

Neither do only they themselves become Slaves, but their Posterity for ever; for whosoever is born of a Woman after she is a Slave, is born a Slave.... [He cites Tacitus to this effect.]

Section 3. Any Thing done to them is unpunishable.

1 But the Effects of this Right are infinite, so that there is nothing that the Lord may not do to his Slave, as *Seneca* the Father said, no Torment but what may be exacted with the utmost Rigour and Severity; so that all manner of Cruelty may be exercised by the Lords upon their Slaves; unless this License is somewhat restrained by the civil law. *It is allowed by all Nations to the Lord, to have Power of Life and Death over his slave*, we are told by *Caius*....

Section 5. The Reason why this was ordained.

1 Now this large Power is granted by the Law of Nations for no other Reason, than that the Captors being tempted by so many Advantages might be inclined to forbear that Rigour allowed to them by the Law, of killing their Prisoners either in the fight, or some Time after....

Sources 513

2 And for the same Reason he has Power to transfer this Right to another, in the same manner as the Property of Goods. This Power also reaches to the Children born in Captivity, because if the Captor had been pleased to have used his utmost Power, he might have prevented their being born; and consequently those born before the Captivity of the Mother (if they are not personally taken) do not become Slaves. And the Reason that by the Law of Nations Children followed the Mother's Condition, without regard to their Father, is because the Cohabitation of Slaves was neither regulated by the Laws, nor maintained in such a manner, that the Mother should be always under the Eye and Guard of the Father, so that it would have been a very difficult Thing to prove who was the Father....

[*He discusses whether those taken in war or their children had the right to escape (they can in limited circumstances) and whether a slave could resist their master (they cannot).*]

Section 9. [On Slavery Among Christians.]

1 But among Christians it is generally agreed, that being engaged in War, they that are taken Prisoners, are not made Slaves, so as to sell them or force them to hard Labours, or to such Miseries as are common to Slaves, and that with Reason; for they are, or should be better instructed by the great Recommender of every Act of Charity, than not to be diverted from the killing of unhappy Persons, unless they may be allowed the Exercise of a somewhat less Cruelty....
2 And what Christians in this Case observe among themselves, the *Mahometans* likewise do among themselves. Yet even among Christians this Custom still continues, that those taken in War are kept till their Ransom be paid, which is set at the Pleasure of the Conqueror, unless it be otherwise agreed upon; but this Right of keeping Prisoners is usually granted to the Captors, except they be Persons of considerable Rank, to whom the State only, or its chief Magistrate has a Right, according to the Custom of most Nations.

[*Above, Grotius explored laws about slavery in light of the law of nations. However, as he detailed in many places, there were several types of law, ranging from natural law to the law of love. Another law might restrain aspects of what was permitted by the law of nations. Similarly, Book 3 contained several chapters on moderation in warfare (3.11–16). The law of nations may permit harsh actions; however, internal moral justice may recommend a more moderate course. In 'Moderation concerning Captives' (3.14), Grotius emphasised the moderating effect of internal justice and divine law on the master-slave relationship.*]

143 *Demands of the Peasants of Austria* (1626)

Keywords: #Rebellion, #War, #Petition, #Toleration, #Property
Region: #Austria
Group: #Lutheran

In 1618, Bohemians rose up against the Habsburg Ferdinand II (Holy Roman Emperor), an event that triggered the Thirty Years' War. The Lutheran majority in Austria above the Enns (upper Austria) allied to the Bohemians. The Catholic Duke Maximilian of Bavaria suppressed these peasants in 1620, and his star continued to rise during the war. He was later elevated to Elector Palatine and Elector of Bavaria. Maximilian attempted to bring the region back into the Catholic fold by promoting the Counter-Reformation, supporting the Jesuits, and repressing the Lutheran faith. When peasants revolted in 1625, 100 years after the **German Peasants' War** (1524–1525), they were initially suppressed with overwhelming force. A year later, a larger group of peasants took up arms again, clearly spelt out their demands, as reproduced below, and they enjoyed some short-lived successes.[203]

Tryntje Helfferich, *The Thirty Years War: A Documentary History* (Indianapolis, IN: Hacket, 2009), 84.

———

The demands of the collected peasantry of Austria above the Enns to His Imperial Majesty consists of the following 12 articles.

1 The word of God.
2 The emperor as ruler, and not the prince [Maximilian] of Bavaria.
3 To remove the governor of Linz [who tried to forcibly re-Catholicise the region].
4 A provincial governor who resides in the province.
5 To place Lutheran judges and mayors in the cities; the Catholics are not to be trusted.
6 To remove prelates from the council and to put in peasants, as is the custom in Tyrol.

Sources 515

7 That the soldiers be expelled legally from the province, for we peasants wish to protect the province.
8 To remove the garrisons from the cities; some money shall be given annually for this.
9 To clear from the province the rabble of Jesuit clergy, in addition to the prelates.
10 A general pardon of all the poor and the rich, of high and low estate.
11 By dint of the capitulation [promising toleration] that Emperor Matthias promised [in 1609], every provincial lord to be able to keep a preacher on his property.
12 All exiles to be entirely restored to their property and be placed once again in peaceful possession of it.

144 *Algonquians and Africans in New Netherland* (1628–1660)

Keywords: #Colonisation, #Land, #Slavery, #War, #Evangelisation, #Missions, #Paternalism
Region: #United States | #Netherlands
Group: #Dutch Reformed | #African, #Indigenous American

The colonial province of New Netherland lasted for a little over a half-century before the English definitively conquered it in 1674. The Dutch settled on the lands of the Lenape, who were part of the linguistic group of the Algonquians. Their homeland (Lenapehoking) encompassed significant portions of what is now New York, Pennsylvania, New Jersey, and Delaware. Like other Protestant groups, the Dutch Reformed entered the region with a sense of cultural and spiritual superiority. Many argued that their presence in these lands should benefit the Lenape by drawing them towards 'civility' and piety. Missionary efforts, however, were slow and frustrating, leading several ministers to advocate a policy of separating Indigenous children from their parents. The Lenape-Dutch relationship was frequently marked by warfare, and sometimes Indigenous groups allied with Europeans (Swedes, Dutch, English) for strategic purposes. By the 1660s, Europeans exerted considerable domination along the coastline and along many of the principal rivers, pushing the Lenape deeper into the interior. Owing to the Dutch, enslaved Africans were also in the colony from early on. The following sources span from 1628 to 1660 and evidence Dutch attitudes towards the Lenape and Africans. The sources reflect on natural law, the possibility of evangelisation, and the supposed benefits of Dutch domination.[204]

1. Albert Eekhof, *Jonas Michaëlius, Founder of the Church in New Netherland, His Life and Work* (Leiden: A. W. Sijthoff, 1926), 110–111; 2, 5. J. Franklin Jameson, ed., *Narratives of New Netherland, 1609–1664* (New York: Charles Scribner's Sons, 1909), 123, 127–130, 329–330; 3–4, 6–7. Hugh Hastings, ed., *Ecclesiastical Records: State of New York* (Albany, NY: James B. Lyon, 1901), I:144, 146–147, 266–267, 326–327, 468–469.

———

Sources 517

1. Jonas Michaëlius to Johannes van Foreest (8 Aug 1628)

[*Jonas Michaëlius was educated in Leiden and ministered in the Netherlands. His plans to serve in Brazil were thwarted by a hostile army and he instead spent some time in Africa before returning to the Netherlands. Another colonial venture needed a minister, and in 1628 he arrived as the first clergyman in New Netherland. Despite struggling in the colony, he worked to bring about moral and religious reform in an outpost of the Dutch Reformed world. This letter recounts the voyage to New Netherland, including the death of his wife, and his initial assessment of the colonies and the Indigenous inhabitants. He then describes the means of acquiring land: what might look like Dutch forbearance and forgiveness was actually a calculated strategy of land dispossession.*]

[You will have been informed] of the whole affair, as well as of many more things, such as the manifold wickedness, devilish tricks, and more than barbarous cruelties of these nations against each other, for they are divided into many tribes. We lack only sufficient people to occupy [the region]. For a small sum of money we can buy from them a large quantity of land, and besides, there are enough old and new causes to be found for taking possession of their land (which can afford us little or no profit) by way of confiscation, on account of much treachery and many offences committed against us. These have never been forgiven them, nor adjusted by any treaty, but have been reserved for a certain purpose, at the propitious time, to make use of them, to the advantage of the Company and this place.

[*The letter then describes the climate, the construction of a fort and the establishment of the first church as well as possible missionary work.*]

Through the Lord's mercy we have begun to found a Christian Church here, about which I have written at greater length [elsewhere], as well as about the fruit of my ministry, which I already perceive, and, with the Lord's blessing, still expect; also of the small possibility I see of leading this blind, perverse, Nation to the true knowledge of God, through Christ.

———

2. Jonas Michaëlius to Adrianus Smoutius (11 Aug 1628)

[*In this letter, Michaëlius recounted the death of his wife, the voyage to New Amsterdam, the foundation of the church and the challenges facing the community. He also reflected at greater length on the Indigenous population, claiming there was scarcely any trace of religion or natural law among them. Although he did not spell out the implications, some legal theorists argued that such people fell outside the norms of international law. He claimed to be unable 'to discover hardly a single good point about them', yet his letter revealed evidence of natural law; namely, the intense affection of parents towards their children. To his frustration, Lenape parents recoiled at the forceable removal of their children, and they helped their children run away.*]

518   *Sources*

As to the natives of this country, I find them entirely savage and wild, strangers to all decency, yea, uncivil and stupid as garden poles, proficient in all wickedness and godlessness; devilish men, who serve nobody but the Devil, that is, the spirit which in their language they call Menitoo [Manitou]; under which title they comprehend everything that is subtle and crafty and beyond human skill and power. They have so much witchcraft, divination, sorcery and wicked arts, that they can hardly be held in any bands or locks. They are as thievish and treacherous as they are tall; and in cruelty they are altogether inhuman, more than barbarous, far exceeding the Africans....

How these people can best be led to the true knowledge of God and of his Mediator Christ, is hard to say. I cannot myself wonder enough who it is that has imposed so much upon your Reverence and many others in the Fatherland, concerning the docility of these people and their good nature, the proper *principia religionis* [rudimentary principles of religion] and *vestigia legis naturae* [vestige of the law of nature] which are said to be among them; in whom I have yet been able to discover hardly a single good point, except that they do not speak so jeeringly and so scoffingly of the godlike and glorious majesty of their Creator as the Africans dare to do. But it may be because they have no certain knowledge of Him, or scarcely any.... Now, by what means are we to lead this people to salvation, or to make a salutary breach among them? I take the liberty on this point of enlarging somewhat to your Reverence.

[*He discusses their language, which he admits some Europeans learn easily. However, he thinks their language is child-like, incoherent and comparable to the biblical peoples of Ashdod (Neh. 13:24) – a pointed reference since this passage forbade intermarriage with non-Israelites.*]

It would be well then to leave the parents as they are, and begin with the children who are still young. So be it. But they ought in youth to be separated from their parents; yea from their whole nation. For, without this, they would forthwith be as much accustomed as their parents to the heathenish tricks and deviltries, which are kneaded naturally in their hearts by themselves through a just judgement of God; so that having once, by habit, obtained deep root, they would with great difficulty be emancipated therefrom. But this separation is hard to effect. For the parents have a strong affection for their children, and are very loth to part with them; and when they are separated from them, as we have already had proof, the parents are never contented, but take them away stealthily, or induce them to run away. Nevertheless, although it would be attended with some expense, we ought, by means of presents and promises, to obtain the children, with the gratitude and consent of the parents, in order to place them under the instruction of some experienced and godly school-master, where they may be instructed not only to speak, read, and write on our language, but also especially in the fundamentals of our Christian religion; and where, besides, they will see nothing but good examples of virtuous living; but they must sometimes speak their native tongue among themselves in order not to forget it, as being evidently a principal means of spreading the knowledge of religion through the whole nation. [*He recounts how God intervenes to purify all Christians from sin and rescue them from the curse of damnation.*] And this I regard so much more necessary, as the wrath and curse of God, resting upon this miserable people, I found to be the heavier. Perchance God may at last have mercy upon them, that the fulness of the heathen may be gradually brought in [Rom. 11:25] and the salvation of our God may be here also seen among these wild savage men. I hope to keep a watchful eye over these people, and to learn as much as possible of their language, and to seek better opportunities for their instruction than hitherto it has been possible to find.

As to what concerns myself and my household affairs: I find myself by the loss of my good and helpful partner very much hindered and distressed – for my two little daughters are yet small; maid servants are not here to be had, at least none whom they advise me to take; and the Angola slave women are thievish, lazy, and useless trash....

———

3. Contract and Call of Rev. John Megapolensis (March 1642)

[*The following sources relate to the sending of a minister, John Megapolensis, to the colony. The contract clearly states that his salary should afford him time to minister to the Lenape, and his official calling anticipated ministry among the Indigenous population.*]

[Contract] Which salary, in order that he and his family shall be able honourably to maintain themselves, and not be necessitated to have resources to any other means [of sustenance]; but by the diligent performance of his duties for the edifying improvement of the inhabitants and the Indians...

[Call to Ministry] Whereas, by the state of the navigation in East and West Indias, a door is opened through the special providence of God, also in New Netherland for the preaching of the Gospel of Jesus Christ for the salvation of all men.... [Having found Rev. Megapolensis worthy, they charge him] to perform the duty of the Gospel to the advancement of God's Holy Name and the conversion of many poor blind men.

May the Almighty God, who hath called him to this ministry, and instilled this good zeal in his heart, to proclaim Christ to Christians and heathens in such distant lands, strengthen him, more and more, in this undertaking....

———

4. Complaints against the West India Company (January 1650)

[*Commerce and conversion were two aims of the Dutch as they expanded globally, and sometimes those interests came into tension. Although the West India Company promoted and defended the Dutch Reformed faith, it gave greater weight to matters of financial advantage. In the following exchange, the WIC was charged with many failings, among them indifference to the*

520   *Sources*

spiritual condition of slaves within their care. The WIC replied that evangelisation was not company business, further adding that the conversion of adults was 'morally impossible'. This exchange again highlights the Dutch focus on children.]

[Charge 18 against the WIC.] The Directors have made no effort to convert to Christianity either Indians, or the Blacks or Slaves, owned by the Company there.

[WIC reply to the charge.] Everyone conversant with the Indians in, and around New Netherland, will be able to say, that it is morally impossible to convert the adults to the Christian faith. Besides, 'tis a Minister's business to apply himself to that, and the Director's duty to assist him therein.

———

5. Bondage and the Benefits of Christianity (1650)

[*For early Dutch colonisers, the term 'Christian' had many meanings. If one were speaking about Catholics, 'Christian' meant 'Protestant' (generic) or 'Reformed' (specific). If one were speaking of about African or Indigenous persons, 'Christian' meant 'European' (generic) or 'Dutch' (specific). This use of language created problems for Protestants who wanted to hold other humans as property and argue that slavery was spiritually beneficial for the enslaved. For centuries, the church argued that Christians should not enslave Christians, often meaning that European Christians should not enslave other European Christians. As Europeans started enslaving more people from Africa and the Americas, they hesitated to release converted slaves or their children. The following source from* The Representation of New Netherland *(1650) was critical of Dutch colonial administrators. The principal author, Adriaen van der Donck, employed the language of 'Christian' in an ethnic or cultural sense, differentiating between Europeans and non-Europeans. However, at one point, he employed 'Christian' in the theological sense, differentiating between the regenerate and unregenerate. He critiqued the colonial administration for keeping the children of African Christians in bondage. The source is important because it shows the decoupling of 'Christian' and 'freedom', meaning that some Christians could remain enslaved, provided they or their ancestors descended from certain people groups. A similar change in language occurred in several Protestant slaveholding regions.[205]*]

The negroes, also, who came from Tamandare [Brazil] were sold for pork and peas, from the proceeds of which something wonderful was to be performed, but they just dripped through the fingers. There are also various other negroes in this country, some of whom have been made free for their long service, but their children have remained slaves, though it is contrary to the laws of every people that any one born of a free Christian mother should be a slave and be compelled to remain in servitude.

[*Dutch ministers claimed they had good reason to deny baptism to African adults or children, as when Henricus Selyns wrote in 1664 that he refused baptism on account of the 'worldly and perverse aims on the part of the said negroes' who merely wanted 'to deliver their children from bodily slavery'.*[206]]

———

6. Evangelisation after Domination (1654)

[*Many European backers of colonial enterprises hoped colonists were reaping material and spiritual rewards. The following letter shows how reports of a great evangelical harvest among the Indigenous population were overblown. Reverends Johannes Megapolensis and Samuel Drisius dispelled sensational accounts. Further, they believed that directly governing the Lenape would be the means to bring them to faith.*]

Revs. Megapolensis and Drisius to the Classis of Amsterdam (16 July 1654)

[*They thank the Classis for helping them keep the Lutheran faith out of New Amsterdam.*]

In addition to this, you make mention in your letter, that you have gathered from our letters, that the knowledge of the Gospel is making great progress among the Indians here. Speaking with all deference, we do not know or think that we have furnished any such intelligence in our letters. We greatly wish, indeed, that such were the state of things among the Indians, but as yet, there is little appearance of it. It is indeed true that a sachem of the Indians has sojourned for a length of time among us at the Manhattans, who was diligent in learning to read and write, which he learned to do tolerably well. He was also instructed in the principle grounds of the Christian faith, and publicly joined in recitations on the catechism by Christian children. We gave him a Bible that he might peruse it and teach his own countrymen from it. We hoped that in due time he might be the instrument of accomplishing considerable good among the Indians. But we acknowledge that he has only the bare knowledge of truth, without the practice of godliness. He is greatly inclined to drunkenness, and indeed, is not better than other Indians. We do not indeed expect much fruit of religion among these barbarous nations, until they are brought under the government of Europeans, as these latter increase in numbers....

[*Another lengthy letter (5 Aug 1657) underscored the lack of progress with the Lenape, arguing that the success of the gospel depended on government intervention: they could 'see no way to accomplish it, until they are subdued by the numbers and power of our people, and reduced to some sort of civilisation'.*]

———

7. Sins that Provoke God (1660)

[*This final source is an official proclamation urging colonists to humble themselves before God. It is similar to other fast-day proclamations produced in*

522   *Sources*

the Protestant world, particularly by the Reformed. Such proclamations tried to make sense of hardship by answering questions about how God communicated through calamity. First, how did one know God was angry? They appealed to physical ailments and Indigenous warfare as evidence of divine chastisement. Second, why was God angry? They cited sins like breaking the Sabbath or adultery. Third, what was the remedy? Like every fast proclamation, the people must return to God. Such proclamations offer a moral assessment of the body politic, and the sins they mention are as illuminating as the sins they omit. In this case, God was angry at 'swearing', but not at the injustice perpetrated against the Lenape. God was provoked by 'feasting', but not by using enslaved Africans to prepare those feasts. Such omissions were typical for the period, and to modern sensibilities, they appear like straining the gnat (repenting of cursing) and swallowing the camel (accepting slavery). However, such proclamations also suggest something deeper: most colonists did not consider their practice of land dispossession or slavery to be sinful.]

Proclamation Appointing a Day of General Fasting and Prayer (issued 23 February 1660)

Respectful, Dear, Faithful.

Whereas it has pleased Almighty God, the just Judge of heaven and the whole earth, to visit us, or at least many of us, justly for our sins, the cause of all punishment, with hot fevers, heavy colds, giddiness of the head and many other diseases, the province in general with threatened invasions and attacks by our neighbours on the territories, streams and rivers, long possessed by us, with rumours of war and its immediate consequences, murder and arson by the savage barbarous natives committed here as well as principally on our friends, countrymen and fellow-inhabitants on the Esopus [First Esopus War], which though the righteous but not less merciful God has mitigated and so directed, that it did not happen, against our expectation, in the worst manner and according to the evil intentions of the barbarians and has made it cease for the present desiring doubtless our penitence and turning away from our crying and God irritating sins, as the abominable desecration of his Sabbath and His Name by swearing and cursing, our indifference and negligence regarding his service, our drunkenness, feasting, voluptuousness, adultery, deception and other heinous sins, which prevail among us to our shame before Christian neighbours and barbarous natives, from which if we do not turn away, we can only expect, that like others we shall perish and that not the tower of Siloa [Luke 13:4] but the wrath of God will fall upon us from heaven and envelop us in flames for our greater punishment, if we do not change....

145 Robert Filmer, *Patriarchal Rule in Home and State* (c.1628)

Keywords: #Authority, #Government, #Liberty, #Family, #Equality, #Democracy, #Natural Law, #Ten Commandments
Region: #England
Group: #Church of England

Robert Filmer (c.1588–1653) is known for his staunch defence of the divine right of kings. He was educated at Cambridge and knighted by James I in 1619. Filmer opposed emerging political theories about the relationship between authority and consent, as well as budding notions of freedom. He understood kingship in the context of fatherhood, and he ascribed great authority to fathers. The government and the family were two important institutions, and there was considerable debate over how the nature of authority in one sphere corresponded to authority in the other. Fathers, it was assumed at the time, had considerable power over their families. Their right over family members derived from nature and was confirmed by sacred writ. Some who would have defended a patriarchal household, like Catholic theologians Robert Bellarmine and Francisco Suárez, or Protestant theologians like **George Buchanan**, thought there was a different relationship, a more limited one involving some measure of consent, between monarch and subject.

For Filmer, monarchical power was rooted in nature and derived directly from God, and thus, the people could not limit their sovereign or resist him. This position was welcomed by many in England's church hierarchy, but it put him at odds with Puritans who wanted a Reformed church and limited monarchy, and they imprisoned him during the English Civil War. He derived his ideas from a reading of the Hebrew Bible, and especially the stories of Adam and Noah, as well as from the theories of Jean Bodin. He applied these ideas to English history and put them in the service of royal absolutism.[207] *Patriarchia*, excerpted below, was likely written before the English Civil War, but it was not published. Other published works that argued for unlimited monarchical power include *The free-holders grand inquest touching our soveraigne lord the King and his Parliament* (1648), *The anarchy of a*

524 *Sources*

limited or mixed monarchy (1648), and *The necessity of the absolute power of all kings: and in particular, of the King of England* (1648). All these were published the year before the execution of Charles I.

Patriarcha, or, The natural power of Kings by the learned Sir Robert Filmer (London: Walter Davis, 1680), 2–4, 21–24. Text modernised by the editors.

———

Chapter 1: That the First Kings were Fathers of Families

Since the time that school-divinity began to flourish, divines and other learned men maintained a common opinion:

> *Mankind is naturally endowed and born with freedom from all subjection, and at liberty to choose the form of government it please: And that the power which any one man has over others, was at first bestowed according to the choosing of the multitude.*

This teaching was first hatched in the schools, and has been fostered by all succeeding papists as good divinity. The divines also of the Reformed churches have entertained it, and the common people everywhere tenderly embrace it, as being most suitable to fleshly interests, for that it generously distributes a portion of liberty to the lowest of the multitude, who magnify liberty, as if the height of human felicity was only found there, never remembering That the desire for liberty was the first cause of the fall of *Adam* [Gen. 3].

However much this vulgar opinion has lately secured a great reputation, yet it is not to be found in the ancient fathers and doctors of the primitive church: It contradicts the doctrine and history of the holy Scriptures, the constant practice of all ancient monarchies, and the very principles of the law of nature. It is hard to say whether it is more erroneous in divinity or dangerous in policy....

This desperate assertion whereby kings are made subject to the *censures* and *deprivations of their subjects* follows (as the authors of it conceive) as a necessary consequence from that former position of the supposed *natural equality and freedom of mankind and liberty to choose what form of government it please*....

In all kingdoms or commonwealths in the world, whether the prince is the supreme father of the people, or the true heir of such a father, or whether he comes to the crown by usurpation, or by election of the nobles, or by the people, or by any other way; or whether some few or a multitude govern the commonwealth: yet still the authority that is in one, or in many, or in all these, is the only right and natural authority of a supreme father. There is and always shall be continued to the end of the world, a natural right of a supreme father over every multitude, although by the secret will of God, many at first do most unjustly obtain the exercise of it.

To confirm this natural right of *regal* power, we find in the *Decalogue*, that the law which enjoins obedience to kings is delivered in the terms of *Honour thy father*, as if all power were originally in the father. If obedience to parents is immediately due by a *natural law*, and subjection to princes, but by the mediation of a *human ordinance*; what reason is there that the laws of *nature* should give place to the laws of men? as we see the power of the father over his child, gives place, and is subordinate to the power of the magistrate.

If we compare the natural rights of a father with those of a king, we find them the same, without any difference at all, but only in the latitude or extent of them: as the father extends his care over one family, so the king as a father over many families preserves, feeds, clothes, instructs and defends the whole commonwealth. His war, his peace, his courts of justice, and all his acts of sovereignty tend only to preserve and distribute to every subordinate and inferior father, and to their children, their rights and privileges; so that all the duties of a king are summed up in a universal fatherly care of his people.

146 Gustav II Adolf, *On Marching to War* (1630)

Keywords: #War, #Intervention
Region: #Sweden, #Germany
Group: #Lutheran

Gustav II Adolf (r.1611–1632) is often remembered as a fighter in the mould of biblical warriors, a practical statesman who elevated the status of Sweden, and a stalwart defender of Protestantism in his own country and abroad. His reign was marked by religious, political, and military reform, such that Sweden outperformed the political dominance of the Duchy of Poland-Lithuania and the Kingdom of Denmark. His decision to enter the Thirty Years' War in 1630 cemented his reputation as Protestantism's defender. While the protection of the Protestant faith was the stated justification, he certainly had other motives for expanding Swedish power.[208] In the first selection reproduced below, Gustav II Adolf described his military aims before saying farewell to his country. He called on God to be with him as he worked to defend Protestantism in general, and the Elector of Brandenburg in particular. However, as the second selection shows, the Elector was unsure about the intrusion of a large foreign army. Gustav tried to clarify his intentions through a representative, but in so doing, he demanded that the Protestant princes decide whether they would be on the side of God or of the devil.

Readings in European History, vol. 2, ed. James H. Robinson (Boston, MA: Ginn and Co., 1906), 207–211.

———

Farewell to the Swedish Estates (May 1630)

I call on the all-powerful God, by whose providence we are all assembled, to witness that it is not by my own wish, or from any love of war, that I undertake this campaign. On the contrary, I have been now for several years goaded into it by the imperial party, not only through the reception accorded to our emissary to Lübeck, but also by the action of the general in aiding with his army our enemies, the Poles, to our great detriment. We have been urged, moreover, by our harassed brother in law [the Elector of Brandenburg] to undertake this war, the chief object of which is to free our oppressed brothers in the faith from the clutches of the pope, which, God helping us, we hope to do.

[*He then addresses the different classes of society individually (counsellors of the kingdom, knights, priests, burghers, and farmers), exhorting them to fulfil the role God has called them to.*]

Reply to the Ambassador from Brandenburg (July 1630)

I have received your explanation of the grounds on which my honoured brother-in-law seeks to dissuade me from this war. I confess I should have expected a different sort of embassy, since God has brought me thus far, and since I have come into this land for no other purpose than to free it from the thieves and robbers who have so plagued it, and first and foremost, to help his Excellency out of his difficulties. Does his Excellency then not know that the emperor and his followers do not mean to rest till the Evangelical religion is wholly rooted out of the empire, and that his Excellency has nothing else to expect than being forced either to deny his religion or leave his country? Did he think by prayers and beseechings and such like means to obtain something different?...

I seek not my own advantage in this war nor any gain, save the security of my kingdom; I can look for nothing but expense, hard work, trouble, and danger to life and limb....

I tell you plainly that I will know or hear nothing of 'neutrality'; his Excellency must be either friend or foe. When I reach his frontier he must declare himself either hot or cold. The fight is between God and the devil. If his Excellency is on God's side, let him stand by me; if he holds rather with the devil, then he must fight with me, there is no third course – that is certain....

147 John Winthrop, *A Model of Christian Charity* (1630)

Keywords: #Colonisation, #Community, #Charity, #Land, #Property, #Poverty, #Natural Law, #International Law
Region: #England, #United States
Group: #Church of England, #Puritan

John Winthrop (1588–1649) was born in Edwardstone, Suffolk, and studied at Cambridge. He was a gentleman of good reputation, and his family had links across the Puritan Atlantic world. He was involved in planning the colony of Massachusetts Bay and was chosen to be its governor in 1629. Before leaving, his *Reasons to Be Considered for...the Intended Plantation in New England* (1629) justified the acquisition of land that was deemed unused, provided a 'sufficient' amount was left for Algonquians. He sailed to the colony in 1630 and played a prominent role in the **Pequot War,** as well as in debates about political representation and accountability. He presided over the famous trial of **Anne Hutchinson,** which was part of a controversy over the relationship between grace and the law (Antinomian Controversy). He also defended restrictions on the immigration of non-conformists, arguing that the colony had a duty to provide security and to prioritise unity over liberty. Although he opposed **Roger Williams'** ideas, Winthrop maintained a relatively positive working relationship with him throughout his life. Winthrop's voluminous journals and letters are invaluable resources for the study of early America.

Winthrop is best known for *Christian Charity: A Model Hereof* (1630), possibly delivered as a sermon on board the *Arbella.* Although this discourse looms large in contemporary American political thought, it had little impact on colonial America and was largely forgotten until the Cold War. Today it provides a central pillar for the claim that the United States would have entered into a covenant with God. The sermon also contained the oft-misunderstood assertion that the colonists would be a 'City upon a Hill', a claim that means something different in recent memory than it did in 1630. Both of these ideas appear towards the end of Winthrop's Model where he warned colonists against turning their back on the lofty promises they made to God and each other. But what were those promises? From the beginning of the sermon, Winthrop described God's ordering all of society so that some were rich and others poor. Although such providentialism could undergird a calloused fatalism, Winthrop argued that God-ordained differences were an invitation to costly charity. Throughout, Winthrop reflected on the political implications of Christian love. The discourse contains much of the idealism of one about to embark on a new experiment in godly community. The colony's behaviour – and that of Winthrop – often fell far short of that model.[209]

Collections of the Massachusetts Historical Society (Boston, MA: Charles C. Little, 1838), 3rd series 7:33–35. Text modernised by the editors.

———

Christian Charity:

A Model hereof

God Almighty, in his most holy and wise providence, hath so disposed of the condition of mankind, as in all times some must be rich, some poor, some high and eminent in power and dignity; others mean and in submission.

The Reason hereof.

1 *Reason*. First, to hold conformity with the rest of his world, being delighted to show forth the glory of his wisdom in the variety and difference of the creatures, and the glory of his power in ordering all these differences for the preservation and good of the whole; and the glory of his greatness, that as it is the glory of princes to have many officers, so this great king will have many stewards, counting himself more honoured in dispensing his gifts to man by man, than if he did it by his own immediate hands.

2 *Reason*. Second, that he might have the more occasion to manifest the work of his Spirit: first upon the wicked in moderating and restraining them: so that the rich and mighty should not eat up the poor nor the poor and despised rise up against and shake off their yoke. Secondly. In the regenerate, in exercising his graces in them, as in the great ones: their love, mercy, gentleness, temperance, etc.; in the poor and inferior sort: their faith, patience, obedience, etc.

3 *Reason*. Third, that every man might have need of others, and from hence they might be all knit more nearly together in the bonds of brotherly affection. From hence it appears plainly that no man is made more honourable than another or more wealthy, etc., out of any particular and singular respect to himself, but for the glory of his creator and the common good of the creature, man. Therefore God still reserves the property of these gifts to himself as he calls wealth, *his gold and his silver* (Ezek. 16:17), and he claims their service as his due, *honour the Lord with thy riches*, etc. (Prov. 3:9). – All men being thus (by divine providence) ranked into two sorts, rich and poor; under the first are comprehended all such as are able

530 *Sources*

to live comfortably by their own means duly improved; and all others are poor according to the former distribution. There are two rules whereby we are to walk one towards another: justice and mercy. These are always distinguished in their act and in their object, yet may they both concur in the same subject in each respect; as sometimes there may be an occasion of showing mercy to a rich man in some sudden danger or distress, and also doing of mere justice to a poor man in regard of some particular contract, etc. There is likewise a double law by which we are regulated in our conversation towards another; in both the former respects, the law of nature and the law of grace, or the moral law or the law of the gospel, to omit the rule of justice as not properly belonging to this purpose otherwise than it may fall into consideration in some particular cases. By the first of these laws, man as he was enabled so withal is commanded to love his neighbour as himself (Mark 12:31). Upon this ground stands all the precepts of the moral law, which concerns our dealings with men. To apply this to the works of mercy; this law requires two things. First, that every man afford his help to another in every want or distress. Second, that he perform this out of the same affection which makes him careful of his own goods, according to that of our Saviour, *Whatsoever ye would that men should do to you* (Matt. 7:12). This was practised by Abraham and Lot in entertaining the angels and the old man of Gibeah. The law of grace or of the gospel hath some difference from the former; as in these respects, First, the law of nature was given to man in the estate of innocency; this of the gospel in the estate of regeneracy. Second, the former propounds one man to another, as the same flesh and image of God; this as a brother in Christ also, and in the communion of the same Spirit, and so teaches to put a difference between Christians and others. *Do good to all, especially to the household of faith* [Gal. 6:10]; upon this ground the Israelites were to put a difference between the brethren of such as were strangers though not of the Canaanites.

Third, the Law of nature would give no rules for dealing with enemies, for all are to be considered as friends in the state of innocency, but the gospel commands love to an enemy. Proof. *If thine enemy hunger, feed him; Love your Enemies, do good to them that hate you* (Matt. 5:44).

This law of the gospel propounds likewise a difference of seasons and occasions. There is a time when a Christian must sell all and give to the poor, as they did in the apostles' times. There is a time also when Christians (though they give not all yet) must give beyond their ability, as they of Macedonia [2 Cor. 8:3]. Likewise, community of perils calls for extraordinary liberality, and so doth community in some special service for the church. Lastly, when there is no other means whereby our Christian brother may be relieved in his distress, we must help him beyond our ability rather than tempt God in putting him upon help by miraculous or extraordinary means.

This duty of mercy is exercised in the kinds, giving, lending and forgiving....

148 *Battle Hymn from the Thirty Years' War* (1631)

Keywords: #War
Region: #Sweden, #Germany
Group: #Lutheran

The genre of Battle Hymns was popular during the Reformation, and often reached back explicitly to the Book of Psalms in the Hebrew Bible. Many of these psalms dealt with issues of persecution, injustice, warfare, and the desire for God to avenge wrongs. Christians across the centuries have used the Psalms, and other portions of scripture, in the context of warfare. They have used them to lament and to afflict atrocities, and as such, battle hymns carry some of the deepest contradictions of the Protestant imagination. There are many accounts of people singing before, during, and after a battle, especially in the literature from the wars of the early modern period. The following hymn was in fashion during the Thirty Years' War. **Gustav II Adolf** had reportedly sung a similar hymn before engaging in the battle of Lützen in 1632, which Sweden won, but at the cost of his life. In memory, the king was not only the defender of Protestantism, he was now viewed as a martyr as well.[210]

Lyra Germanica, trans. Catherine Winkworth (New York: Stenford, 1857), 17–18.

———

Fear not, O little flock, the foe
Who madly seeks your overthrow,
    Dread not his rage and power.
What though your courage sometimes faints,
His seeming triumph o'er God's saints
    Lasts but a little hour.

Be of good cheer; your cause belongs
To Him who can avenge your wrongs,
    Leave it to Him our Lord.

532 Sources

Though hidden yet from all our eyes,
He sees the Gideon who shall rise
    To save us, and His word.

As true as God's own voice is true,
Not earth nor hell with all their crew
    Against us shall prevail.
A jest and by-word are they grown;
God is with us, we are His own,
    Our victory cannot fail.

Amen, Lord Jesus, grant our prayer;
Great Captain, now Thine arm make bare;
    Fight for us once again!
So shall the saints and martyrs raise
A mighty chorus to Thy praise,
    World without End. Amen.

149 Johan Crell, *The End of Miracles and the Beginning of Toleration* (1632)

Keywords: #Toleration, #Persecution, #Violence
Region: #Poland | #Germany
Group: #Polish Brethren, #Socinian, #Unitarian

Johan Crell (1590–1633) was a German theologian who ministered in the Polish city of Raków. The death of Sigismund III Vasa likely inspired his *A Vindication of Liberty of Religion* (1632). Poland's reputation as a land of tolerance and peaceful coexistence was waning during this king's tenure. The legal status of Protestants eroded quickly, and the country was about to elect a new king. The *Pax Dissidentium* (1573), an oath taken by the king, bound the sovereign to 'preserve and maintain peace and quiet among those that differ with regard to religion (*dissidentes de religione*)' and to ensure that magistrates did not oppress people on account of their religion. For the Catholic monarch and the catholic majority, this peace agreement was not a high priority. Those favouring liberty of conscience made formal demands of the government, and Crell likely had these demands in mind when he wrote the *Vindication*.

Crell employed an unusual tactic when pushing Catholics towards toleration. Rather than speak as if he was right, he referred to himself as the one with the wrong beliefs. Protestants and the Polish Brethren were the 'heretics', and he was the 'tare' in the field masquerading as 'wheat' (Matt. 13:24–30). If Catholics plucked him up, they might uproot some of their co-religionists. Thus, his arguments for toleration did not depend on Catholics considering him orthodox. Instead, he offered Catholics reasons that he hoped they could accept, namely that their own tradition taught that tolerating a heretic was permissible, practical, and godly. Crell's literary trope must be remembered when reading the treatise, as his suggestion is of course that those in error may be the true Christians. The lengthy *Vindication* puts forward many of the arguments for toleration, and it was translated into English in 1647 at the height of the **British Civil Wars**.[211]

The following selection comes from the latter part of the book, where he discussed the miracles of ancient biblical Israel. Debates about toleration frequently veered into discussions of miracles. **Roger Williams, Thomas**

534　*Sources*

Hobbes, Samuel Rutherford, and **John Locke** all had lengthy discussions on the political implications of the supernatural because it was believed that miracles had coercive power (i.e., witnessing a miracle might compel faith).[212] Tolerationists like Crell made an epistemic argument for toleration based on the miracles of the Hebrew Bible. In sum, the Israelites had good reasons to believe they heard from God because of the miraculous voice from Sinai, the visible presence in the tabernacle, etc. Yet, because Christian faith did not rely on ongoing miracles, Christians could not claim to speak for God in the same way. This conclusion had important implications for violence in God's name: whereas Israel had good reasons to believe God commanded violence, Christians did not.

A LEARNED And exceeding well-compiled Vindication of Liberty of RELI-GION: Written by Junius Brutus in Latine, And Translated into English by N. Y. (1646), 48–53. Text modernised by the editors.

———

But some may object, saying that God commanded those under the Law to punish with death those who worship strange and false gods. They may say that in such a case, God wants men to be forced to the true religion, and there was no regard to the idea that religion ought to be free. Many, by such force, may be driven to lie or be compelled to do something against their conscience.

[*Crell answers that God, the Lord of all, is also the Lord of conscience and can demand as he wills. He conceded that the Hebrew Bible gave evidence of the compelling of faith. Like many before him, he argues that the Jewish faith was primarily concerned with outward matters, and thus outward measures could be employed in matters of faith. Such coercion was permissible because God commanded it. He is aware that someone could claim God gave a similar call for coercion in the present, and this leads him to discuss why the Jewish people had good reasons to believe that God had spoken.*]

For God appeared openly from the very beginning in Mount Sinai, showing Himself to be the only God, in the sight of all the people, and published His Law unto them so that no man could doubt that He was both their only God and to be worshipped as their only God, and that the law of Moses came from Him. Thus it came to pass that all the people, none making any opposition at all, made a covenant with God through Moses concerning that law. And then, after the law was established, God promised that He would at times raise up Prophets for the people of Israel, by whom the Jews might ask His advice, and find out His mind, not only concerning matters pertaining to religion, but even such things as belong to the commonwealth, yea and such as concern household affairs.... Besides other prophesies and forewarnings, God ordained an ordinary way of asking His counsel by the priests Ephod, or Urim and Thummim, as the holy Scripture calls it. And He moreover revealed secret and hidden matters to such as sought out His will by lot, and showed what they were to do: and as often as the people followed God's counsel, all things succeeded prosperously with them; so that the event itself declared, those answers came from God.

The state of things was thus, as if God had certainly been a king among the people of Israel, even in civil and earthly matters, dwelling in the tabernacle as in a certain kingly palace, and abiding in the ark, and from thence informing the people of his will by the priests, or other prophets, as servants who were to wait near his person. He gave answers about undertaking and waging war, about choosing captains and commanders, and other such matters. He very often showed wonders to declare that he personally dwelt in the midst of this people....

But the disposition of religion is far otherwise now that God is no longer sought on earth, but in heaven, and took away those manifest signs of his presence. He does not uphold and preserve the religion which he ordained in such a conspicuous and open manner; does not stir up prophets, does not give answers, but acts and orders all things more secretly, making a greater trial of men's faith. Presently, men fall more easily into error, and violence is offered to the conscience if one tries to make them abandon their error with threats of punishment; if one forces him to adopt a truth which is not demonstrated by such clear testimonies. These people are forced to hide their true beliefs, which is hateful to God, when they are compelled by force to embrace a religion they are not convinced of (however true that religion is).

People have erred when they thought it fitting to suppress heretics by violence; even those who sought a middle way between legal severity and Christian gentleness have failed to obtain both. For God in former times did not spare apostates and worshipers of false gods or those with contempt for his law, but commanded them to be slain without mercy. This punishment was not used to remedy their error but as revenge for their unpardonable wickedness and disobedience.

Some who think heretics should be harshly dealt with argue that they should be spared because they were led astray; however, receiving clemency is conditioned on renouncing their error, and they only renounce the error because failure to do so will be punished. Such people pretend the Catholic religion, they do not actually approve it.

This approach may not destroy those with an evil opinion concerning God and matters belonging to religion, it only hinders them from professing it outwardly, which the law never intended. But those who punish or kill those whose conscience will not let them renounce error, they neither perform the duty of Christian meekness nor obtain the end thereof (namely, that the erroneous person is brought to the right path and restored).

To sum up; by doing this, they tolerate the worse sort of person and destroy the better. The better and more virtuous person, when they are not convinced of an error, will not renounce it for fear of wounding their conscience and offending God. They are better than those who condemn something against their own conscience, and even if they are wrong, they condemn something they believe to be true and in accordance with God's word.

150 *Religion and Military Discipline in Sweden* (1632)

Keywords: #War, #Morality, #Blasphemy, #Witchcraft, #Capital Crime
Region: #Sweden
Group: #Lutheran

Renowned Protestant military commanders like Gustav II Adolf in Sweden and **Oliver Cromwell** in England employed religious repertoires in their military endeavours. Both leaders were known to sing **Battle Hymns** while on campaign, and they viewed faith as essential to well-ordered military operations. Religious discipline complemented the military discipline that they instilled in soldiers. This was important, because improving the ethical standards of warfare contributed to their claims about just warfare. The following document comes from the Swedish rules of war, and it was translated into English by someone sympathetic to the aims of **Gustav II Adolf**. The English edition also featured prayers that were common in the military, as well as more practical things, such as military discipline, organisation, and strategy. The document contains 117 military regulations. The first 16 articles relate to religion, and the remaining 101 to hierarchy and military discipline. The ordering is intentional: holiness and submission to God were essential to an orderly, efficient, and successful army.[213]

William Watts, trans., *The Swedish Discipline, Religious, Civile, and Military* (London: John Dawson, 1632), 40–41. Text modernised by the editors.

———

1 Seeing therefore that all our welfare and prosperity proceeds from Almighty God; and that it is all men's duty to fear and serve him above all: We straightly hereby charge all manner of Persons whatsoever, that they by no means use any kind of *Idolatry*, *Witchcraft*, or *Enchanting* of *Arms*.... And if any herein be found faulty, he shall be proceeded against according to God's law and the [law of] Sweden...

2 If any shall blaspheme the name of God, either drunk or sober, and the thing be by two or three witnesses proved against him, he shall be put to death without all mercy.

Sources 537

3 If any shall presume to deride or scorn God's word or Sacraments, and be taken in the fault; they shall forthwith be convened before the *Consistory* or *Commission Ecclesiastical*, to be in [the] presence of the *Commissioners* examined: by whom if he be found guilty and condemned; he shall lose his head without all mercy....

5 And to the end that God's word be by no means neglected, our will is, that public Prayers be every day said both morning and evening throughout the whole leaguer [camp]....

[*Points 6–10 relate to the proper order of prayers and services, and the penalties should the clergy, soldier or merchants transgress these rules.*]

151 *Hero Worship, Humility and the Death of Gustav II Adolf (1632)*

Keywords: #War
Region: #Sweden | #Germany
Group: #Lutheran

After the death of **Gustav II Adolf** at the Battle of Lützen in 1632, he was venerated as a Protestant martyr. The following pamphlet appeared soon in response, rebuking the worship of heroes as detracting from the worship of God. The pamphlet looked semi-official and likely came from someone in the Swedish chancellery. The document is important for several reasons. First, it evidenced the fear of a fracturing Protestant cause after the king's death. Second, it showed the extent to which the king had become an object of veneration. The author challenged those worshipping the king, latently suggesting that the king died because of the people's idolatry. However, the author used sacrificial language to describe the death. The king would have been 'sacrificed to Lord Jesus' and would have played a redemptive role similar to Jesus: 'his royal blood was spilled and his life and body laid down for the Protestant German electors and estates, to preserve their religion and to regain their lost liberty'.[214]

"Victorious before Death, in Death, and After Death" (1632), in Hans Medick and Benjamin Marschke, *Experiencing the Thirty Years War: A Brief History with Documents* (Boston, MA: Bedford/St. Martin's, 2013), 148–150.

———

We cannot thank God the Almighty enough for this glorious and exceedingly great victory. On the enemy's side, as the prisoners attest, on the battlefield the dead lay on top of one another half as high as a man.... However, this came to nothing, considering the death of our glorious, most Christian, and in all the world most highly praised king.... So his blessed soul was sacrificed to Lord Jesus, and his royal blood was spilled and his life and body laid down for the Protestant German electors and estates, to preserve their religion and to regain their lost liberty....

The Almighty lend his grace that all the German Protestant electors and estates take this work to heart and gratefully acknowledge the glorious king's deeds and proven loyalty; and that in the future they, by combining their bodies, goods, and blood, and with God's strength, may continue and complete the holy work regarding their religion and liberty, which our most blessed king has established so well and placed in their hands...However, should they separate (though may God in his mercy prevent it), and on other advice divide themselves, then it would be as His Glorious Royal Majesty prophesied before his death, namely, that our religion and freedom would be finished...

In this account I cannot omit the following words, which His Blessed Royal Majesty often said, and repeated again three days before the battle to [his personal chaplain] Dr. Fabricius in Naumburg:

My dear Doctor, things are all good and everything is going as hoped, but I worry, I worry, because everyone venerates me so much and, so to say, they take me for a god. God will punish me for this. But God knows that it does not please me. It is going as dear God wants it, I know, and he will continue things through to completion, because it glorifies his name....

From all of this it is really tangible, that it is we, but rather God, who is the master over our wills, lives and efforts. And we can become even more patient and console ourselves that our king lost his life in the highest grade of immortal fame, because he was and remained victorious *ante mortem, in mortem, and post mortem* [before death, in death, and after death].

152 Jan Amos Komenský, *Politics, Piety and Universal Childhood Education* (c.1632)

Keywords: #Social Welfare, #Education,
Region: #Czech Republic | #Poland, #Sweden, #England, #Hungary
Group: #Unity of Brethren, #Moravian

The early reform movement developed a strong interest in improving social welfare and education. Some efforts remained in the proposal stage, but others were enacted. For example, **Martin Luther** argued that just as the church needed educated clergy, so the temporal authority needed an educated population. He said in 1530 that 'it is the duty of the temporal authority to compel its subjects to keep their children in school, especially the promising ones'.[215] The systematic effort to reform education dates back to Jan Amos Komenský (1592–1670), also known as John Comenius. He was a Czech-born pastor in a Unity of Brethren (*Unitas Fratrum*) congregation, a group that had roots in the Hussite movement and would later form part of the Moravian Church.

Komenský's life changed with the outbreak of the **Thirty Years' War**. One of the flashpoints that sparked that war was the famous Defenestration of Prague (1618), where Czech nobles had thrown Habsburg officials out the window. Bohemian Protestant resistance was initially successful, but they were defeated at the Battle of the White Mountain (1620). The victors rescinded earlier decrees of toleration and sought to bring subjugated regions back into the Catholic fold. As many as 200,000 peasants, nobles, and intellectuals fled, and Komenský was one of them. As an exile, he spent time in Poland, Sweden, England, and Hungary.[216]

During his lifetime, Komenský enjoyed an international and transatlantic reputation, and he is often called the 'Father of Modern Education'. Excerpts from his famous work, *The Great Didactic* (published in Czech around 1632), are shown below. In its prefatory remarks, he described the noble creation of humans and their subsequent fall. Spiritual redemption came through Christ, but paradise was restored on earth by means of education – an argument that would later be made by progressive and 'social gospel' Christians. Komenský did not only try to organise, systematise, and unify all branches of knowledge; his work focused on how to best communicate knowledge to children and

Sources 541

bring about their moral and social improvement. England's Parliament invited him to apply his methodology there, but the **British Civil Wars** led to the abandonment of these plans. Later, John Winthrop invited him to be the first president of Harvard. Although many regions wanted his time, his work focused on the educational system in Sweden and Hungary. After the disappointing end to the Thirty Years' War (because the 1648 **Peace of Westphalia** did not bring toleration for the Bohemian Brethren), Komenský became the last bishop of the *Unitas Fratrum*. Another war, this time between Sweden and Poland, led to his exile in the Netherlands, where he remained for the rest of his life.[217]

M. W. Keatinge, *The Great Didactic of John Amos Comenius: Now for the First Time Englished* (London: Adam and Charles Black, 1896), 163–170.

———

Dedicatory Letter

To all superiors of human society, to the rulers of states, the pastors of Churches, the parents and guardians of children, grace and peace from God the Father of our Lord Jesus Christ in the Holy Ghost.

God, having created man out of dust, placed him in a Paradise of desire, which he had planted in the East, not only that man might tend it and care for it, but also that he might be a garden of delight for his God.

For as Paradise was the pleasantest part of the world, so also was man the most perfect of things created. In Paradise each tree was delightful to look at, and more pleasant to enjoy than those which grew throughout the earth. In man, the whole material of the world, all the forms and the varieties of forms were, as it were, brought together into one in order to display the whole skill and wisdom of God.

Paradise contained the tree of the knowledge of good and evil; man had the intellect to distinguish, and the will to choose between the good and the bad. In Paradise was the tree of life. In man was the tree of Immortality itself; that is to say, the wisdom of God, which had planted its eternal roots in man.

And so each man is, in truth, a Garden of Delights for his God, as long as he remains in the spot where he has been placed. The Church too, which is a collection of men devoted to God, is often in Holy Writ likened to a Paradise, to a garden, to a vineyard of God. But alas for our misfortune! We have at the same time lost the Paradise of bodily delight in which we were, and that of spiritual delight, which we were ourselves. We have been cast out into the deserts of the earth, and have ourselves become wild and horrible wildernesses. We were ungrateful for the gifts, both of the body and of the soul, with which God had so richly provided Paradise; with right therefore have we been deprived of them and been dowered with calamity.

But glory, praise, honour, and blessing for everlasting to our merciful God who abandoned us for a while but did not thrust us from Him for ever....

542 *Sources*

The garden of the Church, the delight of God's heart, blooms anew. [*But it blooms imperfectly and is in danger of deterioration.*]

With most men such a dullness of wit is predominant, instead of the understanding through which we ought to be equal to the angels, that they know no more about those things which are worthy of our attention than do the beasts. Instead of the circumspection with which those who are destined for eternity ought to prepare themselves for it, there reigns such forgetfulness, not only of eternity but also of mortality, that most men give themselves up to what is earthly and transient, yea, even to the death that stands before them. Instead of the godly wisdom through which it has been given to us to know, to honour, and to enjoy the One who is the height of all goodness, there has arisen a horrible shrinking from that God in whom we live, move, and have our being, and a foolish conjuration of His holy name. Instead of mutual love and purity, reign hatred, enmity, war, and murder. Instead of justice, we find unfairness, roguery, oppression, theft, and rapine; instead of purity, uncleanliness and audacity of thought, word, and deed; instead of simplicity and truth, lying, deception, and knavery; instead of modesty, pride and haughtiness between man and man.

But in spite of all this, there remains for us a twofold comfort. First, that God keeps the eternal Paradise in readiness for His chosen ones, and that there we shall find a perfection, more complete and more durable than that first one which we lost.... Another consolation consists in this, that here below also God continually renews the Paradise of the Church, and turns its deserts into a garden of delights.... Perchance even now, after such a bloody war and after such devastation, the Father of mercy looks upon us graciously: how thankfully should we approach Him, and ourselves take care of our own interests, working by those ways and means which the most wise God, the Ordainer of all things, will show us.

The most useful thing that the Holy Scriptures teach us in this connection is this, that there is no more certain way under the sun for the raising of sunken humanity than the proper education of the young. [*He surveys scripture to make this point. It is easier to train a child aright than to set aright a crooked adult tree.*]

Busy yourselves, ye governors, ye faithful servants of Jesus Christ, and utterly destroy evil with the sword that is entrusted to you, with the two-edged sword of speech! Ye have seen that early youth is the best time to attack the evils of the human race; that the tree which is to thrive for ages is best planted when quite young; that Sion is most easily raised on the site of Babylon when the living building-stones of God, the young, are early broken, shaped, and fitted for the heavenly building. If we wish to have well-ordered and prosperous Churches, states, and households, thus and in no other way can we reach our goal.

153 Targeting Civilians in the Pequot War (1637)

Keywords: #War, #Violence, #Colonisation, #Slavery
Region: #United States
Group: #Puritan | #Indigenous American

Political and religious repression in England continued to make it attractive to relocate to the New World. Separatists established a small colony at Plymouth in 1620, with Puritans settling Massachusetts Bay Colony in earnest a decade later (**John Winthrop**). Additional colonies emerged: Connecticut in 1636, Providence in 1636 (**Roger Williams**), and New Haven in 1638. Each time the English expanded, the probability of clashes with Indigenous communities increased.

In the mid-1630s, the killing of an Englishman by Indigenous persons led to calls for legal prosecution, even though the dead Englishman was a notorious troublemaker who had likely been engaged in kidnapping. However, disagreements, misunderstandings, and differing ways of trying to remedy injustice led the English and Indigenous communities into open conflict (the Pequot War of 1636–1638). The English eventually came to believe that the entire Pequot tribe of southern Connecticut was guilty either of shedding blood or of shielding the guilty from prosecution. Bloodguilt, in the English mind, even spread to women, children, and the elderly. The English decided to stamp out the threat. They marched to southern Connecticut, surrounded a Pequot settlement, and massacred its civilians. The English thought their actions were just; however, they also thought that their actions were holy: they decimated the Pequot settlement like the biblical people of Amalek.

The following selections reproduce arresting theological statements from two military leaders engaged in the Pequot War: John Mason and John Underhill. Praise and thanksgiving burst from their writings like the flames from the engulfed settlement. In John Mason's account, the Pequot suffered like the enemies of Israel in the Psalms. With regard to the civilian deaths, John Underhill remarked that scripture was ambiguous about targeting women and children. But he did not want to debate the doctrine: the synod could be called after the cemetery was filled. In the third source, Roger Williams (who

544   *Sources*

largely supported the war but not all of the conduct in the war) interacted with similar biblical verses in a letter to **John Winthrop**. However, he arrived at a different conclusion. One should not base controversial ethical decisions on texts that are mystical or otherwise unclear.[218]

John Mason, *A Brief History of the Pequot War* (Boston, 1736), 14, 20–22; John Underhill, *Newes from America* (London: Peter Cole, 1638), 39–40; "Roger Williams to John Winthrop" (15 July 1637), in *The Correspondence of Roger Williams*, ed. Glenn W. LaFantasie, 2 vols. (London: Brown University Press, 1988), I:101–103. Texts modernised by the editors.

———

John Mason's Providential Account of the Fire and Massacre

[God was seen] burning them up in the Fire of his Wrath [Ps. 21:9], and dunging the Ground with their Flesh [Zeph. 1:17]: It was the *LORD'S* Doings, and it is marvellous in our Eyes [Ps. 118:23]! It is *HE* that hath made his Work wonderful, and therefore ought to be remembered [Ps. 111:4]....

Thus we may see, How the Face of *GOD* is set against them that do Evil, to cut off the Remembrance of them from the Earth [Ps. 34:16].... Blessed be the *LORD GOD* of *Israel*.... Let the whole Earth be filled with his Glory [Ps. 72:18–19]! Thus the *LORD* was pleased to smite our Enemies in the hinder Parts, and to give us their Land for an Inheritance [Ps. 78:55, 66]: Who remembered us in our low Estate, and redeemed us out of our Enemies' Hands [Ps. 136:23–24]: Let us therefore praise the *LORD* for his Goodness and his wonderful Works to the Children of Men [Ps. 107:8]!...

I still remember a Speech of Mr. [Thomas] HOOKER at our going aboard; THAT THEY SHOULD BE BREAD FOR US [Num. 14:9]. And thus when the LORD turned the Captivity of his People, and turned the Wheel upon their Enemies; we were like Men in a Dream; then was our Mouth filled with Laughter, and our Tongues with Singing; thus we may say the LORD hath done great Things for us among the Heathen, whereof we are glad. Praise ye the LORD [Ps. 126:1–3]!

John Underhill's Justification of the Slaughter

[I]t is reported by themselves, that there were about 400 souls in this Fort, and not above five of them escaped out of our hands. Great and doleful was the bloody sight to the view of young soldiers that never had been in War, to see so many souls lie gasping on the ground so thick in some places, that you could hardly pass along. It may be demanded, Why should you be so furious (as some have said) should not Christians have more mercy and compassion? But I would refer you to *David's* war, when a people is grown to such a height of blood, and sin against God and man, and all confederates in the action, there he has no respect to persons, but harrows them, and saws them, and puts them to the sword, and the most terriblest death that may be [2 Sam.

12:31]: sometimes the Scripture declares women and children must perish with their parents [Exod. 20:5; Josh. 7:25–26]; some-time the case alters [Ezek. 18:21]: but we will not dispute it now. We had sufficient light from the word of God for our proceedings.

Roger Williams' Letter to John Winthrop on Guilt in War

Truly, Sir, to speak my thoughts in your ear freely, I bless the Lord for your merciful dealing, etc., but fear that some innocent blood cries at Connecticut [where the war took place]. Many things have been spoken to prove the Lord's perpetual war with Amalek extraordinary and mystical; but [2 Kings 14:5–6] is a bright light discovering the ordinary path wherein to walk and please him. If the Pequots were murderers ... yet not comparable to those treacherous servants that slew their lord, Joshua [Joash], King of Judah, and type of Jesus, yet the fathers only perish in their sin, in the place quoted, etc. The blessed Lamb of God wash away iniquity and receive us graciously.

154 French Reformed Churches, *On the Legality of Slavery* (1637)

Keywords: #Slavery
Region: #France | #Africa, #Americas, #India
Group: #Huguenot

The Reformed in France enjoyed relative toleration since the Edict of Nantes (13 April 1598). King Henry IV, a former Protestant, granted concessions to the Huguenots after he had solidified his political control. He was interested in restoring public peace, and wanted both sides to move beyond enmity and conflict. The Reformed could worship according to their conscience in certain areas, but under certain conditions. However, political privileges were revoked after a Huguenot uprising in the late 1620s. Religious toleration remained in place until 1685, when Louis XIV of France revoked the Edict. The Reformed Churches of France held 29 national synods from 1559 to 1659, often under the watchful eye of a royal representative. The following excerpt comes from their 27th synod held in Alençon in 1637, which is particularly interesting because of its interest in the topic of slavery.

The topic of slavery occasionally surfaced in Reformed synods across the continent. For example, at the Synod of Dort (1618–1619), participants worried that manumitting baptised slaves would prompt masters to withhold the gospel, keeping the slaves in perpetual bondage to sin. The synod did not decide on the matter, allowing individual slave holders to decide on the implications of a slave receiving spiritual liberty through Christ.[219] At the time, bondage was ubiquitous in the early modern world. Not only were Europeans enslaved in North Africa and the Ottoman Empire, but also French Catholics used Protestants as galley slaves. Protestants also enslaved other people, and La Rochelle had been a Protestant hub for the slave trade. At the time of the synod of Alençon, the Protestant world was moving in multiple directions on the issue of slavery. For example, Samuel Rushworth objected in 1635 to slavery on Christian grounds and helped enslaved people escape.[220] Two years later, the Puritans of New England engaged in the **Pequot War** – a war that introduced Indigenous slavery into New England and paved the way for the enslavement of Africans.

Pro-slavery arguments would largely win out at the synod of Alençon. They acknowledged that slavery was widely accepted in Europe and determined that it was not outlawed by God's word. However, they objected to the selling of slaves to 'Infidels'. As Christians had argued for centuries, Alençon decreed that slavery should be tempered by 'Christian Charity' and urged those who owned human flesh to 'take special Care of their precious immortal Souls'. In the late eighteenth century, when the abolitionist movement in Britain was gaining steam, pro-slavery authors cited the decision at Alençon to argue that Protestantism support for slavery had a long and distinguished history.[221]

John Quick, *Synodicon in Gallia Reformata, or, the Acts, Decisions, Decrees, and Canons of thouse famous National Councils of the Reformed Churches in France*, vol. 2 (London: J. Richardson, 1692), 348. Text modernised by the editors.

———

Men may have a Right to buy or keep Slaves, and this is not condemned by the Word of God, nor is it abolished by the Preaching of the Gospel in the overwhelming majority of *Europe*, and although there has insensibly been brought in a Custom to the contrary, and that Merchants purchase and dispose of them as of their proper Goods and Chattels, especially such as traffic on the Coasts of *Africa* and the *Indies*, where this Commerce is permitted, do buy from the Barbarians, either by way of Exchange of Goods, or for ready Money, Men and Women-Slaves, who being once in their power and Possession, they do again openly sell in the Market, or barter them away unto others. This assembly confirming that Canon made on this Occasion by the Provincial Synod of *Normandy*, doth exhort the Faithful not to abuse this their Liberty contrary to the Rules of Christian Charity, nor to transfer these poor Infidels unto other Hands besides those of Christians, who may deal kindly and humanely with them; and above all, may take special Care of their precious immortal Souls, and see them instructed in the Christian Religion.

155 Anne Hutchinson, *Female Authority and Divine Revelation* (1637)

Keywords: #Heresy, #Revelation, #Antinomianism, #Exile, #Women, #Prophecy
Region: #United States
Group: #Puritan

Anne Hutchinson (1591–1643) is perhaps the most notorious female from Puritan New England. She arrived in Boston in 1634 and was banished three years later towards the end of the **Pequot War**. She made her way to Narragansett Bay where **Roger Williams'** newly established settlement provided a haven. In 1642, she moved again to what is now the Bronx, where she was killed by American Indians. Her notoriety stems from her influence as a religious leader during her short stay in Massachusetts Bay Colony. She was a follower of John Cotton, one of New England's most revered ministers who emphasised the free nature of God's grace. Hutchinson started leading groups of women (and perhaps men) as they commented on sermons, critiqued ministers, and discussed theology. Female leadership was already controversial, and some feared that Hutchinson's teachings were furthering antinomianism (the 'Free Grace' Controversy).

Hutchinson was arrested by the colony's authorities and stood trial in November 1637. During the trial, she was non-compliant, questioned her accusers, and returned some of their questions to them. Hutchinson's self-disclosures towards the end of her trial highlighted the threat she posed to stability. Not only did she claim to speak from scripture, but also she claimed that God gave her immediate revelation. As Michael Winship notes, 'authorities worried that "immediate" could mean without the medium of the scriptures altogether, as [believed by] the **Anabaptists of Münster**.... It could signal the end of the Bible as the foundational source of religious truth.... It could also signal the end of all moral restraint, as well as the need for ministers or authorities of any kind, as people did whatever their divine voices told them to'. The following excerpt comes from the end of her trial, and thus does not deal with the propriety of female leadership. Hutchinson recounted her religious uncertainty occasioned by the tumults of religion in England and then New England. Many on the court would have been able to sympathise with aspects of her religious journey. However, her claim to immediate revelation, coupled with a warning for the all-male court and a declaration of imminent divine vindication, was a step too far.[222]

Charles Francis Adams, ed., *Antinomianism in the Colony of Massachusetts Bay* (Boston, MA: Prince Society, 1894), 268–284.

—

Mrs. Anne Hutchinson:

If you please to give me leave I shall give you the ground of what I know to be true. Being much troubled to see the falseness of the constitution of the church of England, I had like to have turned separatist; where-upon I kept a day of solemn humiliation and pondering of the thing; this scripture was brought unto me – he that denies Jesus Christ to be come in the flesh is antichrist. This I considered of and in considering found that the papists did not deny him to be come in the flesh, nor we did not deny him – who then was antichrist? Was the Turk antichrist only? The Lord knows that I could not open scripture; he must by his prophetical office open it unto me. So after that being unsatisfied in the thing, the Lord was pleased to bring this scripture out of the Hebrews. He that denies the testament denies the testator, and in this did open unto me and give me to see that those which did not teach the new covenant had the spirit of antichrist, and upon this he did discover the ministry unto me; and ever since, I bless the Lord, he hath let me see which was the clear ministry and which the wrong. Since that time I confess I have been more choice and he hath left me to distinguish between the voice of my beloved and the voice of Moses, the voice of John the Baptist and the voice of antichrist, for all those voices are spoken of in scripture. Now if you do condemn me for speaking what in my con-science I know to be truth I must commit myself unto the Lord.

550   *Sources*

Mr. Increase Nowel [Secretary]:   How do you know that was the spirit?

Mrs. Hutchinson: How did Abraham know that it was God that bid him offer his son, being a breach of the sixth commandment?

Thomas Dudley [Dep. Gov.]:   By an immediate voice.

Mrs. Hutchinson: So to me by an immediate revelation.

Mr. Dudley: How! an immediate revelation.

Mrs. Hutchinson: By the voice of his own spirit to my soul. I will give you another scripture (Jer. 46:27–28) – out of which the Lord showed me what he would do for me and the rest of his servants. But after he was pleased to reveal himself to me I did presently like Abraham run to Hagar. And after that he did let me see the atheism of my own heart, for which I begged of the Lord that it might not remain in my heart, and being thus, he did show me this (a twelvemonth after) which I told you of before. Ever since that time I have been confident of what he hath revealed unto me. [*She then discoursed on Daniel, warned of the rise and fall of powers, and expressed confidence that Daniel's God would also rescue her from her adversaries*]. Therefore, I desire you to look to it, for you see this scripture fulfilled this day and therefore I desire you as you tender the Lord and the church and commonwealth to consider and look what you do. You have power over my body but the Lord Jesus hath power over my body and soul, and assure yourselves thus much, you do as much as in you lies to put the Lord Jesus Christ from you, and if you go on in this course you begin you will bring a curse upon you and your posterity, and the mouth of the Lord hath spoken it.

Mr. Dudley: What is the scripture she brings?

Mr. Israel Stoughton [Assistant]:   Behold I turn away from you.

Mrs. Hutchinson: But now having seen him which is invisible I fear not what man can do unto me.

John Winthrop [Governor]:   Daniel was delivered by miracle; do you think to be deliver'd so too?

Sources 551

Mrs. Hutchinson:	I do here speak it before the court. I look that the Lord should deliver me by his providence. [*The court then recounted where Mrs. Hutchinson reportedly claimed revelations, and then discussed the theology of hearing from God as well as the propriety of expecting a miracle. Her sympathetic minister, John Cotton, was pushed to denounce her talk of miracles. She ultimately said she expected God to act via providence, not via miracles. Having distanced herself from miracles, Governor Winthrop then pushed the connection between her claims to immediate revelation and societal instability. Cotton then insisted that if she was claiming miracles and revelations independent of scripture, then she was deluded. The court then discussed historical examples of the danger of posed by Anabaptists and 'Enthusiasts'.*]
Mr. Dudley:	These disturbances that have come among the Germans have all been grounded upon revelations, and so they that have vented them have stirred up their hearers to take up arms against their prince and to cut the throats of one another, and these have been the fruits of them, and whether the devil may inspire the same into their hearts here I know not, for I am fully persuaded that Mrs. Hutchinson is deluded by the devil, because the spirit of God speaks truth in all his servants.
Mr. Winthrop:	I am persuaded that the revelations she brings forth is delusion. *All the court but some two or three ministers cry out, we all believe it – we all believe it.* [*Some attempts were made to halt the process that seemed headed towards imprisonment or banishment. William Coddington called into question the legality of some of the proceedings, before turning to the supposed illegality of her actions.*]
Mr. Coddington:	I beseech you do not speak so to force things along, for I do not for my own part see any equity in the court in all your proceedings. Here is no law of God that she hath broken nor any law of the country that she hath broke, and therefore deserves no censure.... [*Coddington ultimately charged the elders with breaking God's rules in how they have proceeded against Mrs. Hutchinson. The court proceeded to debate the charges against her, and all but three found her guilty of a crime worthy of banishment.*]

552 *Sources*

Mr. Winthrop: Mrs. Hutchinson, the sentence of the court you hear is
                      that you are banished from out of our jurisdiction as be-
                      ing a woman not fit for our society, and are to be impris-
                      oned till the court shall send you away.
Mrs. Hutchinson: I desire to know wherefore I am banished?
Mr. Winthrop: Say no more. The court knows wherefore and is satisfied.

156 Godfried Udemans, *Slavery as Godly Commerce* (1612, 1638)

Keywords: #Commerce, #Trade, #Slavery, #Capital Crime, #Evangelisation, #Missions, #Paternalism, #Ten Commandments
Region: #Netherlands, #Global
Group: #Dutch Reformed | #Islam, #Indigenous, #Non-Christians

Godfried Udemans (1581/1582–1649) was a Calvinist minister in Zeeland, one of the Dutch provinces that became heavily involved in the slave trade. His writings are of particular interest to the study of the Protestant slave trade, as he built on notions of just war, authority, and mission. Although he supported the trade slave, he came to think that Protestant masters ought to be better than their Catholic counterparts. This is shown in two excerpts: in *The Practice of Faith, Hope and Love* (1612), Udemans discussed relations between superiors and subordinates. The book was written towards the beginning of Dutch expansion, and he did not seem particularly concerned with discussing the treatment of foreign slaves. Rather, his principal concern was that relations between Christian masters and servants would be aligned with justice and holiness. In *The Spiritual Helm* (1638), he dealt more profoundly with slavery, arguing that slavery should only result from just war, and that masters had certain obligations towards their slaves.[223]

(1) Godefridus Udemans, *The Practice of Faith, Hope and Love*, trans. Annemie Godbehere, ed. Joel R. Beeke (Grand Rapids, MI: Reformation Heritage, 2012), Kindle Loc. 4727–4733, 6572–6578, 7206–7219. (2) Godefridus Udemans, *'t Geestelyk roer van 't Coopmans Schip* (1638), 2nd ed. (Dordrecht: Boels 1640). Translated by Mariëtta van der Tol.

———

1. Excerpt from *The Practice of Faith, Hope and Love* (1612)

Masters and mistresses should not treat their servants as slaves but as free people, whose souls have been saved by Christ Jesus. In their bodies, servants are not slaves but free citizens. In this they are like the rich. Thus, masters and mistresses should not reign in tyranny over the bodies of good Christians, as is the custom of the Turks today. They should treat them in all

554 *Sources*

reasonableness and kindness as children of God. They should also remember that they (masters and mistresses) have a Master in heaven, who will treat their souls as they treat their servants (Eph. 6:9). They should also not overburden their servants but give them work that they can manage, according to their capabilities. They should also teach them the true faith and the fear of God, admonishing them and punishing their shortcomings in a fatherly fashion. [*In addition, servants should have free time, adequate pay, sustenance and clothing.*]

[*In his discourse on the eighth commandment against theft, Udemans discussed the theft of persons.*]

Abduction is stealing or seizing a person, whether young or old, for profit. In the Old Testament, people who could provide a service were sold like cows and horses. According to God's law, a thief of servants had to pay for them with his life. Deuteronomy 24:7 says, 'If a man be found stealing any of his brethren of the children of Israel, and maketh merchandise of him, or selleth him; then that thief shall die; and thou shalt put evil away from among you'. [*He notes how people abduct and maim children who are forced to beg. Girls are exploited and abducted for sexual purposes, a violation of several commandments.*]

[*In his discussion of the tenth commandment against covetousness, Udemans again discusses slavery.*]

These are a few examples of what this commandment tells us not to covet.... Observe that servants are included here as temporal goods that belong to others. That is because the Jews of former times had male and female slaves, as the heathen and the Turks do today. These slaves were bought and sold for money like cows and horses. Praise God that slavery has been abolished among Christians because of Christian rulers such as Constantine the Great. All true Christians are now free in soul by faith in Christ Jesus (1 Cor. 7:22) and in body because of the authority and privileges they have received from Christian princes. The servants of Christians are not slaves, but free people. They are not bound beyond the contract of work that they or their masters have made, and which they are obliged to fulfil with good consciences, as they are able.

2. Excerpt from *The Spiritual Helm* (1640)

Godfried Udemans, *The Spiritual Rudder of the Trader's Ship: that is, how the trader and sailing merchants should conduct their business in peace and in war, before God and people, on the water and on the land, especially among the heathen in East and West India: to the glory of God, the edification of the congregations, and the salvation of their souls: furthermore for the temporal good of the Fatherland, and their family, by Godfried Udemans, Minister of the Word in Zierikzee.*

Art 6: Through his death, our saviour Jesus Christ has set us free from the spiritual slavery of the devil, and from sin (John 8:26). As the Son sets you free, you are truly free (John 2:14–15). Since the children partake in flesh and blood, so he too became partaker of the father so that through his death, he would nullify those who held the power of death, that is, the devil: and would release all who had lived with the slavery of the fear of death all their lives. However, with regards to physical slavery, thereof have we not been released by the Son of God, because the faithful servants are admonished everywhere to obey their master, not only the reasonable ones, but also the harsh ones: comforting themselves with the spiritual freedom, which they obtained through the Lord Jesus Christ, like the free persons (1 Cor. 7:21–22, Eph. 6:5–8, Col. 3:22–25, 1 Tim. 6:2, Phil. 16).

Art 7: Nevertheless, all Christians must strive after physical freedom, to serve the Lord Christ, with steady constancy (1 Cor. 7:21). If you are called as a servant, do not worry; but if you could become free, do that. Because a slave is more closely and strongly tied to his Master, than a woman to her husband: even so, the Apostle praises virginity, since it is becoming to serve the Lord with steady constancy, and without impediment (1 Cor. 7:35). How much more appropriate and becoming is the physical freedom: for this reason, all Christians, and especially the free Dutch people, must highly estimate this treasure, because it is one of the greatest treasures under the sun (Exod. 20:2, Ps. 81:7).

Art 8. This physical freedom was first granted by the Christian emperors, and the Kings, during a thousand years, especially the Kings of France, and that from love, and to honour the Christian Religion: even more, since the false Prophet Mahometh, in order to spread his heinous sect, promised physical freedom to all those who would follow his Law (Stet Rivet, in Exod. 21: 2–4. Item/I. de Serres anno 724).

Art 9. Moreover, since all Christians, who have been born from Christians, are born with this freedom, they should not be made slaves by other Christians, or be sold in perpetuity (Stet Codicis lib 1, Tit. 10), with the exception of Christians who become Mohammedans, or who serve the Turks or Saracens against the Christians: they may be judged to be worse than unbelievers (1 Molanus lib. 3 de Canonicis, chapt 32, Aijala book 1, chap. 1). With regards to the Turkish or Spanish tyrants, who deprive Christians of their freedom with violence, they will have to give an account before God. So will the Antichrist and his accomplices, who trade in the bodies and souls of human beings (Rev. 18:13).

Art 10. With regards to the Heathen and the Turks, they may be used by Christians as slaves, as long as they have been captured in a just war: or bought for a fair price from her parents, or another virtuous Master, like it is said, that normally happens in Angola. Because this is in line with the Law of God (Lev. 25:44–46; see 1 Monalus, de Canonicis book 3, ch. 37).

Art 11. We have no right to wage offensive wars with the Indians: but only to protect ourselves, as long as they have not been offended and provoked by us, or if they seek to prevent a peaceful settlement, like they have done more than once because of the Spanish and the Portuguese (Deut. 2:25).

556 Sources

Art 12. If Christians make use of heathen slaves, they must treat them in accordance with Holy Scripture, in reasonableness and kindness, like the Christian Religion teaches: That is, they must first take responsibility for the care of their souls, that they may be converted to the right belief, like Abraham, the father of all believers, cared for his servants (Gen. 17:23–27). And the merchant Cornelius, cared for for his servants and soldiers, his blood relative, and some friends (Acts 10:7–24). As to the body, they must rule over them, remembering that they too have a Lord in Heaven, without regard for status (Eph. 6:9, Col. 4:1). And otherwise, when he (the slave) is abused or tyrannised by their Masters, then the Lord grants the permission to walk away, and he does not want, that when one of these poor slaves seek refuge, anyone betrays them, or surrenders them into the hands of their master (Deut. 23:15–16, Prov. 30:10). Hence, Johannes Molanus, being a Papist, rightly rebukes all those Christians, who commit cruelty to their slaves. And also, since our ancestors (he says), and almost the entire Christian world, had demonstrated such kindness to their slaves, that they, for Christ's sake, granted them physical freedom (book 3 of the Canonicis, chap 32). Cruelty is especially unbecoming for the Dutch, who tend to be kind by nature, and for this reason had been more ready than other Christians, to grant slaves freedom, like he narrates in the same book (chap. 34), and proves that with the Ordinance of Lady Margriet, Countess of Flanders, and following the advice of the High Council of Mechelen, passed on to Emperor Charles on 7 March 1521, about the question of a certain Moor named Simon, who had been the slave of a Portuguese, and who had run away from his Master, which master had requested the Emperor in a secret audience, that the slave would be surrendered to him: but the Council of Mechelen advised that the request of the Master had been unfounded, since under the old customs of our Nation, slavery had since long ceased in our Low Countries, and that all people receive protection of their freedom here. About this wrote N. Clenardus from Fez to the Prior of Tongerloo: I believe (he said), that in Brabant and the other territories that belong to the Emperor outside of Spain, no slaves ought to be held, but that they are immediately released, also against the will of their Master.

Art 13. The Christians are not allowed to bring Indian slaves into a miserable condition, in soul or in body, like they were before, but they can bring them into a better condition. For this reason, they should not sell them to the Spanish, the Portuguese, or other cruel people, who are tyrannical to their souls and bodies: because this violates love and justice (Mat 7:12). All that you wish for others to do to you, so will you treat him also, since that is in accordance with the Law and the Prophets (Prov. 10:12). The righteous man has mercy on his cattle: however, the heart of the godless is merciless. If we show mercy to our cattle, we should show even more mercy to our servants, (Prov. 30:10).

Sources 557

Art 14. Faithful slaves, especially those who become faithful Christians, must be fairly rewarded and after a number of years released, so that they do not become discouraged, and may be even more lured to the Christian faith. Because this way they become our Brothers, like Onesimus (Phil. 16), and similarly, they ought to be treated like Brothers, as it was stated in Art 9. This is in accordance with the Law of God (Exod. 21:2, Lev. 25:48, Deut. 15:12, Jer. 34:8–9. Thus we are not allowed to rule over our brothers harshly, but we ought to fear our God (Lev. 25:43–46). And when such a faithful slave becomes free, we ought not to let him leave empty-handed from our house [Deut. 15:13], but we should give him something so that he can build up his life. With regard to the timing of their release, this cannot be more reasonably calculated than it has been given by the Lord, that is, seven years, to be sure, to be counted from their conversion to the Christian faith, since from that time has he become our Brother.

Art 15. The way of trading under the Pope, especially under the Spanish and the Portuguese, with the souls and the bodies of human beings, not only of Indian slaves, but also the Moores, and even of faithful Christians,...is a cursed and antichristian trade, which one will not be able to justify before God or before reasonable people (Rev. 18:14). [*He then goes on to discuss the complaints of Bartholome de la Casas.*]

Art 16. As we come to a conclusion, we shall add a beautiful sentence from Augustine (book 4 of the Civitate, chap. 3). A righteous man, he says, is free, even if he were a slave; but an unrighteous man is a slave, even if he were a King: because he is a slave, not only of people, but (what counts heavier) of as many masters as he has flaws. Let this comfort the faithful slaves, and serve as a warning to the godless Masters....

157 *Women's Right to Liberty of Conscience* (1638–1641)

Keywords: #Marriage, #Women's Rights, #Women, #Domestic Abuse, #Freedom of Religion, #Conscience, #Covenant, #Tyranny, #Authority, #Submission, #Servants
Region: #United States, #England
Group: #Puritan, #Leveller

Shortly after **Roger Williams** fled into what is now Rhode Island, he established a small plantation where he sought to maintain reasonable relations with local American Indians, recognising their rights to the land. He named the colony Providence due to God's providential care in his 'distress'. The only colony in New England with a religious name would be the first to promote religious freedom. Williams desired 'it might be for a shelter for persons distressed of conscience'.[224] An early 1636 agreement between the settlers of Providence made the public good central to governance based on consent: We 'do promise to subject ourselves in active and passive obedience to all such orders or agreements as shall be made for public good of the body in an orderly way'.[225] An appeal from a local woman named Jane Verin concerning her freedom of conscience made it into the official records of the colony.

The first source is a 1638 letter from Roger Williams to John Winthrop recounting a case between Joshua Verin and Providence Plantation. Verin did not attend religious services, as was his right. However, Jane Verin attended the services despite her husband's proscriptions. He even resorted to physical abuse to keep her from Christian fellowship. Joshua's free exercise of conscience, it was argued from scripture in his defence, allowed him to constrain his wife's actions. On 21 May 1638, the court argued that Joshua was in 'breach of a covenant for restraining of the liberty of conscience', and thus, he was deprived of the right to vote.[226] Although Joshua simply left the colony in protest, the court's decision was important. As Edward J. Eberle notes, this

> is the first known record recognising a woman's freedom of conscience in America. It thus appears to be the first time a legal precedent was

established supporting the right of a woman to act according to her conscience, independent of her husband.[227]

The second source dates to three years later and from the other side of the Atlantic. During the British Civil Wars, men and women debated the nature and extent of submission to political and religious authority. As England slid into war, Katherine Chidley (fl.1616–1653) became an important female author over the next decade. In the following source from 1641, she pushed against a Presbyterian minister, Thomas Edwards, who wanted to see a centralised church establishment. In defending congregational independence and religious toleration, Chidley grappled with the implications for marriage. She argued that a wife's conscience was independent of her husband, even as she asserted the husband's authority in civil and bodily matters. Over the next decade, Chidley published widely and became a leading female voice for the Levellers, an important group in the history of natural rights, democracy, and egalitarianism (see the 1647 **Agreement of the People**).[228] Jane Verin and Katherine Chidley, in different ways, carved out an inviolable space for conscience, and such arguments eventually played a part in securing greater agency and autonomy in civil matters.

(1) Roger Williams to John Winthrop (27 May 1638), in John Russell Bartlett, ed., *The Letters of Roger Williams* (Providence, RI: Narragansett Club, 1874), 94–96; (2) Katherine Chidley, *The justification of the independant churches of Christ being an answer to Mr. Edwards his booke* (London, 1641), 26.

———

1. Joshua Verin *v.* Jane Verin

Sir, we have been long afflicted by a boisterous and desperate young man, Philip Verin's son of Salem [Massachusetts], who as he has refused to hear the word [of God] with us (which we do not molest him for) these 12 months, so because he could not draw his wife, a gracious and modest woman, to the same ungodliness with him, he has trodden her under foot tyrannically and brutishly: which she and we bearing with this a long time, though with his furious blows, her life was in danger, at the last the majority of us voted to discard him from our civil freedom, or disfranchise, etc.

———

2. Katherine Chidley against Thomas Edwards

Next you [Thomas Edwards] say O! how will this take away that power and authority which God has given to Husbands, Fathers, and Masters, over wives, children, and servants.

560 Sources

To this I answer, O! that you would consider the text in 1 Cor. 7[:13] which plainly declares that the wife may be a believer, and the husband an unbeliever, but if you have considered this text, I pray you tell me, what authority this unbelieving husband has over the conscience of his believing wife; It is true he has authority over her in bodily and civil respects, but not to be a Lord over her conscience; and the like may be said of fathers and masters, and it is the very same authority which the Sovereign has over all his subjects, and therefore it must reach to families: for it is granted that the King has power (according to the Law) over the bodies, goods, and lives of all his subjects; yet it is Christ the King of Kings who reigns over their consciences: and thus you may see it takes away no authority which God has given to them.

158 Anna Maria van Schurman, *Whether a Woman Should be Educated in Politics and Government* (1638)

Keywords: #Education, #Women's Rights, #Women
Region: #Netherlands
Group: #Labadists | #Dutch Reformed

Anna Maria van Schurman (1607–1678) 'was not merely one of the most learned women of her time', writes Amanda C. Pipkin, 'but rather one of the most learned humans of all time'. She knew 15 languages, including Hebrew, Latin, Greek, and Arabic and was skilled in several branches of the arts. Her publications span from 1638 until her death in 1678, writing on a broad range of topics. She was born into a wealthy Calvinist noble family, and her father had recognised her aptitude for learning early on. When Von Schurman was young, family members connected her with leading ministers and scholars like **William Ames** and Gijsbertus Voetius. She quickly built a reputation for her erudition. Within the Reformed community, there was precedence for Calvinist leaders investing in promising noblewomen. Voetius famously allowed her to attend seminary lectures, sitting in a booth that kept her out of the sight of the male students at the University of Utrecht. She used her education and influence to improve the learning of women and men, but her example did not lead to more women being allowed to attend university.[229]

The following selection comes from *The learned maid; or, Whether a maid may be a scholar? A logick exercise* (Latin 1638; English 1639, French 1646). In this work, Von Schurman argued for the proposition that a Christian woman should receive a robust education. This education should be undertaken for God's glory and for the benefit of her family and the betterment of women. Her society valued widespread literacy (in keeping with the Reformation), and some advocated the education of women (in keeping with many humanists). In the following excerpt, Von Schurman explored which subjects were most fitting for the female scholar. Although education about law, the military, and public speaking were 'less proper and less necessary' for a woman, she argued that women should not be 'excluded from such

562 Sources

Scholastic knowledge or Theory; especially not from understanding the most noble Doctrines of *Politics* or Civil Government'.

Anna Maria van Schurman, *The learned maid; or, Whether a maid may be a scholar? A logick exercise* (London: John Redmayne, 1659), 1–6. Text modernised by the editors.

———

The Learned *Maid*. A Logical Exercise upon this Question:

Whether a Maid may be a Scholar?

We hold the *Affirmative*, and will endeavour to argue for it.

We must examine the subject and the predicate of this question.

By a *Maid* or *Woman*, I mean one who is a *Christian*, and not in Profession only, but is genuinely so.

By a *Scholar*, I mean one who is given to the study of *Letters*, that is, the knowledge of *Languages*, *Histories* and all kinds of Learning, both the higher learning entitled *Faculties*; and the inferiour called *Philosophy*. We only except *Scriptural Theology*, properly so named, as that which uncontroversially belongs to all Christians.

When we enquire, *whether she may be*, we mean whether it is *convenient*, that is, expedient, fit, decent.

Having defined the *words*, the *Things* are to be distinguished also. For some *Maids* are *ingenious*, others *not so*: some are *rich*, some *poor*: some *engaged* in Domestic cares, others at *liberty*.

The studies of a *Scholar* are either *universal*, when we give ourselves to all sorts of Learning: or *particular*, when we learn some one Language or Science, or one distinct Faculty.

Wherefore we make use of these Limitations:

First, concerning the *Subject*; our *Maid* should be endowed with some *wit* and have some aptitude for learning.

Second, she should be provided with necessities so that her lack of wealth is not a hindrance. I mention this because few have the good fortune of having Parents who personally educated them, and hiring Teachers is expensive.

Third, her situation must allow for spare hours free from her general and special Calling, that is, from the Exercises of Piety and household Affairs. Children may find time because they have few cares and responsibilities. Older women may be celibate or have servants, if they are wealthy, who can help with domestic duties.

Fourth, the goal of her education should not be vainglory, ostentation, or unprofitable curiosity: but rather the general goal of God's Glory and the salvation of her own soul; that she may become more virtuous and happy, and that she may (if she has the responsibility) instruct and direct her Family, and also be useful (as far as possible) to her whole Sex.

Sources 563

Next, *Limitations* of the *Predicate*: *Scholarship* or the study of *Letters*. I affirm that all honest Disciplines, or the whole of the liberal Arts and Sciences (as it properly benefits and adorns Mankind) is well suited for our *Christian Maid*: yet the manner of learning should accord with the Dignity and Nature of every Art or Science and be suited to the capacity and condition of the Maid herself. The education should follow a fitting order, place and time so that the subjects properly fit together. Special attention should be given to those Arts that closely relate to *Theology* and *Moral Virtue* and are subservient to them. These are *Grammar*, *Logic*, *Rhetoric* (especially *Logic, The Key of all Sciences*): then *Physics, Metaphysics, History*, etc., and also Languages, particularly *Hebrew* and *Greek*. All of these facilitate a deeper understanding of *Holy Scripture* (to say nothing of other Books). Other areas of study, like *Mathematics* (and also *Music*) *Poetry, Painting* and other liberal Arts may be undertaken as an embellishment to learning or for recreation.

Finally, we will consider the study of Law, Military Discipline, and Oratory in the Church, Court, or University, deeming them less proper and less necessary. And yet we do not argue that our *Maid* should be excluded from such Scholastic knowledge or Theory; especially not from understanding the most noble Doctrines of *Politics* or Civil Government.

When we say a Maid may be a Scholar, we clearly do not consider Learning to be a necessary prerequisite for eternal salvation: nor is learning the very *Essence* of Happiness in this life: but it is very useful, contributing to the integrity and perfection thereof. In this regard, the contemplation of excellent things will foster a greater Love of God while contributing to everlasting Felicity.

Therefore let our Thesis or Proposition stand: A Maid *may be a Scholar.*

159 *Begrudged Toleration in New Netherland (1638–1674)*

Keywords: #Colonisation, #Church-State Relations, #War, #Freedom of Religion, #Toleration, #Pluralism
Region: #United States | #Netherlands, #Sweden, #England
Group: #Dutch Reformed | #Lutheran, #Church of England, #Roman Catholic

Toleration in New Netherland emerged as a practical means of handling the presence of religious 'others', rather than as a promotion of pluralism. Partly owing to warfare with the Lenape in the 1630s and 1640s, colonists made little effort to evangelise, and the few ministers present in the colony were often more concerned with warding off other Protestant groups. They often conceptualised toleration as freedom of conscience, freedom from compulsion in religion, or freedom to worship within the home, not the freedom to practise other faiths publicly. Even so, concepts like freedom of conscience were elastic, and they accommodated considerable diversity of practice. Over time, some degree of toleration emerged, but often with significant constraints.[230] The following documents span the history of New Netherland. They reveal the Atlantic, and indeed global nature of debates about the extent of toleration in Dutch territories.

1–2, 5, 8. E. B. O'Callaghan, ed., *Documents Relative to the Colonial History of the State of New-York, Procured in Holland, England and France by John Romeyn Brodhead* (Albany, NY: Weed, Parsons and Company, 1856), I:110–113, 119–123, 607–609; III:216–219 (Text modernised by the editors); 3–4, 6–7. Hugh Hastings, ed., *Ecclesiastical Records: State of New York* (Albany, NY: James B. Lyon, 1901), I:138–139, 318–319, 333–334, 358–359.

———

1. Proposed Articles for the Colonisation and Trade of New Netherland

(2 September 1638)

[*Although Dutch colonisation predated these 1638 articles, they were drawn to attract more people to settle in the area. The document offers colonisation proposals, including freedom of conscience.*]

2 And inasmuch as it is of the highest importance, that, in the first commencement and settlement of this population, proper arrangement be made for Divine worship, according to the practice established by the government of this country, Religion shall be taught and preached there according to the Confession and formularies of union here publicly accepted in the respective churches, with which everyone shall be satisfied and content, without, however, it being inferred from this, that any person shall be hereby in any wise constrained or aggrieved in his conscience, but every man shall be free to live up to his own in peace and decorum; provided he avoid frequenting any forbidden assemblies or conventicles, much less collect or get up any such; and further abstain from all public scandals and offences, which the magistrate is charged to prevent by all fitting reproofs and admonitions, and if necessary, to advise the Company, from time to time, of what may occur herein, so that confusions and misunderstandings may be timely obviated and prevented....

5 Equal justice shall be administered, in all civil and criminal matters, to all inhabitants and others who frequent that country, according to the form of procedure, and the laws and customs already made, or to be hereafter enacted....

8 Each householder and inhabitant shall bear such tax and public charge as shall hereafter be considered proper for the maintenance of Clergymen, comforters of the sick, schoolmasters and such like necessary officers....

----

2. Proposed Freedoms and Exemptions for New Netherland (19 July 1640)

[*Whereas the 1638 articles gave some latitude for freedom of conscience, the updated 1640 Freedoms and Exemptions made it clear that only the Dutch Reformed could openly worship.*]

And no other Religion shall be publicly admitted in New Netherland except the Reformed, as it is at present preached and practiced by public authority in the United Netherlands; and for this purpose the Company shall provide and maintain good and suitable preachers, schoolmasters and comforters of the sick.

----

566   *Sources*

3 Conditions under which a party of English people may come and settle in New Netherland (6 June 1641)

[*Francis Doughty was a footloose English Presbyterian minister. He was critical of Charles I, settled in Massachusetts Bay around the time of the Pequot War and left under pressure for his beliefs about infant baptism. He then became the first Presbyterian minister in New Amsterdam. In 1641 he was granted permission to settle in New Netherland along with many congregants. Dutch ministers and magistrates swore an oath to uphold the established Reformed faith, and allowing Reformed (Presbyterian) foreigners to worship openly was largely unproblematic.*]

Whereas a good number of respectable English people with their preachers have petitioned for permission to settle here and live among us, asking that the conditions may be communicated to them, therefore we have resolved to send them the following terms

First, they will be obliged to take the oath of allegiance to their High Might[iness] the States and to the West India Company, under whose protection they are to live here.

2 They shall have free exercise of their religion.
3 As to their political government, if they desire a Magistrate, they may nominate three of four of their ablest men, from whose number the Governor of New Netherland will select him, who is to be their Magistrate, having final jurisdiction in all civil cases up to 40 guilders, cases for higher amounts may be appealed to the Governor and Council of New Netherland and criminal jurisdiction up to (i.e., not including) capital punishment.
4 They shall not build fortifications without permission....

———

4. Maintaining a Religious Monopoly (1653)

[*The following 1653 letter shows the tight grip ministers wanted to keep on public worship in New Netherland and that keeping a religious monopoly was an important strategy for church growth. Responding in February 1654, the Classis of Amsterdam said the desire for a Lutheran pastor 'grieves us', and the Classis intervened with the result that Directors denied the Lutheran's request and ordered the governor, Peter Stuyvesant, to stifle 'similar petitions ... in the most civil and least offensive way'.*]

Revs. Megapolensis and Drius to the Classis of Amsterdam (6 Oct 1653)

Reverend, Pious and Learned Fathers in Christ

We acknowledge with grateful hearts the favour of God, the good will of the Directors, and the zealous care of your Reverend body, for the defence, and maintenance of the Reformed Religion in this foreign land, which is under the privileged government of the Honourable Company, and which has obligated the Governor by oath, in their commission to him, to permit no other religion than the Reformed.

We have hitherto enjoyed the full benefit of our religion in this province. But recently, on the 4th of October last, it happened that certain Lutheran residents here, prepared and presented a certain request to our Governor, (asking for) permission to call a Lutheran Minister out of Holland, and also to organise separately and publicly a congregation and church. This would tend to the injury of our church, the diminution of hearers of the Word of God, and the increase of dissensions, of which we have had a sufficiency for years past. It would also pave the way for other sects, so that in time our place would become a receptacle for all sorts of heretics and fanatics....

For as long as no other religion than the Reformed has been publicly allowed, all who wish to engage in public worship come to our service. By this means it has happened that several, among whom are some of the principal Lutherans, have made a profession of religion, and united with us in the Lord's Supper....

---

5. Capitulation between the Honourable Valiant Johan Risingh, Governor of New Sweden and the Honourable Peter Stuyvesant, Director-General over New Netherland (15 September 1655)

[*This source comes from the end of the colony of New Sweden (1655). In the terms of capitulation, the Dutch promised to allow Lutherans to remain along with a teacher of the Augsburg Confession. Even with this stipulation, Lutherans struggled for another decade to win the right to worship openly. The Dutch Reformed Church was still far from embracing pluralism, as evidenced by Johannes Megapolensis' 1655 complaint about the Jewish community and the laws against Quakers that gave rise to the Flushing Remonstrance (1657).*]

8. Should there be any Swedes or Fins disinclined to depart, Governor Risingh shall be at liberty to admonish them to leave, and if inclined to accompany him on such admonition, they shall not be detained or prevented by the General, and those who will, then, remain here, and earn their living in the country, shall enjoy the freedom of the Augsburg Confession, and one person to instruct them therein.

---

6. Conscience, Coercion and Illegal Church Meetings (1656)

[*In early 1656, Revs. Johannes Megapolensis and Samuel Drisius informed the Director General and Council of New Netherland about illegal religious meetings on Long Island. The official response is reproduced below.*]

568   *Sources*

Action of the Director General and Council of New Netherland on Conventicles (1 February 1656)

The Director General and Council have been credibly informed [of these illegal gatherings.] This is contrary to the general rules, political and ecclesiastical of our Fatherland; and besides, such gatherings lead to trouble, heresies and schisms.

Therefore, to prevent this, the Director General and Council strictly forbid all such public or private conventicles and meetings [and they impose fines for participants.]

The Director General and Council, however, do not hereby intend to force the consciences of any, to the prejudice of formerly given patents, or to forbid the preaching of God's Holy Word, the use of Family Prayers, and divine services in the family; but only all public and private conventicles and gatherings, be they in public or private houses, except the already mentioned usual, and authorised religious services of the Reformed....

——

7. Petition of Lutherans for Public Worship (24 October 1656)

[*The absorption of New Sweden into New Netherland left the Dutch with few options regarding toleration: they could expel all Lutherans, allow them to worship within their homes or grant them the right to worship publicly. Reformed ministers largely wanted the second option. The Classis of Amsterdam, writing in August and October of 1656, were even grieved by limited toleration and feared it would open the door for more latitude in religious matters. Many Lutherans were also dissatisfied. In the following petition, they asserted their conformity to government orders while claiming the right to public worship.*]

To the Noble, Very Worshipful, the Honourable Director-General and High Council of New Netherland:

We the united adherents of the Unaltered Augsburg Confession residing here in New Netherland, with all respect, do show, that we have obediently acted upon your Honours prohibitive order published by edict, and have not gathered anywhere to hold divine services with reading and singing; nevertheless our friends in the Fatherland, acting in our behalf, have petition the Noble, Honourable Lords of the West India Company, our Patroons, in reference to this matter. Upon their petition, they have obtained from their Lordships, as they reported to us, in a full meeting, a resolution and decree that the doctrines of the Unaltered Augsburg Confession should be tolerated in the West Indies and New Netherland under their jurisdiction, in the same manner as in the Fatherland under its praiseworthy government.

We turn therefore to your Noble Honours, your Worships, knowing us to be humble and obedient subjects, and pray, that henceforth we may not be hindered in our services. These with God's blessing we intend to celebrate, with prayer, reading and singing, until, as we hope and expect, a qualified person shall come next spring from the Fatherland to be our minister and teacher, and remain here as such....

[After this petition, and even after learning a Lutheran minister was allowed by the 1655 Articles of Capitulation, the Classis of Amsterdam in May and June of 1657 sought to restrict Lutheran worship. In July 1657, Revs. Johannes Megapolensis and Samuel Drisius loudly protested the arrival of a Lutheran minister, an event that turned the united and peaceful colony into a 'Babel of confusion' that, by Satan's design, 'obstruct[ed] the march of truth in its progress'. The Mayor and Alderman of New Amsterdam promptly questioned the Lutheran minister and restricted him from 'public or private' worship. Megapolensis and Drisius pushed for his removal from the colony in an August 1657 letter. Lutherans signed another petition in protest in October 1657, and the threatened Lutheran minister also petitioned the Governor and Council. They again ordered him to depart.]

———

8. Duke of York [fut. James II], Instructions for Governor Edmund Andros, Lieutenant Governor of Long Island, New York. Windsor (1 July 1674)

[In 1664, New Amsterdam capitulated to English forces. The terms of surrender guaranteed that 'The Dutch shall enjoy the liberty of consciences in Divine Worship and church discipline'. In the previous half-century, the Dutch Reformed struggled with the West India Company over the nature and extent of toleration, always assuming it was the Reformed who granted liberty of conscience to others. Now the English set the policy. The Lutherans of New York quickly petitioned the new governor, Richard Nicolls, who promptly granted them a charter to worship freely. In the early 1670s, the Dutch temporarily regained control of New Amsterdam, but their grip on power did not last. By the time of the final source from 1674, New Netherland had permanently passed into English hands. As part of the terms of surrender, the Dutch secured toleration within New York.]

11. You shall permit all persons of whatever Religion to quietly inhabit within the precincts of your jurisdiction, without giving them any disturbance or disquiet whatsoever, for or by reason of their differing opinions in matter of Religion: Provided they give no disturbance to the public peace, nor molest or disquiet others in the free exercise of their religion.

160 Amalia Elisabeth, *Fighting for Freedom of Thought and Religion in Germany* (1639)

Keywords: #Freedom of Religion, #Conscience, #War, #Women
Region: #Germany
Group: #Reformed

The **Thirty Years' War** was a conglomeration of overlapping conflicts animated by divergent grievances, war aims, and conditions for peace. Since the beginning, attempts were made to broker peace, but usually, these efforts only involved a subset of the belligerents. The 1635 Peace of Prague was one such attempt. It was signed by Ferdinand II (Holy Roman Emperor) and the Lutheran John George I (Elector of Saxony), and the peace encompassed most German princes. Those not included, like Landgrave Wilhelm of Hesse-Cassel, continued fighting. When he died in 1637, his wife picked up the mantle of opposition. The decisions of Landgravine Amalia Elisabeth (1602–1651) greatly shaped the course of the war and the nature of **The Peace of Westphalia** (1648), and she helped secure the legal recognition of Calvinism in Germany.

In the late 1630s, she sought to negotiate peace with the Emperor (now Ferdinand III) through a mediator, Elector of Mainz. In the process of mediation, the religious clauses of the agreement were modified to the detriment of Calvinists. Some civil and religious authorities thought the reworked agreement sufficiently protected the Reformed. Amalia Elisabeth – with 'eyes wide open' – objected. The following letter was written to the Hessian council, who were more willing to accept trade-offs. She thought that compromising on religious protection betrayed the initial aims of the Hessians. The Emperor offered some concessions, but they were not as robust as those granted to others in the Peace of Prague. Amalia Elisabeth believed assent would leave Calvinists vulnerable, and she refused to back down from her demands. Before long, the Hessians were allied again with Catholic France and Lutheran Sweden in their armed opposition of the Emperor.[231]

Tryntje Helfferich, *The Thirty Years War: A Documentary History* (Indianapolis, IN: Hacket, 2009), 200–201.

———

Sources 571

Letter from Amalia Elisabeth to the Hessian Vice Chancellor and Privy Council, January 5, 1639.

Our noble, steadfast, very learned, and especially dear ones:

We have heard in depth not only from Commissioner Horn, who presented a detailed oral report of what occurred during his and the count of Solms' recent trip to Mainz [concerning the religious stipulations in the peace agreement]....

After, however, the contrary came to light in such a way that one could quite plainly sense how we and our co-religionists were regarded on account of our religion, we justly had all the more reason to keep our eyes wide open. We also had to consider carefully and pursue zealously, with a fervent prayer to God, how we might then not only save our conscience and rescue so many thousand souls, but also free ourselves from such an enormously heavy responsibility and from the critical judgement that we must be prepared to withstand from God, all the world, and dear posterity, both during our life and after our death.

This had been the sole principal work with which our most honoured, dearly beloved lord and spouse, of most praiseworthy memory, concerned himself from the beginning of this war up until his blessed final end. For this reason he took up and bore arms, withstood so much trouble, effort, and danger, and finally lost his life. Furthermore, the land incurred the most extreme ruin and irrecoverable damage, and the subjects spent their lives, limbs, and property in order to assure freedom of thought and the free exercise of their traditional religion, and to preserve the same for their children and descendants. So should one now consider this matter so negligently, and not even get out of it an assurance in mere words that one ought to be allowed, quietly and untroubled, the public free exercise of religion?

161 Massachusetts Bay Colony, *Body of Liberties* (1641)

Keywords: #Law, #Church-State Relations, #Violence, #Liberty, #Rights, #Domestic Abuse, #Animals, #Slavery, #Capital Crimes, #Sexuality, #Witchcraft
Region: #United States
Group: #Church of England, #Puritan, #Congregationalist

New England Puritans quickly set about reforming both church and state. Sometimes, these changes stemmed from desperation or necessity, and, other times, from the desire to be free from political constraints. Many important reforms were formulated in *A Model of Church and Civil Power* (produced by several ministers in 1635) and *How Far Moses [His] Judicials Bind Mass[achusetts]*, written by John Cotton in the mid-1630s. These documents informed the *Body of Liberties* (1641), excerpted below, as well as *The Book of the General Lawes and Libertyes* (1648). The *Body of Liberties* often tempered English Common Law with Mosaic Law, in many ways making English law more egalitarian and humane. It adopted a two-kingdoms framework in which the spiritual and temporal powers were not only distinguished, but sacredly boundaried. Thus, they tried to recover the pre-Constantinian understanding of the relationship between church and state. The two could work together to promote civil and religious flourishing, but magistrates were not in positions of ecclesiastical authority – or vice versa. As with any attempt to revise centuries-old practices, there was often a gap between theory and practice, and there was considerable diversity among the churches themselves.

Although New Englanders were often circumspect about openly tampering with monarchical power, neither the king nor the state held authority over the church. Within the church, power was moving in the direction of individual congregations that were often organised through restrictive covenants and directed by lay governance. Many towns witnessed increased male leadership in deciding ecclesiastical matters and increasing male participation in civil matters. Congregations supported the church voluntarily through tithing, rather than through taxes as had been done in England. Marriage and funerals became civil affairs. Colonists gained new protections against the coercive power of the state, and women were protected from physical abuse in the home. It also detailed laws for other unfree individuals: servants of

Sources 573

European descent. They drastically reduced the number of capital crimes by bringing law into greater conformity with the Hebrew Bible. In keeping with prior English law, transgressions of sexual mores were punishable, sometimes by death. Compared to other colonies, New England was restrained, and executions were never carried out for many of the crimes listed below.[232]

The 'Body of Liberties' is often cited because it sanctioned slavery for 'lawful Captives taken in just wars' – a common practice in the Christian and non-Christian world at the time. However, it also said that 'If any man steals a man or mankind, he shall surely be put to death'. New Englanders already enslaved Indigenous people as a result of the **Pequot War**, as well as a few Africans. However, in 1646, a number of African slaves arrived in Massachusetts, who were deemed to be stolen. The General Court decried the 'heinous and crying sin of manstealing', and ordered their return at the colony's expense. These actions were taken to 'deter all others' from manstealing, and the court ordered that a letter of 'indignation' be sent to Africa. The 'Body of Liberties' thus reveals a complicated attitude towards slavery, and it would be decades before a hereditary, race-based chattel slavery fully developed.[233]

William H Whitmore, ed., *The Colonial Laws of Massachusetts* (Boston, MA: Rockwell and Churchill, 1890), 32–61 (33, 47, 51–59). Text modernised by the editors.

———

1 No man's life shall be taken away, no man's honour or good name shall be stained, no man's person shall be arrested, restrained, banished, dismembered, nor in any way punished, no man shall be deprived of his wife or children, no man's goods or estate shall be taken away from him, nor any way damaged under colour of law, or countenance of authority, unless it is done by virtue or equity of some expressed law of the country warranting the same, established by a General Court and sufficiently published, or in case of the defect of a law in any particular case by the word of God. And in capital cases, or in cases concerning dismembering or banishment, according to that word to be judged by the General Court....

Rites, Rules and Liberties concerning Judicial Proceedings

45 No man shall be forced by torture to confess any crime against himself nor against any other person unless it is done in some capital case where he is first fully convicted by clear and sufficient evidence to be guilty, after which if the cause is of that nature, that it is very apparent there are other conspirators, or confederates with him, then he may be tortured, yet not with such tortures as are barbarous and inhumane.

46 For bodily punishments, we allow amongst us none that are inhumane, barbarous or cruel....

574 Sources

58 Civil authority has the power and liberty to see the peace, ordinances and rules of Christ observed in every church according to his word, so it is done in a civil and not in an ecclesiastical way.

59 Civil authority has the power and liberty to deal with any church member in a way of civil justice, notwithstanding any church relation, office, or interest.

60 No church censure shall degrade or depose any man from any civil dignity, office, or authority that he shall have in the commonwealth.

61 No magistrate, juror, officer, or other man shall be bound to inform, present or reveal any private crime or offence, wherein there is no peril or danger to this plantation or any member of it, when any necessity of conscience binds him to secrecy grounded upon the word of God, unless it is in cases where testimony is lawfully required.

62 Any shire or town shall have the liberty to choose their deputies whom and where they please for the General Court, so be it they are free men and have taken an oath of fealty, and inhabit in this jurisdiction.

65 No custom or prescription shall ever prevail amongst us in any moral cause, our meaning is that we will not maintain anything that can be proved to be morally sinful by the word of God.

Liberties of Women

79 If any man at his death shall not leave his wife a competent portion of his estate, upon just complaint made to the general court, she shall be relieved.

80 Every married woman shall be free from bodily correction or stripes by her husband unless it is done in his own defence upon her assault....

Liberties of Servants

85 If any servants shall flee from the tyranny and cruelty of their masters to the house of any freeman of the same town, they shall be protected there and sustained till due order is taken for their relief....

87 If any man smite out the eye or tooth of his male or female servant, or otherwise maim or much disfigure him, unless it is by mere accident, he shall let them go free from his service. And shall have such further recompense as the court shall allow him.

88 Servants that have served diligently and faithfully to the benefit of their masters seven years, shall not be sent away empty....

Liberties of Foreigners and Strangers

89 If any people of other nations professing the true Christian religion shall flee to us from the tyranny or oppression of their persecutors, or from famine, wars, or the like necessary and compulsory cause, they shall be entertained and succoured amongst us, according to that power and prudence God shall give us.

Sources 575

90 If any ships or other vessels, be they friend or enemy, shall shipwreck upon our Coast, no violence or wrong shall be done to their persons or goods. But their persons shall be harboured, and relieved, and their goods preserved in safety till authority may be certified thereof, and shall take further order therein.

91 There shall never be any bond slavery, villeinage or captivity amongst us, unless it is lawful captives taken in just wars, and such strangers as willingly disguise themselves or are sold to us. And these shall have all the liberties and Christian usages which the law of God established in Israel concerning such persons morally requires. This exempts none from servitude who shall be judged thereto by authority.

Of the Brute Creature

92 No man shall exercise any tyranny or cruelty towards any brute creatures which are usually kept for man's use.

Of Capital Laws

94 Capital Laws

1 If any man after legal conviction shall have or worship any other God, but the lord God, he shall be put to death. [Deut. 13:6, 10; 17:2, 6; Exod. 22:20]

2 If any man or woman is a witch (that is, has or consults with a familiar spirit), they shall be put to death. [Exod. 22:18; Lev. 20:27; Deut. 18:10]

3 If any person shall blaspheme the name of God, the Father, Son, or Holy Ghost, with direct expression, presumptuous or high-handed blasphemy, or shall curse God in the like manner, he shall be put to death. [Lev. 24:15–16]

4 If any person commits any wilful murder, which is manslaughter, committed upon premeditated malice, hatred, or cruelty, not in a man's necessary and just defence, nor by mere accident against his will, he shall be put to death. [Exod. 21:12; Numb 35:13–14; 30:31]

5 If any person slays another suddenly in his anger or cruelty of passion, he shall be put to death. [Num. 25:20–21; Lev. 24:17]

6 If any person shall slay another through guile, either by poisoning or other such devilish practice, he shall be put to death. [Exod. 21:14]

7 If any man or woman lay with any beast or brute creature by carnal copulation, they shall surely be put to death. And the beast shall be slain and buried and not eaten. [Lev. 19:23]

8 If any man lay with mankind as he lay with a woman, both of them have committed abomination, they both shall surely be put to death. [Lev. 19:22]

9 If any person commits adultery with a married or espoused wife, the adulterer and adulteress shall surely be put to death. [Exod. 20:14]

576 *Sources*

10 If any man steals a man or mankind, he shall surely be put to death. [Exod. 21:16]

11 If any man raise up by false witness, knowingly and with the purpose of taking away any man's life, he shall be put to death. [Deut. 19:16, 18–19]

12 If any man shall conspire and attempt any invasion, insurrection, or public rebellion against our commonwealth, or shall endeavour to surprise any town or towns, fort or forts therein, or shall treacherously and perfidiously attempt the fundamental alteration and subversion of our frame of polity or government, he shall be put to death.

Ecclesiastical Liberties

95 A declaration of the liberties the Lord Jesus has given to the churches.

1 All the people of God within this jurisdiction who are not in a church way, and be orthodox in judgement, and not scandalous in life, shall have full liberty to gather themselves into a church estate. Provided they do it in a Christian way, with due observation of the rules of Christ revealed in his word.

2 Every church has full liberty to exercise all the ordinances of God according to the rules of Scripture.

3 Every church has free liberty of election and ordination of all their officers from time to time, provided they are able, pious and orthodox.

4 Every church has free liberty of admission, recommendation, dismissal, and expulsion, or deposal of their officers, and members, upon due cause, with free exercise of the discipline and censures of Christ according to the rules of his word.

5 No injunctions are to be put upon any church, church officers or member in point of doctrine, worship or discipline, whether for substance or circumstance besides the institutions of the Lord.

8 All churches have the liberty to deal with any of their members in a church way that are in the hand of justice. So long as they do not hinder the course thereof.

9 Every church has the liberty to deal with any magistrate, deputy of court or other officer who is a member in a church way in case of apparent and just offence given in their places, so long as it is done with due observance and respect.

10 We allow private meetings for edification in religion amongst Christians of all sorts of people. So long as it is done without just offence both for number, time, place, and other circumstances.

11 [*It makes provision for ministers to discuss controversial matters*] … And that nothing is concluded and imposed by way of authority from one or more churches upon another, but only by way of brotherly conference and consultations. That the truth may be searched out to the satisfying of every man's conscience in the sight of God according to his word….

162 *Solemn League and Covenant of Scotland* (1643)

Keywords: #War, #Church-State Relations, #Covenant
Region: #Scotland
Group: #Presbyterian | #Roman Catholic

In the late 1630s, Charles I and his Scottish Presbyterian subjects rapidly became estranged. Charles wanted to dictate national and ecclesiastical matters from London, while Presbyterians desired to restore power over Scottish politics, citing limitations to the power of the king based on scripture. Matters came to a head after the Archbishop of Canterbury, William Laud (episcopal Church of England), imposed a new prayerbook to replace the one by **John Knox**. A riot ensued in Edinburgh in July of 1637, followed by widespread protests and petitions. The Scots appointed Alexander Henderson (a Presbyterian minister) and Archibald Johnston of Wariston (a lawyer) to draw up a National Covenant that protected and purified the church by limiting kingly power.[234] In February 1638, the Covenant was signed, garnering widespread support from the population. Ministers like **Samuel Rutherford** pushed for the abolition of episcopacy and the Restoration of purified Presbyterianism, the position taken by the General Assembly in Glasgow (Nov 1638).[235] Those who subscribed to the Covenant (Covenanters) then clashed militarily with Charles I (The Bishops' Wars, 1639–1640).

Charles I needed money to defeat the Scots, but Parliament had the power of the purse. However, Charles had been ruling without consulting Parliament during the lengthy Personal Rule 1629–1640. Parliament had accumulated numerous civil and religious grievances that they wanted redressed before supplying funds. Furthermore, many Parliamentarians sympathised with the plight of the Scottish Protestants. English ministers wrote the Scottish General Assembly (12 July 1641) and praised God for 'so miraculously prospering your late endeavours' against the king.[236] By August 1642, the English Parliament was at war with their king. Parliament needed military assistance, and Scotland was a natural ally. Scottish support was conditioned up the adoption of some Covenanter principles. A military and religious alliance was sealed when the Lords and Commons of England signed the Solemn

578   *Sources*

League and Covenant in September 1643. This Covenant, partly reproduced below, bound both parties to root out traces of Catholicism in church and state. Although both agreed that national reform should be done 'according to the Word of God', they disagreed over how to interpret it.[237]

A Solemn League and Covenant (Aberdeen, 1643). Text modernised by the editors.

———

Come; let us join ourselves to the Lord in a perpetual Covenant, that shall not be forgotten (Jer. 50:5).

Take away the wicked from before the King: and his Throne shall be established in righteousness (Prov. 25:5).

And all Judah rejoiced at the Oath: for they had sworn with all their heart, and sought Him with their whole desire; and He was found by them: and the Lord gave them rest round about (2 Chron. 15:15).

A Solemn League and Covenant, For Reformation, And Defence of Religion, The Honour and Happiness of the King, and the Peace and Safety of the three Kingdoms of Scotland, England, and Ireland.

We, Noblemen, Barons, Knights, Gentlemen, Citizens, Burgess, Ministers of the Gospel, and Commons of all sorts in the Kingdoms of Scotland, England, and Ireland, by the Providence of God, living under one King; and being of one reformed Religion; Having before our eyes the Glory of God, and the advancement of the Kingdom of our Lord and Saviour Jesus Christ, the Honour and Happiness of the King's Majesty, and his Posterity, and the true public Liberty, Safety, and Peace of the Kingdoms; wherein everyone's private condition is included; And calling to mind the treacherous and bloody Plots, conspiracies, attempts, and practices of the enemies of God, against the true Religion, and Professors thereof in all places, especially in these three Kingdoms ever since the Reformation of Religion, and how much their rage, power and presumption are of late, and at this time increased and exercised; whereof the deplorable state of the Church and Kingdom of Ireland, the distressed estate of the Church and Kingdom of England, and the dangerous estate of the Church and Kingdom of Scotland are present and public testimonies; We have now at last (after other means of Supplication, Remonstrance, Protestations and Sufferings) for the preservation of ourselves and our Religion from utter ruin and destruction, according to the commendable practice of these Kingdoms in former times, and the example of God's people, in other Nations, After mature deliberation, resolved and determined to enter into a mutual and solemn League and Covenant; Wherein we all subscribe, and each one of us for himself, with our hands lifted up to the most high God do Swear:

1 That we shall sincerely, really, and constantly through the Grace of God, endeavour in our several places and callings, the preservation of the Reformed Religion in the Church of Scotland in Doctrine, Worship, Discipline

and Government, against our common Enemies, The Reformation of Religion in the Kingdoms of England and Ireland, in Doctrine, Worship, Discipline, and Government, according to the Word of God, and the example of the best Reformed Churches; And shall endeavour to bring the Churches of God in the three Kingdoms, to the nearest conjunction and Uniformity in Religion, Confession of Faith, Form of Church-government, Directory for Worship and Catechising; That we and our posterity after us, may as Brethren, live in Faith and Love, and the Lord may delight to dwell in the midst of us.

2 That we shall in like manner, without respect of persons, endeavour the Extirpation of popery, prelacy (that is, Church Government, by Archbishops, Bishops, [etc.]) Superstition, Heresy, Schism, Profaneness, and whatsoever shall be found to be contrary to sound Doctrine, and the power of Godliness; Lest we partake in other men's sins, and thereby be in danger to receive their plagues; And that the Lord may be one, and his Name one in the three Kingdoms.

3 We shall with the same sincerity, reality, and constancy, in our several vocations endeavour with our estates and lives mutually to preserve the Rights and Privileges of the Parliaments, and the Liberties of the Kingdoms, And to preserve and defend the King's Person and Authority, in the preservation and defence of the true Religion, and Liberties of the Kingdoms; That the world may bear witness with our consciences of our Loyalty, and that we have no thoughts or intentions to diminish His Majesty's just power and greatness.

4 We shall also with all faithfulness endeavour the discovery of all such as have been, or shall be Incendiaries, Malignants, or evil instruments, by hindering the Reformation of Religion, dividing the King from his people, or one of the Kingdoms from another, or making any faction, or party amongst the people contrary to this League and Covenant, That they may be brought to public trial, and receive condign punishment, as the degree of their offences shall require or deserve, or the supreme Judicatories of both Kingdoms respectively, or others having power from them for that effect, shall judge convenient....

163 Edmund Calamy, *Souldier's Pocket Bible* (1643)

Keywords: #War, #Hebrew Bible
Region: #England
Group: #Church of England, #Presbyterian, #Puritan

During the **British Civil Wars**, all sides argued in print that their cause was just and holy. Some of this literature was aimed at those who engaged in fighting, seeking to persuade them to take up arms or instead lay them down. *The Souldier's Pocket Bible* (1643) was printed for Parliament's soldiers and was produced under the direction of Edmund Calamy (1600–1666), a prominent English minister who advocated for Presbyterianism at the Westminster Assembly of Divines. The tract did not try to convince the soldier that the cause was just, for other publications had thoroughly argued that point. Rather, it tried to show them how the godly should face the prospect of killing or dying in battle. They needed to know they were fighting God's cause and that God would not abandon them in life or in death. The ideal combatant confessed their sin, recognised their weakness and dependence on God, and gave all the glory to God for the outcome of war.[238]

The full scriptural canon would have been cumbersome for those facing the cannon. As the cover page reads, *The Souldier's Pocket Bible* was intended to 'supply the want of the whole Bible'. However, most of the passages were drawn from the Hebrew Bible, with Moses featuring in the central role. Christ, however, was mentioned nowhere. The pocket Bible was one of many devotional texts for those engaging in war, and it has been reproduced for other conflicts, like the American Civil War.

Edmund Calamy, *Souldier's Pocket Bible* (London, 1643). Text modernised by the editors.[239]

———

The Soldier's Pocket Bible: Containing the most (if not all) those places contained in holy Scripture, which do show the qualifications of his inner man, that is a fit Soldier to fight the Lord's Battles, both before he fight, in the fight, and after the fight; Which Scriptures are reduced to several heads, and fitly

Sources 581

applied to the Soldier's several occasions, and so may supply the want of the whole Bible, which a Soldier cannot conveniently carry about him: And may also be useful for any Christian to meditate upon, now in this miserable time of War.

This Book of the Law shall not depart out of thy mouth, but thou shalt meditate therein day and night, that thou may observe to do according to all that is written therein, for then thou shalt make thy way prosperous, and have good success (Josh. 1:8).

A Soldier must not do wickedly (Deut. 23:9; Luke 13:4; Lev. 26:27, 37; Deut. 28:25).

A Soldier must be valiant for God's Cause (1 Sam. 18:17; 2 Sam. 10:12; 1 Sam. 17:47).

A Soldier must deny his own wisdom, his own strength, and all provision for war (Prov. 3:5; 1 Sam. 2:9; Ps. 44:6; 33:16; Eccl 8:8; 2 Chron. 20:12).

A Soldier must put his confidence in God's Wisdom and strength (Eph. 6:10; Job 12:13; Ps. 68:35; 46:1; 2 Chron. 25:8; Ps. 71:16; 1 Sam. 17:45).

A Soldier must pray before he goes to fight (Neh. 4:9; Judg. 16:28; 2 Sam. 15:31; Jas 1:5; Ps. 119:34; 86:16; 35:1; Judg. 10:15).

A Soldier must consider and believe God's gracious promises (2 Chron. 20:20; Deut. 20:4; Exod. 14:14; 2 Kings 17:39; Dan. 3:17; 1 Chron. 17:10; Isa. 41:12; 54:17).

A Soldier must not fear his enemies (Deut. 20:1; 3:22; 2 Chron. 32:7–8; Isa. 7:4; Matt. 10:28).

A Soldier must love his enemies as they are his enemies and hate them as they are God's enemies (Matt. 5:44; 2 Chron. 19:2; Ps. 139:21–22).

A Soldier must cry unto God in his heart in the very instant of the battle (2 Chron. 13:14; 14:11; 18:31).

A Soldier must consider that sometimes God's people have the worst in battle as well as God's enemies (1 Sam. 11:25; Eccl 9:2; Josh. 7:4; Judg. 6:2; 1 Sam. 4:10; Exod. 17:11; Lam 1:16).

Soldiers and all of us must consider that though God's people have the worst yet it comes of the Lord (Isa. 42:24; Amos 3:6; Judg. 4:2; Lam 1:14; 2:7).

For the iniquities of God's people they are delivered into the hands of their enemies (Deut. 29:24–25; Josh. 7:10–11; Jer. 40:2–3; 50:6–7; Lam 3:39).

Therefore both Soldiers and all God's people upon such occasions must search out their sins (Lam 3:40; Josh. 7:13).

Especially let Soldiers and all of us upon such occasions search whether we have not put two little confidence in the Arm of the Lord, and too much in the arm of flesh (Jer. 2:13, 37; 17:5).

And let Soldiers and all of us consider, that to prevent this sin, and for the committing of this sin, the Lord has ever been accustomed to give the victory to a few (Judg. 7:2; 7:7; 20:15–46; 2 Chron. 13:3–17; 14:8–11).

And let Soldiers, and all of us know, that the very nick of time that God has promised us help is when we see no help in man (Gen. 22:14; Exod. 14:13;

582   *Sources*

2 Chron. 20:12; 2 Chron. 20:17; Deut. 32:35–36; 2 Cor. 12:9; Zech. 4:6; Ps. 12:5; Isa. 33:10).

Wherefore if our Forces are weakened, and the enemy strengthened, then let Soldiers and all of us know that now we have a promise of God's help which we had not when we were stronger, and therefore let us pray more confidently (Isa. 33:2; Deut. 33:7; Ps. 142:4–5; 22:11; 97:8; 35:2; 79:9).

And let Soldiers, and all of us know, that if we obtain any victory over our enemies, it is our duty to give all the glory to the Lord, and say [the following verses] (Exod. 15:3–7; Ps. 118:23; Josh. 10:14; Mic. 7:7; 2 Cor. 1:10; 1 Cor. 29:13; Ezra 9:13–14; Ps. 116:9; 119:106).

164 György I Rákóczi, *Reasons for Going to War* (1644)

Keywords: #War, #Conscience, #Freedom of Religion
Region: #Romania, #Hungary | #Sweden
Group: #Reformed | #Lutheran, #Roman Catholic, #Islam

The **Thirty Years' War** (1618–1648) 'was an extremely complex event', Peter Wilson argues, and 'it was not primarily a religious war'. This second claim seems counterintuitive since his book explores the central importance of religion at every stage of the conflict in forming identities, describing grievances and articulating war aims. Like other wars, there were personal grudges, economic incentives, concerns about ancient privileges, and debates about the nature and the extent of submission. However, the great and small states of Europe were increasingly concerned with the balance of power, and many were willing to cross confessional divides to ensure that power was kept in check.

György I Rákóczi (1593–1648), the Hungarian Calvinist ruler of the Principality of Transylvania, illustrates this complex dynamic rather well. In late 1643, he allied with Sweden (Lutheran), possibly with the view of gaining the Polish crown, and agreed to bring Transylvania back into the war. In the following source from 1644, Rákóczi explains to the Hungarian nobility why he is going to war with the Habsburgs (Catholic) in Upper Hungary. In the opening, he claims to champion the 'precious...liberty of the soul and body'. However, Rákóczi was not strong enough to fight on his own, and he curried favour from the Ottomans (Muslim) and received financial support from France (Catholic). He secured the Peace of Linz in 1645, in which the Habsburg Empire granted religious freedom to Protestants in Hungarian lands, as well as some political privileges, enabling the cultural flourishing of Transylvania. The art of bargaining was equally understood by surrounding powers, and in the same decade, both the Ottomans and the Habsburg Empire would again establish control in the region, ending with the firm rule of the Habsburg Empire after the Battle of Vienna in 1683.[240]

György I Rákóczi, *The Declaration of, Manifesto of George Racokzkie, Prince of Transylvania, to the States and Peeres of Hungarie; Together With*

584 *Sources*

the reasons added thereunto of his modern taking up of Armes the 17. Of February, Anno 1644 (London: Edward Blackmore, 1644), 6. Text modernised by the editors.

———

Wherefore we could suffer this no longer, nor see the apparent ruin and perdition of our native country and the oppression of our nation....

We take God the Lord the searcher of all hearts as our witness, and we dare write it also to your Lordships in very truth, that we have taken up arms not for our own profit, nor out of a desire of revenge, neither also for those manifold wrongs and injuries done unto us, nor lastly out of an intention to reform or persecute Religion, much less to extirpate the same: But that we only intend to erect again the statutes and laws of the kingdom, to re-establish the same, and to proceed according to the same, insomuch that everyone without fear, trouble, let or hindrance may openly profess and exercise that same wherein his conscience is appeased, and thereby also safely to enjoy the corporal liberty, because to domineer and rule over consciences does not belong to men, but to God alone....

165 John Milton, *Freedom of the Press* (1644)

Keywords: #Freedom of the Press, #Education, #Censorship, #Heresy, #Coercion
Region: #England
Group: #Puritan | #Islam

John Milton (1608–1674) was born in London and educated at Cambridge University. As England slid towards war, he began publishing against episcopacy. During the **British Civil Wars,** he became an apologist for the Parliamentary cause, including the regicide and the experimental politics of the Interregnum. He was nearly executed after the Restoration, and his later works were less overtly political. Milton is best known for his epic poems *Paradise Lost* and *Paradise Regained,* but he was also a polymath and polemicist who wrote on theology, divorce, war, politics, toleration, free speech, and history. Milton was one of the most eloquent spokesmen for the freedom of the press. In 1637, during a time when Charles I ruled without Parliament, the dreaded Star Chamber tightened the press regulations. The Long Parliament (convened in late 1640) abolished the Star Chamber and High Commission in 1641. With the lapse of censorship, a deluge of books, pamphlets, and broadsides flooded the market, many of them containing controversial ideas. Many Parliamentarians initially welcomed the relaxation of censorship because it aided their cause against the king. As Parliament gained power, they grew wary of the destabilising nature of unregulated print, and in 1643, Parliament decided to clamp down on printing again.

Milton was incensed and penned one of his most famous works: *Areopagitica; a speech of Mr. John Milton for the liberty of unlicens'd printing, to the Parlament of England* (1644). Although he vigorously critiqued censorship, he did not think there should be an unlimited licence for printing: some ideas were intolerable, but repression should be reserved only for what was known to corrode civil and religious society. In the following selection from *Areopagitica,* Milton compared the destruction and suppression of books to murder. Those who censored were partaking in a centuries-old practice, and censors often suppressed the truth. He argued from scripture that it could be

586   *Sources*

beneficial to interact with unorthodox ideas. Sometimes, reading what was false highlighted the nature of the truth, and keeping people from supposedly dangerous ideas was rarely effective. The struggle for truth required a free press. If one only printed what was orthodox out of a fear of printing error, then humanity would never progress in knowledge. The possibility of error was necessary for arriving at genuine knowledge, just as Adam's potential to fall was essential to his ability to exercise virtue.[241]

John Milton, *Areopagitica*, ed. Richard C. Jebb (Cambridge: Cambridge University Press, 1918), 5–7, 15–21, 43–50. Text modernised by the editors.

———

I do not know what should prevent me from presenting you with an example that shows both the love of truth that you eminently profess and the uprightness of your judgement which does not desire to be partial to yourselves; by considering again that order which you have ordained 'to regulate printing: that no book, pamphlet, or paper shall henceforth be printed, unless the same is first approved and licensed by such', or at least by the person appointed for the task…. That clause about licensing books, the one we thought was removed when the church hierarchy was done away with, I shall address in a homily where I will demonstrate several things to you: First, you would not want to be associated with those who invented the licensing of books; Second, how we should think about reading in general, whatever sort of books they are; Third, that this order will not be successful in suppressing scandalous, seditious, and libellous books; Last, that this order will primarily discourage all learning and hinder the pursuit of truth, not only by discouraging and blunting our abilities in the things we already know, but also by hindering and cropping further discoveries, both in religious and civil wisdom.

I do not deny that the church and commonwealth should be greatly concerned and keep a vigilant eye on how books behave, as they also do with men; and thereafter to confine, imprison, and do sharp justice on them as evildoers; for books are not completely dead, containing a potency of life in them that is as active as the soul that gave birth to the book; rather, books preserve as in a vial the purest efficacy and extraction of the living intellect that bred them. I know books are as lively and as vigorously productive as those fabled dragon's teeth: being sown up and down, they may spring from the ground as armed men. And yet, on the other hand, unless caution is used, as good almost kill a man as kill a good book: whoever kills a man kills a reasonable creature, God's image; but he who destroys a good book, kills reason itself, kills the image of God, as it were, in the eye. Many a man lives as a burden to the earth; but a good book is the precious life-blood of a master-spirit, embalmed and treasured up on purpose for a life beyond life. It is true, no age can restore a life, and there is perhaps no great loss in this; and revolutions of ages seldom recover the loss of a rejected truth, and because they lack this truth the whole nation is worse off. Therefore, we should be cautious about persecuting the living labours of public men, how we spill that seasoned life of man that is preserved and stored in books; since we see that a kind of homicide may be thus committed, sometimes a martyrdom; and if the persecution extends to the whole print run of the book, a kind of massacre, whereof the execution ends not in the slaying of an elemental life, but strikes at that ethereal and fifth essence, the breath of reason itself; slays an immortality rather than a life....

[1]

[*Milton argues that the Greeks had a relatively relaxed attitude towards books and only noticed them when they were 'blasphemous and atheistic, or libellous'. He then gives examples of this point, also noting similarities and differences with Rome. After the conversion of emperors to Christianity, books were sometimes condemned and burned. Ministers occasionally warned against heterodox books that were already in circulation, but they usually did not prohibit them. Over time the church increasingly saw itself as regulator – and destroyer – of heterodox works, culminating in the persecutions against Reformers (Wycliffe and Huss), censorship by the Inquisition and attacks on early Protestants. Someone might argue that censorship had a bad origin, but it performed a public good. Milton argued that drawing good from bad was akin to alchemy.*]

[2]

Not to insist upon the examples of Moses, Daniel, and Paul, who were skilful in all the learning of the Egyptians, Chaldeans, and Greeks, and this probably could not have been so without reading all sorts of their books.... When Julian the Apostate...made a decree forbidding Christians from studying heathen learning, [*Christians thought this proscription to be the worst of persecutions. He then gives examples of those who continued to read and value non-Christian works. Through a food analogy, he challenges the notion that these books necessarily defile the reader.*] 'To the pure, all things are pure' [Titus 1:15]; not only meats and drinks, but all kind of knowledge, whether of good or evil: the knowledge cannot defile, nor consequently the books, if the will and conscience is not defiled. For books are like meats and foods; some of good, some of evil substance; and yet God in that biblical vision said without exception, 'Rise, Peter, kill and eat' [Acts 10:13]; leaving the choice to each man's discretion. Wholesome meats to an impaired stomach differ little or nothing from unwholesome; and the best books to a naughty mind become occasions for evil. Bad meats will scarcely breed good nourishment in the healthiest concoction; but herein there is a difference with bad books, that to a discreet and judicious reader they serve in many ways to discover, to confute, to forewarn, and to illustrate. What better witness of this point could I produce than one of your own who is now sitting in Parliament, the chief of learned men reputed in this land, Mr. John Selden; whose volume of natural and national laws proves, not

588 Sources

only by great authorities brought together, but by exquisite reasons and theorems almost demonstrated mathematically, that all opinions, yes, errors, known, read, and collated, are a great service and assistance toward the speedy attainment of what is truest. [*God has left it to* 'every grown man' *to oversee his own intellectual diet.*] Solomon informs us that much reading is a weariness to the flesh; but neither he, nor other inspired authors, tell us that such or such reading is unlawful; yet certainly had God thought good to limit us herein, it would have been much more expedient to have told us what was unlawful, than what was wearisome. As for the burning of those Ephesian books by St. Paul's converts [Acts 19:18–20], it is replied, the books were magic, the Syriac so renders them. It was a private act, a voluntary act, and leaves us to a voluntary imitation: the remorseful men burnt their own books; this example does not mean the magistrate has a similar appointment; these men practised the books, another person might perhaps have read them in some useful way. We know that good and evil grow up together almost inseparably in the field of this world [Matt. 13:14–20]; and the knowledge of good is so involved and interwoven with the knowledge of evil, and in so many cunning resemblances hardly to be discerned, that those confused seeds which were imposed upon Psyche as an incessant labour to cull out, and sort asunder, were not more intermixed. It was from the rind of one tasted apple that the knowledge of good and evil, as two twins cleaving together, leaped forth into the world [Gen. 2:17]. And perhaps this is that doom which Adam fell into of knowing good and evil; that is to say, of knowing good by evil. As, therefore, the state of man now is; what wisdom can there be to choose, what self-restraint to forbear, without the knowledge of evil? He who can apprehend and consider vice with all her baits and seeming pleasures, and yet abstain, and yet distinguish, and yet prefer that which is truly better, he is the true wayfaring Christian. I cannot praise a fugitive and cloistered virtue unexercised and unbreathed, that never sallies out and seeks her adversary but slinks out of the race, where that immortal garland is to be run for, not without dust and heat. We surely do not bring innocence into the world, rather we bring impurity; that which purifies us is trial, and trial is by what is contrary.... And this is the benefit which may be had from books promiscuously read. But of the harm that may result hence, three kinds are usually reckoned. [*Milton responds to three objections: first, that censorship cuts off the infectious spread of ideas; second, that reading bad books is needlessly walking into temptation; third, that reading bad books is a waste of time.*]

[3]

[*Milton argues that those who start censoring books would, if they were consistent, end up censoring all of life: music, dance, architecture, diet, fashion, public houses and private conversations. Such government power would be destructive of society, and appeals to imagined societies like*

Francis Bacon's New Atlantis *or Thomas More's* Utopia *are ill-suited to governance.*] It is a great art to discern in what situations the law is to restrain and punish, and in what things persuasion only is to work.... There are many who complain that divine Providence allowed Adam to transgress [Gen. 2–3]. Foolish tongues! when God gave him reason, he gave him freedom to choose, for reason is but choosing; otherwise he would have been a mere artificial Adam, such an Adam as he is only in motions. We do not highly value the obedience, love, or gift that is the product of force; God, therefore, left him free, set before him a provoking object continually before his eyes; herein consisted his merit, herein the right of his reward, the praise of his abstinence. For what reason did he create passions within us and put pleasures around us, but that these rightly tempered are the very ingredients of virtue? They who think they can remove sin by removing the matter of sin are not skilful observers of humans; rather, it increases under the very act of diminishing, though some part of it may for a time be withdrawn from some persons, it cannot from all, in such a universal thing as books are; and when this is done, yet the sin remains entire. If you take all the treasure from a covetous man, he is left with one jewel because you cannot bereave him of his covetousness. Banish all objects of lust, confine all youth with the severest discipline that can be exercised in any hermitage, you cannot make those chaste who did not enter in that condition: such great care and wisdom is required for the right managing of this point. Suppose we could expel sin by this means; by expelling sin we would also expel virtue: for it is the same with both of them: remove that, and you remove them both. This justifies the high providence of God, who, although he commands temperance, justice, and restraint, yet he pours out before us an overabundance of all desirable things, and gives us minds that can wander beyond all limit and satisfaction. Why, then, should we be rigorous in a manner that is contrary to God and nature, by abridging or making scarce those means, which freely permitted books are, that are both a trial of virtue and an exercise of truth? It would be better to learn that a frivolous law restrains such thing, uncertainly and equally bringing about both good and evil. Were I the one choosing, a little bit of good should be preferred over the forcible hindrance of evil. For God surely esteems the growth and completion of one virtuous person more than the restraint of ten vicious ones....

[4]

[*Milton then focuses on the harm done by censorship to learning. First, the church hierarchy complained that unlicensed printing would destroy learning. The opposite is the case, and involving censors creates impediments to the articulation, improvement and preservation of ideas. Second, censorship evidences a very low opinion of the people whose faith and loyalty are considered so weak that exposure to controversial opinions will shake them.*

590   *Sources*

Third, censorship shows a low estimation of the work of ministers and the power of their ministry to keep people in the faith. Galileo was censured by ecclesiastics and the church was discredited and learning stifled.]

[d.] Our faith and knowledge thrives by exercise, just like our limbs and complexion. Truth is compared in Scripture to a streaming fountain; if her waters do not flow in a perpetual progression, they sicken into a muddy pool of illegible conformity and tradition. A man may truly be a heretic; and if he believes things only because his pastor says so or the assembly so determines, without knowing other reasons, even though his belief is true, yet the very truth he holds becomes his heresy. [*People in different stations would find different reasons to conform under pressure. They offload responsibility for their religious opinions to authority. Ministers, too, are lulled to sleep by licensing – and the need to stay abreast of controversial publications will rouse them from slumber.*]

I will explore a deeper matter. The licensing of books is detrimental and brings about an incredible loss, more than if an enemy at sea should block all our havens, ports, and creeks, it hinders and retards the importation of our richest merchandise, truth: moreover, it was first established and put in practice by antichristian malice and mystery with the purpose of extinguishing, if it were possible, the light of Reformation, and to settle falsehood; little differing from that policy used by the Turk to uphold his Alcoran by the prohibition of printing. It is not to be denied, but gladly confessed, that we are to send our thanks and vows to heaven, louder than most nations, for that great measure of truth which we enjoy, especially in those main points between us and the Pope, with his appendages, the prelates: but he who thinks we are to pitch our tent here, and have attained the utmost prospect of Reformation that the mortal looking glass can show us till we come to beatific vision, that man by this very opinion declares that he is still far short of truth.

Truth indeed came once into the world with her divine Master, and was a perfect shape most glorious to look on: but when he ascended, and his apostles after him were laid asleep, then deceivers quickly arose who ... took the virgin Truth, hewed her lovely form into a thousand pieces, and scattered them to the four winds. From that time on, the sad friends of Truth ... went up and down, gathering limb after limb wherever they could find them. We have not yet found them all, Lords and Commons, nor shall we ever, until her Master's second coming; he shall bring together every joint and member, and shall mould them into an immortal feature of loveliness and perfection. Do not allow these licensing prohibitions to stand at every place of opportunity forbidding and disturbing those who continue searching, who continue to show respect to the torn body of our martyred saint. We boast of our light; but if we unwisely look on the sun itself, it beats us into darkness.... The light we have gained was given to us, not so that we would stare at it forever, but that by it we might press onward and discover things that are more remote from our knowledge. It is not the unfrocking of a priest, the unmitring of a bishop, and the removing of him from off the Presbyterian shoulders that will make us a happy nation: no; if we do not look into and reform other great things concerning the church or the economic or political rule of life, it is as if we have looked so long upon the blazing beacon of Zwingli and Calvin that we are completely blind. Some perpetually complain of schisms and sects, and consider it a great calamity that any man dissents from their maxims. It is their own pride and ignorance that causes the disturbance, these people will neither hear with meekness nor can they convince others, yet they think all must be suppressed which does not accord with their understanding. The troublers and dividers of unity are those who neglect and do not permit others to unite those severed pieces which are still lacking from the body of Truth. To be still searching for what we do not know by what we know, joining truth to truth as we find it (for her whole body is homogenous and proportional), this is the golden rule in theology as well as in arithmetic, and brings the best harmony in a church; not the forced and outward union of cold, neutral, and inwardly divided minds.

166 Particular Baptists, *The First London Confession of Faith* (1644)

Keywords: #Church-State Relations, #Confession of Faith, #Authority, #Submission
Region: #England
Group: #Baptist | #Church of England, #Puritan

A variety of English Baptists emerged from English Calvinism as frustrations arose over the moderate reforms of **Elizabeth I** and **James VI and I**. These included separatist Baptists, known as the Brownists, named after Robert Brown. Congregations emerged in England and the Netherlands. **John Smyth**, who arrived in Amsterdam in 1608 with a congregation, formed the first Anglophone Baptist congregation. Smyth and his followers moved away from **John Calvin's** orbit and towards the teachings of **Jacobus Arminius**. He eventually entered the Dutch Anabaptist stream, joining the Mennonite church. **Thomas Helwys**, an English follower of Arminius, led a congregation back to England, where they became known as 'General Baptists'. Helwys, who was combative in word and print, was imprisoned and died in jail in 1616. Particular Baptists, a distinct group that dates back to London in 1616, retained an affinity for Puritanism and Reformed thought. In 1644, seven 'Particular Baptist' congregations in London drafted a confession of faith, excerpted below. The origin of the Anabaptists and the Baptists was different, but the latter could not shake the association with the violence of the **Münsterites**.

In 1640, England's established Protestants increased the persecution of London's Particular Baptists, and verbal assaults came from contented Episcopalians and from Puritans. Baptists were slandered as divisive and unorthodox opponents of civil authority, who sowed seeds of rebellion and practised sexual perversion under the cloak of pure worship. During the British Civil Wars, such accusations were hurled at many groups. The following confession aimed to convince detractors that these accusations were not only unfounded, but also that Baptists had much in common with Reformed perspectives on church and state. Some of the sections about magistracy were updated during the tumults of the 1640s to 1680s.

Sources   593

During the Interregnum, many Baptists came to advocate Republicanism and often supported the reforms of **Oliver Cromwell's** regime. By the time of the Restoration in 1660, these seven London churches had grown to about 130 scattered congregations throughout the British Isles (minus Scotland). However, Baptists became associated with Thomas Venner's failed Fifth Monarchist uprising in 1661, and the Restoration regime persecuted them alongside other groups like the **Quakers**, Presbyterians, and Congregationalists.[242]

The Confession of Faith, Of those Churches which are commonly (though falsly) called Anabaptists (London: Matthew Simmons, 1644), in *Baptist Confessions of Faith*, ed. William Joseph McGlothlin (Philadelphia, PA: American Baptist Publication Society, 1911), 171–189 (186–189). Text modernised by the editors.

———

47.

And although the particular Congregations are distinct and several Bodies, every one a compact and knit City in itself; yet are they all to walk by one and the same Rule, and by all convenient means to have the counsel and help of one another in all necessary affairs of the Church, as members of one body in the common faith under Christ their only head (1 Cor. 4:17; 14:33, 36; 16:1; Matt. 28:20; 1 Tim. 3:15; 6:13–14; Rev. 22:18–19; Col. 2:6, 19; 4:16).

48.

That a civil Magistracy is an ordinance of God set up by God for the punishment of evildoers, and for the praise of them that do well; and that in all lawful things commanded by them, subjection ought to be given by us in the Lord: and that we are to make supplication and prayer for Kings, and all that are in authority, that under them we may live a peaceable and quiet life in all godliness and honesty (Rom. 13:1–4; 1 Pet. 2:13–14; 1 Tim. 2:2).

49.

The supreme Magistracy of this Kingdom we believe to be the King and Parliament freely chosen by the Kingdom, and that in all those civil Laws which have been acted by them, or for the present is or shall be ordained, we are bound to yield subjection and obedience unto in the Lord, as conceiving ourselves bound to defend both the persons of those thus chosen, and all civil Laws made by them, with our persons, liberties, and estates, with all that is called ours, although we should suffer at their hands on account of not actively submitting to some Ecclesiastical Laws, which they might conceive to be their duty to establish which we for the present could not see, nor our consciences could submit unto; yet are we bound to yield our persons to their pleasures.

594   *Sources*

50.

And if God should provide such a mercy for us, as to incline the Magistrate's hearts so far to tender our consciences, as that we might be protected by them from wrong, injury, oppression and molestation, which for a long time we formerly groaned under by the tyranny and oppression of the Hierarchy of Prelates, which God through mercy has made this present King and Parliament wonderfully honourable, as an instrument in his hand, to throw down; and we thereby have had some breathing time, we shall, we hope, look at it as a mercy beyond our expectation, and conceive ourselves further engaged to forever bless God for it (1 Tim. 1:2–4; Ps. 126:1; Acts 9:31).

51.

But if God withholds the Magistrate's allowance and furtherance herein; yet we must notwithstanding proceed together in Christian communion, not daring to give place to suspend our practice, but to walk in obedience to Christ in the profession and holding forth this faith before mentioned, even in the midst of all trials and afflictions, not accounting our goods, lands, wives, children, fathers, mothers, brethren, sisters, yea, and our own lives dear unto us, so we may finish our course with joy: remembering always that we ought to obey God rather than men, and grounding upon the commandment, commission and promise of our Lord and master Jesus Christ, who as he has all power in heaven and earth, so also has promised, if we keep his commandments which he has given us, to be with us to the end of the world: and when we have finished our course, and kept the faith, to give us the crown of righteousness, which is laid up for all that love his appearing, and to whom we must give an account of all our actions, and no man is able to discharge us of the same (Acts 2:40–41; 4:19, 5:28–29, 41; 20:23; 1 Thess. 3:3; Phil. 1:27–29; Dan. 3:16–17; 6:7, 10, 22–23; Matt. 28:18–20; 1 Tim. 6:13–15; Rom. 12:1–8; 1 Cor. 14:37; 2 Tim. 4:7–8; Rev. 2:10; Gal. 2:4–5).

52.

And likewise unto all men is to be given whatsoever is their due; tributes, customs, and all such lawful duties, ought willingly to be paid and performed by us, our lands, goods, and bodies, to submit to the Magistrate in the Lord, and the Magistrate is to be in every way acknowledged, reverenced, and obeyed, according to godliness; not because of wrath only but for conscience sake. And finally, all men are so to be esteemed and regarded, as is due and meet for their place, age, estate and condition (Rom. 13:5–7; Matt. 22:21; Titus 3; 1 Pet. 2:13; Eph. 5:21–22; 6:1, 9; 1 Pet. 5:5).

53.

And thus we desire to give unto God that which is God's, and unto *Cesar* that which is *Cesar's*, and unto all men that which belongs unto them, endeavouring to have always a clear conscience void of offence towards God, and towards man. And if any take what we have said, to be heresy, then we along with the Apostle do freely confess, that after the way which they call heresy, we worship the God of our Fathers, believing all things which are written in the Law and in the Prophets and Apostles, desiring from our souls to renounce all heresies and opinions which are not after Christ, and to be steadfast, unmovable, always abounding in the work of the Lord, as knowing our labour shall not be in vain in the Lord (Matt. 22:21; Acts 24:14–16; John 5:28; 2 Cor. 4:17; 1 Tim. 6:3–5; 1 Cor. 15:58–59).

1 Corinthians 1:24

Not that we have dominion over your faith, but are helpers of your joy: for by faith we stand.

167 Roger Williams, *The Bloody Tenent of Persecution* (1644)

Keywords: #Toleration, #Persecution, #Coercion, #Conscience, #Church-State Relations, #Pluralism,
Region: #United States
Group: #Puritan, #Baptist, #Seeker | #Judaism, #Islam, #Roman Catholic

Roger Williams (c.1603–1683) is one of the most important figures in the Anglo-American history of political and religious pluralism. He was apprenticed to **Edward Coke** at a young age, which put him in the highest echelons of the English administration. He trained for the ministry at Cambridge, but eventually fled to New England to escape increasing pressure to conform to the Stuart-backed Church of England. Although New England Puritans initially embraced him, he was reprimanded for raising the standards of purity too high. His advocacy of Indigenous property rights and his controversial stance towards the Stuarts caused further suspicion. Shortly before the **Pequot War**, he was expelled from Massachusetts Bay and founded Providence (in what became known as Rhode Island). He built upon good relations with the Narragansett sachemship and championed Providence as a refuge for 'soul liberty'. Williams was the first to attempt a serious and sympathetic study of Algonquian language, culture, and beliefs. *A Key into the Language of America* (1643) criticised English 'Christians' for their actions towards Algonquians. He frequently argued that American Indians were morally superior, even as he worked to convert them to Christianity.

His settlement offered 'a shelter for persons distressed of conscience',[243] and other exiles like **Anne Hutchinson** and the **Quakers** flocked there. In 1638, the settlement affirmed **Women's Right to Liberty of Conscience**, even when her conscience went against the will of her husband. William's settlement stood on shaky legal grounds, and the nearby colonies of Massachusetts Bay, Plymouth, and Connecticut challenged its right to exist; they anticipated the demise of Williams' political experiment with toleration. Williams knew he was experimenting, but he was convinced that toleration could foster prosperity and stability. Scripture and theology were ubiquitous in his two-volume correspondence and six-volume collected works.

The following selection comes from *The Bloody Tenent of Persecution for Cause of Conscience* (1644), his best-known work. At the opening of this lengthy treatise, Williams distilled his argument: he linked toleration with the person and work of Christ and argued that Christ even demanded the toleration of anti-Christians. Provided people obeyed the government in civil matters, wide latitude should be allowed for differences of conviction. The **Charter of Rhode Island** (1663) placed this colonial 'experiment' on firmer legal footings.[244]

Roger Williams, *The Bloudy Tenent of Persecution for Cause of Conscience* (1644), front matter. Text modernised by the editors.

———

1 The blood of hundreds of thousands of Protestant and Papist souls, spilt in the wars of present and former ages on account of their respective consciences, is not required nor accepted by Jesus Christ the Prince of Peace.
2 Compelling Scriptures and arguments are throughout the book proposed against the Doctrine of Persecution for cause of conscience.
3 Satisfactory answers are given to Scriptures, and objections produced by Mr. [John] Calvin, [Theodore] Beza, Mr. [John] Cotton, and the Ministers of the New England Churches, and others former and later, who claim to prove the Doctrine of Persecution for cause of Conscience.
4 The Doctrine of Persecution for cause of Conscience, is proved guilty of all the blood of the souls crying for vengeance under the altar [Rev. 6:10].
5 All Civil States, with their officers of justice in their respective constitutions and administrations are proved essentially civil, and, therefore, not judges, governors or defenders of the spiritual or Christian state and worship.
6 It is the will and command of God that (since the coming of his Son the Lord Jesus) a permission of the most Paganish, Jewish, Turkish or Antichristian consciences and worships should be granted to all men in all nations and countries: and they are only to be fought against with that sword which is only (in soul matters) able to conquer, namely, the sword of God's Spirit, the word of God.
7 The state of the land of Israel, their kings and people in peace and war, is proved to be figurative and ceremonial, and is no pattern nor precedent for any kingdom or civil state in the world to follow.
8 God does not require uniformity of religion to be enacted and enforced in any civil state; this enforced uniformity (sooner or later) is the greatest cause of civil war, ravishing of conscience, persecution of Christ Jesus in his servants, and of the hypocrisy and destruction of millions of souls.
9 In holding to an enforced uniformity of religion in a civil state, we must necessarily disclaim our desires and hopes of the Jew's conversion to Christ.

598 Sources

10 An enforced uniformity of Religion throughout a Nation or civil state, confounds the civil and religious, denies the principles of Christianity and civility, and denies that Jesus Christ has come in the flesh.

11 The permission of consciences and worships other than that which a state professes, only can (according to God) procure a firm and lasting peace (good assurance being taken according to the wisdom of the civil state for uniformity of civil obedience from all sorts.)

12 True civility and Christianity may both flourish in a state or kingdom, notwithstanding the permission of diverse and contrary consciences, either of Jew or Gentile.

168   Samuel Rutherford, *Lex, Rex, or, The Law and the Prince* (1644)

Keywords: #Government, #Authority, #Magistrate, #Election, #Equality, #War, #Resistance
Region: #Scotland | #England
Group: #Presbyterian

Samuel Rutherford (c.1600–1661) is perhaps the most influential political thinker to emerge from the Scottish Reformation. After studying in Edinburgh, Rutherford taught there as regent of humanity and became an influential preacher. In 1636, he was banished to Aberdeen for opposing the *Articles of Perth* (1618), an attempt by **James VI and I** to bring the Scottish church into greater alignment with the Church of England. English dominance over Scottish church practice created enormous tensions that erupted in a riot in Edinburgh (1637), the signing of a National Covenant (1638), the abolition of episcopacy by the Glasgow Assembly (1638), and the Bishops' Wars between Scotland and England (1639–1640), events that contributed to the more widespread conflict known as the **British Civil Wars** (1638–1660). Rutherford's public career spanned these tumultuous years, becoming a prominent Covenanter from the late 1630s until his death shortly after the 1660 Restoration. He participated in witch trials in the 1640s, defended Presbyterianism in the **Westminster Assembly**, preached before the army, Parliament, and Charles II, defended resistance to Charles I (*Lex Rex*, 1644), and denounced toleration (*A Free Disputation against Pretended Liberty of Conscience*, 1649).

Rutherford wrote *Lex, Rex* (1644) against Royalists who were not only intellectual opponents in the realm of ideas but also physical enemies on the battlefield during the British Civil Wars. It was one of many treatises on resistance that emanated from British presses in the 1640s. This treatise employed complex and wide-ranging arguments on 'the origins of government', 'the relation between king and people', 'the relationship between king and law, placing *rex* firmly under *lex*', and the right to 'the defensive wars of the Scots', as summarised by John Coffey. Rutherford placed particular emphasis on the Hebrew Bible and found arguments for natural law, covenants between the

600 *Sources*

people and their leaders, and grounding for the magistrate's duties to establish and defend the true faith. At the Restoration of the Stuarts in 1660, *Lex Rex* was banned, and Rutherford was summoned for treason, but he died before appearing before Parliament. His ideas continue to influence arguments about the people's right to choose, resistance to authority, and the government's role in fostering faith, particularly in the United States.

The following selection relates to biblical kingship. Although he argued that there was a natural equality between all people, some were destined by circumstances for poverty and others for rule. Israel's kings were not merely chosen by God; rather, in the Hebrew Bible, the people's choice was always necessary, sometimes referring to the Israelites as choosing through 'Parliament, and a Convention of the States'. The power to rule came through the people's choice: they freely chose who would rule over them, set the limits of the ruler's authority, and set conditions for rule (the covenant or contract). The one chosen by the people was also invested with power by God, but with greater authority came greater accountability. If rulers violated conditions, the community could revoke their delegated authority since they retained their rights. The implications for the British Isles were evident and detailed accordingly in later chapters.[245]

Samuel Rutherford, *Lex, Rex: The Law and the Prince: A Dispute for the Just Prerogative of King and People* (London: John Field, 1644), 9–16. Text modernised by the editors.

———

Question IV. Whether the king is only and immediately from God and not from the people.

That this question may be clearer, we set down these Considerations.

1 The question is, Whether the Kingly Office itself comes from God; I conceive it is, and flows from the people, not by formal institution; as if the people had by an act of reason, devised and thought out such a power: God ordained the power; it is from the people only by a virtual emanation, meaning that a community having no Government at all, may ordain a King, or appoint an Aristocracy. But the question is, concerning the designation of the person? Why is it that this man, rather than that man, is crowned King? And why is it, from God immediately and only, that this man rather than that man, and this race or family rather than that race and family is chosen for the Crown? Or is it from the people also, and their free choice? For the Office of Pastor and Doctor is from Christ only; but that John rather than Thomas is the Doctor or the Pastor, is from the will; and choice of men, the Presbyters and people.

2 The Royal power is in the people in three ways; (1) Radically and virtually, as in the first subject. (2) *Collative vel communicative*, by way of free donation, they giving it to this man and not to that man, that he may rule

over them. (3) *Limitatè*; They giving it in such a way that these three acts remain with the people; (1) That they may measure out, by ounce weights, so much Royal power, no more and no less. (2) So as they may limit, moderate, and set banks and boundaries to the exercise. (3) That they give it out, *conditionatè*, upon this and that condition, that they may take again to themselves what they gave out, upon condition, if the condition is violated: The first I conceive is clear, (1) because if every living creature has radically in themselves a power of self-preservation to defend themselves from violence, as we see Lions have paws and some beasts have horns or claws; men being reasonable creatures, united in society, must have the power of warding off violence in a more reasonable and honourable way, in the hands of one or more Rulers, to defend themselves by Magistrates. (2) If all men are born, with reference to civil power, alike; (for no man comes out of the womb with a Diadem on his head, or a Sceptre in his hand) and yet men united in a society may give a crown and sceptre to this man, and not to that man; then this power was in this united society, but it was not in them formally, for they should then all have been one King, and so both above and superior, and below and inferior to themselves, which we cannot say: therefore this power must have been virtually in them, because neither man, nor a community of men, can give that which they neither have formally, nor virtually in them. (3) Royalists cannot deny that Cities have the power to choose and create inferior Magistrates, therefore, many united Cities have the power to create a higher Ruler; for Royal power is only the united and superlative power of inferior Judges, in one greater Judge, whom they call a King.

Second Conclusion. The power of creating a King out of a man, is from the people, (1) Because those who may create this man a King, rather than that man, they have power to appoint a King. For a comparative act, consider that if a man has a power to marry this woman, not that woman; we may strongly conclude, therefore he hath power to marry. The people made Omri King and not Zimri; and his son Ahab rather than Tibni the son of Ginath (1 Kgs 16). Nor can it be replied that the power the people used was unlawful, for that cannot elude the argument, for the people made Solomon King, and not Adonijah (1 Kgs 1), though Adonijah was the elder brother; they say that 'God extraordinarily made the Office, and designed that Solomon be King, the people had no hand in it, but approved God's fact'. Answer. This is what we say, God by the people, by Nathan the Prophet, and the servants of David, and the States crying 'God save King Solomon' made Solomon King; and here is a real action of the people. God is the first Agent in all acts of the Creature, where a people makes a choice of a man to be their King, the States do nothing under God but create this man, rather than another man; and we cannot here find two actions, one of God, another of the people; but in one and

602   *Sources*

the same action; God by the people's free suffrage [vote] and voice creates such a man King, passing by many thousands of other people, and the people are not passive in the action, because by the authoritative choice of the States, a private man who is not a man is made into a public person and a crowned King: 'Hushai said to Absalom, "No, the one whom the Lord and this people, and all the men of Israel choose, his will I be, and with him will I abide"' (2 Sam. 16:18); 'The men of Israel said to Gideon, "Rule thou over us"' (Judg. 8:22); 'The men of Shechem made Abimelek King' (Judg. 9:6)....

2   If God regulates his people in making such a man King, not another man, then he thereby insinuates that the people have a power to make such a man King, and not another man. But God regulates his people in making a King. Therefore the people have a power to make one man a King, not another man. The Proposition is clear, because God's Law does not regulate a *non-ens*, a mere nothing, or an unlawful power; nor can God's holy Law regulate an unlawful power, or an unlawful action, but quite abolish it, and prohibit it; the Lord does not set down rules and ways about how men should not commit Treason, but the Lord commands loyalty and simply interdicts [prohibits] treason. 2. If people then have more power to create a King over themselves, than they had to make Prophets, then God forbidding them to choose such a man for their King, should say as much to his people; as if he would say, I command you to make Isaiah and Jeremiah Prophets over you, but not these and those other men. This certainly should prove that not only God, but also the people with God made Prophets; I leave this to the consideration of the godly. The Prophets were immediately called by God to be Prophets, whether the people consented to having them as Prophets, or not. Therefore God immediately and by himself sent the Prophets, not the people; but though God extraordinarily designed some men to be Kings, and anointed them by his Prophets, yet they were never actually installed Kings until the people made them Kings. I prove the assumption:

When you shall say, "I will set a King over me, like all the nations round about me". You shall set him as King over you whom the Lord your God shall choose, one from amongst your brethren shall you set King over you, you may not set a stranger over you, who is not your brother....

(Deut. 17:14–15)

3   Scripture clearly says that the people made the King, though under God: 'The men of Shechem made Abimelech King' (Judg. 9:6); 'And all the people went to Gilgal, and there they made Saul King before the Lord' (1 Sam. 11:15); 'We will not make any King' (2 Kings 10:5). This would have been

an irrational speech to Jehu, if both Jehu and the people held the Royalist's Tenet, that the people had no power to make a King, nor any active or causative influence therein; but that God immediately made the King. 'All these came with a perfect heart to make David King in Hebron; and all the rest were of one heart to make David King' (1 Chron. 12:38); on these words [the Swiss Reformed theologian Ludwig] Lavater says that Magistrates are now to be chosen in the same way; today God by an immediate Oracle from Heaven appoints the Office of a King; but I am sure he does not immediately signify the man, but only marks him out to the people, as one who has the most royal endowments, and the due qualifications required in a lawful Magistrate, by the Word of God: 'Men of truth, hating covetousness', etc. (Exod. 18:21); men who will judge causes betwixt their brethren righteously, without respect of persons (Deut. 1:16–17); Saul was chosen out of the Tribes according to the Law of God (1 Sam. 10:21); they might not choose a stranger (Deut. 17:15), and [many] Popish Writers think that Saul was not only anointed with Oil, first privately by Samuel (1 Sam. 10:1–2), but also at two other times before the people, once at Mizpah, and another time at Gilgal by a Parliament, and a Convention of the States, and Samuel judged the voices of the people so essential to making a King, that Samuel does not acknowledge him formally as King (1 Sam. 10:7–8, 17–19), though he honoured him, because he was to be King (1 Sam. 9:23–24), while the Tribes of Israel and Parliament were gathered together to make him King according to God's Law (Deut. 17) as is evident. For Samuel caused all the Tribes of Israel to stand before the Lord, and the Tribe of Benjamin was taken (1 Sam. 10:20); the Law provided one of their own, not a stranger to reign over them; and because some of the States of Parliament did not choose him, but being children of Belial, despised him in their heart (10:27), therefore after King Saul, by that victory over the Ammonites, had conquered the affections of all the people fully (10:10–11). Samuel would have his coronation and election by the Estates of Parliament renewed, at Gilgal, by all the people, to establish him King (11:14–15). 2. The Lord by Lots revealed the Tribe of Benjamin. 3. The Lord revealed the man, by name, Saul the son of Kish, when he hid himself amongst the stuff [10:20–22], that the people might do their part in the creation of a King, whereas Samuel had anointed him before; but the Text says expressly that the people made Saul King, and [many authors] do all hence conclude that the people under God, make the King.

I see no reason why William Barclay should here distinguish a power of choosing a King, which he grants that the people have, and a power of making a King, which he says is only proper to God. Answer. Choosing a King is either a comparative crowning of this man, not that man; and if the people have this, it is a creating of a King under God who principally disposes of Kings and Kingdoms: and this is enough for us. The lack of this,

604 *Sources*

made Zimri no King: and those whom the Rulers of Jezreel at Samaria (2 Kings 10) refused to make Kings, no Kings. This election of the people made Athaliah a Princess: the removal of it, and translation of the crown by the people to Joash, made her no Princess (2 Kings 8, 11): for I beseech you, what other calling of God has a race of a family, and a person to the crown, but only the election of the States? There is now no voice from heaven, no immediately inspired Prophets, such as Samuel and Elisha, to anoint David, not Eliab; Solomon, not Adoniah. The mighty or the heroic spirit of a Royal faculty of governing, is, I grant, from God only, not from the people: but I suppose that does not make a King; for then many sitting on the throne this day, should be no Kings; and many private persons should be Kings. If he means by the people's choosing, nothing but the people's approbative consent, posterior to God's act of creating a King; let them show us an act of God making Kings, and establishing royal power in one family, rather than in another family; which is prior to the people's consent, distinct from the people's consent, I believe there is none at all.

4 Hence I argue: If there is no calling or title on earth to tie the Crown to a particular Family and Person, other than the suffrage of the people; then the line of such a family, and the persons now, have no calling of God, no right to the crown, but only by the suffrage of the people, except we say that there is no lawful Kings on earth now, when Prophetic unction and designation to Crowns have ceased, contrary to express Scripture (Rom. 13:1–3; 1 Pet. 2:13–17)....

5 If the Lord's immediate designation of David, and his anointing by the divine authority of Samuel, made David formally King of Israel without the election of the people, then there were two Kings in Israel at one time; for Samuel anointed David, and so he was formally King, upon the ground laid by Royalists, that the King has no royal power from the people: and David after he was anointed by Samuel, several times called Saul the Lord's anointed, and that by the inspiration of God's spirit, as we and Royalists both agree. Now two lawful supreme Monarchs in one Kingdom, I consider to be most repugnant to God's truth, and sound reason; for they are as repugnant as two most Highs, or as two Infinites.... But certainly God's dispensation in this warrants us to say no man can be formally a lawful King, without the suffrage of the people [and he gives the example of Saul, David and Solomon]. Therefore, there flows something from the power of the people, by which he who is not King, now becomes a King, formally, and by God's lawful call; whereas before the man was no King, but as touching all royal power was a mere private man. And I am sure birth must count for less than God's designation to a crown, as is clear. Adoniah was older then Solomon, yet God would have Solomon, the younger by birth, to be King, and not Adoniah....

Sources 605

6 I think Royalists cannot deny but a people ruled by Aristocratic Magistrates, may elect a King, and a King so elected is formally made a lawful King by the people's election, for of six persons who are apt and gifted to reign, what makes one a King, and not the other five? Certainly God disposing the people to choose this man and not another man, it cannot be said but that God gives the Kingly power immediately, and by him King's reign, that is true. The Office is immediately from God, but now the question is, what is it that formally applies the Office and Royal Power to this Person rather than to the other five. Nothing can here be dreamed of, but God inclining the hearts of the States to choose this man and not that man.

169 Massachusetts Bay, *American Indians and Blasphemy* (1646)

Keywords: #Coercion, #Blasphemy, #Punishment, #Coercion, #Capital Crime, #Natural Law, #Colonisation
Region: #United States
Group: #Puritan | #Indigenous American

The **Pequot War** (1636–1638) drew English and Algonquian communities closer. As their orbits neared, the English became more comfortable with passing legislation pertaining to Indigenous communities. In September 1646, **John Eliot** began preaching to Algonquians, and these efforts would develop into the Praying Indian towns that he wrote about in *The Christian Commonwealth*. However, the initial response to his preaching was unenthusiastic. Shortly after Eliot started preaching, Massachusetts Bay passed important legislation relating to Algonquians and Eliot's mission. Parts of the 4 November 1646 legislation are reproduced below, and they show how the state supported these missionary efforts. They also encouraged him to establish a community wherein Algonquians could be taught 'orderly' living and to draw up laws that would train them in 'civility'.

At this time, Massachusetts Bay enacted several laws relating to blasphemy and idolatry. The acts applied to Algonquians who had 'submitted' in 1644 to the government of Massachusetts Bay. Algonquians had their own reasons for moving closer to the English politically and religiously, and these reasons ranged from strategic military alliances to genuine curiosity about the gospel. There is an ironic nature to these Acts. Increased discipline stemmed from perceptions of increased similarity. The closer the English perceived the Algonquians to be – and proximity was measured by their standards of piety and civility – the more Algonquians were treated like Englishmen. In Puritan New England, that could include church discipline, excommunication, fines, imprisonment, or even execution. To become Christian entailed submitting to the disciplinary regime of colonial rule. In this case, that meant that blasphemy was a capital offence for English and Algonquian alike.

The reception of this legislation is notable, for there is no evidence that Algonquians were ever indicted or convicted of blasphemy, although three

Englishmen were convicted under its terms. Richard Cogley suggests that Massachusetts Bay passed these blasphemy laws 'in order to placate God rather than to force the Indians to accept the missionary work'. The Act itself, partly reproduced below, reveals some of the ambiguity surrounding the difference between promoting and compelling faith. Spreading godliness 'by the sword' was unwarranted, it claimed, but a godly society could not tolerate blasphemy.[246] In the early years of Eliot's mission, some critics in Old and New England noted how little effort had been expended towards one of the stated aims of colonisation, namely to bring Algonquians into the story of Christianity. In July 1649, Parliament passed *An Act for the promoting and propagating the Gospel of Jesus Christ in New England*. Harvard established an Indian College in the mid-1650s where the Bible was translated into Algonquian (1663). However, as the English worked to 'civilise' and evangelise Algonquians, they divided loyalties and challenged traditional authority, contributing to tensions that would later erupt (King Philip's War, 1675–1676).

Nathaniel B. Shurtleff, ed., *Records of the governor and company of the Massachusetts bay in New England* (Boston, MA: W. White, 1853), II:176–80 (176–177). Text modernised by the editors.

———

An Act of 4 November 1646

Against Blasphemy in the Name of God

Albeit faith is not brought about by the sword, but by the word, and therefore such pagan Indians as have submitted themselves to our government, though we would not neglect anything that helps to bring them on to grace, and the means of it, yet we do not compel them to the Christian faith; nevertheless, seeing the blaspheming of the true God cannot be excused by the ignorance or infirmity of human nature, the eternal power and Godhead being known by the light of nature and the creation of the world [Rom. 1:19–20], and common reason requires every state and society of men to be more careful of preventing the dishonour and contempt of the most high God (in whom we all consist) than of any mortal princes and magistrates, it is therefore ordered and decreed, by the Court, for the honour of the eternal God, whom we only worship and serve, that no person within the jurisdiction, whether Christian or pagan, shall wittingly and willingly presume to blaspheme his holy name, either by wilful or obstinate denying the true God, or his creation or government of the world, or shall curse God, or reproach the holy religion of God, as if it were but a politic device to keep ignorant men in awe, nor shall utter any other eminent kind of blasphemy, of the like nature and degree; if any person whatsoever, within our jurisdiction, shall break this law they shall be put to death.

608 *Sources*

It is ordered and decreed by this Court, that no Indian shall at any time powwow, or perform outward worship to their false gods, or to the devil, in any part of our jurisdiction, whether they are those who dwell here, or shall come hither. If any shall transgress this law, the powwower is to pay [a fine] and every assistant countenancing, by his presence or otherwise (being of the age of discretion) [shall pay a lesser fine].

[*They then ordain fines against those spreading damnable heresies (fellow Europeans are the primary target). They detail fines for non-attendance at church, or for those who disturb the order of the church. They make provisions for evangelical work among American Indians, endeavouring to spread Christianity and 'civility' among them. Returning to punishments, they then spell out the consequences for reproaching ministers of the word of God. In keeping with the Hebrew Bible, they ordain capital punishment for children who strike their parents and for incorrigible, rebellious sons. They then detail the punishments for many lesser crimes.*]

170 An Agreement of the People for the Restoration of Native Rights (1647)

Keywords: #Authority, #Law, #War, #Natural Rights, #Church-State Relations, #Democracy, #Conscience, #Freedom
Region: #England
Group: #Leveller

In 1637–1638, England's dreaded Court of Star Chamber flogged and imprisoned John Lilburne (1615–1657) for his involvement in a published attack on England's established church. His plight became a cause célèbre for those disillusioned with Charles I's governance. Supporters in Parliament facilitated his release, and he fought for Parliament until a clash with the Presbyterian vision of church and state forced his resignation. He possessed a unique ability to provoke the ire of a wide range of authorities, and many of his supporters grew wary of his unwieldy pen. He spent much of the rest of his life imprisoned by various authorities for his radical views on the 'freeborne' rights of Englishmen. Later in life, Lilburne became a Quaker, renounced the use of the temporal sword, and died in prison.[247]

Along with Richard Overton and William Walwyn, Lilburne became a leader of the 'Levellers' – a loosely organised movement named by their enemies who argued that they wanted to level political, economic, and religious distinctions. Women like **Katherine Chidley** played an important role in asserting that they also had an interest in good governance. From 1647, Leveller ideas flourished in the New Model Army, and hopes for change were placed on the military. However, that army was eventually called upon to suppress mutinous Leveller opposition to Parliament in 1649. The following document, *An agreement of the people* (1647), outlined Leveller plans for church and state. It asserted 'native Rights'. Among these, they demanded regular elections of representatives who remained subordinate to the people. They wanted religious matters to be left to the individual conscience, and they argued that forced military service violated the freedom of the individual and that laws should apply to all, regardless of rank.

An agreement of the people for a firme and present peace, upon grounds of common-right and freedome; as it was proposed by the agents of the five

610   *Sources*

regiments of horse; and since by the generall approbation of the Army, of-
fered to the joynt concurrence of all the free commons of England (London,
1647), 1–6. Text modernised by the editors.

———

Having by our late labours and hazards made it appear to the world at how
high a rate we value our just freedom, and God having so far owned our
cause, as to deliver the enemies thereof into our hands: We now hold ourselves bound in mutual duty to each other, to take the best care we can for
the future, to avoid both the danger of returning into a slavish condition,
and the chargeable remedy of another war: for as it cannot be imagined that
so many of our country-men would have opposed us in this quarrel, if they
had understood their own good; so may we safely promise to ourselves, that
when our common rights and liberties shall be cleared, we will work to dis-
appoint the endeavours of those who seek to make themselves our masters:
since therefore our former oppressions, and scarce-yet-ended troubles have
been occasioned, either by the lack of frequent national meetings in council,
or by rendering those meetings ineffectual; We are fully agreed and resolved,
to provide that hereafter our representatives are neither left to an uncertainty
for the time, nor made useless for the ends for which they are intended: In
order whereunto we declare:

I   That the people of England being at this day very unequally distributed
    by counties, cities, and boroughs, for the election of their deputies in par-
    liament, ought to be more indifferently proportioned, according to the
    number of the inhabitants: the circumstances whereof, for number, place,
    and manner, are to be set down before the end of this present parliament.
II That to prevent the many inconveniences apparently arising from the
    long continuance of the same persons in authority, this present parlia-
    ment be dissolved upon the last day of September, which shall be in the
    year of our Lord, 1648.
III That the people do of course choose for themselves a parliament once in
    two years....
IV That the power of this, and all future representatives of this nation, is
    inferior only to the power of those who choose them, and extends, with-
    out the consent or concurrence of any other person or persons; to the
    enacting, altering, and repealing of laws; to the erecting and abolishing
    of offices and courts; to the appointing, removing, and calling to account
    magistrates, and officers of all degrees; to the making of war and peace,
    to the treating with foreign states: And generally, to whatsoever is not
    expressly, or implied to be reserved by the represented to themselves.

Sources 611

Which are as follows:

1 That matters of religion, and the ways of God's worship, are not at all entrusted by us to any human power, because therein we cannot remit or exceed a tittle of what our conscience dictates to be the mind of God, without wilful sin: nevertheless, the public way of instructing the nation (so it is not compulsive) is referred to their discretion.
2 That the matter of impressing and constraining any of us to serve in the wars is against our freedom; and therefore, we do not allow it in our representatives; the rather, because money (the sinews of war) is always at their disposal, they will never want numbers of men, apt enough to engage in any just cause.
3 That after the dissolution of this present parliament, no person will be at any time questioned for anything said or done in reference to the late public differences, otherwise than in execution of the judgements of the present representatives, or House of Commons.
4 That in all laws made or to be made, every person may be bound alike, and that no tenure, estate, charter, degree, birth, or place, confers any exemption from the ordinary course of legal proceedings, whereunto others are subjected.
5 That as the laws ought to be equal, so they must be good, and not evidently destructive to the safety and well-being of the people.

These things we declare to be our native Rights, *and therefore are agreed and resolved to maintain them with our utmost possibilities, against all opposition whatsoever....*

171 *The Westminster Confession of Faith* (1647)

Keywords: #Church-State Relations, #Confession of Faith, #Conscience, #Liberty, #Government, #Authority, #Punishment, #War, #Natural Law
Region: #England | #Scotland
Group: #Church of England, #Puritan, #Presbyterian, #Congregationalist

Throughout the 1640s, Scotland and the English Parliament were at war with Charles I. They entered a military and religious alliance when the Lords and Commons of England were in the **Solemn League and Covenant** in September 1643. Both parties covenanted to purge church and state of any vestiges of Catholicism so as to bring their nations into greater conformity with scripture. The Westminster Assembly (1643–1653) aimed to settle their doctrinal disagreements, including on the relationship between church and state. The Scots were confident that a thorough examination of scripture would lead to the acceptance of Presbyterianism, and many Puritan ministers in England wanted this outcome. However, Puritan ministers, especially those returning from New England, jeopardised the possibility of consensus by advocating for a more radical option, namely to organise the churches congregationally. Although the Assembly produced the Westminster *Confession of Faith* (1647), the Anglo-Scottish alliance unravelled at its moment of triumph. The confession never formed the basis for the established Church of England, and thus, its impact on English Protestantism was more indirect. However, this confession has been and still is a cornerstone for many Reformed denominations. As with the **Thirty-Nine Articles**, churches in America altered the section on the magistrate.[248]

The Creeds of Christendom, vol. III: The Evangelical Protestant Creeds, ed. Philip Schaff (New York: Harper and Brothers, 1887), 600–673 (643–645, 655–657). The text was heavily annotated with scriptural references, which are omitted from this edition.

———

Sources 613

Chapter 20: Of Christian Liberty, and Liberty of Conscience.

I   The liberty which Christ hath purchased for believers under the gospel consists in their freedom from the guilt of sin, the condemning wrath of God, the curse of the moral law; and in their being delivered from this present evil world, bondage to Satan, and dominion of sin, from the evil of afflictions, the sting of death, the victory of the grave, and everlasting damnation; as also in their free access to God, and their yielding obedience unto him, not out of slavish fear, but a childlike love and willing mind. All which were common also to believers under the law; but under the New Testament the liberty of Christians is further enlarged in their freedom from the yoke of the ceremonial law, to which the Jewish Church was subjected; and in greater boldness of access to the throne of grace, and in fuller communications of the free Spirit of God, than believers under the law did ordinarily partake of.

II God alone is Lord of the conscience, and hath left it free from the doctrines and commandments of men which are in any thing contrary to his Word, or beside it in matters of faith or worship. So that to believe such doctrines, or to obey such commands out of conscience, is to betray true liberty of conscience; and the requiring of an implicit faith, and an absolute and blind obedience, is to destroy liberty of conscience, and reason also.

III They who, upon pretence of Christian liberty, do practice any sin, or cherish any lust, do thereby destroy the end of Christian liberty; which is, that, being delivered out of the hands of our enemies, we might serve the Lord without fear, in holiness and righteousness before him, all the days of our life.

IV And because the power which God hath ordained, and the liberty which Christ hath purchased, are not intended by God to destroy, but mutually to uphold and preserve one another; they who, upon pretence of Christian liberty, shall oppose any lawful power, or the lawful exercise of it, whether it be civil or ecclesiastical, resist the ordinance of God. And for their publishing of such opinions, or maintaining of such practices, as are contrary to the light of nature, or to the known principles of Christianity, whether concerning faith, worship, or conversation; or to the power of godliness; or such erroneous opinions or practices, as, either in their own nature, or in the manner of publishing or maintaining them, are destructive to the external peace and order which Christ hath established in the Church; they may lawfully be called to account, and proceeded against by the censures of the Church, and by the power of the Civil Magistrate. (pp. 643–645).

614   *Sources*

Chapter 22: Of the Civil Magistrate.

I   God, the Supreme Lord and King of all the world, hath ordained civil magistrates to be under him, over the people, for his own glory and the public good, and to this end hath armed them with the power of the sword, for the defence and encouragement of them that are good, and for the punishment of evil-doers.

II It is lawful for Christians to accept and execute the office of a magistrate when called thereunto; in the managing whereof, as they ought especially to maintain piety, justice, and peace, according to the wholesome laws of each commonwealth, so, for that end, they may lawfully, now under the New Testament, wage war upon just and necessary occasion.

III The civil magistrate may not assume to himself the administration of the Word and Sacraments, or the power of the keys of the kingdom of heaven: yet he hath authority, and it is his duty to take order, that unity and peace be preserved in the Church, that the truth of God be kept pure and entire, that all blasphemies and heresies be suppressed, all corruptions and abuses in worship and discipline prevented or reformed, and all the ordinances of God duly settled, administered, and observed. For the better effecting whereof he hath power to call synods, to be present at them, and to provide that whatsoever is transacted in them be according to the mind of God.

IV It is the duty of people to pray for magistrates, to honour their persons, to pay them tribute and other dues, to obey their lawful commands, and to be subject to their authority, for conscience' sake. Infidelity or difference in religion doth not make void the magistrate's just and legal authority, nor free the people from their due obedience to him: from which ecclesiastical persons are not exempted; much less hath the Pope any power or jurisdiction over them in their dominions, or over any of their people; and least of all to deprive them of their dominions or lives, if he shall judge them to be heretics, or upon any other pretence whatsoever. (655–657)

172 Mary Pope, *A Treatise of Magistracy* (1647)

Keywords: #Authority, #Women, #Family, #Law, #War, #Obedience
Region: #England
Group: #Church of England, #Puritan | #Leveller

During the British Civil Wars, Mary Pope (fl.1622–1653) penned several works that addressed the settling of church and state. Although she sympathised with the Royalist cause, she dedicated *A treatise of magistracy* (1647) to both sides, king and Parliament. Her own views on politics and religion were complex, and she made appeals to Christians on the basis of their shared faith, sometimes invoking prophetic authority for her utterances. She argued for the rights of the king over the church, at times equating the king with law. She, however, was not uncritical of the king and his cause. This work was both a treatise and a petition, and, understandably, it was not well received in Parliament (they arrested the person who delivered the work). Pope also wrote against the army and against the **Levellers**, and she opposed religious toleration and popular sovereignty. The following excerpts, from *A treatise of magistracy*, come from her dedication to King Charles I and her second dedication to Parliament. In it, she emphasised familial relations. The king is the father, and the people should be submissive to him as to God. The king is also a marriage partner, and he should not become estranged from his people. It is remarkable for the degree to which she is comfortable instructing and admonishing the powers that be, whether that be the king, Parliament, religious leaders, or the people themselves.[249]

A treatise of magistracy, shewing, the magistrate hath beene, and for ever is to be the cheife [sic] officer in the Church, out of the Church, and over the Church; and that the two Testaments hold forth (1647), dedication. Text modernised by the editors.

———

616 *Sources*

To the Most High and Mighty Prince, Charles

You are God's Representative here on earth, deriving your title from God's own Name, and God has said in his Word, you are supreme, and have your title in these Kingdoms, to be the defender of the faith, and so a nursing Father to the Church [Isa. 49:23]; And seeing your children the Church, and Common-wealth are, and have been, in a deplored and confused condition [on account of the Civil Wars], because God's order has not been observed, and God's Lawes and Ordinances have not been held forth in the purity of the power of them by you, and those that were sent of you. But gracious Prince, if you desire the God of heaven to be on your side, then you must turn to the Law and Testimony, and hear what that says: And may it further please your Majesty to call to mind the counsel that the old godly men that stood before *Solomon* gave to *Rehoboam's* son, and if *Rehoboam* had observed the words of his Grandfather *David*, it would not have fared with him as it did, which was this, *He that rules over men, must be just, ruling in the fear of the Lord* (2 Sam. 23:3)....

[T]hose whom God has already joined together, let no man put asunder [Mark 10:9]; but God has made you King Charles supreme head, in and over these [three waring] Kingdoms, therefore let no one dare to make void this manifest act of God, or keep you our King and people asunder any longer....

To the Right Honourable Lords and Commons Assembled in Parliament

...Now this is that which the Parliament of Heaven calls for at your hands, that you should hold forth and present to your Father and Prince, the royal Law of the great God of heaven, and in it the Law of our Land, which were made upon it, and by which Laws he was crowned our King, to rule and govern us by, and we by the self-same Law have made a reciprocal promise, to obey him our parent in the Lord; and it is commanded by God that parents should not provoke their children to wrath, but bring them up in the fear and nurture of the Lord: but if parents should not do so, but provoke their children to wrath, there is no new truth that teaches children to erect Laws to regulate their parents, but that Law, that the great God has set over both parents and children....

173 *Slavery in Dutch Brazil (1637–1650)*

Keywords: #Colonisation, #Paternalism, #Slavery, #Evangelisation, #Missions, #War, #Trade
Region: #Brazil, #Netherlands
Group: #Dutch Reformed | #Indigenous American

After the Dutch West India Company (WIC) was licensed, they took the colony of Brazil from the Portuguese in 1630, expelled the Catholic orders, but allowed Jews to worship privately. The toleration of Jews is largely ascribed to their financial stake in the colony, but it also reflects the differing standards between toleration in Europe and in the colonies. The WIC was directly involved in the trade of over 20,000 enslaved persons in the 1630s and 1640s. Due to competition with Portuguese Catholics, the Dutch put more effort into evangelism in Dutch Brazil than anywhere else in the Atlantic world, although they grew sceptical of the capacity of slaves to understand and embrace the Christian message. During the First Anglo-Dutch War (1652–1654), Portugal seized the opportunity to re-conquer Brazil. As part of the lead-up to the Second Anglo-Dutch War (1665–1667), the English took control of New Amsterdam, now known as New York. Although the Dutch kept colonies across the globe, they increasingly moved away from founding colonies and protecting trade through mercantilism. Private companies proliferated, and they were trading across empires, bringing much of the wealth back to the Dutch Republic.[250] The sources reproduced below reveal Dutch views of the people they encountered in the colonies. Attitudes towards Indigenous populations in Latin America echoed the tropes that native populations would be barbarous, sexually illicit, and led by their passions. For this reason, some argued that it was to their benefit to be enslaved.

1–2. Hugh Hastings, ed., *Ecclesiastical Records: State of New York* (Albany, NY: James B. Lyon, 1901), I:112, 191; 3a–b. Caspar van Baerle, *History of Brazil Under the Governorship of Count Johan Maurits of Nassau, 1636–1644*, ed. Blanche T. van Berckel-Ebeling Koning (Tallahassee: University Press of Florida, 2011), 1–3, 181; 4. Klaus Koschorke, Frieder Ludwig and Mariano Delgado, eds., *A History of Christianity in Asia, Africa, and Latin*

618   *Sources*

America, 1450–1990: A Documentary Sourcebook (Grand Rapids, MI: Eerdmans, 2007), 338–339.

---

1 Baptism of Children (16 Nov 1637)
[*Because baptism brought the initiate into the Christian family, the Classis of Amsterdam urged greater caution and circumspection.*]

Acts of the Classis of Amsterdam

Touching the baptism of unbaptised children of Brazilians, negroes and others: Inasmuch as this matter has been referred to the Synod, (of North Holland,) and has been acted on by them, their actions will be sent over, (to Brazil.) At the same time they will be told, that so far as our Classis is concerned, she has much wished that the casus had been somewhat more specifically stated, and particularly.... It had really also the intention to question the children of Brazilians, before they were adopted, and so passed over into familiam Christianorum.

---

2. Education

[*The Synod of North Holland discussed reports of the state of the church in the East and West Indies.*]
From the churches of the West Indies we have nothing in particular, except that the instruction of the Brazilians progresses very well; that they have found a school teacher for the Negros, of whom they have good hopes of success.... But they complain much of the scarcity of ministers....

3a Caspar van Baerle dedication to the former Governor-General of Brazil, Johan Maurits, Count of Nassau, 1647

[*The theologian and historian Caspar van Baerle (1584–1648) dedicated his* History of Brazil *to the former colonial governor. In glowing terms, he praised the piety and humanity of this leader. Indigenous Americans, by contrast, were portrayed as cannibals.*]
If the country were capable of speech and could address you, it would surrender itself to you. You have shown exemplary courage defending and enlarging the territory conquered by the Dutch....

The barbarians [of antiquity] have sharpened their weapons against a civilised and morally conscious people. Our nation took up arms against a wild, ferocious people that shuns any form of humanity, and considers devouring one's fellow man as honourable....

You were a light in a world of darkness, a compatriot of a foreign and wandering tribe, a guide in the wilderness, and a ruler to the most wildly different and exotic people. With the help of Mars who rules in battle you brought the word of Christ, who rules over man's soul....

Your piety and religious moderation will be witnessed by a people divided by different forms of belief and religious practice. Your sense of justice will be praised by the rulers of neighbouring cities and regions will speak of your clemency and humanity.... Thanks to your compassion, which sprang from the sorrow you often felt as you witnessed the destruction occasioned by warfare, you pitied its sad ruin and treated it with mercy.... Although taking up arms against sacred deities is to be deplored, building churches – the spiritual home of the citizens – cannot be sufficiently praised. This reflects not only your love of your creator, but of mankind's image, made in God's likeness, as well.

———

3.b Caspar van Baerle on Slavery, 1647

[Baerle did not approve of everything colonists did. Profit-hungry colonists resorted to slavery, an act that corrupted the Reformed faith and violated the Imago Dei of the enslaved.]

Now that the desire for profit has increased even among Christians who accept the pure and reformed faith, a way has been opened for war and arms. We have returned to the custom of buying and selling human beings – although they are created in God's likeness and redeemed by Christ, the Lord of the universe – who are not slaves due to a fault of nature or ingenuity. These days, now that Christians rule in Brazil, a slave might lament and exclaim, 'Oh Jupiter, oh ye gods, what a miserable fate it is to be the slave of a foolish master!' For it happens quite often that the wise man serves a fool, the honest man a thief, and the clever man a stupid one, and that a touch of divine wisdom will be conferred on another not by a defect of nature, but by a capricious fate.

———

4 Comment on Slavery in a Dutch Church Record, c.1650

[This final source is a church record from around 1650. It, again, reveals a very negative opinion of Indigenous Americans and uses derogatory language to disparage them. The church recommended paternalism and slavery as an antidote to immature libertinism. Missionary work alone, they argued, was ineffective in 'civilising' them, and they recommend removing Indigenous children from their parents.]

Their religious views form a peculiar mixture of idolatry, superstitions and that which Catholic missionaries taught them. A few Indians know the articles of faith and the Lord's Prayer but only in their own language....

Would not a mild, legally organised slavery be much better for this uncontrollable society than the unrestrained freedom for which it is not yet mature?

620   *Sources*

The Tapúya must be under a civilised nation; otherwise, they will serve evil. On the request of the W.I.C., we sent missionaries to the savages. But where are the fruits of their efforts and labour? The Redskins still frolic in the hideous evils of prostitution and alcoholism, and do not think about curbing their passions. There is only one way to gradually tame them. One must take the children from them and educate the Indian boys and girls as Christians at the company's expense.

174 *The Windsor Prayer Meeting and the Execution of the King* (1648)

Keywords: #War, #Rebellion, #Authority, #Capital Crime, #Tyranny
Region: #England
Group: #Puritan, #Independent

One of England's most notorious prayer meetings occurred at Windsor Castle from 29 April to 1 May 1648. Parliamentary army leaders devoted three days to understanding God's will as the country slid into civil war again. By the final day, it was clear that war was imminent. They blamed Charles I for renewing hostilities. Defeating the king was not enough, many thought, because he would try to muster troops again. Parliament needed a more decisive settlement. When they first took up arms in 1642, no one imagined (or desired) executing the king or **abolishing of the monarchy**. The prayer meeting at Windsor was an important step towards the unthinkable. When news of renewed hostilities reached those in prayer, the leaders in Windsor Castle turned to the Hebrew Bible and appealed to the concept of bloodguilt. If they were victorious in battle, these subjects would hold their king personally responsible for the bloodshed of the 1640s. Patricia Crawford notes how 'blood guilt' could be a 'levelling idea' that erased distinctions between subject and sovereign. Because anyone could stand guilty of the offence, 'a king polluted by blood could be a king no more'.[251] They called Charles 'that man of blood', and this identification influenced the trial and execution of the king in January 1649. After the regicide, Royalists countered this charge, laying the bloodguilt on Parliamentary leaders like **Oliver Cromwell**. Being a 'man of blood', in other words, was a capital and damnable offence. However, one prominent Puritan minister to Parliament, Peter Sterry, embraced the title when justifying the 1649 conquest of Ireland: David and Christ were men of blood, and if Parliament wanted to build God's kingdom on earth, they needed to become comfortable with shedding blood.[252]

William Allen, *A Faithful Memorial of that Remarkable Meeting of Many Officers of the Army in England, at Windsor Castle, in the Year 1648* (London: Printed for Livewel Chapman, at the Crown in Popes-head Alley, 1659), 4–5. Text modernised by the editors.

———

622 Sources

In the year 1647, you [Lieutenant-General Charles Fleetwood] may remember, we in the army were engaged in actions of a very high nature, leading us to very untrodden paths, both in our contests with the then parliament, as also conferences with the king. [*Many people were dissatisfied with the army and the direction of the country, and they were searching for the causes of God's displeasure.*]

We agreed to meet at Windsor Castle, about the beginning of 1648, and there spent one day together in prayer, inquiring into the causes of that sad situation. Coming to no further result that day beyond that it was still our duty to seek; and on the next day, we met again in the morning, where many spoke from the Word, and prayed; and the then Lieutenant-General [Oliver] Cromwell pressed very earnestly, on all there present, for a thorough consideration of our actions as an army, as well as to our personal conduct as private Christians, to see if any iniquity could be found in them; and what it was, that if possible, we might find out, and so remove the cause of such sad rebukes, as were upon us by reason of our iniquities, as we judged at that time....

...[God] directed our steps, and presently we were led, and helped to a clear agreement amongst ourselves, without any dissenting, that it was the duty of our day, with the forces we had, to go out and fight against those potent enemies, which that year in all places appeared against us, with an humble confidence in the name of the Lord only, that we should destroy them; also enabling us then, after seriously seeking his face, to come to a very clear and joint resolution, on many grounds at large then debated amongst us, that it was our duty, if ever the Lord brought us back again in peace, to call Charles Stuart, that man of blood [Num. 35:33; 2 Sam. 16:7–8], to an account, for that blood he had shed, and mischief he had done, to his utmost, against the Lord's cause and people in these poor nations: and how the Lord led and prospered us in all our undertakings this year, in this way, cutting his work short in righteousness, making it a year of mercy equal, if not transcendent to, any since these wars began, and making it worthy of remembrance by every gracious soul, who was wise to observe the Lord and the operations of his hands; I wish may never be forgotten; bringing us together again, from all parts shortly after, with admiration; each ones heart as it were filled with the wonders beheld, and occasion given to all to say each to the other, Lo, what hath God wrought! The king's armies were broken in all places, most of his strongholds were taken: the king himself was in discussions with that parliament, and both of them desired a conclusion; yet they were hindered by an over-ruling providence, and the king was so infatuated, disputing small matters until he loses everything, and himself with it, and is carried away from his place of treaty to a prison, in order to be executed, which suddenly followed accordingly; and all this was done within less than three quarters of a year, even to the astonishment of ourselves, and others watching at home and abroad; yes, our enemies were made to say, 'God was truly amongst us', and therefore they could not stand against us.

175 Congregationalists of New England, *The Cambridge Platform* (1648)

Keywords: #Church-State Relations, #Magistrates, #Authority, #Coercion, #Ten Commandments, #Punishment, #Excommunication, #Natural Law
Region: #United States | #England
Group: #Congregationalists, #Puritan

When civil war broke out in the British Isles, immigration to New England began to reverse, and those returning to Old England sometimes brought controversial ideas with them. The Westminster Assembly of Divines was already struggling to define orthodoxy when the injection of New England congregationalism further jeopardised the need for religious unity. Presbyterians urged English Congregationalists (Independents) to put forward an authoritative statement of their beliefs, and they offloaded this task on their New England brethren. Delegates met in Cambridge, Massachusetts, home to Harvard College.

The *Cambridge Platform* (1648) incorporated much of the theology of the **Westminster Confession of Faith** (1647), but it differed on ecclesiastical polity and church-state relations. The Platform was full of tension. Churches were to be funded by voluntary donations, but coercion would be necessary if funds were not sufficiently forthcoming. Magistrates should not imitate the authority of biblical leaders and prophets, but those leaders were exemplars who were worthy of their emulation. Church and state were separate, but magistrates had the duty to enforce both Tables of the Ten Commandments. Churches were not bound to adopt the Cambridge Platform, but magistrates should coerce straying congregations, citing Joshua's handling of idolatrous tribes. The document touched on a variety of issues, like the precise nature between spiritual and physical punishment and whether excommunication carried civil punishments. The excommunicated were deemed so far outside Christianity that they could be treated as 'heathens', welcomed to attend church, and treated with civility.[253]

Williston Walker, *The Creeds and Platforms of Congregationalism* (New York: Charles Scribner's Sons, 1893), 220–21, 228, 233–237. Text modernised by the editors.

624　*Sources*

Chapter 11: Of the Maintenance of Church Officers

The apostle concludes that necessary and sufficient maintenance is due unto ministers of the word: from the law of nature and nations, from the law of Moses, the equity thereof, as also the rule of common reason (1 Cor. 9:15; Matt. 9:38, 10:10; 1 Tim. 5:18).

4. Not only members of churches, but *all that are taught in the word* (Gal. 6:6), are to contribute unto him that teaches, in all good things. In case congregations are defective in their contributions, the deacons are to call upon them to do their duty (Acts 6:3–4): if their call is not sufficient, the church, by her power, is to require it of their members, and where church-power through the corruption of men, does not, or cannot attain the end, the magistrate is to see that the ministry is duly provided for, as appears from the commended example of Nehemiah 13:1. The magistrates are nursing fathers, and nursing mothers, and stand charged with the custody of both Tables....

Chapter 14: Of Excommunication and Other Censures

6. Because excommunication is a spiritual punishment, it does not prejudice the excommunicated person in, nor deprive him of, his *civil rights*, and therefore touches not princes, or other magistrates, in point of their civil dignity or authority. And, the excommunicated person, being but as a publican and a heathen (1 Cor. 14:24–25), and heathens are lawfully permitted to come to hear the word and assemblies; we acknowledge therefore the like liberty of hearing the word, may be permitted to excommunicated persons, that is permitted unto heathen. And because we are not without hope of his recovery, we are not to account him as an enemy but to admonish him as a brother.

Chapter 16: Of Synods

3. Magistrates have the power to call a synod, by calling to the churches to send for their elders and other messengers, to counsel and assist them in matters of religion (2 Chron. 29:4–11): but yet the constituting of a synod is a church act, and may be transacted by the churches, even when civil magistrates may be enemies to the churches and to church assemblies (Acts 15).

Chapter 17: Of the Civil Magistrates' Power in Ecclesiastical Matters

It is lawful, profitable and necessary for Christians to gather themselves into church estate and therein to exercise all the ordinances of Christ according to the word, although the consent of the magistrate could not be had thereunto (Acts 2:41–47, 4:1–3)....

2　Church-government stands in no opposition to the civil government of commonwealths (John 18:36), nor does it challenge the authority of civil magistrates in their jurisdictions; nor in the slightest weaken their hands in governing (Acts 25:8); but rather strengthens them, and furthers the people in yielding more hearty and conscionable obedience unto them....

3 The power and authority of magistrates is not to be used for the restraining of churches or any other good works, but for the helping in and furthering thereof (Rom. 13:4; 1 Tim. 2:2); and therefore, the consent and countenance of magistrates when it may be had, is not to be slighted, or lightly esteemed; but on the contrary; it is part of that honour due unto Christian magistrates to desire and crave their consent and approbation therein: which being obtained, the churches then proceed in their way with much more encouragement, and comfort.

4 It is not in the power of magistrates to compel their subjects to become church-members and to partake at the Lord's table....

5 As it is unlawful for church-officers to meddle with the sword of the magistrate, so it is unlawful for the magistrate to meddle with the work that is proper to church-officers. The acts of Moses and David, who were not only princes, but prophets, were extraordinary; therefore, they are not imitable (Matt. 20:25–26). Against such usurpation, the Lord witnessed by smiting Uzziah with leprosy for presuming to offer incense (2 Chron. 26:16–17).

6 It is the duty of the magistrate, to take care of matters of religion and to improve his civil authority for the observing of the duties commanded in the first and second Tables. They are called Gods (Ps. 82:6). The end of the magistrate's office (1 Tim. 2:1–2) is not only the quiet and peaceable life of the subject in matters of righteousness and honesty but also in matters of godliness, yea of all godliness. [*They offer examples of biblical kings who were praised for supporting religion and those denounced for failing to do so.*]

7 The object of the power of the magistrate are not things that are merely inward and so not subject to his cognisance and view, such as unbelief or hardness of heart, erroneous opinions that are not vented; but only such things as are acted by the outward man. [*The magistrate should also not compel people to act in ways that are contrary to God's word.*]

8 Idolatry, blasphemy, heresy, venting corrupt and pernicious opinions that destroy the foundation, openly show contempt for the preached word, prophane the Lord's day, disturb the peaceable administration and exercise of the worship and holy things of God, and the like, are to be restrained, and punished by civil authority (Deut. 13; 1 Kgs 20:28–42; Dan. 3:29; Zech. 13:3; Neh. 13:21; 1 Tim. 2:2; Rom. 13:4).

9 If any church one or more shall grow schismatical, rending itself from the communion of other churches, or shall walk incorrigibly or obstinately in any corrupt way of their own, contrary to the rule of the word; in such case, the magistrate is to put forth his coercive power, as the matter shall require. The tribes on this side of the Jordan intended to make war against the other tribes for building the altars of witness, whom they suspected to have turned away therein from following of the Lord (Josh. 22).

176 *Religious Clauses of the Peace of Westphalia* (1648)

Keywords: #Church-State Relations, #Pluralism, #War, #Treaty, #Peace
Region: #Europe
Group: #Roman Catholic, #Lutheran, #Catholic

The Peace of Westphalia was a collection of several agreements that were concurrently signed in Münster and Osnabrück at the end of the Thirty Years' War (1618–1648). They were the culmination of a long series of negotiations between frequently shifting alliances. Throughout the war, European powers became increasingly concerned with the 'balance of power', and unlikely religious bedfellows often aligned in an effort to tip the scales. Although religion was often not the dividing line on the battlefield, finding a long-term religious settlement was one of the main aims of the negotiations. Although many expressed hopes for Christian unification in the longer term, provisions were made for a measure of coexistence.

The Peace reaffirmed the formula *cuius regio, eius religio* from the **Peace of Augsburg (1555)**. This principle allowed the princes to determine the religion within their territories; however, at Westphalia, the scope of this princely power became more restricted, affording Catholic and Lutheran religious minorities greater rights. The Reformed, too, were incorporated in this agreement, by extension. Pope Innocent X objected to the Peace in the Bull *Zelo Domus Dei* (1648). The fact that Catholic powers largely ignored the pope's objections spoke volumes about the changing nature of religious authority. The Peace is often considered a watershed moment in the history of nation-states and of international relations. Without downplaying its significance, recent scholarship has emphasised the abiding influence of historical Christendom on the new political entities.[254] The following excerpt comes from the Treaty of Osnabrück, made between the Emperor and Sweden.[255]

A General Collection of Treatys, Manifesto's, Contracts or Marriage, Renunciations, and other Publick Papers, from the Year 1495, to the Year 1717, 2nd ed. (London, J.J. Knapton, et al., 1732), II:374–445 (390–391, 404–405, 410, 415). The final article comes from Sidney Z. Ehler and John B. Morrall, ed.

Sources 627

and trans., *Church and State through the Centuries: A Collection of Historic Documents with Commentaries* (New York: Biblo and Tannen, 1967), 193.

———

Article V. Now whereas the Grievances of the one and the other Religion, which were debated amongst the Electors, Princes and States of the Empire, have been partly the Cause and Occasion of the present War, it has been agreed and transacted in the following manner.

Section 1. That the Transaction settled at Passau in the Year 1552 and followed in the Year 1555 with the Peace of Religion, according as it was confirmed in the Year [1566] at Augsburg, and afterwards in diverse other Diets of the sacred Roman Empire, in all its Points and Articles agreed and concluded by the unanimous Consent of the Emperor and Electors, Princes and States of both Religions, shall be maintain'd in its Force and Vigour, and sacredly and inviolably observed. But those things that are appointed by this Treaty with Consent of both parties, touching certain Articles of the said Transaction which are troublesome and litigious, shall be looked upon to have been observed in Judgement and otherwise, as a perpetual Declaration of the said Pacification, until the Matter of Religion can, by the Grace of God, be agreed upon, and that without stopping short for the Contradiction and Protestation of any one whatsoever, Ecclesiastical or Secular, either within or without the Empire, in any time whatsoever: all which Oppositions are by virtue of these Presents declared null and void. And as to all other things, That there be an exact and reciprocal Equality amongst all the Electors, Princes and States of both Religions, conformably to the State of the Commonweal, the Constitutions of the Empire, and the present Convention: so that what is just of one side shall be so of the other, all Violence and Force between two Parties being forever prohibited....

Section 28 [34]. It has moreover been found good, that those of the Confession of Augsburg, who are Subjects of the Catholics, and the Catholic Subjects of the States of the Confession of Augsburg, who had not the public or private Exercise of their Religion in any time of the year 1624 and who after the Publication of the Peace shall profess and embrace a Religion different from that of the Lord of the Territory, shall in consequence of the said Peace be patiently suffered and tolerated, without any Hindrance or Impediment to attend their Devotions in their Houses and in private, with all Liberty of Conscience, and without any Inquisition or Trouble, and even to assist in their Neighbourhood, as often as they have a mind, at the public Exercise of their Religion, or send their Children to foreign Schools of their Religion, or have them instructed in their Families by private Masters; provided the said Vassals and Subjects do their Duty in all other things, and hold themselves in due Obedience and Subjection, without giving occasion to any Disturbance or Commotion. In like manner Subjects, whether they be Catholics, or of the Confession of Augsburg, shall not be despised anywhere upon account of

628 *Sources*

their Religion, nor excluded from the Community of Merchants, Artisans or Companies, nor deprived of [common things like the right to bury the dead]: so that in these and all other the like things they shall be treated in the same manner as Brethren and Sisters, with equal Justice and Protection....

Section 41 [50]. The Magistrates of the one and the other Religion shall severely forbid any person to impugn in any place, in public or in private, by preaching, teaching, disputation, writing or consulting, the Transaction of Passau, the Peace of Religion, and, above all, the present Declaration or Transaction....

But besides these Religions, no other shall be received or tolerated in the Sacred Roman Empire.

Article VIII. And in order to prevent for future all Differences in the Political State, all and every of the Electors, Princes, and States of the Roman Empire shall be established and confirmed in their ancient Rights, Prerogatives, Liberties, Privileges, free Exercise of their Territorial Right, as well in Spirituals and Temporals, Seiagneuries, Regalian Rights, and in the possession of all these things, by virtue of the present Transaction, that they may not be molested at any time in any manner, under any pretext whatsoever....

Art. XVII, sec. 3. Against this Treaty or any article or clause of it no objections may at any time be put forward, listened to or admitted, whether (they be derived from) Canon or Civil Law, general or particular, Conciliar decrees, privileges, indults, edicts, commissions, prohibitions, orders, decrees, rescripts, legal cases, sentences given at any time, judicial decisions, Imperial and other capitulations, rules or exemptions of religious Orders, protests past or future, contradictions, appeals, investitures, treaties, oaths, renunciations, pacts of any kind, or the Edict of 1629 or the Treaty of Prague with its appendices, or Papal Concordats or the Interim of 1548, or any other political statutes or ecclesiastical decrees, dispensations, absolutions, or any other objections, under whatever name or pretext they may be put forward, nor henceforth may any legal processes or actions, whether inhibitory, petitionary or possessory, be recognised against this Treaty.

177 *Act Abolishing the Office of King in England* (1649)

Keywords: #Monarchy, #Parliament, #Authority, #Tyranny, #Law, #Commonwealth, Election
Region: #England | #Ireland, #Scotland, #Wales
Group: #Puritan, #Congregationalist

By January 1649, Charles I was captured, and his forces were defeated. The newly organised 'Rump Parliament' rapidly remade politics. When the king's trial commenced, he refused to recognise the legality of the proceedings. He was charged with failing to protect the 'rights and liberties' of his people and of usurping 'unlimited and tyrannical power to rule', all the while shedding prodigious blood in his unjust cause.[256] On the 27th, he was condemned to death by the High Court. 'Treason' was ordinarily reserved for a crime *against the king*, but Parliament was redefining it as a crime against 'the State' or 'the people'.[257] Right before his execution on the 30th, Charles walked directly under 'The apotheosis of James I', a Rubens painting of his father (**James VI and I**) that Charles commissioned. It was 'perhaps the supreme expression of Charles's vision of absolute monarchy'.[258] Meant to cement the divine origin of monarchy, the painting could also be interpreted as a parable of how the mighty fell.

When the executioner severed Charles I's head, Londoners who gathered outside Whitehall Palace groaned deeply. The regicide put an end to the debate about what to do with the defeated king, and everyone knew Parliament had chosen the most controversial option: it was a theologically significant moment for British Protestantism. On the official day of humiliation, 31 January, **John Owen** preached an apocalyptical sermon about how England was entering a new phase in the establishment of God's kingdom, as Parliament continued remoulding England's political structures. The following extract comes from an Act that abolished the monarchy (introduced on 15 February and passed on 17 March 1649). Two days later, England was declared a Commonwealth and Free State.

630   *Sources*

An Act for the Abolishing the Kingly Office in England, Ireland, and the Dominions Thereunto Belonging (London: Edward Husband, 19 March 1648 [1649]). Text modernised by the editors.

———

Whereas Charles Stuart, late King of England, Ireland, and the Territories and Dominions thereunto belonging, has by the authority derived from Parliament, been, and is hereby declared to be justly condemned, adjudged to die and put to death, for many treasons, murders, and other heinous offences committed by him, by which Judgement he stood and is hereby declared to be attainted[259] of High Treason, whereby his Issue and Posterity, and all others pretending Title under him, are become incapable of the said Crowns, or of being King or Queen of the said Kingdom or Dominions, or either or any of them: Be it therefore Enacted and Ordained, and it is Enacted, Ordained and Declared by this present Parliament, and by the authority thereof, That all the people of England and Ireland, and the Dominions and Territories thereunto belonging, of what degree or condition soever, are discharged of all Fealty, Homage and Allegiance which is or shall be pretended to be due unto any [of the late king's relations. His relatives also forfeit their possessions in lands, property and titles]. And whereas it is and has been found by experience, that the Office of a King in this Nation and Ireland, and to have the power thereof in any single person, is unnecessary, burdensome and dangerous to the liberty, safety and public interest of the people, and that for the most part, use has been made of the Regal power and prerogative, to oppress, impoverish and enslave the subject; and that usually and naturally any one person in such power, makes it his interest to encroach upon the just freedom and liberty of the people, and to promote the setting up of their own will and power above the Laws, that so they might enslave these Kingdoms to their own Lust: Be it therefore Enacted and Ordained by this present Parliament, and by Authority of the same, That the Office of a King in this Nation, shall not henceforth reside in, or be exercised by any one single person; and that no one person whatsoever, shall or may have, or hold the Office, Style, Dignity, Power or Authority of King of the said Kingdoms and Dominions, or any of them, or of the Prince of Wales, Any law, statute, usage or custom to the contrary thereof in any wise notwithstanding. [*It was then made high treason to aid or abet a restoration of the monarchy.*] And whereas by the abolition of the kingly Office provided for in this Act, a most happy way is made for this Nation (if God see it good) to return to its just and ancient right, of being governed by its own Representatives or National meetings in Council, from time to time chosen and entrusted for that purpose by the people, It is therefore Resolved and Declared by the Commons assembled in Parliament, That they will put a period to the sitting of this present Parliament, and dissolve the same so soon as may possibly stand with the safety of the people that has entrusted them, and with what is absolutely necessary for the

Sources 631

preserving and upholding the Government now settled in the way of a Commonwealth; and that they will carefully provide for the certain choosing, meeting and sitting of the next and future Representatives, with such other circumstances of freedom in choice and equality in distribution of Members to be elected thereunto, as shall most conduce to the lasting freedom and good of this Commonwealth: And it is hereby further Enacted and Declared, notwithstanding any thing contained in this Act, no person or persons of any condition and quality ... shall be discharged from the obedience and subjection which he and they owe to the Government of this Nation, as it is now Declared, but all and every of them shall in all things render and perform the same, as of right is due unto the supreme authority hereby declared to reside in this and the successive Representatives of the people of this Nation, and in them only.

178 John Milton, *Biblical Israel and God's Displeasure at Monarchy* (1649)

Keywords: #Magistrate, #Authority, #Tyranny, #Natural Right, #Election, #Covenant, #Submission, #Punishment, #Rebellion, #Commonwealth
Region: #England
Group: #Puritan, #Independent

England's Parliament executed Charles I in January 1649 and quickly set about political reform. At every step, John Milton's pen justified the actions of a kingless state. In February, *The Tenure of Kings and Magistrates* argued that authority ultimately lay in the people's hands. Then, his *History of Britain* offered a new rendering of the nation's past, often linking spiritual with physical decline. Parliament encouraged Milton to write on the conquest of Ireland. In *Observations Upon the Articles of Peace with the Irish Rebels*, he vented anger at English Episcopalians, Irish Catholics, and Scottish Presbyterians who recoiled at the regicide. Especially in death, the king had many supporters. *Εἰκὼν Βασιλική* (King's Image), a popular book attributed to the late king, portrayed Charles I as a Christ-like martyr for the nation. Milton responded with *Ἐικονοκλάστης* (Image Breaker). The king was not a martyr but a persecutor; he did not suffer violence but merited just retribution for the shed blood of so many Protestants.

The new nation needed a new political theology, and Milton provided that in *The Tenure of Kings and Magistrates*, excerpted below. Milton emphasised Israel's divinely granted choice of their form of government. The people could elevate someone to kingship or dethrone them, irrespective of the behaviour of that individual. If the people's choice of a particular king was providential, why not their removal? Milton's interpretation of Israel's choice of a king was deeply indebted to rabbinic interpretation; to texts that were translated in the early modern period and widely read by Christian scholars and ministers. According to some rabbis, Deuteronomy 17 and 1 Samuel 8 showed God's displeasure with monarchies because they entailed a rejection of God's rule. A republican-style government with God as king was the original model. For Milton and others writing at this time of governmental experimentation, a Hebrew-style republic was not merely one option among many, but it was God's original and preferred mode of organising society.[260]

Sources 633

John Milton, *The Tenure of Kings and Magistrates Proving that it Is Lawfull, and Hath Been Held So Through All Ages, For Any Who Have the Power, to Call to Account a Tyrant, or Wicked King, and After Due Conviction, to Depose and Put the Author* (London: Matthew Simmons, 1649), 13–16, 36–37. Text modernised by the editors.

———

It follows lastly that since the king or magistrate holds his authority from the people, both originally and naturally for their good in the first place, and not his own, then may the people as frequently as they shall judge it for the best, either choose him or reject him, retain him or depose him though no tyrant, merely by the liberty and right of free-born men to be governed as seems to them best. This, though it cannot but stand with plain reason, shall be made good also by Scripture: 'When you come into the Land which the Lord your God gives you, and shall say "I will set a king over me like all the nations around me"' (Deut. 17:14). These words confirm that the right of choosing, yes, of changing their own government is granted to the people by God himself. And therefore when they desired a king, though then under another form of government, and though their changing displeased him [God], yet he that was himself their King, and rejected by them, would not be a hindrance to what they intended, further than by persuasion, but that they might do therein as they saw good (1 Sam. 8), only he reserved to himself the nomination of who should reign over them.

Neither did that exempt the king as if he were only accountable to God, though anointed by his special command. Therefore 'David first made a covenant with the elders of Israel, and so was anointed king by them' (1 Chron. 11:3). And Jehoiada the priest, in making Jehoash king, made a Covenant between him and the people (2 Kings 11:17). Therefore when *Rehoboam* at his coming to the crown, rejected those conditions which the Israelites brought him, hear what they answer him: 'what portion have we in David, or inheritance in the son of Jesse. See to thine own house David' (1 Kgs 12:16). And for the like conditions not performed, all Israel before that time deposed Samuel [1 Sam. 8:7]; not for his own default, but for the misgovernment of his sons. But some will say to both these examples, it was wrongly done. I answer that not the latter because it was expressly allowed them in the law to set up a king if it pleased them; and God himself joined with them in the work; though in some sort it was at that time displeasing to him, in respect of old Samuel who had governed them uprightly....

Therefore kingdom and magistracy, whether supreme or subordinate, is called a 'human ordinance' (1 Pet. 2:13), and we are taught that it is the will of God that we should submit to it, insofar as they punish evil doers and encourage those who do well. 'Submit', says he, 'as free men' (1 Pet. 2:16). And 'there is no power but of God', says Paul (Rom. 13:1), which is as much as to say that God put it into man's heart to find out that way at first

634 *Sources*

for common peace and preservation, approving the exercise thereof; else it contradicts Peter who calls the same authority an ordinance of man. It must also be understood of lawful and just power, else we read of great power in the affairs and kingdoms of the world permitted to the Devil: for says he to Christ, 'all this power will I give you and the glory of them, for it is delivered to me, and to whomsoever I will, I give it' (Luke 4:6): neither did he lie, nor did Christ contradict what he affirmed: for we read how the Dragon gave to the beast his power, his seat, and great authority (Rev. 13:4).... . Therefore when Saint Paul tells us of magistrates, he means those who are not a terror to the good but to the evil, such as do not bear the sword in vain, but are to punish offenders and encourage the good (Rom. 13:3)....

And it is worth pointing out that kings appeal to Scripture to boast of the justness of their title saying, that they hold it immediately of God, yet they cannot show the time when God set the throne on them or their forefathers, but only when the people chose them. Since God frequently ascribes to himself the casting down of princes from the throne, why, by the same reason, should it not be thought lawful, and as much from God, when this is done by the people upon a just cause. For if it is necessarily a sin for them to depose, it may as likely be a sin to have elected. And on the contrary, if the people's act in election is argued by a king, saying it is an act of God and the most just title to enthrone him, why may not the people's act of rejection also be understood by the people as the act of God, and the most just reason to depose him? So we see that the title and just right of reigning or deposing, as it related to God, is found in Scripture to be all one; visible only in the people, and depending merely upon justice and demerit....

But God, as we have cause to trust, will put other thoughts into the people and turn them from looking after these firebrands [who oppose the new government], of whose fury and false prophecies we have enough experience; and from the murmurs of new discord will incline them to hearken rather with upraised minds to the voice of our supreme magistracy, calling us to liberty and the flourishing deeds of a reformed common-wealth; with the hope that as God was heretofore angry with the Jews who rejected him and his form of government to choose a king, so that he will bless us, and be propitious to us who reject a king to make him [God] our only leader, and supreme governor in the conformity as near as may be to his own ancient government; if we have the worth in us to entertain the sense of our future happiness, and the courage to receive what God vouchsafed to us: wherein we have the honour to precede other nations who are now labouring to be our followers.

179 Alexander Ross, *The Alcoran of Mahomet* (1649)

Keywords: #Censorship, #Freedom of the Press, #War
Region: #England | #Ottoman Empire
Group: #Church of England | #Islam, #Puritan

The Ottoman and Holy Roman Empires both claimed to be the imperial heirs of Rome. After Constantinople fell to the Ottomans in 1453, the Roman Church feared its fate might be similar to that of the Orthodox. The Ottomans were a potent force in the early Reformation, politically and imaginarily, as they continued to be framed as the 'other' to Roman Christianity, inducing fear across the continent. The year after his *Ninety-Five Theses*, Luther critiqued the call for an unholy offensive war against the Turks. In *Exsurge Domine*, a Bull against Luther's teachings, Pope Leo X misinterpreted the nascent Reformer as arguing for non-resistance to Turkish invasion. Luther defended resistance in *On War against the Turk* (1529), although he was principally concerned with sins that provoked divine wrath. Ottoman advances influenced the Diet of Augsburg in 1530 and the emergence of the Protestant party: the 1521 conquest of Belgrade (Ottoman victory), the 1526 Battle of Mohács (Ottoman victory), and the 1529 siege of Vienna (Ottoman withdrawal).[261]

As the Ottoman military threat continued to increase, there was a greater desire to learn about their culture and religion. Humanist education incorporated Hebrew and Greek, and many learned Arabic and translated texts. In 1543, Theodor Bibliander edited a Latin translation of the Qur'an, and Luther provided a preface. Not only Luther expressed very positive views about the Ottomans and about Islam, but he also disparaged them. In this preface, he claimed to be living at 'the extreme end of the ages', a time of heightened spiritual warfare:

> We must fight on all fronts against the ranks of the devil. In this age of ours how many varied enemies have we already seen? Papist defenders of idolatry, the Jews, the multifarious monstrosities of the Anabaptists, **Michael Servetus,** and others. Let us now prepare ourselves against Muhammad.

636   *Sources*

In this fight, 'it is of value for the learned to read the writings of the enemy in order to refute them more keenly'.[262]

The Qur'an was first published in English in 1649 after the Parliamentarians executed Charles I. It was translated from French by Charles' chaplain, Alexander Ross. The new Commonwealth regime halted the printing, arrested the printer, and called Ross to appear before the Council of State. Publication was allowed to resume. In the publication, Ross vented derogatory views on Muhammad, the Qur'an, and Muslims. He also attacked the heretical English regime that killed his king, describing Muslims as morally superior to Puritan radicals. He argued that the Qur'an had no inherent appeal, and it was only accepted due to ignorance, the desire for power, or the fear of the sword. He refuted the objection that it was dangerous to publish the Qur'an in English, offering many reasons why such a translation was beneficial. In reason 11, he used Muslim virtues to shame Commonwealth England. Reason 12 was expressly political: Christians should learn about the faith of those they fought against, if only to refute their beliefs or better arm themselves.[263]

Alexander Ross, *The Alcoran of Mahomet...Newly Englished* (London: Randal Taylor, 1688), d3–4. Text modernised by the editors.

———

11   [I]f Christians will but diligently read and observe the laws and histories of the *Mohammedans*, they may blush to see how zealous they are in the works of devotion, piety, and charity, how devout, cleanly, and reverent in their mosques, how obedient to their priests, that even the great Turk himself will attempt nothing without consulting his Mufti: how careful are they to observe their hours of prayers five times a day wherever they are, or however employed? how constantly do they observe their Fasts from morning till night a whole month together; how loving and charitable the Muslims are to each other, and how careful they are towards strangers may be seen by their hospitals, both for the poor and for travellers: if we observe their justice, temperance, and other moral virtues, we may truly blush at our own coldness, both in devotion and charity, at our injustice, intemperance, and oppression: doubtless these men will rise up in judgement against us; and surely their devotion, piety, and works of mercy are main causes of the growth of *Mohammedans*, and on the contrary, our neglect of religion, and looseness of conversation, is a main hindrance to the increase of Christianity; is it not a shame that they should read over their *Alcoran* once every month, and we scarce read over the Bible in all our life? that they shall give such reverence to their *Alcoran*, as to honour the very camel that carried it to *Mecca*, and to lay up for holy relics the napkins and handkerchiefs that rubbed off the sweat from his skin; and we shall prefer lascivious poems, and wanton

ballads to the sacred word of Almighty God? do we not make ourselves unworthy of such an inestimable treasure?

12 The *Turks* are our neighbours, and their territories border upon the dominions of Christendom: there have been continual wars, and they will continue between us: it concerns every Christian who makes conscience of his ways to examine the cause, and to look into the grounds of this war, whether they be just or not, which cannot be known but by reading the *Alcoran* in which we see the *Mohammedans* to be the enemies of the cross of Christ, in denying his death, and of his divinity also, in that they deny his Godhead: we shall find so many passages in it that are repugnant to, and destructive of Christian religion, that Christian princes are bound to oppose the enemies thereof; after the example of those glorious emperors, *Constantine*, who made war against the heathen princes (*Maxentius, Maximinus* and *Licinius*), of *Theodosius* the elder against the tyrant *Eugenius* the worshipper of *Hercules*, of *Theodosius* the younger against the *Saracens*, of *Honorius* against the *Goths*, all enemies of Christ, by whose assistance they got notable victories, and glorious triumphs.

180 Gerrard Winstanley, *On the True Levelling of Social Difference* (1649)

Keywords: #Land, #Economics, #Poverty, #Equality, #Slavery, #Authority, #Communal Living, #Revelation, #War, #Violence, #Love
Region: #England
Group: #Digger | #Leveller, #Puritan, #Quaker

Gerrard Winstanley (1609–1676) was born to a modest English family in Wigan and, by 1638, was a freeman of the Merchant Taylors' Company. The outbreak of war hurt his fledgling business, and he turned to farming. It is unclear when his political and religious radicalism developed, but when it did, the land formed a central component. Like many of his contemporaries, the politics of the late 1640s fostered intense eschatological speculation. In print and practice, he theorised about new ways of organising communities. His agenda went beyond that of the **Levellers**, founding the community that would become known as the 'Diggers'. His communal experiments began at St George's Hill (Surrey) and spread to several other regions across England. They thought they were living in a time of renewal, returning society to its propertyless state before the fall of humanity in the garden of Eden. These communities did not last long, partly owing to increasing pressure from Parliamentarians. After the Restoration in 1660, Winstanley served in an Anglican congregation as a churchwarden, and later, he had ties with **Quakers**.

The following extract comes from the opening of *The True Levellers Standard Advanced* (1649), attributed to Winstanley. The latter parts of the publication surveyed biblical history, charged England with crimes that stemmed from impure religion, and described the Edenic community at St George's Hill. The Restoration of Eden would not come through the force of arms, it argued, but by the sweat of their brow in the fields as they shared the bounty of the earth in Christian charity. They claimed a special mission by the voice and revelation of God. Their community was the start of the fulfilment of prophecies given to the Jews, and they viewed their actions through an expectant eschatological frame. Winstanley had many of the same concerns for the oppressed as **Thomas Müntzer**, and he coupled this concern with an emphasis on the voice of God and eschatological expectation. However,

Sources 639

unlike Müntzer, he was unwilling to use force to bring about his experiment in communal living.[264]

Gerrard Winstanley, et al., *The True Levellers Standard ADVANCED: OR, The State of Community opened, and Presented to the Sons of Men* (London, 1649). Text modernised by the editors.

———

A Declaration to the Powers of England, and to all the Powers of the World, Showing the Cause why the Common People of England have begun, and Consented to Dig up, Manure, and Sow Corn upon George-Hill in Surrey; by those that have Subscribed, and thousands more that give Consent.

In the beginning of time, the great Creator Reason, made the earth to be a common treasury, to preserve beasts, birds, fishes, and man, the lord that was to govern this creation; for man had domination given to him, over the beasts, birds, and fishes [Gen. 1–2]; but not one word was spoken in the beginning, That one branch of mankind should rule over another.

And the reason is this, every single man, male and female, is a perfect creature of himself; and the same Spirit that made the globe, dwells in man to govern the globe; so that the flesh of man being subject to Reason, his Maker, has him within himself for his Teacher and Ruler, therefore he does not need to look outside himself for any other teacher and ruler, for he does not need any man to teach him, for the same anointing that ruled in the Son of Man, teaches him all things.

But since human flesh (that king of beasts) began to delight in the objects of the creation, more than in the Spirit Reason and Righteousness, who manifests himself as the indweller in the five senses (hearing, seeing, tasting, smelling, feeling); then he fell into blindness of mind and weakness of heart, and searched abroad for a teacher and ruler: And so selfish thoughts took possession of the five senses, and ruling as king in the internal room of reason, and working with covetousness, he set up one man to teach and rule over another; and thereby killed the Spirit, and man was brought into bondage, and became a greater slave to his own kind, than the beasts of the field were to him.

And hereupon, the earth (which was made to be a common treasury of relief for all, both beasts and men) was hedged in and enclosed by the teachers and rulers, and the others were made servants and slaves: And that earth that is within this creation to be a common store-house for all, is bought and sold, and kept in the hands of a few, whereby the great creator is mightily dishonoured, as if he were a respecter of persons [Rom. 2:11], delighting in the comfortable livelihood of some, and rejoicing in the miserable poverty and desperate condition of others. From the beginning it was not so....

But for the present state of the old world that is burning up like parchment in the fire, and wearing away, we see proud imaginary flesh, which is the wise Serpent, as it rises up in the flesh and gets dominion and some rule

640   *Sources*

over others, and so forces one part of the creation, man, to be a slave to another; and thereby the Spirit is killed in both. The one looks upon himself as a teacher and ruler, and so is lifted up in pride over his fellow creature: The other looks upon himself as imperfect, and so is dejected in his Spirit, and looks upon his fellow creature of his own image, as a lord above him.

And thus Esau, the man of flesh, which is covetousness and pride, has killed Jacob, the Spirit of meekness and righteous government in the light of Reason, and rules over him: And so the earth that was made a common treasury for all to live comfortably upon, becomes, through man's unrighteous actions one over another, to be a place, wherein one torments another.

Now the great creator, who is the Spirit Reason, suffered himself thus to be rejected, and trodden under foot by the covetous proud flesh, for a limited time; therefore he says,

> The Seed out of whom the creation proceeded, which is myself, shall bruise this Serpent's head [Gen. 3:15], and restore my creation again from this curse and bondage; and when I, the King of Righteousness, reigns in every man, I will be the blessing of the earth, and the joy of all nations.

And since the coming in of the stoppage, or the A-dam [a dam blocking the Spirit of Peace and Liberty] the earth has been enclosed and given to the elder brother Esau, or man of flesh, and has been bought and sold from one to another; and Jacob, or the younger brother, that is to succeed or come forth next, who is the universal spreading power of righteousness that gives liberty to the whole creation, is made a servant.

And this elder Son, or man of bondage, has held the earth in bondage to himself, not by a meek law of righteousness, But by subtle selfish councils, and by open and violent force; for wherefore is it that there is such wars and rumours of wars in the nations of the earth? And wherefore are men so mad to destroy one another? But only to uphold civil propriety of honour, dominion and riches one over another, which is the curse the creation groans under, waiting for deliverance [Rom. 8:19–22].

But when the earth becomes a common treasury again, as it must, for all the prophesies of scriptures and Reason are circled here in this community, and mankind must have the law of righteousness once more written in his heart, and all must be made of one heart, and one mind [e.g., Jer. 31:33; Ezek. 11:19–20; Heb. 8:10].

Then enmity will cease in all lands, for none shall dare to seek dominion over others, neither shall any dare to kill another, nor desire more of the earth than another; for he that will rule over, imprison, oppress, and kill his fellow creatures, under any pretence, is a destroyer of the creation, and an actor of the curse, and walks contrary to the rule of righteousness: Do, as you would have others do to you [Matt. 7:12]; and love your enemies [Matt. 5:43–48], not in words, but in actions....

181 Johanna and Ebenezer Cartwright, *Petition for the Readmission of the Jews* (1649)

Keywords: #Toleration, #Women, #Exile, #Violence
Region: #Netherlands, #England
Group: #Anabaptist | #Judaism, #Puritan, #Independent

England expelled the Jews in 1290, but some managed to remain and worshipped covertly. Until the seventeenth century, there was little desire to see them return to England. One of the most important figures in England's change of attitude was **Oliver Cromwell**, although his relationship with Jews was complex. In 1648, Cromwell expressed a desire for 'union and understanding between godly people (Scots, English, Jews, Gentiles, Presbyterians, Independents, Anabaptists, and all)'. He also had economic reasons to want their readmission. Cromwell organised a conference at Whitehall in 1655 where participants debated Jewish readmission, partly in response to the advocacy of Rabbi Menasseh ben Israel (1604–1657). The conference ended inconclusively, but it was followed by a spate of antisemitic publications. Protestants who held more positive attitudes were often animated by theopolitical expectancy, namely the hope that the conversion of the Jews would usher in a long-awaited millennium. Similar hopes were placed on the 'Jewish' Algonquians of New England by **John Eliot** and others.

The Whitehall Conference was the culmination of disparate calls for change over the last few decades.[265] Shortly before the execution of Charles I, an English Anabaptist mother and son petitioned for the readmission of the Jews: Johanna and Ebenezer Cartwright. They had lived alongside Jews in the Dutch Republic and sent their petition from Amsterdam. They claimed that the wrath of God was against England for historical violence done against England's Jews. They called for a reversal of expulsion so that they could live in England and even for their repatriation to the land of promise. This petition also hinted at the possibility of conversion, but this was not the primary aim of readmission or a requirement for it.[266]

Johanna and Ebenezer Cartwright, *The Petition of the Jewes* (London: George Roberts, 1649). Text modernised by the editors.

———

To the Right Honourable, Thomas Fairfax, (His Excellency) England's General, and the Honourable Council of War, Convened for God's Glory, Israel's Freedom, Peace, and Safety,

The humble Petition of Johanna Cartwright, Widow, and Ebenezer Cartwright her Son, freeborn of England, and now Inhabitants of the City of Amsterdam.

Humbly Shows,

That your petitioners being conversant in that city [Amsterdam], with and among some of Israel's race, called Jews, and growing sensible of their heavy out-cries and clamours against the intolerable cruelty of this our English nation, exercised against them by that (and other) inhumane exceeding great massacre of them, in the reign of Richard the [First], king of this land, and their banishment ever since, with the penalty of death to be inflicted upon any of their return into this land, that by discourse with them, and serious perusal of the prophets, both they and we find, that the time of her call draws nigh; whereby they together with us, shall come to know the Emanuel, the Lord of life, light, and glory; even as we are now known of him, And that this nation of England, with the inhabitants of the Netherlands, shall be the first and readiest to transport Israel's sons and daughters in their ships to the land promised to their forefathers, Abraham, Isaac, and Jacob, for an everlasting inheritance.

For the glorious manifestation whereof, and pious means thereunto, your petitioners humbly pray that the inhumane cruel statute of banishment made against them may be repealed, and they, under the Christian banner of charity and brotherly love, may again be received and permitted to trade and dwell amongst you in this land, as now they do in the Netherlands.

By which act of mercy, your petitioners are assured of the wrath of God, will be much appeased towards you, for their innocent blood shed, and they thereby daily enlightened in the saving knowledge of him, for whom they look daily and expect as their King of eternal glory, and both their and our Lord God of salvation (Christ Jesus.) For the glorious accomplishing whereof, your petitioners do, and shall ever address themselves to the true Peace, and pray; etc.

This petition was presented to the General Council of the Officers of the Army, under the command of His Excellency, Thomas Lord Fairfax, at White-Hall on Jan. 5. And favourably received with a promise to take it into speedy consideration when the present more public affairs are dispatched.

182 A Petition of Women to the English Parliament (1649)

Keywords: #Women, #Women's Rights, #Freedom of Speech, #Equality, #Execution, #Petition, #Law, #Tyranny, #Censorship
Region: #England
Group: #Leveller | #Puritan, #Congregationalist

Owing to a lapse in censorship laws in 1641, the British Civil Wars witnessed a dramatic rise in the number of publications. Women, too, found new opportunities to voice their concerns and grievances. 'During the civil war decade, women published 112 pamphlets of a political nature, despite their lack of training in classical political rhetoric'.[267] Petitioning became a common way for women to address specific grievances, and they sometimes offer glimpses into the ways women responded to the political ideas of their time. Petitioners often rooted their demand to be heard in their distinct experiences and sufferings as women – highlighting how the upheavals of the 1640s and 1650s impacted them. The documents addressed concerns to institutions like Parliament or persons like Queen Henrietta Maria or Oliver Cromwell. Female publications ranged from the practical to the prophetic, from religious to political. Their petitions were often ignored by those in power, although some leaders belittled the female voice in public discourse. The pamphlets also aimed at wider audiences, and some were reprinted in newsbooks. Female petitioners often adopted a humble and submissive demeanour, even while making demands of those in power as Esther had done. They supported several different causes and could embrace the establishment or want to see it remodelled.

Women in the London area wrote the following petition to the House of Commons, following the harsh crackdown on Levellers in 1649. These women objected to intolerance on the basis of scripture, English history, the jurisprudence of **Edward Coke**, and the existence of universal rights. The petition has been attributed to **Katherine Chidley** (fl.1616–1653), an important author among the Levellers. 'In a number of petitions from 1642 to 1653, Leveller-inspired women defended the spiritual and political interests of subjects, the toleration of non-conformist religion, and – above all – the

644   *Sources*

individual's freedom of conscience', write Jacqueline Broad and Karen Green. In this 1649 petition, 'These women assert their equal interest (as women compared to men) in the protection of civil liberties'.[268] The relationship between these Civil War petitions and the later feminist or liberal traditions is complicated and contentious.

To the Supreme Authority, the Commons of England Assembled in Parliament The Humble Petition of Divers Well-Affected Women of the Cities of London and Westminster, the Borough of Southwark, Hamblets, and Parts Adjacent. Affecters and Approvers of the Petition of Sept. 11. 1648 (London: s.n., 1649). Text modernised by the editors.

———

To The Supreme Authority of England, The Commons Assembled in Parliament.

The humble Petition of diverse well-affected Women of the Cities of London and Westminster, the Borough of Southwark, Hamlets.

Shows,

That since we are assured of our creation in the image of God [Gen. 1:26–27], and of an interest in Christ, equal to men [e.g., Gal. 3:28], as also of a proportionable share in the freedoms of this commonwealth, we cannot but wonder and grieve that we should appear so despicable in your eyes, as to be thought unworthy to petition, or represent our grievances to this honourable House.

Do we not have an equal interest with the men of this nation in those liberties and securities contained in the *Petition of Right* [1628] and other good laws of the land? Are any of our lives, limbs, liberties, or goods to be taken from us more than from men, but by due process of law, and conviction of 12 sworn men of the neighbourhood?

And can you imagine us to be so sottish or stupid as to not perceive or be sensible when daily those strong defences of our peace and welfare are broken down and trod under-foot by force and arbitrary power?

[*They object to remaining silent and homebound while husbands and male friends are unjustly imprisoned or killed.*] Shall the blood of war be shed in time of peace? Doth not the word of God expressly condemn it? Doth not the *Petition of Right* [1628] declare, *That no person ought to be judged by martial law (except in times of war) and that all commissions given to execute martial law in times of peace are contrary to the laws and statutes of the land?* Does not Sir Edward Coke, in his chapter on murder in the third part of his *Institutes*, consider it good law (and Parliament also acknowledge it to be good) *That for a general or other officers of an army in time of peace to put any man (although a soldier) to death by appeals to martial law, it is absolute murder in that general?* And has it not by this House in the case of the late Earl of Strafford been adjudged high treason? And are we Christians, and shall we sit still and keep at home, while such men as have born continual testimony against the injustice of all times and unrighteousness of men are picked out and delivered up to the slaughter, and yet must we show no sense of their sufferings, no tenderness or affections, no bowels or compassion, nor bear any testimony against such an abominable cruelty and injustice?

Have such men as these continually hazarded their lives, spent their estates and time, lost their liberties, been as a guard by day, and as a watch by night; and when for this they are in trouble and greatest danger, persecuted and hated even to the death; and should we be so basely ungrateful, as to neglect them in the day of their affliction? No, far be it from us: Let it be accounted folly, presumption, madness, or whatsoever in us, whilst we have life and breath, we will never leave them, nor forsake them, nor ever cease to importune you (having yet so many hopes of you, as of the unjust Judge mentioned in Luke 18, to obtain justice, if not for justice sake, yet for importunity) or to use any other means for the enlargement and reparation of those who are left alive; and for justice against such as have been the cause of Mr. Lockiers death: Nor will we ever rest until we have prevailed, that we, our husbands, friends, and servants, may not be liable to be abused, violated, and butchered at men's wills and pleasures. But if nothing will satisfy but the blood of those just men, those constant undaunted asserters of the people's freedoms will satisfy your thirst, drink also, and be glutted with our blood, and let us all fall together: Take the blood of one more, and take all: slay one, slay all.

And therefore, again, we entreat you to review our last petition on behalf of our friends mentioned above and not to slight the things therein contained because they are presented unto you by the weak hand of women, it being a normal thing with God, to work mighty effects by weak means [1 Cor. 1:27]: For we are not at all satisfied with the answer you gave unto our husbands and friends, but do equally remain liable to those snares laid in your declaration, that makes the abetters, of the book laid to our friends charge, no less than traitors, when as hardly any discourse can be touching the affairs of the present times, but falls within the compass of that book: So that all liberty of discourse is thereby utterly taken away, and there can be no greater slavery than this.

Nor shall we be satisfied; however you deal with our friends, except you free them from their present extrajudicial imprisonment and the use of force against them, and give them full reparations for their forceable attachment, etc. And leave them from first to last, to be proceeded against by the due process of law, and give them respect, in keeping with their good and faithful service to the commonwealth.

Our houses are made worse than prisons to us, and our lives worse than death; the sight of our husbands and children are matters of grief, sorrow, and affliction to us, until you grant our desires, and therefore, if you ever intend any good to this miserable nation, do not harden your hearts against petitioners, nor deny us in things so evidently just and reasonable, as you would not be dishonourable to all posterity.

183 *Colonisation and Slavery in Dutch South Africa (1649–1685)*

Keywords: #Colonisation, #War, #Violence, #Slavery, #Land
Region: #South Africa
Group: #Dutch Reformed

The Khoekhoe inhabited the southern tip of Africa, and their first encounter with Europeans dates to 1488. Early interactions often involved trade and sometimes violence. The Dutch were one of many European powers who used the region to restock vessels coming from or going to the Indian Ocean or Southeast Asia. Five short sources give insight into Dutch-Indigenous relationships in the region now known as South Africa.[269]

D. Moodie, trans. and ed., *The Record; or, a Series of Official Papers Relative to the Condition and Treatment of the Native Tribes of South Africa*, vol. 1. 1649–1720 (Cape Town: A. S. Robertson, 1838), 4, 124, 200–201, 387, 396–397.

———

[1 Reasons for Establishing a Permanent Settlement]

Remonstrance, in which is briefly set forth and explained, the service, advantage, and profit, which will accrue to the United Chartered East India Company, from making a Fort and Garden, at the *Cabo de Boa Esperance*.

26 July 1649

[In this first source from 1649, Leendert Janz and Nicolaas Proot gave reasons why the Dutch should establish a permanent settlement on the Cape, among them being the glory of God and the good of Africans. Towards the end, the Remonstrance turns to a religious purpose that might follow in the wake of financially investing in the Cape. In 1652 three ships commanded by Jan van Riebeeck arrived on the coast and established a fort at Table Bay. This station was another point in a vast and powerful global trading network run by the **Dutch East India Company** *(VOC). As the fort grew*

into a expansive colony, trade partnerships with the Khoekhoe turned to dominance and dispossession.]

...The refreshments procured at the Cape by the passing ships, would also cause a material saving to the Company in the issue of provisions. That the said natives would easily learn the Dutch language is evident....

By maintaining a good correspondence with them, we shall be able in time to employ some of their children as boys and servants, and to educate them in the Christian Religion, by which means, if it pleases God Almighty to bless this good cause, as at Tayouan and Formosa, many souls will be brought to God, and to the Christian Reformed Religion, so that the formation of the said Fort and Garden, will not only tend to the gain and profit of the Honourable Company, but to the preservation and saving of many men's lives, and what is more, to the magnifying of God's holy name, and to the propagation of his gospel, whereby, beyond all doubt, your Honours' trade over all India will be more and more blessed....

This is briefly what we had to propose and to remonstrate to your Honours, for the benefit of the Honourable Company...meanwhile, heartily praying that the Almighty will be pleased to bless your Honours with wisdom and understanding, so that you may direct, not this alone, but all the Company's affairs in such a manner that it may tend to the glorifying of God's holy name, the establishment of the church of Christ, and your individual honour and reputation, etc., etc.

Leendert Janz

N. Proot

Amsterdam, 26th July 1649

———

[2 Journal of Commander Jan van Riebeeck].

[*This second source, from the journal of van Riebeeck in 1658, blended slavery, education and the inculcation of Christianity.*]

April 17 1658.

Begun holding school for the young slaves – the chaplain (*siekentrooster*) was charged with this duty of the *crankbesoeker* [visitor or comforter of the sick] the rather because he could read the true Holland Dutch, fluently and well; to stimulate the slaves to attention while at school, and to induce them to learn the Christian prayers, they were promised each a glass of brandy and two inches of tobacco, when they finish their task; all their names were also taken down, those who had no [Christian?] names had names given to them.... (p.124)

———

648   *Sources*

[3 First Khoekhoe–Dutch War]

[*In a third source from 1660, Pieter Sterthemius advised van Riebeeck on how to proceed in the First Khoekhoe–Dutch War. The document evidences a remarkably low opinion of the Khoekhoe, and Sterthemius tried to temper van Riebeeck's desire for revenge. Another Khoekhoe-Dutch war occurred in the 1670s and was one of many factors that contributed to the collapse of Khoekhoe power.*]

Extracts from a Memorandum for the guidance of Commander J. Van Riebeeck, until further Orders from Holland or Batavia.

March 12 1660.

...Recommending you above all to persevere in your exertions, until the true object of our masters in taking possession here, shall have been attained, and this will not be the case until the cultivation of the soil (which, thanks to God, has this year succeeded beyond all expectation, in spite of the war with the Hottentoo [a pejorative name for the Khoekhoe]...) is prosecuted with zeal and in real earnest....

But, as to your proposal of revenging ourselves upon them after peace and reconciliation, I should conceive that it might, indeed, be easily effected; but then, whether it be permitted, as consistent with our obligations as Christians, and whether we are accordingly at liberty to act thus towards these irrational and blinded men, and according to the proverb, to repay them in the same coin – is very much to be doubted; besides that I should deem that course one which would not redound to our credit, nor would it be sufficiently dignified towards them, for it would seem as if we could do nothing to them in any other way; such a course these savages could not reconcile with justice, and therefore would have good cause to regard us with suspicion hereafter, and never to trust us again. I should therefore deem it best to allow past events to pass unnoticed, and to try whether we cannot convince them by kindness – should that fail – there will be opportunities enough of making them pay for both offences together....

Pieter Sterthemius

———

[4 Making Africans Loyal to the Dutch]

Extracts of Considerations for the information and guidance of Commander Van der Stell, by Governor-General R. van Goens.

24 April 1682

[*In a fourth source from 1682, Governor-General Rijcklof van Goens disparaged the Khoekhoe and brushed aside their claims to the land. The colony needed to expand and he gave advice on where and how to go about it. He argued that paternalistic policies and introducing 'civilisation' would make Africans more loyal.*]

This space comprises a great extent of country, which is (to all appearance) inhabited, or wandered over (*door geloopen*) by none but various tribes of poor ignorant Hottentots in their migratory mode of life, but still it is abundantly stocked with oxen, cows, steers, elands, harts, sheep, all kinds of deer, hares, birds, and other useful animals. The Company and the burgers being thus supplied with abundance of land, – time, and the future condition of the Company and the Fatherland, will point out what else is necessary.... It would be a very desirable thing if we could induce the Hottentots to adopt some kind of civilised habits, and thus teach them to be faithful to us, which would give us much security in such an emergency (*i.e.*, an invasion by any European power); but of this there appear as yet but slender hopes, from the great barbarism and rude manners of those people. What may be effected upon those ignorant men in time, and with skilful management, depends upon the will of Providence but nothing will be accomplished by any kind of severity; and it will be necessary to exhibit much patient forbearance, discretion, and, especially, affability.

———

[5 Paternalism and Perpetual Slavery]

[*This final source from 1685 frankly discussed the permanent and heritable status of the enslaved. Christians were to use their authority as 'foster fathers' to bring enslaved peoples to the knowledge of Christ.*]

Extracts of Instructions for the Commander Simon van der Stell.

16 July 1685

The greatest advantage that the Company expects in this country, consists in fixing here a good Colony and peopling it with our own countrymen....

The labour of the Company's slaves also produces much profit, and holds out equal hopes for the future; but these poor men must be looked upon with other eyes, for they are the Company's own people, not hirelings; they cannot quit the service of their master when tired, but are bound, not only for all their lives, but for those of their children and descendants. The better we make them, the fitter will they be to perform their duty, the more will they love their masters, and the more faithful will they prove to our nation. They are heathens, ignorant of the true God; and we, in whose power are their bodies – we may almost say, their lives – are Christians. It would be a shame to us, whose part it is to take good care of our irrational domestic cattle, if we permitted men to run wild, and left them in a worse condition than when in their fatherland. Our masters are the foster fathers (*vochter heeren*) of Christ's church, and if we fail to employ the means in our hands, and do not

650 *Sources*

exert every endeavour to bring, these men to the knowledge of the redeeming faith – we shut the doors of that church. How do we know what God, in his mercy, has determined as to these people, and what will not foreign nations say to our shame, if we allow them to live together by hundreds, like brutes, in utter licentiousness, and do not provide herein as for our own countrymen?

H. A. Van Rheede.

184 John Eliot, *The Christian Commonwealth among Algonquians* (c.1649)

Keywords: #Government, #Church-State Relations, #Covenant, #Ten Commandments, #Family, #Marriage, #Punishment #Colonisation, #Evangelisation, #Missions
Region: #United States
Group: #Puritan | #Indigenous American, #Judaism

John Eliot (1604–1690) was born in England and studied at Cambridge University before coming under the ministry of Thomas Hooker. Hooker preached an important farewell sermon to what he saw as England in decline, *The Danger of Desertion* (preached 1631). He later founded Connecticut Colony and influenced the *Fundamental Orders of Connecticut*, one of the foundational documents in the history of constitutional democracy in America. He also advocated for a confederacy of colonies. Under mounting ecclesiastical pressure, Eliot fled to the newly formed colony of Massachusetts Bay and began his ministry there. He was involved in justifying **Roger Williams'** banishment, questioned **Anne Hutchinson,** and was nearly selected as chaplain for the **Pequot War** (1636–1637). He is best known for furthering the education of English, American Indians, and Africans alike. With the help of several Indigenous persons, including John Sassamon and James Printer, he translated the Bible into Algonquian, and it was the first Bible printed in the Americas. Eliot ministered among the American Indians for four decades and was sometimes called the 'Apostle to the Indians'. He organised 'praying towns', Algonquian communities that implemented English and Christian principles. Praying Towns were greatly disrupted by King Philip's War (1675–1676), and both Indigenous and Christian leaders often mistreated Indigenous converts.

While Eliot's co-religionists in the British Isles experimented with new forms of government, he did so among Christian Algonquians. Eliot turned to the Hebrew Bible for political guidance, and this coincided with debates about the Jewish nature of American Indians, as famously argued in Thomas Thorowgood's *Jewes in America, or, Probabilities that the Americans are of that race* (1650). In *The Christian Commonwealth*, Eliot reached back to Moses and forward to the eschaton to construct a unique political theory.

652   *Sources*

He described a restored utopian Christian government as inaugurated among the Praying Indians, crucially relocating this civilisation among an identifiable, non-English, population. Written much earlier, around the execution of Charles I in 1649, this work was published around the Restoration (1660), and authorities soon banned it. Eliot retracted the work. Under similar pressure, **Richard Baxter** (Eliot's friend) similarly printed and retracted his political treatise, *A Holy Commonwealth* (1659).[270]

The Christian Commonwealth: Or the Civil Policy of the Rising Kingdom of Jesus Christ (1659), 1–4, 21–22. Text modernised by the editors.

Chapter 1

It is the commandment of the Lord that a people should enter into covenant with the Lord to become his people, even in their civil society, as well as in their church-society (Deut. 29:10–13). Whereby they submit themselves to be ruled by the Lord in all things, receiving from him, both the platform of their government and all their laws; which when they do, then Christ reigns over them in all things, they being ruled by his will, and by the word of his mouth (Isa. 33:22).

The substance of this covenant, and subjection of themselves unto the Lord, to be ruled by him in all things, is this. That they humbly confess their corruption by nature, and lost condition; that they acknowledge the free grace (Deut. 26:1–12) of God, in their redemption by Christ, and in the promulgation of the gospel unto them, and making application thereof effectually unto their souls: and therefore the Lord has showed his everlasting love unto them, and caused them inwardly by faith, to give up themselves unto him, to be forever his, to love, serve, and obey him, in all his word and commandments: so now they do outwardly, and solemnly with the rest of God's people join together so to do in their civil polity, receiving from the Lord, both the platform of their civil government, as it is set down (in the essentials of it) in the holy scriptures; and also all their laws, which they resolve through his grace, to fetch out of the Word of God, making that their only *Magna Carta*; and accounting no law, statute or judgement valid, further than it appears to arise and flow from the Word of God.

Those who with a lively faith enter into or walk in this covenant perform every act (wherein they are free from temptation) of civil conversation among men (1 Cor. 10:31) by faith in obedience unto God. Instructing, that all should do so, who take this covenant; and if they do not, they are guilty of breach of covenant, before God. A willing subjection of a man's self to Christ in this covenant is some hopeful sign of some degree of faith in Christ and love to God; and as a good preparative for a more near approach to Christ in church-fellowship and covenant: he that is willing to serve Christ by the polity of the second Table [of the Ten Commandments] in civil matters, is in some degree prepared to serve him, by the polity of the first Table in ecclesiastical matters.

The Child is implicitly comprehended in the father's covenant (Deut. 29:14–15), the wife is explicitly comprehended in her husband's, insomuch that in her widowhood she and her family are one, under the order of the government of God.

The particular form of government which is approved by God and instituted by *Moses* among the sons of Israel (Exod. 18:23–24) – and is profitable to be received by any nation or people that reverences the command of God and trembles at his Word – is this; that they choose (Exod. 18:21) for themselves rulers of thousands (Exod. 18:25; Deut. 1:15), of hundreds, of fifties and of tens, who shall govern according to the pure, holy, righteous, perfect and good Law of God (Deut. 1:17; 2 Chron. 19:6; Ezek. 44:24), written in the Scriptures of the Old and New Testament.

Chapter 5

The duties of all the rulers of the civil part of the kingdom of Christ, are as follows.

The office and duty of all rulers is to govern the people in the orderly and seasonable practice of all the commandments of God, in actions related to political matters, whether of piety and love to God, or of justice and love to man with peace.

Hence they are keepers of both Tables [of the Ten Commandments] and are to ensure that all the commandments of God are observed, as to compel men to their undoubted duty, and punish them for their undoubted sins, errors and transgressions.

A case, a duty, a sin, is said then to be undoubted, when either it is expressly, or by generally approved consequence, commanded or forbidden in the Scriptures; or when it has passed the circuit of God's polity, and received its final determination according to the Scriptures; unto which not to submit, is capital presumption.

Hence again, rulers are eminently concerned to maintain the purity of religion, with all care and power; holiness, truth, and peace being deeply concerned herein.

Hence again, all rulers must be skilful in the Scriptures; they must read and meditate on the same all the days of their life, that thereby they may be enabled to do their office faithfully and religiously so long as they live.

Hence again, they are to give counsel and command for the well-ordering of all the public affairs of their people; both in the education of youth, whether in schools or other occupations; in walking in their callings, in their neighbourhood, commerce and converse with men, in subjecting themselves to government, with religion, justice and peace.

185 Oliver Cromwell, *Plea to Avoid War* (1650)

Keywords: #War, #Conscience, #Toleration, #Covenant
Region: #England, #Scotland
Group: #Independent, #Puritan | #Presbyterian

As England had just executed Charles I, the Scots were outraged at the murder of their Scottish king and the violation of England's sworn loyalty to the **Solemn League and Covenant**. In response to the killing, Scotland declared Charles II as King of all Great Britain. England understood this as a thinly veiled threat: Scotland would restore the Stuarts to the English throne and institute a Presbyterian form of government. This possibility was intolerable for those who were convinced that the Stuarts trampled on ancient liberties and believed that God had led England into greater religious pluralism. As a result, Oliver Cromwell launched a pre-emptive strike against his theological brethren in Scotland.

Oliver Cromwell composed the following letter upon his march against Scotland. He desperately tried to convince the Kirk that he was submissive to the leading of God and that God had providentially chosen against the Stuart monarchy. His letter was passionate, urging the Scots to assume the best about their fellow Protestants and former military allies. It evidences much of the tension in Cromwell's mind: he was certain of God's leading, but also entertained doubt. He suggested greater toleration, and was willing to use force to bring it about. The Kirk would not be persuaded. The battle of Dunbar in 1650 was a clash between two Reformed armies who claimed to represent nations built upon the pure word of God – and in effect, both appealed to a trial by battle wherein God would providentially decide. The vastly superior Scottish army suffered a catastrophic defeat – a loss that had a lasting impact on Presbyterianism and on the relationship between Scotland and England.[271]

Thomas Carlyle, *Oliver Cromwell's Letters and Speeches* (Boston, MA: Standard, 1899), 175–178.

To the General Assembly of the Kirk of Scotland; or, in case of their not sitting, To the Commissioners of the Kirk of Scotland: These.

Musselburgh, 3d August, 1650.

Sirs,

Your *Answer to the Declaration of the Army* we have seen. Some godly Ministers with us did, at Berwick, compose this *Reply*; which I thought fit to send you.

That you or we, in these great Transactions, answer the will and mind of God, it is only from His grace and mercy to us. And therefore, having said as in our Papers, we commit the issue thereof to Him who disposeth all things, assuring you that we have light and comfort increasing upon us, day by day; and are persuaded that, before it be long, the Lord will manifest His good pleasure so that all shall see Him; and His People shall say, *This is the Lord's work, and it is marvellous in our eyes: this is the day that the Lord hath made; we will be glad and rejoice therein.* – Only give me leave to say, in a word, 'thus much:'

You take upon you to judge us in the things of our God, though you know us not, though in the things we have said unto you, in that which is entitled the Army's Declaration, we have spoken our hearts as in the sight of the Lord who hath tried us. And by your hard and subtle words you have begotten prejudice in those who do too much, in matters of conscience, – wherein every soul is to answer for itself to God, – depend upon you. So that some have already followed you, to the breathing-out of their souls [in a recent skirmish]: 'and' others continue still in the way wherein they are led by you, – we fear, to their own ruin.

And no marvel if you deal thus with us, when indeed you can find in your hearts to conceal from your own people the Papers we have sent you; who might thereby see and understand the bowels of our affections to them, especially to such among them as fear the Lord. Send as many of your Papers as you please amongst ours; they have a free passage. I fear them not. What is of God in them, would it might be embraced and received!-One of them lately sent, directed *To the Under-officers and Soldiers in the English Army*, hath begotten from them this enclosed Answer; which they desired me to send to you: not a crafty politic one, but a plain simple spiritual one; – what kind of one it is God knoweth, and God also will in due time make manifest.

And do we multiply these things [written declarations], as men; or do we them for the Lord Christ and His People's sake? Indeed we are not, through the grace of God, afraid of your numbers, nor confident in ourselves. We could, – I pray God you do not think we boast, – meet your Army, or what you have to bring against us. We have given, – humbly we speak it before our God, in whom all our hope is, – some proof that thoughts of that kind prevail not upon us. The Lord hath not hid His face from us since our approach so near unto you.

656   *Sources*

Your own guilt is too much for you to bear: bring not therefore upon yourselves the blood of innocent men, – deceived with pretences of King and Covenant; from whose eyes you hid a better knowledge! I am persuaded that divers of you, who lead the People, have laboured to build yourselves in these things; wherein you have censured others, and established yourselves 'upon the Word of God'. Is it therefore infallibly agreeable to the Word of God, all that *you* say? I beseech you, in the bowels of Christ, think it possible you may be mistaken. Precept may be upon precept, line may be upon line, and yet the Word of the Lord may be to some a Word of Judgement; that they may fall backward and be broken, and be snared and be taken! There may be a spiritual fulness, which the World may call drunkenness; as in the second Chapter of the *Acts* [2:13–15]. There may be, as well, a carnal confidence upon misunderstood and misapplied precepts, which may be called spiritual drunkenness. There may be a *Covenant* [i.e., the National Covenant] made with Death and Hell [Isa. 28:15]! I will not say yours was so. But judge if such things have a politic aim: To avoid the overflowing scourge [Isa. 28:15]; or, To accomplish worldly interests? And if therein we [i.e., you] have confederated with wicked and carnal men, and have respect for them, or otherwise 'have' drawn them in to associate with us, Whether this be a Covenant of God, and spiritual? Bethink yourselves; we hope we do.

I pray you read the 28th of Isaiah, from the 5th to the 15th verse. And do not scorn to know that it is the Spirit that quickens and giveth life.

The Lord give you and us understanding to do that which is well-pleasing in His sight. Committing you to the grace of God, I rest,

Your humble servant,

Oliver Cromwell

186 Thomas Hobbes, *Political Obedience and Eternal Salvation* (1651)

Keywords: #Church-State Relations, #War, #Rebellion, #Authority, #Submission, #Revelation, #Magistrate, #Law, #Natural Law
Region: #England
Group: #Church of England | Non-Christian

Thomas Hobbes (1588–1679) was born in Malmesbury, the son of a Church of England minister, and educated at Oxford University. His tutoring for the famous Cavendish family took him on the first of many European tours. He served as a secretary to Francis Bacon and was distantly involved in early colonial efforts in Virginia. Hobbes gained notoriety through his political works, written against the backdrop of conflict in the British Isles. Fearing prosecution, he spent the 1640s and the early 1650s in France. Hobbes imagined to create social stability through the recognition of a single absolute sovereign over both church and state. His political philosophy, and the way he related these theories with scripture, earned him contempt and the charge of promoting atheism, facilitating immorality and despotism. He is perhaps best known for a dismal view of humanity that undergirded a limited scope for human freedom in his thought. Much of his political philosophy, particularly in the third and fourth parts of *Leviathan*, aimed to sway English Protestants towards a re-evaluation of politics through an interaction with scripture, and especially the Hebrew Bible.

The third part of *Leviathan* explored the 'Christian Common-Wealth'. The following selection comes from the capstone chapter of that section, and it dealt with the weightiest matter of eternal damnation or salvation. Hobbes recognised that fears about damnation had important implications for authority, submission, politics, and war. If God commanded that Christians obey God and their civil sovereign, what happened when the two authorities disagreed? Hobbes argued that humans should follow God. However, as he did throughout *Leviathan*, he was suspicious of humans who claimed to speak for God and doubted their ability to accurately discern God's voice. Because God no longer communicates through special revelation, one is left with the voice of their sovereign as 'their Supreme Pastor'.

658   *Sources*

Hobbes also drastically reduced the requirements for salvation in an attempt to remove the tension between obedience to God and human authority. Only two things were necessary: obedience and faith. God rewarded the desire to obey divine laws, even if the Christian might err in this regard. If Christians acted wrongly, that error was not eternally held against them. He also simplified the economy of salvation, arguing that only one doctrine was necessary, belief that Jesus is the Christ. Christians could believe this one point when they live under a godly sovereign, an errant 'Christian' sovereign or an unbelieving one. Even if the sovereign led the subjects astray in smaller matters of doctrine, and even if the Christian acted wrongly out of obedience to his sovereign, this obedience could not hinder salvation.[272]

Thomas Hobbes, *Leviathan, or, The Matter, Forme, and Power of a Common Wealth, Ecclesiasticall and Civil* (London: Andrew Crooke, 1651), 321–324, 330–331. Text modernised by the editors.

——

Part III: Of a Christian Common-Wealth

Chapter 43: *Of what is* necessary *for a Man's Reception into the Kingdom of Heaven.*

The most frequent pretext of sedition and civil war in Christian-wealths has long proceeded from a difficulty, not yet sufficiently resolved, of simultaneously obeying God and man when their commandments contradict. It is clear that when a man receives two contrary commands and knows that one of them is from God, he ought to obey that one, and not the other, though the other command comes from his lawful sovereign (whether a monarch or a sovereign assembly) or his father. The difficulty consists in this: when men are commanded in the name of God, in many cases they do not know if the command is from God, or if the one commanding abuses God's name for personal benefit. This was the case in the church of the Jews, where many false prophets sought reputation with the people by feigned dreams and visions; so there have been in all times in the church of Christ, false teachers that seek reputation with the people by fantastical and false doctrines; and with this reputation (as is the nature of ambition) to govern them for their private benefit.

But this difficulty of obeying both God and the civil sovereign on earth – to those who can distinguish between what is *necessary* and what is not *necessary* for their *reception* into the *kingdom of God* – is insignificant. For if the command of the civil sovereign is of such a nature that obedience is possible without forfeiting eternal life; disobedience is unjust; and the precept of the apostle takes place; *Servants obey your masters in all things* [Col. 3:22]; and, *children obey your parents in all things* [Col. 3:20]; and the precept of our Saviour, *The Scribes and Pharisees sit in Moses' chair, all therefore they shall say, that observe, and do* [Matt. 23:1–3]. But if the command is of such a

Sources   659

nature that obedience brings damnation to eternal death, then it would be madness to obey, and the counsel of our Saviour takes place, *Fear not those that kill the body, but cannot kill the soul* (Matt. 10:28). Therefore, all men who want to avoid worldly punishments that are inflicted for disobedience to their earthly sovereign, and those who want to avoid other-worldly punishment for disobedience to God, need to be taught to distinguish between what is, and what is not necessary for eternal salvation.

All that is necessary *for salvation*, is contained in two virtues, *faith in Christ* and *obedience to laws*. The latter of these, if it were perfect, were enough for us. But because we are all guilty of disobedience to God's law, not only originally in Adam but also actually by our own transgressions, there is required at our hands now, not only *obedience* for the rest of our time, but also a *remission* of past sins; which remission is the reward of our faith in Christ. That nothing else is necessarily required for salvation is manifest from this, that the kingdom of heaven is shut to none but to sinners; that is to say, to the disobedient, or transgressors of the law; nor to them if they repent and believe all the articles of Christian faith that are necessary for salvation.

The obedience required at our hands by God, who accepts in all our actions the will for the deed, is a serious attempt to obey him; and is called also by all such names as signify that attempt. And therefore obedience is sometimes called by the names of *charity* and *love*, because they imply a will to obey; and our Saviour himself considers our love to God and to one another a fulfilling of the whole law: and sometimes by the name of *righteousness*; for righteousness is but the will to give to every one his own, that is to say, the will to obey the laws: and sometimes by the name of *repentance*; because to repent, implies a turning away from sin, which is a return of the will to obedience. Whosoever therefore genuinely desires to fulfil the commandments of God, or truly repents of his transgressions, or who loves God with all his heart, and his neighbour as himself, has all the obedience necessary to his reception into the kingdom of God: For if God should require perfect innocence, no flesh could be saved.

But what commandments are those that God has given us? Are all those laws which were given to the Jews by the hand of Moses, the commandments of God? If they are, why are Christians not taught to obey them? If they are not, what others are so, besides the law of nature? For our Saviour Christ has not given us new laws, but counsel to observe those we are subject to; that is to say, the laws of nature, and the laws of our several sovereigns: Nor did he make any new law to the Jews in his Sermon on the Mount, but only expounded the laws of Moses, to which they were subject before. Therefore the laws of God are the laws of nature, whereof the principal is, that we should not violate our faith, that is, a commandment to obey our civil sovereigns whom we constituted over us, by mutual pact one with another. And this law of God that commands obedience to the civil law, commands by consequence obedience to all the precepts of the Bible; which (as I have proved in the

660   *Sources*

previous chapter) is there only law, where the civil sovereign has made it so; and in other places but counsel; which a man at his own peril, may without injustice refuse to obey.

Knowing what obedience is necessary for salvation and to whom it is due; we now consider faith, whom, and why we believe; and what articles or points must be believed by those who shall be saved. And first, for the person whom we believe, because it is impossible to believe any person before we know what he says, it is necessary that he is one whom we have heard speak. The person therefore, whom Abraham, Isaac, Jacob, Moses and the prophets believed, was God himself, who spoke to them supernaturally: And the person, whom the apostles and disciples that conversed with Christ believed, was our Saviour himself. But of those to whom neither God the Father nor our Saviour ever spoke, it cannot be said that the person whom they believed was God. They believed the apostles, and after them the pastors and doctors of the church who recommended to their faith the history of the Old and New Testament: so that the faith of Christians ever since our Saviour's time, has had for its foundation, first, the reputation of their pastors, and afterward, the authority of those who made the Old and New Testament the rule of faith; which none could do but Christian sovereigns; who are therefore the supreme pastors, and the only persons, whom Christians now hear speak from God; except those God supernaturally speaks to in these days[, which Hobbes argues elsewhere no longer happens]. But because there are many false prophets *gone out into the world*, other men are to examine such spirits *whether they be of God, or not* (1 John 4:1). And therefore, seeing the examination of doctrines belongs to the supreme pastor, persons without special revelation are to believe (in every Common-wealth) their supreme pastor, that is to say, the civil sovereign.

[*He bifurcates knowledge of religious truths from the belief that they are true, arguing that Christians believe because they are taught to do so. They believe because faith comes through the teaching of their ministers. He then reduces the necessary articles of faith to one doctrine.*]

The (*Unum Necessarium*) only article of faith that Scripture makes necessary for salvation is this: that *Jesus is the Christ*. By the name of *Christ* is understood the king whom God promised by the prophets of the Old Testament to send into the world to reign (over the Jews, and over other nations that believe in him) under himself eternally; and to give them that eternal life, which was lost by the sin of Adam....

Having shown what is necessary for salvation; it is not hard to reconcile our obedience to God with our obedience to the civil sovereign; who is either Christian or infidel. If he is a Christian, he allows the belief of this article, that *Jesus is the Christ*; and of all the Articles that are contained in or are deduced from it: which is all the faith necessary to salvation. And because he is a sovereign, he requires obedience to all his own civil laws; in which also are contained all the laws of nature, that is, all the laws of God: for besides

Sources 661

the laws of nature, and the laws of the church, which are part of the civil law (for the church that can make laws is the common-wealth), there are no other divine laws. Therefore, those who obey their Christian sovereign are not hindered from believing or from obeying God. But suppose that a Christian King should from this foundation, *Jesus is the Christ*, draw some false conclusions, that is to say, make some superstructure of hay or stubble, and command the teaching of the same; yet seeing St. Paul says, he shall be saved [1 Cor. 3:15]; much more shall he be saved who teaches them by the ruler's command; and much more yet, he that teaches not, but only believes his lawful teacher. And in case a subject is forbidden by the civil sovereign to profess some of his opinions, upon what just ground can he disobey? Christian kings may err in deducing a consequence, but who shall judge? Shall a private man judge when the question is of his own obedience? Or shall any man judge but he that is appointed by the church, that is, by the civil sovereign that represents it? Or if the Pope or an apostle judge, may he not err when deducing a consequence? Did not one of the two, St. Peter or St. Paul, err concerning the superstructure, when St. Paul confronted St. Peter to his face [Gal. 2:11–13]? There can therefore be no contradiction between the laws of God and the laws of a Christian common-wealth.

And when the civil sovereign is an infidel, every subject that resists him sins against the laws of God (for such as are the laws of nature) and rejects the counsel of the apostles, that admonishes all Christians to obey their princes, and all children and servants to obey their parents and masters in all things [e.g., Rom. 13:2; Eph. 6:1–8; Col. 3:20–22]. And for their *faith*, it is internal and invisible; they have the licence that Naaman had [2 Kings 5], and need not put themselves into danger for it. But if they do, they ought to expect their reward in heaven, and not complain about their lawful sovereign; much less make war upon him. For he that is not glad of any just occasion for martyrdom does not have the faith he professes, but only pretends in order to disguise his disobedience. When an infidel king knows he has a subject who waits for the second coming of Christ that precedes the conflagration of the present world, a subject who intends to obey him (who is intent on believing that Jesus is the Christ), a subject who thinks he is bound to obey the laws of that infidel king (which all Christians are obliged in conscience to do), what infidel king would be so unreasonable that he would persecute or execute such a subject?

And this shall suffice, concerning the kingdom of God and ecclesiastical policy. I do not claim to advance my own position but only to show the consequences that seem to me deducible from the principles of Christian politics (which are the Holy Scriptures), in confirmation of the power of civil sovereigns and the duty of their subjects. And in making arguments from Scripture, I have endeavoured to avoid texts whose interpretation are obscure and to avoid arguing about interpretation; and to put forward only plain interpretations that agree with the harmony and scope of the whole Bible; which

662 Sources

was written for the re-establishment of the kingdom of God in Christ. For it is not the bare words, but the scope of the writer that gives the true light, by which any writing is to be interpreted; and they that insist upon single texts, without considering the main design, can derive nothing from them clearly; but rather by casting atoms of Scripture like dust before men's eyes, they make everything more obscure than it is; an ordinary artifice of those who seek their own advantage rather than the truth.

187 Doll Allen, *Petition of an Enslaved Christian Girl in Bermuda* (1652)

Keywords: #Colonisation, #Slavery, #Freedom, #Women
Region: #Bermuda
Group: #Church of England?, #Puritan?

Bermuda's permanent settlement by the English dates back to a 1609 shipwreck, and it was established as a Puritan colony in 1612. Like other Separatist or Puritan colonies (e.g., **Plymouth, Massachusetts Bay** and Providence Island), enslaved labour became an important part of their colony. Bermuda led the way in tobacco exportation, and they imported enslaved persons of African and American Indian descent. Four decades after the Puritans established Bermuda, the daughter of an enslaved woman and a white settler challenged the system that held her in bondage. Doll Allen's petition is reproduced below. She lived with her father, William, who could have legally treated her like any other slave. While it is unclear how he viewed her status, he educated her and introduced her to Christianity, a faith that she embraced. Local magistrates tried to remove her from her father and redefine her slave status as 'perpetual'. These actions prompted her direct appeal to the Bermuda Company.

Much of the justification for slavery rested on the premise that those enslaved had been taken in a 'just war', but this could not apply to Doll since she was born after her mother was captured. Therefore, Doll's petition also questioned whether slave status could be inherited, as scholars like **Hugo Grotius** maintained. Her status was also partly determined by religious difference and justified by the claim that enslavement might prove spiritually beneficial.[273] Doll's conversion complicated justifications for slavery. She appealed to shared faith as a factor that differentiated her from 'heathen' slaves. She was allowed to live with her father, and her life after 1659 is unknown. Michael Jarvis writes:

> Her case was especially complex because Barbados lawmakers had recently recognised religion as a criteria to differentiate Christian (de facto white) servants from Negro (de facto heathen) slaves. If baptism and

664   *Sources*

Christian education negated continued bondage, then a large portion of Bermuda's enslaved population could justifiably claim freedom.... A mulatto teenager's petition thus threatened to destabilise the institution of slavery as it had locally developed over the past three decades.[274]

J. H. Lefroy, ed., *Memorials of the Discovery and Early Settlement of the Bermudas or Somers Islands, 1511–1687* (London: Longmans, Green, and Co., 1879), 34. Text modernised by the editors.

———

At a General Court of the Somer Islands Company held at the accustomed place in Watling Street (Tuesday the 5th of October, 1652).

The petition of Doll Allen setting forth how her father, William Allen, out of his tender care and Fatherly affection, did bring her up from the cradle unto 15 years of age, during which time she had the privilege of Christian people, and now being at a Woman's estate is taken from her father, and reputed a perpetual slave, and therefore she prays that the Honourable Company, since it has pleased God to set a distinction between her and the heathen negroes, by providentially allotting her birth among Christians, and making her free on account of the ordinances of Christ, that they will be pleased to restore to her that freedom which is due to her father's right, and give her liberty to dispose of herself in such service as she may find most proper to her condition.

188 Frederick William, *On Tolerating Contentious Protestants* (1652)

Keywords: #Toleration, #Pluralism, #Freedom of Religion
Region: #Germany
Group: #Reformed, #Calvinist | #Lutheran

Frederick William, the 'Great Elector' of Brandenburg (1620–1688), came to power in 1640 at a low point for his dynasty. Sweden had entered the Thirty Years' War, and their forces continued to occupy much of the Elector's lands. He entered into a truce with Sweden, and at the **Peace of Westphalia** (1648), Sweden demanded and received land in compensation for their military involvement. The Great Elector also benefited from the Peace. Westphalia reaffirmed the statement from the 1555 **Peace of Augsburg** that allowed the prince to set religious policy within their land (*cuius regio, eius religio*). Westphalia, unlike Augsburg, extended this privilege to Reformed princes, and Frederick William was a Calvinist. The following document dates to a few years after Westphalia. It evidences some of the tensions involved in trying to fairly treat those of a different Protestant faith. His concern about Lutherans was simple: should a sovereign elevate people to positions of leadership when they might undermine loyalty to the state?[275]

W. F. Reddaway, *Select Documents of European History, Vol 2: 1492–1715* (London: Methuen, 1930), 188–189.

———

As for the exercise of the Augsburg Confession, it is clear and undeniable that the Estates enjoy it unhindered, and we never supposed that the least among them thought otherwise, nor have they any ground for the slightest complaint or infringement, least of all of exclusion from public or ecclesiastical office or from universities and schools.... The most numerous and considerable appointments in the principal Colleges are rather in the hands of the Lutherans than the Calvinists. We believe that no Lutheran Elector or prince in the whole Roman Empire can be found who would act towards the Calvinists with our impartiality.... If peace-loving theologians could be found (a great rarity to-day) who could restrain their untimely and needlessly bitter

666 Sources

zeal so as to refrain from unchristian reviling, slander and condemnation in school and pulpit, we should not hesitate to give them places in the theological faculty also. But the Lutheran Estates cannot seriously suppose that we should commit the young men who will serve in church and state to teachers who revile, slander and condemn our religion and thereby make us hated by our subjects. Thereby we should burden our conscience.

189 Mary Cary, *Twelve Humble Proposals to the Supreme Governours of the Three Nations* (1653)

Keywords: #Tax, #Eschatology, #Magistrate, #Education, #Justice, #Law, #Land, #Women
Region: #England, #Economics, #Charity
Group: #Fifth Monarchist | #Puritan, #Presbyterian

Little is known about Mary Cary (fl.1620–1653) – also known by the surname Rande. She wrote during the British Civil Wars and Interregnum, and resided in London during the period of her writing. Eschatological interpretations of the wars pervaded her earlier works, and towards the end of her publishing career, she became a Fifth Monarchists. The 'Fifth Monarchists' derived their name from prophecies in Daniel and Revelation. This apocalyptically minded group grew out of Puritanism during the British Civil Wars and sought to bring about the 'Rule of the Saints'. Some embraced violence as a means of constructing dominion on grace and ushering in the millennial age where Christ would directly reign on earth. Cary vigorously argued for the saint's right to preach and utter prophesies – irrespective of training, sex, and governmental authorisation.

She offered counsel through her writings to the nation – instructing both high and low in the demands of God. In her works, she advocated for the poor and for freedom of conscience. She argued that the state should tolerate sects and that the sects should tolerate each other and recognise other Christian groups as (albeit imperfect) followers of God. In *Twelve Humble Proposals*, she championed the right of individuals to propose governmental reforms. Among her proposals, she advocated relief for the poor, the reform of the universities so that the poor could attend, the use of English in legal discourse, and awarding magisterial qualifications based on character, rather than not financial standing.[276]

Extracts from Mary Cary [Rande], *Twelve Humble Proposals to the Supreme Governours of the Three Nations Now Assembled at Westminster* (1653). Text modernised by the editors.

668 *Sources*

1 Proposal. That the supreme governors always would remember those who Rule over men must be just, ruling in the fear of God.
2 Proposal. That they would always remember that Jesus Christ must now reign, and so act as those that are officers deputed by him.
3 Proposal. That they would make it all their care to do service for Christ in their place and leave the care of themselves and their posterity wholly to him.
4 Proposal. That they would be speedy in doing the work of Christ: 'made hast and delayed not to keep thy righteous judgements' (Ps. 119:60).
5 Proposal. That they would zealously endeavour to propagate the gospel.

  1 That tithes be abolished.
  2 That blind Priests may have no encouragement to mislead poor souls.
  3 That the Pastors and gifted brethren of all the churches of Christ in the nation be desired to preach in public meeting places.
  4 That two or three parishes be reduced to one
  5 That godly Presbyterians and all other godly preachers may have free liberty alike to preach.
  6 That such as are magistrates, and all others that are gifted, and of holy and godly conversations, be desired to preach.
  7 That the universities be newly modelled.
  8 That some ways of maintenance out of the public treasury be provided for Gospel preachers, but not by way of compulsion from the people.

6 Proposal. That the poor be seriously considered, and speedily provided for, being a work the Lord requires special care should be taken of it.
7 Proposal. That those of lower status may have as much or more favour shown them in courts of justice or otherwise than the richest sort.
8 Proposal. That commissioners be appointed to dispatch all businesses and redress all grievances of people in the respective counties where they live.
9 Proposal. That all unprofitable and strife-increasing and substance-devouring laws, and lawyers be abolished and abandoned.
10 Proposal. That none be henceforth constituted justice of the peace or administrators of justice but such as are men fearing God and hating covetousness.
11 Proposal. That no officer that serves the common-wealth in such employments as are not hazardous to their lives or healths be allowed more than 200£ per annum. [*This allowed people to be paid for government work, but not to be made rich by it.*]
12 Proposal. That no more of the lands belonging to the Common-wealth [confiscated in the late war] be henceforth sold, but reserved to the people taxes and excise and custom [by leasing the land out].

The *unworthy servant of Christ and his people*, M. R.
  London, July 7th 1653.

190 Roger Williams, *Toleration and Compulsion in the Ship of State* (1655)

Keywords: #Toleration, #Pluralism, #Coercion, #Conscience, #Commonwealth, #Obedience, #Liberty
Region: #United States
Group: #Puritan, #Baptist, #Seeker | #Roman Catholic, #Judaism, #Islam, #Non-Christians

Roger Williams wrote voluminously about the freedom of conscience, and some worried that his ideas would eventually lead to anarchy. Williams cautioned against libertinism and antinomianism throughout his writings. In the following letter, he offered a vivid illustration of toleration in the metaphor of the 'ship of state'. Whatever religion the passengers onboard adhered to, they should not be compelled to worship or be prohibited from it. The captain, however, was responsible for justice and good order and may steer the ship, demand pay for transport, or compel those onboard to follow the laws.

John Russell Bartlett, ed., *The Letters of Roger Williams* (Providence, RI: Narragansett Club, 1874), 278–279.

———

To the Town of Providence.

[Providence, January, 1655]

That ever I should speak or write a tittle, that tends to such an infinite liberty of conscience, is a mistake, and which I have ever disclaimed and abhorred. To prevent such mistakes, I shall at present only propose this case: There goes many a ship to sea, with many hundred souls in one ship, whose weal and woe is common, and is a true picture of a commonwealth, or a human combination or society. It hath fallen out sometimes, that both papists and protestants, Jews and Turks, may be embarked in one ship; upon which supposal I affirm, that all the liberty of conscience, that ever I pleaded for, turns upon these two hinges – that none of the papists, protestants, Jews, or Turks, be forced to come to the ship's prayers or worship, nor compelled from their own particular prayers or worship, if they practice any. I further add, that I

670 *Sources*

never denied, that notwithstanding this liberty, the commander of this ship ought to command the ship's course, yea, and also command that justice, peace and sobriety, be kept and practiced, both among the seamen and all the passengers. If any of the seamen refuse to perform their services, or passengers to pay their freight; if any refuse to help, in person or purse, towards the common charges or defence; if any refuse to obey the common laws and orders of the ship, concerning their common peace or preservation; if any shall mutiny and rise up against their commanders and officers; if any should preach or write that there ought to be no commanders or officers, because all are equal in Christ, therefore no masters nor officers, no laws nor orders, nor orders nor punishments; – I say, I never denied, but in such cases, whatever is pretended, the commander or commanders may judge, resist, compel and punish such transgressors, according to their deserts and merits. This if seriously and honestly minded, may, if it so please the Father of lights, let in some light to such as willingly shut not their eyes. I remain studious of your common peace and liberty.

Roger Williams

191 *Resenting and Restricting the Jewish Community of New Netherland (1655–1656)*

Keywords: #Exile, #Refugee, #Toleration, #Colonisation
Region: #United States | #Netherlands, #Brazil
Group: #Dutch Reformed | Judaism, #Roman Catholic, #Mennonite, #Lutheran, #Puritan

The first recorded Jewish person in the Americas was invited by **Elizabeth I** to join the ill-fated Roanoke expedition because of his expertise in mining. In 1586, he returned to London, where he was charged with 'blasphemy' a few years later, and his fate remains unknown. When **Dutch Brazil** fell back into the hands of the Portuguese in 1654, many who lived and traded there sought refuge in other Dutch colonies. Nearly two dozen Jewish refugees arrived in 1654, and it was thought that they came from Brazil. The governor, Peter Stuyvesant, protested their presence to officials from the West India Company, but the refugees appealed to the Jewish community in Holland to plead their case. Around this time, Reverend Megapolensis also wrote to his ecclesiastical superiors in Holland, and his letter is reproduced below. Both Stuyvesant and Megapolensis rehearsed antisemitic tropes in an attempt to ensure that **freedom of religion in New Netherland** did not extend to Jewish persons. The West India Company thought otherwise, although they did so because of financial interests rather than warm affections, as the second source indicates. Similarly, the authorities of New Netherland only tolerated Quakers after other inhabitants protested the un-Christian behaviour (**Flushing Remonstrance, 1657**). As the end of Megapolensis' letter indicates, he also loathed other tolerated Protestants in the colony.[277]

1. Jacob Rader Marcus, ed., *The Jew in the American World: A Source Book* (Detroit, MI: Wayne State University Press, 1996), 32; 2–4. Hugh Hastings, ed., *Ecclesiastical Records: State of New York* (Albany, NY: James B. Lyon, 1901), I:338, 348–349, 352.

———

672   *Sources*

1. Rev. Johannes Megapolensis, New Amsterdam, to the Classis, the Governing Board of the Dutch Reformed Church, Amsterdam, Holland, March 18, 1655.

...Last summer some Jews came here from Holland, in order to trade. Afterwards some Jews, poor and healthy, also came here on the same ship with D[omine Theodorus] Polheijmis. It would have been proper that these had been supported by their own nation, but they have been at our own charge, so that we have had to spend several hundred guilders for their support. They came several times to my house, weeping and bewailing their misery, and when I directed them to the Jewish merchant [Jacob Barsimson?] they said that he would not lend them a single stiver. Now again in the spring some have come from Holland, and reported that a great many of that lot would yet follow and then build here their synagogue. This causes among the congregation here a great deal of complaint and murmuring. These people have no other God than unrighteous Mammon, and no other aim than to get possession of Christian property, and to win all other merchants by drawing all trade towards themselves. Therefore, we request your Reverences to obtain from the Lords Directors that these godless rascals, who are of no benefit to the country, but look at everything for their own profit, may be sent away from here. For, as we have here Papists, Mennonites and Lutherans among the Dutch; also many Puritans or Independents, and many Atheists and various other servants of Baal among the English under this Government, who conceal themselves under the name of Christians; it would create a still greater confusion, if the obstinate and immovable Jews came to settle here.

———

2. Directors in Holland to Peter Stuyvesant (26 April 1655)

[*Governor Stuyvesant was disinclined to allow any religious diversity. In the following letter, authorities in Holland urged to open up New Netherland to the Jews.*]

We would have liked to agree to your wishes and request, that the new territories should not be further invaded by people of the Jewish race, for we foresee from such immigration the same difficulties, which you fear; but after having further weighed and considered this matter, we observe, that it would be unreasonable and unfair, especially because of the considerable loss, sustained by the Jews in the taking of Brasil and also because of the large amount of capital, which they have invested in shares of this Company. After many consultations we have decided and resolved upon a certain petition made by said Portuguese Jews, that they shall have permission to sail to and trade in New Netherland, and to live and remain there, provided the poor among them shall not become a burden to the Company or the community, but be supported by their own nation. You will govern yourself accordingly.

———

Sources 673

3. Classis of Amsterdam to the Consistory of New Netherland
(26 May 1656)

[*They lament that the missionary work among Indigenous communities has not had the success they hoped and then comment on the growing religious pluralism in the colony.*]

From [your silence] we conclude that the Lutherans must have abandoned their intention of procuring a minister of their persuasion. Our Rev. Classis, indeed, looked into this matter as an affair of great consequence; for the Mennonists and English Independents, of whom there is said to be not a few there, might have been led to undertake the same thing in their turn, and would probably have attempted to introduce public gatherings. In fact we are informed that even the Jews have made request of the Hon. Governor, and have also attempted in that country to erect a synagogue for the exercise of their blasphemous religion. Out of all these things, indeed, there would have arisen a very Babel. One cannot contemplate, without great emotion of soul, how greatly a pastor's labour would have been increased under such circumstances, and beset with obstacles, and what difficulties would have arisen to interfere with their good and holy efforts for the extension of the cause of Christ. The Hon. Directors appear to have acted in this matter in a very Christian manner. Let us then – we here in this country and you there – employ all diligence to frustrate all such plans, that the wolves may be warded off from the tender lambs of Christ.

———

4. Failure of Peter Stuyvesant to Follow Orders Concerning the Jews
(14 June 1656)

[*Authorities in the Netherlands were not pleased that Governor Stuyvesant insufficiently followed repeated orders concerning the Jews, also disapproving of his mistreatment of Lutherans. Since he failed to carry out general orders, they detailed the rights that Jewish communities had in New Netherland, including those related to worship, trade, owning houses and establishing communities. The following order sought to bring greater conformity across the Atlantic in how Jewish communities were treated in Dutch lands. However, after this letter, in April 1657, authorities in New Amsterdam denied Jacob Cohin Henrdricus' request to open a bakery and Asser Levy's request to be admitted as a Burgher (a position he held in Amsterdam).*]

Honourable, Vigorous, Pious, Dear, Faithful:

We have seen and heard with displeasure, that against our orders of the 15th of February 1655, issued at the request of the Jewish or Portuguese nation, you have forbidden them to trade to Fort Orange and the South River; also the purchase of real estate, which is granted them without difficulty here in this country; and we wish it had not been done and that you had obeyed our orders, which you must always execute punctually and with

674 *Sources*

more respect: Jews or Portuguese people however shall not be employed in any public service, (to which neither are they admitted in this city), nor allowed to have open retail shops; but they may quietly and peacefully carry on their businesses as before, and exercise in all quietness their religion within their houses, for which end they must without doubt endeavour to build their houses close together in a convenient place on one or the other side of New Amsterdam – at their own choice – as they have done here.

192 Michael Wendeler, *Politics of the Turkish Republic* (1655)

Keywords: #Tyrant, #Republic, #Common Good, #Empire, #Absolutism, #International Relations, #Treaty
Region: #England | #Turkey
Group: #Lutheran | #Islam, #Roman Catholic

Michael Wendeler (1610–1671) studied philosophy, mathematics, and astronomy in Wittenberg before pursuing further theological education. He taught at Wittenberg from 1637 and held successive positions in philosophy, ethics, moral philosophy, and theology. He wrote widely, including on Jewish and Muslim political thought. The following selection comes from Wendler's treatise on the political government of the Ottoman Empire. Much as Luther had done over a century earlier, he framed Ottoman military power through an eschatological lens, connecting Ottoman with Catholic 'tyranny' in the war against the church of Christ. Wendler compared the Turkish republic to the threefold Aristotelian ordering of governments, identifying that regime as an inherently unstable 'tyranny'. He argued that such a form of government preyed upon the unhappy people who groaned under it. The apparent success of the empire was not attributable to the wisdom or justice of the Ottomans themselves. Rather, God allowed them a modicum of success to chastise Christians.

A similar argument appears in the literature of colonial interactions in the Americas: positive Indigenous qualities were attributed to divine restraint, negative qualities to satanic influence. Wendler presented the Ottoman Empire as a threat (because of their worldliness) and inconsequential (because their strength was owing to divine chastisement). He spent considerable time arguing against Machiavelli and his affinity for Turkish politics, arguing that the resistance theory of *Vindiciæ Contra Tyrannos* (1579) would be the proper antidote. Finally, he argued that the Turk could not be trusted in war or peace, but that the pope was even worse. Thus, Wendler showed how talk of the vices and virtues of non-Christians could be used as a polemical tool against Catholics.[278]

676 *Sources*

Mehmet Karabela, *Islamic Thought Through Protestant Eyes* (New York: Routledge, 2021), 246–253.

———

Tyranny, the worst of all states, is farthest from a kingdom; since it is opposed to the highest good. Along with Aristotle, I judge a tyrant by how much he contributes to the public good. A tyrant is the opposite of a king. It is the duty of a king to give his full attention to the state; a tyrant is one who neglects and subverts the public good for the sake of his own convenience. The resulting vices follow from this inversion of the public good.....

The Turkish Sultan is properly called a monarch: not a king however, but rather a *dominus* or a tyrant, for these two terms are easily interchangeable. I would say that the Turk is a *dominus*; Jean Bodin says that according to their laws only the caliph, the High Priest, can openly lay claim to domination, or call himself the *dominus* of any household....

Such an empire should not be long-lasting: it is violent, and everyone hates it, even those who live in the highest honour. Therefore, I will try to explain why it has endured so long. That tyranny has now persevered for 355 years. It was founded by the hard work and fraud of Osman in 1300. This empire is long-lasting and savage; I do not attribute its strength to the domination of an unjust barbarian, but to the punishment of a divine godhead, mutual hatred and wars with their neighbours....

From all these things that I have recounted, it is certain how unlucky and weak the Turkish Empire was. It lasted so long not because of their rulers' counsel, but because of God's anger and their neighbours' discord. If these two means of preserving the longevity of the Turkish state did not exist, it would most certainly have been weak, short, and defenceless against all invaders.

Therefore, politicians who recommend this way of ruling to German princes err enormously. What the inauspicious Niccolò Machiavelli advocated in the previous century is well known to all learned men. In particular, the way this monstrous man advocates for a hypocritical prince can be seen from Chapter 8 onward. Indeed, throughout *The Prince*, Machiavelli seems to concern himself with opportunistically attributing to the good prince everything that Aristotle said about the Sophist's way of preserving tyranny....

The dogmas in [Machiavelli's work] are so horrible that they need no refutation. Anyone who has been steeped in their first letters and any sort of piety can refute this new and absurd doctrine. But anyone who does not know how to oppose these dogmas should read [*Vindiciæ contra tyrannos* (1579)]. He disputes Machiavelli's evil arts, depraved advice, and false and pestiferous doctrine....

Although the Turkish Empire became an absolute tyranny in all degrees, it is properly called a republic, since my definition of a republic agrees with

Aristotle's description, which does not distinguish between a good republic and a bad one....

Finally I must say a few words about the Turks' judicial system and treaties. The handing down of judgements among the Turks is quick, but not just. For their highest judge, knowledgeable in law, and of a grand old age, judges cases on the spot. Appeals can be made to a *kadı* [judge], who in dubious cases seeks the opinion of a *Muftī* [jurist]. But since the Turks still have few written laws, the judges have great influence on sentencing. Hence, the Turkish judges never judge promptly without bribes, and they have hands in the pockets of the litigants on both sides. This causes the calamitous oppression of the poor and the whole republic. For those who afflict the poor are so powerful, especially if they are eminent, that they cannot be punished without damage to the empire.

Almost all treaties are measured by their usefulness. For this reason, no one is an ally to the Turks. They do not comply with treaties, except when it pleases them, on the grounds that they believe it sacred to destroy their enemies in any way....

Our political officials and writers are not the only ones who desire treaties with heretics, but the Turks do as well during times of great necessity. Georg Schönborner was in a great uproar, constantly urging that such treaties should be completely forbidden. On top of that, political elites point out that we could enter a treaty less safely with the Pope than with a Turk. This is because Papists equivocate, and their oaths are vain, due to the ready acquittal of the Jesuits, and also because of the difficulty of the Successor [Pope], who denies that the law can constrain him. If the number of pages permitted, I would say more about this tyrannical republic.

193 *The Confession of the Waldenses* (1655)

Keywords: #Confession of Faith, #Government, #Persecution, #Intervention, #Violence
Region: #Italy, #France, #England
Group: #Waldensian

Protestant Reformers claimed to be the 'true' church who opposed the 'false' church based in Rome. If this were true, the 'false' church had an ancient lineage and the true church was relatively young. Protestantism thus posed an intellectual problem to European Christianity, particularly because it appeared as if God had not preserved the church over the centuries, as Protestants believed. This intellectual hurdle was easily answered by many Protestants because they argued that even in times of darkness, God would have preserved a remnant of true Christians. These included Peter Waldo (Waldensians), John Wycliffe (Luddites), and Jan Hus (Hussites) who were seen by Protestants as forerunners of the Reformation. By the early sixteenth century, Waldensians entertained similar ideas as Martin Luther, although there were some meaningful differences relating to the role of good works in salvation. They also overlapped with the teachings of some radical Reformers, most notably their rejection of violence and critique of Christians in power. However, they ended up aligning with the Swiss Reformed in 1532, although the Waldensians tended to emphasise an ethics based on the Sermon on the Mount over the Reformed emphasis on doctrine.

As Catholic regions sought to stamp out heterodoxy in the second half of the sixteenth century after the Council of Trent, the Waldensians suffered increased persecution and many abandoned their position on non-resistance. In the first half of the seventeenth century, there was a large Waldensian presence in southern France and northern Italy. The 1655 massacre of 1,700 Waldensians prompted outrage across Europe, and **Oliver Cromwell** and **John Milton** helped to secure the Restoration of their rights. The following source was produced shortly after the 1655 massacre as part of a campaign for international aid. The Waldensians presented themselves as true Christians who were worthy of sympathy and support from international Protestantism.[279]

The Creeds of Christendom, vol. III: The Evangelical Protestant Creeds, ed. Philip Schaff (New York: Harper and Brothers, 1887), 757–770 (757, 767–769).

A Brief Confession of Faith of the Reformed Churches of Piedmont

Published with their Manifesto on the occasion of the frightful massacres of the year 1655.

Having understood that our adversaries, not contented to have most cruelly persecuted us, and robbed us of all our goods and estates, have yet an intention to render us odious to the world by spreading abroad many false reports, and so not only to defame our persons, but likewise to asperse with most shameful calumnies that holy and wholesome doctrine which we profess, we feel obliged, for the better information of those whose minds may perhaps be preoccupied by sinister opinions, to make a short declaration of our faith, such as we have heretofore professed as conformable to the Word of God; and so every one may see the falsity of those their calumnies, and also how unjustly we are hated and persecuted for a doctrine so innocent.

We believe,

XXVI. That this Church can not fail, nor be annihilated, but must endure forever

XXXII. That God hath established kings and magistrates to govern the people, and that the people ought to be subject and obedient unto them, by virtue of that ordination, *not only for fear, but also for conscience' sake,* in all things that are conformable to the Word of God, who is the King of kings and the Lord of lords.

And for a more ample declaration of our faith we do here reiterate the same protestation which we caused to be printed in 1603, that is to say, that we do agree in sound doctrine with all the Reformed Churches of France, Great Britain, the Low Countries, Germany, Switzerland, Bohemia, Poland, Hungary, and others, as it is set forth by them in their confessions; as also in the Confession of Augsburg, as it was explained by the author, promising to persevere constantly therein with the help of God, both in life and death, and being ready to subscribe to that eternal truth of God with our own blood, even as our ancestors have done from the days of the Apostles, and especially in these latter ages.

Therefore we humbly entreat all the Evangelical and Protestant Churches, notwithstanding our poverty and lowness, to look upon us as true members of the mystical body of Christ, suffering for his name's sake, and to continue unto us the help of their prayers to God, and all other effects of their charity, as we have heretofore abundantly experienced, for which we return them our most humble thanks, entreating the Lord with all our heart to be their rewarder, and to pour upon them the most precious blessings of grace and glory, both in this life and in that which is to come. Amen.

194 John Phillips, *Humanitarian Conquest in the Caribbean* (1656)

Keywords: #Intervention, #Colonisation, #War, #Slavery
Region: #England, #Dominican Republic, #Haiti, #Jamaica, #Spain
Group: #Puritan | #Roman Catholic, #Indigenous American, #African

Colonising Protestants defined themselves not only against the Indigenous 'other', but also against the colonising 'other'. For them, Spain exemplified ungodly and unjust colonisation, and a large body of Protestant literature rehearsed anti-Catholic tropes, such as the 'Black Legend'. A persistent theme running through Protestant colonisation – a theme found across several denominations, nations, and centuries – was that Protestant colonisation was more restrained and humane than its Catholic counterpart. At the root of this belief lay the conviction that the Protestant presence in the Americas should be physically and spiritually beneficial for the Indigenous inhabitants.[280] The following source from 1656 shows an example of this thinking Puritan Parliamentarians had recently defeated Charles I in battle and executed him for treason. They then subdued Ireland and Scotland and also defeated the Dutch. While some advocated an attack on Rome, others sought to overturn Catholic colonies overseas. Propelled by a chain of victories, **Oliver Cromwell** launched an ambitious plan to topple Spain's global empire by capturing the island of Hispaniola (Dominican Republic and Haiti).

A century earlier, the Spanish Dominica priest Bartolomé de las Casas detailed atrocities in the Americas and called for greater rights for Indigenous persons. Cromwell believed the Spanish were ripe for providential judgement. He hoped that enslaved peoples would rise up when they saw the Spanish came under attack. The campaign was unsuccessful, but England did capture Jamaica. The following source comes from *Tears of the Indians* (1656), a translation of Las Casas' account of Spanish atrocities by John Phillips. Phillips, who was a nephew of John Milton, dedicated his translation to Oliver Cromwell, urging him and the English people to take vengeance on violent Spaniards. This work contained several woodcuts, and there was a striking resemblance to other images of violence: namely, the persecuted in *Foxe's Book of Martyrs* and those slain in the Thirty Years' War, in colonial

Virginia and during the 1641 rebellion in Ireland. In all of these cases, illustrations provided a visual feast of atrocity, victimisation, and bloodshed that seemed to cry out for divine vengeance. In Phillips' rendering, Cromwell matches the militant virtue of David, Joshua, and Jehu, and the Spaniards exceed the wickedness of the Canaanites and Ahab.[281]

John Phillips, *Tears of the Indians* (London, 1656). Text modernised by the editors.

———

Deuteronomy 29:15

Therefore thine eye shall have no compassion; but life for life, tooth for tooth, hand for hand, foot for foot.

To His Highness, Oliver [Cromwell], Lord Protector of the Commonwealth of England, Scotland and Ireland, with the dominions thereto belonging.

May it please your Highness,

I have here laid prostrate before the throne of your justice, above 20 millions of the souls of the slaughtered Indians; whose forced departure from their bodies, cruelty itself compassionates. Yet I think I hear a sudden stillness among them; the cry of blood ceasing at the noise of your great transactions, while you arm for their revenge. By this it is apparent that Your Highness well observes the will of the Most High, using your vast power and dignity only for the advancement of His glory among the nations: while the divine deity bequeathes you back again immediate recompense; crowning you, like his holy warrior, *David*, with the highest degree of earthly fame. Therefore he hath inspired Your Highness with a prowess like that of *Joshua*, to lead His armies forth to battle; and a zeal more devoutly fervent than that of *Jehu*, to cut off the idolater from the earth. Which divine virtues appear so eminent in you, that there is no man, who opposes not himself against heaven, but extols your just anger against the bloody and popish nation of the Spaniards, whose superstitions have exceeded those of *Canaan*, and whose abominations have excelled those of *Ahab*, who spilt the blood of innocent *Naboth*, to obtain his vineyard.

And now, may it please Your Highness, God having given you a full victory over your enemies in this land, and a fixed establishment, by the prosperous and total quelling of those determined spirits; certainly, there is no true Englishman who does not lift up his eyes to heaven with thanks to Almighty God, that you have made the land so happy, as to be the admiration of other nations, who have laid themselves at your feet for alliances, as knowing your wonderful successes both by sea and land.

Pardon me, great Sir, if next my zeal to heaven, the loud cry of so many bloody massacres, far surpassing the popish cruelties in *Ireland* [since the rebellion of 1641], the honour of my country, of which you are as tender as

682 *Sources*

of the apple of your own eye, hath induced me, out of a constant affection to your highness service, to publish this relation of the *Spanish Cruelties*; whereby all good men may see and applaud the justness of your proceedings: being confident that God, who hath put this great design into your hands, will also be pleased to give it a signal blessing; which is the prayer of

Your Highness
most faithful and most obedient Servant,
J. Phillips.

195 James Harrington, *Commonwealth of Oceana* (1656)

Keywords: #Authority, #Equality, #Absolutism, #Balance of Powers, #Church-State Relations, #Common Good, #Law, #Conscience, #Commonwealth
Region: #England
Group: #Church of England

The Commonwealth of Oceana (1656) has had an outsized impact on early modern political theory in Europe and the United States, but comparatively little is known about its author, James Harrington (1611–1677). He was a country gentleman in England's Midlands who remained aloof throughout the First English Civil War. During Charles I's lengthy captivity, he attended the king and remained close to him for a while. He seems to have rejected both the **Leveller** egalitarianism of many in the Puritan army and the Episcopal establishment favoured by Charles. Harrington had visited Venice and highly esteemed republican government. Slightly earlier republican works were written by Sir Henry Vane and Marchmont Nedham. Throughout *Oceana*, Harrington responded to **Thomas Hobbes's *Leviathan*** – a book that had many detractors after publication in 1651. Harrington was sympathetic to Machiavelli's political realism and his high esteem for human reason. He agreed with many Renaissance authors that the path forward required a resurrection of pre-gothic precedents. He culled positive and negative examples from across sacred and secular history, particularly from the ancient 'commonwealths' of the Hebrews, Greeks, and Romans. He was unconventionally Christian, and his deep admiration for ancient non-Christian polities stirred suspicions.

Oceana was written, in part, to explain why the English monarchy was dissolved, but its immediate context was the disappointment of the short-lived English Commonwealth (1649–1653) that resulted in the protectorate of Oliver Cromwell. England provided the thinly veiled reference point for the imagined civilisation of Oceana, and the fictional nature of the work has led to it being classified as utopian. Harrington urged those victorious in the British Civil Wars to seize the opportunity afforded by the collapse of the

684 *Sources*

government and remake society in a republican mould. The now-dissolved British monarchy was supported by medieval deference for hierarchy, nobility, and vast inequalities of wealth. He argued that there should be limits on the accumulation of wealth and the destitution of the poor. Political stability rested on rightly distributed property and the division of powers. If regular elections rotated the office-bearers, the government would be more dynamic and less corrupt.[282]

James Harrington, *The Commonwealth of Oceana*, ed. Henry Morley (London: George Routledge & Sons, 1887), 44–48.

———

But let a commonwealth be equal or unequal, it must consist, as has been shown by reason and all experience, of the three general orders; that is to say, of the senate debating and proposing, of the people resolving, and of the magistracy executing. Wherefore I can never wonder enough at Leviathan, who without any reason or example, will have it that a commonwealth consists of a single person, or of a single assembly....

But to finish this part of the discourse, which I intend for as complete an epitome of ancient prudence, and in that of the whole art of politics, as I am able to frame in so short a time

The two first orders, that is to say, the senate and the people, are legislative, whereunto answers that part of this science which by politicians is entitled 'of laws;' and the third order is executive, to which answers that part of the same science which is styled 'of the frame and course of courts or judicatories'. A word to each of these will be necessary.

And first for laws: they are either ecclesiastical or civil, such as concern religion or government.

Laws, ecclesiastical, or such as concern religion, according to the universal course of ancient prudence, are in the power of the magistrate; but, according to the common practice of modern prudence, since the Papacy, torn out of his hands.

But, as a government pretending to liberty, and yet suppressing liberty of conscience (which, because religion not according to man's conscience can to him be none at all, is the main), must be a contradiction, so a man that, pleading for the liberty of private conscience, refuses liberty to the national conscience, must be absurd.

A commonwealth is nothing else but the national conscience. And if the conviction of a man's private conscience produces his private religion, the conviction of the national conscience must produce a national religion. Whether this be well reasoned, also whether these two may stand together, will best be shown by the examples of the ancient commonwealths taken in their order.

In that of Israel the government of the national religion appertained not to the Priests and Levites, otherwise than as they happened to be of the Sanhedrim or senate, to which they had no right at all but by election. It is in this capacity therefore that the people are commanded, under pain of death, 'to hearken to them, and to do according to the sentence of the law which they should teach [Deut. 17:10];' but in Israel the law ecclesiastical and civil was the same, therefore the Sanhedrim, having the power of one, had the power of both. But as the national religion appertained to the jurisdiction of the Sanhedrim, so the liberty of conscience appertained, from the same date, and by the same right, to the prophets and their disciples; as where it is said, 'I will raise up a prophet,.... and whoever will not hearken to My words which he shall speak in My name, I will require it of him [Deut. 18:10]'. The words relate to the prophetic right, which was above all the orders of the commonwealth; whence Elijah not only refused to obey the king, but destroyed his messengers with fire [2 Kings. 1]. And whereas it was not lawful by the national religion to sacrifice in any other place than the Temple, a prophet was his own temple, and might sacrifice where he would, as Elijah did at Mount Carmel [1 Kgs. 18]. By this right John the Baptist and our Saviour, to whom it more particularly related, had their disciples, and taught the people, whence is derived our present right of gathered congregations; wherefore the Christian religion grew up according to the orders of the commonwealth of Israel, and not against them. Nor was liberty of conscience infringed by this government, till the civil liberty of the same was lost, as under Herod, Pilate, and Tiberius, a three-piled tyranny.

To proceed, Athens preserved her religion, by the testimony of Paul, with great superstition.... Nevertheless, if Paul reasoned with them, they loved news, for which he was more welcome; and if he converted Dionysius the Areopagite, that is one of the senators, there followed neither any hurt to him, nor loss to Dionysius [Acts 17:34]. And for Rome, if Cicero, in his most excellent book 'De Natura Deorum', overthrew the national religion of that commonwealth he was never the farther from being consul. But there is a meanness and poorness in modern prudence, not only to the damage of civil government, but of religion itself; which admits not of sensible demonstration..., engage to believe no otherwise than is believed by my Lord Bishop, or Goodman Presbyter, is a pedantism that has made the sword to be a rod in the hands of schoolmasters; by which means the Christian religion is the farthest of any from countenancing war, there never was a war of religion but since Christianity, for which we are beholden to the Pope; for the Pope not giving liberty of conscience to princes and commonwealths, they cannot give that to their subjects which they have not themselves, whence both princes and subjects, either through his instigation or their own disputes, have introduced that execrable custom, never known in the world before, of fighting for religion, and denying the magistrate to have any jurisdiction concerning it, whereas the magistrates losing the power of religion loses the liberty of conscience, which in that case has nothing to protect it....

To come to civil laws: if they stand one way and the balance another, it is the case of a government which of necessity must be new modelled; wherefore your lawyers, advising you upon the like occasion to fit your government

686 *Sources*

to their laws, are no more to be regarded than your tailor if he should desire you to fit your body to his doublet. There is also danger in the plausible pretence of reforming the law, except the government be first good, in which case it is a good tree, and (trouble not yourselves overmuch) brings not forth evil fruit; otherwise, if the tree be evil, you can never reform the fruit, or if a rot that is naught bring forth fruit of this kind that seems to be good, take the more heed, for it is the ranker poison. It was nowise probable, if Augustus had not made excellent laws, that the bowels of Rome could have come to be so miserable eaten out by the tyranny of Tiberius and his successors. The best rule as to your laws in general is, that they be few. Rome, by the testimony of Cicero, was best governed under those 12 tables.... You will be told, that were the laws be few, they leave much to arbitrary power; but where they be many, they leave more, the laws in this case, according to Justinian and the best lawyers, being as litigious as the suitors. Salon made few, Lycurgus fewer laws; and commonwealths have the fewest at this day of all other governments.

Now to conclude this part with a word *de judiciis*, or of the constitution or course of the courts; it is a discourse not otherwise capable of being well managed by particular examples, both the constitution and course of courts being divers in different governments, but best beyond compare in Venice, where they regard not so much the arbitrary power of their courts but the constitution of them, whereby that arbitrary power being altogether unable to retard or do hurt to business, produced and must produce the quickest despatch, and the most righteous dictates of justice that are perhaps in human nature.

196 Richard Baxter, *Directions to Justices of the Peace* (1657)

Keywords: #Church-State Relations, #Authority, #Magistrate, #Punishment, #Justice, #Law, #Morality, #Commonwealth, #Poverty
Region: #England
Group: #Presbyterian

Born in Shropshire, England, Richard Baxter (1615–1691) entered the ministry as the British Isles slid into civil war. While serving as a chaplain to the Parliamentary forces, he grew alarmed by radical ideas emerging within the army. He is known as an attentive and thorough Presbyterian minister at Kidderminster. His works were widely read throughout the Atlantic world, and **John Eliot** translated *A Call to the Unconverted* into Algonquian. Many of Baxter's writings contained important comments on government, conflict, and the events of his day. For example, *A Christian Directory* (1673) included extensive discussions of war, submission, slavery, and politics. Baxter published his most important political work, *A Holy Commonwealth* (1659), as the Commonwealth government was falling apart. This work provided an invaluable window into the motivations that led him to support Parliament, and he argued that resistance might be justified in some circumstances. Although Baxter disagreed with **James Harrington's** *Oceana*, both works theorised about an ideal society and how to bring that society about. The Hebrew Bible loomed large in Baxter's political thought, as it did in Eliot's *The Christian Commonwealth* (1659). After the Restoration, Baxter was periodically persecuted for his nonconformity. He retracted *A Holy Commonwealth* in 1670, and Oxford University ordered it to be burned in 1683.[283]

Commonwealths would struggle to be holy if the magistrates were unholy. Baxter wrote the following source, *Directions to justices of peace* (1657), 'at the request of a Magistrate'. It contained little of the theory and nuanced reasoning that would later appear in his longer works on politics and ethics. It was a direct and concise application of Christian principles to the daily life of leaders. It was printed as a broadside, a single-sided document that might be put on a wall for display. Baxter argued for a close relationship between the church and state. His ministry was known for the effort he put into visiting

688 *Sources*

his parishioners rather than remaining aloof. Similarly, he urged magistrates to be proactive and vigilant as they searched for vice and resisted the temptations to pervert justice.

Richard Baxter, *Directions to Justices of Peace* (London: Robert White, 1657). Text modernised by the editors.

———

I shall suppose that you begin with God, in the public hearing of his word for your direction, and by fasting and prayer to beg his blessing on your endeavours, and I must suppose that you are *resolved to do God's will when you know it*. Yet be very jealous of your own heart, lest there be any latent reserves; for *in this is your greatest danger* (Jer. 42:1–5; 43:1–4).

Direction 1. *Remember the original and nature of authority*: It is a beam from the sovereign authority of God; it can have no lower spring: as there can be no being but from God's being (Rom. 13:1–6). You are all God's officers. The sense of this will teach you: (1) Whose *work* you have to do, and to abhor the doctrine that would make you so humanly focused as to have nothing to do in matters of religion, or of concerns about the soul. (2) And whose *will* you must consult. (3) And to take heed of *abusing* so Divine a thing, by negligence or misuse. (4) And to use your authority *reverently* and *religiously*, and not carelessly as if it were a common thing. As ministers must speak with reverence because they are God's messengers, so you must rule with pious reverence because you are God's officers. (5) Nor must *others* be allowed to *despise* your authority because it is from God and is necessary to the common good. (6) And this will teach you to look to *God* for protection, approbation, encouragement and reward.

Direction 2. *Be sure that your ultimate end is God* and, next to that, the *public good*. Let the pleasing and honouring of God, and the benefit of men be the very thing that you intend and seek: and not any carnal pleasure in your own exaltation, power or honour. If you do the best works for *self*, and not for God, you debase them and lose them; and make them sins, and you serve yourself and not God in them; and your reward will be accordingly. Be exceedingly vigilant about your hearts: for *selfishness* is deep rooted; it is the common cause of man's perdition, and the sin that overturns the governments of the earth and destroys the governors. Look not at sin only as a troubler of the nation and wrong to men, but as an offence to God and a cause of damnation. Do all your work with respect to God and everlasting life. It is the Pope's device to make men believe that magistrates are only concerned with men's bodies and temporal affairs, except as executioners of his decrees....

Direction 4. *Do not forget the two great aims of your work: To encourage the good and be a terror and avenger to the evil* (Rom. 13). And therefore you should not be the *same* to persons that are not the *same*; but be a Lamb to the Lambs, and a Lion to the Wolves (Ps. 18:25–26). God, who is no respecter of persons, is still the greatest Distinguisher of persons....

Direction 5. *Never make the law an instrument of evil: Set not the letter against the sense: interpret not the sense to be against the end.* As the sense is the law, so the end informs the means and is above it. The law of the land may restrain you from doing some good that the law of God commands to the sovereign rulers: but it cannot warrant you to do any evil. There is no power but from God and God gives none against himself (Rom. 13:4).

Direction 6. *See that you are the person you would have others be. Be examples of holiness, temperance and righteousness to all the people....*

Direction 7. *Decide to do good with all your skill, care and industry.* Have no restriction but your own ability. Study it, and make it your daily work to do all the good you can: You have an office to discharge, and the work is not of secondary importance. Abhor the principles and spirit that entice magistrates to shift off all the displeasing and troublesome work and to do no more than is thrust upon them, and they know not how with honour to avoid. If you know of unlicensed or abusive alehouses or other wickedness that calls for redress; do not wait until you are urged, and conviction is offered you; but make enquiry and procure the convicted, and do not think it is below you or too much to search for vice, and do all within your power to suppress it. If the laws of the land do not necessitate that you do this, God's law does and by this law you shall be judged. (1) Is not sin God's enemy? (2) Have you not taken up arms against it by a double engagement as Christians and as Magistrates? (3) Does it not bring down judgements, and is it not the fire in our thatch, and the plague of the Common-wealth? ...

Direction 8. *Do not think that doing your duty will come without many temptations:* See therefore that you are fortified with self-denial and resolution: Those who are punished by you will complain, every sinner will have a friend who solicits you for an exemption from the penalty. Your own selfishness will tempt you to be partial to your friends, to gentlemen, and to those who may do you a pleasure or a displeasure. If you cannot deny both self and all for Christ, you cannot be true to him (Luke 14:26, 33). Be resolved that God must be pleased if that means everyone else will be displeased. You are captains in Christ's army against sin and satan and therefore must excel in courage (Josh. 1:7; 1 Chron. 22:13; 28:10, 20; 2 Chron. 15:7; 19:6–7). He that cannot deny his friend, or self, will deny God (1 Sam. 2:29–30). Have greater pity, more for the nation and men's souls than the body of a sinner (Prov. 19:18; 23:13–14). If punishment will do the *sinner* no good, it will restrain many others, and so is due to the Common-wealth.

Direction 9. *Remember still that your opportunity will be short:* both of office and life: and therefore be up and doing, lest you give a dreadful account of your stewardship; as an unprofitable servant that bore the sword in vain and only passed the time sitting in the seat and wearing the clothes of a magistrate....

Direction 11. Do not *defraud the poor of anything that the law has made their due....*

690 *Sources*

Direction 12. *Let zeal and prudence go together*. Do not listen to the *impious* who would destroy your zeal and plunge you into mortal guilt, on the pretence of prudence and moderation: Nor yet to any who would draw you to rash imprudent actions, on pretences of piety or zeal. In cases where your duty is plain, go through with it, whatever it costs you: But in cases that are too hard for you, if it is a difficulty concerning the law, consult with those skilful in the law (lest the malicious take advantage of your mistakes). If there is a doubt about the laws of God, advise with some judicious ministers of Christ, whose office it is to teach you, and rule by God's word, as it is yours to command and rule them by the sword. It is never well, but where magistrates and ministers go together, each knowing his proper place and work (Mal. 2:6–7; Deut. 17:8–9, 12; 1 Cor. 4:1; 1 Thess. 5:12; Heb. 13:7, 17, 24).

Proverbs 29:2.

When the righteous are in authority, the people rejoice but when the wicked rule, the people mourn.

197 *Flushing Remonstrance Against Persecuting Religious Outsiders* (1657)

Keywords: #Conscience, #Freedom of Religion, #Church-State Relations, #Pluralism, #Toleration, #Persecution
Region: #United States
Group: #Dutch Reformed | #Quakers, #Presbyterian, #Independent, #Baptist, #Islam, #Judaism

Quakers were persecuted in Old and New England, and some moved nearer to the Dutch settlements out of a desire for safety and with the purpose of evangelisation. As elsewhere, their presence was largely unwelcome. Their religious tenets were deemed incompatible with authority and societal stability. In New Netherland, they were forbidden to preach, and it was against the law to take a Quaker into one's home, even for a night. In November 1656, legal action was taken against an English Baptists in Flushing (present-day Queens, New York). When authorities clamped down on Quakers in Flushing in 1657, the people recoiled at this religious persecution, and they defended the rights of Quakers. In the first source, the Flushing Remonstrance, they argued that they could not support persecuting Quakers or several other groups who were also children of Adam. Toleration was the glory of the Dutch, and the same should be true of New Netherland. Furthermore, Christ had hated persecution in his name, and the Remonstrants said Christians should even look for the presence of Christ in persons from other denominations. The second excerpt shows the response of the magistrates to this petition and demonstrates how the inhabitants of Flushing put themselves at risk for defending Quakers.[284]

"Ecclesiastical Records of the State of New York," published by The State of New York, under the supervision of Hugh Hastings, State Historian (Albany, N.Y., 1901), I:412–413; *The Friends' Intelligencer*, vol. no. 1 (1838): 85–86. Text modernised by the editors.

———

692 *Sources*

The Flushing Remonstrance

Remonstrance of the Inhabitants of Flushing, Long Island, against the Law Against Quakers and the Subsequent Proceedings by the Government Against Them and Others for Favouring Quakers.

Right Honourable,

You have been pleased to send up unto us a certain prohibition or command, that we should not receive or entertain any of those people called Quakers because they are considered by some to be seducers of the people; for our part, we cannot condemn them in this case, neither can we stretch out our hands against them to punish, banish or persecute them, for out of Christ, God is a consuming fire, and it is a fearful thing to fall into the hands of the living God [Heb. 10:31]; we desire therefore in this case not to judge lest we be judged [Matt. 7:1], neither to condemn lest we be condemned, but rather let every man stand and fall to his own. Master we are bound by the law to do good unto all men, especially to those of the household of faith [Gal. 6:10]; and though for the present we seem to be insensible of the law and the lawgiver; yet when death and the law assault us: If we have not our advocate to seek, who shall plead for us in this case of conscience between God and our own souls; the powers of this world can neither attack us neither excuse us, for if God justify who can condemn [Rom. 8:33–34], and If God condemn there is none can justify; and for those jealousies and suspicions which some have of them [the Quakers] that they are destructive unto magistracy and ministry that cannot be; for the magistrate has the sword in his hand and the minister has the sword in his hand as evidenced by those two great examples which all magistrates and ministers are to follow Moses and Christ; whom God raised up maintained and defended against all the enemies both of flesh and spirit, and therefore that which is of God will stand, and that which is of man will come to nothing [Acts 5:38]: and as the Lord hath taught Moses, or the civil power, to give an outward liberty in the state by the law written in his heart designed for the good of all and can truly judge who is good and who is evil, who is true and who is false, and can pass definitive sentence of life or death against that man which rises up against the fundamental law of the States General, so he hath made his ministers a savour of life unto life, and a savour of death unto death [2 Cor. 2:16].

The law of love, peace and liberty in the states extending to Jews, Turks and Egyptians, as they are considered the sons of Adam, which is the glory of the outward State of Holland; so love, peace and liberty extending to all in Christ Jesus, condemns hatred, war and bondage; and because our Saviour says it is impossible but that offence will come, but woe be unto him by whom they comes [Luke 17:1], our desire is not to offend one of his little ones in whatsoever form, name or title he appears in, whether Presbyterian, Independent, Baptist or Quaker; but shall be glad to see anything of God in any of them: desiring to do unto all men as we desire all men should do unto us, which is the true law of both church and state; for our Saviour says this is the law and the prophets [Matt. 7:12]; Therefore if any of these said persons come in love unto us, we cannot in conscience lay violent hands upon them, but give them free access into our town and houses as God shall persuade our consciences; and in this we are true subjects both of the church and state; for we are bound by the law of God and man to do good unto all men, and evil to no man; and this is according to the patent and charter of our town given unto us in the name of the States General which we are not willing to infringe and violate, but shall hold to our patent and shall remain your humble subjects the inhabitants of Vlissingen; written the 27th of December in the Year 1657.

———

Response from Magistrates

We, director-general and council in New Netherland, having maturely considered the mutinous orders and resolutions adopted by the sheriff, clerk, magistrates, and the majority of the inhabitants of the village Vlissingen, signed on the 27th of December, 1657, and delivered a few days after to the director-general by the sheriff, Tobias Fecco, by which resolution they not only contemn, infringe, and oppose the aforesaid order of the director-general and council against the Quakers, and other sectarians, daring to express themselves in so many words, that they cannot stretch out their arms against them [Quakers], to punish, banish, or persecute them by imprisonment; that they, so as God shall move their consciences, will admit each sectarian in their houses and villages, and permit them to leave these again, which, as said before, is contrary to the orders and placards of the director-general and council, and directly in opposition of these; a case, indeed, of the worst and most dangerous tendency, as treading, absolutely, the authority of the director-general and council under their feet, and, therefore, well deserved to be corrected and punished, for an example to others, with the total annihilation of the privileges and exemptions which were granted from time to time ... to the aforesaid village; and besides this, with a corporal punishment and banishment of each one who signed the aforesaid mutinous resolution. But the director-general and council, in the hope of greater prudence in the future, are actuated towards their subjects more by mercy than by the extremes of rigorous justice; more so, as they were inclined by several circumstances to believe that many, yea, the majority, were encouraged by the previous signatures of the sheriff, clerk, and some of the magistrates. Wherefore, the director-general and council pardon, remit, and forgive this transgression against the authority of the director-general and council....

[*The magistrates then seek to prevent disobedience, including by limiting town-hall meetings and providing for better religious education.*]

198 Edward Sexby and Silius Titus, *Killing No Murder* (1657)

Keywords: #Violence, #Revelation, #Justice, #Tyrant, #Authority, #Consent, #Submission
Region: #England
Group: #Leveller

Edward Sexby (c.1616–1658) fought under **Oliver Cromwell** in the early stages of the English Civil War and in the New Model Army after its formation. He became a **Leveller** spokesman representing Puritan radicals within the army. He was involved in the Putney Debates (1647), which discussed the incorporation of wider suffrage into a new national constitution. After the regicide, he served Parliament in various functions, sometimes falling from their favour. The Commonwealth sent him to France in an effort to leverage internal factions for the benefit of England. After Cromwell became Lord Protector in 1653, Sexby grew disillusioned with the government and conspired against him. He tried to unite discontented persons of various political and religious persuasions, providing them with arguments about resistance and assassination. The following work, *Killing No Murder* (1657), was published under the name of William Allen, but was likely produced by Sexby and Silius Titus, along with other possible contributors. Titus' allegiances shifted several times during the war. He was a Presbyterian supporter of Parliament who then became a Royalist. Sexby was arrested in 1657 and died in the Tower of London in 1658.

This short work argued that Catholics could assassinate a head of state when sanctioned to do so by the pope. English Protestants recently killed their head of state, but they did so through a legal trial.[285] *Killing No Murder* argued that anyone could take divine vengeance into their own hands. The tract stirred controversy and was followed by unsuccessful attempts to kill Cromwell. In the following excerpt, Sexby argued from scripture that biblical assassins were models and that the Christian assassin did not need a miraculous commission from God. Second, he argued that the people did not tacitly consent to Cromwell's government, and therefore, his regime was illegitimate.[286]

Sources 695

William Allen, *Killing Noe Murder. Briefly Discoursed in Three Quaestions* (1657). Text modernised by the editors.

———

The law of God itself decreed certain death (Deut. 17:17) to that man that would act presumptuously and submit to no decision of justice. Who can read this and think a tyrant ought to live? But certainly, neither that nor any other law would have any effect if there were no way to execute it. But in a tyrant's case, process and citation have no place, and if we will only have formal remedies against him, we are sure to have none. There is small hope of justice when the malefactor has the power to condemn the judge.

Therefore, the only remedy against a tyrant is Ehud's dagger [Judg. 3:21], without which all our laws were fruitless, and we helpless. This is that high court of justice where Moses brought the Egyptian [Exod. 2:11–12]: whether Ehud brought Eglon: Samson the Philistines [Judg. 16:28–30]: Samuel Agag [1 Sam. 15:33]: and Jehoiada the she tyrant Athaliah [2 Kings 11:15]....

Objection 1: That these examples out of Scripture are of men that were inspired of God, and they therefore had that call and authority for their actions, which we cannot pretend to have, so that it would be unsafe for us to turn their actions into examples, except we had similar justifications.

Objection 2: That there is now no opposition made to the government of his Highness [Cromwell], that because the people continued to work and trade at home and abroad, making use of the laws and appealing to his Highness' courts of justice: That all this argues the people's tacit consent to the government; and that this government is now to be considered lawful, and the people's obedience voluntary.

Solution 1: I answer with learned [John] Milton that if God commanded these things, this is a sign they were lawful and commendable. But secondly, as I observed in the relations of the examples themselves; Neither Samson nor Samuel alleged any other cause or reason for what they did, but retaliation, and the apparent justice of the actions themselves. Nor had God appeared to Moses in the bush when he slew the Egyptian; nor did Jehoiada allege any prophetic authority or other call to do what he did, but that common call which all men have, to do all just actions that are within their power, when the ordinary course of justice ceases.

Solution 2: If commerce and petitioning authority were enough to argue that the people consented, thus giving tyranny the name of government, then no tyranny would have lasted more than a few weeks. Certainly, we then wrongly call Caligula and Nero 'Tyrants', and those who conspired against them were 'rebels'; unless we believe that during their entire reign, the people in Rome kept their shops shut and did not open their temples or courts. With no less absurdity, we imagine that during the whole 18 years when Israel served Eglon and six years that Athaliah reigned, the Israelites refrained from trading, petitioning or other public acts: otherwise, Ehud and Jehoiada were both traitors, the one for killing his king, the other his queen.

199 Congregational Churches of England, *The Savoy Declaration* (1658)

Keywords: #Conscience, #Liberty, #Magistrate, #Violence, #War, #Censorship, #Blasphemy, #Submission, #Heresy
Region: #England
Group: #Congregational

As the British Civil Wars progressed, success and failure contributed to the fragmenting of the 'godly party'. Towards the beginning of the wars, Presbyterians and Puritans found common cause in church and state, culminating in military cooperation on the battlefield and theological debates at the **Westminster Assembly**. As England's Parliament grew ascendant in their war against Charles I, a gulf emerged between those who wanted a Presbyterian settlement and Independents who wanted to model their congregational structure on New England. Most Presbyterians desired a limited monarchy under Charles I, and many Independents advocated holding Charles accountable for crimes against God and humanity, as discussed at the 1648 **Windsor Prayer meeting**. The war against Charles I untuned the string of authority in church and state, and, hark, what discord followed. English Protestantism fragmented into ever smaller and more alarming groups, notably the **Levellers, Diggers, Quakers,** and Fifth Monarchists. After the execution of Charles I, England struggled to find a lasting and satisfactory political or religious settlement, leading to a *de facto* measure of religious pluralism.

Many Independents remained close to **Oliver Cromwell**'s regime, and some tried to bridge the divide between Independents and Presbyterians. In 1658, Independent Congregationalists sought to draw up a confession of faith that might serve as the basis for a national church. Representatives from around 120 congregations gathered at the Savoy Palace (Westminster). Several had taken part in the Westminster Assembly of Faith in the 1640s. Prominent Congregationalists like **John Owen,** with some moderate Presbyterians in attendance, tried to hammer out Congregational distinctives. Their theology was informed by Calvinism and affirmed much of the *Westminster Confession*. On matters of church polity, it was indebted to the 1648 Cambridge Platform, drawn up by New England divines.[287]

The following excerpt from the Savoy Declaration relates to a Christian's freedom of conscience and the relationship with the civil magistrate. The first section opens with a discussion of liberty in the Hebrew Bible and Christian Scriptures, arguing that both testaments enshrined freedom. True faith must be free of human compulsion, and blind obedience undermined conscience and reason. However, Christian liberty did not entail the liberty to sin. The section on civil magistracy opened conventionally, rooting human government in the divine ordinance. Christians could hold civil authority and partake in just wars; an unsurprising conclusion given their involvement in the British Civil Wars. Magistrates had a duty to foster true faith and punish blasphemy while also protecting the right to theological disagreement; a delicate balancing act. The conclusions of this 1658 assembly were overshadowed by political events, most notably the death of Oliver Cromwell. The government devolved to his son Richard, whose sympathies lay with Presbyterianism. However, his regime quickly unravelled. Although the Restoration of the Stuarts in 1660 blunted the Savoy Declaration's impact on England, it was embraced by the Synod of Massachusetts (1680), and it also influenced the Saybrook Platform (1708).[288]

Congregational Church in England and Wales, *A Declaration of the Faith and Order Owned and Practised in the Congregational Churches in England; Agreed Upon and Consented Unto by their Elders and Messengers in their Meeting at the Savoy, Octob. 12. 1658* (London, 1659), 15, 17–18.

———

Chapter 21: Of Christian Liberty, and Liberty of Conscience.

The Liberty which Christ hath purchased for Believers under the Gospel, consists in their freedom from the guilt of sin, the condemning wrath of God, the rigour and curse of the Law, and in their being delivered from this present evil world, bondage to Satan, and dominion of sin, from the evil of afflictions, the fear and sting of death, the victory of the grave, and everlasting damnation; as also in their free access to God, and their yielding obedience unto him, not out of slavish fear, but a child-like-love, and willing mind: All which were common also to Believers under the Law, for the substance of them; but under the New Testament the liberty of Christians is further inlarged in their freedom from the yoake of the Ceremonial Law, the whole Legal administration of the Covenant of Grace, to which the Jewish Church was subjected, and in greater boldness of access to the Throne of Grace, and in fuller communications of the free Spirit of God, then Believers under the Law did ordinarily partake of.

II God alone is Lord of the Conscience, and hath left it free from the Doctrines and Commandments of men, which are in any thing contrary to

698 *Sources*

his Word, or not contained in it; so that to believe such Doctrines, or to obey such Commands out of conscience, is to betray true Liberty of Conscience; and the requiring of an implicit faith, and an absolute and blind obedience, is to destroy Liberty of Conscience, and Reason also.

III They who upon pretence of Christian Liberty, do practise any sin, or cherish any lust, as they do thereby pervert the main design of the Grace of the Gospel to their own destruction; so they wholly destroy the end of Christian Liberty, which is, that being delivered out of the hands of our enemies, we might serve the Lord without fear, in holinesse and right-eousnesse before him all the dayes of our life.

CHAP. XXIV. Of the Civil Magistrate.

God the supreme Lord and King of all the World, hath ordained civil Magistrates to be under him, over the people for his own glory and the publique good: And to this end hath armed them with the power of the Sword, for the defence and incouragement of them that do good; and for the punishment of evil-doers.

II It is lawful for Christians to accept and execute the Office of a Magistrate, when called thereunto: in the management whereof, as they ought specially to maintain Justice and Peace, according to the wholsome Laws of each Common-wealth; so for that end they may lawfully now under the New Testament wage war upon just and necessary occasion.

III Although the Magistrate is bound to incourage, promote, and protect the Professors and Profession of the Gospel, and to manage and order civil administrations in a due subserviency to the interest of Christ in the World, and to that end to take care that men of coroupt minds and conversations do not licentiously publish and divulge Blasphemy and Errors, in their own nature subverting the faith, and inevitably destroying the souls of them that receive them: Yet in such differences about the Doctrines of the Gospel, or ways of the worship of God, as may befal men exercising a good conscience, manifesting it in their conversation, and holding the foundation, not disturbing others in their ways or worship that differ from them; there is no warrant for the Magistrate under the Gospel to abridge them of their liberty.

IV It is the duty of people to pray for Magistrates, to honour their persons, to pay them Tribute and other dues, to obey their lawful commands, and to be subject to their Authority for conscience sake. Infidelity, or difference in Religion, doth not make void the Magistrates just and legal Authority, nor free the people from their obedience to him: from which, ecclesiastical persons are not exempted, much lesse hath the Pope any power or jurisdiction over them in their dominions, or over any of their people, and least of all to deprive them of their dominions, or lives, if he shall judge them to be Hereticks, or upon any other pretence whatsoever.

200 Pieter Corneliszoon Plockhoy, An Ideal and Loving Society (1659)

Keywords: #Colonisation, #Family, #Love, #Poverty, #Servants, #Slavery
Region: #United States, #Netherlands
Group: #Mennonite

Pieter Corneliszoon Plockhoy (c.1625–c.1664) was born in Zierikzee in the Dutch province of Zeeland. He was part of a Mennonite community and entered Amsterdam's intellectual and artistic life in his early twenties. He stirred controversy for some of his beliefs on politics and religion, particularly regarding polygamy. Plockhoy thought **Oliver Cromwell's** England fostered social reform. He moved there in 1658 and wrote several appeals to Cromwell and the English – laying out his ideas for an ideal community. He thus joined the chorus of **Levellers, Diggers, Quakers,** Fifth Monarchists, and others who fervently advocated for social and religious reform. Unlike many of them, he decided to plant his society in the Americas. He gained an audience with Cromwell but did not receive the backing he desired. As England grew more hostile to ideas like his at the Restoration, Plockhoy sought backing from Amsterdam for his commonwealth.

The Dutch settled Zwaanendael (Valley of Swans, in present-day Delaware) in the early 1630s, but the settlement was destroyed by the Algonquians. A few decades later, Plockhoy and 24 families established another short-lived settlement in 1663. The Algonquians did not recognise Dutch claims to the land, frustrating Plockhoy's ideal settlement from the start. The community was soon snuffed out by the English in 1664 as part of the Second Anglo-Dutch War. It is likely that the inhabitants were driven from their land, killed, or sold into slavery in Virginia. Plockhoy may have outlived the settlement by several decades, but evidence of his life after 1664 is sparse.[289] The following extract comes from the introduction to one of his works that laid out the plans for his godly society.

Pieter Corneliszoon Plockhoy, *A Way Propounded to Make the Poor in These and Other Nations Happy, by Bringing Together a Fit, Suitable, and Well Qualified People Unto One Houshold-Government, or Little-Common-Wealth* (London: G. C., 1659), 3–4. Text modernised by the editors.

700 *Sources*

A way propounded to make the poor in these and other nations happy, etc.

Having seen the great inequality and disorder among men in the world, that not only evil governors or rulers, covetous merchants and tradesmen, lazy, idle and negligent teachers, and others, have brought all under slavery and bondage: But also a great number of the common handy-craft men, or labourers (by endeavouring to decline, escape or cast off the heavy burden) do fill all things with lies and deceit, to the oppressing of the honest and good people, whose consciences cannot bear such practises, therefore I have (together with others born for the common welfare) designed to endeavour to bring four sorts of people, whereof the world chiefly consists out of several sects into one family or household-government, *viz.* husband-men, handy-crafts people, mariners, and masters of arts and sciences, to the end that we may better reject the yoke of temporal and spiritual *Pharaohs*, who have long enough domineered over our bodies and souls, and that we may set up again (as in former times) righteousness, love and brotherly sociableness, which are scarcely to be found anywhere, in order to convince those who place all greatness only in domineering, and not in well-doing, contrary to the pattern and doctrine of the Lord Jesus, who came not to be served but to serve, and gave his life a ransom for many [Matt. 10:28]; appointing his kingdom unto his apostles, as it was appointed to him from his father, answering them when they murmured, who after his departure should be the greatest amongst them, said; *If any among you would be greatest, let him be the servant of all* [Luke 22:26]. In direct opposition and contradiction to the world where they are counted as the greatest who have most servants, and not they that do most service to others, and therefore the world's greatness and the greatness of Christians differ as light and darkness, whereas true Christians being merciful do endeavour to ease men's burdens, instead thereof, others (as if there were not trouble enough in the world) are still making the burden heavier with new devices setting themselves forth daily, in their sight as if their design were to vex and grieve poor people (and stir them up to impatience) with their excess and riot.

201 Andrzej Wissowatius and Joachim Stegman, *Preface to the Racovian Catechism* (1659)

Keywords: #Conscience, #Freedom of Religion, #Confession of Faith
Region: #Poland | #England
Group: #Unitarian, #Socinian

In the mid-1560s, the Reformed Church in Poland split, and the Minor Reformed Church came to advocate an antitrinitarian theology that would later become known as Unitarianism. These ideas flourished among a community that was comprised of exiles in Raków. From 1597, **Fausto Sozzini** (1539–1604) emerged as a leader of this radical community, and his name became a scare word among theologians and magistrates across Europe. He advocated free religious choice, challenged prevailing conceptions of church and state, and rejected the use of the sword by Christians. After his death, his followers systematised and published his teachings in the *Racovian Catechism* (Polish, 1605).

Poland was once home to considerable religious pluralism, but Catholicism was returning to dominance. Religious minorities felt the pressure, and they had few places to relocate. As Sarah Mortimer notes, Socinians struggled to carve out a space in a Europe torn between Catholics and the major Protestant branches: 'German and Dutch theologians believed that Socinian arguments weakened the ability of the Protestants to withstand this Catholic threat, something which helps to explain the often lurid terms in which they denounced Socinus and his followers'.[290] A Latin edition of the *Racovian Catechism* was published in 1609 and dedicated to **King James VI and I** of England, likely out of a desire that this powerful Protestant monarch would protect them. However, James expressed disdain for the document.[291]

The Catechism was revised and expanded several times over the following century. In particular, during the Civil Wars in the 1650s, heterodox or novel religious ideas gained a hearing. In this climate, the *Racovian Catechism* was published in English in 1652. Ministers closely aligned with Parliament, like **John Owen**, denounced the work. Parliament suppressed it because it 'doth contain matters that are Blasphemous, Errronious and Scandalous'.[292] Many in England who wanted greater latitude for differences in beliefs and

702 *Sources*

practices still thought Socinian teachings were beyond the bounds. The following preface was written by Andrzej Wissowatius and Joachim Stegman and appeared before a 1659 edition of the Catechism.

Thomas Rees, ed., *The Racovian Catechism, with Notes and Illustrations* (London: Longman, et al., 1818), xcv–xcvi, ciii–civ.

———

It is not without just cause that many pious and learned men complain at present also, that the Confessions and Catechisms which are not put forth, and published by different Christian Churches, are hardly any thing else that apples of Eris, trumpets of discord, ensigns of immortal enmities and factions among men. The reason of this, that those Confessions and Catechisms are proposed in such a manner that the Conscience is bound by them, that a yoke is imposed upon Christians to swear to the words and opinions of men; and that they are established as a Ruler of Faith, from which, every one who deviates in the least is immediately assailed by the thunderbolt of an anathema, is treated as a heretic, as a most vile and mischievous person, is excluded from heaven, consigned to hell, and doomed to be tormented with infernal fires.

Far be from us this disposition, or rather this madness. Whilst we compose a Catechism, we proscribe nothing to any man: whilst we declare our own opinions, we oppress no one. Let every person enjoy the freedom of his own judgement in religion; only let it be permitted to us also to exhibit our view of divine things, without injuring or calumniating others. For this is the golden Liberty of Prophesying which the sacred books of the New Testament so earnestly recommended to us, and wherein we are instructed by the example of the primitive apostolic church. 'Quench not the spirit', says the apostle (1 Thess. 5:19–20)....

But neither do we ask for this [liberty of prophesying] without limitation and restriction; but wish it to be restrained by the reins of Piety, Charity and Prudence. Piety demands that nothing should be said or done against conscience; that nothing be uttered reproachful to God and Christ, or contrary to his glory and commands. Charity teaches us that no one should be injured, that scandal, calumnies, railing accusations against our neighbour, invidious and unfair representations of the opinions of others, should be avoided: – and in the other hand, that our equity, gentleness, and modesty

———

Chapter 4: *Of a Common-wealth in General, and Civil Power Civil.*

1

Therefore to proceed, observe that a community is like a matter without form in respect of something that it must receive, yet a matter and a subject disposed and *in proxima potentia* to receive a form to perfect it: and this form is what we call a Common-wealth, a polity, a state, wherein we may observe four things. (1) That it is an order. (2) An order of superiority and subjection: this is the general nature of it. (3) An order of superiority and subjection in a community. (4) Such an order tending to the peace and happiness of a community....

[On this fourth point, he notes:] Because there may be such an order in a community of wicked men and devils, if that might be called a community, where the association is unjust, as properly it cannot; therefore it must be such an order as tends to and contributes directly to the peace and happiness of the community. An unjust order cannot do this. To better understand this, you must know that all spiritual and temporal communities are grounded upon that commandment of God, *Love your Neighbour as yourself* [Lev. 19:18; Mark 12:31]: where that word neighbour may truly signify a single person, yet it includes a notion of society.... This neighbour, therefore, is either a single person, yet as a society, or collective as in a family, kindred, congregation, corporation or community. This love is the true cause of all association and is the special duty of all parties associated. A common-wealth is grounded upon a branch of that great love, the fifth commandment [Exod. 20:12], which presupposing superiority and subjection, in respect of power, requires certain duties of the parties superior and subject both in a greater and lesser society. And because these duties cannot be performed in great societies, except this order be settled, therefore by that commandment, all communities are bound, so far as they are able, to erect a form of government. In this respect, polities are from God, not only allowing and approving them, nor merely as enabling men, but commanding them to be enabled to establish and preserve them established, for the better manifestation of his glory and their own greater temporal and spiritual good. From this, it is evident that both civil and ecclesiastical politics belong unto theology and are but a branch of the same.

[He argues that superiority and subjection are linked, and the act of creating a sovereign simultaneously creates subjugation].

4

Majestas est maxima in civitate potestas; majesty is the greatest power in a community, (1) Its *potestas,* power. (2) *Maxima in civitate, potestas est ius imperandi,* power is a right, to govern. It's *ius* a right, and in itself is always just, and is from some propriety, and as the absolute propriety, so the absolute power of all things is from God, and there is no power but derived from him. It's not physical but moral, and so *nomen iuris,* and may be considered as a faculty or habit, which qualifies the subject to do something which one that hath no power cannot do. The proper act of it is to govern, and in governing to command, so as to bind the subject party to obedience or punishment. This *imperium* or command is an act of the will, and presupposes some act of the understanding, and must necessarily be ineffectual and

704 Sources

in vain without a sufficient coactive force. And because the understanding may be ignorant or erroneous, the will unjust, the coactive force act accordingly: therefore the understanding of a superior as such, ought to be directed by wisdom, his commanding will by justice, and his executive force by both. And that act of power which is not thus directed is not properly an act of power, nor is any such command binding. Therefore the apostles refused to obey the charge and command of the *Jewish rulers* [Acts 5:29] when it was devoid both of wisdom and justice, and it was so much the more invalid because it was contrary to an express command of a superior Lord and Master, even Jesus Christ. This power is an excellency, and makes the party invested with it like unto *God*: and the greater it is, the greater the excellency of him who has it; though it is in itself good and just, as being from God; or rather the power of God in the intellectual creature, yet it may be exercised either too little or too much. For one that is invested with it may do less or more than his power warrants him; nay, he may act contrary to the rules of divine wisdom and justice. And such is the imperfection of man, that there is no perfect government in the world, but that God supplies all defects and aberrations. *For the Judge of all the world will do right* [Gen. 18:25]; and in the final judgement will complete all justice, and reward every man according to his works [Rom. 2:6], so that everything in any person, man or angel, will be judged.

[*He then discourses on the views of various theorists about the rights of majesty and sovereignty*].

8

Leaving everyone to his own method, I will, with submission to better judgement,

make bold to deliver my own.

[*Majesty is real which is the power to constitute, abolish, alter, reform forms of government: and it is personal which concerns foreign affairs, peace, war, treatises, embassies; and the regulation of religion and human law.*][293]

I. Therefore, majesty is real [and] personal.

Real majesty is in the community, and is greater than personal, which is the power of a Common-wealth already constituted. For, as you have heard before, this form of a Common-wealth is virtually in it before it is constituted, and their consent is the very foundation of it. And this consent, whether mediate or immediate, tacit or express, is so necessary, that although a people is conquered, yet the victor cannot govern them as men without their consent: Even more, when God designed immediately, first *Saul*, then *David*, yet the election and consent of the people did concur with and follow upon the Divine designation [1 Sam. 9–10; 16; 2 Sam. 5]. As this real majesty is a power to model a state, so its always inherent and can never be separated; insomuch, that when a form of government is dissolved, or there shall be a failure of succession, the power of the sovereign devolves unto them by the law of nature, or rather it was always in the people. As this community has the power of constitution, so it hath of dissolution, when there shall be a just and necessary cause.... subjects as subjects cannot do it, because of their subjection and obligation, whereas the community as a community is free from any obligation to any particular form, either from the laws of God, natural or positive, or from their own consent or oaths: And although the people in this consideration are bound by both the natural and positive laws of God to constitute a government, if they can, yet they are not bound to this form or that. Another act of this majesty in the community is, when they see it necessary and just and they have not only power but the opportunity to do it, to alter the form of the government: this act, as with us, is above the power of a parliament, which may have personal, yet cannot have this real majesty. For a parliament necessarily presupposes a form of government already agreed upon, whereby they are made the subject of personal sovereignty. Therefore they cannot alter or take away the cause whereby they have their being, nor can they meddle with the fundamental laws of the constitution, which if it once cease, they cease to be a parliament. If the government is dissolved, and the community still remains united, the people may make use of such an assembly as a parliament to alter the former government, and constitute anew; but this they cannot do as a parliament, but considered under another notion, as an immediate representative of a community, not of a Common-wealth, and thus considered, the assembly may constitute a government, which as a parliament cannot do, which always presupposing the constitution, as such, can act only in and for the administration. That community is wise which does, and happy which can keep their majesty so due unto them, as to limit their personal sovereigns, so as not to suffer them to take it from them, and assume it to themselves.

[*He goes on to describe 'personal majesty' – or majesty residing in persons. These persons are bound to seek the common good and have certain powers, for example, pertaining to war and peace.*]

10

This personal majesty and sovereignty acts within the Common-wealth, and with the subjects as subjects. With these it acts, (1) In matters of religion. For [the magistrate is the guardian of both books],[294] Where by magistrate, we must not understand officers, but supreme governors, as the word is taken largely by many authors, especially such as profess theology. For it is the duty, as it is the right of civil sovereign to order matters of religion, and that in the first place, so far as it tends unto or concerns the peace and happiness of a state, which depends much upon the establishment, profession and practice thereof. As they must order it, so they must not only constantly and sincerely profess, practise it themselves, but as sovereigns protect and defend their subjects in the profession and exercise of the same, so far as their coactive force and sword may justly do it. This should be their first and principal

706   *Sources*

work, which they should do, not only for the good of the people, but their own happiness, success and establishment in the throne. They are not to associate as priests or *presbyters*, nor arrogate the power of making canons, ordination, excommunication, absolution, and such like acts, which are purely spiritual, yet they may make civil laws concerning those things, and execute the same, and also ratify by civil acts the ecclesiastical canons; and punish such as shall violate the same. Yet this right presupposes that the religion, which they establish and maintain is true and instituted from heaven. It's true, that the consciences of men are subject only unto God, and to him alone are they answerable for their secret thoughts and opinions, which men can have no certain cognisance of. Yet if they introduce errors in religion or blasphemies, and seek by communicating them by word or writing to seduce, pervert or infect others, they disturb the peace of the state, offend God, and bring God's judgements from heaven upon themselves, who are guilty of such sins, and upon the sovereign and the subject of that state where they live. And in this case, though the consciences cannot be forced, yet their estates, persons, and lives are liable to the sword, and, in that respect, they may and ought to be punished by the sword of justice. This is so a right of civil sovereigns that we never read of any state of civilised people without laws concerning religion and the worship of a deity. I confess, this branch of civil power is not rightly placed, nor is the method exact, because it comes in under the heads of legislation and jurisdiction, the matter of both which are religion, men's persons, estates, and lives.

[*He closes the chapter by discussing the right to legislate and to execute laws, following this with a discussion of jurisdiction and the nature of sovereignty.*]

202 George Fox, *Friends Must Refuse Violence* (c.1660)

Keywords: #Non-Violence, #War, #Peace
Region: #England
Group: #Quaker

The Society of Friends (Quakers) grew out of the tumults of the British Civil Wars, and many early Friends fought in the Puritan forces. Their distinctive doctrine of principled pacifism took time to develop, and the principle was not initially absolute or entirely accepted among Friends. The Friends emerged from the ministry of several persons, and foremost among them was George Fox (1624–1671). He was born into a working-class Puritan family in Leicestershire and started searching for an inner light in the early 1640s. His message was deemed a political and religious threat, and as with many groups with unconventional practices who claimed divine inspiration, Fox experienced persecution. He was imprisoned in Derby from 1650 to 1651 and refused a commission in **Oliver Cromwell's** Parliamentary forces. He travelled widely as a missionary throughout England, the European continent, and the Americas. Around the world, Friends faced persecution, banishment, imprisonment, or execution, but persecution often hardened resolve and drew in converts.

The following letter likely comes from a pivotal moment for anglophone Protestantism – the 1660 Restoration of the Stuarts after a period of Puritan rule (some give the document a later date). As Puritans gained and lost power, religious offshoots proliferated: **Levellers, Diggers, Quakers,** and (most worrying of all) Fifth Monarchists. For groups like the Fifth Monarchists, obedience to God led them to take up arms against the government in an attempt to usher in the anticipated reign of Christ on earth. The Quakers adopted a different attitude towards violence. The following document from George Fox may have been produced around the Restoration in an attempt to differentiate the Friends from the Fifth Monarchists. Both groups believed they were living through eschatologically significant times, both thought most 'Christians' in England were not following Christ, and

708   *Sources*

both emphasised a divine revelation. Whereas the Fifth Monarchists embraced violence, Fox warned Friends that they must refuse the physical sword. His warning was a reminder that pacifism was not yet settled doctrine. Fox's apocalypticism was evident in his gendered language of fighting against the 'whore' from Revelation, but he insisted that this fight must be spiritual and that physical weapons disqualified one from the kingdom of Christ.[295]

Hugh Barbour and Arthur O. Roberts, eds., *Early Quaker Writings, 1650–1700* (Grand Rapids, MI: Eerdmans, 1973), 406–407.

———

All friends everywhere, keep out of plots and bustling and the arm of the flesh: for all that is among Adam's son in the fall, where they are destroying men's lives like dogs and beasts and swine, goring, rending and biting one another, and destroying one another, and wrestling with flesh and blood [Eph. 6:12]. From whence arises wars but from lust and killing [Jas 4:1]? ... And ye are called to peace [Col. 3:15], therefore follow it. And Christ is that peace, and Adam is in the fall. For all that pretend to fight for Christ, they are deceived, for his kingdom is not of this world [John 18:36]; therefore his servants doth not fight. Therefore fighters are not of Christ's kingdom, and are without Christ's kingdom, for his kingdom stands in peace and righteousness. And so fighters are in the lust, and all that would destroy men's lives are not of Christ's mind, who comes to save men's lives. Christ's kingdom is not of this world, it is peaceable; and all that be in strifes are not of his kingdom, and all such as pretend to fight for the Gospel (the Gospel is the power of God, before the devil or fall of man was), which are ignorant of the gospel, and all that talk of fighting for Sion, are in darkness, for Sion needs no such helpers. And all such as profess themselves to be ministers of Christ and Christians, and go beat down the whore [Rev. 17] with outward carnal weapons, the flesh and the whore are got up in themselves in a blind zeal.... [T]he beating down of the whore must be by the inward rising of the sword of the spirit within. All such as pretend Christ Jesus and confesseth him and runs into carnal weapons, wrestling with flesh and blood, they throw away Christ's doctrine, and flesh is got up in them, and they are weary of their sufferings; and such as would revenge themselves be out of Christ's doctrine; and such as would be stricken on one cheek, and would not turn the other [Luke 6:29] be out of Christ's doctrine, and such as do not love one another [John 13:34] and love enemies [Matt. 5:44] be out of Christ's doctrine. And therefore you that be heirs of the blessings of God, which was before the curse and fall was, come to inherit your portions.

Sources 709

Notes

1 Famous and infamous works that bear on politics include the following: *The Freedom of a Christian* (1520), *Temporal Authority: To What Extent It Should Be Obeyed* (1523), *Open Letter to the Princes of Saxony Concerning the Rebellious Spirit* (1524), *Admonition to Peace: A Reply to the Twelve Articles of the Peasants in Swabia* (1525), *Against the Robbing and Murdering Hordes of Peasants* (1525), *An Open Letter on the Harsh Book Against the Peasants* (1525), *Whether Soldiers, Too, Can Be Saved* (1526), *On War Against the Turk* (1529), *Dr. Martin Luther's Warning to His Dear German People* (1531), *On the Jews and Their Lies* (1543). For background on Luther's political thought, see Francis Oakley, "Christian Obedience and Authority, 1520–1550", in *The Cambridge History of Political Thought, 1450–1700*, ed. J.H. Burns (Cambridge: Cambridge University Press, 2008), 159–192 (174).

2 Heinz Scheible, "Melanchthon, Philipp", in *The Oxford Encyclopedia of the Reformation*, ed. Hans J. Hillebrand (Oxford: Oxford University Press, 1996), https://www.oxfordreference.com/view/10.1093/acref/9780195064933.001.0001/acref-9780195064933-e-0922 (accessed 9 October 2023).

3 Francis Oakley, "Christian Obedience and Authority, 1520–1550", in *The Cambridge History of Political Thought, 1450–1700*, ed. J.H. Burns (Cambridge: Cambridge University Press, 2008), 159–192 (174).

4 See letters in Preserved Smith and Charles M. Jacobs, trans. and eds., *Luther's Correspondence and Other Contemporary Letters* (Philadelphia, PA: Lutheran Publication Society, 1918), II:81–86 (quotes at 81, 82, and 84 respectively).

5 For background, see Carlos M. N. Eire, *Reformations: The Early Modern World, 1450–1650* (New Haven, CT: Yale University Press, 2016), 190–199.

6 For background on early Reformation approaches to poverty, see Carter Lindberg, *Beyond Charity: Reformation Initiatives for the Poor* (Minneapolis, MN: Fortress, 1993).

7 Andreas Karlstadt, *Whether One Should Proceed Slowly* (1524), in *The European Reformations Sourcebook*, ed. Carter Lindberg, 1st ed. (Malden: Blackwell, 2000), 86–87.

8 Luther, *Letter to the Christians at Strassburg in Opposition to the Fanatic Spirit* (1524), in *The European Reformations Sourcebook*, ed. Carter Lindberg, 1st ed. (Malden: Blackwell, 2000), 87.

9 Martin Luther, *Against the Heavenly Prophets* (1525), in *The European Reformations Sourcebook*, ed. Carter Lindberg, 1st ed. (Malden: Blackwell, 2000), 63–64 (64); Letter to the Princes of Saxony (July 1524), in *The European Reformations Sourcebook*, ed. Lindberg, 88. For background on Karlstadt, see Michael G. Baylor, ed., *The Radical Reformation* (Cambridge: Cambridge University Press, 1991), 263–264; and Ulrich Bubenheimer, "Bodenstein Von Karlstadt, Andreas", in *The Oxford Encyclopedia of the Reformation*, ed. Hans J. Hillebrand (Oxford: Oxford University Press, 1996), https://www.oxfordreference.com/view/10.1093/acref/9780195064933.001.0001/acref-9780195064933-e-0159 (accessed 9 October 2023).

10 J. M. Porter, *Luther: Selected Political Writings* (Minneapolis, MN: Fortress, 1974), 51.

11 Francis Oakley, "Christian Obedience and Authority, 1520–1550", in *The Cambridge History of Political Thought, 1450–1700*, ed. J.H. Burns (Cambridge: Cambridge University Press, 2008), 159–192 (168).

12 Karl-Heinz zur Mühlen, "Two Kingdoms", in *The Oxford Encyclopedia of the Reformation*, ed. Hans J. Hillebrand (Oxford: Oxford University Press, 1996), https://www.oxfordreference.com/view/10.1093/acref/9780195064933.001.0001/acref-9780195064933-e-1431 (accessed 9 October 2023).

710 *Sources*

13 Summary adapted from Matthew Rowley, "Forgetting and Remembering the Reformation's First Female Pamphleteer", Remembering the Reformation, n.d., https://remref.hist.cam.ac.uk/research/forgetting-and-remembering-reformations-first-female-pamphleteer (accessed 9 October 2023); Peter Matheson, ed., *Argula von Grumbach: A Woman's Voice in the Reformation* (Edinburgh: T&T Clark, 1995).

14 Mark A. Noll, *Confessions and Catechisms of the Reformation* (Repr., Vancouver, BC: Regent College, 2001), 37–38. For background, see Bruce Gordon, *Zwingli: God's Armed Prophet* (New Haven, CT: Yale University Press, 2021), 96–98.

15 Summary drawn from Bruce F. Gordon, *Zwingli: God's Armed Prophet* (New Haven, CT: Yale University Press, 2021), 96–98; Matthew J. Tuininga, *Calvin's Political Theology and the Public Engagement of the Church: Christ's Two Kingdoms* (Cambridge: Cambridge University Press, 2017), 41–44.

16 Ole Peter Grell, "Scandinavia", in *The Reformation World*, ed. Andrew Pettegree (London: Routledge, 2000, 257–276; Harry Lenhammar, "Vasa, Gustavus", in *The Oxford Encyclopedia of the Reformation*, ed. Hans J. Hillebrand (Oxford: Oxford University Press, 1996), https://www.oxfordreference.com/view/10.1093/acref/9780195064933.001.0001/acref-9780195064933-e-1461 (accessed 9 October 2023).

17 See documents in Carter Lindberg, ed., *The European Reformations Sourcebook*, 1st ed. (Malden, MA: Blackwell, 2000), 84–90.

18 Luther, *Admonition to Peace: A Reply to the Twelve Articles of the Peasants of Swabia* (1525), in *The European Reformations Sourcebook*, ed. Carter Lindberg, 1st ed. (Malden, MA: Blackwell, 2000), 93–95 (94).

19 Carlos M.N. Eire, *Reformations* (New Haven, CT and London: Yale University Press), 268.

20 Ulrich Bubenheimer, "Müntzer, Thomas", in *The Oxford Encyclopedia of the Reformation*, ed. Hans J. Hillebrand (Oxford: Oxford University Press, 1996), https://www.oxfordreference.com/view/10.1093/acref/9780195064933.001.0001/acref-9780195064933-e-0971 (accessed 9 October 2023).

21 Walter Klaassen, "Grebel, Conrad", in *The Oxford Encyclopedia of the Reformation*, ed. Hans J. Hillebrand (Oxford: Oxford University Press, 1996), https://www.oxfordreference.com/view/10.1093/acref/9780195064933.001.0001/acref-9780195064933-e-0596 (accessed 9 October 2023).

22 For background, see Walter Rauschenbusch, "The Zurich Anabaptists and Thomas Münzer", *The American Journal of Theology* 9, no. 1 (1905): 91–106.

23 Michael G. Baylor, *The German Reformation and the Peasants' War: A Brief History with Documents* (Boston, MA: Bedford/St. Martins, 2012), 4.

24 Peter Blickle, "Twelve Articles", in *The Oxford Encyclopedia of the Reformation*, ed. Hans J. Hillebrand (Oxford: Oxford University Press, 1996), https://www.oxfordreference.com/display/10.1093/acref/9780195064933.001.0001/acref-9780195064933-e-1430?rskey=bmTSKk&result=1 (accessed 9 October 2023).

25 James Harvey Robinson, *Readings in European History* (Boston, MA: Ginn & Company, 1906), II:99.

26 Luther, *Admonition to Peace. A Reply to the Twelve Articles of the Peasants of Swabia* (1525), in *The European Reformations Sourcebook*, ed. Carter Lindberg, 1st ed. (Malden, MA: Blackwell, 2000), 93–95.

27 Scriptural citations in parentheses are from the version in Michael G. Baylor, ed., *The Radical Reformation* (Cambridge: Cambridge University Press, 1991), 231–238.

28 For background, see Hans Jürgen Goertz, "Thomas Müntzer: Revolutionary in a Mystical Spirit", in *Profiles or Radical Reformers: Biographical Sketches from Thomas Müntzer to Paracelsus*, ed. Hans Jürgen Goertz (Scottsdale, PA: Herald, 1982), 29–44.

Sources 711

29 Summary drawn from Michael G. Baylor, *The German Reformation and the Peasants' War: A Brief History with Documents* (Boston, MA: Bedford/St. Martins, 2012), 76, 93–97, 115–127 (quote at 115).

30 Summary drawn from Anna Marie Johnson, "Rhegius, Urbanus", in *Dictionary of Luther and the Lutheran Traditions*, ed. Timothy J. Wengert (Grand Rapids, MI: Baker, 2017), 644–645; B. Ann Tlusty, *Augsburg during the Reformation Era: An Anthology of Sources* (Indianapolis, IN: Hacket, 2012), 17–18.

31 Document in B.J. Kidd, ed., *Documents Illustrative of the Continental Reformation* (Oxford: Clarendon, 1911), 453–454.

32 Robert C. Walton, "Zurich", in *The Oxford Encyclopedia of the Reformation*, ed. Hans J. Hillebrand (Oxford: Oxford University Press, 1996), https://www.oxfordreference.com/display/10.1093/acref/9780195064933.001.0001/acref-9780195064933-e-1550?rskey=CQlG6v&result=1 (accessed 9 October 2023).

33 Bruce Gordon, *Zwingli: God's Armed Prophet* (New Haven, CT: Yale University Press, 2011), 190.

34 For background, see Timothy J. Demy, Mark J. Larson and J. Daryl Charles, *The Reformers on War, Peace, and Justice* (Eugene, OR: Pickwick, 2019), Kindle Loc. 191–691.

35 Trygve R. Skarsten, "Odense, Diets of", in *The Oxford Encyclopedia of the Reformation*, ed. Hans J. Hillebrand (Oxford: Oxford University Press, 1996), https://www.oxfordreference.com/display/10.1093/acref/9780195064933.001.0001/acref-9780195064933-e-1017?rskey=GuKBWK&result=1 (accessed 9 October 2023).

36 Martin Schwarz Lausten, "The Early Reformation in Denmark and Norway, 1520–1559", in *The Scandinavian Reformation: From Evangelical Movement to Institutional Reform*, ed. Ole Peter Grell (Cambridge: Cambridge University Press, 1995), 12–41 (12–27).

37 Michael G. Baylor, ed., *The Radical Reformation* (Cambridge: Cambridge University Press, 1991), 172, fn. 2. Biographical details come from Baylor, *The Radical Reformation*, 270; and C. Arnold Snyder, "Sattler, Michael", in *The Oxford Encyclopedia of the Reformation*, ed. Hans J. Hillebrand (Oxford: Oxford University Press, 1996), https://www.oxfordreference.com/display/10.1093/acref/9780195064933.001.0001/acref-9780195064933-e-1250?rskey=BGoBxs&result=1 (accessed 9 October 2023); Martin Haas, "Michael Sattler: On the Way to Separatism," in *Profiles or Radical Reformers: Biographical Sketches from Thomas Müntzer to Paracelsus*, ed. Hans Jürgen Goertz (Scottsdale, PA: Herald, 1982), 132–143.

38 Patrick Hayden-Roy, "Denck, Hans", in *The Oxford Encyclopedia of the Reformation*, ed. Hans J. Hillebrand (Oxford: Oxford University Press, 1996), https://www.oxfordreference.com/display/10.1093/acref/9780195064933.001.0001/acref-9780195064933-e-0402?rskey=PPns8q&result=1 (accessed 9 October 2023).

39 For background, see Daniel Liechty, *Early Anabaptists Spirituality: Selected Writings*, ed. Daniel Liechty (New York: Paulist, 1994), 111–112.

40 Ingun Montgomery, "Västerås, Diet of", in *The Oxford Encyclopedia of the Reformation*, ed. Hans J. Hillebrand (Oxford: Oxford University Press, 1996), https://www.oxfordreference.com/display/10.1093/acref/9780195064933.001.0001/acref-9780195064933-e-1463?rskey=C0C0EY&result=1 (accessed 9 October 2023). See also Ole Peter Grell, "Scandinavia", in *The Reformation World*, ed. Andrew Pettegree (London: Routledge, 2000), 257–276; Harry Lenhammar, "Vasa, Gustavus", in *The Oxford Encyclopedia of the Reformation*, ed. Hans J. Hillebrand (Oxford: Oxford University Press, 1996), https://www.oxfordreference.com/view/10.1093/acref/9780195064933.001.0001/acref-9780195064933-e-1461 (accessed 9 October 2023).

712 *Sources*

41 Ingun Montgomery, "Västerås, Diet of", in *The Oxford Encyclopedia of the Reformation*, ed. Hans J. Hillebrand (Oxford: Oxford University Press, 1996), https://www.oxfordreference.com/display/10.1093/acref/9780195064933.001.0001/acref-9780195064933-e-1463?rskey=C0C0EY&result=1 (accessed 9 October 2023).

42 Christof Windhorst, "Balthasar Hubmaier: Professor, Preacher, Politician", in *Profiles or Radical Reformers: Biographical Sketches from Thomas Müntzer to Paracelsus*, ed. Hans Jürgen Goertz (Scottsdale, PA: Herald, 1982), 144–157; James M. Stayer, "Hubmaier, Balthasar", in *The Oxford Encyclopedia of the Reformation*, ed. Hans J. Hillebrand (Oxford: Oxford University Press, 1996), https://www.oxfordreference.com/display/10.1093/acref/9780195064933.001.0001/acref-9780195064933-e-0685?rskey=dE2Fmj&result=1 (accessed 9 October 2023).

43 For background, see Eric Lund, "Tyndale, William", in *Encyclopedia of Martin Luther and the Reformation*, ed. Mark A. Lamport (New York: Rowman & Littlefield, 2017), 780–781; Donald Dean Smeeton, "Tyndale, William", in *The Oxford Encyclopedia of the Reformation*, ed. Hans J. Hillebrand (Oxford: Oxford University Press, 1996), https://www.oxfordreference.com/display/10.1093/acref/9780195064933.001.0001/acref-9780195064933-e-1432?rskey=e8HW8f&result=1 (accessed 9 October 2023).

44 Carlos M. N. Eire, *Reformations: The Early Modern World, 1450–1650* (New Haven, CT: Yale University Press, 2016), 216, 241.

45 Summary drawn from Bruce Gordon, *Zwingli: God's Armed Prophet* (New Haven, CT: Yale University Press, 2021), 212–226; Bruce Gordon, "Switzerland", in *The Encyclopedia of Protestantism*, ed. Hans J. Hillebrand (London: Routledge, 2004), 1836–1840.

46 Summary drawn from Kurt K. Hendel, "Bugenhagen, Johannes", in *Encyclopedia of Martin Luther and the Reformation*, ed. Mark A. Lamport (New York: Rowman & Littlefield, 2017), 94–96; "Bugenhagen, Johannes (1485–1558)", in *The Encyclopedia of Protestantism* (London: Routledge, 2004), 314.

47 Overview drawn from James M. Estes, *Godly Magistrates and Church Order: Johannes Brenz and the Establishment of the Lutheran Territorial Church in Germany, 1524–1559* (Toronto, ON: Center for Reformation and Renaissance Studies, 2001), 1–20.

48 For background, see Jarkko Tontti, "Olaus Petri and the Rules for Judges", *Associations: Journal for Social and Legal Theory* 4, no. 1 (2000): 113–128; Trygve R. Skarsten, "Petri, Olaus and Laurentius", in *The Oxford Encyclopedia of the Reformation*, ed. Hans J. Hillebrand (Oxford: Oxford University Press, 1996), https://www.oxfordreference.com/display/10.1093/acref/9780195064933.001.0001/acref-9780195064933-e-1085?rskey=AbW7WA&result=1 (accessed 9 October 2023).

49 Joy Margaret Kammerling, "Andreas Osiander and the Jews of Nuremberg: A Reformation Pastor and Jewish Toleration in Sixteenth-Century Germany" (PhD diss., University of Chicago, 1995), 283, https://hdl.handle.net/10027/16794 (accessed 9 October 2023).

50 For background, see James M. Estes, *Whether Secular Government Has the Right to Wield the Sword in Matters of Faith. A Controversy in Nürnberg over Freedom of Worship and the Authority in Spiritual Matters* (Toronto, ON: Center for Reformation and Renaissance Studies, 1994), 9–36.

51 Thorkild C. Lyby, "Copenhagen, Confession of", in *The Oxford Encyclopedia of the Reformation*, ed. Hans J. Hillebrand (Oxford: Oxford University Press, 1996), https://www.oxfordreference.com/display/10.1093/acref/9780195064933.001.0001/acref-9780195064933-e-0356?rskey=IXpoTS&result=2 (accessed 9 October 2023); Trygve R. Skarsten, "Tausen, Hans (1494–1561)", in *The Encyclopedia of Protestantism*, ed. Hans J. Hillebrand (London: Routledge, 2004), 1844–1845.

Sources 713

52 Summary drawn from Helmar Junghans, "Augsburg Confession", in *The Oxford Encyclopedia of the Reformation*, ed. Hans J. Hillebrand (Oxford: Oxford University Press, 1996), https://www.oxfordreference.com/display/10.1093/acref/9780195064933.001.0001/acref-9780195064933-e-0077?rskey=dqTE5j&result=2 (accessed 9 October 2023); Grantley McDonald, "Augsburg", in *Encyclopedia of Martin Luther and the Reformation*, ed. Mark A. Lamport (New York: Rowman & Littlefield, 2017), 43–46.

53 Summary drawn from Cynthia Grant Bowman, "Luther and the Justifiability of Resistance to Legitimate Authority", *Journal of the History of Ideas* 40, no. 1 (1979): 3–20; Quentin Skinner, *The Foundations of Modern Political Thought* (Cambridge: Cambridge University Press, 1978) II: Kindle Loc. 4051–4250.

54 For documents, see M.J. Spalding, *The History of the Protestant Reformation* (Louisville, KY: Webb & Levering, 1860), I:482–491.

55 Thomas A. Brady, Jr., "Schmalkald League", in *The Oxford Encyclopedia of the Reformation*, ed. Hans J. Hillebrand (Oxford: Oxford University Press, 1996), https://www.oxfordreference.com/display/10.1093/acref/9780195064933.001.0001/acref-9780195064933-e-1266?rskey=jKsAWj&result=1 (accessed 9 October 2023).

56 Hans-Peter Hasse, "Blarer, Ambrosius", in *The Oxford Encyclopedia of the Reformation*, ed. Hans J. Hillebrand (Oxford: Oxford University Press, 1996), https://www.oxfordreference.com/display/10.1093/acref/9780195064933.001.0001/acref-9780195064933-e-0154?rskey=IlsE45&result=1 (accessed 9 October 2023).

57 Bruce Gordon, *Zwingli: God's Armed Prophet* (New Haven, CT: Yale University Press, 2021), 232–239.

58 Alec Ryrie, *Unbelievers: An Emotional History of Doubt* (Cambridge, MA: Belknap Press, 2009), 26–30.

59 Jerome Friedman, "Servetus, Michael", in *The Oxford Encyclopedia of the Reformation*, ed. Hans J. Hillebrand (Oxford: Oxford University Press, 1996), https://www.oxfordreference.com/display/10.1093/acref/9780195064933.001.0001/acref-9780195064933-e-1292?rskey=oJXbja&result=1 (accessed 9 October 2023); Bruce Gordon, *Calvin* (New Haven, CT: Yale University Press, 2009), 217–232.

60 Summary drawn from John Witte Jr., "An Evangelical Commonwealth: Johannes Eisermann on Law and the Common Good", in *Caritas et Reformatio: Essays in Honor of Carter Lindberg*, ed. David M. Whitford (St. Louis, MO: Concordia Publishing House, 2002), 73–87. He was known by several names, including Joannes Ferrarius Montanus.

61 Lowell H. Zuck, *Christianity and Revolution: Radical Christian Testimonies, 1520–1650* (Philadelphia, PA: Temple, 1975), 90–93. See also Carter Lindberg, ed., *The European Reformations Sourcebook*, 1st ed. (Malden, MA: Blackwell, 2000), 136–137.

62 For background, see Willem de Bakker, Michael Driedger and James Stayer, *Bernard Rothmann and the Reformation in Münster, 1530–35* (Kitchener, ON: Pandora, 2009).

63 Hans Hillerbrand, *The Reformation: A Narrative History Related by Contemporary Observers and Participants* (Grand Rapids, MI: Baker, 1972), 255–257.

64 Hastings Robinson, *Original Letters Relative to the English Reformation* (Cambridge: Cambridge University Press, 1847), II:556–557.

65 For documents, see M.J. Spalding, *The History of the Protestant Reformation* (Louisville, KY: Webb & Levering, 1860), I: 482–491.

66 Gary K. Waite, "Simons, Menno", in *The Oxford Encyclopedia of the Reformation*, ed. Hans J. Hillebrand (Oxford: Oxford University Press, 1996), https://www.oxfordreference.com/display/10.1093/acref/9780195064933.001.0001/acref-9780195064933-e-0929?rskey=slejgL&result=1 (accessed 9 October 2023).

67 On Calvin's identity as a foreigner and 'refugee', see Robert. R. Vosloo, "The Displaced Calvin: 'Refugee Reality' as a Lens to Re-examine Calvin's Life, Theology and Legacy", *Religion & Theology* 16 (2009): 35–52.

714   *Sources*

68   Bruce Gordon, *John Calvin's Institutes of the Christian Religion: A Biography* (Princeton, NJ: Princeton University Press, 2016), 17. Editions: 1536 Basel (Latin), 1539 Strasbourg (Latin), 1541 Geneva (French), 1543 Geneva (Latin), 1545 Geneva (French), 1550 Geneva (Latin), 1559 Geneva (Latin), and 1560 Geneva (French). See Bruce Gordon, *John Calvin's Institutes of the Christian Religion: A Biography* (Princeton, NJ: Princeton University Press, 2016), 227.

69   Bruce Gordon, *John Calvin's Institutes of the Christian Religion: A Biography* (Princeton, NJ: Princeton University Press, 2016), 24.

70   For background, see Mary B. McKinley, "Marie Dentière (1495–1561): In Defense of Women", in *Women Reformers of Early Modern Europe: Profiles, Texts, and Contexts*, ed. Kirsi I. Stjerna (Minneapolis, MN: Fortress, 2022), 23–30; Irena Backus, "Dentière, Marie", in *The Oxford Encyclopedia of the Reformation*, ed. Hans J. Hillebrand (Oxford: Oxford University Press, 1996), https://www.oxfordreference.com/display/10.1093/acref/9780195064933.001.0001/acref-9780195064933-e-0405?rskey=hmUsCJ&result=1 (accessed 9 October 2023).

71   Gary K. Waite, "Joris, David", in *The Oxford Encyclopedia of the Reformation*, ed. Hans J. Hillebrand (Oxford: Oxford University Press, 1996), https://www.oxfordreference.com/display/10.1093/acref/9780195064933.001.0001/acref-9780195064933-e-0743?rskey=p5V2C2&result=1 (accessed 9 October 2023).

72   For background, see *Peter Riedemann's Hutterite Confession of Faith*, trans. and ed. John J. Friesen (Walden; NY: Plough Publishing House, 2019).

73   Jeannine E. Olson, "Calvin and Social-Ethical Issues", in *Cambridge Companion to Calvin*, ed. Donald K. McKim (Cambridge: Cambridge University Press, 2004), 153–172.

74   Martin Luther, *That Jesus Was Born a Jew* (1523), as quoted in *A Reformation Sourcebook: Documents from an Age of Debate*, ed. Michael W. Bruening (New York: University of Toronto Press, 2017), 256–257.

75   R. Po-Chia Hsia, "Jews", in *The Oxford Encyclopedia of the Reformation*, ed. Hans J. Hillebrand (Oxford: Oxford University Press, 1996), https://www.oxfordreference.com/display/10.1093/acref/9780195064933.001.0001/acref-9780195064933-e-0728?rskey=Kd5pDC&result=1 (accessed 9 October 2023).

76   See, for example, Susan C. Karant-Nunn and Merry E. Wiesner-Hanks, *Luther on Women: A Sourcebook* (Cambridge: Cambridge University Press, 2003), 193.

77   Luther's even more antisemitic work, *On the Ineffable Name and Lineage of Christ*, was not translated into English until 1992. See Christopher J. Probst, *Demonizing the Jews: Luther and the Protestant Church in Nazi Germany* (Indianapolis: Indiana University Press, 2012), 50.

78   Dainora Pociūtė, "Abraomas Kulvietis. Humanistic Origins of the Early Reformation in the Grand Duchy of Lithuania" (2011), https://www.academia.edu/38220974/Abraomas_Kulvietis_Humanistic_Origins_of_the_Early_Reformation_in_the_Grand_Duchy_of_Lithuania?auto=citations&from=cover_page (accessed 9 October 2023). See also Kęstutis Daugirdas, "The Reformation in Poland-Lithuania as a European Networking Process", *Church History and Religious Culture* 97 (2017): 356–368; Antanas Musteikis, *The Reformation in Lithuania: Religious Fluctuations in the Sixteenth Century* (New York: Columbia University Press, 1988).

79   Matt Young, *The Life and Times of Aonio Paleario: Or, A History of the Italian Reformers in the Sixteenth Century Illustrated by Original Letters and Unedited Documents, 2 Vols.* (London: Bell and Daldy, 1860).

80   George Huntston Williams, *History of the Polish Reformation* (Minneapolis, MN: Fortress, 1995), 49.

81   Background drawn from John N. King, "Coverdale, Miles", in *The Oxford Encyclopedia of the Reformation*, ed. Hans J. Hillebrand (Oxford: Oxford University Press, 1996), https://www.oxfordreference.com/display/10.1093/acref/9780195064933.001.0001/acref-9780195064933-e-0373?rskey=g0wI2l&

Sources 715

result=1 (accessed 9 October 2023). See also Carlos M. N. Eire, *Reformations: The Early Modern World, 1450–1650* (New Haven, CT: Yale University Press, 2016), 320–336.

82 David Loades, "Cranmer, Thomas", in *The Encyclopedia of Protestantism*, ed. Hans J. Hillebrand (London: Routledge, 2004), 528–531; David Scott Gehring, "Cranmer, Thomas", in *Encyclopedia of Martin Luther and the Reformation*, ed. Mark A. Lamport (New York: Rowman & Littlefield, 2017), 175–177.

83 Jason Lavery, *Reforming Finland: The Diocese of Turku in the Age of Gustav Vasa, 1523–1560* (Leiden: Brill, 2017), 1–21; Kaisa Häkkinen, *Spreading the Written Word: Mikael Agricola and the Birth of Literary Finnish*, trans. Leonard Pearl (Helsinki: Finnish Literature Society, 2016). See also Simo Heininen, "Agricola, Mikael', in *Encyclopedia of Martin Luther and the Reformation*, ed. Mark A. Lamport (New York: Rowman & Littlefield, 2017), 8–9.

84 For background, see Diarmaid MacCullough, *The Boy King: Edward VI and the Protestant Reformation* (New York: Palgrave, 2001); Dale Hoak, "Edward VI of England", in *The Oxford Encyclopedia of the Reformation*, ed. Hans J. Hillebrand (Oxford: Oxford University Press, 1996), https://www.oxfordreference.com/display/10.1093/acref/9780195064933.001.0001/acref-9780195064933-e-0454?rskey=A36ZhD&result=1 (accessed 9 October 2023).

85 Carlos M. N. Eire, *Reformations: The Early Modern World, 1450–1650* (New Haven, CT: Yale University Press, 2016), 321–337. See also Mark Stoyle, *A Murderous Midsummer: The Western Rising of 1549* (New Haven, CT: Yale University Press, 2022).

86 David Scott Gehring, "Cranmer, Thomas", in *Encyclopedia of Martin Luther and the Reformation*, ed. Mark A. Lamport (New York: Rowman & Littlefield, 2017), 175–177.

87 For background, see Martin Bucer, *De Regno Christi*, in *Melanchthon and Bucer*, ed. Wilhelm Puck (Philadelphia, PA: Westminster, 1969), 155–173; Martin Greschat, "Bucer, Martin", in *The Oxford Encyclopedia of the Reformation*, ed. Hans J. Hillebrand (Oxford: Oxford University Press, 1996), https://www.oxfordreference.com/display/10.1093/acref/9780195064933.001.0001/acref-97801950649 33-e-0200?rskey=2AwQzg&result=1 (accessed 9 October 2023).

88 David VanDrunen, "The Use of Natural Law in Early Calvinist Resistance Theory", *Journal of Law and Religion* 21, no. 1 (2005/2006): 143–167.

89 David W. Leinweber, "Luther, A Biography", in *Encyclopedia of Martin Luther and the Reformation*, ed. Mark A. Lamport (New York: Rowman & Littlefield, 2017), 442–448.

90 Kirsi Stjerna, *Women and the Reformation* (Malden, MA: Blackwell, 2009), 51–70.

91 For background, see Irvin B. Horst, "Menno Simmons: The New Man in Community", in *Profiles or Radical Reformers: Biographical Sketches from Thomas Müntzer to Paracelsus*, ed. Hans Jürgen Goertz (Scottsdale, PA: Herald, 1982), 203–213; Gary K. Waite, "Simons, Menno", in *The Oxford Encyclopedia of the Reformation*, ed. Hans J. Hillebrand (Oxford: Oxford University Press, 1996), https://www.oxfordreference.com/display/10.1093/acref/9780195064933.001.0001/acref-9780195064933-e-0929?rskey=slejgL&result=1 (accessed 9 October 2023).

92 David Loades, "Latimer, Hugh", in *The Oxford Encyclopedia of the Reformation*, ed. Hans J. Hillebrand (Oxford: Oxford University Press, 1996), https://www.oxfordreference.com/display/10.1093/acref/9780195064933.001.0001/acref-9780195064933-e-0799?rskey=PI7vHB&result=1 (accessed 9 October 2023); Carlos M. N. Eire, *Reformations: The Early Modern World, 1450–1650* (New Haven, CT: Yale University Press, 2016), 330–330.

93 For background, see Bruce Gordon, *Calvin* (New Haven, CT: Yale University Press, 2009), 228–232; Roland H. Bainton, *Concerning Heretics: Whether They*

716 *Sources*

    Are to Be Persecuted and How they Are to Be Treated: A Collection of the Opinions of Learned Men Both Ancient and Modern (New York: Columbia, 1935).

94 Jill Raitt, "Bèze, Théodore De", in *The Oxford Encyclopedia of the Reformation*, ed. Hans J. Hillebrand (Oxford: Oxford University Press, 1996), https://www.oxfordreference.com/display/10.1093/acref/9780195064933.001.0001/acref-9780195064933-e-0143?rskey=66UOM1&result=1 (accessed 9 October 2023). On his response to later violence in France, see Scott M. Manetsch, *Theodore Beza and the Quest for Peace in France, 1572–1598* (Leiden: Brill, 2000).

95 For background, see J. Wayne Baker, "Bullinger, Heinrich (1504–1575)", in *The Encyclopedia of Protestantism*, ed. Hans J. Hillebrand (London: Routledge, 2004), 314–316; Bruce Gordon and Emidio Campi, eds., *Architect of Reformation An Introduction to Heinrich Bullinger, 1504–1575* (Eugene, OR: Wipf and Stock, 2019).

96 W.J.T. Kirby, *Zurich Connection and Tudor Political Theology* (Boston, MA: Brill, 2007), 29.

97 W.J.T. Kirby, *Zurich Connection and Tudor Political Theology* (Boston, MA: Brill, 2007), 724–725. For a possible interpretation of Calvin's changing warfare beliefs in later life, see Jon Balserak, *John Calvin as a Sixteenth Century Prophet* (Oxford: Oxford University Press, 2014).

98 George Huntston Williams, *History of the Polish Reformation* (Minneapolis, MN: Fortress, 1995), 13.

99 Stanislas Lubieniecki, *History of the Polish Reformation*, trans. and ed. George Huntston Williams (Minneapolis, MN: Fortress, 1995), 131.

100 Stanislas Lubieniecki, *History of the Polish Reformation*, trans. and ed. George Huntston Williams (Minneapolis, MN: Fortress, 1995), 117–119.

101 Noel Malcolm, *Useful Enemies: Islam and the Ottoman Empire in Western Political Thought, 1450–1750* (Oxford: Oxford University Press, 2019), 79, 92–93.

102 "Thomas Cranmer to John A. Lasco" (4 July 1548), in *The Works of Thomas Cranmer*, ed. G. E. Duffield (Appleford: Sutton Courtenay Press, 1964), 311–313.

103 For background, see Wacław Urban, "Łaski, Jan", in *The Oxford Encyclopedia of the Reformation*, ed. Hans J. Hillebrand (Oxford: Oxford University Press, 1996), https://www.oxfordreference.com/display/10.1093/acref/9780195064933.001.0001/acref-9780195064933-e-0796?rskey=THGZ8y&result=1 (accessed 9 October 2023); Zbigniew Pasek, "Łaski, Jan", in *Encyclopedia of Martin Luther and the Reformation*, ed. Mark A. Lamport (New York: Rowman & Littlefield, 2017), 408–411.

104 "Christoper Mont to Heinrich Bullinger" (2 Oct 1567), in *The Zurich Letters*, ed. Hastings Robinson (Cambridge: Cambridge University Press, 1845), II:168–170 (169); Robert M. Kingdon, "Calvinism and Resistance Theory, 1550–1580", in *The Cambridge History of Political Thought, 1450–1700*, ed. J.H. Burns (Cambridge: Cambridge University Press, 2008), 193–218 (210).

105 Robert M. Kingdon, "Calvinism and Resistance Theory, 1550–1580", in *The Cambridge History of Political Thought, 1450–1700*, ed. J.H. Burns (Cambridge: Cambridge University Press, 2008), 193–218.

106 Summary drawn from Roger A. Mason, ed., *Knox: On Rebellion* (Cambridge: Cambridge University Press, 1994), xvii–xxi.

107 "John Knox to Elizabeth I" (20 July 1559), in *John Knox: The First Blast of the Trumpet against the Monstrous Regiment of Women (1558)*, ed. Edward Arber (Westminster: Archibald Constable and Co., 1895), 57–60.

108 For example, in a 1555 letter to John Calvin, David Whitehead and others said "that outrageous pamphlet of Knox's [An Admonition to Christians] added much oil to the flame of persecution in England". See Hastings Robinson, *Original*

Letters Relative to the English Reformation: Written During the Reigns of King Henry VIII., King Edward VI., and Queen Mary: Chiefly from the Archives of Zurich (Cambridge: Cambridge University Press, 1864), II:756–763 (761).

109 Summary drawn from Jenny Wormald, "Knox, John", in *The Oxford Encyclopedia of the Reformation*, ed. Hans J. Hillebrand (Oxford: Oxford University Press, 1996), https://www.oxfordreference.com/display/10.1093/acref/9780195064933.001.0001/acref-9780195064933-e-0774?rskey=WBD3B K&result=1 (accessed 9 October 2023).

110 Summary drawn from Carole Levin, "Queen Elizabeth I (1533–1603): Religion and Beliefs", in *Women Reformers of Early Modern Europe: Profiles, Texts, and Contexts*, ed. Kirsi I. Stjerna (Minneapolis, MN: Fortress, 2022), 131–137; Norman Jones, "Elizabeth I (1533–1603)", in *The Encyclopedia of Protestantism*, ed. Hans J. Hillebrand (London: Routledge, 2004), 660–661.

111 Bruce Gordon, *Calvin* (New Haven, CT: Yale University Press, 2009).

112 Summary drawn from Richard Mulcaster, from *The Queen's Majesty's Passage Through the City of London* (1559), in *Voices of the English Reformation: A Sourcebook*, ed. John N. King (Philadelphia: University of Pennsylvania Press, 2004), 332–344 (quote at 338).

113 For documents, see Charles E. Bennett, ed., *Laudonniere & Fort Caroline* (Repr.; Tuscaloosa: University of Alabama Press, 2001).

114 Matthew J. Tuininga, *Calvin's Political Theology and the Public Engagement of the Church: Christ's Two Kingdoms* (Cambridge: Cambridge University Press, 2017), 84–85.

115 David Norton, "English Bibles from c.1520 to c.1750", in *The New Cambridge History of the Bible: From 1450–1750*, ed. Euan Cameron (Cambridge: Cambridge University Press, 2016), 305–344 (315–319, 328–329). Quote on 316.

116 Matthew Rowley, "From Witness to Warrior: Remembering the Red Sea in British Warfare, 1560–1660", Remembering the Reformation (July 2019), https://remref.hist.cam.ac.uk/research/witness-warrior-remembering-red-sea-british-warfare-1560-1660.html (accessed 9 October 2023).

117 For background, see Carlos M. N. Eire, *Reformations: The Early Modern World, 1450–1650* (New Haven, CT: Yale University Press, 2016), 356–364; James Kirk, "Scottish Confession", in *The Oxford Encyclopedia of the Reformation*, ed. Hans J. Hillebrand (Oxford: Oxford University Press, 1996), https://www.oxfordreference.com/display/10.1093/acref/9780195064933.001.0001/acref-9780195064933-e-1279?rskey=1nYHwM&result=3 (accessed 9 October 2023).

118 Background drawn from Ingun Montgomery, "Erik XIV", in *The Oxford Encyclopedia of the Reformation*, ed. Hans J. Hillebrand (Oxford: Oxford University Press, 1996), https://www.oxfordreference.com/display/10.1093/acref/9780195064933.001.0001/acref-9780195064933-e-0479?rskey=TQD o7b&result=1 (accessed 9 October 2023); Janet Glenn Gray, "The Calvinist Struggle for Recognition in Sweden", *Fides et Historia* 39, no. 2 (2007): 79–95 (85); Ole Peter Grell, "Exile and Tolerance", in *Tolerance and Intolerance in the European Reformation*, ed. Ole Peter Grell and Bob Scribner (Cambridge: Cambridge University Press, 1996), 164–181 (176–179).

119 Summary drawn from A. Gordon Kinder, *Casiodoro de Reina: Spanish Reformer of the Sixteenth Century* (London: Tamesis, 1975), 18–38; Sabine Hiebsch, "De Reina, Casiodoro", in *Encyclopedia of Martin Luther and the Reformation*, ed. Mark A. Lamport (New York: Rowman & Littlefield, 2017), 192–193.

120 Summary from Torrance Kirby, "Political Theology: The Godly Prince", in *A Companion to Peter Martyr Vermigli*, ed. Torrance Kirby, Emidio Campi and Frank A. James III (Leiden: Brill, 2009), 401–421 (quote at 401); Marvin W. Anderson, "Vermigli, Peter Martyr", in *The Oxford Encyclopedia of the Reformation*,

718 Sources

ed. Hans J. Hillebrand (Oxford: Oxford University Press, 1996), https://www.oxfordreference.com/display/10.1093/acref/9780195064933.001.0001/acref-9780195064933-e-1471?rskey=qG4Cnq&result=1 (accessed 9 October 2023).

121 E.g., "To Edward VI" (January 1551); "To Edward VI" (4 July 1552); "To the King of Poland" (5 December 1554); "To the King of Poland" (24 December 1555); "To the King of Navarre" (14 December 1557); "To William Cecil" (29 January 1559); "To William Cecil" (c. May 1559); "To the King of France" (28 January 1561); "To the King of Navarre" (May 1561); "To the King of Navarre" (December 1561). See also Charmarie Jenkins Blaisdell, "Calvin's Letters to Women: The Courting of Ladies in High Places", *The Sixteenth Century Journal* 13, no. 3 (Autumn, 1982): 67–84.

122 Summary from Krisi Stjerna, *Women and the Reformation*, 1st ed. (Malden, MA: Blackwell, 2008), 158–174; cf. Kathleen M. Llewellyn, "Jeanne D'Albret (1528–1572)", in *Women Reformers of Early Modern Europe: Profiles, Texts and Context*, ed. Kirsi I. Stjerna (Minneapolis, MN: Fortress, 2022), 177–183.

123 Description from Sebastian Castellio, *Advice to a Desolate France*, trans. Wouter Valkhoff (Grand Rapids, MI: Acton Institute, 2016).

124 For background on martyrdom, John Foxe and his *Acts and Monuments*, see Brad S. Gregory, *Salvation at Stake: Christian Martyrdom in Early Modern Europe* (Cambridge, MA: Harvard University Press, 1999). On martyrdom in New England, see Adrian Chastain Weimer, *Martyrs' Mirror: Persecution and Holiness in Early New England* (Oxford: Oxford University Press, 2011).

125 Daniel Timmerman, "From Zurich to Westminster: Covenant as Structuring Principle in Reformed Catechisms", in *Covenant: A Vital Element of Reformed Theology*, ed. Hans Burger, Gert Kwakkel and Michael Mudler (Leiden: Brill, 2021), 232–253.

126 John W. Nevin and John W. Proudfit, *The Heidelberg Catechism. The Mercersburg Understanding of the German Reformed Tradition* (Eugene, OR: Wipf and Stock, 2021).

127 For biographical details, see Sascha Salatowsky, "Ochino, Bernardino", in *Encyclopedia of Martin Luther and the Reformation*, ed. Mark A. Lamport (New York: Rowman & Littlefield, 2017), 569–570; Elizabeth G. Gleason, *Reform Thought in Sixteenth-Century Italy* (Ann Arbor, MI: Scholars Press, 1981), 35–37.

128 Gary Remer, *Humanism and the Rhetoric of Toleration* (*University Park*, PA: The Pennsylvania State University Press, 1996).

129 A. Keller, "Aconcio, Jacopo [Jacobus Acontius] (c. 1520–1566/7?), Theologian and Military Engineer", *Oxford Dictionary of National Biography*, https://doi.org/10.1093/ref:odnb/69 (accessed 9 October 2023).

130 Jenny Wormald, "Buchanan, George", in *The Oxford Encyclopedia of the Reformation*, ed. Hans J. Hillebrand (Oxford: Oxford University Press, 1996), https://www.oxfordreference.com/display/10.1093/acref/9780195064933.001.0001/acref-9780195064933-e-0201?rskey=njX9f8&result=1 (accessed 9 October 2023).

131 John Coffey, "George Buchanan and the Scottish Covenanters", in *George Buchanan: Political Thought in Early Modern Britain and Europe*, ed. Caroline Erskine and Roger A. Mason (London: Routledge, 2012), 189–203 (199).

132 E.g., George Huntston Williams, *History of the Polish Reformation* (Minneapolis, MN: Fortress, 1995), 57.

133 Summary drawn from Joseph Henry Crooker, *The Winning of Religious Liberty* (Boston, MA: Pilgrim, 1918), 80–81.

134 Michael W. Bruening, *A Reformation Sourcebook: Documents from an Age of Debate* (New York: University of Toronto Press, 2017), 264–265.

135 Donald J. Ziegler, *Great Debates of the Reformation* (New York: Random House, 1969), 243–245.

Sources 719

136 Geoffrey Treasure, *The Huguenots* (New Haven, CT: Yale University Press, 2013), 156.
137 Summary drawn from David Potter, ed., *The French Wars of Religion: Selected Documents* (London: Macmillan, 1997), 96–97; Kathleen M. Llewellyn, "Jeanne D'Albret (1528–1572)", in *Women Reformers of Early Modern Europe: Profiles, Texts and Context*, ed. Kirsi I. Stjerna (Minneapolis, MN: Fortress, 2022), 177–183.
138 Summary from Krisi Stjerna, *Women and the Reformation*, 1st ed. (Malden, MA: Blackwell, 2008), 158–174; Kathleen M. Llewellyn, "Jeanne D'Albret (1528–1572)", in *Women Reformers of Early Modern Europe: Profiles, Texts and Context*, ed. Kirsi I. Stjerna (Minneapolis, MN: Fortress, 2022), 177–183.
139 Summary drawn from Hans J. Hillerbrand, "Erastus, Thomas (Lüber) (1524–1583)", in *The Encyclopedia of Protestantism*, ed. Hans J. Hillebrand (London: Routledge, 2004), 680–681; Eric Nelson, *The Hebrew Republic: Jewish Sources and the Transformation of European Political Thought* (Cambridge, MA: Harvard University Press, 2011), 92–94 (quote at 92).
140 E. J. Hutchinson and Korey D. Maas, "Introduction", in *On the Law of Nature: A Demonstrative Method*, ed. Niels Hemmingsen, trans. E. J. Hutchinson (Grand Rapids, MI: CLP Academic, 2018), xi–xlii.
141 Summary drawn from David Potter, ed., *The French Wars of Religion: Selected Documents* (London: Macmillan, 1997), 99–100; Kathleen M. Llewellyn, "Jeanne D'Albret (1528–1572)", in *Women Reformers of Early Modern Europe: Profiles, Texts and Context*, ed. Kirsi I. Stjerna (Minneapolis, MN: Fortress, 2022), 177–183.
142 Lech Szczucki, "Poland", in *The Encyclopedia of Protestantism*, ed. Hans J. Hillebrand (London: Routledge, 2004), 1500–1507; Zbigniew Pasek, "Sandomierz Agreement", in *Encyclopedia of Martin Luther and the Reformation*, ed. Mark A. Lamport (New York: Rowman & Littlefield, 2017), 674–675.
143 Summary drawn from Martin van Gelderen, *The Dutch Revolt* (Cambridge: Cambridge University Press, 1993), ix–xviii.
144 Lyle D. Bierma, "Ursinus and the Theological Landscape of the Heidelberg Catechism", in *The Spirituality of the Heidelberg Catechism*, ed. Arnold Huijgen (Göttingen: Vandenhoeck & Ruprecht, 2015), 9–24 (9).
145 Diarmaid MacCullough, *Thomas Cranmer* rev. ed. (New Haven, CT: Yale University Press, 1996), 372.
146 Summary drawn from Ronald Bond, ed., *Certain Sermons or Homilies (1547) and a Homily Against Disobedience and Wilful Rebellion (1570): A Critical Edition* (Toronto: University of Toronto Press, 1987), 40–44; Diarmaid MacCullough, *Thomas Cranmer* rev. ed. (New Haven, CT: Yale University Press, 1996), 372.
147 Kelly Digby Peebles, "Jeanne d' Albret (1528–1572): Reformer and Queen", in *Women Reformers of Early Modern Europe: Profiles, Texts, and Contexts*, ed. Kirsi I. Stjerna (Minneapolis, MN: Fortress, 2022), 177–183.
148 Peter Newman Brooks, "Thirty-Nine Articles of Religion", in *The Encyclopedia of Protestantism*, ed. Hans J. Hillebrand (London: Routledge, 2004), 1886–1889.
149 George Huntston Williams, *The Radical Reformation*, 3rd ed. (Ann Arbor, MI: Sixteenth Century Essays & Studies, 1995), 1139–1141.
150 Summary drawn from Donald R. Kelley, "Hotman, François", in *The Oxford Encyclopedia of the Reformation*, ed. Hans J. Hillebrand (Oxford: Oxford University Press, 1996), https://www.oxfordreference.com/display/10.1093/acref/9780195064933.001.0001/acref-9780195064933-e-0679?rskey=OXIs4f&result=1 (accessed 9 October 2023).
151 For background, see Ralph E. Giesey, ed., and J.H.M. Salmon, trans., *Francogallia by Fraçois Hotman* (Cambridge: Cambridge University Press, 1972).

720 *Sources*

152 Background on Grindal and prophesyings from Michael P. Winship, *Hot Protestants: A History of Puritanism in England and America* (New Haven, CT: Yale University Press, 2019), 26–32, 41–42. David Hall, *The Puritans: A Translatlantic History* (Princeton, NJ: Princeton University Press, 2019), 44–48, 70–71, 151–152.

153 Summary drawn from L. J. Andrew Villalon, "Niccolò Machiavelli", in *The Oxford Encyclopedia of the Reformation*, ed. Hans J. Hillebrand (Oxford: Oxford University Press, 1996), https://www.oxfordreference.com/display/10.1093/acref/9780195064933.001.0001/acref-9780195064933-e-0861?rskey=GeJ3fI&result=1 (accessed 9 October 2023); J. H. Burns and Mark Goldie, eds., *The Cambridge History of Political Thought, 1450–1700* (Cambridge: Cambridge University Press, 1991), 675.

154 Innocent Gentillet, *A Discourse …Against Nicholas Machiavell the Florentine*, trans. Simon Patrick (London: Adam Islip, 1602), 80.

155 Primary sources related to Hutter and Riedemann can be found in Michael G. Long, ed., *Christian Peace and Nonviolence: A Documentary History* (Maryknoll, NY: Orbis, 2011), 81–83; cf. Abraham Friesen, "Hutter, Jacob", in *The Oxford Encyclopedia of the Reformation*, ed. Hans J. Hillebrand (Oxford: Oxford University Press, 1996), https://www.oxfordreference.com/display/10.1093/acref/9780195064933.001.0001/acref-9780195064933-e-0696?rskey=ByH2fR&result=1 (accessed 9 October 2023). Summary drawn from Peter Walpot, *The Christian and the Sword*, trans. Elizabeth Bender et al., ed. Art Wiser and Leonard Gross (Robertsbridge: Plough, 2011), v–xi.

156 A.E.M. Janssen, "Het verdeelde Huis", in *De Unie van Utrecht. Wording en werking van een verbond en een* verbondsactie, ed. S. Groeneveld and H.L.Ph. Leeuwenberg (The Hague: Martinus Nijhoff, 1979), 101–135.

157 Luc Panhuysen, "De Unie van Utrecht: Visie, Improvisatie en Grootspraak", *Historisch Nieuwblad* 7 (2012), https://www.historischnieuwsblad.nl/nl/artikel/29185/de-unie-van-utrecht.html (consulted 7 April 2017); Koenraad W. Swart, *Willem van Oranje en de Nederlandse Opstand 1572–1584* (The Hague: SDU, 1994), 161–162; P.J. Blok, "Brief van den Utrechtsen burgemeester Aernt Dircxsz van Leijden over zijne zending naar den prins van Oranje", *BMHG* 41 (1920): 232–246 (244).

158 George Garnett's scholarly edition provided helpful clarifications (*Brutus: Vindiciae, contra tyrannos, Or, Concerning the Legitimate Power of a Prince over the People, and of the People over a Prince* [Cambridge: Cambridge University Press, 2010], xix–lxxvi.

159 Lech Szczucki, "Sozzini, Fausto", in *The Encyclopedia of Protestantism*, ed. Hans J. Hillebrand (London: Routledge, 2004), 1794–1796; Peter Brock, "Faustus Socinus Against War: From the First Chapter of the Third Part of His Reply to Jacobus Palaeologus (1581)", *The Mennonite Quarterly Review* 70 (1996): 419–430.

160 Background drawn from Martin van Gelderen, *The Dutch Revolt* (Cambridge: Cambridge University Press, 1993), ix–xviii.

161 Alan G. R. Smith, "Cecil, William", in *The Oxford Encyclopedia of the Reformation*, ed. Hans J. Hillebrand (Oxford: Oxford University Press, 1996), https://www.oxfordreference.com/display/10.1093/acref/9780195064933.001.0001/acref-9780195064933-e-0257?rskey=CAIwRD&result=1 (accessed 9 October 2023). See also W. MacCaffrey, "Cecil, William, first Baron Burghley (1520/21–1598)", *ODNB*; Brett Usher, *William Cecil and Episcopacy, 1559–1577* (London: Routledge, 2017).

162 A. Payne, "Hakluyt, Richard (1552?–1616)", *ODNB*.

163 Jerzy Kloczowski, *A History of Polish Christianity* (Cambridge: Cambridge University Press, 2000), 113.

Sources 721

164 Frank C. Senn, "Sigismund III Vasa", in *The Oxford Encyclopedia of the Reformation*, ed. Hans J. Hillebrand (Oxford: Oxford University Press, 1996), https://www.oxfordreference.com/display/10.1093/acref/9780195064933.001.0001/acref-9780195064933-e-1301?rskey=ej7tU2&result=1 (accessed 9 October 2023).

165 For background, see Oliver O'Donovan and Joan Lockwood O'Donovan, *From Irenaeus to Grotius: A Sourcebook in Christian Political Thought* (Grand Rapids, MI: Eerdmans, 1999), 743–745; Dairmaid MacCulloch, *Reformation: Europe's House Divided, 1490–1700* (New York: Penguin, 2003), 502–508.

166 For background, see Trygve R. Skarsten, "Sweden", in *The Encyclopedia of Protestantism*, ed. Hans J. Hillebrand (London: Routledge, 2004), 1827–1833; Trygve R. Skarsten, "The Reception of the Augsburg Confession in Scandinavia," *The Sixteenth Century Journal* 11, no. 3 (1980): 87–98; Eric Lund, "Nordic and Baltic Lutheranism", in *Lutheran Ecclesiastical Culture, 1550–1675*, ed. Robert Kold (Leiden: Brill, 2008), 411–454.

167 Timeline drawn from Alberico Gentili, *The Wars of the Romans: A Critical Edition and Translation of De Armis Romanis*, ed. Benedict Kingsbury and Benjamin Straumann, trans. David Lupher (Oxford: Oxford University Press, 2011), xxvi–xxvii.

168 Valentina Vadi, *War and Peace: Alberico Gentili and the Early Modern Law of Nations* (Leiden: Brill 2020), 201.

169 David Hall, *The Puritans: A Translatlantic History* (Princeton, NJ: Princeton University Press, 2019), 172–177.

170 Tara Alberts, *Conflict and Conversion: Catholicism in Southeast Asia, 1500–1700* (Oxford: Oxford University Press, 2013), 7.

171 Summary drawn from Charles H. Parker, *Global Calvinism: Conversion and Commerce in the Dutch Empire, 1600–1800* (New Haven, CT: Yale University Press, 2022), 10, 14, 25, 34 (quotes from 129 and 202 respectively). Timeline drawn from Peter Borshberg, ed., *Journal, Memorials and Letters of Cornelis Matelieff de Jonge: Security, Diplomacy and Commerce in 17th-century Southeast Asia* (Singapore: NUS Press, 2015), xxxi–xxxv. Further background on the treaty drawn from Borshberg, *Journal, Memorials and Letters of Cornelis Matelieff de Jonge*, 421–422.

172 Summary from Hans Medick and Benjamin Marschke, eds., *Experiencing the Thirty Years War: A Brief History with Documents* (Boston, MA: Bedford, 2013), 31–32; and from Eric Lund, ed., *Documents of Lutheranism* (Minneapolis, MN: Fortress Press, 2002), 260, 280.

173 Overview drawn from Brian P. Levack, ed., *The Witchcraft Sourcebook*, 2nd ed. (London: Routledge, 2015), 59–60, 74, 102, 112, 146, 352, 366–384. On William Perkins, see M. Jinkins, "Perkins, William (1558–1602)", *ODNB*; William Brown Patterson, *William Perkins and the Making of a Protestant England* (Oxford: Oxford University Press, 2014); Joel R. Beeke and Greg Salazar, eds., *William Perkins: Architect of Puritanism* (Grand Rapids, MI: Reformation Heritage Books, 2019).

174 For background, see A. Boyer, "Coke, Sir Edward (1552–1634)", *ODNB*; Allen D. Boyer, *Sir Edward Coke and the Elizabethan Age* (Stanford: Stanford University Press, 2003).

175 For documents, see Herbert H. Rowen, ed., *The Low Countries in Early Modern Times: A Documentary History* (New York: Harper & Row, 1972), 127–142.

176 Hugo Grotius, *The Truth of the Christian Religion*, trans. John Clarke, ed. Maria Rosa Antognazza (Indianapolis, IN: Liberty Fund, 2012), 116–119, 167, 246 (quote at 30).

722 *Sources*

177 Charles H. Parker, *Global Calvinism: Conversion and Commerce in the Dutch Empire, 1600–1800* (New Haven, CT: Yale University Press, 2022), 203. For background, see Stephen C. Neff, *Hugo Grotius: On the Law of War and Peace* (Cambridge: Cambridge University Press, 2012), xiii–xxxv.

178 See Benjamin J. Kaplan, "Arminius, Jacobus", in *The Oxford Encyclopedia of the Reformation*, ed. Hans J. Hillebrand (Oxford: Oxford University Press, 1996), https://www.oxfordreference.com/display/10.1093/acref/9780195064933.001.0001/acref-9780195064933-e-0061?rskey=IZbVIj&result=1 (accessed 9 October 2023); Carl Bangs, *Arminius: A Study in the Dutch Reformation* (Eugene, OR: Wipf and Stock, 1985), 335–336.

179 For background, see Johann P. Sommerville, *King James VI and I: Political Writings* (Cambridge: Cambridge University Press, 1994), xv–xxviii.

180 Description drawn from John Roth and James Stayer, eds., *A Companion to Anabaptism and Spiritualism, 1521–1700* (Leiden: Brill, 2007).

181 For a longer defence of these positions, see Thomas Helwys, *An advertisement or admonition, unto the congregations, vvhich men call the new fryelers in the lowe Countries* (1611), 55–84.

182 For background, see Alexandra Walsham, *Charitable Hatred: Tolerance and Intolerance in England, 1500–1700* (Manchester: Manchester University Press, 2006), 23, 183–187, 232–234; John Coffey, *Persecution and Toleration in Protestant England, 1558–1689* (Essex: Pearson, 2000), 55, 61, 70, 113, 214.

183 Background from Warren M. Billings, ed., *The Old Dominion in the Seventeenth Century: A Documentary History of Virginia, 1606–1700*, Rev. ed. (Chapel Hill: University of North Carolina Press, 2007), 1–8.

184 John Coffey, *Persecution and Toleration in Protestant England 1558–1689* (London: Routledge, 2000), 112–113.

185 David Hall, *The Puritans: A Translatlantic History* (Princeton, NJ: Princeton University Press, 2019), 196–205.

186 For background, see Alexandra Walsham, *Charitable Hatred: Tolerance and Intolerance in England, 1500–1700* (Manchester: Manchester University Press, 2006), 234, 241–243; John Coffey, *Persecution and Toleration in Protestant England, 1558–1689* (Essex: Pearson, 2000), 60.

187 Summary drawn from Johannes Althusius, *The Politics of Johannes Althusius*, trans. and ed. Frederick S. Carney (London: Eyre & Spottiswoode, 1964), quote at 4; Johannes Althusius, *On Law and Power*, ed. Stephen Grabill, John Witte Jr., and Jeffrey Veenstra (Grand Rapids, MI: Christian Library Press, 2013).

188 Johannes Althusius, *The Politics of Johannes Althusius*, trans. and ed. Frederick S. Carney (London: Eyre & Spottiswoode, 1964), "Preface to the First Edition" (1603), 4.

189 Summary from Crawford Gribben, *The Rise and Fall of Christian Ireland* (Oxford: Oxford University Press, 2021), 88–121.

190 Summary drawn from Wayne P. Te Brake, *Religious War and Religious Peace in Early Modern Europe* (Cambridge: Cambridge University Press, 2017).

191 Summary of Pareus' life and Romans commentary drawn from Daniel John Toft, "Shadows of Kings: The Political Thought of David Pareus, 1548–1622" (PhD diss.; University of Wisconsin-Madison, 1970), 9–10, 185–251.

192 Nicolaas H. Gootjes and Nicolaas Hendrik Gootjes, *The Belgic Confession: Its History and Sources* (Grand Rapids, MI: Baker Academic, 2007).

193 P.J. Hoedemaker, *Article 36 of the Belgic Confession VINDICATED against Dr. Abraham Kuyper, 1901*, trans. R. Alvarado (Aalten: Pantocrator Press, 2019).

194 John Coffey, *Persecution and Toleration in Protestant England 1558–1689* (London: Routledge, 2000), 110–114.

195 Summary from David Hall, *The Puritans: A Transatlantic History* (Princeton, NJ: Princeton University Press, 2020), 203.

Sources 723

196 The Avalon Project: Documents in Law, History and Diplomacy, https://avalon.law.yale.edu (accessed 9 October 2023).

197 Paul Douglas Lockhart, *Sweden in the Seventeenth Century* (Basingstoke: Palgrave, 2004), 22–37.

198 On James' political thought, see Johann P. Sommerville, *King James VI and I: Political Writings* (Cambridge: Cambridge University Press, 1994), xv–xxviii.

199 "Andrew Ferris, 'Vile and Clamorous Reports' from New England", *Early American Literature* 54, no. 2 (2019): 381–412.

200 K. Sprunger, "Robinson, John (1575/6?–1625)", *ODNB*; Timothy George, *John Robinson and the English Separatist Tradition* (Macon, GA: Mercer University Press, 1982).

201 S.C. Neff, ed., *Hugo Grotius: On the Law of War and Peace* (Cambridge: Cambridge University Press, 2012), xxxvii.

202 On the difference between these ways of relating violence and theology, see Matthew Rowley, *Godly Violence in the Puritan Atlantic World* (Woodbridge: Boydell & Brewer, 2024), chap. 3.

203 Summary adapted from Tryntje Helfferich, *The Thirty Years War: A Documentary History* (Indianapolis, IN: Hacket, 2009), 82–83.

204 For background, see Albert Eekhof, *Jonas Michaëlius, Founder of the Church in New Netherland, His Life and Work* (Leiden: A. W. Sijthoff, 1926); J. Franklin Jameson, ed., *Narratives of New Netherland, 1609–1664* (New York: Charles Scribner's Sons, 1909); Hugh Hastings, ed., *Ecclesiastical Records: State of New York* (Albany, NY: James B. Lyon, 1901), vol. I.

205 Some of this shift detailed in Katharine Gerbner, *Christian Slavery: Conversion and Race in the Protestant Atlantic World* (Philadelphia: University of Pennsylvania Press, 2018).

206 J. Franklin Jameson, ed., *Narratives of New Netherland, 1609–1664* (New York: Charles Scribner's Sons, 1909), 408.

207 Summary drawn from Johann P. Sommerville, ed., *Sir Robert Filmer: Patriarchia and Other Writings* (Cambridge: Cambridge University Press, 1991), ix–xxiv.

208 Summary from Paul Douglas Lockhart, *Sweden in the Seventeenth Century* (New York: Palgrave MacMillan, 2004), 22–55.

209 Matthew Rowley, "Reverse-Engineering the Covenant: Moses, Massachusetts Bay and the Construction of a City on a Hill", *Journal of the Bible and its Reception* 8, no. 2 (2021): 209–227. See also Abram Van Engen, *City on a Hill: A History of American Exceptionalism* (New Haven, CT: Yale University Press, 2020).

210 Summary drawn from Paul Douglas Lockhart, *Sweden in the Seventeenth Century* (New York: Palgrave MacMillan, 2004), 22–55. The hymn has variously been attributed to Michael Altenburg, Gustav II Adolf and Jacobus Fabricius; Standford W. Reid, "The Battle Hymns of the Lord Calvinist Psalmody of the Sixteenth Century", *Sixteenth Century Essays and Studies* 2 (1971): 36–54.

211 Summary drawn from George Huntston Williams, *The Polish Brethren: Documentation of the History and Thought of Unitarianism in the Polish-Lithuanian Commonwealth and in the Diaspora, 1601–1685* (Missoula, MO: Scholars Press, 1980), 337–341.

212 Matthew Rowley, "Authority, Toleration and Miracles in the Writings of Roger Williams, Thomas Hobbes and John Locke", in *Miracles, Political Authority and Violence in Medieval and Early Modern History*, ed. Matthew Rowley and Natasha Hodgson (London: Routledge, 2022), 190–212.

213 Summary from Tryntje Helfferich, *The Essential Thirty Years War: A Documentary History* (Indianapolis, IN: Hackett, 2015), 53.

214 Hans Medick and Benjamin Marschke, *Experiencing the Thirty Years War: A Brief History with Documents* (Boston, MA: Bedford/St. Martins, 2013), 148.

724 *Sources*

215 Martin Luther, *A Sermon on Keeping Children in School* (1530), in *The European Reformations Sourcebook*, ed. Carter Lindberg, 1st ed. (Malden: Blackwell, 2000), 67–82 (82).

216 Jan Bažant, Nina Bažantová and Frances Starn, eds., *The Czech Reader: History, Culture, Politics* (Durham, NC: Duke University Press, 2010), 83.

217 Simon S. Laurie, *John Amos Comenius, Bishop of the Moravians: His Life and Educational Works. Vol. 2* (Syracuse, NY: C.W. Bardeen, 1892); Andrea Sterk, "Comenius, John (1592–1670)", in *The Encyclopedia of Protestantism*, ed. Hans J. Hillebrand (London: Routledge, 2004), 483–484.

218 For background, see Matthew Rowley, *Godly Violence in the Puritan Atlantic World* (Woodbridge: Boydell & Brewer, 2024), chap. 4.

219 Katharine Gerbner, *Christian Slavery: Conversion and Race in the Protestant Atlantic World* (Philadelphia: University of Pennsylvania Press, 2018), 23.

220 Alison Games, *The Web of Empire: English Cosmopolitans in an Age of Expansion, 1560–1660* (Oxford: Oxford University Press, 2008), 71–72. See entry for April 20 1635 in W. Noel Sainsbury, ed., *Calendar of State Papers Colonial, America and West Indies: Volume 1, 1574–1660* (London: Her Majesty's Stationery Office, 1860), 201–206.

221 Seymour Drescher, *Abolition: A History of Slavery and Antislavery* (Cambridge: Cambridge University Press, 2009), 67; citing G. Francklyn, *An Answer to the Reverend Mr. Clarkson's Essay* (London: Logographic Press, 1789), xv–xvi.

222 Summary from Michael P. Winship, *The Times and Trials of Anne Hutchinson: Puritans Divided* (Lawrence: University Press of Kansas, 2005), quote on 112; Amy Schrager Lang, *Prophetic Woman: Anne Hutchinson and the Problem of Dissent in the Literature of New England* (Oakland: University of California Press, 1987).

223 Adapted from Joris van Eijnatten, "War, Piracy and Religion: Godfried Udemans' Spiritual Helm (1638)", in *Property, Piracy and Punishment: Hugo Grotius on War and Booty in De iure praedae*, ed. Hans Blom (Leiden: Brill, 2009), 192–214.; Katharine Gerbner, *Christian Slavery: Conversion and Race in the Protestant Atlantic World* (Philadelphia: University of Pennsylvania Press, 2018), 23–24; Charles H. Parker, *Global Calvinism: Conversion and Commerce in the Dutch Empire, 1600–1800* (New Haven, CT: Yale University Press, 2022), 82, 203–204.

224 John Russell Bartlett, ed., *Records of the Colony of Rhode Island and Providence Plantations in New England, 10 Vols* (Providence, RI: A. C. Greene and Brothers, 1856–1865) I:22.

225 John Russell Bartlett, ed., *Records of the Colony of Rhode Island and Providence Plantations in New England, 10 Vols* (Providence, RI: A. C. Greene and Brothers, 1856–1865) I:14.

226 John Russell Bartlett, ed., *Records of the Colony of Rhode Island and Providence Plantations in New England, 10 Vols* (Providence, RI: A. C. Greene and Brothers, 1856–1865) I:16.

227 Edward J. Eberle, "Another of Roger William's Gifts: Women's Right to Liberty of Conscience: *Joshua Verin v. Providence Plantations*", *Roger Williams University Law Review* 9 (2004): 399–407 (400).

228 Jacqueline Broad and Karen Green, *A History of Women's Political Thought in Europe, 1400–1700* (Cambridge: Cambridge University Press, 2009), 140–161.

229 Summary from Amanda C. Pipkin, *Dissenting Daughters: Reformed Women in the Dutch Republic, 1572–1725* (Oxford: Oxford University Press, 2022), 97–132 (quoted at 98).

230 Summary drawn from Evan Haefeli, *New Netherland and the Dutch Origins of American Religious Liberty* (Philadelphia: University of Pennsylvania Press, 2012), 1–19; Charles H. Parker, *Global Calvinism: Conversion and Commerce*

Sources   725

in the Dutch Empire, 1600–1800 (New Haven, CT: Yale University Press, 2022), 7, 47–48, 78, 118.

231 Summary from Tryntje Helfferich, The Thirty Years War: A Documentary History (Indianapolis, IN: Hacket, 2009), 198; Tryntje Helfferich, The Iron Princess: Amalia Elisabeth and the Thirty Years War (Cambridge, MA: Harvard University Press, 2013), 1–2, 124–139.

232 Daniel Allen Hearn, Legal Executions in New England: A Comprehensive Reference, 1623–1960 (Repr., Jefferson, NC: McFarland, 2015), 2.

233 Summary drawn from David Hall, The Puritans: A Transatlantic History (Princeton, NJ: Princeton University Press, 2020), 228–236. The 1646 quotations are from Nathaniel B. Shurtleff, ed., Records of the Governor and Company of the Massachusetts Bay in New England, 5 Vols (Boston, MA: William White, 1853–1854) II:168. For the wider background on slavery, see Margaret Ellen Newell, Brethren by Nature: New England Indians, Colonists, and the Origins of American Slavery (Ithica, NY: Cornell University Press, 2015).

234 Ian Gentles, The English Revolution and the Wars in the Three Kingdoms, 1638–1652 (London: Routledge, 2007), 9.

235 John Coffey, Politics, Religion and the British Revolutions: The Mind of Samuel Rutherford (Cambridge: Cambridge University Press, 1997), 48–49.

236 "English Ministers to the Scottish General Assembly" (12 July 1641), New College Library (University of Edinburgh), MSS BAILL. 1.2. ff.1214–1215.

237 For additional background, see Matthew Rowley, Godly Violence in the Puritan Atlantic World (Woodbridge: Boydell & Brewer, 2024), chap. 5 and 7.

238 Summary from David J. Appleby, "Soldier's Bible", in Puritans and Puritanism in Europe and America: A Comprehensive Encyclopedia, ed. Francis J. Bremer and Tom Webster (Santa Barbara, CA: ABC-CLIO, 2005), 548–549. On the wider context of Puritan warfare, see Matthew Rowley, Godly Violence in the Puritan Atlantic World (Woodbridge: Boydell & Brewer, 2024).

239 Below each reference, the relevant verse was reproduced for the soldier. The editors omitted the scriptural text, which seems closer to the Geneva Bible than the Authorized Version. References appear in the order that they appear in the text, and several have been corrected by the editors.

240 Summary from Peter H. Wilson, The Thirty Years War: Europe's Tragedy (Cambridge, MA: Harvard University Press, 2011), 8–9, 696 (quote at 8–9).

241 For background, see G. Campbell "Milton, John (1608–1674), ODNB; Martin Dzelzainis, "John Milton, Areopagitica", in A Companion to Literature from Milton to Blake, ed. David Womersley (Oxford: Blackwell, 2000): 151–158.

242 Summary drawn from Michael A.G. Haykin, "Separatists and Baptists", in The Oxford History of Protestant Dissenting Traditions, Volume I, ed. John Coffey (Oxford: Oxford University Press, 2020), 113–138.

243 John Russell Bartlett, ed., Records of the Colony of Rhode Island and Providence Plantations in New England, 10 Vols (Providence, RI: Crawford Green, 1856–1865), I: 156.

244 For background, see Teresa M. Bejan, Mere Civility Disagreement and the Limits of Toleration (Cambridge, MA: Harvard University Press, 2017); Matthew Rowley, "'All Pretend an Holy War": Radical Beliefs and the Rejection of Persecution in the Mind of Roger Williams', The Review of Faith & International Affairs, 15, no. 2 (2017), 66–76.

245 Summary drawn from John Coffey, Politics, Religion and the British Revolutions: The Mind of Samuel Rutherford (Cambridge: Cambridge University Press, 1997), 1–61, 146–187 (quote at 152).

246 Summary drawn from Richard W. Cogley, John Eliot's Mission to the Indians Before King Philip's War (Cambridge, MA: Harvard University Press, 1999), 40–43 (quote on 42).

726 *Sources*

247 Andrew Sharp, *The English Levellers* (Cambridge: Cambridge University Press, 1998), vii–xxii, 206–207.
248 For background, see volume one of Chad Van Dixhoorn, ed., *Minutes and Papers of the Westminster Assembly, 1643–52* (Oxford: Oxford University Press, 2012).
249 Catie Gill, "Pope, Mary", *Oxford Dictionary of National Biography*, https://doi.org/10.1093/ref:odnb/69153 (accessed 9 October 2023).
250 Summary drawn from Charles H. Parker, *Global Calvinism: Conversion and Commerce in the Dutch Empire, 1600–1800* (New Haven, CT: Yale University Press, 2022), 7, 41–46, 109; Michiel van Groesen, "Introduction", in *The Expansion of Tolerance: Religion in Dutch Brazil (1624–1645)*, ed. Michiel van Groesen, Jonathan Israel and Stuart B. Schwartz (Amsterdam: Amsterdam University Press, 2007), 6–11.
251 Patricia Crawford, "Charles Stuart, That Man of Blood", *Journal of British Studies* 16, no. 2 (1977): 41–61. Quotes on 50 and 42 respectively.
252 For background, see Matthew Rowley, *Godly Violence in the Puritan Atlantic World* (Woodbridge: Boydell & Brewer, 2024), chap. 6.
253 Summary drawn from David Hall, *The Puritans: A Transatlantic History* (Princeton, NJ: Princeton University Press, 2020), 330–331; Michael P. Winship, *Hot Protestants: A History of Puritanism in England and America* (New Haven, CT: Yale University Press, 2019), 175–177.
254 David Onnekink, ed., *War and Religion after Westphalia, 1648–1713* (London: Routledge, 2009).
255 Summary drawn from Derek Croxon and Anuschka Tischer, *The Peace of Westphalia: A Historical Dictionary* (Westport, CT: Greenwood, 2002), xiii–xx.
256 Victor Stater, *A Political History of Tudor and Stuart England: A Sourcebook* (London: Routledge, 2002), 144–145.
257 C. Russell, "The Theory of Treason in the Trial of Stratford", *The English Historical Review* 80 (1965): 30–50.
258 David L. Smith, *A History of the Modern British Isles, 1603–1707: The Double Crown* (Oxford: Blackwell, 1998), 163.
259 'Attainted' is a legal status related to bloodguilt that proscribes children from inheriting.
260 For background, see Eric Nelson, "Talmudical Commonwealthsmen and the Rise of Republican Exclusivism", *The Historical Journal* 50, no. 4 (2007): 809–835.
261 Adam S. Francisco, "Crusade, Pacifism, and Just War: Responses to Ottoman Imperialism in the Early Reformation Era", *The Muslim World* 107, no. 4 (2017): 621–631.
262 Sarah Henrich and James L. Boyce, "Martin Luther – Translations of Two Prefaces on Islam: Preface to the *Libellus de ritu et moribus Turcorum* (1530), and Preface to Bibliander's Edition of the Qur'an (1543)", *Word & World* 16, no. 2 (1996): 250–266 (263, 266).
263 Nabil Matar, *Islam in Britain, 1558–1685* (Cambridge: Cambridge University Press, 1998), 73–80.
264 J. Davis and J. Alsop, "Winstanley, Gerrard (bap. 1609, d. 1676)", *ODNB*.
265 For example, Henry Finch and the publisher William Gouge were imprisoned by James VI and I for a 1621 work that called for a policy change. The text argued that if the Jewish people were to return, they needed to convert to Christianity. See source in *Global Reformations Sourcebook: Convergence, Conversion, and Conflict in Early Modern Religious Encounters*, ed. Nicholas Terpstra (New York: Routledge, 2021), 124–127.
266 Summary drawn from Kenneth Austin, *The Jews and the Reformation* (New Haven, CT: Yale University Press, 2020), 195–204 (Cromwell quote at 196).

Sources   727

267 Jacqueline Broad and Karen Green, *A History of Women's Political Thought in Europe, 1400–1700* (Cambridge: Cambridge University Press, 2009), 140–161 (144).

268 Jacqueline Broad and Karen Green, *A History of Women's Political Thought in Europe, 1400–1700* (Cambridge: Cambridge University Press, 2009), 142, 51.

269 Summary drawn from Robert Ross, "Khoesan and Immigrants: The Emergence of Colonial Society in the Cape, 1500–1800", in *The Cambridge History of South Africa, Volume 1: From Early Times to 1885*, ed. Carolyn Hamilton, Bernard K. Mbenga and Robert Ross (Cambridge: Cambridge University Press, 2009), 168–201 (168–182).

270 Kristina Bross, *Dry Bones and Indian Sermons: Praying Indians in Colonial America* (London: Cornell University Press, 2004); Matthew Rowley, *Godly Violence in the Puritan Atlantic World* (Woodbridge: Boydell & Brewer, 2024), chap 4 and 8.

271 Summary drawn from Matthew Rowley, *Godly Violence in the Puritan Atlantic World* (Woodbridge: Boydell & Brewer, 2024), chap. 7. See also R. Scott Spurlock, *Cromwell and Scotland: Conquest and Religion, 1650–1660* (Edinburgh: John Donald, 2007).

272 For background, see Matthew Rowley, "Authority, Toleration and Miracles in the Writings of Roger Williams, Thomas Hobbes and John Locke", in *Miracles, Political Authority and Violence in Medieval and Early Modern History*, ed. Matthew Rowley and Natasha Hodgson (London: Routledge, 2022), 190–212; Noel Malcolm, "Hobbes and Spinoza", in *The Cambridge History of Political Thought, 1450–1700*, ed. J. H. Burns and Mark Goldie (Cambridge: Cambridge University Press, 1991), 530–557.

273 In a later petition, some enslaved Africans argued that conversion and baptism set them free. On the 13 November 1669, a proclamation by Sir John Heydon vigorously asserted the benefit accruing to slaves through their enslavement by Christians, and they were commanded by God to submit in all things. See J. H. Lefroy, ed., *Memorials of the Discovery and Early Settlement of the Bermudas or Somers Islands, 1511–1687* (London: Longmans, Green, and Co., 1879), II:293–294.

274 Summary drawn from Michael J. Jarvis, *Isle of Devils, Isle of Saints: An Atlantic History of Bermuda, 1609–1684* (Baltimore, MD: Johns Hopkins University Press, 2022), 1–17, 244–245 (quotes at 39, 244–245).

275 Summary drawn from Derek Croxon and Anuschka Tischer, *The Peace of Westphalia: A Historical Dictionary* (Westport, CT: Greenwood, 2002), 98–99.

276 On Cary and the wider context of female prophecy, see Elizabeth Bouldin, *Women Prophets and Radical Protestantism in the British Atlantic World, 1640–1730* (Cambridge: Cambridge University Press, 2015).

277 For background, see Jacob Rader Marcus, ed., *The Jew in the American World: A Source Book* (Detroit, MI: Wayne State University Press, 1996).

278 Summary drawn from Mehmet Karabela, *Islamic Thought through Protestant Eyes* (New York: Routledge, 2021), 243–246.

279 Summary drawn from David Lumpp, "Waldensians", in *Encyclopedia of Martin Luther and the Reformation*, ed. Mark A. Lamport (New York: Rowman & Littlefield, 2017), 815–817.

280 Ennis B. Edmonds, and Michelle A. Gonzalez, *Caribbean Religious History: An Introduction* (New York: New York University Press, 2010), 65; Matthew McCullough, *The Cross of War: Christian Nationalism and U.S. Expansion in the Spanish-American War* (Madison: University of Wisconsin Press, 2014).

281 For background, see Carla Gardina Pestana, *The English Atlantic in an Age of Revolution, 1640–1661* (Cambridge, MA: Harvard University Press, 2004); idem, *The English Conquest of Jamaica: Oliver Cromwell's Bid for Empire* (Cambridge, MA: Harvard University Press, 2017).

728   *Sources*

282   Summary drawn from J.G.A. Pocock, ed., *James Harrington: The Common-wealth of Oceana and A System of Politics* (Cambridge: Cambridge University Press, 1992), vii–xxiv; Blair Worden, "English Republicanism", in *The Cambridge History of Political Thought, 1450–1700, ed.* J. H. Burns and Mark Goldie (Cambridge: Cambridge University Press, 1991), 443–475 (450–455).

283   Summary drawn from William Lamont, ed., *Baxter: A Holy Commonwealth* (Cambridge: Cambridge University Press, 1994), ix–xxi.

284   For background, see Evan Haefeli, *New Netherland and the Dutch Origins of American Religious Liberty* (Philadelphia: University of Pennsylvania Press, 2012), 156–185.

285   On tyrannicide as a divine act, see Julien Le Mauff, "The Sword of God: Tyrannicide as a Providential and Miraculous Event from Medieval Debates to Early Modern Religious Conflicts", in *Miracles, Political Authority and Violence in Medieval and Early Modern History*, ed. Matthew Rowley and Natasha Hodgson (London: Routledge, 2022), 123–136.

286   For background, see Alan Marshall, "Edward Sexby", *Oxford Dictionary of National Biography*, https://doi.org/10.1093/ref:odnb/25151 (accessed 9 October 2023). Quotations from Gary S. De Krey, *Following the Levellers, Volume Two: English Political and Religious Radicals from the Commonwealth to the Glorious Revolution, 1649–1688* (London: Palgrave Macmillan, 2018), 150.

287   On the political life of John Owen, including his involvement in the Savoy Declaration, see Crawford Gribben, *John Owen and English Puritanism: Experiences of Defeat* (Oxford: Oxford University Press, 2016).

288   Summary drawn from Francis J. Bremer, "Savoy Assembly", in *Puritans and Puritanism in Europe and America: A Comprehensive Encyclopedia*, ed. Francis J. Bremer and Tom Webster (Santa Barbara, CA: ABC-CLIO, 2005), 533–534.

289   Biographical details can be found in Bart Plantenga, "The Mystery of the Plockhoy Settlement in the Valley of Swans", *Mennonite Historical Bulletin* 62, no.1 (2001): 4–13.

290   Overview from Sarah Mortimer, *Reason and Religion in the English Revolution: The Challenge of Socinianism* (Cambridge: Cambridge University Press, 2010), quote at 40.

291   Ariel Hessayon and Diego Lucci, "The Supposed Burning of the Racovian Catechism in 1614: A Historiographical Myth Exposed", *History* 107 (2022): 25–50 (28).

292   Parliament of England and Wales, *Votes of Parliament Touching the Book Commonly Called the Racovian Catechism* (London: John Field, 1652).

293   Translation from Conal Condren, *George Lawson's Politica and the English Revolution*, rev. ed. (Cambridge: Cambridge University Press, 2002), 47.

294   Translation from Conal Condren, *George Lawson's Politica and the English Revolution*, rev. ed. (Cambridge: Cambridge University Press, 2002), 50.

295   For background, see Hugh Barbour and Arthur O. Roberts, eds., *Early Quaker Writings, 1650–1700* (Grand Rapids, MI: Eerdmans, 1973), 32–38, 406.